Mason County, West Virginia Marriages, 1806 to 1915

Compiled and Edited by

Julie Chapin Hesson
with
Sherman Gene Hesson
& Jane J. Russell

Copyright © 1997 by Julie Chapin Hesson
All Rights Reserved.

Printed for
Clearfield Company, Inc. by
Genealogical Publishing Co., Inc.
Baltimore, Maryland
1997

Reprinted for
Clearfield Company, Inc. by
Genealogical Publishing Co., Inc.
Baltimore, Maryland
2000, 2003

International Standard Book Number: 0-8063-4673-6

Made in the United States of America

For Gene, my Sweet Prince: your love, your inspiration, your support, and most of all, your faith in me, have made this work possible.....you truly are "the wind beneath my wings."

~~ Julie
September 1996
Lebanon, Tennessee

Acknowledgments

Any compilation of this type doesn't happen without a great deal of assistance from many other people, and my sincere gratitude goes to the following:

Mason County Clerk, **Diana Cromley**, and her very helpful and friendly staff--**Rice Tarbott, Bev Whittington, Dawn Gandee, Nadene Pearson** and **Dottie Campbell**, all of whom made me eagerly anticipate each new trip to the Mason County Courthouse; **Ruth and Rush Finley** and their daughter **Marcia**, proprietors of the historic Lowe Hotel in downtown Point Pleasant, WV, whose warm hospitality and transportation assistance was deeply appreciated; **Janice Deel and friends** of Gallipolis, OH, whose help with my disabled vehicle was most gratifying; and our dear cousins in Hartford, Mason County, **Don and Annie Warth**, whose hospitality and assistance from the very beginning were, and forever will be, remembered with appreciation and love.

Last, but far from least, we are indebted to computer guru extraordinaire and friend, **Ron House**, without whose constant technical expertise, not one page of this book would exist.

Introduction

During the compilation of this volume, I have been asked, frequently, what prompted this endeavor. My wonderful husband of twelve years, Sherman Gene Hesson, was born in Mason County, as were his parents and grandparents. In attempting to obtain marriage documentation on one set of his great-grandparents, I went to the Mason County Courthouse in Point Pleasant, West Virginia. There, I discovered that the early marriage indexes, having been copied decades ago, were in many instances incorrectly or inconsistently spelled; some entries were duplicated, many were abbreviated and/or incomplete, and still others were omitted entirely.

In addition to missing names and dates, whole segments of the larger alphabetical listings, due to lack of adequate pages, were scattered throughout other letter divisions. Thus, a thorough name search became an exercise in confusion for anyone unfamiliar with the arrangement of the entries.

This volume was created in an effort to provide the first-ever comprehensive index of Mason County's 11,100+ earliest marriages. By comparing index entries with the original licenses and ministers' returns, we have obtained what we believe is the most complete index possible.

The original (or older) series of volumes was numbered 1-12 and encompassed licenses issued between 1806 and 1887. The second or newer series of volumes began with number 5 and ran parallel with the older series, but with a span of some 18 to 23 years apart. Volume 10, page 318, for instance, carries an 1880 older series entry and a 1903 new series entry.

We have used the genealogically correct "2-3-4" (2-digit day, 3-letter month, 4-digit year) date format to eliminate any confusion. In the colon-separated references, volumes are the left 2-digits, and page numbers are to the right of the colon. When only license dates were given, an asterisk precedes the date; double asterisks denote licenses which were not used.

With any work of this type and size, mistakes are inevitable, due to interpretation of the various handwritten scripts and the occasional typographical error, but every effort has been made to eliminate errors and to ensure accuracy. Please bear in mind that many names were spelled phonetically, so all possible variant spellings should be considered when seeking an individual's marriage record.

PAGE CUT FROM BOOK	1881	10:439
PAGE CUT FROM BOOK	1881	10:440
PAGE CUT FROM BOOK	1882	11:103
PAGE CUT FROM BOOK	1882	11:104
ABBOT, WILLIAM & McGUIRE, ELIZABETH	03 MAY 1830	01:031 5
ABBOTT, B LEE & THIVENER, CARRIE I	11 MAY 1913	14:144
ABBOTT, CHARLES E & LEPORT, JENNIE	12 FEB 1906	11:265
ABBOTT, CHARLES E & CASTO, HARRIET	08 NOV 1904	10:634
ABBOTT, WILLIAM THOMAS & PICKENS, IVA ELLEN	20 NOV 1892	06:438
ABLES, ALEXANDER & STATTS, HANNAH	20 JAN 1830	01:022
ABLES, F P & HECK, ELLA M	28 FEB 1912	13:492
ABSTEN, LAWRENCE & STOVER, MIRTIE BLANCHE	24 SEP 1914	15:281
ABSTEN, WILBERT & KEEFER, GUSSIE	09 OCT 1909	12:525
ACKLEY, JEREMIAH & WRIGHT, CHARLOTTE	28 OCT 1830	01:023
ADAM, ARCHBOLE T & DUFFER, SARAH	19 APR 1868	05:173
ADAMS, ALFRED L & WALLACE, CARRIE E	06 MAR 1900	09:091
ADAMS, ALVIN & STOUT, MARTHA J	01 SEP 1881	11:010
ADAMS, C MARION & OLDAKER, MINNIE A	02 JUL 1902	10:102
ADAMS, CHARLES & HAMBRICK, ELLA	05 OCT 1887	05:103
ADAMS, CHARLES W & BYERS, SALLIE N	03 MAR 1897	08:042
ADAMS, ELIJAH & GOULD, ELLA	26 DEC 1888	05:332
ADAMS, FRANK & MASON, MARGARET	12 DEC 1909	12:564
ADAMS, GEORGE WILLIAM & HANNIS, JENNIE L	17 JAN 1900	09:066
ADAMS, H E & YOUNG, KATHRYN A	14 JUL 1910	13:105
ADAMS, JACOB & ADAMS, ESTHER	30 SEP 1869	06:092
ADAMS, JAMES A & BIRD, ELIZABETH	27 SEP 1881	11:002
ADAMS, JAMES A & HAMBRICK, GRACE	27 JUN 1896	07:576
ADAMS, JAMES F & DOOLEY, REBECCA J	15 APR 1896	07:529
ADAMS, JAMES GOMER & WOYAN, MAGGIE MAY	19 MAR 1913	14:107
ADAMS, JAMES W & ELLIS, SUSAN ELIZABETH	12 JAN 1865	03:216
ADAMS, JOHN & BUMGARNER, HAGAR ELIZABETH	*28 NOV 1853	02:005
ADAMS, JOHN WILLIAM & COLLINS, BLANCHE	12 NOV 1901	09:446
ADAMS, JOSEPH & DALTON, ELLEN C	15 NOV 1909	12:546
ADAMS, JOSHUA A & McCOY, SARAH F	*22 SEP 1858	02:011
ADAMS, LEWIS S & DEWEES, MARTHA J	22 FEB 1875	08:205
ADAMS, MARTIN L & FARLEY, ANNIE L	30 APR 1876	08:349
ADAMS, ROBERT J & McCOMB, MALINDA J	19 JAN 1887	12:468
ADAMS, ROBERT LEE & DAVIS, OLIVE EDITH	18 APR 1900	09:108
ADAMS, SAMUEL H & MEADOWS, MAHALA A L	01 APR 1873	07:339
ADAMSON, GEORGE E & SCOTT, ANNIE L	13 SEP 1911	13:375
ADDISON, RUSH & CRAIG, SALLIE	01 JAN 1884	11:447
ADKINS, ADAM & CASTO, HARRIET	13 MAR 1909	12:384
ADKINS, ALEXANDER & THOMPSON, NORA	04 JUL 1894	07:110
ADKINS, ALEXANDER & ROHRABAUGH, EFFIE	28 AUG 1898	08:352
ADKINS, ALFRED P & WHITTINGTON, NANNIE A	20 MAR 1880	10:227
ADKINS, ARTHUR LEWIS & McGRAW, GEORGIANNIE	08 NOV 1888	05:301
ADKINS, CLARK S & CHAPMAN, MARY	05 DEC 1894	07:201
ADKINS, EMORY W A & MORROW, ALICE CLARINDA	13 JAN 1886	12:279
ADKINS, ERNEST MANFIELD & RAY, RETHIE	27 APR 1907	11:519
ADKINS, ERVIN B & WEAVER, DOROTHY	20 JAN 1893	06:473
ADKINS, ERVIN & WEAVER, DORTHA S	14 SEP 1903	10:352
ADKINS, GEORGE TAYLOR & FRY, IVA GENEVA	25 AUG 1892	06:390
ADKINS, GEORGE W & IRVIN, ELLA MAY	11 APR 1899	08:505
ADKINS, IRA & CRAIG, ANNIE	10 APR 1909	12:398
ADKINS, JOHN M & BLAKEMORE, MARGARET A	21 DEC 1881	11:082
ADKINS, JOHN T & FRY, INA M	27 JAN 1907	11:492
ADKINS, SPENCER & GLOVER, CAROLINE	*20 OCT 1852	02:003

Names	Date	Ref
ADKINS, STEPHEN E & HYSELL, MAGGIE	29 OCT 1884	12:085
ADKINS, WILLIAM A & PLANTS, SUSIE	13 SEP 1907	12:010
ADKINS, WILLIAM B & PERRY, MARY S C	28 DEC 1876	09:014
ADKISON, CHARLES H & PEARSON, ORA E	15 NOV 1911	13:418
AEIKER, DENVER P & McLEOD, CHRISTIE	25 APR 1909	12:402
AEIKER, HUGH & PAGE, NEVADA MAY	25 OCT 1910	13:190
AGEE, T EMMET & MEADOWS, ETHEL JEANNESS	12 FEB 1911	13:265
AILER, W C & BRADLEY, CAROLINE	18 JUN 1886	12:340
AILES, JOHN L & GREEN, MARY J	23 OCT 1881	11:036
ALDERMAN, CORNLY D & ELLENWOOD, ETHEL C	28 DEC 1906	11:484
ALDERMAN, JAMES P & DEWEESE, LAURA M	19 FEB 1897	08:047
ALDERSON, GEORGE & SEWELL, AMANDA	09 DEC 1869	06:122
ALDERSON, ROBERT P & LONG, LUCY E	22 FEB 1906	11:272
ALESHIRE, ALLEN F & SAYRE, ELIZABETH F	25 DEC 1878	10:026
ALESHIRE, ELMER & FORBES, MOLLIE	14 NOV 1903	10:409
ALESHIRE, JAMES & MEDLEY, SALLIE	13 AUG 1894	07:132
ALESHIRE, JAMES & WHITTAKER, LAURA E	13 APR 1907	11:518
ALESHIRE, SHERMAN & FRASHER, LULA	05 NOV 1905	11:198
ALEXANDER, ADONIJAH E & TAYLOR, SELAH D	07 JUN 1903	10:300
ALEXANDER, JAMES P & POFFENBARGER, JEANNETTE	09 JUN 1897	08:100
ALEXANDER, JOHN E & ROLLINS, SARAH E	16 JUL 1873	08:012
ALEXANDER, JOHN T & HAYMAN, ANNIE	04 SEP 1878	09:305
ALEXANDER, JOSEPH T & SMITH, JULIA	12 OCT 1870	07:014
ALEXANDER, JOSEPH T & RISON, GUSSIE	04 APR 1914	15:170
ALEXANDER, SAMUEL & COLLINS, SARAH	31 MAR 1875	08:224
ALEXANDER, VERGIL B & HALEY, VERGIE H	13 NOV 1907	12:065
ALEXANDER, VIRGIL L & ADKINS, GENERVA	03 MAR 1901	09:298
ALEXANDER, WILBUR & GIST, MAY	23 DEC 1896	08:020
ALEXANDER, WILLIAM H & WARNER, RUBY E	02 OCT 1907	12:027
ALFORD, CHARLES A & TAYLOR, MARY A	22 MAY 1898	08:311
ALFORD, EARLY W & EDMONDS, MISSOURI	25 DEC 1913	15:101
ALFORD, WILLIAM & WAUGH, NANCY CATHARINE	*06 DEC 1853	02:004
ALLEMANG, HARRY H & YOUNG, HANNAH A	07 FEB 1901	09:287
ALLEN, ALEXANDER N & RUSK, SUSAN L C	23 JAN 1879	10:046
ALLEN, ALFRED E & LARIMER, LYDE E	05 SEP 1882	11:192
ALLEN, CLINT & KEEFER, SARAH LIZZIE	26 JUN 1910	13:101
ALLEN, EDGAR M & BURDETT, FLORA M	22 JUN 1898	08:324
ALLEN, FRANK & ROUSH, SALLIE M	24 JUN 1906	11:348
ALLEN, GEORGE & WHITNEY, MARY	*10 NOV 1856	02:009
ALLEN, JAMES A & JONES, NETTIE	02 JUL 1904	10:556
ALLEN, JESSE A & TORRENCE, ANNA M	07 JUN 1887	05:039
ALLEN, JESSE M & KING, MARY E	29 JUL 1880	10:282
ALLEN, JOHN & GREENLEE, LOUISA	24 DEC 1831	01:025
ALLEN, JOHN W & KIRBY, HENRIETTA	09 JAN 1879	10:040
ALLEN, LEWIS DAVIS & JACOBS, VIRGINIA	*11 APR 1879	10:074
ALLEN, LEWIS D & LONG, NANCY E	21 JUL 1879	10:101
ALLEN, LON M & CLARK, HELEN M	03 NOV 1886	12:412
ALLEN, OSCAR & LAWSON, AMANDA	26 JAN 1912	13:474
ALLEN, REUBEN H & NUTTER, TOLA	02 JUN 1895	07:312
ALLEN, RICHARD JOSEPH & LEDERER, LENA	23 MAY 1888	05:227
ALLEN, THOMAS M & ALLEN, EMMA E	21 DEC 1881	11:074
ALLEN, WILLIAM & JONES, MARY	17 NOV 1865	04:072
ALLEN, WILLIAM J & MAUPIN, SALLIE G	*23 MAR 1857	02:009
ALLEN, WILLIAM L & TAYLOR, NANNIE	26 SEP 1896	07:622
ALLENSWORTH, GEORGE W & REYNOLDS, MINERVA	25 FEB 1873	08:079
ALLINDER, BURKE H & WAMSLEY, MAUDE E	17 DEC 1911	13:437
ALLISON, S M & ROGERS, BERTHA E	20 OCT 1912	14:017
ALTICE, MORTON D & BOYCE, ANNIE L	12 JUN 1864	03:188

Names	Date	Reference
ALVERT, EDWARD & WARD, NANCY	20 APR 1820	01:007
AMBERGER, ELMER & FUGATE, MAYME	23 AUG 1913	15:018
AMBLER, ISAAC & EISHER, LYDIA A	31 DEC 1868	06:024
AMES, JESSE & MAYES, MARTHA J	27 SEP 1864	03:197
AMOS, BENJAMIN J & SWANN, MAUD O	18 FEB 1891	06:063
AMOS, CHARLES F & ANGUISH, LAURA	23 APR 1887	05:015
AMOS, CLINTON D & ANKROM, MAGGIE	29 APR 1888	05:219
AMOS, FRANKLIN & DONOHUE, ADALINE	23 MAR 1898	08:276
AMOS, GEORGE & FERGUSON, JUNIA	30 OCT 1887	05:132
AMOS, GILBERT B & KNAPP, CAROLINE	14 APR 1842	01:037
AMOS, JOSHUA & CREMENES, MARY	03 JUN 1847	01:048
AMOS, WILLIAM B & GRAHAM, IDA B	25 OCT 1914	15:298
AMOS, WILLIAM P & MILLER, MARGARET J	18 APR 1872	07:212
AMOSS, JOHN & CHOEN, MATILDA	23 JUN 1836	01:029
AMSBARY, DON CARLOS & AYRES, MARILLA T	*18 MAR 1838	02:032
AMSBARY, HAMLET & BOWERS, LAVINA	12 JAN 1873	07:305
AMSBARY, SENECA & AYRES, AURELIA J	1838	01:041
AMSBARY, WILLIAM & DUNN, ANN E	13 FEB 1873	07:319
AMSBERRY, HORACE H & BLAIN, MARY J	*19 MAR 1858	02:011
AMSBERRY, WM & EVERETT, POLLY	15 MAY 1823	01:008
AMSBERY, JOSEPH E & BAKER, CLARA	19 JUN 1898	08:322
AMSBURY, FRANCIS E & BEARD, LUCY C	02 MAR 1848	01:048
ANDERSON, ANDREW & BOICE, MARY	29 SEP 1825	01:014
ANDERSON, ASEL & PEASE, MARY JANE	*18 AUG 1855	02:007
ANDERSON, GEORGE J & ADAMS, ESTA	13 SEP 1914	15:261
ANDERSON, JAMES & HUGHS, SUSANNA	07 SEP 1826	01:015
ANDERSON, JAMES & HUGHES, MARY	11 NOV 1891	06:223
ANDERSON, JAMES & COSSIN, (Mrs) MARY C	07 MAR 1913	14:102
ANDERSON, JAMES PAUL & HART, MARY	08 JUL 1906	11:356
ANDERSON, JOHN & LEWIS, ELIZABETH A	23 JAN 1849	01:049
ANDERSON, JOS & STANLEY, NANCY	25 FEB 1823	01:008
ANDERSON, JOSEPH & HARTLEY, BIRDIE	13 JUN 1895	07:316
ANDERSON, LEWIS & WILEY, CATHARINE	*01 MAR 1852	02:002
ANDERSON, SAMUEL & EDMUNDS, SOPHIA J V	23 FEB 1862	03:050
ANDERSON, THOMAS & THOMPSON, MARGARET S	05 NOV 1870	07:021
ANDERSON, THOMAS C & MOURNING, LUELLA BLANCHE	25 JUN 1900	09:146
ANDERSON, WILEY & KIMBERLING, HARRIET	06 APR 1876	08:342
ANDERSON, WILLIAM & HOWELL, ELIZABETH	27 NOV 1878	08:414
ANDREWS, GEORGE F & JOHNSTON, (Mrs) LOUISA	*17 SEP 1852	02:003
ANDREWS, GEORGE & FISHER, AMANDA	*25 SEP 1857	02:010
ANDREWS, JOHN W & GOSNAY, LOTTIE	07 JAN 1886	12:277
ANGEL, HENRY I & TAYLOR, ANN	31 JAN 1878	09:206
ANGUS, WILLIAM & VANMATER, MARIA	02 JUN 1864	03:187
ANKRUM, ALEXANDER P & DARST, SARA D	*15 JAN 1856	02:007
ANKRUM, BURTON L & EDWARDS, ORA M	17 DEC 1902	10:209
APPLETON, EDWARD & EDWARDS, DELILA	09 AUG 1827	01:016
ARBUCKLE, JAMES H & EASTHAM, ELIZABETH	13 APR 1881	10:397
ARCHER, JAMES N & LUTE, SARAH E	09 OCT 1884	12:070
ARCHER, JOHN M & JORDAN, ROSA	02 MAY 1906	11:309
ARCHER, ROBERT LAMLEY & KNIGHT, IRMA LOUISE	20 SEP 1893	06:608
ARCHER, STEPHEN P & KRAFT, CLARA E	11 JUL 1900	09:160
ARKLE, THOMAS & WHITE, ALMA	28 JUN 1910	13:104
ARMSTEAD, EDWARD & NOARK, MINNIE	06 OCT 1897	08:169
ARMSTEAD, EDWARD OTHO & PAGE, EMMA	15 DEC 1889	05:494
ARMSTEAD, EDWARD O & CRAIG, LETTIE	15 DEC 1904	10:669
ARMSTEAD, JAMES WILLIAM & LEWIS, SEJUS ALMEDA	15 NOV 1889	05:480
ARMSTEAD, TILLMAN & JOHNSON, SALLIE	08 APR 1896	07:524
ARMSTEAD, WILLIAM & JORDEN, HANNAH	09 OCT 1871	07:131

Names	Date	Ref
ARMSTRONG, ANDREW J & KING, JANE	28 FEB 1867	05:031
ARMSTRONG, BENJAMIN A & THORNTON, MARY	26 OCT 1878	09:342
ARMSTRONG, FLOYD & FRY, MARTHA A	13 NOV 1875	08:282
ARMSTRONG, JAMES L & VAN MATRE, LIZZIE E	21 DEC 1907	12:094
ARMSTRONG, JOHN W C & HOOFF, MARY F	30 DEC 1874	08:200
ARMSTRONG, JOSEPH E & HAWKINS, ZERELDA C	30 MAR 1878	09:226
ARNOLD, CLERMONT E & PLANTS, NANCY ANN	01 JAN 1868	05:126
ARNOLD, CLERMONT E & ROUSH, NETTIE M	16 DEC 1895	07:455
ARNOLD, CLAREMONT E & WISE, MAUD	25 DEC 1900	09:266
ARNOLD, GEORGE & MAYES, ROSSETTA	13 SEP 1902	10:154
ARNOLD, THEODORE & HERSMAN, EDITH	04 DEC 1909	12:561
ARNOTT, GEORGE A & LOVE, OLIVE M	17 NOV 1910	13:209
ARNOTT, JOHN & McCALLISTER, ELIZABETH	12 DEC 1887	05:155
ARNOTT, OTIS & ROUSH, BIRDIE M	24 APR 1905	11:080
ARRINGTON, EDWARD & MAYS, IDA	05 NOV 1902	10:182
ARRINGTON, GIDEON HENKLE & HENRY, MAMIE FRANCES	16 OCT 1887	05:120
ARRINGTON, ISAAC N & MAYES, VANSIE	31 MAR 1900	09:103
ARRINGTON, JOSIAH & LONG, ELIZABETH	*30 DEC 1852	02:003
ARRINGTON, ROBERT L & PIERCE, ELLEN	13 MAY 1891	06:107
ARTHUR, CHARLES W & CLENDENEN, LUCINDA L	*14 SEP 1858	02:011
ARTHUR, EDWARD & JORDAN, CLARISSA	*15 DEC 1858	02:011
ARTHUR, ISAAC L & GIBBEAUT, MINNIE F	22 FEB 1911	13:273
ARTHUR, JAMES T & SHELINE, RUTHIE	02 APR 1899	08:494
ARTHUR, JOHN V & WRAY, MARGARET V	22 FEB 1874	08:100
ARTHUR, JOHN & JOHNSON, LUCINDA	07 JUN 1882	11:159
ARTHUR, LAFAYETTE & PATTERSON, MAHALA	19 OCT 1865	04:063
ARTHUR, WILLIAM T & BATES, MARY	02 DEC 1894	07:200
ASBERRY, CHARLES JOSEPH & WAMSLEY, MARY ALICE	22 SEP 1894	07:158
ASBERRY, THOMAS & SHELINE, ELIZA Z	26 NOV 1866	05:005
ASBERRY, WILLIAM & DEVOIR, ALICE	03 OCT 1884	12:067
ASBURY, ADAM C & SIMMS, ELLA	22 OCT 1894	07:174
ASBURY, HARRY B & SMITH, MAY O	24 DEC 1891	06:258
ASBURY, WILLIAM & FENTEN, ALICE	11 AUG 1901	09:383
ASH, HARRY V & LEWIS, GOLDIE E	08 JAN 1914	15:122
ASHBURN, GEORGE P & ZERKLE, ELNORA	03 JAN 1914	15:116
ASHBY, OLIVER & SMITH, (Mrs) ANNIE	23 DEC 1909	12:578
ASHER, ANTHONY W & BIRD, SARAH D	23 MAR 1890	05:528
ASHWORTH, JAMES A & TAYLOR, LUCY J	23 FEB 1871	07:052
ASKEW, J S & ZAPF, BARBARA	17 APR 1887	05:012
ASKEW, JAMES & LEMASTER, CATHARINE	*09 OCT 1874	08:170
ASKEW, JEREMIAH S & BARGER, MARY A	26 FEB 1891	06:068
ASTON, JAMES & GLASS, RACHEL	11 FEB 1873	07:322
ATEN, DON OWENS & WITHERS, EDNA A	10 AUG 1912	13:580
ATEN, JOHN GIBB & FRY, NELLIE MAY	12 JUN 1906	11:340
ATENS, WILLIAM G & McMANN, HANNAH	21 NOV 1875	08:300
ATHEY, THOMAS ALBERT & BOOTH, ESTER	29 DEC 1887	05:171
ATHEY, WALTER L & GROVER, NELLIE ANNIS	20 SEP 1912	14:005
ATKESON, C W & BROWN, ANYTIS C	05 AUG 1847	01:048
ATKESON, THOMAS & BROWN, VIRGINIA H	1836	01:040
ATKESON, WILLIAM & BOYLES, LOUISA G	10 AUG 1837	01:030
ATKINS, CHARLES W & McFADDEN, SARAH C	08 MAR 1882	11:125
ATKINS, JAMES & WALLIS, LULLA	06 APR 1899	08:498
ATKINS, JUNE & SHIFLET, IDA	05 AUG 1908	12:222
ATKINS, THOMAS & DUVALL, NANCY E	13 FEB 1881	10:375
ATKINSON, CHARLES A & WILLIAMS, RHODA	*14 JUN 1860	02:014
ATKINSON, DERIAS & WILLIAMS, FRANCES E	*11 OCT 1860	02:014
ATKINSON, GEORGE H & MOREHEAD, LUCINDA	01 JAN 1863	03:093
ATKINSON, HILAS L & WOLF, NORA	23 NOV 1898	08:413

ATKINSON, JAMES J & HILL, MARY M	02 MAR 1882	11:118
ATKINSON, JOSEPH & FROST, ANNA	08 OCT 1914	15:290
ATKINSON, LLOYD & WARNER, AMY	24 NOV 1912	14:030
ATKINSON, WILLIAM & HARRISON, NANCY	07 MAR 1839	01:032 5
ATKINSON, WILLIAM & GARDNER, ALFRETTA	17 MAR 1872	07:204
ATKINSON, WILLIAM C & RAYBURN, EMMA	05 FEB 1899	08:462
ATKINSON, WILLIAM N & SMITH, MARY	28 JAN 1875	08:209
ATKINSON, ZEBEDEE & RAYBURN, JENNETTE	*13 AUG 1885	12:209
ATKISON, JERRY & LITCHFIELD, BESSIE LEE	10 AUG 1913	15:006
ATWELL, E R & INAW-WOCKHWOE, PRAIRIE FLOWER	05 FEB 1910	13:006
AULT, ANDREW F & GREENLEE, SARAH C	04 APR 1878	09:238
AUMILLER, GIDEON & OLIVER, NANCY	10 APR 1834	01:028
AUMILLER, NOAH & GRAHAM, SARAH E	25 APR 1876	08:348
AUMILLER, SAMUEL R & GRINSTEAD, MARY F	01 JUL 1914	15:228
AUMILLER, SPENCER H & KAY, MARGARET L	*24 SEP 1857	02:010
AUMILLER, SPENCER H & BOYCE, SARAH	31 DEC 1865	04:090
AUSTIN, ALFRED A & HART, MARIA	31 JUL 1871	07:106
AUSTIN, ARCH & BARKER, EDNA	19 DEC 1909	12:570
AUSTIN, ARTHUR & RHOADES, MAUD	11 FEB 1900	09:080
AUSTIN, CLARENCE D & POWELL, LALLAH	24 DEC 1914	15:353
AUSTIN, EARL B & BATES, VIRGIE L	12 JUL 1902	10:112
AUSTIN, FURMAN H & THOMAS, EFFIE J	26 OCT 1913	10:391
AUSTIN, HORTON & GLISSPY, DORA E	02 MAY 1875	08:237
AUSTIN, JOHN P & BROWN, ANNA F	23 SEP 1869	06:079
AZBELL, HENRY & ROBSON, GOLDIE M	15 MAY 1901	09:343
BABLE, WILLIAM D & LUELLEN, MYRTIE	24 NOV 1904	10:646
BACCHUS, N V & COLSTON, MOSELLA H	24 JUN 1913	14:185
BACHELOR, CHARLES W & ROSE, ELIZABETH A	25 DEC 1877	09:178
BACKUS, W R & BLACKBURN, SYLVIA GALE	*20 JUN 1910	13:093
BADER, EDWARD & OLIVER, MARY E	29 JUL 1891	06:151
BADGELEY, WILLIAM F & MEADOWS, SARAH C	03 FEB 1873	07:310
BADGLEY, DRURY F & KING, SARAH E	24 AUG 1876	08:379
BADGLEY, ENOCH WILLSON & SMITH, SARAH MARGARET	06 SEP 1889	05:449
BADGLEY, GEORGE & BOWMAN, ELIZABETH	15 OCT 1902	10:172
BADGLEY, HENRY V & SMITH, CHRISTENA E	29 JUL 1894	07:125
BADGLEY, LAUNICE F & WARNER, HALLIE N	16 JUL 1893	06:565
BADGLEY, MARION A & WOLF, VIRGINIA	*12 DEC 1896	08:015
BADGLEY, MARRION A & WOLF, VIRGINIA	09 MAY 1898	08:303
BADGLEY, VANNIE A & DAVIS, SYLVIA E	04 JUL 1911	13:337
BAIER, JACOB D & McCAULEY, IDA M	07 OCT 1891	06:203
BAIER, LEWIS H & KINTZEL, MAGGIE D	30 APR 1893	06:531
BAILES, GEORGE V & FLORAY, ISADORE E	25 OCT 1914	15:305
BAILES, HARVEY & MARTIN, DORA	06 JUL 1905	11:126
BAILES, HUGH S & SLADE, HARRIET	05 DEC 1897	08:208
BAILES, JOHN CURTIS & TUCKER, MADDY	06 OCT 1912	14:013
BAILES, JOSIAH D & CLAGG, SARAH A S	09 JUN 1877	09:096
BAILES, ROSS C & HUDSON, ANNA	24 JAN 1903	10:230
BAILEY, EDGAR & LOVE, ANNETTA	08 NOV 1877	09:154
BAILEY, EDWARD & NEALE, REGINA	28 APR 1877	09:067
BAILEY, EDWIN & HAMILTON, ALVINA	10 APR 1905	11:074
BAILEY, HARVEY D & RYAN, MARY	09 JUL 1865	04:024
BAILEY, HENRY F & COLLINS, ELIZABETH	18 JUN 1883	11:359
BAILEY, JAMES & BEAVER, OLLA	13 MAY 1906	11:311
BAILEY, JAMES & PAYNE, PAMELIA		01:027
BAILEY, JAMES & PAYNE, PAMELIA	1832	01:039
BAILEY, JAMES A & WARNER, MARTHA F	13 DEC 1900	09:247
BAILEY, JAMES E & MASON, MARGARET	28 JUN 1868	05:195
BAILEY, JOHN & PERRY, ELIZABETH	25 OCT 1872	07:276

Name	Date	Ref
BAILEY, LONIE & HELLAM, ROSELLA	29 JAN 1906	11:258
BAILEY, ROBERT W & HILL, FORRIA	24 NOV 1895	07:433
BAILEY, WILLIAM M & McELVAIN, JULIA A	09 MAR 1870	06:164
BAILS, EMMET & WARNER, ELLEN L	17 MAR 1881	10:389
BAILS, HARRY & KELLEY, JULIA A	05 SEP 1878	09:310
BAILS, JOSIAH D & SIDERS, LISETTA	14 FEB 1885	12:140
BAILS, LEWIS P & RAY, MARY	31 MAR 1909	12:391
BAILS, STANTON & STEPHENS, PARMELIA	30 DEC 1881	11:093
BAIRD, ANDREW & CHARLES, MARY C	25 NOV 1885	12:260
BAIRD, HAYES & MAYES, RETHA ELLEN	08 OCT 1900	09:218
BAKER, ABRAHAM & McGUIRE, ANN	14 FEB 1849	01:050
BAKER, ABRAHAM & SAYRE, SYLVIA	01 JUN 1913	14:160
BAKER, ARTHUR STROAT & PINNICK, MARTHA ELIZABETH	22 SEP 1886	12:390
BAKER, ARTHUR S & PINNICK, MARTHA E	22 SEP 1886	12:398
BAKER, BENJAMIN F & ROBERTS, ELIZA J	20 APR 1870	06:180
BAKER, CLEAS J & BEATTIE, MAGGIE	08 MAR 1881	10:379
BAKER, ELI J & LAINE, LILLIE	08 JAN 1898	08:242
BAKER, ELI V & BOWERS, ELLEN	17 FEB 1878	09:216
BAKER, GEORGE & McCLURE, MAGGIE C	17 MAY 1908	12:177
BAKER, GEORGE C & YAUGER, BYANTHA	05 OCT 1898	08:379
BAKER, GEORGE C & LIVINGSTON, TACY C	07 SEP 1903	10:356
BAKER, HARRY & BRIGHT, LUELLA	10 MAR 1911	13:289
BAKER, J G & BARR, DIANAH	21 JUL 1898	08:337
BAKER, JASPER C & BARR, NANCY B	04 NOV 1897	08:189
BAKER, JOHN G & BUTCHER, LYDA J	12 SEP 1910	13:156
BAKER, JOHN J & HENSON, SARAH	28 MAY 1876	08:358
BAKER, JOHN M & HARPER, MARTHA J	25 JUN 1880	10:272
BAKER, MOSES L & STONE, ORA	19 SEP 1908	12:266
BAKER, RICHARD & PERRY, MARGARET	13 JAN 1875	08:202
BAKER, SAMUEL & HEWIT, CAROLINE	05 OCT 1871	07:128
BAKER, SAMUEL I & PAINTER, ISA	10 SEP 1901	09:400
BAKER, SAMUEL V & BATEMAN, IDELLA	06 AUG 1899	08:589
BAKER, V & CULVER, M B	19 DEC 1909	12:571
BAKER, WILLIAM A & BENNETT, EDITH B	28 DEC 1902	10:218
BALCH, JOSEPH & BETTINGER, KATHARINE	20 MAY 1895	07:297
BALDWIN, ALBERT J & PLATT, MATILDA	19 DEC 1881	11:055
BALDWIN, CHARLES R & LEWIS, MARY JANE	26 DEC 1833	01:028
BALDWIN, JAMES A & McQUAID, MARY E P	20 NOV 1899	09:022
BALES, GEORGE & CLARK, MAY G	10 NOV 1907	12:064
BALL, ANDREW T & SCARBERRY, MARTHA J	07 SEP 1884	12:053
BALL, C C & CHAMBERS, MATTIE	17 AUG 1905	11:134
BALL, DAVID G & WOODY, VIOLA	14 SEP 1898	08:363
BALL, DAVIS H & McCALLISTER, ORPHA	*03 NOV 1858	02:011
BALL, ELIAS & KAY, EVA C	23 AUG 1883	11:390
BALL, GURTY E & FRY, IVY M	05 MAY 1903	10:283
BALL, GURTY E & BALL, CORA F	30 JAN 1908	12:123
BALL, GURTY E & SMITH, RACHEL	01 MAR 1911	13:281
BALL, HARRISON EDGAR & MEADOWS, ABIGAIL	25 FEB 1881	10:377
BALL, HARRISON E & FLETCHER, LEFAVOR	09 JAN 1901	09:275
BALL, IRA WESLEY & BEARD, MARY AMSY	13 MAR 1888	05:194
BALL, ISAAC H & WALLIS, SARAH E	08 SEP 1867	05:079
BALL, JAMES & LOVE, MARTHA ANN	18 NOV 1847	01:047
BALL, JAMES & BALLINGER, RIXEY	28 NOV 1889	05:487
BALL, JAMES E & CREMEENS, BERTHA D	15 AUG 1894	07:135
BALL, JAMES E & MILLER, DELTA V	21 NOV 1909	12:548
BALL, JAMES H & WAUGH, SARAH ELLEN	29 APR 1890	05:550
BALL, JAMES R & HART, FIDELIA	25 APR 1872	07:217
BALL, JAMES W & LOCK, JULIA A	06 MAY 1861	03:004

BALL, JOHN H & COBB, ELLA	06 MAR 1873	07:331
BALL, JOHN W & HOFFMAN, LAURA A	13 JUN 1872	07:234
BALL, LEWIS T & YEAGER, ANNA L	31 DEC 1893	07:034
BALL, OTHER L & JORDAN, MAGGIE M	06 DEC 1899	09:028
BALL, ROBERT H & SOMERVILLE, MARY ANN	*10 SEP 1855	02:007
BALL, ROY & ROWSEY, MYRTLE M	13 APR 1912	13:508
BALL, THOMAS & HOGG, JULIA ANN	21 AUG 1828	01:018
BALL, THOMAS & BLESSING, MARY ANN	04 APR 1850	01:052
BALL, THOMAS E & GEORGE, MARY F	08 DEC 1863	03:209
BALL, THOMAS H & DAILEY, GRACE E	09 SEP 1900	09:194
BALL, WESTLY & JONES, ELIZABETH	21 DEC 1826	01:015
BALL, WILLIAM E & HOFFMAN, SARAH A	08 JAN 1871	07:041
BALL, WILLIAM M & ADKINS, NORA	25 JUL 1895	07:348
BALL, WILLIAM P & STATEN, ROZELLA	10 DEC 1889	06:126
BALLARD, LEWIS & WEIRS, ANN	08 JUN 1891	06:123
BANDY, EDWARD L & CHERRINGTON, LILLIE	30 AUG 1907	11:603
BANKER, MORREL D & DELANEY, LEE D	03 JUL 1907	11:568
BANKS, CHARLES & GILES, MILLIE	18 MAY 1911	13:319
BANKS, EDWARD D & WATKINS, MAGGIE	18 MAY 1907	11:522
BANKS, MORGAN J & BROWN, ALICE M	05 APR 1905	11:069
BANNISTER, PEYTON & BARNITT, ELIZABETH	1830	01:024
BANNISTER, THOMAS & GWYNN, ANNIE	08 OCT 1895	07:402
BARBEE, ANDREW R & THOMPSON, M A G	*17 MAY 1852	02:003
BARBER, BYRON C & SHREWSBURY, HATTIE C	29 SEP 1896	07:620
BARBER, LEWIS & BOARDMAN, MARY J	04 OCT 1895	07:400
BABER, MARTIN & JONES, ELIZABETH ANN	21 JUN 1843	01:037
BABER, TIMOTHY L & COUCH, SARAH R	30 NOV 1882	11:261
BARCUS, RICHARD W & CROUSE, MYRTLE	15 SEP 1906	11:407
BARGAR, ERASTUS C & HAYS, IVA G	**09 APR 1898	08:287
BARGER, JAMES R & COLEMAN, IDA MAY	29 APR 1899	08:520
BARKER, EDWARD RAY & CARTWRIGHT, HELEN RUTH	23 FEB 1913	14:095
BARKER, GEORGE & SAXTON, MIRTY	22 FEB 1890	05:526
BARKER, ORIS & CUNNINGHAM, MARY E	03 NOV 1913	15:024
BARKER, ROBERT L & LEWIS, MYRTIE	02 FEB 1893	06:482
BARKER, VIRGIL & HOLLEY, EVA	03 SEP 1905	11:163
BARKER, WILLIAM H & WOODS, LETHA M	08 SEP 1885	12:220
BARKER, WILLIAM T & HAYMAN, HARRIET A	29 DEC 1878	10:033
BARNARD, ELIAS & SARGENT, MARY D	27 JUN 1872	07:240
BARNES, THERON & WAGGENER, MILLY	*23 OCT 1851	02:002
BARNET, WILLIAM & ALLEN, BETSY	01 MAY 1817	01:003
BARNETT, A A & ROBINSON, (Mrs) MAUD	03 FEB 1912	13:478
BARNETT, A J & STONE, BELLE I	26 DEC 1910	13:237
BARNETT, BENJAMIN B & NEWMAN, MARGARET E	24 OCT 1878	09:341
BARNETT, CAMDEN C & PICKENS, BERTIE V	15 FEB 1900	09:081
BARNETT, EDGAR H & MURRAY, MAUDE	13 OCT 1910	13:183
BARNETT, ELLIOTT E & HILL, MARTHA ANN	*02 APR 1855	02:006
BARNETT, ELVA R & WRAY, SADIE F	08 JAN 1909	12:357
BARNETT, IRA R & WRAY, SADIE F	26 JAN 1909	12:356
BARNETT, FISHER & HYATT, REBECCA JANE	*03 DEC 1860	02:014
BARNETT, FRANCIS L & BARNETT, GEORGIANA	21 NOV 1889	05:484
BARNETT, FRANCIS LINCOLN & COSSIN, GEORGIA	27 JUL 1901	09:371
BARNETT, GEORGE WASHINGTON & HALL, LURY ELLA	25 DEC 1895	07:467
BARNETT, HARRY B & STEWART, NELLIE	02 JUN 1906	11:332
BARNETT, HENRY & SCANTLING, MARGARET	14 JAN 1869	06:028
BARNETT, JAMES & OLDAKERS, REBECCA ANN	01 JAN 1846	01:046
BARNETT, JAMES L & LEMASTER, ARABELL	04 NOV 1886	12:414
BARNETT, JOHN & CARTER, NANCY	1831	01:025
BARNETT, JOHN ELSWORTH & STOVER, MARY CATHARINE	25 DEC 1892	06:455

BARNETT, JOHN W & HILL, ROXY ANN	*01 NOV 1856	02:009
BARNETT, LEON R & SCHOOLS, LOVINE F	27 NOV 1910	13:215
BARNETT, LEWIS & BOYD, MATILDA	16 JUN 1886	12:337
BARNETT, OLIVER P & CARTER, MARY E	06 APR 1876	08:343
BARNETT, ROBERT & RAYBURN, BETSEY	11 NOV 1824	01:010
BARNETT, ROBERT & BOORUM, EMILY	1838	01:032
BARNETT, SAMUEL & GREENLEE, REBECCA ANN	*30 JAN 1854	02:005
BARNETT, SHERMAN BEVERLY & HILL, RUCY BELLE	01 JUN 1890	05:566
BARNETT, STEPHEN & LEWIS, PRISCILLA	*05 MAY 1891	06:104
BARNETT, THOMAS & STEELE, MARY M	27 MAR 1870	06:170
BARNETT, WILLIAM & FONLY, SUSAN	10 FEB 1828	01:017
BARNETT, WILLIAM & HARRISON, MARY	24 FEB 1848	01:048
BARNETT, WILLIAM & MARTIN, ELIZABETH M	30 APR 1865	04:010
BARNETT, WILLIAM & ARNOLD, SUSAN	10 MAR 1889	05:365
BARNETT, WILLIAM & WINGET, ALMA	09 NOV 1899	09:010
BARNETT, WILLIAM A & LITTLE, ELIZABETH	22 NOV 1866	05:003
BARNETT, WILLIAM U & LOVETT, PHEBE	21 NOV 1839	01:032 5
BARNETT, WINTEN W & PIERCE, MARY	28 JUL 1892	06:377
BARNEY, JAMES & STEEL, JANE	26 SEP 1872	07:266
BARNHOUSE, JEREMIAH & HUGHES, ANNIE ROSETTA	29 MAY 1887	05:030
BARNITT, WILLIAM & FONLY, SARAH	1831	01:026
BARR, FRANK C & WALKER, LAURA	25 NOV 1909	12:544
BARR, ISAAC & CAMPBELL, MARY	06 JAN 1825	01:012
BARR, LOUIS A & WEATHERS, DAISY	16 OCT 1909	12:531
BARR, WILLIAM & SEBRELL, BLANCHE	11 FEB 1897	08:043
BARRETT, DANIEL & MARTIN, MARY A	29 DEC 1870	07:036
BARRETT, DANIEL & HARRIGAN, REBECCA A	25 DEC 1881	11:085
BARRETT, PATRICK & WILSON, ANNABELLA	22 APR 1873	07:313
BARRETT, WILLIAM H & CLAGG, SARAH F	29 JAN 1880	10:203
BARRETT, WILLIAM H & PICKENS, VIOLA	15 MAR 1896	07:512
BARRINGER, GEORGE A & KIRKPATRICK, MARTHA E	18 APR 1895	07:281
BARRINGER, GEORGE WASHINGTON & McGREW, IDELLA	30 JUN 1889	05:419
BARRINGER, PETER & CROOKHAM, LULA	17 AUG 1910	13:132
BARRINGER, WILLIAM & ROUSH, BARBARA	03 DEC 1835	01:030
BARROWS, E L & RIPLEY, ANNA	13 NOV 1883	11:423
BARROWS, FRANKLIN A & HILL, VENITIA E	02 JAN 1879	10:038
BARROWS, GEORGE A & HEREFORD, MARY A	27 DEC 1871	07:163
BARROWS, GEORGE A & DEAL, IRENA B	27 JUL 1903	10:325
BARROWS, HERMAN E & JAMES, MYRTLE B	01 FEB 1893	06:481
BARROWS, ISAAC P & ALLEN, MINNIE M	01 JAN 1891	06:038
BARROWS, ISAAC P & RIFFLE, SARAH M	19 FEB 1905	11:046
BARTLES, HENRY FREDRICK & ROUSH, MARTHA	25 OCT 1891	06:211
BARTHALP, JNO & VAN MATRE, MARTHA	22 DEC 1836	01:030
BARTLETT, ASA J & DENNIE, ALICE J	*25 OCT 1906	11:438
BARTLETT, GRANT & LAWSON, EVA A	20 MAY 1891	06:111
BARTLETT, RICE H & SWON, SARAH	*21 NOV 1855	02:007
BARTLETT, SYLVANUS C & FRY, EFFA M	30 AUG 1896	07:598
BARTON, ELZA D & BARROWS, BESSIE E	31 DEC 1895	07:476
BARTON, GEORGE R & QUILLEN, MATTIE C	13 OCT 1880	10:311
BARTON (Dr), THOMAS H & NEWMAN, MARTHA M	*07 SEP 1853	02:004
BARTRAM, EDWARD G & MAYES, MINNIE	07 APR 1896	07:525
BARTRAM, MILTON & STEELE, LILLIE M	14 JAN 1900	09:065
BARTRAM, SAMUEL F & HOBBS, BERTHA	16 JUN 1905	11:111
BARTRUM, ALBERT & ASBERY, FANNIE CAMPBELL	15 FEB 1889	05:354
BARTRUM, DAVID & WAMSLEY, MARY ALICE	13 MAR 1900	09:096
BARTRUM, GEORGE H & SULLIVAN, MAGGIE F	19 APR 1905	11:079
BASHORE, FRANK & REFSNYDER, ERMA	12 MAY 1906	11:314
BASKETT, JESSE A & BEALE, SARAH E	*29 OCT 1850	02:001

BASS, EPHRAIM & HOVER, (Mrs) MARY	*17 OCT 1857	02:010
BASS, EPHRAIM & MOOR, JANE	10 MAR 1868	05:153
BASS, FRANCIS M & RICKARD, MARY C	26 DEC 1878	10:025
BASS, FRANKLIN P & MOORE, ELIZABETH	04 JUN 1871	07:093
BASS, FRANKLIN P & ROUSH, LAURA	25 DEC 1882	11:273
BASS, GEORGE M & RICKARD, BARBARA E	27 AUG 1885	12:216
BASS, GEORGE W & GIBBS, MARY E	30 JUN 1878	09:280
BASS, GEORGE W & WHEELER, ELLEN	25 SEP 1892	06:414
BASS, JAMES & CUNDIFF, MARY FRANCES	16 OCT 1890	05:623
BASS, JAMES A & CONOWAY, FANNIE	22 JUL 1877	09:110
BASS, JEREMIAH & YEAGER, MATILDA	19 SEP 1875	08:273
BASS, JOHN D & CAMPBELL, ELIZABETH	30 JUN 1876	08:262
BASS, JOSEPH G & ZURKLE, CANILLA	24 DEC 1885	12:270
BASS, LEWIS E & MOORE, MERLEY	01 AUG 1909	12:471
BASS, PHILIP S & COOPER, RACHEL F	28 OCT 1882	11:235
BASS, PHILIP SHERIDAN & WOODY, MAMIE AUGUSTA	20 FEB 1889	05:358
BASS, ROBERT O & MORNING, SARAH	03 DEC 1910	13:219
BASS, TAYLOR HARRISON & KLASS, ALICE E	30 JUN 1892	06:358
BASS, THOMAS HENRY & FRY, SARAH FRANCES	29 DEC 1897	08:226
BASS, WILLIAM H & ANDERSON, ISABELLE	23 FEB 1871	07:055
BASS, ZOAS HENSLEY & EDWARDS, IDA MAY	28 AUG 1887	05:082
BATEMAN, BOYD & LONG, LEARNER	27 OCT 1907	12:054
BATEMAN, DOCK & WHITTINGTON, BETTIE	22 FEB 1900	09:089
BATEMAN, EDWARD HOMER & HALL, MALINDA CATHARINE	13 SEP 1891	06:182
BATEMAN, GEORGE & LEMASTERS, NORMA MAY	17 JUL 1914	15:243
BATEMAN, GROVER C & JORDAN, MURTLE L	24 DEC 1906	11:481
BATEMAN, JOHN & DABNEY, MARY E	21 JUL 1872	07:247
BATEMAN, JOHN H & MAYSE, ELIZABETH T	*10 DEC 1855	02:007
BATEMAN, JOHN W & CASEY, MAHOLA V	03 OCT 1880	10:306
BATEMAN, JOHN WILBERT & DAWES, IRENE	17 SEP 1893	06:607
BATEMAN, LEWIS H & GILLISPIE, SARAH E	26 FEB 1891	06:065
BATEMAN, ROBERT W & TERRY, SARAH C	05 DEC 1894	07:203
BATEMAN, SAMUEL S & SHIELDS, SARAH E	22 SEP 1884	12:059
BATEMAN, THOMAS & McCALLISTER, IDILLA	21 NOV 1885	12:255
BATEMAN, WILLIAM & WITHERS, MARY JANE	22 OCT 1840	01:032.5
BATERAL, COLUMBUS C & McGARVEY, LUCINDA	*22 JUL 1850	02:003
BATES, CHARLES W & DAIGH, ELLA M	25 JUN 1898	08:325
BATES, ED L & THOMAS, VIRGIE	18 JUN 1896	07:568
BATES, EDWARD M & FROST, LENA	16 FEB 1894	07:049
BATES, FLEMING & ROBERTS, LOUISA	07 JAN 1873	07:304
BATES, JOHN W & RAYBOULD, ANNA E	09 JUL 1907	11:576
BATES, LEMUEL & MORROW, EMILY J	05 NOV 1882	11:242
BATES, LEMUEL & WAMSLEY, NANCY M	22 FEB 1892	06:289
BATES, WILLIAM & HENRY, ADALINE	16 JAN 1878	09:201
BATEY, JAMES & SANDERS, MAGGIE	15 FEB 1897	08:039
BATEY, JOSPHY M & BOARD, CORA	20 AUG 1902	10:132
BATTERSON, ELMER C & DUNCAN, ALICE	12 FEB 1891	06:054
BATTERSON, JOSEPH & McBRIEN, JANE	*25 AUG 1859	02:013
BATTIE, ANDREW WILSON & SMITH, REBECCA	21 APR 1892	06:326
BATTRELL, CHARLES H & COSSIN, MATILDA	24 DEC 1896	08:021
BATTRELL, FRANCIS E & McDERMITT, CHLOE A	*09 APR 1860	02:014
BATTRELL, JOHN W & BURNSIDE, MARY	*12 NOV 1859	02:013
BATTRELL, WILLIAM E & WALKER, AMELIA M	23 OCT 1895	07:413
BATY, JAMES & ROUSH, ROSA	17 APR 1884	12:004
BAUER, FRANK & MILLS, ELLEN	01 MAR 1887	12:486
BAUER, FREDERICK J & MARTIN, MARY M	31 DEC 1878	10:037
BAUER, VALLIE & DURST, ELIZABETH R	18 DEC 1912	14:056
BAUM, JOHN J & NEVILLE, SAMANTHA J	08 DEC 1873	01:067

Names	Date	Ref
BAUMAN, LINDSEY & OVERSHINER, MARGARET	19 JUN 1836	01:029
BAUMGARNER, CALVIN S & FIELDS, MARY	05 JUL 1856	04:138
BAXTER, CHANCELLOR H & GILL, GARNET E	31 JUL 1907	11:586
BAXTER, WM H & MARTIN, ADDA	17 SEP 1890	05:614
BAYRUN, REESE G & BOYER, MARY M	25 MAY 1873	07:351
BAYS, HARRISON & FETTY, GERTIE	30 APR 1912	13:507
BAYS, HERBERT E & VANCE, LEOLA	24 DEC 1905	11:232
BAYS, JOSEPH C & SHULER, SAMARIA	**09 DEC 1912	14:049
BAYS, J C & SHULER, SAMARIA	14 DEC 1913	15:086
BEABOUT, WM H & HILL, GEORGIA	20 MAY 1913	14:151
BEAGLE, DAVID & SMITH, MARTHA J E	03 NOV 1877	09:150
BEAL, GEORGE & GINDER, MARY	12 NOV 1900	09:237
BEALE, CHARLES T & STEENBERGEN, ELLEN D	30 MAY 1872	07:228
BEALE, JAMES M & WILEY, JANE R	17 NOV 1852	02:007
BEALE, RICHARD & WILSON, HANNA	09 JAN 1818	01:004
BEALE, WILLIAM & MOORE, LAVINA	*20 DEC 1852	02:003
BEALL, NEIL PRESTON & LUSHER, BONNIE ELIZABETH	09 OCT 1913	15:042
BEARD, ADAM G & CROUCH, SARAH E	*31 OCT 1872	08:051
BEARD, ADDISON M & GREENLEE, MARY J	19 NOV 1874	08:185
BEARD, CALVIN JABEZ Jr & KINCADE, MARY MARTHA	29 DEC 1887	05:165
BEARD, CHARLES THOMAS & ROWSEY, ELLEN FRANCES	09 JUL 1890	05:588
BEARD, J C & DALTON, MARGUERITE	24 NOV 1911	13:428
BEARD, JABEZ & CROUCH, MARTHA JANE	*14 MAR 1856	02:008
BEARD, JABEZ C & CAUFMAN, LOIS A	16 AUG 1903	10:338
BEARD, JOHN & STEELE, SALLIE ANN	*09 MAR 1858	02:010
BEARD, JOHN & DINGY, CORA	27 MAY 1896	07:556
BEARD, JOHN C & WILLIAMSON, ELIZABETH	19 MAY 1914	15:197
BEATGOOD, JOHN & HAYSE, LIDDIA	(no date)	01:027
BEATTIE, ANDREW W & RAY, OSA	14 APR 1900	09:322
BEATTIE, JAMES & KING, SUSAN	03 SEP 1908	12:224
BEATTIE, JOHN W & STUTLER, MINNIE	13 OCT 1907	12:037
BEAVER, GEORGE N & WHITT, SUSANNA M	12 NOV 1889	05:478
BEAVER, GRANT & LANIER, MARIA Z	04 OCT 1908	12:276
BEAVER, V & AMSBARRY, SARAH F	13 OCT 1898	08:384
BEAVER, RICHARD & RUNNION, MARTHA J	03 DEC 1872	07:296
BEAVER, RICHARD M & PURDY, CORNELIA M	09 MAY 1899	08:531
BEAVER, WASHINGTON S & MYERS, SOPHRONIA C	07 DEP 1880	10:299
BEAVER, WILLIAM EDISON & SAYRE, KATHERINE	30 MAY 1913	14:162
BEAVER, WILLIAM S & McCOY, MENA	16 FEB 1895	07:254
BEBBY, ELIJAH & WRIGHT, MARY	09 FEB 1820	01:006
BEBEE, DANIEL CONTEC & SANNS, NETTIE MASON	23 JUN 1901	09:360
BECHTLE, CHARLES E & DABNEY, GERTRUDE L	21 SEP 1904	10:603
BECHTLE, GRANVILLE M & HALFHILL, LOLA A	07 OCT 1905	11:181
BECHTLE, WILBUR M & SHELINE, SYBILL D	18 NOV 1910	13:211
BECK, ALFRED & CROSSLEY, ELIZABETH	21 SEP 1881	11:021
BECK, DANIEL & WARD, ELIZABETH	18 MAR 1826	01:013
BECK, SAMUEL K & LEMASTERS, MARY	02 JUN 1909	12:423
BECKET, JOHN & JONES, MARY	25 JUL 1816	01:004
BECKETT, HENRY M & MOORE, MATTIE A	04 OCT 1905	11:184
BECKNER, MICHAEL & STANLEY, HANNAH	05 APR 1909	12:396
BECKWITH, ALFRED & AMOSS, JANE	26 APR 1836	01:029
BECKWITH, GLEN E & SAYRE, EVA	15 JUL 1908	12:215
BEHAN, ISAAC & ANDERSON, ANN	02 MAR 1838	01:032
BELKNAP, FRANK L & ROSEBERRY, ROSALIE	01 JAN 1893	06:463
BELL, CHARLES & DEEM, MARY M	20 SEP 1871	07:121
BELL, CHARLES W & BLACKWELL, CORA	14 SEP 1882	11:205
BELL, CHARLES WILLIAM & JACKSON, ANNIE	09 MAY 1909	11:528
BELL, FRANCIS R & DAY, CARRIE H	25 OCT 1897	08:181

Names	Date	Ref
BELL, JOSEPH G & BUSH, MYRTLE D	09 OCT 1901	09:420
BELL, ROBERT F & KUHN, NINA A	18 JAN 1914	15:119
BELL, ROBERT PIERRE & STEINBACH, KATHERINE LEONORA	01 JUN 1909	12:421
BELLER, CHARLES PETER & SMITH, FANNY	07 APR 1889	05:379
BELLER, JOHN EDWARD & BEHAN, GRACE	13 OCT 1889	05:118
BELLER, WILLIAM ELISHA & WILLIAMS, MARY C (BURNELL)	30 SEP 1891	06:197
BELTZ, ADAM & HARDY, MARGARET A	01 MAR 1871	07:059
BENJAMIN, ARTHUR & BRYAN, JOANNA ALICE	20 JUL 1896	07:583
BENNER, JOHN H & OLDAKER, MARGARET	24 SEP 1878	09:320
BENNET, (Dr) JESSE & FOWLER, HARRIET	17 FEB 1833	01:028
BENNETT, BENJAMIN & HILL, JOSEPHINE	27 FEB 1863	03:114
BENNETT, CARL & DURST, LIZZIE A	*23 NOV 1908	12:313
BENNETT, CHARLES H & SPENCER, ELLEN A	13 AUG 1879	10:111
BENNETT, CRAYTON & KIMBERLING, JOANNA	17 DEC 1874	08:106
BENNETT, EDWARD A & OLIVER, ETHEL PEARL	10 AUG 1901	09:381
BENNETT, FRANK & GARDNER, MARY	25 DEC 1899	09:049
BENNETT, GEORGE W & MONROE, VIRGINIA	03 NOV 1898	08:399
BENNETT, HARRY B & HOWARD, MARILL K	10 AUG 1913	15:007
BENNETT, HENRY & JONES, JOSEPHINE	10 JUL 1892	06:367
BENNETT, JOHN J & NEALE, LOU	05 FEB 1885	12:134
BENNETT, LEWIS E & RIFFLE, NELLIE J	26 APR 1897	08:081
BENNETT, MACK & HOLLAND, NELLIE G	24 OCT 1898	08:394
BENNETT, RICHARD & ROOT, ANNETTE	07 APR 1868	05:162
BENNETT, SOLOMON S & WOOD, ANNIE E	23 JUN 1904	10:546
BENNETT, WAID & SMITH, SARAH	14 JUN 1900	09:141
BENSON, JOHN & CLONCH, MARTHA	21 SEP 1904	10:604
BENTZ, FRED M & POWELL, TESSA	28 OCT 1911	13:404
BENTZ, JONAS W & JONES, INEZ	24 FEB 1897	08:052
BERKLEY, ALFRED W & DODSON, TENA	02 SEP 1900	09:182
BERKLEY, FREDRICK H & BLAND, SUSAN M	31 DEC 1905	11:240
BERKLEY, HARVEY Z & FOWLER, ELIZABETH C	25 NOV 1903	10:415
BERKLEY, WILLIAM H & EADS, MARY J	10 AUG 1871	07:108
BERRIDGE, CARL & THEVENIN, EMMA	27 MAY 1902	10:079
BERRIDGE, CHRISTOPHER & DAUGHERTY, VIRGINIA C	27 FEB 1849	01:051
BERRY, ALBERT J & RIFFLE, SADIE	25 NOV 1911	13:426
BERRY, WILEY & WITHERS, SARAH L	05 JUL 1886	12:353
BESSIE, OWEN & McCOY, ANGELINE	15 JAN 1893	06:470
BETTINGER, C A & THOMAS, ELIZABETH	10 OCT 1883	11:409
BETZING, JOSEPH & O'NEILL, CLARA E	03 NOV 1901	09:437
BIBBEE, PAUL H & ROUSE, SARAH F	21 OCT 1891	06:208
BICHMAN, WILLIAM & MEES, ANNA MARGARET	20 JAN 1901	09:280
BICKEL, CHAD W & BAKER, MARGARET	04 JUL 1878	09:283
BICKEL, NEWTON D & ORR, EVA C D	18 DEC 1902	10:227
BIGGS, ALVIN D & DECKER, FANNY L	30 OCT 1914	15:309
BIGGS, BENJAMIN & RICHARDSON, ELIZA H	*22 DEC 1856	02:009
BILLINGSLEY, RICHARD & GILLIS, CORA B	27 FEB 1892	06:297
BILLINGSLY, BENJAMIN & BARRETT, MARY E	30 DEC 1893	07:033
BIRCH, HENRY & OLDACRE, JANE	19 APR 1827	01:016
BIRCHFIELD, CHARLES & HAWKINS, LAURA	09 JUN 1914	15:215
BIRCHFIELD, ELI & POTTS, DORA	04 FEB 1908	12:125
BIRCHFIELD, GEORGE & SMITH, EVALINA	06 SEP 1900	09:197
BIRCHFIELD, GEORGE E & ECKARD, SALLIE R	14 SEP 1907	12:011
BIRCHFIELD, HENRY S & HUGHES, ELIZABETH W	05 FEB 1890	05:515
BIRCHFIELD, JAMES C & COMPSTON, MAGGIE R	28 MAY 1899	08:544
BIRCHFIELD, JAMES M & SAUER, EDITH MAY	24 SEP 1913	15:039
BIRCHFIELD, JOHN & HAYES, SARAH	22 MAY 1908	12:181
BIRCHFIELD, JOHN & LEMASTER, BLANCH	30 DEC 1914	15:363
BIRCHFIELD, NATHANIEL Jr & LEWIS, AMERICA	16 FEB 1868	05:141

Name	Date	Ref
BIRCHFIELD, NATHEN J & COLLINS, SARAH	20 NOV 1907	12:071
BIRCHFIELD, OSCO & ROBINSON, ELIZABETH	28 SEP 1895	07:395
BIRCHFIELD, SELDON & SHELINE, MARY	30 OCT 1898	08:397
BIRCHFIELD, THOMAS & GLASSBURN, MAGGIE C	09 AUG 1905	11:145
BIRCHFIELD, WADE H & DUNN, ELIZA J	17 MAY 1881	10:414
BIRCHFIELD, WILLIAM G & MARTIN, NORA C	08 MAR 1906	11:277
BIRD, CHARLES W & BROWN, MARY	13 OCT 1863	03:137
BIRD, WILLIAM C & FOWLER, VICTORIA	01 JAN 1882	11:092
BIRD, WILLIAM G & CABLE, HATTIE M	07 JUN 1899	08:548
BIRTHISEL, FRANK H & THOMAS, NORA	15 APR 1900	09:110
BISHOP, ELSWORTH M & CHERINGTON, DELLA M	09 MAY 1908	12:176
BISHOP, VIRGIL B & MILLER, MINNIE J	21 OCT 1885	12:242
BITGOOD, JOHN T & HAYSE, LYDIA	1832	01:039
BITZ, CHARLES M & POLSLEY, ELIZA V	25 APR 1894	07:079
BIXLER, WM L W & LAVENDER, (Mrs) ADDA M	12 MAR 1911	13:290
BLACK, ALEXANDER & IRVIN, ROSIE	17 MAR 1895	07:269
BLACK, CHARLES R & GRIMM, FLOSSIE M	03 JUL 1908	12:205
BLACK, DAVIS & ROWSEY, DELILAH M	13 APR 1893	06:520
BLACK, EDWARD E & SAYRE, (Mrs) IVA M	17 JUN 1912	13:547
BLACK, EMBERSON & BLACK, MARY B	29 APR 1905	11:081
BLACK, JACOB & AMOS, ELIZABETH	05 OCT 1847	01:048
BLACK, JAMES O & WARTENBURG, CORA M	29 APR 1905	11:084
BLACK, JAMES R & CHAPMAN, SARAH C	26 MAR 1899	08:486
BLACK, JEFFERSON & CREMEANS, REBECCA J	04 APR 1887	05:009
BLACK, JEROME & BUSH, LILLIE	19 OCT 1899	08:362
BLACK, JOHN & ROLLINS, ANGELINE	19 OCT 1876	08:400
BLACK, JOHN A & BUMGARNER, GEORGIA G	16 OCT 1906	11:431
BLACK, JOSEPH & HAYMAN, ALMIRA	31 OCT 1872	07:283
BLACK, KYE & SMITH, ANNIE	18 FEB 1906	11:267
BLACK, LEANDER & HOLLY, ETTIE V	10 DEC 1891	06:243
BLACK, PETER A & BARRETT, ANNA M	19 NOV 1872	07:290
BLACK, PETER ALEXANDER & EGAN, CORA JACKSON	*26 DEC 1891	06:264
BLACK, PETER A & POLK, ETTIE	18 JUN 1892	06:351
BLACK, PHILIP & HUMPHREYS, ELIZABETH	29 SEP 1872	07:268
BLACK, RALPH W & EDWARDS, MARY	15 AUG 1869	06:083
BLACK, RICHARD J & HESSEN, TEXA ANN	25 FEB 1899	08:471
BLACK, WILSON & WEAVER, MARY V	10 OCT 1875	08:286
BLACKBURN, CECIL C & RUNION, HATTIE	21 JAN 1914	15:126
BLACKBURN, J H & SHIVELY, EMMA	23 DEC 1911	13:447
BLACKBURN, JAMES A & DURST, SUSAN	09 MAY 1869	06:059
BLACKBURN, WILLIAM E & CLICK, CHARLOTTIE	27 DEC 1899	09:053
BLACKMORE, CHARLES W & POWELL, FANNIE BELLE	14 AUG 1898	08:341
BLACKWELL, BEVERLY & TEMPLES, HANNA J	25 DEC 1871	07:169
BLACKWELL, JAMES R & EVANS, LIZZIE	30 APR 1912	13:523
BLACKWELL, WILLIAM & BRONAUGH, MARY A	12 AUG 1819	01:006
BLACKWOOD, CHARLES KENTON & NEALE, MARGARET LEWIS	27 JUN 1900	09:148
BLAGG, DONALD O & KNOPP, ANNIE L	01 JUL 1909	12:445
BLAIN, BYRD O & AUSTIN, DONLEY	08 NOV 1908	12:302
BLAIN, C E & LOCKHART, KATE C	19 AUG 1913	15:013
BLAIN, CALVIN R & PIERSON, EFFIE M	25 FEB 1903	10:246
BLAIN, CHARLES A & SHANK, MINA M	16 JAN 1897	08:037
BLAIN, CHARLES B & GWYNN, DESSA M	25 DEC 1881	11:066
BLAIN, FONNIE E & AUSTIN, EFFIE A	05 NOV 1905	11:196
BLAIN, FRANCIS ELLSWORTH & ROLLINS, LOUISA EVALINE	19 MAY 1889	05:399
BLAIN, HUGH DAIGH & JOHNSON, LAURIE ELLEN	08 OCT 1895	07:403
BLAIN, STERLING P & LOCKHART, EMMA	07 NOV 1894	07:184
BLAIN, WILLIAM H & SWISHER, ELLA	26 JAN 1882	11:102
BLAIN, ZERAH & DAIGH, AMANDA	*04 SEP 1854	02:005

BLAIN, ZERAH T J & MULFORD, MARY J	19 SEP 1877	09:131
BLAINE, JAMES G & HUMPHREYS, E GRACE	03 SEP 1905	11:156
BLAKE, ANDREW H & SUMMERS, SUSAN ANN	05 AUG 1834	01:028
BLAKE, CHARLES H & TOLLIVER, EVA	17 FEB 1912	13:482
BLAKE, CHARLES I & SUMMERS, AMANDA	24 DEC 1880	10:357
BLAKE, CLARENCE B & BLETNER, ELLEN MAE	08 MAY 1910	13:057
BLAKE, CLAUDE & HOLLEY, DORCAS	26 OCT 1904	10:622
BLAKE, CYRUS T & McCLAIN, MARGARET J	06 JUN 1861	03:006
BLAKE, GEORGE W & FERGUSON, HESTHER	10 NOV 1877	09:155
BLAKE, GEORGE W & LEPORT, JENNIE	09 SEP 1908	12:256
BLAKE, GROVER & WAUGH, MARY	18 JUN 1902	10:089
BLAKE, JOHN C & BURCHARD, FLORA	21 MAY 1871	07:086
BLAKE, JOHN E & ROUSH, ICIE	13 MAY 1901	09:338
BLAKE, JOHN L & McCOLLISTER, MARY J	10 AUG 1865	04:037
BLAKE, JOHN L & MEADOWS, DAISY	14 MAR 1909	12:381
BLAKE, JOHN W & HOLLY, MARY	*19 JUL 1860	02:014
BLAKE, MILES L & HALL, MARIETTA	03 JUN 1868	05:184
BLAKE, MORDECAI & DAVIES, MARY	24 DEC 1888	05:330
BLAKE, WHIRLEY W & JARVIS, STELLA	14 NOV 1909	12:541
BLAKE, WILLIAM & BRYAN, SARAH A	06 MAY 1872	07:222
BLAKE, WILLIAM H & HOGSETT, CLARA E	31 OCT 1893	06:637
BLAKEMORE, ISAAC & GREENLEE, MARY	*05 MAY 1860	02:014
BLAKENSHIP, WILLIAM H & WILLIAMS, JOSEPHINE	*01 NOV 1860	02:014
BLAND, GEORGE W & PICKENS, ALLIE M	14 APR 1910	13:042
BLAND, J WALTER & BASS, ELCA M	23 OCT 1909	12:534
BLAND, JOHN ELDRIDGE & ELLIOTT, SALINDA CATHERENE	06 APR 1884	11:478
BLAND, ROBERT L & MOORE, FRANCES R	23 JUN 1897	08:116
BLANE, ISAIAH & BUCKLE, JANE D	*04 OCT 1859	02:013
BLANKENSHIP, LEWIS & FOREMAN, MARY A	12 APR 1872	07:214
BLANKENSHIP, SYLVESTER & HESSON, ELLA	05 FEB 1905	11:039
BLAZER, HARRY B & HANNAN, MARY E	01 NOV 1890	05:635
BLAZER, MILLARD F & HEREFORD, VIRGINIA E	29 NOV 1877	09:160
BLAZER, THURMAN J & JOHNSON, LILLIE F	25 DEC 1908	12:342
BLESSING, BENJAMIN F & RICE, HATTIE E	22 JAN 1879	10:045
BLESSING, CALVIN T & BOARD, SARAH J	19 JAN 1868	05:148
BLESSING, CHARLES E & OHLINGER, MARY L	29 DEC 1897	08:230
BLESSING, GEORGE GILMORE & RHUSS, TRYPHENA	04 JUL 1892	06:360
BLESSING, GEORGE L & RICKARD, SUSANNA	28 JUN 1842	01:038
BLESSING, GEORGE L & BOARD, ELLA G	30 AUG 1881	11:007
BLESSING, GEORGE LATHAM & McDANIEL, VIOLA FRANCES	02 JUL 1890	05:580
BLESSING, JOHN A & GIBBS, ELVIRA	06 JUN 1850	01:052
BLESSING, JOHN F & WEIGAND, GERTRUD M	04 JUL 1894	07:112
BLESSING, LEWIS A & RAY, ELIZA E	30 MAY 1878	09:266
BLESSING, OSON G & ROLLINS, ETHA J	28 MAY 1895	11:098
BLESSING, ROBERT T & ROUSH, SEVILLA E	21 AUG 1907	11:592
BLESSING, SAMUEL JOSEPH & FRY, LIZZIE MAY	23 MAY 1900	09:132
BLESSING, THOMAS E & FRY, ALLIE M	28 OCT 1903	10:390
BLESSING, THOMAS Z & RAYBURN, LUCY C	12 JUL 1885	12:195
BLESSING, W B & BLAND, LAURA A B	27 MAY 1891	06:119
BLESSING, WILLIAM A & FRY, HANNAH F	02 JUL 1899	08:567
BLESSING, WILLIAM B & MAUPIN, JULIA J	24 MAY 1874	08:125
BLETNER, CHRISTOPHER & GRESS, MARGARET E	05 APR 1913	14:114
BLETNER, EDWARD & WOLF, LIZZIE	04 APR 1872	07:207
BLETNER, FREDRICK EDWARD & MUMAW, ELIZABETH SEICHRIST	16 DEC 1891	06:250
BLETNER, KARL & CAMPBELL, ALICE BEATRICE	25 MAR 1909	12:389
BLISS, WILLIAM G M & SWALLOW, MATTIE E	*04 MAR 1879	10:061
BLOOM, NATHAN & SMITH, GRACE	07 NOV 1882	11:246
BLOOMER, CHRISTOPHER & PIERCY, ELIZABETH	1833	01:039

Names	Date	Ref
BLOSFIELD, FRANK HENRY & GIBBS, SARAH ANN	16 APR 1884	12:007
BLUME, HENRY C & SINES, ELLEN V	04 MAR 1893	06:499
BOARD, ALBERT C & COTTRILL, ROSE	19 FEB 1907	11:497
BOARD, CHARLES SHERIDAN & SELBY, IVA E	05 OCT 1893	06:617
BOARD, DAVID A & SENNITT, FRANKIE O	17 APR 1912	13:516
BOARD, DENCIL W & WEIGAND, ARTIE E	23 DEC 1906	11:472
BOARD, GEORGE & PARSONS, ELIZABETH	11 MAR 1825	01:014
BOARD, GEORGE & PARSONS, ELIZABETH	16 MAR 1825	01:012
BOARD, JAMES & BUSH, LULA	05 JAN 1888	05:176
BOARD, JNO & CASTO, NANCY	10 MAY 1821	01:008
BOARD, JOHN H & FISHER, HENRIETTA	08 JAN 1914	15:117
BOARD, ORVIL S & COLEMAN, THINCY M	25 DEC 1905	11:229
BOARD, WILLIAM M & TURLEY, MARY E	29 SEP 1897	08:159
BOARD, WILLIAM W & HAYMAN, MARTHA C	17 MAR 1878	09:228
BOARD, WILLIAM W & WILSON, NANCY C	30 JUN 1883	11:367
BOARDMAN, BENJAMIN FRANKLIN & FOWLER, DORISCA	13 JAN 1902	10:003
BOARDMAN, BENJAMIN & JEFFERS, OMA	09 MAR 1905	11:055
BOARDMAN, CHARLES A & WEIRS, MARY L	24 DEC 1880	10:356
BOARDMAN, GEORGE & GILLASPIE, EMMA	19 FEB 1901	09:292
BOARDMAN, JOHN & JEFFERS, MARTHA	06 SEP 1896	07:605
BODEN, JAMES & JONES, OLIVIA	1833	01:039
BODIE, THOMAS H & JOHNSON, CLARA E	19 SEP 1901	09:410
BOGGESS, ADAM & HALL, JANE	07 MAR 1833	01:028
BOGGESS, ANDREW LEWIS & YEAGER, ALBERTA	19 SEP 1895	07:387
BOGGESS, ANDREW S & RIFFLE, LAVINIA	05 AUG 1878	09:294
BOGGESS, BENJAMIN & BROWN, MARY	28 MAR 1844	01:038
BOGGESS, BENJAMIN A & CRAFT, NANCY ANN	26 NOV 1903	10:419
BOGGESS, BENJAMIN F & RAYBURN, RUTHA F	04 MAR 1869	06:038
BOGGESS, CHRISTOPHER W & RIFFLE, FANNIE	26 JAN 1871	07:047
BOGGESS, ERNEST J & YEAGER, ELIZA	08 APR 1908	12:154
BOGGESS, JAMES & CHATTIN, MARTHA A	18 APR 1877	09:064
BOGGESS, JAMES & FADELEY, MARY JANE	13 OCT 1892	06:423
BOGGESS, JAMES & RUGH, CLARISA	22 JUL 1895	07:349
BOGGESS, JAMES MONROE & BABLE, MARGARET ESTHER	07 AUG 1884	12:044
BOGGESS, JOHN A & LOVE, MARY ISABELLE	17 JAN 1867	05:021
BOGGESS, JOHN R & McCOY, EDDA	02 DEC 1906	11:458
BOGGESS, LEWIS & GRIM, DOROTHY	*17 DEC 1858	02:011
BOGGESS, OSCAR & LEWIS, LILLIE	14 NOV 1894	07:190
BOGGESS, ROBERT O & SOMERVILLE, REBECCA	24 DEC 1868	06:021
BOGGESS, ROBERT OSBURN & GRAY, RACHEL MARIA	07 MAR 1889	05:366
BOGGESS, WILLIAM & DOWER, JOSIE	24 NOV 1909	12:551
BOGGS, ANDERSON & HOWARD, MISTA M	02 OCT 1897	08:165
BOGGS, JAMES A & GILL, LAVINA	09 JUL 1872	07:244
BOGGS, JOSIAH C & LEMASTER, LOUISA	11 OCT 1829	01:020
BOGGS, OSCAR & LANIER, LUELLA	26 FEB 1909	12:371
BOICE, AUGUSTIN & ARNDT, MARY H	16 MAR 1911	13:495
BOLDS, ALBERT & HILL, ELLEN	06 SEP 1876	08:386
BOLES, ALEXANDER & JIVIDEN, LUVERNIA	11 NOV 1907	12:066
BOLES, ALFERD & BURDETTE, LONA NAOMI	28 DEC 1911	13:455
BOLES, J W & BALES, ELLA	08 MAR 1908	12:140
BOLES, JOHN & GREENLEE, HARRIET	13 APR 1873	07:312
BOLES, ROBERT & WHEELER, MAHALA	22 OCT 1876	08:403
BOLES, ROBERT A & HILL, LENA R A	07 SEP 1900	09:198
BOLES, WILLIAM M & DUVALL, REBECCA J	15 AUG 1877	09:118
BOLIN, LIFE & DYE, MURL	03 AUG 1914	15:250
BOLLES, FREDERICK & YOUNG, AGNES	25 APR 1889	05:391
BOND, JAMES & STEVENS, ISABEL	19 NOV 1876	08:413
BONECUTTER, ARTHUR W & WAMSLEY, ANNIE	15 JUN 1906	11:341

Name	Date	Ref
BONECUTTER, FREDERICK R & PATTERSON, DAISY	05 JUN 1904	10:531
BONECUTTER, PHILIP H & LEE, KATIE	15 NOV 1903	10:408
BONECUTTER, PHILIP H & MARTIN, LUCY F	20 DEC 1913	15:095
BONET, WILLIAM & GIBBS, ADA A	25 DEC 1880	10:359
BONNET, WILLIAM & KEARNS, MAHALA B	25 DEC 1885	12:272
BONNETT, ANDREW M & PICKENS, VICTORIA	15 MAY 1880	10:258
BONNETT, H & GREENLEE, MARGARET	15 NOV 1885	12:251
BOOKER, GEORGE & BOOKER, MELINDA	17 SEP 1819	01:004
BOOTH, EVERETT E & YOUNG, ANNIE M	25 DEC 1895	07:460
BOOTH, FRANK & DAVIS, CARRIE	14 MAY 1898	08:306
BOOTH, HARVEY & HOLLEY, EMMA	25 MAY 1898	08:314
BOOTH, JAMES W & WORKMAN, MARY M	03 FEB 1875	08:208
BOOTH, JOHN W & LLOYD, MAGGIE A	19 APR 1880	10:241
BOOTH, PONTIUS P & SHIFTLETT, ELLA	05 DEC 1902	10:201
BOOTH, PRESTON & HARRIGAN, SARAH	22 JUN 1875	08:250
BOOTH, SIDNEY S & WALKER, CARRIE	07 MAY 1911	13:317
BOOTH, THOMAS A & SCHOLZ, ELLENOR	20 JUN 1905	11:114
BOOTHE, HARVEY & WORKMAN, MARY	*07 MAY 1897	08:092
BORAM, ISAAC & BRIAN, POLLY	JUL 1807	01:002
BORDEN, FREDERIC & WILSON, SARAH	03 OCT 1877	09:137
BORUM, ZACHARIAH & AMSBARY, RUTH	1840	01:032 5
BOST, CHARLES H & KING, FLOSSIE E	24 DEC 1906	11:478
BOSTER, CHRISTOPHER C & CHICK, FEDILIA	*23 DEC 1890	06:031
BOSTER, GROVER C & MESSICK, ETHEL M	19 FEB 1911	13:271
BOSTIC, GEORGE & CASH, ANNIE M	27 JUN 1906	11:351
BOSTICK, HARLEY A & BELL, PEARL	17 JUL 1914	15:246
BOSTICK, JOHN F & CORNS, MARY	27 NOV 1907	12:078
BOSTON, DANIEL & ZIRKLE, ADDIE L	29 NOV 1911	13:429
BOSTON, DANIEL W & WATKINS, JULIA A	08 MAR 1881	10:385
BOSTON, GEORGE W & SHULTZ, HARRIET	26 MAY 1883	11:344
BOSTON, JOHN D & SHIRLEY, FLORIDA FRANCES	16 NOV 1913	15:070
BOSTON, SAMUEL M & BLESSING, FANNIE L	17 DEC 1888	05:321
BOSWELL, CREED & FARGO, IRENA	01 JUL 1827	01:016
BOSWELL, THOMAS F & STEEL, (Mrs) MARY	*11 SEP 1854	02:005
BOSWORTH, EDWARD M & NOE, ELIZABETH	10 DEC 1907	12:085
BOSWORTH, URSON & JOHNSON, CORA	19 APR 1903	10:271
BOTTS, WILLIAM C & EASTHAM, LIZZIE F	14 NOV 1888	05:306
BOWCOTT, EDWARD & TANNER, NORA	14 MAR 1897	08:061
BOWCOTT, LEWIS & WILLIAMS, STELLA	10 JUL 1904	10:559
BOWDENOT, TOBIAS & LOYD, RICHMOND	17 AUG 1826	01:015
BOWEN, ALBERT & GOBLE, VADIE	12 OCT 1903	10:384
BOWEN, CHARLES W & WESTBAY, ELIZABETH A	17 SEP 1840	01:035
BOWEN, CHRISTOPHER C & JONES, MARTHA	10 NOV 1864	03:205
BOWEN, JAMES A & BOWMAN, ELLA	06 DEC 1902	10:202
BOWEN, JOHN M & BROWN, VERLIE	05 DEC 1914	15:340
BOWEN, JOHNSON & HOLLEY, EVALINE	26 OCT 1875	08:281
BOWEN, WILLIAM & TEMPLETON, ADALADE	13 MAR 1845	01:044
BOWERS, GEORGE & KIESLING, MINA	16 JUN 1878	09:275
BOWERS, HOWARD H & RUSSELL, JESSIE	09 JUL 1913	14:192
BOWERS, ULYSES GRANE & HAWKINS, JANE ANN	18 APR 1889	05:381
BOWERS (Dr), JACOB A & MILLER, NANCY R	17 MAR 1908	12:145
BOWLES, BERTIE L & BURDETT, EMMA J	23 DEC 1895	07:462
BOWLES, FRANCIS M & HAYES, ERNA A	05 SEP 1893	06:597
BOWLES, JOHN & BOWLES, NANCY J	02 JUN 1881	10:418
BOWLES, LONESS AMBROS & ROUSH, ALICE S	03 JUL 1888	05:242
BOWLES, WILSON E & MILLER, EVA D	05 JAN 1905	11:026
BOWLEY, WILLIAM & SIMPSON, SUSANNA	18 MAY 1826	01:015
BOWLING, JAMES M & COURTS, JULIA A	25 MAR 1869	06:045

Name	Date	Ref
BOWLING, JOE M & LASLEY, HATTIE E	28 JUL 1882	11:182
BOWLING, JOHN & BARTLEY, MINERVA J	*04 NOV 1890	06:001
BOWLS, MARTIN & HARPOLE, JEMESONA	06 APR 1826	01:015
BOWMAN, GEORGE ALLEN & FLETCHER, EMILY JANE	*14 APR 1902	10:056
BOWMAN, LINSEY & WAUGH, METY	30 AUG 1885	12:217
BOWMAN, LINZEY & St CLARE, JOSEPHINE	20 DEC 1889	05:496
BOWMAN, ROBERT & WAUGH, SOPHA A	20 NOV 1879	10:166
BOWMAN, ROBERT J & CASEY, MARTHA A	04 MAY 1884	12:013
BOWN, FRED S & KNIGHT, LILLIE B	02 SEP 1890	05:610
BOWYER, A H & GRAHAM, DICIE E	09 OCT 1912	14:011
BOWYER, CHARLES C & PARSONS, KITTY B	17 SEP 1879	10:130
BOWYER, GEORGE C & MILLER, MARY S	*17 MAR 1853	02:004
BOWYER, SOLOMON S & GRAHAM, ELIZABETH J	30 NOV 1876	08:415
BOWYER, U S GRANT & WATSON, CHARLOTTE EMMA	28 SEP 1892	06:415
BOYCE, JAMES & BOYCE, VIRGINIA	30 OCT 1904	10:623
BOYCE, RALPH R & PIERSOL, (Mrs) LEOTA	01 MAY 1910	13:044
BOYCE, STEPHEN & SAYRE, SARAH	28 NOV 1824	01:011
BOYD, ALEXANDER & CALLISON, NELLY	22 MAY 1807	01:001
BOYD, DANIEL & OHLINGER, SARAH	13 FEB 1870	06:151
BOYD, JAMES M & GRIMMETT, MAGGIE J	10 MAR 1891	06:074
BOYER, ABRAHAM C & McKERN, BARBARA E	*07 SEP 1870	06:224
BOYER, DAVID & BAILES, LUCETTA	26 JUN 1892	06:350
BOYER, S S & DURST, MARY	08 NOV 1866	04:167
BOYER, STEPHEN C & GRAHAM, SARAH E	04 MAY 1879	10:085
BOYLE, J W & WOODLEY, EMMA	23 JAN 1913	14:085
BOYLES, CHARLES & DAVIS, EMELINE	22 FEB 1880	10:213
BOYLES, ELI F & DAYWAULT, MARY	19 AUG 1907	11:590
BOYLES, JOHN W & PROFFITT, MARGARET A V	29 AUG 1880	10:290
BOYLES, SAMUEL & GARDNER, JUDY WEST	29 DEC 1867	05:125
BOYLES, SAMUEL & McDANIEL, MARTHA	07 JUL 1900	09:158
BOYLES, SIMEON A & PROFFITT, SOPHIA J F	03 FEB 1881	10:372
BOZWELL, THOMAS L & RIFFLE, CATHARINE	07 OCT 1850	01:051
BOZZELL, PEASLEY & McDANIEL, CAROLINE	1831	01:024
BRACEWELL, JOHN & CLENDENIN, REBECCA	01 AUG 1869	06:068
BRACEY, JOHN S & McDANIEL, ANNIE	05 MAY 1895	07:298
BRADBURN, JOSEPH & MACKLEY, ANN	18 OCT 1809	01:002
BRADFORD, COLUMBUS G & McILVEEN, MARY	*28 JUL 1886	12:365
BRADY, THOMAS J & LEWIS, HANNAH	23 MAY 1898	08:313
BRAGG, EDGAR & BRAGG, EMMA B	08 SEP 1908	12:254
BRALEY, CARSY D & HANLY, GRACE	*30 APR 1906	11:304
BRALEY, PEARL & HAMILTON, BLANCHE	22 FEB 1905	11:048
BRAMBLE, GEORGE THORNTON & AMOS, ADELLA	10 NOV 1886	12:420
BRANDANS, STUART & BROWN, CAROLINE	15 MAR 1829	01:019
BRANDON, FRANCIS & LITCHFIELD, LUCINDA	01 MAY 1840	01:033
BRANNAN, ADAM J & PLANTS, MARY J	09 JUN 1870	06:196
BRANNAN, GEORGE S & TAYLOR, ELECTA V	05 APR 1891	06:091
BRANNAN, JOHN S & EDWARDS, SALLIE	23 APR 1904	10:508
BRANNON, JOHN S & FOGLESONG, JANE C	16 DEC 1866	05:008
BRANNON, OTHO & KIMBERLING, SALLIE A	29 DEC 1898	08:445
BRANNON, WILLIAM A & KNAPP, ALMIRA	02 DEC 1894	07:197
BRECKMAN, MASSON C & HUGHES, NELLIE B	06 OCT 1909	12:521
BREITENSTEIN, LAWRENCE & CAYLOR, MARY	21 APR 1842	01:036
BRENT, WILLIAM & LEWIS, JENNET	04 JUL 1823	01:012
BREWER, CALVIN A & ESTILL, ALFORATA V	02 DEC 1868	06:014
BREWER, HENRY & DONOHUE, EMMA A	02 JAN 1913	14:080
BREWER, JAMES & GARDNER, ESTELLA B	28 MAY 1883	11:347
BRICKLE, ROBERT I & HOWELL, ETTA	31 OCT 1893	06:640
BRICKLES, SAMUEL J & HUDNALL, LILLIE B	23 DEC 1912	14:063

BRIDGET, WILLIAM & YEAGER, SARAH	09 DEC 1847	01:048
BRIGGS, JOHN & KEARNS, MARGARET	17 OCT 1878	09:335
BRIGHT, CHARLES CANTREL & KERWOOD, FLORA M	28 OCT 1889	05:472
BRIGHT, EMMONS S & MILLER, CHARLESANNA R M	11 SEP 1867	05:081
BRIGHT, GEORGE O & MINK, GIRTIE	*11 JUL 1908	12:208
BRIGHT, HEROLD EMMONS & GREENLEE, GEORGIE BELLE	23 SEP 1903	10:370
BRIGHT, JAMES S & JEFFERS, FANNIE	16 DEC 1908	12:328
BRIGHT, JESSE J & CAPEHART, MARY A	24 MAY 1876	08:356
BRIGHT, JESSE J & McCULLOCH, SARAH V	24 MAY 1881	10:415
BRIGHT, JOHN P & BRIGHT, LUELLA	30 SEP 1908	12:279
BRIGHT, MATHEW W & NIBERT, ALTA	15 NOV 1900	09:238
BRIGHT, PHILLIP S & LANIER, MATILDA JANE	08 APR 1899	08:501
BRIGHT, ROBERT W & FOWLER, REBECA E	05 AUG 1892	06:584
BRIGHT, STEPHEN & PILES, EMILY J	25 DEC 1886	12:451
BRINKER, A J & ROUSH, REBECCA A	01 MAY 1878	09:252
BRINKER, DAVID HOMER & JONES, ANAMA ELIZABETH	05 DEC 1888	08:313
BRINKER, ELMER E & McCARTY, NANNIE	29 NOV 1896	08:008
BRINKER, ELMER E & WEIGAND, ABBIE E	15 APR 1908	12:156
BRINKER, GEORGE W & FISHER, FLORA L	20 OCT 1897	08:175
BRINKER, JEROME & SAYRE, VIRGINIA H	07 AUG 1869	06:071
BRINKMEIER, THEODORE & COLLET, KATIE	18 NOV 1890	05:630
BRISTOL, C W & LEE, GRACE M	13 JUN 1913	14:189
BRITGETT, BERT B & VICKERS, MAUD	24 DEC 1899	09:035
BRITTON, EDWARD W & GIBBS, FLORENCE E A	26 APR 1893	06:529
BRITTON, THOMAS W & BOWERS, CATHARINE	25 JAN 1877	09:026
BROADHURST, WILLIAM J & HALL, MARY A	02 JUL 1882	11:169
BROCK, JOHN & SMITH, NANCY E	02 SEP 1880	10:294
BROFFORD, ROBERT & LEMASTER, MARY A	26 SEP 1896	07:621
BRONAUGH, ADDISON & PEYTON, SUSAN F	OCT 1839	01:034
BRONAUGH, THOMAS J & HENDERSON, NANCY	1832	01:026
BROOKE, WILLIAM M & LYNCH, MAE ELIZABETH	28 APR 1914	14:183
BROOKS, HARRY A & FRENCH, ELNORA	10 OCT 1911	13:393
BROOKS, LEWIS F & WESSEN, MINERVA	01 MAY 1845	01:044
BROOKS, STEPHEN F & STRIBLING, SARAH	27 AUG 1907	11:600
BROSIUS, DAVID L & LEE, ESTELLA H	27 FEB 1862	03:052
BROWDER, WILLIAM H & GEORGE, MARGARET B	20 OCT 1863	03:139
BROWEN, HIRAM & BLAIN, MARY	14 AUG 1879	10:109
BROWN, ALBERT S & EDWARDS, EVA LEE	10 AUG 1901	09:380
BROWN, ALFRED & PAIN, ELIZABETH	29 MAR 1827	01:016
BROWN, ANTHONY & ROTHGEB, NANCY J	10 APR 1897	08:075
BROWN, BENJAMIN F & YAUGER, SARAH	06 FEB 1880	10:207
BROWN, CHARLES W & SIMPKINS, SARAH R	03 NOV 1872	07:284
BROWN, CHARLES W & LOVE, MARY V	11 DEC 1895	07:447
BROWN, DANA & PHILIPS, SADDIE	24 APR 1906	11:299
BROWN, DANIEL M & ROUSH, WYOMA	01 JUN 1904	10:528
BROWN, DANIEL W & LEMASTER, MARGARETTA L	11 OCT 1883	11:410
BROWN, EARL & BAKER, E LOUISE	16 NOV 1912	14:029
BROWN, ED & TAYLOR, MARY E	13 DEC 1890	06:018
BROWN, ELIAS & ISAACS, MALINDA	18 JAN 1881	10:367
BROWN, ELLIOT & HATCHER, MARY	10 MAY 1825	01:011
BROWN, ELMER E & SAYRE, EFFA E	06 JUL 1907	11:573
BROWN, EPHRAIM & WATKINS, MAGGIE	27 NOV 1873	08:057
BROWN, FRIEND & CAMP, AMELIA	09 FEB 1826	01:012
BROWN, GEORGE & ROUSH, ELSIE	31 DEC 1905	11:239
BROWN, GEORGE WINFIELD & SAUNDERS, ALICE	05 APR 1893	06:516
BROWN, GEORGE W & DORSEY, SALLIE	28 MAY 1908	12:188
BROWN, GIDEON & MAHAFFY, SALLY	*12 DEC 1884	12:109
BROWN, HARRY & BUSH, BIRDIE	24 MAY 1910	13:072

Names	Date	Ref
BROWN, HENRY C & DURST, EMELINE R A	24 NOV 1869	06:105
BROWN, HUGH & LONG, MARY M	17 APR 1851	02:001
BROWN, ISAAC C & MORSE, IDA M	17 JUL 1886	12:361
BROWN, JAMES & ROBSON, ISABELLA	28 DEC 1873	08:083
BROWN, JAMES F & ROSE, ANNA B	22 FEB 1891	06:064
BROWN, JAMES R & HOGG, SARAH L	10 NOV 1880	10:325
BROWN, JOHN & KNIGHT, KATE	*20 FEB 1856	02:008
BROWN, JOHN & McCOLLISTER, MARTHA	20 JUN 1865	04:018
BROWN, JOHN & WURNEL, JANE	27 JUN 1819	01:004
BROWN, JOHN B & STEWART, ADDA B	12 OCT 1869	06:096
BROWN, JOSEPH & WALLIS, FLORENCE EMILY	08 APR 1891	06:094
BROWN, JOSEPH A & MASH, HATTIE	18 MAR 1891	06:081
BROWN, JOSEPH G & HOFFMAN, INA	22 SEP 1901	09:412
BROWN, LEWIS W & PETTY, IDA L	04 JAN 1883	11:286
BROWN, MAJOR & GREENLEE, INGABY	*03 MAR 1860	02:013
BROWN, MAJOR ED & EGGENSWILLER, MILLIE	13 NOV 1890	06:006
BROWN, MANLY & KNIGHT, REBECCA	29 OCT 1870	07:019
BROWN, MARLON E & HARPER, ELIZABETH	19 MAY 1868	05:180
BROWN, MILBURN & ZERCKLE, SARAH	23 OCT 1911	13:402
BROWN, MILES O & RUTTENCUTTER, WILHELMINA F	22 JUN 1910	13:091
BROWN, NELSON & HENNIGAN, NANCY J	21 FEB 1887	12:478
BROWN, NELSON & AMSBERRY, LAVINA	29 MAY 1892	06:342
BROWN, RAYMOND M & SCHOOLS, BESS I	04 JUN 1911	13:326
BROWN, ROBERT & FORREST, CATHERINE	21 SEP 1905	11:175
BROWN, SAMUEL & LONG, EMILY SUSAN	*25 JAN 1853	02:003
BROWN, SAMUEL H & SANDERS, CATHARINE A	*31 MAR 1859	02:012
BROWN, SAMUEL T & VARIAN, ORA V	03 OCT 1900	09:207
BROWN, SIMON KLYDE & WARD, BERTHA ALAMEDA	1909	12:506
BROWN, THOMAS & CRINER, ELLA MAY	02 SEP 1907	11:604
BROWN, VAN B & RAYBURN, MATTIE S	21 DEC 1887	05:158
BROWN, VICTOR C & GIBBS, BERTHA A	25 JUL 1906	11:371
BROWN, W E & BOBO, ELSIE	09 OCT 1909	12:523
BROWN, WALTER EMORY & KENNEY, DORA	25 JUL 1889	05:427
BROWN, WILLIAM & LONG, ELIZABETH	*06 FEB 1854	02:005
BROWN, WILLIAM A & WINDON, SUSAN M	25 MAR 1862	03:056
BROWN, WILLIAM A & ERRETT, MAY R	21 JUL 1914	15:242
BROWN, WILLIAM AUGUSTUS & PARKER, MARY ANN	24 NOV 1842	01:037
BROWN, WILLIAM C & CRAIG, KITTY K	1843	01:042
BROWN, WILLIAM J & KIRKER, BIRDIE	26 APR 1894	07:080
BROWN, WM & RICKARD, MARGT	*21 NOV 1859	02:013
BROWNE, WALTER D & RHODES, FRANCES	02 JUN 1912	13:539
BROWNELL, LEW H & BARNETT, DORA A	12 AUG 1893	06:585
BRUCE, RILEY & FARLEY, HESTER	25 MAR 1880	10:225
BRUCE, WILLIAM & WARD, MARY	10 JAN 1885	12:126
BRUCKELMEYER, FREDERICK & McHONE, MARY	08 SEP 1903	10:348
BRUCKER, WILBER & EARWOOD, PEARLIE	03 DEC 1902	10:200
BRUFF, COLLINS W & RAY, STELLA DEL	04 DEC 1911	13:369
BRUMFIELD, MILLARD R & HESSON, MERTIE	05 NOV 1905	11:197
BRUMLEY, HOWARD E & DAVIS, ROSA L	05 AUG 1904	10:568
BRUNFIELD, WILLIAM & BRUNFIELD, EMRYNE	15 JUL 1899	08:578
BRYAN, ALBERT GORDON & BLAKE, OSIE	28 DEC 1889	05:506
BRYAN, ALLEN M & SHELTON, JOANA	06 JAN 1872	07:177
BRYAN, ANDREW & MEIGS, PARSHONEA	01 JUN 1809	01:002
BRYAN, ANDREW G & MORRIS, MARY	*01 AUG 1857	02:010
BRYAN, CHARLES L & POLSLEY, KATE ALICE	25 NOV 1897	08:207
BRYAN, DANIEL R & CHAPMAN, MADLAIN MAY	28 NOV 1900	09:240
BRYAN, HENRY & COVINGTON, LUCY R	04 MAY 1902	10:067
BRYAN, JAMES H & HAWKINS, JULIA E	07 DEC 1898	08:428

BRYAN, JAMES W & JONES, ELIZABETH G	28 JAN 1874	08:093
BRYAN, NATHANIEL L & SIMPSON, MARY MARGARET	01 JUN 1897	08:105
BRYAN, NIMROD & HUNTER, MARY F	05 AUG 1891	06:156
BRYAN, WILLIAM WESTON & MIDDLECOFF, IDA	10 JUN 1888	05:234
BRYAN, WILLIAM W & TULLY, LIZZIE G	30 APR 1901	09:330
BUCK, FLOYD & LEGG, MATTIE	30 OCT 1905	11:194
BUCK, LORENZO & ATKINSON, VIRGINIA M	30 MAR 1873	07:309
BUCK, MARIDA & STEWART, VILETTA	11 SEP 1873	08:026
BUCK, MILLARD & HAYES, LILLIE E	01 APR 1911	13:300
BUCK, OSCAR & McCALL, DESSIE	23 SEP 1912	14:007
BUCK, SAMUEL E & WHITT, MARTHA F	03 MAR 1901	09:299
BUCK, WALTER & WERNER, EMMA	28 FEB 1905	11:052
BUCK, WILLIAM & GRIMM, FLORENCE	25 DEC 1908	12:341
BUCKALEW, EDGAR OLIVER & SEE, EMMA	28 SEP 1891	06:195
BUCKHANAN, RICHARD A & PERRY, ROSE B	12 DEC 1887	05:156
BUCKLE, CHARLES F & CHAPMAN, CARRIE A	03 SEP 1906	11:402
BUCKLE, FRED T & FOWLER, (Mrs) DAISY	30 OCT 1911	13:407
BUCKLE, FREDRICK & CASEY, LULA	13 OCT 1906	11:427
BUCKLE, JAMES FRIEND & JORDAN, ALICE	23 JAN 1887	12:469
BUCKLE, JESSE JAMES & SHANK, EVA F	23 DEC 1914	15:350
BUCKLEY, SAMUEL B & HOWELL, MARY A	02 JAN 1873	07:303
BUFFINGTON, ALFRED FRANKLIN & LIEVING, ADDIE	24 AUG 1887	05:076
BUFFINGTON, JAMES R & MILLER, ANN ELIZA	*05 NOV 1850	02:001
BUFFINGTON, JAMES R & MILLER, ELLENOR B	*21 AUG 1855	02:007
BUFFINGTON, JOSEPH W & ROUSH, CARIE	29 AUG 1889	05:441
BUFFINGTON, RICHARD & BROWN, MARY	28 APR 1818	01:005
BUFFINGTON, THOMAS W & McDANIEL, SARAH E	08 FEB 1899	08:465
BULLINGTON, WILLIAM & HOOD, MARY P	03 JAN 1873	07:308
BUMGARDNER, CURTIS & SAYER, MAY	14 MAR 1900	09:095
BUMGARDNER, LEWIS J & ROUSH, SARA A	13 MAR 1892	06:304
BUMGARDNER, OSCAR & BARROWS, MARY E	06 NOV 1901	09:440
BUMGARDNER, THOMAS F & BASS, NETTIE	*19 JAN 1912	13:471
BUMGARNER, BERT E & BUMGARNER, CARRIE B	07 DEC 1905	11:206
BUMGARNER, C S & SHANK, ELLA F	21 JUN 1883	11:358
BUMGARNER, CALVIN & AUMILLER, FANNIE	08 JUN 1865	04:014
BUMGARNER, CHARLES & BROWN, REBECCA	*17 JAN 1853	02:003
BUMGARNER, CLARENCE & MILLER, ALSONA	10 FEB 1895	07:244
BUMGARNER, CLYDE MARTIN & FIELDS, IDA FLORENCE	26 SEP 1900	09:212
BUMGARNER, DAVID & OLIVER, MARY ANN	*20 DEC 1852	02:003
BUMGARNER, DAVID & MITCHELL, MARGERY	16 NOV 1871	07:148
BUMGARNER, ELMER & JOHNSON, ORA	*12 JAN 1903	10:225
BUMGARNER, ELMER & JOHNSON, ORA	24 OCT 1903	10:387
BUMGARNER, FRANKLIN & BASS, LILLY MAY	28 FEB 1885	12:146
BUMGARNER, GEORGE FREMONT & WASHINGTON, FANNIE	17 SEP 1890	05:613
BUMGARNER, GEORGE F & WOOD, EFFA B	24 MAR 1898	08:277
BUMGARNER, GILBERT & ARNOLD, ELIZABETH	11 DEC 1909	12:565
BUMGARNER, J T & BYRNE, ANNIE E	25 FEB 1891	06:067
BUMGARNER, JAMES & ROHRABAUGH, MILLIE LOURAS	22 APR 1890	05:547
BUMGARNER, JEREMIAH & JOHNSON, VERNICIA	24 DEC 1879	10:182
BUMGARNER, JOHN & ROUSH, SARAH	26 MAR 1846	01:044
BUMGARNER, JOHN & STRICKLAND, JULIA MAY	14 DEC 1897	08:213
BUMGARNER, JOHN J & ROUSH, ALMERIA	17 JUN 1877	09:099
BUMGARNER, JOHN W & SOMERVILLE, CATHARINE B	18 MAR 1865	04:019
BUMGARNER, MARTIN M & ROUSH, ARTA	08 JAN 1883	11:296
BUMGARNER, MILLARD & McMILLEN, JENNIE	28 APR 1881	10:405
BUMGARNER, REZIN Jr & YEAGER, MARY	05 SEP 1844	01:044
BUMGARNER, SAMUEL J & McMILLIN, MARGARET	24 DEC 1876	09:008
BUMGARNER, SETH & CAPEHART, MARY ANN	*23 JUL 1856	02:008

Names	Date	Ref
BUMGARNER, TAYLOR & HOFFMAN, SARAH C	29 DEC 1886	12:453
BUMGARNER, THOMAS & TAYLOR, ANGELINE	08 SEP 1868	05:209
BUMGARNER, THOMAS M & WILLIAMS, GWENDOLINE	17 FEB 1912	13:486
BUMGARNER, TOBIAS P & ROUSH, LIZZIE F	29 OCT 1899	09:003
BUMGARNER, WILLARD & ROUSH, EMMA L	05 APR 1893	06:518
BUMGARNER, WILLIAM & HUMPHRIES, MARY	*19 FEB 1861	02:015
BUMGARNER, WINFIELD & FOWLER, LAURA C	09 DEC 1880	10:342
BURCH, WILLIAM & OLDAKERS, DEBORAH	1831	01:024
BURCH, ZIBA & WALLACE, PATSY	1832	01:027
BURCH, ZIBA & WALLACE, PATSY	1832	01:039
BURCHAM, WILLIAM & HOLLEY, CAROLINE	22 JAN 1892	06:279
BURCHERD, CHARLES & WILSON, SARAH V	23 NOV 1901	09:449
BURCHFIELD, ELIAS A & EDWARDS, JANE	11 SEP 1878	09:308
BURCHFIELD, HARRISON & WEARS, NORA	27 APR 1909	12:404
BURCHFIELD, WILLIAM G & GATES, OLA	*13 AUG 1875	08:265
BURCHFIELD, WILLIAM G & WOODS, FLORENCE	15 DEC 1877	09:168
BURD, HILLARY & WHITTINGTON, RHODA	29 JAN 1846	01:046
BURDETT, CHARLES E & ROUSH, NORAH	26 MAY 1908	12:185
BURDETT, CLARENCE M & SAYRE, ROSA	13 OCT 1906	11:426
BURDETT, E H & BUXTON, MARY	27 NOV 1886	12:429
BURDETT, GUY & KNAPP, ERMA A	24 DEC 1914	15:355
BURDETT, J WALLACE & JOHNSON, EDNA ADA	07 JAN 1914	15:118
BURDETT, MARK & BOWLES, EFFIE	19 OCT 1882	11:223
BURDETT, PEARL T & CONNER, CARRIE V	09 OCT 1906	11:422
BURDETT, THEODORE M & GOBE, LIZZIE A	24 DEC 1896	08:025
BURDETT, WILLIAM C & HANSON, NELLIE	08 NOV 1899	09:009
BURDETTE, LOGAN & STANLEY, GEORGIA	25 OCT 1907	12:052
BURDETTE, WILLIAM S & HADSELL, (Mrs) LUCIE	06 JAN 1909	12:351
BURGE, JOSHUA G & GANDEE, MARY C	11 APR 1878	09:243
BURGESS, EDGAR G & HARPER, IMOGENE	23 MAR 1868	05:154
BURGESS, WALTER & TURNER, CLARINDA	02 AUG 1909	12:472
BURGESS, WYATT & PARKER, MARTHA	01 JUL 1897	08:120
BURK, THOMAS & LEWIS, MARTHA R	23 DEC 1877	09:172
BURK, WILLIAM & CUNNINGHAM, CARRIE	23 AUG 1897	08:146
BURKE, S L & RAMBOW, DORIS S	02 DEC 1912	14:041
BURKETT, HIRAM & DIXON, (Mrs) MAUDE A	23 FEB 1911	13:278
BURKS, CREED & STANLEY, LIZZIE	*05 SEP 1894	07:148
BURKS, GEORGE W & WALKER, RHODA	22 JUN 1884	12:031
BURKS, ROBERT L & FIERBAUGH, LONA	24 DEC 1900	09:252
BURNETT, WILLIAM H & LOVETT, PHEBE	21 NOV 1839	01:035
BURNETTE, GRIFFEN & DAVIS, ELIZABETH	21 SEP 1826	01:013
BURNIDER, AUGUSTUS F & FISHER, IVIE L	14 OCT 1906	11:429
BURNS, CHRISTOPHER COLUMBUS & ROUSH, NETTIE	27 JUL 1896	07:584
BURNS, DANIEL & DENNY, MINNIE A	03 SEP 1895	07:376
BURNS, HARVEY & LAMBERT, PRISCILLA	05 JAN 1887	05:017
BURNS, HUBERT E & SPANN, BERTHA	26 APR 1897	08:085
BURNS, HOWARD & SINES, MARY E	07 JUL 1907	11:574
BURNS, JAMES & CASEY, LUCY	08 OCT 1882	11:221
BURNS, JOHN M & BRYANT, JENEVIEVE E	17 APR 1913	14:126
BURNS, JULIUS H & HUDSON, SARAH F	24 SEP 1911	13:384
BURNS, PETER F & CASTO, MINTA M	26 JUL 1897	08:133
BURNS, WARREN B & KNAPP, EFFIE E	25 JUN 1904	10:550
BURNS, WILLARD & HILL, BESSIE L	18 OCT 1913	15:053
BURNSIDE, E A & MORRIS, MINNIE B	22 FEB 1886	12:296
BURNSICE, WILLIAM & SMITH, SARAH C	02 NOV 1907	12:059
BURRELL, MARTIN & HOLLEY, LINA	23 DEC 1909	12:576
BURRIS, ALONZO & TEFORD, MARY J	16 JUN 1880	10:266
BURRIS, ANDERSON & SMITH, NANCY	*15 DEC 1853	02:004

BURRIS, CHARLES & LONG, LILLIE	25 AUG 1897	08:148
BURRIS, CHARLES P & SNYDER, DRILLIE	17 FEB 1895	09:255
BURRIS, DANIEL & ADKINS, JANE F	25 MAR 1883	11:315
BURRIS, EDWARD W & DAVIS, MARY M	02 JUL 1914	15:232
BURRIS, FRANK & ROUSH, CALLIE	27 SEP 1908	12:267
BURRIS, GEORGE & KINCAID, NANCY	19 OCT 1843	01:038
BURRIS, GEORGE & KNIGHT, (Mrs) SARAH JANE	*27 DEC 1855	02:007
BURRIS, JAMES A & BOARD, SYLVIA N	08 AUG 1906	11:381
BURRIS, JASPER E & SCARBERRY, JULIA E	30 SEP 1896	07:624
BURRIS, JOHN & KINCADE, ELLEN	16 AUG 1848	01:050
BURRIS, JOHN & BOARD, NANCY	08 MAY 1909	12:408
BURRIS, JOHN H & ROUSH, ELZADIE	13 FEB 1904	10:477
BURRIS, LEWIS & KNAPP, ROSY	16 OCT 1901	09:424
BURRIS, LUTHER & ELLIOTT, MARY	14 JAN 1897	08:035
BURRIS, THOS & DENNY, MARY F	11 AUG 1891	06:161
BURROWS, ELI & ROUSH, EDA	08 JUL 1880	10:277
BURROWS, ELMER S & RUSSELL, ORA	16 AUG 1913	15:011
BURROWS, GEORGE W & GOODNITE, ANGELINE	25 JAN 1889	05:344
BURROWS, JAMES W & GOODNITE, DRUZILLA	21 FEB 1898	08:263
BURROWS, LUTHER & CLARK, MINERVA	30 JUL 1887	05:065
BURROWS, TOM & NEVILLE, (Mrs) MARY D	15 APR 1911	13:309
BURTON, ALFRED & MASON, ISABELLA	26 DEC 1897	08:228
BURTON, ERNEST M & BEABOUT, CARRIE E	03 DEC 1913	15:082
BURTON, ISHMAEL & ADAMS, GERTRUDE J	23 JUN 1904	10:545
BURTON, ISHMAEL & EMBREE, (Mrs) BLANCHE	24 AUG 1911	13:362
BURTON, JOHN & PATRICK, MAGGIE	26 APR 1896	07:536
BURTON, JOSEPH & COTTLE, LUELLA G	28 OCT 1881	11:040
BURTON, JOSEPH & CHAFIN, CLARA	27 NOV 1903	10:421
BURTON, LEVI & TULLY, ANNIE	13 APR 1878	09:244
BURTON, SAMUEL & DORNICK, MARY	15 APR 1881	10:399
BURTON, SMITH & BROWN, LAURA	11 JAN 1894	07:037
BUSH, ADAM & MARTIN, MARY	01 DEC 1864	03:212
BUSH, ANDREW & JORDAN, ELIZABETH	09 JUN 1872	07:323
BUSH, BRADY & EADS, IDA	22 APR 1903	10:276
BUSH, CHARLES F & PLANTS, OLLIE	21 JUN 1903	10:306
BUSH, CORNELIUS & PECK, LAVINIA	*25 JUL 1854	02:005
BUSH, GEORGE F & OLIVER, MARY	25 MAY 1887	05:028
BUSH, G F & HARMAN, (Mrs) S B	28 FEB 1910	13:017
BUSH, HARVEY & CUTCHALL, LOTTIE B	24 SEP 1898	08:368
BUSH, HARVEY & HALSEY, NANCY	06 OCT 1899	08:628
BUSH, HUTTON & KING, SUSIE	19 DEC 1912	14:059
BUSH, JAMES R & CHURCH, MARY	24 OCT 1880	10:316
BUSH, JAMES W & CAMPBELL, SARAH A	14 SEP 1871	07:119
BUSH, JAMES W & JORDAN, JENNIE P	14 NOV 1876	08:410
BUSH, JOHN & CRAFT, MARY	10 NOV 1903	10:404
BUSH, JOHN G & RUGGLES, ELIZABETH	17 FEB 1895	07:251
BUSH, JONAH M & HODGES, STELLA M	21 AUG 1907	11:593
BUSH, JORDAN & MOODESPAUGH, KATIE	22 OCT 1896	07:634
BUSH, JOSIAH & RIFFLE, MALINDA	20 MAR 1862	03:053
BUSH, LEW R & JEFFERS, SARAH E	13 JUN 1905	11:109
BUSH, WILLIAM & TURNBULL, WILLIE M	04 JUL 1886	12:349
BUTCHER, ARTHUR GRANT & STEPHENSON, LENA LEOTIE	28 AUG 1888	05:266
BUTCHER, BENJAMIN FRANKLIN & MOLDEN, EMMA	31 AUG 1912	13:593
BUTCHER, CHARLES E & LEWIS, MATTIE A	08 NOV 1887	05:137
BUTCHER, CHARLES EDWIN & FRY, HATTIE CLEMENTINE	01 FEB 1888	05:182
BUTCHER, FLOYD E & CARR, (Mrs) BLANCHE	24 APR 1913	14:133
BUTCHER, GEORGE & APPLEWHITE, LIZZIE	20 MAY 1906	11:301
BUTCHER, JAMES & MASON, MARY	14 SEP 1893	06:603

BUTCHER, JOHN & KLINGER, ELLEN	09 AUG 1883	11:388
BUTCHER, JOHN O & MYERS, (Mrs) NELLIE ANN	05 NOV 1914	15:317
BUTCHER, WILLIAM A & INVERN, VIELLA	09 JUN 1878	09:274
BUTLER, AUSTIN D & FOX, LUCY J	23 MAR 1873	07:333
BUTLER, BENJAMIN F & SISSON, MARIA E	19 JUN 1866	04:133
BUTLER, CHAS E & BRYAN, JENCIE	24 SEP 1891	06:187
BUTTERS, WATSON C & SCHMANFER, INEZ	24 JUN 1909	12:440
BUXTON, ARTHUR & STOVER, IVEY L	16 DEC 1900	09:249
BUXTON, CHARLES & PICKENS, MARY M	38 NOV 1894	07:196
BUZZART, FRANCIS H & GORDON, (Mrs) MARY K	*31 MAR 1855	02:006
BYER, CHARLES & THOMAS, SAVILLA	01 APR 1886	12:312
BYER, EARL H & KNAPP, NELLIE	27 MAR 1910	13:032
BYERS, MAXWELL C & McCULLOCH, JANET	28 NOV 1906	11:460
BYRNE, JOHN B & ARMSTRONG, ABBIE	29 JUN 1879	10:097
BYRNE, MICHAEL & O'LEARY, MARGARET	17 FEB 1895	07:253
BYRNE, THOMAS M & KAY, HANNAH	13 OCT 1869	06:098
BYUS, ANDERSON & JORDEN, NANCY	*07 NOV 1859	02:013
BYUS, BARNEY P & ROGERS, IDA E	24 OCT 1902	10:176
BYUS, BENNET Jr & DOSS, PENELOPE SUSAN	28 MAY 1862	03:066
BYUS, CALUB L & JORDAN, A L	04 JUL 1893	06:566
BYUS, DAVID C & FIRST, MAY	02 SEP 1896	07:599
BYUS, GEORGE E & GARDNER, MARY A	26 DEC 1894	07:225
BYUS, GEORGE MONROE & JORDAN, MARGARET EMEZETTA	26 OCT 1879	10:150
BYUS, JOHN & HAYES, CORA	21 MAY 1892	06:339
BYUS, W A & PAULY, (Mrs) TERESA	08 NOV 1914	15:318
BYUS, WARREN & WAUGH, DORA	25 JAN 1899	08:458
BYUS, WILLIAM A & MORRIS, CATHARINE A	30 DEC 1869	06:137
CABELL, HEWITT L & CABLE, BESSIE S	15 NOV 1893	07:007
CABELL, W W & HEREFORD, KATE	20 APR 1886	12:319
CADLE, OTHO M & KING, DORA	04 MAY 1899	08:524
CADY, JAMES W & BROWN, LUCY M	08 OCT 1906	11:423
CAHOON, JAMES & BENSON, MARY E	12 MAR 1886	12:300
CAHOON, JAMES & EWING, SARAH E	11 MAY 1905	11:091
CAIN, ANDREW J & KNOPP, ROWENA	14 DEC 1882	11:267
CAIN, ANDREW J & SHINN, VESSIE	01 MAY 1904	10:510
CAIN, JAMES B & SHINN, LONA	07 SEP 1902	10:149
CAIN, JASPER N & KNAPP, VIRGINIA	06 NOV 1879	10:156
CAIN, LABAN H & KNAPP, MARY J	08 JAN 1885	12:121
CAIN, LABAN & PICKENS, ADALINE	11 JUL 1897	08:119
CAIN, RICHARD BEATTIE & KNAPP, SUSAN VIRGINIA	17 NOV 1889	05:481
CAIN, WILLIAM & HERSMAN, MARY	18 NOV 1869	06:108
CAIN, WILLIE A & STRAIGHT, ALMA C	27 SEP 1914	15:280
CALBREATH, WILLIAM J & BOZZELL, ELIZABETH	03 MAR 1842	01:036
CALDERWOOD, HENRY & SPURLOCK, VICTORIA	11 DEC 1901	09:468
CALDWELL, AMOS ALMO & POLLY, EMMA RILLA	01 MAY 1884	12:011
CALDWELL, ANSEL A & LONG, LOUISA	*13 DEC 1858	02:011
CALDWELL, LEWIS L & CARTMILL, ANNIE L	26 NOV 1903	10:417
CALDWELL, MATTHEW & WAUGH, JANE	15 MAY 1842	01:037
CALDWELL, WARREN L & FAUVER, FANNIE	15 SEP 1910	13:160
CALHOON, JOHN M & SIDERS, L MARGARET	17 MAR 1899	08:484
CALHOON, JONN M & SIDERS, LOUISA M	03 JAN 1908	12:114
CALHOUN, HENRY T & SULLIVAN, ADA BLANCH	16 MAR 1892	06:305
CALL, IRA & HAMBRICK, MINNIE	30 JUL 1902	10:123
CALL, MILTON & SAXTON, CAROLINE	17 AUG 1878	09:293
CALL, THOMAS FRANKLIN & DEVORE, ROSIE LEE	21 SEP 1888	05:277
CALL, THOMAS & WOOTEN, MAUD	12 MAY 1904	10:518
CALLAND, GEORGE N & HEATHERINGTON, HULDAH E	12 JUN 1903	14:173
CALLICOAT, GOLDEN E & RAYBURN, ELIZABETH M	14 MAR 1906	11:280

Names	Date	Ref
CALLOWAY, JOHN & FOWLER, BELVIL	24 AUG 1908	12:234
CALVERT, T E & GROVER, LILLIE MAY	15 DEC 1898	08:435
CAMDEN, CHARLES T & PARK, EDITH	13 AUG 1882	11:186
CAMDEN, JOHN T & HAYMON, ALMERIA	26 SEP 1887	05:106
CAMDEN, ROBERT & BROWN, CLARA	27 APR 1895	07:295
CAMP, ABE & WILSON, ELIZA	04 JUL 1905	11:128
CAMP, GEORGE W & EDWARDS, SAMANTHA	25 MAR 1886	12:307
CAMP, HOMER & RICE, ELIZABETH C	24 NOV 1909	12:552
CAMP, J B & MEADOWS, OCIE O	03 DEC 1896	08:009
CAMP, JAMES M & MEADOWS, GUSTIE E	16 SEP 1904	10:597
CAMP, JAMES M, Jr & ANDERSON, MARTHA	07 APR 1842	01:037
CAMP, WILLIAM H & MEADOWS, ELIZABETH	06 SEP 1883	11:397
CAMPBELL, ARCHIE M & ELLISON, EDNA E	29 MAY 1906	11:325
CAMPBELL, DANIEL T & BARR, MAZILLA E	22 FEB 1878	09:218
CAMPBELL, HENRY & COATES, ANGELINE	27 JAN 1867	05:026
CAMPBELL, HENRY & HAWKINS, CATHERINE	19 OCT 1895	07:411
CAMPBELL, HENRY J & CLARK, EVALINE	22 MAY 1895	07:306
CAMPBELL, JAMES & JONES, LOUISA M	01 JAN 1888	08:168
CAMPBELL, JAMES C & YOUNG, CAROLINE	07 JUN 1882	11:355
CAMPBELL, JAMES E & RUSSELL, (Mrs) L MARGARET	24 APR 1913	14:132
CAMPBELL, JOHN R & COTTLE, DORA	26 APR 1881	10:404
CAMPBELL, JOHN W & EAGAN, MATTIE J	27 JUL 1870	06:209
CAMPBELL, JOHN W & JEFFERS, ELIZA	14 JUN 1873	08:004
CAMPBELL, JOSEPH H & JORDAN, JESSIE BLANCHE	29 JUN 1898	08:326
CAMPBELL, JOSEPHUS & LEWIS, SARAH E	19 DEC 1880	10:347
CAMPBELL, JULINS & MILLER, MAMIE BELLE	01 MAY 1910	13:054
CAMPBELL, JULIUS & BARR, SOPHIA	31 OCT 1871	07:142
CAMPBELL, LABAN F & MENAGER, IDA L	24 MAY 1871	07:090
CAMPBELL, ROBERT P & RINGS, MENA	*04 APR 1882	11:135
CAMPBELL, THOMAS H & FRUITH, TILLIE	30 OCT 1892	06:434
CAMPBELL, THORNTON F & RAYBURN, VIOLA B	14 NOV 1883	11:422
CAMPBELL, VIRGIL S & MATHEWSON, JANE H	07 MAY 1913	14:140
CAMPBELL, WILLIAM J & YOUNG, ELLA	17 MAY 1886	12:328
CAMPBELL, WM & BOWLES, ELIZABETH A	19 JAN 1912	13:467
CAMPE, ULYSSES S & HAYMON, ALMENIA	17 DEC 1899	09:032
CAMPFIELD, JAMES & OLDAKER, MARY	29 JAN 1890	05:517
CANADA, WILLIAM R & BURCHFIELD, ZOLA	08 MAR 1896	07:503
CANADY, REUBEN & NUTTER, ROSA	01 MAY 1898	08:297
CANARD, ROBERT F & SIDERS, SARAH E	04 AUG 1895	07:357
CANNADAY, EARL & McCARLEY, ELLA	26 FEB 1914	15:148
CANNON, AUGUSTUS & LILICH, CARRIE	14 DEC 1884	12:102
CANTER, DAVID & GRIMM, MARTHA M	02 JUN 1898	08:317
CANTER, GEORGE W & RINE, MARY E	16 MAR 1887	12:490
CANTER, GEORGE & REYNOLDS, CHRISTINA	23 APR 1898	08:295
CANTER, JONAS & GRAHAM, NORA	23 JUL 1893	06:577
CANTER, U G & RIFFLE, IDA MAY	08 JUL 1902	10:106
CANTERBERRY, JAMES & STILES, BLANCHE	20 AUG 1909	12:485
CANTERBERRY, JOHN & BORAM, TAZY	07 JUN 1809	01:002
CANTERBERRY, JOSEPH C & ELLIOTT, BERTHA	05 MAY 1897	08:090
CANTERBERRY, WILLIAM A & BUSH, CAROLINE	12 NOV 1876	08:409
CAPEHART, ABNEY W & SEGRIST, CAROLINE A	29 DEC 1867	05:127
CAPEHART, CHARLES C & TUCKER, VEVA I	16 SEP 1903	10:354
CAPEHART, EDGAR L & SHANK, ZUA M	19 SEP 1900	09:201
CAPEHART, FRANK H & ZERKLE, ANNIE E	17 JUN 1907	11:555
CAPEHART, GEORGE N & BUSH, DORA	28 SEP 1887	05:107
CAPEHART, GEORGE P & BUMGARNER, MARTHA	01 JAN 1863	03:095
CAPEHART, GEORGE P & SOMERVILLE, ANN	09 FEB 1865	03:220
CAPEHART, J P & SIEGRIST, HANNAH M	*09 JAN 1858	02:010

Name	Date	Ref
CAPEHART, JAMES H & ZIRKEL, ORRILLA	13 OCT 1861	03:026
CAPEHART, LEWIS T & GRAHAM, VICTORIA A	05 MAY 1892	06:331
CAPEHART, SAMUEL J & SHIPLEY, ELLA	22 FEB 1880	10:210
CAPEHART, STEPHEN P & SMITH, HARRIET B	02 SEP 1896	07:600
CAPEHART, THOMAS E & ORD, ELLA	11 JUN 1903	10:304
CAPEHART, LTHOMAS G & BOWLDEN, MARGARET	04 MAY 1876	08:351
CAPEHART, WILLIAM H & GILPIN, SARAH J	13 JUL 1865	04:025
CAPEN, J & CUMPSTON, SALLY	14 SEP 1828	01:021
CAPITO, GOTLIP & PHELPS, MARY E	01 MAY 1879	10:086
CAPITO, GUSTAVE & BETTINGER, LIZZIE	26 APR 1880	10:244
CARDER, GEORGE H & RICE, ELLA B	19 JAN 1905	11:033
CARDER, HOLLIE O & RICE, CORA MAY	24 DEC 1913	15:098
CARDER, L M & ABSTON, SUSAN T	29 APR 1880	10:247
CARGILL, GEORGE W & SHAW, MARY B	*07 NOV 1860	02:014
CARGO, JOSEPH TIMOTHY & JAMES, LAURA	31 MAY 1892	06:345
CARLETON, COLUMBUS & HARPOLD, SUSSIE	27 JAN 1898	08:251
CARLETON, GEORGE R & SEAMANS, LIZZIE G	24 SEP 1895	07:391
CARLIN, JAMES & GOSNAY, MATILDA	14 OCT 1866	04:155
CARLIN, JOHN & WOLF, REBECCA	21 NOV 1868	06:007
CARLYLE, ALVY & HESSON, MARGARET ANN	*18 MAR 1854	02:005
CARLYLE, JOSEPH C & BUTLER, ANNIE M	27 JUN 1894	07:108
CARMAN, FREDERICK B & DEEAN, KATE	08 JAN 1894	07:036
CARNELL, JACOB & DARE, SUSANNA	MAR 1838	01:034
CARNEY, CHARLES & GREEN, ELIZABETH	04 SEP 1823	01:010
CARNEY, JOHN & JIVIDEN, EASTY	20 OCT 1825	01:014
CARNEY, THOMAS & McCOY, LAVINIA	28 DEC 1875	08:314
CARNEY, THOMAS & HAYMAN, NANCY B	07 NOV 1884	12:090
CAROTHERS, JOSEPH A & GRIMM, LILLIE B	29 APR 1893	06:534
CAROTHERS, JOSEPH A & VAN MATRE, VIOLA E	24 JUN 1907	11:561
CARPENTER, CHARLES & FREEMAN, CORA	15 APR 1888	05:209
CARPENTER, FRANK A & RIFFLE, VIRGIE	27 SEP 1907	12:026
CARPENTER, G W & STOW, ALICE K	20 APR 1914	15:178
CARPENTER, JAMES D & SHARP, FLORENCE	11 JAN 1912	13:464
CARPENTER, JASPER & BOARD, ADDA G	19 JAN 1913	14:083
CARPENTER, JEREMIAH & FRIEND, ELLEN	*11 NOV 1858	02:011
CARPENTER, THOMAS P & SHAW, REBECCA T	07 FEB 1867	05:028
CARPENTER, WILLIAM A & WALKER, ETTA	15 JAN 1899	08:455
CARPENTER, WILLIAM H & ROSEBERRY, NETTIE A	20 OCT 1886	12:404
CARR, ALVA O & GREER, GARNET M	30 DEC 1914	15:361
CARR, HOWARD & BOOKER, IDA	17 OCT 1886	12:397
CARR, JACKSON & RYAN, MOLLIE CLEOPATRA	15 SEP 1887	05:093
CARR, JAMES R B & BOARD, MARTHA A	19 JUN 1893	06:557
CARR, JAMES W & WHALEY, MAUD K	03 SEP 1902	10:144
CARR, WILLIAM H & KING, ELIZABETH	23 APR 1868	05:174
CARROLL, JOHN & MINNS, MARY A	07 MAY 1872	07:220
CARROLL, JOHN C & HUNTER, LAURA J	25 DEC 1883	11:435
CARROW, SAMUEL J & FARLEY, BESSIE	02 MAY 1914	15:188
CARSEY, ALONZO & McKINEY, ELIZA J	06 OCT 1894	07:163
CARSEY, CHESLEY B & SELBY, BETHA L	12 SEP 1902	10:155
CARSEY, FRED R & GIST, GLADYS E	26 JUL 1913	14:202
CARSON, BENJAMIN R & SMITH, REBECCA A	19 AUG 1873	08:014
CARSON, JAMES E & CROOKS, ADELIA L	31 DEC 1908	12:347
CART, SAMUEL E & DOSS, ELLA	13 NOV 1904	10:637
CART, WILLIAM A & HUGHES, LAVINA A	28 DEC 1873	08:081
CARTER, DAVID HENRY & DABNEY, MATTIE	25 JUN 1887	05:051
CARTER, DENVER B & CHICK, HARTIE F	22 FEB 1906	11:275
CARTER, JOHN & BOSWELL, JANE	29 FEB 1826	01:013
CARTER, JOHN F & BOWCOTT, NORA E	11 FEB 1903	10:237

CARTER, ROBT & HARRISON, MARY	05 SEP 1839	01:033
CARTMILL, CHARLES N & MUSGRAVE, EMMA C	24 MAY 1896	07:555
CARTMILL, CHARLES S & HARDWICK, FRANCES S	21 DEC 1873	08:077
CARTMILL, DAVID E J & EADS, MARY J	07 SEP 1902	10:147
CARTMILL, E S & RICE, IDA	08 MAR 1891	06:076
CARTMILL, GEORGE W & CHEESBREW, MARY S	03 SEP 1879	10:125
CARTMILL, JAMES A & CHAPMAN, LUCY A	20 MAY 1866	04:122
CARTMILL, JAMES T R & CRINER, LILLIE J	09 OCT 1907	12:033
CARTMILL, JEFF D & HANNAN, NANNIE	25 NOV 1895	07:436
CARTMILL, NAPOLEON B & ZIRCKLE, ADA V	04 DEC 1878	10:019
CARTRIGHT, JOEL & GRAY, ROSANA	08 JAN 1829	01:018
CARTRIGHT, WILLIAM & NICHOLSON, ROENA E	22 JUN 1884	12:024
CARTT, WILLIAM SHERMAN & DOSS, MARY E	10 MAR 1912	13:498
CARTWRIGHT, ALBERT H & EDWARDS, LOUISA	21 MAY 1871	07:088
CARTWRIGHT, FREDRICK G & COLEMAN, MATTIE	11 JUL 1908	12:211
CARTWRIGHT, HARRY A & OLIVER, ANNA GRACE	18 DEC 1908	12:330
CARTWRIGHT, HERMAN & VAN MATRE, JESSIE	03 SEP 1910	13:147
CARTWRIGHT, JESSE & SKIVERS, SABRA	22 JAN 1844	01:042
CARTWRIGHT, LEWIS H & COSSIN, LUCRETIA A	11 JUL 1895	07:338
CASEY, CHARLES & STANLEY, LUCY	21 JUL 1905	11:125
CASEY, CHARLES & WOOMER, (Mrs) ALICE	11 MAY 1914	15:191
CASEY, EDWARD & BUSH, HENRIETTA	05 AUG 1899	08:591
CASEY, EDWARD F & LEWIS, ROSA	25 APR 1911	13:313
CASEY, GEORGE A & LONG, JULIA F	30 DEC 1906	11:486
CASEY, GEORGE T & CARTER, LAVINIA M	17 MAR 1881	10:387
CASEY, ISAAC & PHILIPS, BESSIE	14 SEP 1904	10:587
CASEY, JOHN & RICKARD, MARY	24 FEB 1870	06:158
CASEY, JOHN & RODES, DELLA	23 SEP 1904	10:605
CASEY, JONATHAN & BLAKE, (Mrs) EUNICE	*25 JUN 1855	02:007
CASEY, KELSY & FROST, FANNY	21 NOV 1891	06:229
CASEY, PERCY & BONECUTTER, VIOLA	03 FEB 1909	12:362
CASEY, SAMUEL StCLARE & HANEH, CORA B	06 JUL 1907	11:575
CASEY, WILLIAM C & LONG, NOLA	*01 MAY 1906	11:306
CASH, CHARLES A & HOLLEY, JANE	14 MAY 1901	09:342
CASH, HENRY & BARBER, SADIE	07 OCT 1905	11:185
CASH, JAMES W & CAIN, SARAH E	15 AUG 1878	09:292
CASSEL, WILLIAM H & MEADOWS, CARA MABEL	30 OCT 1913	15:061
CASTO, AUGUSTUS KENISON & ELY, ELLA	28 OCT 1886	12:407
CASTO, BAILES & LEMASTER, MARY E	27 JUL 1893	06:579
CASTO, CHARLES & JEFFERS, PEARL	10 SEP 1898	08:364
CASTO, CHARLES B & DEWEESE, MINERVA J	06 MAR 1897	08:055
CASTO, CHAS C & PARSONS, EFFIE J	04 AUG 1911	13:387
CASTO, CLYDE C & ALLEN, BERTHA E	31 DEC 1912	14:076
CASTO, ELIAS F & BARR, BELINDA J	01 JAN 1880	10:190
CASTO, ELIJAH R & DEWEESE, RACHEL	29 JUL 1830	01:023
CASTO, ENOCH & SMITH, JANE	19 DEC 1867	05:121
CASTO, ENOCH S & LEE, MELISSA	29 OCT 1887	05:134
CASTO, EVERTT & KREBS, CLARA B	29 JUN 1913	14:188
CASTO, FRANCIS M & ANGEL, ALICE	05 NOV 1876	08:406
CASTO, GEORGE W & JOHNSTON, MARGARET F	14 DEC 1878	10:017
CASTO, ISAAC A & BARNETT, ROSANNA M	28 OCT 1873	08:046
CASTO, JAMES & GIBSON, BIRTIE	26 SEP 1899	08:622
CASTO, JAMES N & GRAHAM, ALICE	16 FEB 1873	07:320
CASTO, JEPTHA M & BARR, ROSETTA J	12 JAN 1881	10:365
CASTO, JNO D & McDADE, SUSANNA	20 OCT 1819	01:007
CASTO, JOHN M & PLATT, CHARLOTTE E	21 JUN 1882	11:166
CASTO, JULIUS A & CASTO, MINERVA J	11 MAR 1903	10:253
CASTO, LEVI & WRIGHT, POLLY	10 MAR 1831	01:023

Names	Date	Ref
CASTO, LEWIS M & SAYRE, MARY	02 MAY 1905	11:085
CASTO, LOYD P & BAKER, MINNIE E	11 DEC 1912	14:051
CASTO, MASON & KELLY, MARGUERITE	18 JUL 1913	14:195
CASTO, MOSES M & BAKER, MARIA	27 DEC 1866	05:015
CASTO, MOSES M & STONEKING, JULIA A	03 JUN 1906	11:324
CASTO, ORPHA & HILL, MARY O	26 OCT 1910	13:193
CASTO, OSCAR & SCOYC, ALICE	25 DEC 1907	12:096
CASTO, PERRY E & KEEFER, LAURA M	05 JUN 1904	10:532
CASTO, ROBERT & BARNETT, ELLEN	22 MAY 1862	03:063
CASTO, ROBERT E & LEWIS, MARY C	06 MAR 1893	06:496
CASTO, ROBERT P & WINGER, MARY J	25 AUG 1907	11:598
CASTO, SAMUEL & WARNER, DORA	03 SEP 1901	09:398
CASTO, SAMUEL F & RIFFLE, ANNER L	22 NOV 1906	11:453
CASTO, SOLOMON & WADE, MARTHA	*21 MAR 1855	02:006
CASTO, THEODORE & SIDERS, MARY L	05 AUG 1906	11:380
CASTO, THOMAS & McDADE, NANCY	29 NOV 1825	01:014
CASTO, WILLIAM A & WEAVER, ELLA M	13 JUN 1889	05:412
CASTO, WILLIAM E & HILL, HANNAH M	24 AUG 1893	06:594
CASTO, WILLIAM G & SMITH, CORA A	25 APR 1910	13:052
CAUFMAN, GRANDVILLE HUSTON & HOLDREN, SADIE BELLE	10 MAY 1900	09:127
CAUFMAN, JONAS & DOBYNS, MARY A	12 NOV 1826	01:013
CAUFMAN, JONAS & McDERMIT, CYNTHIA	1836	01:040
CAUFMAN, MARTIN M & ADAMS, LOUISA	03 AUG 1870	06:214
CAUFMAN, WALTER L & SOMMER, CLARA	09 SEP 1903	10:347
CAVIN, DANIEL & AMSBARY, AMELIA M	1838	01:041
CAYLOR, JACOB & ROUSH, MARY	04 MAR 1841	01:043
CAYLOR, JOHN & WINKELBACK, ELIZABETH JANE	22 AUG 1844	01:043
CAZAD, NELSON E & McWHORTOR, MARGARET F	02 JUN 1870	06:194
CAZY, StCLAIR & NEIBERT, JEMIMA	08 MAY 1828	01:017
CEMMIS, GEORGE & NEALE, EMMA E	15 AUG 1880	10:286
CENTERS, BRENT & MALONE, MARY S	09 APR 1902	10:052
CENTERS, JACOB & ROSEBERRY, ELVIRA	18 JUL 1849	01:051
CHAFFIN, WILLIAM & WADE, MARY J	31 DEC 1888	05:335
CHAMBERLAIN, EUGENE & MEEKS, NANCY J	07 OCT 1875	08:283
CHAMBERLAIN, FRANCIS & McINTIRE, SARAH	JAN 1847	01:049
CHAMBERLAIN, JOHN R & KNOPP, MARTHA A C	*24 DEC 1860	02:015
CHAMBERLAIN, LUTHER & VANMATRE, SARAH	08 AUG 1839	01:042
CHAMBERLAIN, LUTHER W & JONES, MARTHA	*04 NOV 1859	02:013
CHAMBERS, CORNELIUS & HARRINGTON, MYRTA	09 NOV 1890	06:002
CHAMBERS, DAVID & BEARD, EMMA	01 MAY 1883	11:321
CHAMBERS, M E & MOORE, NORA F	19 MAR 1898	08:272
CHAMBERS, ULYSSES G & FERGUSON, LEONA P	23 JUN 1895	07:323
CHANCELLOR, EDMUND P & MILLER, RHODA J	*24 JUL 1855	02:007
CHANDLER, ANDREW & GILBERT, JULIA	25 NOV 1875	08:303
CHANDLER, AUGUSTUS & KIRK, SARAH	14 DEC 1876	08:420
CHANDLER, DORMAN & WRIGHT, LUCINDA	21 APR 1881	10:403
CHANDLER, GENERAL W & MEADOWS, PARTHENIA E	22 SEP 1878	09:319
CHANDLER, GEORGE PRESTON & PIERCE, MARY MAGDALANE	15 SEP 1887	05:092
CHANDLER, JAMES L & MEADOWS, JULIA J	16 MAY 1907	11:534
CHANDLER, JOSEPH T & ALDERMAN, LETHA A	15 OCT 1876	08:398
CHANDLER, MATISON & HOLLY, MARY A	16 JAN 1878	09:167
CHANDLER, MOSES & HENRY, LILLY M	24 JUN 1899	08:561
CHANDLER, PHILIP & WOLFORD, EUSTASIA L	27 FEB 1883	11:305
CHANNEY, JOSEPH & BRYANT, JANE	1832	01:026
CHANNEL, JAMES B & WITHROW, LEONA	24 DEC 1901	09:482
CHAPDEAN, CHARLES & FIELDER, ELIZABETH	13 JAN 1887	12:465
CHAPMAN, A F Jr & CAHILL, MARGARET I	03 JUL 1913	14:190
CHAPMAN, A P & MILLER, MARY C	*23 MAY 1859	02:012

CHAPMAN, ALEXANDER & CONRAD, RHODA	08 JAN 1898	08:236
CHAPMAN, ALRICK ALONZO & FETTY, BESSIE	09 OCT 1911	13:390
CHAPMAN, ARCHIE F & GRAHAM, MINNIE F	02 MAY 1914	15:189
CHAPMAN, BRICE H & McCARTY, MYRTIE E	13 APR 1907	11:517
CHAPMAN, CARROLL DANA & MALONEY, MARY ELIZABETH	09 SEP 1912	13:596
CHAPMAN, CHARLES & THAXTON, VALLEY	15 NOV 1909	12:544
CHAPMAN, CHARLES ALONZO & POLK, ETTA	19 AUG 1888	05:257
CHAPMAN, CHARLES F & HILL, ZETTA M	13 FEB 1904	10:476
CHAPMAN, CHARLES F & DUNCAN, ELIZA	26 MAY 1910	13:074
CHAPMAN, CHARLES O & LOVE, GEORGIANNA	24 SEP 1898	08:360
CHAPMAN, CHARLES PETERS & EDWARDS, IDA	*16 JUL 1892	06:370
CHAPMAN, CHARLES SPURGEON & HUTCHINSON, BELLE MARY	20 JUN 1889	05:416
CHAPMAN, CHARLES T & CARPENTER, IDA M	15 AUG 1894	07:131
CHAPMAN, CLARENCE & FOURTH, MADA	03 MAR 1908	12:132
CHAPMAN, EPHRAIM & WALLIS, CATHARINE	06 MAR 1877	09:039
CHAPMAN, FRANK & HANNA, FANNY	15 MAR 1870	06:166
CHAPMAN, FRANK A & BANKS, (Mrs) MARY ALICE	15 JUN 1912	13:546
CHAPMAN, FRANKLIN AMELIUS & HANNA, MARY A	09 OCT 1895	07:405
CHAPMAN, G C & RAYBURN, CLARA, B	30 APR 1914	15:184
CHAPMAN, GEORGE T & SMITH, ETHEL F	23 FEB 1914	15:143
CHAPMAN, GEORGE W & CREMEANS, MATTIE J	17 SEP 1894	07:154
CHAPMAN, HARRY & CASEY, EDNA	16 SEP 1899	08:612
CHAPMAN, JAMES & CARPENTER, MARY	*23 NOV 1858	02:011
CHAPMAN, JAMES A & CONRAD, EMILY	*08 MAR 1899	08:479
CHAPMAN, JAMES F & HARRIS, ELIZA J	06 JUN 1880	10:265
CHAPMAN, JAMES F & ROHBAUGH, SUSAN	04 APR 1893	06:514
CHAPMAN, JAMES H & PAGE, LUCINDA J	31 JUL 1879	10:106
CHAPMAN, JAMES H & ZIMMERMAN, MEDIA A	03 JAN 1911	13:256
CHAPMAN, JAMES L & CHAPMAN, GENEVIA A	01 JUL 1888	05:241
CHAPMAN, JAMES M & STONE, PERMELIA	07 NOV 1844	01:042
CHAPMAN, JOHN F & McCLURE, MARY E	22 AUG 1882	11:191
CHAPMAN, JOHN F & SHANK, NANCY J	26 DEC 1867	05:132
CHAPMAN, JOHN M & RIFE, MARY A	07 JUL 1877	09:069
CHAPMAN, JOHN W & FARLEY, GRACE	19 NOV 1874	08:184
CHAPMAN, JOHN W & MEADOWS, JENNIE A	16 MAY 1902	10:073
CHAPMAN, JOHN W & WILSON, ANNIE	28 AUG 1911	13:366
CHAPMAN, JOHN WESLEY & WRIGHT, MARY ELIZABETH	19 JUL 1888	05:245
CHAPMAN, JOSEPH G & WALKER, MARIA A	29 DEC 1887	05:162
CHAPMAN, JOSEPH M & VILLARS, ROSESRUTHEY	25 MAR 1907	11:508
CHAPMAN, JOSEPH M & CREMEANS, LYDIA	27 MAY 1877	09:086
CHAPMAN, JOSEPH ROW & JOLLY, NORA	26 AUG 1880	10:288
CHAPMAN, LOWRY & RICKARD, DELPHA	22 MAR 1902	10:039
CHAPMAN, LYCURGUS S & HUTCHINSON, AMELIA	20 JAN 1892	06:371
CHAPMAN, MARCUS R & STROBLE, CLARA E	23 NOV 1901	09:454
CHAPMAN, MORRIS ELLIS & LAMBERT, MINNIE	10 FEB 1904	10:473
CHAPMAN, OSCAR L & MORRIS, ARRETTA E	25 NOV 1906	11:457
CHAPMAN, ROBERT C & WITHERS, MINERVA C	28 OCT 1877	09:146
CHAPMAN, ROBERT N & CARSON, SARAH M	08 AUG 1895	07:358
CHAPMAN, ROBERT S & SPURLOCK, LOUISA	02 FEB 1808	12:124
CHAPMAN, ROBERT S & HANNON, LEVENA D	29 MAY 1914	15:207
CHAPMAN, ROBERT S & HARMON, LEVENA D	29 MAY 1914	15:207
CHAPMAN, SHELBY L & CHAPMAN, MARTHA J	27 AUG 1898	08:350
CHAPMAN, SIDNEY M & REA, SARAH J	18 JUL 1897	08:125
CHAPMAN, THOMAS & FERGUSON, ELLA	*05 JUL 1894	07:118
CHAPMAN, THOS J & GILMORE, LIDA F	14 SEP 1912	14:001
CHAPMAN, WADE L & CLATTERBUCK, ETHEL L	05 JAN 1908	12:113
CHAPMAN, WALTER M & GIBBS, MARY C	17 AUG 1891	06:166
CHAPMAN, WILBER V & MOORE, DULCIE E	21 DEC 1902	10:205

CHAPMAN, WILLIAM & ESTES, SARIAH		01:032 5
CHAPMAN, WILLIAM G & JOHNSON, MARY JANE	*20 APR 1852	02:002
CHAPMAN, WILLIAM H & MITCHELL, ANGELINE	08 FEB 1865	03:221
CHAPMAN, WILLIS FRANKLIN & HOPSON, ADALINE	23 NOV 1884	12:097
CHASE, GUY & CHURCH, ELSIE	15 NOV 1905	11:205
CHASE, HENRY F & WINDON, NANCY M	22 NOV 1866	05:002
CHASE, JOHN & KEY, MELINA (MALINDA)	29 MAR 1828	01:021
CHASE, JOHN J & STEWART, WYNNE B	16 AUG 1899	08:597
CHASE, OWEN G & SMITH, ELIZABETH	*22 FEB 1853	02:004
CHATMAN, JOHN C & WARD, MAGGIE MAY	21 JAN 1900	09:068
CHATTIN, JAMES R & STEELE, ABBIE G	27 NOV 1901	09:456
CHATTIN, SQUIRE HILL & KNAPP, ELLA MAY	05 SEP 1889	05:448
CHEATAM, ROBERT & LEE, HANNAH B	06 AUG 1909	12:475
CHEATAM, WILLIAM M & GIBBS, HATTIE K	23 JUN 1909	12:439
CHEESBREW, CLARENCE R & LAYRUE, MABLE	26 DEC 1914	15:359
CHEESBREW, ISAAC H & MAYES, EMMA D	19 DEC 1886	12:440
CHEESBREW, JAMES P & HARDWICK, SARAH M	08 JUN 1876	08:359
CHEESBREW, JOHN H & NOBLE, ETTA F	10 NOV 1883	11:421
CHEESBREW, SAMUEL R & RODGERS, SUSAN M	14 MAY 1882	11:148
CHENOWETH, D B & EDWARDS, FRANCES W	28 JAN 1866	04:100
CHERRINGTON, F E & COFFMAN, KATE	29 FEB 1912	13:490
CHERRINGTON, IRA E & FERGUSON, E VANNA	22 OCT 1890	05:627
CHERRY, ALBERT H & FINDLEY, ELIZABETH	29 AUG 1861	03:015
CHERRY, HENRY & MORGAN, RACHEL	08 APR 1868	05:164
CHESEBREW, JOHN S & MACKLY, VIOLA	24 DEC 1903	10:443
CHESNUTT, LEON L & HAYNES, AURELIA B	24 NOV 1909	12:563
CHESTER, FRANK M & STALNAKER, MURREL M	11 JUL 1907	11:577
CHESTER, GEORGE F & FRY, MARY F	11 MAR 1876	08:333
CHEUVRONT, W A & BROWN, MARY F	20 FEB 1884	11:460
CHILDERS, BENJAMIN F & CARTMILL, FANNIE	24 MAY 1884	12:020
CHILDERS, CHARLES & JAQUES, SUSIE	23 SEP 1898	08:369
CHILDERS, EZEKIEL & FLOWERS, ANNIE A	12 DEC 1902	10:206
CHILDERS, FRANCIS & PARSONS, (Mrs) LUCINDA	*12 NOV 1855	02:007
CHILDERS, FRANK & MILLER, DORA	07 NOV 1912	14:023
CHILDERS, GEORGE H & BATTRELL, MINERVA	09 JUL 1895	07:337
CHILDERS, GRANVILLE & HILL, SPICE A	21 OCT 1888	05:291
CHILDERS, HARVEY & STEWART, SUSAN	10 DEC 1885	12:264
CHILDERS, JOHN & MOSBARG, BETSY	1809	01:004
CHILDERS, JORDAN & SULLIVAN, MARIA A	25 OCT 1882	11:233
CHILDERS, JORDAN & PIERCY, HESTER	1838	01:040
CHILDERS, JOSEPH & FINNY, CATHARINE	1842	01:041
CHILDERS, LAWRENCE E & STEPHENS, MINERVA J	11 FEB 1901	09:289
CHILDERS, MARION W & TILLIS, MALINDA E	15 JUL 1886	12:357
CHILDERS, PERRY A & JONES, PEARL D	19 NOV 1908	12:309
CHILDERS, ROBERT & RIFFLE, MIRIAM	25 AUG 1868	05:207
CHILDERS, ROBERT & HIGGINBOTHAM, MARY A	19 AUG 1897	08:144
CHILDERS, ROBERT & McCOY, SARAH J	20 JUN 1874	08:135
CHILDERS, ROBERT L & JEFFERS, AMANDA E	13 MAR 1869	06:040
CHILDERS, RUFUS J & DOSS, ONA	13 MAR 1901	09:305
CHILDERS, SANFORD & HART, MARY M	27 APR 1889	05:384
CHILDERS, THOMAS & LEWIS, ADA E	20 JUN 1908	12:200
CHILDERS, WILLIAM & WISEMAN, MARY	24 DEC 1885	12:267
CHILDRESS, JOHN & KIMBERLING, BELINDA	11 JUL 1844	01:042
CHILDS, GEORGE E & SAYRE, (Mrs) L N	13 NOV 1910	13:203
CHILDS, GEORGE ERA & ROSEBERRY, ELLA	24 DEC 1891	06:257
CHILDS, GEORGE RICHARD & McDERMITT, RHODA	18 DEC 1890	06:022
CHILDS, GEORGE WILLIAM & KIDWELL, KATIE MAY	13 JUN 1887	05:042
CHILDS, JOHN W & BARNETT, SARAH E	22 MAY 1892	06:341

CHILDS, ROBERT D & McGUFFIN, LILLY B	12 DEC 1886	12:439
CHILDS, RUSSEL IRA & DYE, ALBERTA	08 APR 1914	15 169
CHILDS, SAMUEL W & DAVIS, ELIZABETH	26 APR 1871	07:076
CHILDS, WILLIAM J & RIFFLE, SADIE V	12 JUL 1908	12:209
CHILDS, WILLIAM H & LEWIS, AGNES E	20 SEP 1886	12:388
CHITTENDEN, WM R & SAYRE, SYDNEY	*14 JAN 1857	02:009
CHOEN, CHARLES G & YEAGER, SUSANNA	02 APR 1835	01:029
CHOEN, ROBERT & EVANS, DEBORAH	08 MAY 1842	01:037
CHRIS, JESSE & MEADOWS, NANCY J	15 MAR 1877	09:046
CHRIST, PATRICK L & LONG, MARY	19 MAY 1892	06:338
CHRISTOPHER, EDWARD A & CHRISTOPHER, HARRIET	17 AUG 1904	10:576
CHRISTY, HENRY & HOLLY, MARY	11 JUN 1846	01:045
CHRISTY, JAMES M & APPLETON, SUSAN	19 SEP 1850	02:001
CHRISTY, JOHN M & FOWLER, RHODA	*30 MAY 1896	07:558
CHRISTY, JOSEPH E & DUNCAN, MAGGIE L	27 NOV 1893	07:009
CHRISTY, JOSEPH M & McCUMBER, NORA B	02 FEB 1901	09:266
CHRISTY, PERRY & WOODY, CARRIE	03 JUN 1905	11:104
CHRISTY, SAMUEL J & VAN SICKLE, BETTIE	08 OCT 1898	08:380
CHRISTY, WALTER E & ALEXANDER, LILLIE B	05 OCT 1910	13:175
CHURCH, EDWARD & MOSES, EMMA	23 FEB 1896	07:501
CHURCH, GEORGE A & McFARLAND, ANN ELIZA	11 MAY 1867	05:045
CHURCH, JAMES T & HEARSMAN, VIOLETTA F	06 JAN 1886	12:276
CHURCH, R A & HART, DORA	01 MAY 1914	15:187
CHURCH, WILLIAM & COOPER, MARGARET JANE	28 JUN 1866	04:134
CHURCH, WOODWARD W & HALL, HAZELTINE	18 APR 1872	07:211
CIRCKLE, WILLIAM & HUDSON, MARY E	18 APR 1869	06:049
CIRCLE, CHARLES WESLEY & DAVIS, ORA FLORENCE	03 JUL 1900	09:153
CIRCLE, RAY & HENRY, GARNETT MARIE	01 NOV 1913	15:055
CIRCLE, WESLEY & GOSSETT, EUNICE E	23 DEC 1869	06:133
CLAGG, ALBERT & FARLEY, SIANDA	08 MAY 1901	09:335
CLAGG, ASA O & HUDSON, LIZZIE E	09 APR 1911	13:308
CLAGG, EDWARD & HOLLEY, ELLA	07 FEB 1904	10:467
CLAGG, ERA P & BLAKE, LAURA B	04 OCT 1912	14:019
CLAGG, HARRISON & WARNER, JANE	09 MAR 1878	09:023
CLAGG, JEFFERSON D & SIDERS, MAGGIE M	03 SEP 1885	12:219
CLAGG, JOHN & JOHNSON, FRANCES	1833	01:039
CLAGG, JOHN & JOHNSON, FANNY	1833	01:027
CLAGG, JOHN L & HOLLY, CAROLINE	*23 MAY 1856	02:008
CLAGG, JULIUS J & SMITH, REBECCA JANE	26 SEP 1867	05:086
CLAGG, WALTER E & FLORY, JENCIE	17 MAY 1908	12:146
CLAGG, WALTER E & WARDEN, ORPHE BELLE	05 OCT 1900	09:216
CLAGG, WILLARD & WARDEN, EDITH E	28 NOV 1900	09:243
CLAGG, WILLARD & CHAPMAN, ALMA	*21 NOV 1910	13:212
CLAGG, WILLARD & SAUNDERS, RUBY E	31 DEC 1910	13:251
CLAGG, WILLIAM & HARLER, MARGARET	08 MAY 1901	09:336
CLAGG, WILLIAM & WAMSLEY, WILLIE B	27 JUN 1895	07:325
CLAIG, JULIUS J & DANIELS, MARY A	*26 MAR 1853	02:004
CLARK, (given name missing) & HAYMAN, SURA ANN	05 DEC 1869	06:115
CLARK, CHARLES E & ROUSH, LULU	16 JUN 1896	07:566
CLARK, DAVID A & TURNBULL, MARY E	10 MAY 1886	12:325
CLARK, DAVID SMITH & MYERS, LYDA ANN	30 JUL 1890	05:594
CLARK, ELDON J & VAN METRE, LORENO	15 DEC 1908	12:332
CLARK, FLOYD & JOHNSON, ANNIE	23 MAY 1899	08:538
CLARK, FRANKLIN J & RODGERS, HATTIE E	26 MAR 1905	11:061
CLARK, GEORGE & HOFFMAN, MALINDA	02 FEB 1872	07:188
CLARK, GEORGE A & PICKENS, WINONA	01 DEC 1910	13:216
CLARK, GEORGE F & HOLLAND, ODDIE	24 OCT 1901	09:430
CLARK, HARMAN & RAPPOLD, (Mrs) ADDIE MAY	03 NOV 1913	15:063

Name	Date	Ref
CLARK, JAMES F & GRIER, MARY W	12 OCT 1892	06:424
CLARK, JOSE ALVAH & TOMLINSON, BLANCHE	26 FEB 1889	05:361
CLARK, LESTER & JACKSON, BELVA D	24 DEC 1906	11:477
CLARK, ROBERT & McCARNY, SUSAN	18 JUN 1871	07:096
CLARK, THOMAS H & YOUNG, NEVADA	25 SEP 1907	12:017
CLARK, WILLIAM & CLARK, CHARLOTTE	*09 JUL 1886	12:354
CLARK, WILLIAM A & TUCKER, EMILY L	04 JAN 1878	09:190
CLARK, WILLIAM N & McMULLEN, ELIZA	18 SEP 1826	01:013
CLARK, WILLIAM W & HOFFMAN, BERTHA E	25 JAN 1899	08:457
CLARKE, ALFRED L & ROSE, AUGUSTA ROMAINE	10 JAN 1914	15:124
CLARKE, HARRY H & SHATO, BESSIE B	23 AUG 1911	13:361
CLARKE, HERMAN A & MORRIS, JESSIE F	28 NOV 1883	11:427
CLARKE, P H & WADDELL, MARTHA A	05 SEP 1872	07:258
CLAY, JAMES R & BOWLES, ROSELLA	03 JUL 1869	06:064
CLAYTON, EMETT L & ROUSH, LIZZIE M	21 APR 1908	12:163
CLEEK, ANDREW P & BURNSIDE, CLARIBULL	22 NOV 1894	07:187
CLEEK, GEORGE W & GARNS, MARY	03 NOV 1878	10:001
CLEEK, MINOR V & SALLAZ, LULA O	08 MAR 1908	12:137
CLEEK, THOMAS J & FISHER, MARY M	04 MAR 1903	10:251
CLEEK, THOMAS J & RIFFLE, CYNTHIA F	11 AUG 1909	12:476
CLELAND, VURN D & WINDSOR, MABLE	10 APR 1908	12:155
CLEMENT, ELMER & BLACKSON, MAGGIE B	03 JUL 1908	12:204
CLEMONS, DENNIS JOHNSON & HOLDREN, LIZZIE	27 OCT 1894	07:180
CLENDENEN, (given name missing) & KERWOOD, PRISILLA	*20 MAR 1855	02:006
CLENDENEN, ALEXANDER & YEAGER, ELIZABETH	*27 FEB 1854	02:005
CLENDENEN, BURTON THOMAS & SWISHER, BERTIE LUELLAN	04 JUL 1869	05:421
CLENDENEN, CHARLES & NEEL, SOPHIA	11 DEC 1807	01:001
CLENDENEN, GEORGE M & EDWARDS, MARIA A	14 SEP 1877	09:129
CLENDENEN, ISAAC & DODSON, VIENNA	*27 DEC 1858	02:012
CLENDENEN, JAMES A & LEWIS, REBECCA	21 JUN 1840	01:032 5
CLENDENEN, JAMES E & FOWLER, ELLA	30 DEC 1875	08:315
CLENDENEN, JAMES EDWARD & GARNES, MALISSA ELIZABETH	21 JUL 1890	05:593
CLENDENEN, JAMES R & EDWARDS, SARAH E	16 NOV 1876	08:411
CLENDENEN, LEWIS G & KNOPP, CATHARINE C	29 FEB 1876	08:332
CLENDENEN, LORENZO DOW & McCULLOCH, LYDIA ANNIE	09 JAN 1890	05:509
CLENDENEN, MICHAEL WILLIAM & GOSNAY, ISABELLE	17 OCT 1887	05:122
CLENDENEN, SAMUEL A & STEPHENSON, MARTHA E	15 NOV 1877	09:156
CLENDENEN, WILLIAM M & WINDON, SARAH F	28 FEB 1879	10:059
CLENDENEN, WILLIAM W & SQUIER, SARAH A	31 OCT 1861	03:029
CLENDENIN, GEORGE E & KINCADE, OTTIE L	22 JUN 1912	13:550
CLENDENIN, JAMES E & STERRITT, AGNES A	30 OCT 1862	03:084
CLENDENIN, JOHN A & FISHER, FANNIE	19 SEP 1906	11:415
CLENDENIN, JOSEPH & EDWARDS, FRANCES	03 NOV 1881	11:044
CLENDENIN, JOSEPH B & HAWKINS, MARY E	25 MAR 1875	08:219
CLENDENIN, TAYLOR W & KINCADE, SARAH	11 NOV 1882	11:238
CLENDENIN, WILLIAM T & STEWART, ANNA P	11 FEB 1885	12:138
CLENDINEN, FRANCIS M & DARNEL, OZELLO	21 APR 1864	03:180
CLENDINEN, GIDEON S & DODSON, VIRGINIA F	13 FEB 1863	03:101
CLENDINEN, JAMES S & YEAGER, MARGARET	26 APR 1840	01:050
CLENDINEN, LEANDER & LEWIS, ELIZAGETH	27 SEP 1832	01:025
CLICK, EDGAR L & BAKER, MARY JANE	11 MAR 1909	12:382
CLICK, FREDERICK PHILIP & LUTZE, EMMA	06 SEP 1900	09:196
CLICK, GEORGE & DURST, CHRISTENA	21 JUL 1870	06:208
CLICK, MONROE & RIFFLE, MINNIE	06 APR 1899	08:504
CLICK, ORVIL J & SOMMER, ROSE E	04 MAY 1904	10:515
CLICK, PHILIP & KAPP, LOUISA	09 MAY 1872	07:221
CLICK, REUBEN P & MARTIN, FANNIE J	01 JUL 1872	07:186
CLICK, ROBERT CHRISTOPHER & DURST, FANNY	28 DEC 1887	05:167

CLICK, THOMAS & WALKER, LORA L	19 OCT 1898	08:388
CLIFF, GEORGE W & PHILLIPS, KATE	10 NOV 1890	06:003
CLIFF, JOHN & LITTLE, ROSA E	09 NOV 1881	11:051
CLINE, JESSE & HILL, MARY	30 OCT 1826	01:013
CLINE, WESLEY B & PATTERSON, ROSA	20 SEP 1906	11:413
CLINZING, FRED J & MYERS, HATTIE R	03 NOV 1895	07:418
CLONCH, ABNER & NEWELL, EVA	09 NOV 1910	13:201
CLONCH, ALBERT A & HICKS, ELLA	14 APR 1890	05:541
CLONCH, GEORGE & HAWKINS, ALTHA	02 JAN 1914	15:114
CLONCH, JOHN E & HICKS, IDA	01 AUG 1895	07:355
CLONCH, THOMAS E & FOUT, LAURA	20 MAR 1911	13:292
CLUTTER, JOHN & McCOY, HANNAH	12 SEP 1847	01:047
CLUTTS, CHAS C & McCLURE, LILLIAN	25 JUL 1912	13:569
CLUTTS, JAMES & PORE, MAGGIE E	02 APR 1882	11:132
COAR, DOSSON & GILLIS, ANN	23 NOV 1872	07:292
COATES, CHARLES T & MAUPIN, JENNETTE A	27 AUG 1868	05:206
COBB, AUGUSTUS & ELMORE, RHODA FRANCES	09 JUN 1847	01:047
COBB, GEORGE W & BIRCH, JOSEPHINE	30 MAR 1905	11:064
COBB, HOWARD & SHIVELEY, MARY F	16 NOV 1908	12:307
COBB, JOHN H & VAN MATRE, ELIZA	03 APR 1873	07:340
COBB, JOHN W & HARBOR, MARY M	13 MAR 1896	07:507
COBB, JOHN W & VAUGHAN, NANCY E	08 NOV 1882	11:245
COCHRAN, CHARLES & GLEASON, MARY	17 AUG 1909	12:482
COCHRAN, CHARLES E & MARTIN, MINNIE B	07 MAY 1898	08:304
COCHRAN, HERBERT & HILL, LUCY	06 DEC 1905	11:218
COCHRAN, JAMES E & ADKINS, ELOSHA E	08 DEC 1886	12:435
COCHRAN, JOHN & STRAIT, CORA D	23 SEP 1897	08:164
COCHRAN, JOHN M & BARRET, JENNIE	02 JUN 1883	11:352
COCHRAN, SHERMAN & FORREST, MARY ELLEN	20 MAR 1900	09:068
COCHRAN, SHERMAN & BUCKLEY, AUGUSTA	24 DEC 1891	06:263
COE, JAMES F & PHELPS, NANCY	26 APR 1878	09:251
COEN, W H & KING, STELLA	27 APR 1912	13:521
COFFMAN, CHARLES & YEAGER, SARAH ANN	07 FEB 1887	12:479
COFFMAN, JOHN & HUGHS, MARTHA	23 MAR 1824	01:010
COFFMAN, REUBEN & REYNOLDS, JULIA	01 JAN 1824	01:010
COFFMAN, ZACHARIAH & CROUCH, SUSAN	26 OCT 1839	01:033
COFFMAN, ZACKARIAH & HILL, SALLY	17 JAN 1828	01:017
COHEN, CHARLES W & CHURCH, LOTTIE	23 NOV 1914	15:326
COLDWELL, LUTHER C & JOHNSON, MARGARET J	15 AUG 1861	03:012
COLE, JAMES & HILL, MELISSA	1830	01:024
COLEMAN, ALBERT H & GREER, MARY T	02 AUG 1888	05:253
COLEMAN, ALONZO & SAXTON, MATTIE	18 MAR 1897	08:060
COLEMAN, ANDREW J & BRYANT, SARAH	28 AUG 1912	13:592
COLEMAN, ANDREW J & BRYANT, (Mrs) SARAH	04 SEP 1912	13:595
COLEMAN, ARCHIE J & GIBBS, ETHEL M	04 JUN 1899	08:547
COLEMAN, HENRY S & HOOP, HARRIET E	12 APR 1871	07:073
COLEMAN, ISAAC & CHISHOLM, MARGARET A	26 DEC 1867	05:122
COLEMAN, JACOB & BAILEY, NANCY E	06 JUN 1844	01:038
COLEMAN, JAMES J & FOWLER, EDNA	*11 MAY 1896	07:546
COLEMAN, JAMES J & FOWLER, EDNA	17 AUG 1897	08:142
COLEMAN, JESSE N & CHAFFIN, JESSIE	01 JUL 1909	12:146
COLEMAN, LEE ROY & ELLIS, BERTINE	25 DEC 1912	14:068
COLEMAN, P C & POWELL, LELIA	26 JAN 1910	12:596
COLEMAN, THOMAS G & STEPHENS, LAURA B	24 JUL 1897	08:132
COLEMAN, WILLIAM & CURRY, LENA	07 JUN 1908	12:195
COLEMAN, WILLIAM & WILSON, ELIZA	05 SEP 1875	08:278
COLEMAN, WILLIAM & SATTES, LUTITIA A	05 JUL 1885	12:192
COLEMAN, WILLIAM & LEGUE, SARAH L	21 NOV 1888	05:307

COLEMAN, WILLIAM & KIRK, MARY F	07 OCT 1901	09:418
COLEMAN, WILLIAM & CAREY, SARAH	22 JUL 1897	08:132
COLEMAN, WILLIAM H & DUFF, LOUISA L	09 DEC 1880	10:342
COLEMAN, WILLIAM L & RINE, MARTHA A	07 FEB 1869	06:032
COLLIER, CHARLES & PATCHAL, NANCY A	26 DEC 1877	09:179
COLLIER, CHARLES W & ECKARD, LUCY M	01 JUL 1891	06:133
COLLIN, ANDREW J & HEREFORD, MARIA C	29 NOV 1838	01:031 5
COLLINS, ANDREW & MISNER, ELIZABETH M	06 JUN 1870	06:197
COLLINS, DAVID & THOMAS, ANNIE	05 JUL 1882	11:171
COLLINS, GEORGE W & MYERS, NETTIE F	04 JAN 1894	07:035
COLLINS, GEORGE W & QUEEN, OCTA E	10 AUG 1906	11:384
COLLINS, GIBSON & McCOY, SAMANTHA	07 JAN 1880	10:195
COLLINS, JAMES & SHAY, MARY	17 JAN 1882	11:097
COLLINS, JAMES & ROBSON, ANNIE	20 MAY 1880	10:255
COLLINS, LEE L & VAN MATRE, MOLLIE	27 APR 1988	05:217
COLLINS, TIMOTHY & RHEY, PERMELIA J	02 MAY 1878	09:253
COLLINS, WILLIAM & JONES, JENNIE	30 JAN 1873	07:307
COLSTON, THOMAS & CALLOWAY, LUCY	25 JAN 1880	10:201
COLVILLE, JESSE L & GREER, NANNIE B	18 OCT 1900	09:025
COLVIN, SOLOMON D & FORD, MARY ANN	15 AUG 1875	08:266
COLWELL, ALLEN C & CAIN, EDE A	11 JUL 1905	11:130
COLWELL, ANDREW & SNYDER, DOMINE V	* 04 JUL 1894	07:115
COLWELL, FRANK & McGHEE, KATIE	28 OCT 1897	08:184
COLWELL, JOHN B & DUNCAN, LUCINDA W	*17 SEP 1857	02:010
COLWELL, JOHN W & MAYES, MARY M	06 MAR 1883	11:307
COLWELL, OLIVER B & WALLIS, MARY E	01 APR 1891	06:089
COMBES, JONATHAN B & McFADDEN, MARY A	23 APR 1873	07:317
COMBS, HENRY C & SAYRE, NORA A	25 DEC 1883	11:442
COMBS, S GEORGE & OLDFIELD, MINNIE B	16 DEC 1898	08:292
COMBS, WILLIAM H & SEE, LIZZIE	10 JUN 1911	13:328
COMER, THEODORE & SAMPLES, DELIA A	01 JAN 1875	08:201
COMPSON, JOHN & KERWOOD, LIDA	31 OCT 1887	05:135
COMPSTON, ISAAC N & SIDENSTRICKER, SARAH J	16 JUN 1878	09:273
COMPSTON, JAMES & HOBBS, SARAH E	13 JAN 1883	11:291
COMPSTON, JAMES D & BABBINGTON, SARAH A	24 DEC 1878	10:030
COMSTOCK, FRANK ELMER & NORTON, ANNA	07 OCT 1887	05:114
COMSTOCK, GEORGE O & YOUNG, ALICE R	10 JUN 1874	08:131
CONRAD, WILLIAM ELZIE & HOLLEY, AMY	30 JUL 1908	12:220
CONAWAY, FRED & STEELE, MINNIE	23 JUN 1907	11:560
CONDEE, ASA & GREENLEE, LURETTA	20 OCT 1889	05:466
CONDEE, RALPH & RAYBURN, ELSIE M	19 AUG 1905	11:150
CONDEE, WEB & SMITH, ANNIE MARGARET	21 SEP 1887	05:098
CONGROVE, ZACHARIAH & THOMPSON, CAROLINE	08 OCT 1868	05:218
CONLEY, COLUMBUS F & HILL, ROSA	18 AUG 1889	05:431
CONLEY, COLUMBUS F & WATSON, MARY E	04 APR 1904	10:497
CONLEY, HENRY & SAYRE, ESTELLA	14 JUN 1898	08:321
CONLEY, JOHN W & BUCKHANAN, EMMA L	05 APR 1880	10:231
CONLEY, ROBERT & ROUSH, CATHARINE	18 FEB 1868	05:146
CONLEY, WILLIAM T & SAYRE, LENORA	02 JAN 1884	11:438
CONNER, JNO & ROUSH, HOUMA	*16 JUL 1860	02:014
CONNOLLY, COLUMBUS T & TILLIS, MARTHA	21 JUL 1897	08:127
CONNOLLY, ELIZAH & TAYLOR, MARY E	03 NOV 1909	12:536
CONNOLLY, JOHN & DUNLAP, HESTER	13 MAR 1873	07:332
CONOWAY, CHARLES M & RUSSELL, SARAH	17 JAN 1877	09:024
CONRAD, ANDREW, Jr & CIRCKLE, STELLA	22 SEP 1892	06:411
CONRAD, BAILEY & MEADOWS, SARAH E	02 OCT 1874	08:166
CONRAD, DAVID & BLACK, CATHARINE	12 APR 1838	01:031 5
CONRAD, JACOB H & WALLACE, ROSA BELLE	01 NOV 1895	07:417

Name	Date	Ref
CONRAD, JAMES G & BLACK, ROSE	21 JUN 1896	07:570
CONRAD, JASPER & HOLLEY, MILLIE	05 JUL 1903	10:316
CONRAD, JESSIE & MEADOWS, MANDY B	06 SEP 1908	12:249
CONRAD, JOHN W & ROWLEY, DELIA	20 JUN 1896	07:571
CONRAD, WILLIAM THOMAS & CHAPMAN, MARY F	29 JUL 1891	06:152
CONWAY, JERMIAH W & HANNAH, MARTHA	02 JUN 1867	05:067
COOK, ALFRED L & EDWARDS, IDA A	27 MAR 1910	13:034
COOK, ALLEN C & WALKER, KATIE	04 JUN 1910	13:086
COOK, ANDREW & BARNITT, HANNAH	1832	01:026
COOK, CHARLES A & LEWIS, MINERVA	24 OCT 1886	12:406
COOK, HORACE & VANMATRE, REBECCA	*20 SEP 1853	02:004
COOK, ISRAEL & JEFFERS, ESTHER	*04 SEP 1856	02:008
COOK, JAMES T & MARTIN, MARIA	27 NOV 1877	09:161
COOK, JOHN MYERS & PULLIN, ESMERALDA	01 OCT 1885	12:229
COOK, ROBERT & CLARK, RUTH ADALINE	15 NOV 1888	05:305
COOK, WILLIAM H H & SOWERS, DOLLIE	27 MAR 1886	12:308
COOKE, NORBOURN L & HERSHBARGER, (Mrs) RHODA S	*30 JAN 1854	02:005
COOLEY, CALVIN & CAMDEN, MARY M	14 NOV 1872	07:289
COONROD, LEWIS & HOLLY, LUCINDA	04 FEB 1841	01:036
COOPER, ANDEREW J & HURSHMAN, MARTHA	10 NOV 1875	08:296
COOPER, AUDUBON B & BALTHASER, ADELINE L	16 MAY 1912	13:527
COOPER, CHARLES G & ROUSH, METTIE E	03 APR 1887	05:001
COOPER, DANIEL B & MARTIN, HENRIETTA J	13 JAN 1878	09:199
COOPER, DAVID W & CHAPMAN, MINNIE M	08 DEC 1907	12:090
COOPER, GEORGE A & GIBBS, MARTHA C	06 SEP 1894	07:146
COOPER, GEORGE W & PERRY, ELIZABETH A	02 JUL 1874	08:140
COOPER, GEORGE W & WEST, BETHLEHEM	29 OCT 1879	10:155
COOPER, HAMILTON & SUTTON, MARIA	APR 1840	01:034
COOPER, HENRY & ORRINGTON, IDA M	06 JAN 1896	07:481
COOPER, HENRY C & PIERCE, BLANCH I	14 JUN 1906	11:339
COOPER, ISAAC & PULLINS, NANCY	26 FEB 1824	01:010
COOPER, JACKSON & McCLAIN, ELIZA ANN	31 DEC 1863	03:149
COOPER, JAMES MONROE & CLENDENIN, ANNIE	11 OCT 1893	06:623
COOPER, JOHN & WALKUP, ELIZABETH	02 APR 1849	01:050
COOPER, JOHN L & MULLINS, MARGARET	10 MAY 1868	05:179
COOPER, JOHN W & GREER, CATHARINE	07 MAR 1830	01:019
COOPER, JOSEPH A & KERWOOD, CARRIE M	24 SEP 1882	11:211
COOPER, NELSON & HALL, ADELINE	05 OCT 1878	09:327
COOPER, ROY C & COMSTOCK, GEORGIA B	05 SEP 1911	13:370
COOPER, SAMUEL & ARMSTRONG, ELIZABETH	24 OCT 1875	08:291
COOPER, W E & RODGERS, NELLIE F	10 MAY 1910	13:065
COOPER, WILLIAM & BUMGARDNER, BETSY	04 APR 1808	01:001
COOPER, WILLIAM & WAUGH, SARAH E	19 AUG 1877	09:121
COOPER, WILLIAM H & BISHOP, CAROLINE M	21 SEP 1876	08:391
COOPER, ZACHARIAH & FAUVER, NANCY A	12 AUG 1869	06:073
COOPER, ZACHARIAH & LEMASTER, MARY ELIZABETH	15 APR 1887	05:010
CORBET, MICHAEL & KINNEY, CATHARINE	*29 JUN 1860	02:014
CORBETT, JOHN & ELLIOTT, NANCY	16 DEC 1891	06:247
CORBETT, JOSEPH & RAYBURN, RUTH	18 OCT 1806	01:001
CORBETT, WILLIAM R & MASON, FRANCES M	26 DEC 1895	07:461
CORBIN, ALBERT S & RAY, LELIA A	15 NOV 1893	07:006
CORBIN, RICHARD E & STALNAKER, LIZZIE	28 MAY 1891	06:120
CORDELL, CHARLES & MILLER, MATTIE L	09 MAR 1901	09:302
CORFEE, GEORGE HENRY & TAYLOR, MARY DELILA	20 JUN 1887	05:046
CORFEE, HERBERT B & STUTLER, CLARA B	30 JUL 1913	14:203
CORFEE, JOHN & MILLER, MALINDA R	13 OCT 1880	10:309
CORN, JOSEPH & BURRESS, SALLY	29 NOV 1838	01:031 5
CORN, SAMUEL S & ROGERS, DELIA V	27 DEC 1877	09:180

Name	Date	Ref
CORN, WILLIAM B & KAUFF, BESSIE M	15 NOV 1909	12:543
CORRY, WILLIAM & McNERRY, MARY	29 DEC 1869	06:135
CORWIN, THOMAS & COMER, NONA J	15 DEC 1897	08:214
COSSEN, GEORGE & SMITH, MARGARET E	07 JAN 1869	06:027
COSSET, BERNARD A & KOUNS, MARY	1833	01:027
COSSIN, BURLY J & SMITH, MARY L	31 MAR 1898	08:278
COSSIN, ELI A & KNAPP, EMMA	06 AUG 1902	10:124
COSSIN, GEORGE WALTER & BAKER, MINNIE T	14 OCT 1896	07:629
COSSIN, JACOB & PULLIN, MARY	12 JUN 1872	07:235
COSSIN, JOHN O & McKINEY, LILLIE	18 SEP 1909	12:509
COSSIN, ODUS C & STOVER, ANNIE	25 JUN 1899	08:562
COSSIN, WILLIAM & STONE, ELIZA J	06 NOV 1871	07:143
COSSIN, WILLIAM ALLEN & HAWKINS, VIRGINIA FRANCES	04 OCT 1892	06:417
COSTEN, CLARENCE L & EADS, MABEL RUTH	12 JUN 1912	13:545
COTRELL, WILLIAM & McTHENY, (Mrs) SUSANA	*18 SEP 1854	02:006
COTTEREL, ANDREW & COTTEREL, SARAH	08 MAR 1821	01:009
COTTEREL, ANDREW & COTTEREL, SARAH	08 MAR 1822	01:011
COTTEREL, JESSE & COTTEREL, ANN	16 SEP 1820	01:006
COTTLE, HENDERSON & ATKINSON, MARY E	09 OCT 1881	11:031
COTTRELL, ANDREW J & JIVIDEN, LUCINDA A	12 NOV 1880	10:327
COTTRELL, FRANCIS L & ROSE, RUTH	12 APR 1913	14:124
COTTRELL, THASA & MORROW, VIOLA	12 MAY 1889	05:397
COTTRELL, WILLIAM A & McCARTY, BERTHA M	15 JUL 1895	07:341
COTTRELL, WILLIAM J & THORNTON, MARY	25 MAR 1869	06:042
COTTRILL, ART LEE & LINKHART, ANNIE C	24 NOV 1892	06:446
COTTRILL, CALEB H & PICKENS, MAUDE R	26 JAN 1910	12:595
COTTRILL, ELANTHERN & BAUM, ANNIE E	12 JUL 1908	12:210
COTTRILL, ELIJAH W & DUNLAP, EMMA	18 MAY 1903	10:291
COTTRILL, GEORGE W & GRAHAM, ESSIE EDITH	15 SEP 1909	12:502
COTTRILL, IRA G & COTTRILL, BESSIE A	25 JUN 1904	10:553
COTTRILL, LEE ANDERSON & PICKEN, THEODOSIA	25 DEC 1901	09:477
COUCH, DANIEL & HEREFORD, CATHARINE	27 JAN 1839	01:031 5
COUCH, JAMES H & WAGGONER, HELEN	02 MAY 1844	01:038
COUCH, JOHN R & DAY, SUSAN C	29 SEP 1880	10:305
COUCH, PETER S & EASTHAM, MARY KATE	05 MAY 1868	05:197
COUCH, SAMUEL & MILLER, SALLIE V	02 MAY 1994	07:082
COUCH, SAMUEL & STEENBERGEN, SARAH ANN	05 MAY 1840	01:037
COUGHENOUR, MARLOW S & HARDING, JESSIE E	06 DEC 1894	07:206
COUGHLIN, CORNELIUS & JORDEN, PENELOPE	25 SEP 1862	03:081
COULTER, JAMES & TILLIS, (Mrs) NANCY	*18 MAR 1857	02:009
COULTER, JOHN & KING, MARY J	06 JAN 1887	12:462
COULTER, WILLIAM P & SHANK, CARRIE F	31 DEC 1884	12:117
COUNROD, SAMUEL & CONNER, ANN	06 JUL 1869	06:065
COURSEN, JESSE & BRYAN, SALINA	1833	01:027
COURTNEY, THOMAS E & OSHEL, LENNA G	28 APR 1897	08:086
COUSINS, MORRIS & STRAUTHER, SYNTHA	09 OCT 1880	10:308
COVERT, WILLIAM A B & WADE, ELLA	29 JAN 1895	07:242
COWAN, JAMES BURNETTE & TUCKER, ETHEL L	08 FEB 1912	13:481
COWDERY, WHITNER & WHITESIDE, MAUD	02 AUG 1906	11:378
COX, AUGUSTUS B & LAWRENCE, CORA E	24 JAN 1901	09:283
COX, CHARLES V & CURRY, MARY B	09 AUG 1905	11:146
COX, EDWIN M & SOWASH, BLANCHE J	22 OCT 1914	15:300
COX, FRANK M & SNYDER, GRACE	13 JUN 1913	14:176
COX, WILLIAM T & GARDNER, MARY S	20 JUL 1909	12:462
COZART, ISAAC H & SAYRE, HANNAH	17 JAN 1884	11:449
CRAFT, GEORGE H & McGUFFIN, ORA A	16 SEP 1906	11:410
CRAFT, WILLIAM H & HIGGINBOTHAM, NANCY A	30 OCT 1889	05:474
CRAIG, ALEXANDER & CASH, LUCY JANE	03 NOV 1867	05:102

CRAIG, BENJAMIN K & CLARK MARY A	28 APR 1826	01:013
CRAIG, CHARLES & LEGG, JUNIA	10 SEP 1897	08:157
CRAIG, DANIEL & SCOTT, HARRIET	27 APR 1871	07:082
CRAIG, EDWARD M & COUCH, MARTHA A	17 OCT 1894	07:170
CRAIG, ELMER & HIGGINBOTHAM, EVA G	25 DEC 1906	11:482
CRAIG, EMERY & HAYNES, EARNIE	24 AUG 1908	12:233
CRAIG, GEO & McMULLEN, POLLY	28 NOV 1822	01:008
CRAIG, GEORGE W & HIGGINBOTHAM, WILLIE A	25 DEC 1893	07:030
CRAIG, IRA & McCALL, MIRTIE	03 JUN 1908	11:545
CRAIG, ISRAEL & MULLIN, ANGELINE	13 JAN 1878	09:197
CRAIG, JAMES K & LANGTRY, CATHARINE	15 NOV 1826	01:013
CRAIG, JOHN & JOHNSON, FANNIE	09 JUN 1882	11:161
CRAIG, JOHN & PATTERSON, OLLIE	13 JAN 1886	12:281
CRAIG, JOHN Jr & STRIBLING, MARY	12 NOV 1904	10:642
CRAIG, LEWIS & DOLEMAN, MARIA	18 JAN 1906	11:250
CRAIG, LEWIS E & BURGESS, OATA	13 JUL 1908	12:212
CRAIG, LEWIS RODGERS & NICHOLS, ABBY	21 APR 1889	05:387
CRAIG, MARSHALL & STEEL, MARGARET	20 AUG 1873	08:015
CRAIG, MOSES & CLICK, MARGARET	03 APR 1825	01:012
CRAIG, MOSES & CLICK, MARGARET	03 APR 1825	01:014
CRAIG, ROBERT D & LEWIS, LETITIA	14 JAN 1874	08:091
CRAIG, SAMUEL & HENDERSON, KATIE	19 DEC 1904	11:002
CRAIG, THOMAS & MARRS, ANNIE	14 FEB 1903	10:241
CRAIG, WILLIAM A & JEFFERS, SARAH	07 OCT 1907	12:029
CRAIG, WILLIAM C & TUCKER, ELSABELL	05 FEB 1908	12:126
CRAIG, WILLIAM F & LANGTREE, ANN	04 AUG 1831	01:025
CRALL, AMOS & LIVINGSTON, (Mrs) MALINDA	31 AUG 1913	15:023
CRAMER, CLYDE & HARMON, EFFIE	23 MAY 1907	11:538
CRAMER, EDWARD & STOVERS, NANCY BELLE	24 DEC 1911	13:451
CRAMER, JOHN H & KING, MARY A	14 JUL 1878	09:259
CRANS, JOHN K & NUMAN, SARAH J	14 NOV 1868	06:004
CRANS, M F & CONGROVE, MATTIE E	22 JUL 1891	06:143
CRARY, ARCHIBALD & WHETSTONE, MARY S	10 OCT 1875	08:285
CRAWFORD, CHARLES CHANEY & OWENS, ELIZA	*21 JUL 1853	02:004
CRAWFORD, GEORGE & BROWN, PANELLA	04 MAY 1825	01:012
CRAWFORD, HARLAND & PULLEN, NELLIE	19 OCT 1904	10:614
CRAWFORD, JOHN & SPEARS, LUCINDA	30 APR 1900	09:120
CRAWFORD, JOHN H & RIMMEY, LILLIE D	23 DEC 1897	08:219
CRAWFORD, JOSEPH & LUCKADOE, SALLIE	28 JUN 1902	10:101
CRAWFORD, JOSEPH & LEWIS, BELL	07 DEC 1906	11:468
CRAWFORD, SAMUEL & GIBBS, SARAH P	14 AUG 1871	07:110
CRAWFORD, SYLVESTER G & EDWARDS, VIRGINIA L	26 NOV 1868	06:008
CRAWFORD, WILLIAM & JENKINS, NANCY SUSAN	15 OCT 1891	06:205
CREEL, WILLIAM R & McDANIEL, OLLIE MAY	**20 OCT 1908	12:292
CREEMEANS, ANDREW & POWERS, MARTHA	10 DEC 1840	01:032 5
CREIGH, HAMILTON & ROSE, POLLY	10 NOV 1817	01:003
CREIGH, (Dr) THOMAS & LEWIS, SARAH FRANCES	*11 JAN 1855	02:006
CREMEANS, ALLEN & HAGER, ELLA	23 JAN 1902	10:011
CREMEANS, ALLEN & HOLLEY, FANNIE	12 MAR 1903	10:254
CREMEANS, BALLARD & HOLLEY, ELIZABETH B	13 MAY 1875	08:241
CREMEANS, CHARLES & BRIDGET, MAUDE	13 JUL 1914	15:236
CREMEANS, CLARENCE & HOLLEY, DAISY	24 APR 1903	10:277
CREMEANS, JAMES S & WARD, SARAH E	05 OCT 1884	12:068
CREMEANS, JOSEPH & CREMEANS, ALICE	03 DEC 1886	12:431
CREMEANS, JOSEPH M & VILLARS, LORA L	25 NOV 1906	11:449
CREMEANS, LAWSON V & WALLIS, RUSHIA A	28 FEB 1876	08:330
CREMEANS, PETER & WALDEN, JULIA A E	26 APR 1871	07:079
CREMEANS, PETER & HILL, EFFIE	28 JUL 1903	10:327

CREMEANS, SAMPSON & MEADOWS, ROZELIE	22 SEP 1887	05:100
CREMEANS, WINGATE & SMITH, SARAH	12 FEB 1872	07:192
CREMEANS, ZAN OTRIG & STEPHEN, SARAH M	24 APR 1873	07:349
CREMEENS, A C & SMITH, (Mrs) MARY R	21 JAN 1903	10:229
CREMEENS, BAILEY & EDMONDS, JENNETTE F	*27 AUG 1860	02:004
CREMEENS, CHARLES ALBERT & HOLLEY, LOUISA FRANCES	25 NOV 1891	06:228
CREMEENS, CLARKE & HOLLEY, ZELMA	25 DEC 1913	15:108
CREMEENS, CORNELIUS S & MEADOWS, ANGELINE	24 SEP 1896	07:619
CREMEENS, GALLATIN & MEADOWS, ONA	30 JAN 1913	14:088
CREMEENS, HERMAN & WALLIS, LAURA M	16 OCT 1876	08:394
CREMEENS, JAMES H & LEWIS, MARY	05 NOV 1899	09:008
CREMEENS, JOHN A & JENKINS, JULIA F	*18 DEC 1858	02:011
CREMEENS, PETER & ELKINS, LIZZIE	12 MAR 1904	10:489
CREMEENS, PETER C & AMOS, ROSIE	21 DEC 1904	11:005
CREMEENS, S D & TAYLOR, MARY C	02 MAR 1884	11:465
CREMEENS, WINGATE & LYNN, POLLY	25 JUN 1838	01:032.5
CRINER, ANDREW FOUNTAINE & MILLER, DELIA	20 JAN 1893	06:474
CRINER, ANDREW F & SAUNDERS, BERTHA M	*25 MAY 1904	10:524
CRIPPEN, ELBERT F & MITCHELL, MAUD	28 DEC 1908	12:345
CRIST, JOSEPH H & YOUNG, CORY OCIAL	23 OCT 1913	15:301
CROMLEY, JOSEPH K & DENTON, ANNIE F	17 JAN 1897	08:036
CROMWELL, CHARLES W & BATES, LULU M	21 APR 1890	05:545
CROMWELL, JONAS & BLACKWELL, LULU	11 JUN 1890	05:570
CROOKHAM, DAVID & CAVIT, SARAH	13 OCT 1873	08:036
CROOKHAM, SNELLING S & THOMAS, LANIE	20 MAY 1880	10:263
CROOKS, HIRAM J & RICE, KATIE M	27 NOV 1904	10:647
CROOKS, WALTER W & CARSON, ADA	31 OCT 1906	11:441
CROOKS, WM S & STEPHEN, BETHA C	19 DEC 1880	10:348
CROSS, ELMER E & WARNER, EMMA L	03 JUN 1888	05:232
CROSS, OTHY & JONES, ANNIE B	20 SEP 1906	11:409
CROSSLEY, THOMAS & WITHERS, LULA MARICE	23 SEP 1889	05:458
CROSSLEY, WILLIAM & DIXON, MAGGIE	13 MAR 1889	05:368
CROSSMAN, WILLIAM & RAMSEY, LOUISA	24 SEP 1895	07:390
CROUCH, ISAAC R & HALSTEAD, ANN ELIZA	13 JAN 1858	02:010
CROUCH, JOSEPH & CRINE, PAMELIA	1831	01:024
CROUCH, ROBERT & HENRY, MARY C	*17 DEC 1881	11:073
CROUCH, ROBERT & HENSON, LUELLA	04 MAY 1890	05:552
CROW, GEORGE B & POLSLEY, ELIZA M	25 FEB 1870	06:163
CROWDER, HENRY & MILLS, MARY	15 AUG 1876	08:376
CROWDER, LEWIS & BLACK, MALINDA	03 APR 1877	09:058
CRUM, LEWIS E & KIRK, NANCY C	21 SEP 1887	05:096
CRUMP, ANDREW & FAUBER, JUDA J	22 AUG 1861	03:014
CRUMP, ANDREW J & WAUGH, MARY A	20 JUL 1895	07:345
CRUMP, CHARLES F & CLAGG, MARY	25 DEC 1897	08:229
CRUMP, GUY S & EDWARDS, REBECCA E	24 MAY 1913	14:156
CRUMP, HARRY E & AUSTIN, NEVA I	13 AUG 1910	13:130
CRUMP, JAMES & CALLAHAN, SARAH	20 MAY 1834	01:028
CRUMP, JAMES & HOFFMAN, ELLA	03 FEB 1887	12:470
CRUMP, JAMES E & DOWNS, BERTHA A	17 SEP 1904	10:602
CRUMP, JAMES M & MILLER, MARY B	03 JUL 1897	08:124
CRUMP, JAMES M & HOBBS, BESSIE A	11 JUN 1905	11:108
CRUMP, JAMES MONROE & MASON, CATHARINE A	06 AUG 1887	05:069
CRUMP, JAMES V & GARDNER, CARRIE D	01 NOV 1899	09:004
CRUMP, JOHN & JEFFERS, ELLEN	*03 JAN 1859	02:012
CRUMP, JONN H & FORREST, SALLIE ELIZABETH	11 NOV 1886	12:421
CRUMP, JOHN R & JONES, ELIZABETH	29 DEC 1907	12:101
CRUMP, LESS & JONES, ROSELLA	27 APR 1908	12:171
CRUMP, MANIA A & EDMUNDS, CORA	06 JAN 1909	12:350

CRUMP, SAMUEL & CALLAGHAN, MARY	1831	01:024
CRUMP, VIRGIL & RIFFLE, LAURA SUSAN	03 JUN 1914	15:208
CRUMP, WILLIAM H & GARD, MAGGIE	12 MAR 1894	07:059
CRUZAN, BENJAMIN & LAYONS, CATHARINE	05 OCT 1826	01:015
CRUZAN, ISAAC & HARPOLE, MILLIE	27 DEC 1827	01:020
CRUZAN, JACOB & HESTER, NANCY	19 JAN 1830	01:022
CRYNER, ELZA & SIDERS, NETTIE	11 JAN 1913	14:081
CULLEN, ISRAEL, Jr & MINTURN, DELILAH	*08 DEC 1858	02:011
CULLEN, JAMES M & RICKARD, MARY V	05 APR 1883	11:218
CULLEN, MATHIAS & HARRIS, (Mrs) ANN	*16 JAN 1856	02:007
CULLEN, MATHIAS & ECKARD, MAHALA E	24 JAN 1867	05:023
CULLEN, PERRY D & RIFFLE, MINA L	21 JUN 1910	13:095
CULLEN, SAMUEL P & THORNTON, GEORGIA	06 JUL 1890	05:583
CULLEN, SAMUEL PARK & YONKER, LAVINA FRANCES	08 JUN 1913	14:169
CULVER, WILLIAM & MITCHELL, MARIA	*04 FEB 1861	02:015
CUMMINGS, JOHN & BILLUPS, IDA	07 JUN 1903	10:299
CUMMINS, BENJAMIN HILL & LAWSON, LYDIA J	07 APR 1886	12:315
CUMMINS, MARTIN A & HAWTHORN, SARAH E	11 MAR 1872	07:203
CUMMINS, WILLIAM & CRAWFORD, JANE	20 JUN 1884	12:029
CUMMINS, WILLIAM N & HICKS, ANNIE M	30 MAR 1890	05:534
COMPSON, GEORGE ALLEN & LONG, CATHARINE R	06 APR 1888	05:204
COMPSTON, BENJAMIN H & CHANDLER, RENA	25 DEC 1909	12:580
CUMPSTON, JOHN & HUGHS, MARY	28 JUN 1827	01:020
CUMPTON, LEWIS J & WOLF, EMILY JANE	30 SEP 1889	05:461
CUMSTON, JACOB H & LITCHFIELD, MARY	25 AUG 1907	11:599
CUNDIFF, ALBERT & HALL, LILLIE	07 NOV 1904	10:636
CUNDIFF, CHARLES B & ROBINSON, SARAH	03 JUL 1870	06:205
CUNDIFF, GEORGE W & PORTER, MARTHA	05 MAR 1871	07:061
CUNDIFF, I C & SMITH, A ELLEN	21 MAY 1884	12:015
CUNDIFF, ISAIAH C & KNIGHT, SALLIE F	18 NOV 1894	07:191
CUNDIFF, JAMES H & HENRY, ELLA	14 NOV 1906	11:447
CUNDIFF, JAMES M & POWELL, AZERAH B	04 FEB 1869	06:030
CUNDIFF, JOHN R & KNIGHT, BLANCHE E	11 AUG 1891	06:162
CUNDIFF, JOHN S & TURLEY, JENNIE C	09 DEC 1895	07:446
CUNDIFF, ROBERT ELSWORTH & SURGEON, SARAH ELIZABETH	17 MAY 1896	07:549
CUNDIFF, ROBERT O & HARRIS, MINNIE B	05 SEP 1913	15:025
CUNDIFF, ROBERT T & SCHRAY, MARY	04 OCT 1905	11:183
CUNDIFF, WILLIAM H & LEADMAN, RICEY JANE	20 NOV 1867	05:129
CUNINGHAM, JOHN RILEY & SCHOLL, FRANCES VIRGINIA	13 FEB 1892	06:287
CUNINGHAM, SHERMAN & DORNICK, SHUELLA	23 NOV 1887	05:145
CUNINGHAM, ED & HOFFMAN, EMELINE	06 AUG 1876	08:373
CUNINGHAM, EDMOND & GIBBS, JULIA	22 MAY 1887	05:029
CUNINGHAM, EDMUND & ROUSH, SUSAN	27 SEP 1846	11:046
CUNINGHAM, EMERY G & HESSON, ELIZABETH	18 FEB 1900	09:088
CUNINGHAM, HENRY & BLAKE, MARGARET	JUL 1843	01:043
CUNINGHAM, HENRY & MASON, (Mrs) HELEN	08 FEB 1914	15:139
CUNINGHAM, HENRY I & VINCENT, MARY	15 AUG 1865	04:040
CUNINGHAM, HENRY WALTER & BASS, (Mrs) MURREL	26 MAR 1914	15:163
CUNINGHAM, JAMES A & ZIRKLE, CATHARINE	01 APR 1880	10:229
CUNINGHAM, JAMES & HALL, ELIZABETH	19 JUN 1880	10:271
CUNINGHAM, JOHN HARNESS & SHOOL, FRANCES MOORE	27 OCT 1887	05:130
CUNINGHAM, JOHN R & ROUSH, VIOLA V	04 OCT 1899	08:627
CUNINGHAM, JOHN R & GRAHAM, RUTH E	17 APR 1878	09:246
CUNINGHAM, JOSEPH W & HESSON, BERTHA M	14 JAN 1905	11:029
CUNINGHAM, LOUIS & GIBBS, MARIA	28 JUL 1892	06:376
CUNINGHAM, ORIS G & ROUSH, RHODA	25 DEC 1902	10:216
CUNINGHAM, SEBASTIAN, & RICKARD, VIOLA	31 MAY 1895	07:308
CUNINGHAM, THOMAS & CASTO, MARGARET	17 FEB 1829	01:021

CUNINGHAM, WILLIAM WARNER & ROUSH, NANCY	19 SEP 1878	09:316
CURRY, ISAIAH & KING, CATHARINE	03 AUG 1869	06:070
CURRY, JOHN & McCOY, MARGARET	25 DEC 1878	10:031
CURRY, S F & COLE, CINTHIA A	03 JAN 1871	07:040
CURRY, TIMOTHY, & BOARD, REBECCA	21 NOV 1901	09:452
CURRY, WILBUR & COX, JENNIE	15 AUG 1909	12:463
CURTIS, CLARENCE & FRENCH, DELLA G	12 NOV 1910	13:205
CURTIS, JOHN & MULLIN, BRIDGET	15 APR 1865	03:225
CURTIS, THOMAS N & KERWOOD, ESTELLA A	22 JAN 1991	06:049
CUSHMAN, WILLIAM H & DONNALLY, CORNELIA J	08 AUG 1865	04:034
CUSTARD, JESSE P & GANNON, SARAH	02 APR 1868	05:161
CUSTER, RICHARD D & NEWELL, ANNIE L	20 DEC 1888	05:324
CUTCHALL, GEORGE, & BIRCHFIELD, CLARA	06 APR 1864	03:170
CUTSHALL, ELICK C & BARNETT, DORIS M	02 APR 1908	12:153
CUTTING, ROBERT C & LUSHER, MAE C	01 JUN 1910	13:078
DABNEY, GRANVILLE B & SLAYTON, BLANCHE A	26 SEP 1907	12:025
DABNEY, IRA S & HALFHILL, JULIA C	25 DEC 1890	06:032
DABNEY, ISAAC N & COLVIN, MARGARET J	01 JAN 1874	08:087
DABNEY, JAMES & SHIELDS, ELIZABETH	03 JAN 1828	01:016
DABNEY, JOHN C & WALLACE, MARY C	27 FEB 1868	05:150
DABNEY, JOHN L & CLEEK, ANNIE B	27 DEC 1899	09:056
DABNEY, ROBERT & HAMBRICK, LUCRETIA	19 SEP 1877	09:132
DABNEY, WILLIAM & MORRIS, ANN M	*13 OCT 1856	02:009
DABNY, CLARK C & GARD, CHRISTINA	06 OCT 1875	08:280
DAIGH, JOHN H & CREMEANS, ELIZABETH R	25 NOV 1903	10:413
DAILEY, EARL B & MANLIE, IDA	11 FEB 1911	13:266
DAILEY, H W & FIELD, BERTHA MAY	06 FEB 1913	14:090
DAILEY, JAMES & WITHERS, JENNIE	28 SEP 1898	08:372
DAILEY, JAMES & GIBBS, MARTHA	28 AUG 1912	13:592
DAILEY, JOHN & HOLLEY, MATIE	15 SEP 1909	12:497
DAILEY, LEWIS W & CASTO, MATILDA F	22 AUG 1911	13:360
DAILY, ISAAC M & LIKENS, MARY M	26 SEP 1879	10:128
DAILY, MARTIN & LEWIS, MAUD	22 FEB 1906	11:271
DALEY, JOHN & TROEGER, ROSA MAY	09 APR 1895	07:279
DALEY, PATRICK FRANKLIN & JONES, (Mrs) JANE	22 NOV 1881	11:058
DALTON, ALBERT & MORRISTON, ARAY A	18 JUN 1874	08:134
DALTON, BENJAMIN F & THOMAS, MAY B	03 SEP 1907	12:004
DALTON, JOHN & MAYSE, MARY B	18 NOV 1874	08:058
DALTON, ROBERT E & DOWELL, SARAH A E	20 APR 1904	10:507
DANA, AUGUSTUS & BURCH, MARY	27 MAR 1825	01:012
DANIELS, JOHN R & HOLLY, ELLEN FRANCIS	*13 AUG 1858	02:011
DANIELS, WILLIAM E & ACKLEY, EVA L	13 APR 1907	11:515
DARNELL, ORTON EDWARD & BARBEE, ANN REBECCA	25 DEC 1900	09:265
DARNING, JOHN P & SMITH, EVA L	14 SEP 1898	08:362
DARST, DANIEL & DUNCAN, MARY L	19 JAN 1866	04:099
DARST, DANIEL & CHEESBREW, AILCY C	31 OCT 1891	06:219
DARST, GEORGE T & BALDWIN, MARY	29 JUN 1870	06:203
DARST, HENRY & JOHNSON, ELIZA	*19 JAN 1876	08:320
DARST, JOHN D & WALKER, MARIAH	20 SEP 1900	09:208
DARST, NONROE & BUTRICKS, CLARA F	11 JUL 1906	11:366
DARST, MONROE H & SEARLS, BESSIE F	22 NOV 1911	13:422
DARST, REUBEN & HYATTE, ELLENOR	*01 AUG 1859	02:012
DARST, ROBERT C & MAYSE, EMMA E	16 JUL 1908	12:216
DARST, SAM & TAYLOR, MARY H	12 JAN 1895	07:234
DARST, WILLIAM M & CAVET, NANCY A	31 JAN 1864	03:157
DARST, WILLIAM M & DEVAULT, MARY H	03 JUN 1883	11:350
DASHNER, CHARLES ANDREW & SHY, RUCY HELLEN	10 JUN 1909	12:426
DASHNER, DAVID & WAGGENER, LAVINA	30 DEC 1832	01:027

DASHNER, FRANCIS M & BUFFINGTON, ELLA B	16 MAR 1869	06:041
DASHNER, JOHN J & MILLER, MARGARET E F	23 SEP 1868	05:213
DAUGHERTY, CHARLES & EDWARDS, TILLIE	08 JUL 1899	08:570
DAUGHERTY, HENRY E & THORNTON, TENA	08 OCT 1908	12:280
DAUGHERTY, HIRAM T & CARSON, CORA B	13 FEB 1890	05:518
DAUGHERTY, HOMER VARIAN & FOWLER, ANNIE	22 AUG 1900	09:178
DAUGHERTY, HUGH & GILL, ELNORA	28 DEC 1880	10:186
DAUGHERTY, JAMES C & THORNTON, SARAH J	28 MAY 1882	11:153
DAUGHERTY, JAMES C & LOVE, MARY	30 NOV 1886	12:430
DAUGHERTY, LEWIS & DAUGHERTY, FANNIE	28 SEP 1878	09:324
DAUGHERTY, ROY & GREER, OMA R	05 OCT 1904	10:610
DAVALT, JOHN & CLONCH, ANNIE A	23 DEC 1892	06:456
DAVID, JOHN & MOORE, LEAH	23 APR 1903	10:272
DAVIDSON, CHARLES & SYDENSTRICKER, ELECTA	21 MAR 1893	06:506
DAVIDSON, CHARLES NELSON & O'LEARY, NANNIE	15 MAY 1901	09:340
DAVIDSON, DANIEL S & ASHBY, CLARA E	20 MAY 1901	09:344
DAVIDSON, HENRY A & BASS, MARY P	20 OCT 1872	07:278
DAVIDSON, JOHN J & ARTHUR, LUCINDA A	31 DEC 1887	05:173
DAVIES, THOMAS L & SULLIVAN, FANNIE L	29 SEP 1889	05:459
DAVIN, THOMAS J & SMITH, FININE A	02 JUL 1897	08:121
DAVIS, A PERRY & THORNTON, LAURA A	27 APR 1894	07:078
DAVIS, ALLEN & FLETCHER, ELIZABETH E	27 JUN 1861	03:009
DAVIS, ALLEN BAXTER & HOLLEY, MARTHA ETNA	21 APR 1889	05:382
DAVIS, ARTHUR P & SMITH, FLORA D	12 APR 1905	11:073
DAVIS, CALVIN CLARK & THORNTON, LIEUVANA A	08 DEC 1891	06:242
DAVIS, CHARLES & NEWBY, FLORENCE A	22 DEC 1881	11:072
DAVIS, CHARLES M & CLAGG, MARY F	24 MAR 1893	06:509
DAVIS, CHARLES N & TATE, SARAH	31 DEC 1883	11:445
DAVIS, CHARLES STEPHEN & GRANDSTAFF, EVETH ELZONA	23 JUN 1890	05:513
DAVIS, CHAS R & ROUSH, ICY	17 OCT 1911	13:396
DAVIS, CLYDE & GUNN, M ORA	07 MAR 1913	14:106
DAVIS, CLYDE & GREEN, ORA M	07 MAR 1913	14:106
DAVIS, EDGAR S & MILLER, IDA C A	01 AUG 1891	06:157
DAVIS, EDWARD & HYSELL, LILLIE B	19 NOV 1892	06:441
DAVIS, ELIAS & STREIGHT, JEMIMA	14 JUN 1866	04:130
DAVIS, ELMER F & STAGG, EMMA R	19 AUG 1902	10:134
DAVIS, EPHRAIM & EADS, ANGELINE	14 OCT 1875	08:289
DAVIS, ERNEST H & CANTERBERRY, JULIA B	25 DEC 1899	09:041
DAVIS, EUGENE B & AUMILLER, SUSANNA E	*06 DEC 1851	02:001
DAVIS, FREDRICK & WEAKLEY, ANNIE	23 APR 1895	07:292
DAVIS, GEORGE & DUNCAN, HARRIET M	03 FEB 1879	10:050
DAVIS, GEORGE HENRY & KING, MARY JANE	13 OCT 1892	06:425
DAVIS, HARVEY & MANLEY, ANNA	07 FEB 1909	12:363
DAVIS, HENRY D & MASH, SARAH FRANCES	30 JUL 1910	13:120
DAVIS, JOHN & HUTCHINSON, JANE	29 APR 1868	05:176
DAVIS, JOHN & WALKER, JULIA E	*04 OCT 1860	02:014
DAVIS, JOHN M & ASHBY, JOSEPHINE E	06 DEC 1871	07:150
DAVIS, JOHN P & LEE, NANNIE M	05 JUL 1905	11:129
DAVIS, JOHN R & YEAGER, ALICE	08 NOV 1885	12:248
DAVIS, JOHN S & SWISHER, MARY L	28 OCT 1903	10:396
DAVIS, JOSEPH A & JONES, ORETHA	13 APR 1841	01:034
DAVIS, JOSEPH WILLIAM & VAN MATRE, ALICE	03 SEP 1888	05:268
DAVIS, KIMBERLING & PAGE, MARTHA F	17 JUL 1851	02:002
DAVIS, LEWIS & COLINS, MARY J	26 MAR 1873	07:338
DAVIS, LEWIS & SIMPSON, SUSAN	04 DEC 1898	08:423
DAVIS, NATHAN & RUSSELL, LUCRETIA	25 NOV 1836	01:030
DAVIS, ORIS & NEASE, NANNIE	20 AUG 1910	13:138
DAVIS, P L & MEADOWS, SINA B	20 JUN 1909	12:429

DAVIS, PETER & PONTSLER, REBECCA	02 MAR 1876	08:331
DAVIS, PURLY L & CORFEE, LIZZIE	17 MAR 1878	09:230
DAVIS, STANLEY, EVANS, NELLIE	05 SEP 1908	12:250
DAVIS, THOMAS M & CHAPMAN, MARY ANN	04 DEC 1892	06:451
DAVIS, THOMAS S & JOHNSON, EFFIE L	17 SEP 1906	11:411
DAVIS, W H & DOUGLASS, MARY T	03 MAR 1914	15:152
DAVIS, WILLIAM E & OHLINGER, NANCY	24 AUG 1897	08:147
DAVIS, WILLIAM H & JOHNSON, BETSY E	26 SEP 1872	07:264
DAWSON, GEORGE C & YEAGER, MARY C	31 OCT 1883	11:420
DAWSON, WILLIAM B & ALLIS, NELLIE	04 MAR 1905	11:056
DAY, BENJAMIN & MAYES, MARY A	28 MAR 1838	01:032.5
DAY, BENJAMIN & WAUGH, MARTHA JANE	03 JUL 1850	01:052
DAY, CHARLES F & FOSTER, COLUMBIA A	01 OCT 1875	08:279
DAY, HARRY C & BIRD, IDA C	26 MAR 1910	13:033
DAY, HARRY G & GABBERT, ELMIRA D	27 APR 1905	11:082
DAY, RUSH & BAILEY, MINNIE	17 SEP 1903	10:373
DAY, WILLIAM P & LONG, JULIA M	23 FEB 1903	10:247
DAY, WILSON & ADAMS, MARY J	24 DEC 1873	08:075
DAY, WILSON & LOCKHART, JENNIE F	06 JUN 1883	11:354
DAYLONG, ROBERT W & RIFFLE, KATHARYN	26 JUN 1909	12:442
DAYWALT, HENRY & VANMATRE, MARY	21 FEB 1839	01:031 5
DAYWALT, THOMAS A & DEWUEES, CATHARINE C	*21 JAN 1853	02:003
De GARCELON, JOHN W & SMITH, NINA E	18 OCT 1902	10:175
De VAULT, JAMES T & THORNTON, DELPHIA	15 SEP 1901	09:407
DEAL, ALONZO & KENTZLER, MARY	04 JUL 1878	09:285
DEAL, ELMER & SHARP, WILLIE PEARL	10 JAN 1914	15:123
DEAL, OSCAR & SHARP, MARTINNIE	20 AUG 1902	10:136
DEAN, JOSEPH H & COOK, MARTHA F	19 JUL 1911	13:347
DEAN, SAMUEL B & BOWLING, JULIA A	10 JUL 1876	08:369
DEBALT, JACOB & GREY, CASSANDRA	16 APR 1868	05:169
DECKARD, EDWARD A & JAQUES, MAGGIE	25 DEC 1899	09:047
DECKARD, IRA & BUGG, ROSA	19 JAN 1904	10:462
DECKARD, LAWRENCE L & HOLCOMB, GRACE	04 APR 1911	13:304
DECKER, ARTHUR & SAYRE, EVA	30 NOV 1906	11:464
DECKER, CURTIS & BUGG, MIRTIE	30 MAY 1903	10:296
DECKER, JOHN & POSTON, LUELLA B	30 SEP 1897	08:162
DEEM, ABRAHAM & LOHR, MARY ANN	10 MAR 1864	03:167
DEEM, JOSEPOH & CLARK, SARAH	24 APR 1895	07:290
DEEM, ROY & CONDEE, MABELL	*30 SEP 1910	13:172
DEFOE, CHAS ELMER & MEADOWS, ELIZABETH	11 SEP 1909	12:496
DELBAR, CHARLES F & BRUNER, EMMA	10 AUG 1904	10:573
DELANEY, RILEY E & COOPER, LILLIE B	15 AUG 1901	09:385
DELANEY, SAMUEL & ROUSH, JENNIE B	10 JUL 1883	11:371
DELANEY, SAMUEL & ROUSH, SARAH J	20 NOV 1898	08:409
DENNEY, AUGUSTUS & WELTON, MOLLIE	11 DEC 1904	10:666
DENNEY, HENRY & DENNEY, CYNTHIA	12 DEC 1992	06:453
DENNEY, WILLIAM & ROBERTS, MINNIE F	29 OCT 1903	10:399
DENNIS, WILLIAM & HAMILTON, LOUISA	19 APR 1883	11:327
DENNY, AUGUSTUS, DAYLONG, ANNA E	28 DEC 1876	09:015
DENNY, FRANKLIN S & HART, ELIZABETH	26 JUN 1877	09:101
DENNY, GEORGE W & MAYES, STELLA MARIE	18 SEP 1913	15:037
DENNY, STEWART & MULFORD, MATTIE	03 OCT 1897	08:167
DENNY, ZEPHUS & CONRAD, ORPHA E	27 DEC 1899	09:052
DENTON, JACKSON BRUFF & JEWETT, ANNIE FLORENCE	24 JUN 1886	12:342
DERNBACH, GEO A & NIEMEYER, CATHARINE S	13 JUL 1911	13:345
DEVAULT, ASHBELL GREEN & HOWELL, ELIZA JANE	12 JAN 1893	06:469
DEVAULT, CHARLES E & PARSONS, EMMA L	02 APR 1898	08:281
DEVAULT, ELMUS W & DURST, LORA B	25 NOV 1897	08:202

DEVAULT, ELMUS W & KNAPP, SOPHIA	15 APR 1908	12:159
DEVAULT, HARVEY L & CLICK, AMELIA	16 APR 1893	06:522
DEVOIR, CHARLES W & FLORVA, PHOEBE J	27 DEC 1886	12:449
DEVORE, CORNELIUS C & JEFFERS, RHODA C	22 JUL 1892	06:373
DEVORE, JAMES & BARBER, LILLIE	29 DEC 1903	10:451
DEVORE, ORPHAS & MASH, ROSA MAY	11 JUL 1910	13:109
DEVORE, THOMAS & TONEY, CORA	23 NOV 1914	15:327
DEWEES, CHARLES R & SISSON, FLORENCE M	21 JUN 1874	08:136
DEWEES, GEORGE A & KING, LUCINDA	13 JAN 1864	03:153
DEWEES, HENRY L H & JENKINS, LUCETTA C	24 DEC 1891	06:261
DEWEES, JAMES FRANKLIN & RIEHL, IDA MARY	19 JUN 1909	12:435
DEWEES, JAMES HOWARD & TILLIS, IDA JANE	28 JUN 1887	05:049
DEWEES, WILLMOUTH I & SIDERS, EMELINE	09 JUN 1893	06:562
DEWEES, WINFIELD S & BOWYER, HANNAH	05 OCT 1879	10:137
DEWEESE, CHARLES M & SMITH, NANNIE	08 MAR 1887	12:488
DEWEESE, GEORGE W & HILL, ROSA BELLE	20 NOV 1895	07:429
DEWEESE, JOHN ANDREW & SMITH, MARY JANE	04 JUL 1895	07:335
DEWEESE, JOHN W & MYERS, PHOEBE	26 JUN 1886	12:345
DEWEESE, THOMAS F & BUCK, MEDA	18 APR 1898	08:288
DEWEESE, WILLIAM H & SAYRE, ELLA	22 APR 1900	09:109
DEWESE, JOSHUA & DAYWALT, CATHARINE JANE	09 AUG 1849	01:050
DEWITT, IRA WILSON & GARDNER, CLARA MELINDA	15 MAR 1900	09:097
DeWITT, R D & POWELL, LENA N	26 JUN 1912	13:554
DeWOLF, ARTHUR C & JOHNSON, LAURA J	15 NOV 1902	10:187
DICKEN, ROBERT E & EDWARDS, MURIEL E	13 SEP 1913	15:035
DICKENS, HORACE L & HAYNES, MARY J	24 FEB 1885	12:144
DICKENSON, WILLIAM & NORMAN, DAISY	11 FEB 1902	10:022
DICKERSON, ALBERT & WIMER, IDA	07 NOV 1895	07:423
DICKIN, JOHN & MULFORD, LYDIA	JAN 1843	01:043
DIEFENBACH, EDWARD & CIRCLE, LINNIE M	21 FEB 1889	05:356
DIFENBACH, PHILIP & JENKINS, ELIZABETH	05 SEP 1900	09:184
DIEHL, HENRY & MEES, ELIZABETH	02 DEC 1877	09:163
DIEHL, HENRY M & WOODS, ELEANORE BAIRD	06 JUL 1914	15:229
DIEHL, JOHN F & HOBBS, NINA J	03 SEP 1910	13:148
DIEHL, JOSEPH & CUNDIFF, IDA H	20 SEP 1889	05:454
DILCHER, CHARLES H & RUSSELL, FLORENCE R	25 FEB 1905	11:049
DILCHER, EARL & REEVES, EMMA L	18 OCT 1911	13:395
DILCHER, FRED & ROMINE, CLARA B	16 FEB 1914	15:142
DILCHER, WILLIAM C & RUSSELL, RUTH M	07 MAY 1904	10:516
DILLARD, AYLOR A & SULLIVAN, SALLIE J	08 JUN 1901	09:352
DILLARD, HART & WARD, ORAH	26 MAR 1873	07:336
DILLARD, JNO F & HULBERT, IRENA	26 JUN 1911	13:334
DILLON, OLLIE & DYKE, PEARL	31 OCT 1909	12:537
DILS, WILLIAM S & WILKS, MALINDA	02 MAY 1839	01:032.5
DILTZ, WILLIAM J & WEEKS, MELINDA J	02 MAY 1839	01:042
DILWORTH, BYRON SALATHIEL & KEAN, EMMA FLORENCE	20 OCT 1887	05:126
DINGEY, CHARLES & BATEMAN, ADA	*26 DEC 1895	07:471
DINGEY, ELIJAH & DINGEY, CHARITY A	09 SEP 1886	12:385
DINGEY, ISAAC & ROUSH, LOUISA	*26 SEP 1853	02:004
DINGEY, JAMES R & ROSEBERRY, GEORGIA A	09 MAR 1898	08:266
DINGY, CHARLES & TAYLOR, EFFIE	11 SEP 1896	07:607
DINGY, JAMES R & CARPENTER, MARY	07 JAN 1878	09:194
DINGY, JOHN & ROUSH, SARAH J	*17 APR 1851	02:002
DIXON, JNO O & MARRIS, MARGT J	20 OCT 1878	09:337
DIXON, JOHN O & KERWOOD, EDITH M	06 JUN 1914	15:212
DIXON, MATHEW J & BOBO, MARGARET	16 JUL 1914	15:241
DIXON, WM N & FRANCES, ELIZABETH	18 SEP 1881	11:020
DOBBINS, PEYTON & HALSTEAD, RHODA	23 MAR 1824	01:010

Names	Date	Ref
DOBYNS, PEYTON & FONLY, MARGARET	06 FEB 1830	01:019
DOBYNS, WASHINGTON & CORBIN, MARGARET L	1837	01:040
DODD, STEPHEN T & WETZEL, REBECCA J	*28 JAN 1857	02:009
DODDRICK, JOHN W & McCOY, MARTHA C	12 NOV 1872	07:277
DODSON, ALLIN & WOODY, ELIZA	24 DEC 1845	01:044
DODSON, CHARLES A & FISHER, SARAH S	16 APR 1874	08:113
DODSON, DAVID & MILLER, MINNIE	25 APR 1895	07:293
DODSON, JAMES & SMITH, RACHEL	13 MAR 1910	13:022
DODSON, JOHN G & WHITT, EMMA L	15 JUN 1898	08:320
DODSON, LEWIS & FOWLER, ORILLA	11 AUG 1902	10:126
DODSON, ORIS H & STEWARD, FLOE L	23 DEC 1913	15:106
DODSON, THOMAS M & EDWARDS, RHUHAMA A	03 OCT 1872	07:270
DODSON, WALTER & BOHRAM, ELLA	24 AUG 1905	11:153
DODSON, WILLIAM THOMAS & NEASE, MINNIE FRANCES	16 FEB 1910	13:010
DOLBY, JONAS T & RAIRDEN, HANNAH	31 JUL 1906	11:374
DOLLMIRE, HENRY & GISE, MARGARET	26 FEB 1863	03:105
DOLMAN, DAVID FRANKLIN & THOMAS, ELLA	09 FEB 1888	05:184
DONAHEW, ANDREW F & CHILDERS, DANIE	20 AUG 1902	10:135
DONAHOE, WILLIAM H & RIFFLE, MARY S	23 AUG 1878	09:299
DONNALLY, HUGH M & BARNETT, ROXY A	23 JAN 1867	05:025
DONNALLY, VAN B & WAGGENER, MARY B	02 OCT 1832	01:027
DONNELL, EDWARD & HARKINS, ELLEN	29 MAY 1905	11:102
DONOHEW, ANDREW J & LEMASTER, MARY	23 OCT 1903	10:388
DONOHEW, HIRAM & SMITH, LYDIA	07 MAR 1839	01:031 5
DONOHEW, JESSE Mc & WILSON, EMMA L	03 OCT 1914	15:266
DONOHEW, STEWART & McPHERSON, ADELINE	07 MAR 1839	01:031 5
DONOHUE, CYRUS H & KING, JANE	26 JUL 1901	09:373
DONOHUE, GEORGE WASHINGTON & LONG, MARY CATHARINE	21 JUL 1886	12:359
DONOHUE, JESSIE M & CLICK, LIZZIE	10 NOV 1896	08:003
DONOHUE, JULIUS McNITE & ROUSH, MARY IZETTIE	28 MAR 1900	09:100
DONOHUE, REUBIN E & SHIELDS, DELLA M	11 JUN 1905	11:106
DONOHUE, WESLEY & THORNTON, CHRISTENA	*06 MAR 1860	02:013
DONOHUE, WILLIAM & RYNE, CATHARINE	17 MAY 1891	06:106
DONOVAN, JOSEPH H & TULLY, MINNIE	10 DEC 1898	08:430
DONREY, JOSEPH & ROUSH, SARAH A	*19 SEP 1855	02:007
DOOLITTLE, GEORGE S & COX, ELVIRA	20 APR 1869	06:051
DOOLITTLE, WILLIAM & EADS, MAGGIE	26 AUG 1888	05:265
DORNICK, LEWIS & JONES, OMA	31 DEC 1905	11:234
DORNING HENRY & CONLEY, MARY	15 AUG 1869	06:072
DORSEY, THOMAS & ADDISON, SALLIE	18 DEC 1902	10:210
DOSS, ALFRED & WILSON, JANE	1833	01:039
DOSS, JAMES & WRAY, MARY JANE	14 MAR 1867	05:037
DOSS, JOHN & JOURDEN, NANCY SUSAN	*28 OCT 1852	02:003
DOSS, JOHN A & ASBURRY, EMMA	24 JAN 1899	08:456
DOSS, L & FORTH, ANNA	08 JUN 1902	10:085
DOTT, AMOS M & GREEN, EMMA A	25 DEC 1876	09:010
DOUBT, AMBROSE M & WALLIS, ELIZABETH	22 SEP 1889	05:453
DOUGLAS, ALBERT F & PARRY, REBECCA	25 DEC 1899	09:030
DOUTT, CHARLES R & MEADOWS, LENA	24 FEB 1904	10:480
DOWELL, GEORGE A & HILL, NANCY B	16 NOV 1893	07:008
DOWELL, GEORGE A & KNAPP, RUTH E	01 SEP 1880	10:295
DOWELL, JAMES & WARNER-HALL (Mrs), LUCY	30 MAR 1910	13:035
DOWELL, JAMES R & HOFFMAN, ANNIE G	27 DEC 1905	11:237
DOWELL, JOHN M & HUDSON, SARAH A	10 MAY 1892	06:336
DOWELL, JOHN M & BAILES, EMMA	10 SEP 1902	10:153
DOWELL, JOHN W & BEAVER, MARIETTA	10 SEP 1881	11:201
DOWER, JOHN J & LUSE, CARRIE B	07 JUN 1899	08:546
DOWER, PATRICK & WEAVER, MARIA TERESA	12 MAY 1867	05:046

Couple	Date	Ref
DOWER, STAUNTON M & WINDON, EVA BELLE	31 AUG 1898	08:357
DOWER, JOSEPH S & ROUSH, MARY M	21 MAY 1863	03:116
DOWNEY, SAMUEL W & HYSELL, LUCINDA	18 OCT 1879	10:143
DOWNS, GEORGE W & PUTNEY, MARY E	15 AUG 1903	10:339
DOWNS, ROBERT O & GARTON, FIDELIA M	23 JUL 1868	05:199
DOWNS, ULYSSES & RIFFLE, ESTELLA	05 MAR 1905	11:053
DOWNS, WILLIAM & PARSONS, VESTA J	24 MAY 1862	03:065
DOYLE, HENRY JOHN & JONES, MATTIE LEE	12 MAR 1888	08:208
DRAKE, ROY A & SPROUSE, ETHEL M	15 JAN 1910	12:591
DRESELER, CHAS W & PROSSER, MAHALA M	10 OCT 1822	01:000
DROUILLARD, SIMON B & LONG, EVELINE E	*21 NOV 1850	02:001
DRUGGIN, EARL FORBUS & SKINNIN, ROSE	03 JUL 1900	09:157
DRUMM, WILLIAM & MEEKS, OLLIE	19 JUL 1885	12:197
DRUMMOND, HOMER V & CURRY, MAY	19 DEC 1909	12:572
DUEL, ELON L & HUFF, HENRIETTA	03 JAN 1899	08:446
DUEL, LUTHER L & DECKER, ELIZABETH	01 JAN 1906	11:241
DUFF, ALBERT S & DUFF, SARAH J	17 APR 1873	07:345
DUFF, BERTON & WHITTINGTON, CARRIE	08 DEC 1903	10:425
DUFF, GOVEY H & MORGAN, MINA L	29 JUN 1902	10:099
DUFF, JAMES S & GARTON, SARAH C	22 APR 1874	08:114
DUFF, MEL & BOARD, STELLA	24 DEC 1901	09:475
DUFF, MILFORD E & KOLBE, CLARA L	03 APR 1911	13:302
DUFFE, WILLIAM F & WILLIAMS, ELIZABETH	27 APR 1848	01:048
DUFFER, ALFRED F & JORDAN, MARGARET	*20 DEC 1858	02:011
DUFFER, ELMER L & EVANS, EMOZETTE	26 MAR 1903	10:262
DUFFER, OSCAR & BARRETTE, NAOMA MIRTLE	09 OCT 1913	15:045
DUFFEY, ANDREW & KILLEEN, KATIE	17 JUN 1890	05:571
DUGAN, A & CLARK, ELIZABETH	22 JUN 1884	12:028
DULANY, ARCHIE FRANKLIN & SCHOONOVER, MARY PEARL	02 MAY 1914	15:180
DUMBLE, EARL CRANSTON & MOORE, LYDE MAY	31 OCT 1889	05:475
DUNBAR, F M & FIELDS, IDA V	18 SEP 1883	11:404
DUNCAN, ALBERT S & FOWLER, RHODA	13 MAY 1911	13:318
DUNCAN, BENJAMIN A & POWERS, JEMIMA	02 AUG 1871	07:105
DUNCAN, CHARLES E & RAYNOR, GRACE L	24 AUG 1912	13:588
DUNCAN, CHARLES S & STARBURGH, CLARA	23 AUG 1904	10:585
DUNCAN, CHARLES W & McDANIEL, BELLE	28 JAN 1892	06:283
DUNCAN, FREDRICK J & FLINT, REBECCA	04 NOV 1908	12:295
DUNCAN, JAMES & FISHER, CATHARINE	29 MAR 1877	09:052
DUNCAN, JAMES M & WING, HATTIE	10 AUG 1904	10:572
DUNCAN, JAMES S & BERKLEY, MARTHA J	23 DEC 1869	06:132
DUNCAN, JOHN R & HILL, MARY M	08 NOV 1866	04:168
DUNCAN, JOHN R & WINER, FANNIE	28 APR 1902	10:064
DUNCAN, MILLARD M & COMPSTON, LENA M	04 MAR 1903	10:249
DUNCAN, MOSES & PERSINGER, MARTHA SUSAN	*04 JAN 1853	02:003
DUNCAN, PETER F & NEALE, MARY A	01 OCT 1877	09:135
DUNCAN, ROBERT H & FOWLER, NANNIE	14 NOV 1901	09:447
DUNCAN, SHERMAN F & WATTERSON, BERTHA	*18 MAY 1894	07:094
DUNCAN, WALTER & STOVER, DORA	24 AUG 1898	08:349
DUNCAN, WALTER W & COMPTON, VIRGIE	26 DEC 1809	12:579
DUNCAN, WILLIAM A & WELLS, SUSAN A	31 DEC 1879	10:189
DUNCAN, WILLIAM H & GROVES, REBECCA J	14 FEB 1878	09:214
DUNCAN, JACKSON & PARSONS, ISABELL	05 MAY 1889	05:395
DUNCAN, WORTHY E & STOVER, ELLA	18 SEP 1906	11:414
DUNFIELD, CHARLES C & JEFFRESS, ELIZABETH	1834	01:039
DUNFIELD, JURDAN & FLESHER, RACHAEL	10 APR 1828	01:021
DUNHAM, ALEXANDER LECKY CROW & MORRISON, ALDA B	28 JAN 1900	09:074
DUNLAP, ALBERT & SCARBERRY, LOUISA A	18 JUN 1893	06:559
DUNLAP, ALBERT & CONKLE, NANCY	29 OCT 1899	09:002

Names	Date	Ref
DUNLAP, ISRAEL & GREENLEE, VIRGINIA E	25 JAN 1872	07:183
DUNLAP, JESSE & BURNS, MAGGIE	25 DEC 1901	09:483
DUNLAP, JOHN & DAVIS, ALMIRA	*09 JAN 1858	02:010
DUNLAP, JOHN E & RIFFLE, LOUISA J	08 OCT 1897	08:171
DUNLAP, SAMUEL W & SMITH, BESSIE M	05 JUL 1903	10:315
DUNLAP, WILLIAM & WASHINGTON, FLEETA	23 JUN 1870	06:201
DUNLAP, WILLIAM B & LYONS, EMELINE	24 FEB 1893	06:495
DUNN, A O & HUGHES, LAURA	30 APR 1910	13:050
DUNN, ALBERT W & DEVORE, MAUD A	16 JUL 1910	13:113
DUNN, CHARLES E & KIRK, ELIZA M	17 JUN 1905	11:113
DUNN, EDWIN & MANLEY, RETTIE	27 OCT 1901	09:431
DUNN, EDWIN & LEE, EVIE	22 JUN 1909	12:428
DUNN, FRANCIS MARRION & LANIER, IDA	05 JAN 1887	12:456
DUNN, FRANK & DUNLAP, ELLA	27 JUN 1900	09:149
DUNN, GILBERT J & WORKMAN, VENA E	23 DEC 1913	15:104
DUNN, GRANT & WARD, LECTA M	05 JAN 1898	08:239
DUNN, GRANT & NIBERT, BERTHA M	29 NOV 1905	11:213
DUNN, HEZEKIAH & KNOPP, MARY M	*15 AUG 1859	02:013
DUNN, JAMES & JONES, POLLY	27 NOV 1822	01:008
DUNN, JAMES & McMAHAN, ROSE	13 SEP 1892	06:404
DUNN, JAMES T & CASEY, RHODA A	09 FEB 1872	07:191
DUNN, JOHN I & HESSON, EMMA B	01 DEC 1892	06:450
DUNN, JOHN W & ABRAMS, LIZZIE	21 DEC 1881	11:080
DUNN, JULE & COLEMAN, ETHEL OLEVIA	25 AUG 1910	13:143
DUNN, JULIUS C & LOUDEN, JESSIE E	20 AUG 1908	12:228
DUNN, ROBERT H & CAUFMAN, CYNTHIA A	02 JAN 1872	07:167
DUNN, WILLIAM MARSHALL & LANHAM, ADIE ELIZABETH	24 DEC 1889	05:501
DURST, CHARLES M & HUGHES, NORA A	25 DEC 1914	15:352
DURST, DAVID & BLACKBURN, ELIZABETH CALISTA	*13 DEC 1855	02:007
DURST, DENSEL D & RAINEY, CORA INEZ	05:APR 1914	15:168
DURST, FLOYD S & SHIRLEY, FORREST	20 JAN 1912	13:468
DURST, GEORGE A & McBRIDE, MINA F	15 JUL 1903	10:320
DURST, GEORGE A & McDADE, MARMA	11 MAY 1907	11:530
DURST, HENRY H & STONE, LIZZIE	04 OCT 1879	10:145
DURST, HERSCHEL W & BARNETT, RUTH	23 SEP 1906	11:417
DURST, HOMER O & SINES, NINIE M	15 JUL 1905	11:119
DURST, KINSY & HUGHES, LYDIA	07 MAY 1913	14:139
DURST, PHILIP & ROLLINS, ADA	20 NOV 1908	12:311
DURST, THOMAS D & SHIRLEY, MARY E	02 MAR 1884	11:464
DURST, WILLIAM G & OLIVER, LENA B	21 JUN 1902	10:093
DuVAL, GEORGE A & GILMORE, NELLIE B	23 JAN 1901	09:282
DuVAL, FREDRICK C & CHEESEBREW, CORA M	22 DEC 1904	11:008
DYE, ASA W & SMITH, ALMA K	12 MAY 1914	15:193
DYE, CHARLES KIRTLEY & COLEMAN, JOANNA	27 APR 1890	05:548
DYE, CHARLES T & CRUMP, ALLIE	01 JAN 1910	12:587
DYE, JOHN H & ROUSH, SARAH C	24 OCT 1872	07:280
DYE, WILLIAM H & LAMBERT, JENNIE M	01 MAR 1907	11:501
DYER, ISAAC H & McVEY, ERSA	18 AUG 1911	13:358
DYKE, GEORGE DANA & BRINKER, GERTRUDE	10 NOV 1911	13:414
EADES, CHARLES H & DYE, EMILY	*28 FEB 1853	02:004
EADES, JAMES THOMAS & BROWN, MARGARET	31 DEC 1903	10:458
EADES, JOHN T & McDANIEL, REBECCA	20 APR 1882	11:141
EADS, C W & DUNCAN, FANNIE	04 DEC 1910	13:221
EADS, CHARLES & SIMPKINS, NANCY S	13 FEB 1872	07:195
EADS, CHARLES H & MOURNING, EMILY J	05 APR 1870	06:175
EADS, CHARLES P & MAYS, MARY J	12 SEP 1872	07:261
EADS, CHARLES W & RODGERS, LUELLA E	13 MAR 1898	08:269
EADS, HERBERT & GREENLEE, BERTHA F	02 APR 1905	11:066

EADS, JAMES E & MOURNING, EDITH G	25 DEC 1904	11:009
EADS, JAMES F & CLENDENIN, ELLA	25 DEC 1901	09:484
EADS, JAMES L & BLANKENSHIP, MINNIE B	13 OCT 1907	12:041
EADS, JAMES W & GASKINS, MINNIE M	25 DEC 1896	08:024
EADS, JOHN R & WAUGH, ROSA	11 OCT 1903	10:383
EADS, JOHN W & McQUAID, LILLY	03 OCT 1896	07:625
EADS, JOHN WILLIAM & RIFFLE, CORDELIA F	21 APR 1891	06:098
EADS, JOSEPH & RODGERS, SARAH	15 AUG 1893	06:586
EADS, ODDIE E & DUNCAN, BIRDIE F	14 MAY 1911	13:314
EADS, SAMUEL & GISE, MARY ELLEN	29 MAR 1866	04:112
EADS, WILLIAM & ROACH, MARY	24 NOV 1840	01:035
EADS, WILLIAM & HOWELL, SARAH	13 AUG 1896	07:593
EADS, WILLIAM A & MAYS, ELIZABETH J	14 AUG 1869	06:074
EADS, WILLIAM I & BURROWS, ARENIA M	16 MAR 1891	06:079
EARHART, NATHANIEL & WELTON, ELLA M	24 MAR 1867	05:039
EARLE, PETER & JENNINGS, ELLA	22 JUN 1887	08:048
EARWOOD, AMPUDA & WILLIAMS, ANNIE L	*18 OCT 1887	05:124
EARWOOD, JOHN ALVEY & EARWOOD, BETTIE	21 SEP 1900	09:210
EASTER, CHARLES & PEGRAM, MAGGIE	27 SEP 1904	10:607
EASTER, CHARLES & WRIGHT, LIZZIE C	25 JUL 1907	11:548
EASTHAM, HENRY H & MILLER, WILLIE A	25 OCT 1871	07:137
EASTHAM, HENRY H & McCONIHAY, MATTIE	17 JAN 1898	08:256
EASTHAM, PRESLEY C & LONG, MARY A	*25 JAN 1860	02:013
EASTHAM, WELLINGTON & COUCH, SARAH F	31 OCT 1871	07:140
EATON, ALBERT & KEARNS, SARINA C	*03 NOV 1856	02:009
EBERSBACH, CHARLES & KRAFT, ELLA E	11 NOV 1897	08:196
EBERSBACH, THEODORE & HAWKINS, GRACE P	12 OCT 1913	15:046
EBLIN, BIRT & HENRY, VINA	06 SEP 1897	08:156
EBLIN, SAMUEL & DODSON, ROSE E	22 MAR 1898	08:274
ECCARD, ANDREW & CALDWELL, REBECCA F	29 MAR 1841	01:036
ECKARD, ANDREW & McGINNIS, JOANN P	21 JUN 1868	05:193
ECKARD, ANDREW & ROBERTS, PEGGY	04 MAY 1840	01:035
ECKARD, ANDREW S & GASTON, MILDRED J	12 NOV 1862	03:087
ECKARD, CALVIN J & CULLEN, ALLICE	03 SEP 1862	03:077
ECKARD, CALVIN J & ECKARD, ANN	28 NOV 1867	05:135
ECKARD, CLARENCE O & HALBLIEB, NAOMI A	18 MAR 1908	12:143
ECKARD, DAVID A & POWERS, LOUISA F	16 JUL 1881	10:428
ECKARD, EDGAR L & JOHNSON, IDA M	11 MAR 1897	08:062
ECKARD, GEORGE WILLIAM & GREENLEE, ORA O	30 JUL 1890	05:595
ECKARD, JACOB & RAYBURN, ARABELLA	05 NOV 1879	10:158
ECKARD, JAMES ABRAHAM & CRUMP, MARANDA	15 SEP 1887	05:094
ECKARD, JAMES T & HOGG, INEZ	06 JAN 1895	07:229
ECKARD, JOHN M & LEMASTER, MARGARETTA	*20 DEC 1858	02:011
ECKARD, JOHN T & ARNOLD, PRICY A	28 OCT 1894	07:179
ECKARD, JOHN W & KIRK, TABITHA C	23 OCT 1873	08:045
ECKARD, JOHN W & CARSON, ESTHA E	22 FEB 1911	13:274
ECKARD, JOSEPH W & GILLESPIE, MIRIAM	20 MAY 1880	10:261
ECKARD, JUNIUS N & EMANUEL, MARY M	19 FEB 1874	08:099
ECKARD, JUNIUS NEWTON & JACKSON, HENRIETTA	26 JUL 1885	12:199
ECKARD, ORVILL & FOWLER, ELNORA	12 NOV 1905	11:202
ECKARD, RICHARD E & HALL, CAROLINE	29 DEC 1873	08:084
ECKARD, THOMAS & RIFFLE, ELIZABETH	30 MAY 1844	01:038
ECKARD, WILLIAM & EDWARDS, MAE	09 OCT 1909	12:528
ECKARD, WILLIAM G & LANIER, DIANAH G	06 JUL 1880	10:279
ECKER, HARRY HARISON & WORKMAN, CAREY M	21 SEP 1887	05:095
EDDY, JAMES FRANKLIN & REYNOLDS, NARCISSA J	21 JUN 1885	12:189
EDENS, B A & SANDS, EFFIE E	21 MAY 1912	13:531
EDENS, GEORGE BROWN & RICKARD, SARAH CATHARINE	28 AUG 1890	05:607

EDENS, JOHN V & HENSON, GERMINIA	27 AUG 1908	12:225
EDENS, LEANDER & GRIM, MATILDA A	30 DEC 1880	10:363
EDENS, WILLIAM & LEMASTER, SARAH ANN	04 JUL 1888	05:243
EDENS, WILLIAM J & GRIM, MELISSA J	21 AUG 1882	11:175
EDINGTON, BURT & HARMON, MAY	08 MAR 1908	12:138
EDINGTON, ETHAN A & HARRIS, ORA B	03 JAN 1911	13:257
EDINGTON, JOHN F & WORKMAN, AMANDA	03 OCT 1887	05:112
EDMOND, WILLIAM B & MEADOWS, SARAH E	03 MAR 1886	12:297
EDMONDS, AMOS BENJAMIN & WOLFORD, REBECCA V	29 NOV 1885	12:262
EDMONDS, BEN & CREMEENS, MINTA	27 MAR 1884	11:473
EDMONDS, FENTON & SHIVELEY, NANCY E	20 MAY 1903	08:290
EDMONDS, GEORGE & HAWTHORN, MARY	11 OCT 1879	10:140
EDMONDS, JEREMIAH & HOLLEY, MATTIE J	1907	12:093
EDMONDS, NORDA R & MEADOWS, ADA	11 APR 1906	11:286
EDMONDS, ROLAN E & HARBOUR, ISABELL	28 MAR 1899	08:487
EDMONDS, CARLTON EVERETT & McCALLISTER, AMRY F	04 APR 1886	12:313
EDMUNDS, JAMES B & MINTURN, SARAH A C	*27 OCT 1858	02:011
EDMUNDS, JAMES RILEY & MEADOWS, JENNIE CATHARINE	03 APR 1892	06:318
EDMUNDS, NIMROD & HOLLY, MAUD E	04 MAR 1908	12:134
EDMUNDS, PORTER M & HOLLEY, LYDIA E	21 APR 1881	10:402
EDMUNDS, RILEY J & HOLLEY, SARAH M	*04 MAR 1858	02:010
EDWARDS, ADAM & GRAHAM, CAROLINE	14 FEB 1872	07:198
EDWARDS, ALBERT & VANMATRE, REBECCA SUSAN	02 AUG 1849	01:050
EDWARDS, ARTHUR & SAUNDERS, SARAH A	25 SEP 1878	09:321
EDWARDS, ARTHUR & BROWN, ETHA	09 APR 1902	10:051
EDWARDS, ARTHUR I & NOBLES, ELIZA J	09 NOV 1898	08:403
EDWARDS, BENJAMIN FRANKLIN & DRAKE, IRMA	14 JUN 1907	11:552
EDWARDS, CHARLES S & ROUSH, JEANNETTE	14 OCT 1883	11:412
EDWARDS, CHARLES S & ADAMS, HESTER G	16 APR 1911	13:310
EDWARDS, CHARLES W & RICE, DAISY A	11 AUG 1898	08:342
EDWARDS, CRAWFORD & BOON, MARY E	28 DEC 1871	07:172
EDWARDS, DAVID & MORRISTON, LETHA J	17 JAN 1882	11:099
EDWARDS, DAVID A & THOMAS, SEREPTA J	02 JAN 1879	10:036
EDWARDS, ED & RUSSELL, ANNIE	15 MAY A895	07:304
EDWARDS, EDWARD & DAVIES, MARY	21 OCT 1889	05:468
EDWARDS, ELSWORTH & GLOVER, ANNIE L	02 OCT 1897	08:163
EDWARDS, FRANCIS MARTIN & GRIMM, AMANDA ELLEN	27 MAR 1886	12:309
EDWARDS, FRANK & WILLIAMS, JENNIE	17 MAR 1885	12:152
EDWARDS, GEORGE & GRAY, NANCY	1832	01:026
EDWARDS, GEORGE T & THOMPSON, ADDIE	23 DEC 1906	11:475
EDWARDS, GILBERT B & MILLER, ROSA	20 MAY 1898	08:310
EDWARDS, GODFREY & WOLF, MARY A	10 SEP 1899	08:608
EDWARDS, J Jr & LUTTON, CORDELIA J	25 DEC 1884	12:110
EDWARDS, JACKSON Y & MONTGOMERY, RUBY	27 AUG 1911	13:363
EDWARDS, JACOB & BELLER, MARGARET E	27 AUG 1885	12:213
EDWARDS, JAMES & STAATS, MARY F	01 NOV 1877	09:147
EDWARDS, JAMES C & MEADOWS, AMANDA	11 JUN 1882	11:160
EDWARDS, JAMES LIGHTBURN & FRANCIS, MAMIE	25 APR 1888	05:215
EDWARDS, JAMES M & VANMATRE, MAHALA	10 SEP 1866	04:146
EDWARDS, JAMES R & GERMAN, ELIZA J	16 JUN 1891	06:128
EDWARDS, JAMES T & FOWLER, MARY R	22 OCT 1899	08:634
EDWARDS, JOHN & HOFFMAN, SARAH A	28 AUG 1879	10:116
EDWARDS, JOHN & FARLEY, HELLEN G	03 APR 1887	12:500
EDWARDS, JOHN H & SANDERS, FANNIE E	26 APR 1893	06:528
EDWARDS, JOHN R & GIBBS, NANCY V	15 AUG 1865	04:039
EDWARDS, JOHN THOMAS & VAN MATRE, LOTTIE MAY	25 DEC 1892	06:454
EDWARDS, LEWIS & GIBBS, CHRISTENA CATHARINE	*12 FEB 1855	02:006
EDWARDS, LEWIS A & NELSON, LUCINDA A	*26 FEB 1892	06:295

Name	Date	Ref
EDWARDS, NOAH & HAYES, CORA	06 SEP 1899	08:605
EDWARDS, NORMAN A & COTTON, GRACE R	02 SEP 1907	12:003
EDWARDS, ORUS & EBLIN, NETTIE JANE	24 DEC 1913	15:088
EDWARDS, OWEN & RICE, MARIETTA	1842	01:041
EDWARDS, OWEN & FARGO, HENRIETTA	18 JUN 1827	01:016
EDWARDS, PHILIP R & MONTGOMERY, IDA	28 JUL 1892	06:379
EDWARDS, PHYLETUS & DODSON, CLARISSA	22 SEP 1870	07:006
EDWARDS, RAMIE & ROACH, MARY R	22 JAN 1900	09:070
EDWARDS, RANSALEER & BARNETT, EVELINE	20 MAR 1845	01:045
EDWARDS, RANSLER & MYERS, LOUISA	31 MAR 1863	03:110
EDWARDS, ROBERT & KNAPP, SARAH J	17 FEB 1873	07:326
EDWARDS, ROBERT & BEBEE, ANNIE	20 DEC 1893	07:024
EDWARDS, ROBERT & BIRCHFIELD, NANCY E	27 MAR 1892	06:314
EDWARDS, ROBERT & OLIVER, MARY	22 FEB 1865	03:223
EDWARDS, SAMUEL & DODSON, CAROLINE	04 AUG 1864	03:191
EDWARDS, SAMUEL S & VAN MATRE, PAMELIA ANN	04 NOV 1848	01:048
EDWARDS, SMITH & PULLIN, MARGARET	25 MAR 1841	01:043
EDWARDS, SMITH & CLENDENEN, MARY C	25 FEB 1864	03:163
EDWARDS, SQUIRE R & SHULL, ELIZABETH	09:JUN 1872	07:230
EDWARDS, STROTHER & GIBBS, NANCY ANN	27 MAY 1870	06:193
EDWARDS, THOMAS & OLIVER, SUSANNAH	01 MAR 1865	03:228
EDWARDS, TIMOTHY & SHORT, PAMELA	14 NOV 1874	08:181
EDWARDS, VINSON & GIBBS, MARGARET JANE	*02 SEP 1856	02:008
EDWARDS, W H & LEMASTERS, PRISCILLA	02 APR 1885	12:154
EDWARDS, WALTER W & BASS, LILLIE	03 SEP 1907	12:001
EDWARDS, WILLIAM & SCARBERRY, JEANETTE	05 JUN 1884	12:027
EDWARDS, WILLIAM & WHITEHEAD, DIANA G	*20 DEC 1858	02:011
EDWARDS, WILLIAM A & FOWLER, PAMELIA O	10 AUG 1890	05:597
EDWARDS, WILLIAM W & BOARD, IDA M	24 DEC 1878	10:028
EDWARDS, WOODBERRY G & RICE, ELSIE	18 AUG 1910	13:136
EDWARDS, WOODBERRY GREEN & YAUGER, JENNIE	05 SEP 1880	10:298
EGGENSCHWILER, CHARLES & AUMILLER, ELIZABETH	*04 JAN 1858	02:010
EGGENSCHWILER, CHARLES W & BANKS, MARY M	18 APR 1899	08:510
EGGENSCHWILER, JOHN H & HAVERTY, BLAYNE L	01 SEP 1903	10:341
EHLE, ORLANDO G & RICKARD, SEVILLA B	14 FEB 1900	09:078
EISELSTEIN, FRED W & EPPLE, FREDA L	17 MAR 1910	13:024
EISELSTEIN, VICTOR E & CROY, BESSIE	31 DEC 1906	11:488
EISENBARTH, ELLSWORTH E & BROWN, JENNIE E	10 DEC 1907	12:092
ELIAS, DAVID & HARPER, MARGARET A	06 NOV 1878	09:344
ELIAS, JOHN & FOX, ETHELL	24 OCT 1906	11:428
ELIAS, JOSEPH & DAILEY, MAGGIE	05 APR 1903	10:269
ELIAS, WILLIAM & COOPER, LUCY MATILDA	*21 DEC 1914	15:349
ELKINS, GEORGE & JACKSON, LULLA MAY	07 OCT 1891	06:202
ELLIOTT, ADDISON & DAILEY, EMMA	15 JUN 1902	10:091
ELLIOTT, DECATUR & SHERWOOD, PARMY	02 MAY 1837	01:030
ELLIOTT, JOHN B & HOOD, PEARL MAY	11 SEP 1909	12:500
ELLIOTT, JOSEPH & McDERMITT, HARRIET	21 APR 1872	07:213
ELLIOTT, PHILIP H & ONEAL, ANN	13 APR 1864	03:176
ELLIOTT, STEPHEN D & JACKSON, MARGARET	24 MAR 1870	06:167
ELLIOTT, THOMAS M & ZERCKEL, MARGARET A	12 JUL 1877	09:108
ELLIOTT, WILLIAM T & EDWARDS, SARAH	15 MAR 1891	06:078
ELLIOTT, WILLIAM T & BOILES, JULIA F	11 JUN 1905	11:107
ELLIS, CHARLES E & WOMELDORFF, MINNIE E	05 JAN 1881	10:360
ELLIS, GEORGE & MANICK, SARAH	07 SEP 1876	08:387
ELLIS, JACOB & DUNLAP, ANNIE	07 FEB 1895	07:248
ELLIS, JAMES H & FADELY, LYDIA M	17 OCT 1861	03:027
ELLIS, JAMES H Jr & MILLER, EMMA	29 APR 1880	10:246
ELLIS, JEREMIAH M & DUNN, ELIZA J	09 JUN 1868	05:187

Names	Date	Ref
ELLISON, ALBERT W & TIPPETT, KATE L M	23 DEC 1885	12:269
ELMORE, JOHN & CRAMENES, CATHARINE	10 AUG 1844	01:044
ELSHAM, WILLIAM H & BATES, LYDA E	06 NOV 1908	12:136
ELSWICK, ELI & HEMSLEY, JANE A	29 DEC 1870	07:037
ELSWICK, JOHN & STEPHEN, ELIZA	20 MAY 1863	03:117
ELY, ALFRED L & BEVAN, MARY	11 JAN 1877	09:023
ELY, ALFRED L & KNAPP, MARGARET VIRGINIA	*09 OCT 1855	02:007
ELY, ALRED LERON & HARRISON, MARY ANN	27 JUN 1886	12:343
ELY, GORDON RANDOLPH & YOUNG, CLARA	05 SEP 1913	15:043
ELY, JOHN H & LEWIS, ALICE B	16 JUN 1896	07:567
ELY, MARION F & BUTLER, ANNIE L	16 APR 1882	11:140
ELY, WASHINGTON & EPPLEWHITE, (Mrs) DECIMAY	17 JAN 1888	05:178
ELY, WASHINGTON & MILLS, ANN	06 MAR 1871	07:060
ELY, WILLIAM R H & JENNINGS, IDAH B	(no date)	06:246
EMANUEL, SAMUEL L & CHATTIN, ELIZA G	29 NOV 1883	11:428
EMBLETON, JAMES B & JONES, TIRZAH A	30 OCT 1889	05:473
EMBLETON, JAMES W & BUMGARNER, IDA O	17 SEP 1893	06:606
EMBLETON, ROBERT & NEWBY, MARGARET E	22 SEP 1881	11:071
EMBLETON, ROBERT TOBIAS & STONE, HATTIE MAY	25 OCT 1892	06:432
EMBLETON, THOMAS E & MORRISON, JENNIE	24 DEC 1879	10:177
EMBRY, ARMSTEAD & SNELL, MILDRED A	1839	01:041
ENGLE, BENJAMIN & CLAGG, LAURA B	24 OCT 1901	09:429
ENGLE, CHARLES B & WOLFE, MAGGIE I	21 OCT 1890	05:626
ENGLE, W M & HANNAN, BETTIE F	08 NOV 1898	08:401
ENGLES, CHARLES F & FISHER, NANCY JANE	03 APR 1910	13:036
ENGLISH, JOB & WARTH, MARY	26 JUN 1828	01:021
ENGLISH, JOHN W & LEWIS, FANNIE	05 MAY 1862	03:060
ENGLISH, LEWIS SEHON & HOOVER, JENNIE	06 JUN 1887	05:038
ENGLISH, NATHANIEL & WARTH, HANNAH	13 MAR 1828	01:021
ENICKS, CHARLES H & WOODRUM, BLANCHE	03 AUG 1912	13:575
ENNIS, JOHN C & BROOKS, WINNY	1831	01:026
ENTSMINGER, ALFRED E & McCOY, CORA	12 FEB 1902	10:023
ENTSMINGER, GEORGE A & JIVIDEN, LAVENIA M	02 SEP 1900	09:181
ENTSMINGER, ISAAC & CHILDERS, CATHARINE	13 FEB 1887	12:480
ENTSMINGER, LORENZO D & HUGHES, AMANDA	18 DEC 1873	08:074
ENTWISTLE, JAMES E & THOMPSON, HATTIE M	17 FEB 1904	10:478
EPPLE, GEORGE & SARGENT, IDA F	06 FEB 1888	05:183
EPPLE, JOHN & COTTRILL, ESSTELLA M	01 SEP 1892	06:398
ERETT, JOHN C & HARBOR, ANNIE	25 DEC 1897	08:222
ERRETT, WILLIAM R N & YOUNG, VIRGINIA F	02 DEC 1880	10:334
ERVIN, ANDREW & MITCHELL, CATHARINE	13 OCT 1878	09:333
ERVIN, EDWARD & BARNET, POLLY	09 FEB 1815	01:004
ERVIN, HARRY H & STALEY, MARY A	15 JUL 1907	11:579
ERVIN, JOHN C & NELSON, BERTHA E	04 JUL 1906	11:360
ERWIN, A KYLE & WRIGHT, MARY E	02 MAY 1996	07:542
ERWIN, ANDREW JACKSON & CARPENTER, MARTHA FRANCES	23 MAY 1862	03:064
ERWIN, CECIL & IRVIN, NOLA	27 APR 1902	10:063
ERWIN, ELMER D & O'CONNOR, (Mrs) ALICE J	14 MAY 1913	14:148
ERWIN, ISAAC & McCALLISTER, MARIAN	1836	01:032
ERWIN, JAMES & McCOWN, MARY JANE	1836	01:040
ERWIN, JOHN & JORDAN, MARY JANE	13 APR 1884	12:003
ERWIN, JOHN HENRY JACKSON & NEEDHAM, MARY CATHARINE	18 MAY 1887	05:027
ERWIN, ROBERT & McCALISTER, VIRGINIA	17 AUG 1848	01:046
ERWIN, ROY & THACKER, EMMA M	15 NOV 1910	13:208
ESKEW, ALFRED & STEWART, ANNA	24 AUG 1893	06:592
ESKEW, JAMES M & KIMBERLING, (Mrs) ALICE	21 OCT 1914	15:296
ESKEW, JAMES M & DEARTLE, DELIA	09 JAN 1908	12:117
ESKEW, ROY M & ATKINSON, BEULAH D	21 MAR 1913	14:111

ESTEP, ENOCH & BALDWIN, RUTH	25 FEB 1867	05:029
ESTEP, GEORGE W & BIRCHFIELD, REBECCA J	15 MAR 1896	07:514
ESTEP, PLEASANT L & BIRCHFIELD, SARAH J	24 MAY 1896	07:553
ESTES, GEORGE W & STANLEY, NETTIE E C	23 NOV 1905	11:211
EULER, WILLIAM CASPER & KINTZEL, FLORA	22 APR 1900	09:113
EVANS, EDWARD L & FELLURE, DORA	10 OCT 1914	15:292
EVANS, EPHRAIM & WRIGHT, RHEUAMA	01 FEB 1826	01:014
EVANS, FRANK & HAWKINS, MARY L	31 DEC 1901	09:488
EVANS, HENRY H & ALLEN, ANN E	13 APR 1883	11:323
EVANS, JOHN & GREENLEE, DEBORAH	05 FEB 1828	01:017
EVANS, JOHN & MILLS, MARTHA B	16 SEP 1895	07:366
EVANS, JOHN W & EDEN, STELLA B	13 APR 1914	15:174
EVANS, JONATHAN & STATTS, MARY	09 JAN 1827	01:020
EVANS, WALTER FRANKLIN & HAWK, HELEN MARIE	02 OCT 1909	12:518
EVANS, WALTER M & HESS, EDNA L	26 NOV 1902	10:197
EVERETT, DAY & GREENLEE, PARETHA	18 JAN 1840	01:033
EVERMAN, WILLIAM & BOOTON, RHODA	08 MAR 1820	01:006
EVERS, R A & MILLER, JEANNETTE	15 MAR 1913	14:108
EVERT, HOOTON FRANKLIN & HEAD, CARRIE	13 APR 1907	10:516
EVRETT, ROBERT W & SHANK, MARY F	24 DEC 1890	06:025
EWEN, WILLIAM & ANGEL, LOUISA S	08 DEC 1863	03:146
EWING, CALVIN & GRIM, CYNTHIA	11 APR 1875	08:226
EWING, EDGAR & ARMSTRONG, DAISY M	06 JUN 1906	11:335
EYNON, DAVID & ALLEN, EMMA J	16 FEB 1907	11:495
FABIAN, SAMUEL D & RAWSON, CATHARINE M	11 AUG 1868	05:202
FABIAN, SAMUEL D & BECK, ANNIE M	10 SEP 1884	12:055
FADELEY, MONROE HAMILTON & HOGG, MARY LUCINDA	03 NOV 1892	06:436
FADELY, FRANKLIN W & McNEALEY, DELLA M	12 JUN 1899	08:552
FADELY, GEO & ROBERTSON, ELIZABETH	*07 FEB 1861	02:015
FADELY, GEORGE E & TUCKER, ROSETTA B	12 NOV 1893	07:005
FADELY, JACOB & PEARSON, ELIZABETH J	26 JUL 1866	04:142
FADELY, JOHN FRANKLIN & HAWKINS, PERMELIA	25 DEC 1890	06:023
FADELY, JOSHUA & DAIGH, MINERVA	*18 JAN 1856	02:007
FADELY, MOSES & DAY, EMILY	*05 DEC 1859	02:013
FADLEY, ISAAC & SLACK, ELIZABETH	*20 DEC 1852	02:003
FADLEY, ROBERT E L & CALL, SARAH J	17 JUN 1906	11:342
FAGGIN, HERSCHEL & ERRETT, VIRGINIA FRANCES	08 JAN 1901	09:274
FARGO, LAROTT & EDWARDS, ELIZA	1837	01:040
FARLEY, CALEB & CANTERBERRY, FLORENCE V	21 NOV 1880	10:333
FARLEY, HARRY N & MYERS, BERTHA C	16 DEC 1894	07:212
FARLEY, HARRY W & WEBB, HATTIE	06 DEC 1903	10:424
FARLEY, ISAAC & MEADOWS, CYNTHIA ANN SUSAN	21 DEC 1871	07:155
FARLEY, JESSE C & MILLER, RACHEL	10 AUG 1895	07:363
FARLEY, MOSES & GROVES, MAGGIE J	10 NOV 1881	11:050
FARLEY, SIMON & CIRCLE, MAGGIE	30 DEC 1877	09:184
FARLEY, WILLIAM A & MILLER, MYRTLE	15 JAN 1902	10:007
FARLEY, WILLIAM B & JONES, ARNA	23 APR 1913	14:131
FARLEY, WM CARYL & LYONS, FLORA ALICE	30 SEP 1912	14:010
FARNSWORTH, DAVID & HALL, EDNA	30 MAR 1901	09:314
FARNSWORTH, JOHN W & GREEN, AMANDA C	15 FEB 1900	09:079
FARRON, ROBERT B & EASTHAM, MARGARET	1832	01:026
FAUBER, THOMAS D & HARRIS, ELANOR	14 SEP 1870	06:228
FAUDREE, JOHN ALBERT & EDWARDS, CLARA	18 JUN 1887	05:047
FAUDREE, JOSEPH P & BOOTH, ELIZABETH	18 DEC 1901	09:473
FAUDREE, THOMAS L & BURKS, MATTIE L	01 APR 1891	06:086
FAUDREE, WILLARD O & GILMORE, VENICE	25 AUG 1901	09:393
FAULKNER, JAMES F & RICHARDS, JANNETTE	14 SEP 1911	13:377
FAUVER, JAMES F & BAKER, HESTER H	27 JAN 1901	09:281
FAUVER, THOMAS D & HARRIS, ELENOR	14 SEP 1870	07:003

FAUVER, THOMAS D & NEALE, E V	30 DEC 1874	08:199
FAWCETT, PETER H & DANIEL, NANCY	*02 FEB 1860	02:013
FAWVER, JAMES M & DURST, HANNAH	19 SEP 1867	05:085
FEELER, MICHAEL & GOODWIN, MATILDA	15 FEB 1830	01:019
FEENY, MARK A & FLANAGAN, EMMA C	01 AUG 1894	07:126
FELLOWS, FRANK H & BOWEN, BEATRICE IMO	10 MAY 1900	09:094
FELLURE, HOMER C & HOOTON, EDNA L	13 JUN 1913	14:175
FENIMORE, ANDREW H & FUNK, ANN M	16 OCT 1877	09:140
FENIMORE, THOMAS & GREENLEE, LELIA ANN	*01 AUG 1860	02:014
FENNIMORE, GEORGE McCLELLAN & SMITH, ALMIRA	20 JUN 1885	12:188
FENNIMORE, THOMAS T & KIMBERLING, ELLEN	12 OCT 1875	08:284
FENTON, ARTHUR K & GIBBONS, ELLA J	06 SEP 1897	08:155
FERGUSON, CECIL C & PARSON, MARY A	21 DEC 1910	13:234
FERBUSON, GEORGE A & KIESZLING, MAGGIE M	24 MAY 1891	06:108
FERGUSON, JOHN & GEORGE, POLLY	04 MAY 1830	01:022
FERGUSON, JOHN H & SHIELS, VIRGINIA	25 OCT 1866	04:160
FERGUSON, ORON O & COLEMAN, BESS	08 JUL 1903	10:318
FERGUSON, WILLIAM & MARKHAM, MARY	21 APR 1892	06:325
FERGUSON, WILLIAM A & GREENLEE, HARRIET	05 DEC 1867	05:111
FERGUSON, WILLIAM J & STEWART, MARIE E	14 OCT 1899	08:630
FERRELL, EMERY & DAYLONG, OCEA MYRTLE	22 NOV 1911	13:423
FETTEY, HAMILTON & HOLLEY, LIENARY	13 MAR 1895	07:268
FETTY, AUGUSTUS & TURNER, POLLY ANN	*20 MAR 1852	02:002
FETTY, BALLARD & CHAPMAN, FANNIE	26 NOV 1992	06:444
FETTY, ELMER A & HARLEY, MARY E	25 AUG 1895	07:371
FETTY, ELMER FRANKLIN & DONOHUE, LILLIE ROMA	21 JAN 1914	15:128
FEETY, LEVI & CREMEANS, NARCISSA	01 JUL 1863	03:119
FETTY, LEVI & HOLLY, ELIZABETH	03 NOV 1851	02:002
FETTY, LEVI B & MEADOWS, SEMINET	29 MAR 1880	05:536
FETTY, SAMUEL HARVEY & HUDSON, LUELLA	25 AUG 1887	05:075
FETTY, WILLIAM & MEADOWS, IDORA D	22 SEP 1881	11:018
FICK, ALBERT J & KAUFF, EVA M	11 MAY 1910	13:066
FICK, SAMUEL L & JONES, ANNA G	12 MAR 1914	15:156
FIELD, JOHN A & BUTLER, MAYME	15 APR 1906	11:291
FIELDER, HENRY H & PAINTER, EFFIE	02 JAN 1910	12:589
FIELDER, J A & SHEETS, (Mrs) MARIA	15 OCT 1910	13:184
FIELDER, JOHN J & DUNLOPP, SARAH B	08 SEP 1910	13:152
FIELDER, WILLIAM & BEAVER, ROSY	07 SEP 1901	09:042
FIELDS, CHARLES C & KERBEY, ELLA	26 APR 1886	12:322
FIELDS, CHARLES C & RINGS, MARY M	17 MAY 1891	06:109
FIELDS, DAVID I & MARTIN, CLARA	02 MAR 1902	10:030
FIELDS, DAVID IRA & PARSONS, ESTELLA	*10 APR 1912	13:512
FIELDS, JAMES R & BUMGARNER, MARGARET	*05 MAY 1860	02:014
FIELDS, ROBERT R & RICKARD, HATTIE	24 JUN 1891	06:139
FIELDS, ROBERT RANDOLPH & HARRIS, LIZZIE	09 JUL 1893	06:571
FIELDS, T THURMAN & POST, ELDA	06 NOV 1912	14:024
FIELDS, WILLIAM & GIBBS, MARTHA	21 MAR 1889	05:373
FIELDS, WILLIAM WARREN & CUNDIFF, RHODA	23 DEC 1895	07:469
FIERBAUGH, BIRT C & BONECUTTER, IDA	21 SEP 1899	08:616
FIFE, ROSS & HOOD, BESSIE	26 OCT 1907	12:055
FIFE, WILLIAM & ROSE, AMANDA	01 OCT 1899	08:625
FIGLEY, HOWARD M & PATTON, MINNIE L	22 JUN 1905	11:115
FINARTY, WILLIAM & HANLEY, CAROLINE	12 OCT 1843	01:038
FINDLEY, ALONZO E & MILLER, HELEN E	03 SEP 1896	07:601
FINK, CHARLES H & DIEHL, ROSA M	23 DEC 1908	12:329
FINK, W P & MARKUM, MAUD	10 APR 1913	14:120
FINLEY, ALBERT & CARELL, MAGGIE	26 MAY 1897	08:095

FINLEY, THOMAS & DUNN, ALICE	30 MAR 1892	06:317
FINLEY, THOMAS H & STURGEON, ROSA	09 JUN 1896	07:564
FINNEY, HANNAN B & O'NEAL, JANE	27 NOV 1869	06:112
FINNICUM, ADAM & VINCENT, BERTHA O	30 APR 1898	08:298
FINNICUM, GEORGE W & HURLOW, LIZZIE	26 NOV 1885	12:258
FINNICUM, JOHN & TAYLOR, IZETTA	28 JAN 1886	12:287
FINNICUM, WILLIAM & TAYLOR, EDY ANN	*13 JAN 1851	02:001
FIRST, WILLARD E & CARMAN, CORA E	23 DEC 1911	13:450
FISH, CLIFFORD & SMITH, ADA	19 OCT 1886	12:403
FISH, JOHN E & PENNEBAKER, FLORIDA B	28 APR 1892	06:330
FISHER, ANDREW H & RAYBURN, ANGELINE R	02 JAN 1876	08:316
FISHER, ARTHUR I & WEES, EDITH L	01 NOV 1908	12:296
FISHER, CHARLES M & BIXLER, LULU M	26 MAR 1902	10:042
FISHER, CYRUS E & FOWLER, SARAH	11 AUG 1902	10:127
FISHER, DAVID & ROUSH, MARY	12 FEB 1829	01:018
FISHER, DAVID & JORDAN, MIRTIE	26 MAR 1904	10:498
FISHER, DAVID & KOONTZ, SABINA	29 NOV 1838	01:031 5
FISHER, DAVID & HALEY, HARRIET	12 AUG 1879	10:110
FISHER, DAVID & HELPER, RACHEL	*03 MAR 1851	02:001
FISHER, DAVID W & ROUSH, MARY M	27 OCT 1881	11:037
FISHER, EDWARD EVERETT & HART, VIRGIE AUGUSTA	21 OCT 1908	12:291
FISHER, EZRA W & HOPE, IONA B	16 NOV 1890	06:008
FISHER, G W & SWARZ, (Mrs) ETTIE	24 OCT 1912	14:018
FISHER, GEORGE & FRUITH, ANNIE M	19 SEP 1894	07:155
FISHER, GEORGE G & ROLLINS, LILLIE B	28 DEC 1899	09:057
FISHER, GEORGE MADISON & McMILLEN, MARGARET ELIZABETH	13 SEP 1888	05:273
FISHER, GEORGE W & HOFFMAN, MARY M	11 DEC 1903	10:453
FISHER, GEORGE W & HART, LAVINIA	16 APR 1846	01:044
FISHER, GEORGE W & DOTSON, MARY EVELINE	29 AUG 1867	05:075
FISHER, GEORGE W & LUSE, CYNTHIA J	17 OCT 1861	03:025
FISHER, GIDEON & LEWIS, AMERICA	06 MAR 1864	03:165
FISHER, GIDEON & MORRIS, NANCY	10 OCT 1867	05:091
FISHER, HARRY F & WATTERSON, FLOSSIE J	04 JUL 1912	13:558
FISHER, HENRY J & BOOTON, POLLY	09 MAY 1828	01:018
FISHER, HENRY N & CLENDENIN, ALICE R	27 OCT 1901	09:443
FISHER, HENRY UTT & PICKENS, RUTH ANN	13 SEP 1888	05:272
FISHER, J W & SIDERS, (Mrs) JULIA C	05 NOV 1909	12:538
FISHER, JACOB & RIFFLE, VIRGINIA	*26 DEC 1859	02:013
FISHER, JACOB & VANMATRE, ELIZABETH	31 DEC 1835	01:031
FISHER, JACOB & MELTON, AMANDA	02 NOV 1865	04:065
FISHER, JACOB WILLIAM & JONES, REGINA VIRGINIA	29 OCT 1879	10:149
FISHER, JAMES F & WILLIAMS, MARY	28 SEP 1914	15:283
FISHER, JAMES M & ROUSH, ALICE	*07 SEP 1874	08:159
FISHER, JAMES M & STEVENS, NANNIE	10 JUN 1907	11:584
FISHER, JAMES ROBERT & McMILLEN, SARAH FRANCES	17 MAY 1888	05:225
FISHER, JAMES T & THOMAS, SUSANNAH	08 APR 1877	09:054
FISHER, JOHN & RHOADS, ARIZONA	23 JAN 1895	07:239
FISHER, JOHN & JOHNSTON, SARAH	20 FEB 1812	01:003
FISHER, JOHN ALLEN & PICKENS, SARAH MARGARET	29 DEC 1887	05:266
FISHER, JOHN CLINTON & RUTTENCUTTER, MAGGIE	16 OCT 1887	05:121
FISHER, JOHN M & FRY, LYDIA E	14 JUN 1866	04:131
FISHER, JOSEPH A & BOARD, MARTHA E	22 APR 1885	12:164
FISHER, JOSEPH A & THOMPSON, ESTELLA	09 OCT 1895	07:401
FISHER, MADISON C & RAYBURN, FRANCES	29 AUG 1879	10:119
FISHER, ROBERT & VIERS, SUSAN S	11 JAN 1899	08:450
FISHER, ROBERT M & McDERMITT, MAGGIE B	24 NOV 1887	05:144
FISHER, SALVENIS & ROUSH, VINA MAY	06 MAY 1908	12:173
FISHER, THOMAS H & RAYBURN, SARAH C	27 NOV 1861	03:036

Names	Date	Ref
FISHER, WILLIAM & WHITTINGTON, FRANCES L	08 AUG 1861	03:011
FISHER, WILLIAM ANDERSON & LOVE, FLORA	28 OCT 1893	08:634
FISHER, WILLIAM H & VIERS, SARAH F	24 DEC 1890	06:029
FITCH, ALFRED R & LINKHART, MARY	21 JUN 1893	06:560
FITCH, JOSEPH CLARKE & ROY, ALICE MAY	05 SEP 1900	09:137
FITZSIMMONS, BURTON & FITZSIMMONS, JULIA	04:MAR 1905	11:054
FLEAK, MARION & REED, MARY ANN	15 MAR 1886	10:303
FLEAK, PLATT & HIPSHEAR, MARIA	31 MAY 1894	07:101
FLEMING, ALONZO & REESE, LUNA	23 JUN 1906	11:350
FLEMING, ASHBEL WILLARD & JONES, JENNIE WASHINGTON	08 MAY 1884	12:014
FLEMING, GUY P & ASHLEY, AMANDA	14 SEP 1913	15:033
FLEMING, RILEY A & ROTENBERRY, LUCY	*31 AUG 1853	02:004
FLESHER, ANDREW & HUGH, ANNA	08 APR 1827	01:020
FLESHER, WILLIAM H & SAYRE, SARAH A	28 APR 1868	05:175
FLETCHER, ALEXANDER & TOLIVER, REBECCA J	17 APR 1881	10:398
FLETCHER, ALFRED & CASEY, MARY F	21 SEP 1879	10:132
FLETCHER, EDWARD & DAY, REBECCA J	07 JUN 1871	07:094
FLETCHER, ELIJAH F & MATHENY, ANNA	01 MAY 1901	09:331
FLETCHER, GEORGE W & DEAL, LEFAVOR	*12 FEB 1878	09:224
FLETCHER, JAMES & WOODS, MARGARET T	*22 MAY 1852	02:003
FLETCHER, JAMES & GUNN, NANCY	*12 MAR 1856	02:008
FLETCHER, JOHN F & PIKE, MARY A	25 JAN 1913	14:086
FLETCHER, JOSEPH & LONG, AMANA C	*12AUG 1857	02:010
FLETCHER, LEWIS & KASIE, ELLA J	13 APR 1910	13:041
FLETCHER, NELSON H & WALLIS, SARAH J	02 FEB 1872	07:189
FLETCHER, WILLIAM & TALAFERRO, BARBARA M	24 DEC 1894	07:213
FLETCHER, WILLIAM E & NEEDHAM, MAGGIE J	09 JUL 1882	11:173
FLINN, WILLIAM T & SANDERS, KATIE	07 DEC 1905	11:220
FLINT, GEORGE & LITCHFIELD, ELIZABETH	25 SEP 1898	08:371
FLINT, JAMES F & SADDLER, CYNTHA	23 JUN 1895	07:322
FLINT, JEREMIAH & SIDERS, MARIETTA	*15 SEP 1882	11:206
FLOOD, WILBUR D & GABBERT, ADA F	24 JUN 1903	10:308
FLORA, MARSHAL S & HOLLEY, JINCY	29 NOV 1897	08:205
FLORAY, C & HUGHES, JEMIMA B	15 JAN 1891	06:043
FLORAY, JOHN W & HEDGE, ELECTA	19 OCT 1905	11:191
FLORAY, LEONIDAS M & HUGHES, REBECCA	05 JAN 1991	06:036
FLOWERS, ABIJAH & VANSICKLE, HANNAH	15 FEB 1864	03:158
FLOWERS, DAVID & JORDAN, LILLIE B	16 JUN 1905	11:131
FLOWERS, DAVID V & HUGHES, DIANAH M	03 JAN 1878	09:166
FLOWERS, DAVID V & SAYRE, ELLEN	04 OCT 1902	10:169
FLOWERS, GEORGE E & BATTRELL, VINNIE	26 DEC 1894	07:222
FLOWERS, JASPER V & ABSTEN, ORPHA	23 NOV 1901	09:455
FLOWERS, JOHN W & BAILES, EMMA	0 8 MAR 1891	06:072
FLOWERS, MARTIN W & PULLINS, FRANCES	03 SEP 1902	10:142
FLOWERS, TALLE & HUGHES, SARAH	22 JU N 1902	10:096
FLOWERS, THOMAS W & SLAUGHTER, VIRGINIA E	23 SEP 1903	10:368
FLOWERS, WILLIAM & McDADE, BELLE	26 NOV 1901	09:457
FLOWERS, WILLIAM A & SAYRE, ALZINA	26 DEC 1878	10:020
FLOYD, JOHN SHERMAN & BRADLEY, LOU	25 MAY 1890	05:562
FOGLESON, JAMES W & ECKARD, ELIZABETH	*05 SEP 1854	02:005
FOGLESONG, ALVA G & VARIAN, MINNIE	12 JUL 1900	09:161
FOGLESONG, EDWARD E & MUSGRAVE, MARY L	20 NOV 1897	08:204
FOGLESONG, GEORGE W & VAN SICKLES, SARAH C	16 NOV 1865	04:073
FOGLESONG, GEORGE W & RIFFLE, IDA	09 NOV 1882	11:248
FOGLESONG, JAMES & WADDLE, MARY	08 DEC 1836	01:031
FOGLESONG, JAMES W & RIFFLE, EMMA	09 DEC 1880	10:344
FOGLESONG, JOHN & GIBBS, DELLA	02 SEP 1909	12:491
FOGLESONG, JOHN & ECKARD, MARGARET	*16 SEP 1853	02:004

FOGLESONG, JOHN T & YEAGER, EMMA B	27 APR 1884	12:009
FOGLESONG, JOHN W & PICKENS, EMMA	01 JAN 1908	12:110
FOGLESONG, MARVEN JASPER & KINCADE, MINNIE MAHALA	27 NOV 1895	07:435
FOGLESONG, N L & FINNY, ANNIE L	30 OCT 1884	12:086
FOGLESONG, ROBERT B & CIRCLE, ELLA	01 MAR 1891	06:071
FOGELSONG, SAMUEL & STEWART, MARTHA R	23 DEC 1875	08:308
FOGLESONG, SAMUEL A & FOWLER, CORA	24 DEC 1904	11:012
FOGLESONG, THOMAS & CLENDENEN, NARCISSUS J	16 APR 1868	05:170
FOGLESONG, WILLIAM & KINCADE, MARY A	JAN 1872	07:179
FOGLESONG, WILLIAM E & GREENLEE, SARAH K	31 MAR 1897	08:068
FOGLESONG, WILLIAM GEORGE & McDERMITT, LUCINDA J	13 OCT 1892	06:426
FOGLESONG, WILLIAM H & RUTTENCUTTER, MARTHA K	09 SEP 1908	12:248
FOLDEN, CHRISTOPHER C & DICKEN, EVA MAY	20 MAY 1900	09:130
FOLDEN, DAVID NEWTON & JONES, JENNIE	23 SEP 1894	07:159
FOLDEN, HERDIE R & KENEDY, NELLIE	21 MAY 1906	11:321
FOLDEN, ROY & HOLTE, AUDREY	18 NOV 1814	15:322
FOLDING, RICHARD & ICENHOWER, ELIZA F	20 MAY 1877	09:079
FONER, JAS & MILLER, NANCY	17 AUG 1821	01:008
FOOCE, WM D & FLORA, ELECTA	27 AUG 1912	13:589
FORBES, ARTHUR & KIRKPATRICK, MARY J	*06 AUG 1860	02:014
FORBES, DUNCAN C & BAILEY, SARAH	22 OCT 1863	03:138
FORBES, THOMAS & PONTZLER, ALICE	09 MAR 1874	08:104
FORBES, WAID & JOHNSON, MAY	27 APR 1912	13:477
FORBES, WILLIAM F & FORBES, EVA S	18 JUN 1907	11:556
FORBIS, AMON & HILL, NETTIE M	31 DEC 1910	13:230
FORBIS, JOSEPH & SCANTLING, RHODA A	29 APR 1904	10:511
FORBUS, LEWIS & STOVER, ALZINA	29 SEP 1883	11:408
FORCE, FREDRICK & LEACH, BESSIE	21 DEC 1908	12:333
FORD, GROVER & GILLISPIE, DELLA	26 APR 1903	10:278
FORD, MORRIS L & BANNASTER, MARIA	OCT 1840	01:034
FORD, VERNON HEBB & LONG, ALICE S	12 JUN 1889	05:411
FORD, WILLIAM & SHUMATE, JANE	1840	01:032.5
FOREMAN, A I LEROY & WILSON, ELLENORA	25 DEC 1879	10:178
FOREMAN, E L & STEWART, VICA M	06 DEC 1911	13:434
FOREMAN, ORVEL O & MOODY, EDITH A	28 AUG 1881	11:005
FORNHAUER, AMHERST N & ROWLEY, HANNAH	*14 DEC 1860	02:014
FORREST, HOSEA & WALLIS, MARTHA	*22 OCT 1856	02:009
FORREST, JOHN W & FARGO, LUNA	1834	01:039
FORREST, JOHN W & THORNE, MARY M	30 OCT 1887	05:133
FORREST, PEARL O & STANLEY, MANISE	05 DEC 1894	07:205
FORREST, W N & WOOD, EMMA M	25 OCT 1884	12:080
FORSHEE, DAVID A & GARDNER, BESSIE A	26 APR 1902	10:062
FORTH, CHARLES ALLEN & HENRY, REBECCA FRANCES	03 NOV 1881	11:043
FORTH, GEORGE & GEORGE, SARAH M	26 NOV 1899	09:023
FORTH, WILLIAM & MEADOWS, LETTIE O	25 APR 1910	13:046
FORTUNE, ALBERT S & ROWLEY, LAURA G	21 JUN 1899	08:559
FORTUNE, H C & HOWELL, FRANCES	*07 JUL 1855	02:007
FOSSETT, KANE & WILLIAMS, SALLIE	16 NOV 1890	06:007
FOSTER, CHARLES L & HUDSON, LETHA A	05 MAR 1881	10:381
FOSTER, DANIEL & JORDAN, CYNTHIA	24 FEB 1870	08:154
FOSTER, HOPKINS B & MAUPIN, COLUMBIA A	25 MAR 1874	08:107
FOSTER, JAMES G & STORTZ, ANNIE B	14 JUL 1892	06:372
FOSTER, JAMES WESLEY & KAPP, LOTTIE	05 MAR 1912	13:496
FOSTER, JEREMIAH & AUMILLER, AMANDA	24 DEC 1865	04:091
FOSTER, MONROE & AUMILLER, SARAH	02 DEC 1867	05:105
FOUGHT, ALFRED M & ALLEN, ANNIE	23 OCT 1878	09:339
FOUT, CHARLES & JONES, MARY J	*04 AUG 1875	08:262
FOUT, CHAS J & LEACH, EMMA L	27 JUL 1910	13:117

Names	Date	Ref
FOUT, JOHN & DANKIN, TELITHA	26 AUG 1841	01:036
FOWLER, BENNET & PECK, CYNTHIA	*30 AUG 1860	02:014
FOWLER, CHARLES FORBES & RICE, JONNIE EARNEST	07 APR 1892	06:320
FOWLER, CHARLES N & CREMEANS, ELIZABETH	26 AUG 1904	10:577
FOWLER, CHARLES OTHO & THOMPSON, CARRIE	13 FEB 1901	09:288
FOWLER, CLEVELAND & FISHER, EVALENA	14 APR 1909	12:399
FOWLER, DON C & RICE, ORA E	14 MAY 1905	11:090
FOWLER, EDWARD LEE & LAMBERT, SALLIE B	24 AUG 1900	09:177
FOWLER, ELERY & JEFFERS, DORA	31 MAY 1898	07:557
FOWLER, ELERY & JEFFERS, LIZZIE	09 DEC 1901	09:466
FOWLER, EMORY & COLEMAN, MARY	11 OCT 1908	12:284
FOWLER, GEORGE A & HOBBS, IDA M	07 APR 1904	10:501
FOWLER, HARRY A & McMILLEN, LUSETTA	29 DEC 1904	11:017
FOWLER, HARRY & FLORA, ANNIE	15 MAR 1911	13:282
FOWLER, HOMER B & RODGERS, MINA F	31 MAY 1905	11:101
FOWLER, JAMES C & JEFFERS, IDA MAY	16 MAR 1893	06:502
FOWLER, JAMES C & CONRAD, JULIA B	13 SEP 1905	11:168
FOWLER, JESSE B & LEWIS, EMILY J	16 NOV 1865	04:074
FOWLER, JOHN & SAYRE, AMANDA M	26 MAY 1864	03:183
FOWLER, JOHN & SAYRE, DELILA	24 SEP 1876	08:392
FOWLER, JOHN DANIEL & FISHER, CLARA LOVENIA	02 JUN 1892	06:346
FOWLER, JOHN H & WRIGHT, LILLIAN	06 FEB 1887	12:477
FOWLER, JOHN J & HARRISON, CHRISTENIA E	22 SEP 1869	06:091
FOWLER, JOHN M & BLANKENSHIP, ELLA E	25 MAR 1880	10:228
FOWLER, LEONIDAS & DUNCAN, CORA	05 NOV 1899	09:006
FOWLER, LEONIDAS O & RICKARD, DORA	03 NOV 1904	10:626
FOWLER, LEVI & RAYBURN, POLLY	04 JUL 1833	01:027
FOWLER, LEWIS & STOVER, ARIZONIA	20 SEP 1903	10:355
FOWLER, OTIE S & GLOVER, NANNIE M	12 APR 1906	11:290
FOWLER, RICHARD J & MASON, RACHEL	30 OCT 1873	08:047
FOWLER, ROBERT E & RICE, SARAH E	18 DEC 1895	07:458
FOWLER, ROY C & GLOVER, ROSE A	15 DEC 1907	12:089
FOWLER, SAMUEL C & St CLAIR, MARY A	17 MAY 1885	12:178
FOWLER, THADDEUS C & CONGROVE, NETTIE D	14 JUN 1891	06:129
FOWLER, THOMAS & FISHER, LAVINIA A	29 JUN 1899	08:564
FOWLER, THOMAS G & BUMGARNER, REBECCA E	28 DEC 1871	07:168
FOWLER, WILLIAM & GARDNER, EMALINE C	*07 SEP 1857	02:010
FOWLER, WILLIAM ALLEN & HAWKINS, ADA MAY	30 OCT 1887	05:129
FOWLER, WILLIAM M & LUTTON, SALLIE M	06 MAY 1899	08:528
FOX, CLIO D & HOGG, DAISY L	02 OCT 1897	08:166
FOX, GEORGE E & VAN MATRE, LAURA	14 DEC 1884	11:103
FOX, HENRY BASCOM & ROBSON, LIZZIE	16 OCT 1889	05:465
FOX, JOHN HENRY & GRESHEM, FANNIE	29 JUN 1887	05:052
FOX, ROY & HARRISON, MOLLIE	15 AUG 1912	13:583
FOX, THEODORE & NEWELL, FLORA	17 JUL 1912	13:565
FOX, THOMAS A & FISHER, SARAH	04 MAY 1896	07:543
FOX, THORNTON O & WOODARD, OLEVIA	10 MAY 1902	10:069
FOX, WILLIAM C & EDWARDS, MARY	25 OCT 1885	12:236
FOX, WILLIAM H & BOARD, LUCINDA ISABEL	30 MAY 1866	04:128
FRAKES, ANDREW J & WAUGH, FANNIE H	23 OCT 1891	06:212
FRANCE, CHARLES W & POLLOCK, MARIE	16 NOV 1910	13:206
FRANCE, WILLIAM & MOORE, ANNIE	22 AUG 1903	10:340
FRANCES, THOMAS W & ANDERSON, ISABELLE J	03 DEC 1882	11:263
FRANCESCO, THOMAS & WILSON, LEANAH	16 OCT 1894	07:187
FRANCIS, CHARLES & CORBIT, JENNIE	13 DEC 1885	12:265
FRANCIS, GEORGE P & HAGEMAN, MAY	10 FEB 1901	09:290
FRANCIS, JAMES & OLIVER, ALICE	17 JAN 1894	07:039
FRANCIS, THOMAS P & NUNLEY, MARTHA J	17 SEP 1882	11:208

Names	Date	Ref
FRANKLIN, BENJAMIN Jr & LONG, FRANCES E	05 SEP 1905	11:164
FRANKLIN, CHARLES E & GRICE, MARY C	14 SEP 1864	03:195
FRANKLIN, ERNEST & PRICE, MINNIE B	25 JAN 1905	11:036
FRANKLIN, JAMES & PECK, ITLEY V	09 FEB 1898	08:261
FRANKLIN, JAMES & STEVENSON, MARY F	18 NOV 1905	11:207
FRASHIER, HARRY F & MACKLEY, MARY F	02 JUL 1898	08:330
FRASIER, POPE & MINNICK, MARY J	11 AUG 1841	01:036
FRAZER, COLUMBUS & BALL, ABIGAIL	*29 DEC 1854	02:006
FRAZER, MONTAGUE & WALLACE, MARTHA A	05 OCT 1869	06:078
FRAZIER, CLAUDE A & WRIGHT, MYRTLE E	14 FEB 1912	13:485
FRAZIER, ETHNILE & JONES, GERTRUDE	28 DEC 1901	09:486
FRAZIER, FRANK & GREENLEE, MARTHA	01 JAN 1893	06:466
FRAZIER, FREDRICK & DENNEY, JOSEPHINE	30 MAY 1903	10:295
FRAZIER, LOVE & JONES, GERTIE	08 MAY 1898	08:301
FRAZIER, SAMUEL & GALLASPIE, NANCY	19 AUG 1819	01:005
FRAZIER, WALTER & DUNN, SALLIE	22 SEP 1887	05:097
FRAZIER, WILLIAM & ERWIN, BARBARY	24 NOV 1825	01:012
FRAZIER, WILLIAM A & MEADOWS, VINIE	26 DEC 1900	09:251
FREDRICK, JOHN M & DYER, MILA A	27 NOV 1882	11:259
FREED, JOHN & PINNELL, ELIZA M	*28 JUL 1859	02:012
FREELAND, WM A & MALONE, ANNIE K	22 JUN 1910	13:097
FRENCH, BENJAMIN & SNYDER, LOLA	02 JUN 1876	09:268
FRENCH, JAMES E & PECK, WILLIE	18 APR 1887	05:013
FRENCH, JAMES E & HULL, MARY C	31 AUG 1899	08:602
FRENCH, JAMES J & HARVEY, (Mrs) LEUEMA	*08 NOV 1850	02:001
FRENCH, JAS & HUGHS, LUCY	14 DEC 1820	01:007
FRENCH, JOHN J & GWINN, AMELIA	30 AUG 1883	11:395
FRENCH, JOHN W & CULLEN, MARGARET	11 JUN 1872	07:233
FRENCH, JOSEPH H & MARTIN, PEARL	10 OCT 1901	09:421
FRENCH, THOMAS & MAXWELL, MEHALA	1831	01:024
FRENCH, THOMAS & ROLLINS, ADALINE	12 DEC 1883	11:434
FRIBLING, CHARLES CLAIMUND & HOFFMAN, MAHALA	*05 MAY 1853	02:004
FRICK, CONRAD & ASTON, HENRIETTA	29 APR 1883	11:232
FRICKLER, PHIDLIP & STIDGER, KATE E	29 AUG A882	11:195
FRIDLEY, CHARLES L & HAWKINS, NANCY	07 JUN 1903	10:301
FRIDLEY, CHARLES S & LOVE, PAMELA	11 JUN 1877	09:087
FRIDLEY, GEORGE W & NEWMAN, MATILDA H	05 SEP 1876	08:384
FRIDLEY, JAMES A & SEE, MAGGIE	04 JUL 1906	11:362
FRIDLEY, LEWIS & BENNETT, STELLA	03 SEP 1902	10:145
FRIDLEY, LEWIS N & FRY, LONA	08 MAR 1911	13:287
FRIDLEY, TAYLOR N & MATTOX, SUSAN C	08 OCT 1902	10:171
FRIEBIS, JOSEPH P & SKINNER, AUGUSTA	15 MAR 1912	13:500
FRIEDMAN, JOSEPH Jr & WILLIAMS, SARAH M	28 JAN 1891	06:053
FRIEND, MARTIN & CANTER, CINTHA	20 MAR 1900	09:099
FRIEND, MARTIN & HUDSON, LIZZIE	15 MAY 1906	11:316
FRIESE, FRANK & KAPP, CHARLOTTE	15 NOV 1868	05:225
FRIESE, WILLIAM H & HERDMAN, ALMEDA	16 MAR 1904	10:491
FROIDVEAUX, PEARL & POSTON, PLEASANT	03:MAR 1903	10:250
FROSCHKE, JNO B & LEARY, MARY L	12 DEC 1880	10:346
FROST, GEORGE & BIRCHFIELD, REBECCA J	20 JAN 1879	10:043
FROST, GEORGE H & FISHER, ARTA J	24 DEC 1908	12:339
FROST, ISAAC & CARROLL, MAUD	26 OCT 1901	09:434
FROST, ISAAC & HESSON, BERTHA	04 NOV 1914	15:315
FROST, JOHN & CASTO, ANNIE	05 JAN 1898	08:241
FROST, JOHN & MILLER, MINNIE	16 MAR 1889	05:370
FRUITH, CHRISTOPHER & MANLEY, ELIZABETH	29 SEP 1909	12:514
FRUSH, ANDREW & FRUITH, MAGDALENA	*01 NOV 1877	09:152
FRY, AARON & YEAGER, JANE	*02 OCT 1854	02:006

FRY, ALGER N & GRINSTEAD, IVA	14 DEC 1903	10:429
FRY, AMOS & SPROUT, ADELINE	20 AUG 1863	03:129
FRY, CHARLES E & YEAGER, ETHEL V	06 APR 1907	11:513
FRY, EARL HOMER & CARSEY, IDA LUELLA	25 DEC 1888	05:326
FRY, ELERY & GRAHAM, ALLIE	29 SEP 1909	12:517
FRY, ELERY HOMER & ROUSH, IVA ELIZABETH	30 MAR 1892	06:315
FRY, EMORY B & ROSEBERRY, TESSIE A	19 JUN 1895	07:318
FRY, GIDEON & ROUSH, ANGELINE	05 JAN 1868	05:138
FRY, GIDEON & ZERCLE, ELIZABETH	07 APR 1836	01:030
FRY, GIDEON L & ROUSH, ALICE A	11 FEB 1906	11:263
FRY, HARRISON T & ROUSH, SARAH S	04 DEC 1873	08:066
FRY, HARVEY A & ROUSH, ANNA L	29 NOV 1893	07:013
FRY, HENRY & GILMORE, MARY C	25 APR 1889	05:390
FRY, HENRY KELLIAN & RAY, FANNIE L	11 APR 1900	09:106
FRY, JAMES EDWARD & EDWARDS, MARGARET ANN	30 DEC 1891	06:268
FRY, JESSE FRANKLIN & ROUSH, ANNA	01 JAN 1913	14:079
FRY, JOHN & TAYLOR, CATHARINE	01 FEB 1851	02:001
FRY, JOHN & ZERCLE, ELIZABETH	MAY 1845	01:049
FRY, JOHN Jr & BUMGARNER, SARAH CATHARINE	(no date)	01:049
FRY, JOHN P & CLENDENEN, RUTH A	24 DEC 1876	09:012
FRY, JOHN W & NEASE, SALOME	18 MAY 1848	01:049
FRY, LEWIS F & SAMPLES, KATE M	24 OCT 1882	11:232
FRY, LEWIS G & OLINGER, STELLA E	13 APR 1893	06:521
FRY, MARION & FISHER, ELIZA	13 JUN 1867	05:057
FRY, PETER Jr & MITCHELTREE, ELIZABETH	*11 AUG 1856	02:008
FRY, REUBEN & ROUSH, SYRENA C	12 SEP 1872	07:260
FRY, SAMUEL & ZIRCKEL, MARY	20 APR 1848	01:048
FRY, ULYSSES GRANT & McMILLEN, MAGGIE ALLAH	15 SEP 1892	06:406
FRY, WILLIAM & ROUSH, SARAH C	22 AUG 1872	07:254
FRY, WILLIAM H & LOVE, FANNIE A	30 SEP 1874	08:165
FRY, WILLIAM H & WHALEY, MARY J	27 JUL 1869	09:077
FRY, WILLIAM K & MURRY, NANCY	19 JUN 1838	01:032
FRY, WILLIAM M & ZERKEL, LAURETTA C	06 AUG 1885	12:205
FUDGE, JOHN M & DAVIS, BELLE	27 JUL 1903	10:326
FUKERY, ED & PARISH, DORA	24 NOV 1892	06:045
FULLER, NOAH & KING, EMMA M	22 JUL 1879	10:102
FULLERTON, JOHN S & KITE, GEORGEA	05 AUG 1904	10:570
FULMER, G W & CAVET, MARY	18 JAN 1864	03:154
FULTON, CARL O & SCOTT, MAUDE F	10 NOV 1914	15:320
FULTON, GEORGE W & GUSTLER, NETTIE F	04 DEC 1913	15:083
FULTON, JOHN & PHELPS, NANCY A	09:NOV 1865	04:070
FULTON, L C & WILSON, ELLA	24 AUG 1885	12:203
FULTZ, CHARLES E & RHODES, BARBARA J	16 OCT 1884	12:074
FULTZ, JOHN & BIRTHISEL, ELIZA	*14 APR 1853	02:004
FULTZ, SAMUEL & JANET, MARY E	29 MAY 1872	07:227
FULTZ, SILAS S C & BUMGARNER, MARY CATHARINE	*14 APR 1856	02:008
FUNK, JOHN B & ELY, HULDAH M	02 DEC 1869	06:121
FURGASON, HENRY W & LEWIS, LURA	14 OCT 1885	12:234
FURGET, HARRY RAYMOND & RIMMEY, IDA McK	*08 NOV 1913	15:065
FURGUSON, CHARLES & SAYRE, ELIZABETH E	25 SEP 1881	11:024
FURGUSON, HENRY & PARKER, ANNA	12 NOV 1868	06:001
FURGUSON, WILLIAM H & ELLIS, LUCINDA ANNIE	26 APR 1888	05:216
FURGUSSON, DAVID P & EMORY, MARY JANE	*01 SEP 1851	02:002
GABBERT, HARRISON HANLEY & JEFFERS, NAOMI FRANCES	24 APR 1879	10:079
GABERT, PERRY M & SOMERVILLE, MARY E	19 JAN 1881	10:368
GAHM, KARL & ROBINSON, SUSAN	22 JUL 1877	09:011
GALLAGHER, MICHAEL & WARD, HANNORAH	26 DEC 1882	11:272
GALLAWAY, JAMES N & JOHNSON, BELLE	14 AUG 1896	07:594

Name	Date	Ref
GILLASPIE, NATHANIEL & CAZY, CHARELLA	10 JAN 1828	01:017
GALLOWAY, AUGUSTUS & JOHNSON, MARY ELIZA	27 MAR 1892	06:213
GALLOWAY, LEVI & WHITE, SUSAN	23 MAY 1901	09:347
GAMBLE, SIGEL & HAMBRICK, NORA E	26 SEP 1907	12:020
GANDY, URIAH & BOICE, ELIZABETH	03 AUG 1826	01:015
GARD, JOHN & COLEMAN, IVA	05 AUG 1901	09:376
GARDINER, JOHN & EADS, SALLY	18 SEP 1834	01:028
GARDNER, ALFRED H & WOODRUM, EVA	11 MAY 1874	08:119
GARDNER, ALFRED L & HOFFMAN, RASILLA	27 MAY 1899	08:543
GARDNER, CAMBELL & BIRCHFIELD, SONIA	30 MAY 1907	11:542
GARDNER, CHARLES & RIFFLE, BARBARA	23 JUL 1882	11:176
GARDNER, CHARLES A & CRUMP, EMMA E	28 JUN 1896	07:573
GARDNER, CHARLES WILLIAM LEWIS & FOURCHE, JENNIE	02 MAY 1891	06:102
GARDNER, DON E & RODGERS, MATTIE L	02 DEC 1903	10:423
GARDNER, DON EVERETT & KNOPP, DORA	23 FEB 1901	09:294
GARDNER, GEORGE LONG & ARNETT, ETHEL GRACE	17 DEC 1914	15:345
GARDNER, GEORGE P & MEES, SOPHIA	18 FEB 1900	09:093
GARDNER, GEORGE W & PECK, MARY	06 AUG 1839	01:032
GARDNER, JAMES & SPENCER, MAGGIE	25 DEC 1873	08:082
GARDNER, JAMES A & EADS, KATIE	07 DEB 1903	10:239
GARDNER, JAMES R T & MILAM, MARY R	11 DEC 1879	10:175
GARDNER, JOHN W & KNOPP, MARY L	10 JAN 1878	09:195
GARDNER, JOSEPH & HENRY, EMMA	17 OCT 1900	02:223
GARDNER, LEONARD & ROSEBERRY, SARAH A	10 MAY 1877	09:076
GARDNER, LEONIDAS & WILSON, JANE	14 MAY 1867	05:036
GARDNER, PERRY O & STEWART, CORDELIA F	14 NOV 1879	10:164
GARDNER, PERRY O & PIERCE, DEBBIE K	26 NOV 1884	12:098
GARDNER, PETER & FRIDLEY, LILLIE B	23 DEC 1900	09:256
GARDNER, PETER D & GILLISPIE, LUALLIE	11 DEC 1912	14:052
GARDNER, W M & BOWYER, MAGGIE	09 APR 1911	13:306
GARDNER, WILLIAM & PATTERSON, ELIZA	20 APR 1896	07:532
GARDNER, WILLIAM & JONES, ELLA	03 SEP 1906	11:403
GARDNER, WILLIAM & RODGERS, MARGARET	25 DEC 1913	15:109
GARDNER, WILLIAM HENRY HARRISON & LONG, FANNIE	23 MAR 1892	06:003
GARLAND, GEORGE & JONES, ELLA	03 FEB 1898	08:249
GARLAND, GEORGE & GASKINS, MINNIE C	04 JUL 1893	06:569
GARLAND, JAMES R & FLOWERS, RUHAMA H	26 SEP 1849	01:050
GARLAND, R A & POFFENBARGER, RACHEL	*19 DEC 1860	02:015
GARLAND, WILLIAM & RIFFLE, KATE	31 MAR 1887	12:499
GARLAND, WILLIAM H & ECKARD, HENRIETTA	25 AUG 1901	09:369
GARNES, ERNEST & SMITH, NITA JANE	11 OCT 1913	15:047
GARRISON, JOHN W & NEWELL, GERTRUDE	04 JUL 1903	10:314
GARRISON, WILLIAM T & MARTIN, FLAVIA	28 OCT 1900	09:229
GARVEY, JAMES & THOMAS, IDA M	18 OCT 1884	12:175
GARVIN, SAMUEL HENRY & GOWLIN, NORA A	15 JAN 1902	10:004
GASKINS, BARTHOLOMEW & MOBLY, MARGARET E	26 MAY 1873	07:355
GASKINS, CHARLES P & EDWARDS, SEREPTA A	31 DEC 1890	06:034
GASKINS, CHARLES T & CORN, ELIZABETH F	*09 NOV 1859	02:013
GASKINS, FISHER M & GASKINS, SARAH J	01 JAN 1882	11:094
GASKINS, GEORGE & KIRKER, MAGGIE R	10 SEP 1890	05:611
GASKINS, HENRY J & PATTERSON, AUGUSTA A	23 AUG 1894	07:144
GASKINS, JAMES & JENKINS, MARY ELIZABETH	18 AUG 1887	08:073
GASKINS, JAMES C & SPENCER, ANNIE A	24 MAY 1893	06:545
GASKINS, JAMES H & BUSH, SAMANTHA	*21 NOV 1859	02:013
GASKINS, JAMES HENRY & MISNER, ELIZA JANE	14 AUG 1890	05:600
GASKINS, JAMES R & KIRKER, CARRIE	25 DEC 1890	06:030
GASKINS, JOHN R & SPENCER, SUSANAH	08 MAY 1860	03:005
GASKINS, LEONARD O & ZUSPAN, ANNA E	30 NOV 1913	15:079

GASKINS, LEONARD O & ZUSPAN, ANNA E	30 NOV 1913	15:079
GASKINS, ROBERT H & McDANIEL, FANNIE	03 APR 1909	12:395
GASKINS, SAMUEL R A & FOWLER, GEORGIA A	29 JUN 1882	11:170
GASTEN, WILLIAM J & COLLINS, ELVIRA V	22 APR 1878	09:249
GASTON, CALVIN & COALMAN, SARAH J	16 APR 1874	08:112
GASTON, NAPOLEON B & WEAVER, SARAH	04 NOV 1849	01:051
GASTON, ZACHARIAH & PRIDDY, LUCY JANE	(no date)	01:027
GASTON, ZACHARIAH & PRIDDY, LUCY JANE	1832	01:039
GATES, HEZEKIAH G & FIEDLER, VIOLA	13 SEP 1908	12:251
GATEWOOD, CHAS & ROBINSON, SARAH J	*21 FEB 1859	02:012
GATTON, GROVER & SONDERS, EDNA	18 OCT 1909	12:532
GAY, AMOS H & MARSH, RUBY	30 JAN 1829	01:018
GAY, FRANK & JOLLEY, ELIZABETH	07 NOV 1911	13:142
GEARHART, DANIEL & JOHNSON, REBECCA	*13 AUG 1853	02:004
GEARHART, DANIEL E & HOLDREN, MAHALA	22 NOV 1885	12:256
GEARHART, WILLIAM L & WILLIAMSON, FLORA A	05 DEC 1912	14:043
GEARY, JOHN B & RINE, MALINDA V	21 JUN 1868	05:191
GEBHART, GEORGE E & KRAFT, MARY E	19 SEP 1909	12:507
GEDDES, HORATIO H & PIERCY, NANCY	*22 DEC 1851	02:001
GEE, ASHER B M & WATSON, (Mrs) MARY L	16 FEB 1910	13:011
GEHO, JOHN & BRYMON, MARY ANN	*05 MAY 1855	02:006
GEHO, JOSEPH W & SMITH, MARY A	06 JAN 1879	10:034
GEIS, GEORGE H & PRIODE, LENA J	23 APR 1895	07:291
GENHEIMER, CARL W & QUILLIN, MATTIE	03 SEP 1906	11:404
GEORGE, ALLEN & HARDING, ELLA	18 OCT 1913	15:054
GEORGE, AMMON B & BAILEY, ELLA	16 AUG 1902	10:131
GEORGE, DAVID & JORDEN, MARY M	13 MAY 1875	08:239
GEORGE, JAMES & WALLACE, ANNA	20 JUN 1822	01:009
GEORGE, JAMES & LIVEZEY, ELVIRA C	24 JAN 1907	11:490
GEORGE, JAMES J & HEREFORD, EMELINE C	04 JUN 1868	05:186
GEORGE, JOHN W & WALLACE, VIRGINIA E	26 MAR 1876	08:341
GEORGE, JOSEPH E & HENDERSON, SALLIE A	20 FEB 1868	05:147
GEORGE, JUDSON A & LANHAM, NORA M	31 DEC 1896	08:012
GERLACH, ALBERT C & YAUGER, SARAH C	11 MAR 1896	07:505
GERLACH, ALBERT C & THORNTON, EMMA J	03 APR 1900	09:104
GERMAN, ALBERT & KNAPP, REBECCA J	31 AUG 1882	11:194
GERMAN, ALBERT & SMART, ETTA	01 OCT 1893	06:616
GERMAN, WILLIAM O & LAMBERT, SARAH E	28 DEC 1884	12:115
GEST, CHARLES H & CASEY, NEOLA	22 OCT 1907	12:051
GIBAUT, BAZALEEL & HYATT, ELIZABETH	16 APR 1874	08:111
GIBAUT, HEZEKIAH & MEADOWS, SELAH	08 DEC 1867	05:112
GIBBAUT, GEORGE W & JOHNSON, GEORGIA E	24 JUL 1904	10:564
GIBBEAUT, CHARLES C & STEWART, RUTH A	14 APR 1897	08:076
GIBBEAUT, ODEN OTHER & WHITESIDE, MINNIE F	14 OCT 1890	05:624
GIBBONS, MATHINS S & KNIGHT, IDA R	08 MAY 1883	11:334
GIBBS, A E & LEDERER, KATHREN	10 JAN 1900	09:063
GIBBS, ABRAM & KEARNS, MARY ANN	*06 OCT 1856	02:009
GIBBS, ALBERT & PLANTS, LUCY ELLEN	28 AUG 1890	05:606
GIBBS, ANDREW J & RIGGS, ROSA E	21 JUL 1902	10:114
GIBBS, ANDREW J & JOHNSON, OELLA	17 JAN 1891	06:046
GIBBS, ANDREW L & GREENLEY, HANNAH K	03 JUL 1886	12:350
GIBBS, ANDREW S & CHILDERS, MARY J	15 SEP 1894	07:153
GIBBS, ARCH E, Jr & LILLICH, EMMA	30 DEC 1886	12:458
GIBBS, ARCHA W & CARTWRIGHT, EDITH	12 AUG 1906	11:387
GIBBS, ARCHE & HUMPHREY, MARTHA	*26 OCT 1859	02:013
GIBBS, ARCHIBALD & WHITE, MARINDA	25 DEC 1902	10:212
GIBBS, BENJAMIN F & SCHULL, MARGARET	15 DEC 1878	10:015
GIBBS, BENJAMIN F & GANDEE, LUCINDA E	05 OCT 1879	10:136

GIBBS, CHARLES & RODGERS, EFFY S	01 JUL 1880	10:274
GIBBS, CHARLES GRANT & McKINEY, MINNIE	22 JUN 1893	06:561
GIBBS, CHARLES JEROME & CHAFFIN, IDA CATHARINE	22 SEP 1889	05:456
GIBBS, DAVID & BONNETT, MARY	02 SEP 1905	11:162
GIBBS, DWIGHT L M & FRY, LAURA A	03 JUL 1906	11:353
GIBBS, EDGAR C & KAY, ELIZABETH A	23 AUG 1884	12:048
GIBBS, EDWARD J & MAERZ, JESSE H	31 JAN 1914	15:132
GIBBS, EMERY & YOUNG, TREACY	14 FEB 1909	12:368
GIBBS, ERVIN B & GIBBS, ANNA E	05 AUG 1903	10:330
GIBBS, GEORGE E & COLEMAN, RACHEL V	03 JUL 1895	07:331
GIBBS, HAL & CUNDIFF, SADIE	11 JAN 1906	11:247
GIBBS, HAMILTON & CUNDIFF, MINNIE M	22 DEC 1904	10:667
GIBBS, HARRY CLARENCE & GIBBS, RACHEL FLORENCE	04 JUL 1914	15:231
GIBBS, ISAIAH & BAKER, MARY	25 OCT 1877	09:145
GIBBS, ISAIAH W & BURGIN, LUCINDA	*14 JAN 1861	02:015
GIBBS, JACOB & RICKARD, CATHARINE	17 SEP 1835	01:029
GIBBS, JACOB & KAUFF, REBECCA	12 OCT 1876	08:397
GIBBS, JAMES & HOSCHAR, ATHENIA J	24 DEC 1885	12:268
GIBBS, JAMES E & BROWN, LIZZIE	25 NOV 1896	08:007
GIBBS, JAMES F & MOORE, FLORA	23 DEC 1910	13:240
GIBBS, JOHN H & HOFFMAN, LUCY	24 DEC 1890	06:024
GIBBS, JONAS A & FARLEY, FANNIE M	08 DEC 1880	10:343
GIBBS, JOSEPH F & HART, MARY M	25 JAN 1872	07:182
GIBBS, JOSEPH P & MOURNING, REBECCA N	15 AUG 1911	13:354
GIBBS, JUNIUS R & ROACH, MARY J	12 DEC 1869	06:127
GIBBS, JUNIUS R & BASS, HANNAH E	17 NOV 1881	11:054
GIBBS, LEWMAN L & BICKEL, DINAH E	04 SEP 1864	03:194
GIBBS, LUMAN & STEPHENSON, ELEANOR JANE	DEC 1842	01:043
GIBBS, MARION & GIBBS, ROSANA	10 AUG 1881	10:442
GIBBS, MICHAEL & CARNES, HANNAH	27 JUL 1865	04:029
GIBBS, MILFORD V & LOVE, MABEL IRENE	26 DEC 1914	15:179
GIBBS, MOSES & GIBBS, SARAH A	25 DEC 1879	10:183
GIBBS, ORLAND T & CARTMILL, ORA E	29 SEP 1909	12:156
GIBBS, RICHARD & STAATS, ADDIE	24 DEC 1903	10:436
GIBBS, RILEY F & FRY, IDA E	04 JUL 1904	07:111
GIBBS, ROBERT DRYDEN & SIMS, ELVA MAY	07 SEP 1910	13:146
GIBBS, ROBERT S & BOGGESS, MINNIE	27 AUG 1881	06:173
GIBBS, SAMUEL & STEPHENSON, SUSANNA	25 SEP 1832	01:025
GIBBS, SAMUEL ELIJAH & BASS, SARAH MATILDA	10 JUL 1890	05:590
GIBBS, SANTFORD & SMITH, KATIE	30 DEC 1908	12:346
GIBBS, SHELDON & KLINGINGSMITH, ANNIE	05 JUN 1887	05:037
GIBBS, SHELDON & AUMILLER, SARAH	*21 OCT 1854	02:006
GIBBS, SIMEON & STEEL, HARRIET	09 FEB 1832	01:025
GIBBS, THOMAS E & GRAY, EFFIE E	*28 DEC 1897	08:234
GIBBS, THOMAS J & GRAY, SUSAN E	25 FEB 1880	10:216
GIBBS, WILLIAM A & STOKELY, BLANCHE	03 APR 1903	10:268
GIBBS, WILLIAM L & HAWK, JENNIE	25 DEC 1891	06:251
GIBBS, ZEBULON & VANMATRE, MARIA	10 MAR 1831	01:023
GIBEAUT, SAMUEL & RAYBURN, ANN	10 AUG 1870	06:216
GIBSON, ALEXANDER & WHITTENDON, MARTHA J	24 FEB 1870	06:156
GIBSON, G W & WERNER, SUSIE P	04 MAR 1911	13:284
GIBSON, IRA & HOPE, MARY	13 SEP 1893	06:602
GIBSON, JAMES E & RAYBURN, IDA E	23 DEC 1906	11:471
GIBSON, JAMES H & MIDDLECOFF, KATE L	25 DEC 1884	12:112
GIBSON, JOHN MILLER & HANLY, NANCY CATHARINE	02 JUL 1890	06:577
GIBSON, JOHN ROBERT & McGUFFIN, LUCY MENTOR	05 NOV 1902	10:019
GIBSON, JOHN W & WATSON, MARGARET	19 NOV 1864	03:207
GIBSON, JOHN W & BLAIN, CYNTHIA A	07 AUG 1882	11:184

GIBSON, LEROY M & BLAKE, (Mrs) JANE	12 NOV 1865	04:069
GIBSON, SQUIRE O & ALHANDS, BETTIE	20 FEB 1906	11:273
GIBSON, WILLIAM & FROUNFELTER, CLEMMIE	19 JUL 1886	12:362
GIBSON, WILLIAM L & SMITH, LUELLEN	03 AUG 1899	08:587
GILES, BENJAMIN & INGLES, ELIZABETH	20 JAN 1831	01:123
GILES, JAMES B & JOHNSTON, BERTHA E	29 JUN 1912	13:556
GILES, JAMES F & TUCKER, CAROLINE M	29 JAN 1879	10:048
GILES, MARTIN & CROWN, ELIZA	19 NOV 1882	11:255
GILES, WILLIAM & WALLACE, SALLY	1838	01:041
GILESPIE, FOUNTAIN & SAXTON, LAURA	09 OCT 1907	12:032
GILESPIE, JAMES THOMAS & ROWSEY, PERLINA ANN	03 MAY 1888	05:223
GILFILIN, BRADY O & FROST, SARAH F	08 DEC 1908	12:321
GILFILLEN, JAMES L & HOPE, MATTIE C	19 JUL 1885	12:198
GILKAY, BURTON & WARD, BLANCH	21 JUL 1907	11:583
GILKEY, CHARLES L & CHEADLE, MERVANIA M	20 MAY 1891	06:112
GILKEY, CLINTON & FRENCH, AVA MARIE	18 MAY 1914	15:198
GILKEY, EDWARD & GRAYSON, LIDDIE M	04 JUL 1905	11:122
GILKEY, HOMER & ARNOLD, MARY GERTRUDE	26 SEP 1908	12:270
GILL, FRANCIS M & WILSON, MARY	*02 MAR 1860	02:013
GILL, FRANK E & CARSON, CLARA P	30 NOV 1890	06:013
GILL, JAMES & CHAPMAN, LEDIE	28 OCT 1904	10:621
GILL, LIGHTBURN & EWERS, MAGGIE	27 MAR 1895	07:273
GILL, LON & GREER, EMMA D	16 SEP 1895	07:382
GILL, ULYS & HART, JANNIE	13 JUN 1913	14:177
GILL, WILLIAM & SINES, EVA	*27 APR 1858	02:011
GILL, WILLIAM R & BOGGESS, MARTHA J	30 AUG 1883	11:393
GILLESPIE, ALONZO J & ECKARD, CLARA M	13 JUN 1899	08:550
GILLESPIE, ELZA & WALLACE, MEDA	14 DEC 1912	14:054
GILLESPIE, GROVER C & HOLLEY, LILLY F	03 DEC 1908	12:319
GILLESPIE, JOHN C & BECKETT, LUCY A E	18 JUN 1913	14:183
GILLILAN, HUGH & MARTIN, REBECCA	24 JAN 1811	01:003
GILLILAN, SAMUEL & HOLLOWAY, BETSEY A	1831	01:026
GILLILAND, GEORGE & STORY, MANTIE	30 AUG 1883	11:394
GILLIS, ROGER & CHENEY, EMMA V	15 NOV 1868	06:005
GILLIS, THOMAS & WARD, MARY E	30 DEC 1901	09:487
GILLISPIE, CLAYTON, & SMITH, MARTHA	04 AUG 1910	13:122
GILLISPIE, ELZA & STONEROCK, MATTIE M	12 AUG 1914	15:253
GILLISPIE, FRANK & HUGHES, MAY	25 AUG 1908	12:229
GILLISPIE, THOMAS BROWN & LAMBERT, IDA MAY	14 JUN 1893	06:554
GILLOM, ALFRED & GREEN, MARIA	12 MAY 1878	09:261
GILMORE, JOHN & REYNOLDS, MARIA	23 SEP 1819	01:006
GILMORE, VICTOR R & SHURZ, DARLIE D	07 SEP 1899	08:606
GILMORE, WILLIAM & CORNWELL, MARGARET	04 SEP 1925	01:012
GILPIN, THOMAS J & BOOTH, LAURA S	05 JUN 1879	10:095
GILSON, ISAAC & CHAPMAN, MARY V	18 NOV 1882	11:254
GILSON, JOHN & GUY, AMANDA M	*01 DEC 1851	02:001
GINTHER, GEORGE WOLF & BROWN, MATTIE VIRGINIA	17 NOV 1887	05:139
GINTHER, JACOB & GRADY, LORETTA	30 SEP 1882	11:217
GINTHER, PHILIP & JACKSON, ALICE	21 JAN 1896	07:491
GINTHER, PHILIP & KNIGHT, NORA	17 OCT 1885	12:239
GINTHER, WILLIAM W & OLIVER, FANNIE	06 SEP 1900	09:192
GUARD, AMEDEE R & MUSGRAVE, ANNIE LEE	02 SEP 1894	07:147
GISE, JOSEPH E & HOBBS, LEOTI	24 APR 1894	07:076
GISE, WILLIAM FREDERICK & WOYAN, MINNIE MONA	22 MAY 1907	11:536
GISE, WILLIAM H & GARDNER, JOSEPHINE	24 MAR 1870	06:172
GIST, DANIEL P & SAYRE, CLARA A	13 JAN 1866	12:278
GIST, NATHAN V B & EGGLESTON, HATTIE E	20 NOV 1867	05:134
GLASENKAMP, FREDERICK & OLIVER, MAGDALINE	23 JUN 1881	10:422

GLASPIE, JOHN & LEMASTER, LIZZIE	24 JUL 1893	06:578
GLASS, HENRY & JACKSON, JENNIE	25 NOV 1894	07:195
GLASSBURN, ALEXANDER & VARIAN, MATILDA	12 AUG 1832	01:025
GLASSBURN, HARRY H & NELSON, ORA E	21 OCT 1914	15:299
GLASSBURN, JAMES E & JOHNSON, ANNIE	08 MAY 1899	08:530
GLASSBURN, JAMES E & HIGGINBOTHAM, MADALINE E	17 MAY 1913	14:149
GLASSBURN, JESSE B & SCHNEIDER, ANNA C	25 AUG 1910	13:144
GLASSBURN, WILLIAM E & FIRST, LILLIAN V	26 DEC 1908	12:343
GLEASON, JOHN & JONES, LAURA ALICE	25 DEC 1912	14:069
GLENN, ABRAHAM & MELTON, MARY M L	20 OCT 1886	12:405
GLENN, ALVAROE & ROLLINS, DOROTHY E	22 SEP 1867	05:082
GLENN, CHARLES & WARNER, BESSIE	21 JUL 1907	11:582
GLENN, FRANKLIN & FOURTH, ESSIE	14 SEP 1913	15:031
GLENN, JOSHUA P & CLARK, LAURA S	31 AUG 1904	10:588
GLENN, THOMAS M & KECK, ATTIE A	15 JAN 1902	10:006
GLENN, THOMAS MARSHALL & GOETING, LOUISE	24 DEC 1888	05:331
GLENN, VALENTINE & CHAPMAN, SARAH	23 MAR 1896	07:519
GLOECKNER, ALBERT G & RAYBURN, MARY E	23 AUG 1913	15:019
GLOVER, CHARLES & MORRIS, CORA E	06 DEC 1897	08:209
GLOVER, JESSE W & HARMON, ANN E	11 MAR 1886	12:299
GLOVER, JOHN K & HUGHES, MARGARET B	20 JUL 1902	10:113
GLOVER, SAMUEL & HARDWICK, ORA	11 SEP 1909	12:498
GLOVER, WILLIAM & STEEL, LOUISA	*24 JAN 1859	02:012
GLOVER, WILLIAM & GREER, LYDIA J	17 OCT 1879	10:148
GODLEY, EDWARD H & YEAGER, BARBARA	02 NOV 1841	01:036
GODLEY, JOHN & MIDDLECOFF, MARY MARGARET	20 OCT 1847	01:048
GODLY, JOHN & MEEK, ELENOR	*24 MAR 1860	02:014
GODLY, MARTIN & ROSEBERRY, JANE	OCT 1822	01:008
GOE, EZRA H & COULTER, CATHARINE E	07 AUG 1906	11:383
GOES, WILLIAM F & GREEN, SARAH	26 NOV 1871	07:149
GOETTING, CHARLES & VOLLBURN, CAROLINE	04 JUL 1874	08:145
GOFFORD, JOHN & CAZAD, AMY	18 SEP 1830	01:023
GOGGINS, PATRICK & BOOTH, LOUISA	07 JAN 1863	03:097
GOINS, WILLIAM & CHRISTY, JENNIE	*08 JUN 1874	08:128
GOLDEN, PHILIP & BLAIR, MARY	28 DEC 1870	07:035
GOODALL, ALONZO C & MONROE, GEORGIA A	10 JUL 1898	08:333
GOODALL, BERMOND & WORKMAN, CLARA C	20 MAR 1879	10:070
GOODALL, JAMES B & COLVIN, RACHEL A	28 JUL 1882	11:179
GOODKNIGHT, WASHINGTON & ROUSH, DELILA	JAN 1849	01:049
GOODNIGHT, CHARLES & ROUSH, RUTH V	29 JAN 1912	13:475
GOODNIGHT, JOHN & ROUSH, SARAH ANN	26 AUG 1886	12:380
GOODNOW, WILLIAM M & CASTO, ANNIE B	27 MAY 1908	12:189
GOODRICH, CLAUDE S & WADDELL, IRENE	16 JUN 1869	06:057
GOODRICH, GODFREY BENJAMIN & NORRIS, MARY C	19 MAY 1885	12:179
GOODWIN, ARTHUR & MUSGRAVE, CLARA BELLE	22 SEP 1914	15:277
GOOLDING, JAMES A & WATERSON, MARIA	14 APR 1895	07:266
GORDNER, JOHN & McGUNIGAL, ANNA	10 SEP 1901	09:404
GORDON, BAKER & HAWLEY, MABEL	02 AUG 1913	15:002
GORDON, CHARLES & DEWITT, LEOTA JANE	06 JUN 1899	08:549
GORDON, EDWARD & TAYLOR, EMMA	08 NOV 1894	07:182
GORDON, EMORY & COOPER, IDA	10 JUN 1904	10:533
GORDON, HARVEY & MAYES, ANNA	30 SEP 1892	06:416
GORDON, HASE & JORDAN, MAGGIE	26 MAY 1900	09:134
GORDON, PETER & GORDON, ELIZA	28 APR 1900	09:119
GORDON, SAMUEL TAYLOR & DAVISON, JENNIE R	14 SEP 1888	05:279
GORMAN, CORNELIUS & YAUGER, RACHEL	16 APR 1871	07:072
GORMAN, DANIEL & AMES, RACHAEL	*17 JUL 1856	02:008
GORMAN, SAMUEL & WOLF, MARGARET	22 AUG 1823	01:009

Name	Date	Reference
GOSLEY, JOHN & HOWELL, JANE	*02 JUL 1856	02:008
GOSNAY, ROBERT & ROUSH, OLIVIA J	27 NOV 1901	09:460
GOSNEY, JOHN H & TURNER, MARY	29 MAR 1901	09:328
GOSSETT, A LAMONT & YONKER, EMMA F	30 NOV 1892	06:447
GOSSETT, DAVID W & BURROWS, LAVINIA	22 NOV 1866	05:001
GOSSETT, GRANT & ROUSH, SERENA F	01 MAY 1894	07:084
GOTSCHALL, H G & MOLDEN, VALLIE V	18 JUN 1913	14:182
GOULD, ADDIS J & HUDSON, DOSHIA K	17 SEP 1903	10:359
GOULD, CARL R & GORDON, BESSIE M	18 MAR 1912	13:503
GOULD, FRANKLIN & ASBERRY, SARAH CATHARINE	02 JUL 1892	06:361
GOULD, NATHANIEL & GEORGE, JOSEPHINE	03 SEP 1896	08:361
GOULDING, JOHN B & BEVAN, MAGGIE	17 JAN 1878	09:200
GOWEL, JACOB & BARTZEL, MARY	*16 NOV 1857	02:010
GOWER, JACOB W & REYNOLDS, ADALINE	16 MAR 1876	08:338
GRADY, GEORGE H & ESKEW, MARY	04 DEC 1905	11:217
GRAHAM, ARTHUR HOWARD & PARSONS, BERTIE	16 JAN 1896	07:486
GRAHAM, ARTIE & GIBBS, FANNIE F	27 SEP 1906	11:420
GRAHAM, C C & HIVELEY, JENNIE	09 JUL 1913	14:193
GRAHAM, GEORGE & CAMPBELL, LAVINIA	28 DEC 1879	10:184
GRAHAM, HORACE B & ROUSH, ADUTH E	06 JAN 1895	07:231
GRAHAM, HUGH J & ROLLINS, CHRISTENA A	21 AUG 1877	09:119
GRAHAM, JAMES & STRIBLING, RACHEL	07 MAY 1878	09:255
GRAHAM, JAMES F & ROUSH, PHEBE JANE	18 NOV 1875	08:297
GRAHAM, JEREMIAH & GOODNIGHT, SUSAN	31 DEC 1880	10:204
GRAHAM, JOHN & LIKEN, SARAH C	26 SEP 1878	09:323
GRAHAM, JOHN A & RIGGS, LELIA M	04 JUN 1882	11:163
GRAHAM, JOHN M & CARTMILL, NANCY J	*05 SEP 1857	02:010
GRAHAM, JOHN T & PULLIN, NANNIE E	20 FEB 1890	05:524
GRAHAM, JOSEPH P & FOWLER, SALLIE	08 JUN 1910	13:080
GRAHAM, JOSEPH P & GRIMM, EMMA R	17 JUL 1895	07:343
GRAHAM, LEWIS & ROUSH, ORILLA	08 JUL 1880	10:278
GRAHAM, LEWIS N & PECK, ANNA	08 MAR 1899	08:478
GRAHAM, RICHARD & JOHNSON, MARY	01 FEB 1874	08:094
GRANT, JOHN F & IRWIN, MARY I	20 APR 1898	08:293
GRANT, WASHINGTON & THORNTON, ESTHER	26 SEP 1874	08:163
GRAVES, HOMER R & KERN, MARGARET	23 SEP 1903	10:367
GRAY, ANDREW & LANIER, HATTIE MAY	08 SEP 1914	15:269
GRAY, GEO & PONTZLER, MARGT	*15 SEP 1858	02:011
GRAY, GEORGE & WEARS, MARTHA	21 OCT 1847	01:048
GRAY, GEORGE & BENNETT, CORA	23 DEC 1894	07:215
GRAY, GEORGE W & CLARK, MARY C	26 APR 1896	07:535
GRAY, JAMES & CARTRITE, MARY	1842	01:041
GRAY, JAMES W & ROUSH, ISABEL	28 NOV 1872	07:298
GRAY, JASPER & STOVER, SARAH ESTHER	23 APR 1912	13:518
GRAY, JOHN & BYRNE, ANNIE	23 NOV 1897	08:199
GRAY, JOHN & RIFFLE, EMMA E	30 DEC 1900	09:270
GRAY, PETER & DASHNER, MARY	28 MAY 1837	01:030
GRAY, ROBERT & HOPSON, SOPHRONIA	15 DEC 1825	01:012
GRAY, STRICK & SANDERS, QINNIE D	28 AUG 1889	05:437
GRAY, THOMAS B & ZERCKEL, SARAH J	26 OCT 1880	10:315
GRAY, WILLIAM & KNAPP, REBECCA J	14 JUN 1899	08:551
GRAY, WILLIAM & SHARROCK, ELIZABETH	01 JAN 1835	01:029
GRAY, WILLIAM R & ROUSH, IDA	18 OCT 1898	08:382
GRAY, WILLIAM ROBERT & LOVE, SARAH KATHARINE	21 DEC 1887	05:159
GRAY, ZACH & KIRKPATRICK, JULIAN	27 MAY 1847	01:047
GREATHOUSE, DAVID G & CUMMINS, VIRGINIA	24 DEC 1871	07:160
GREEN, CHARLES & DAVIS, FRANCES	26 JUL 1887	05:064
GREEN, CULVER A & LOCKE, IVA E	26 DEC 1899	09:055

GREEN, EDWARD & PARSONS, SARAH	14 SEP 1826	01:015
GREEN, EDWARD TYLER & BARNETT, MARY EDYSINE	11 NOV 1885	12:249
GREEN, EMERY & FERGUSON, MINNIE	19 SEP 1900	09:204
GREEN, HENRY & MORRISON, EARLY JANE	07 MAY 1874	08:118
GREEN, JOHN & NOTT, LEOTA	02 DEC 1899	09:027
GREEN, JOSEPH & WILES, MARY A	25 SEP 1866	04:152
GREEN, RUSH C & CURTIS, ELIZABETH	02 JUN 1881	10:419
GREEN, TAYLOR & COLE, ISABELLA	01 NOV 1877	09:149
GREEN, TEMPLE H & STEELE, BELLE	25 OCT 1899	08:640
GREEN, THOMAS & CUTLER, ANNA	06 NOV 1878	10:005
GREEN, WILLIAM IRVIN & HOLSTEIN, MARCY ELLEN	30 SEP 1900	09:213
GREENE, WILLIAM E & TAYLOR, MARY B	20 SEP 1876	08:390
GREENLEE, ANDREW & LEWIS, RACHEL G	09 APR 1876	08:336
GREENLEE, ANDREW M & PICKENS, MISSOURI B	02 JAN 1880	10:191
GREENLEE, CHARLES HENRY & McCULLOUCH, MARY E	21 OCT 1903	10:336
GREENLEE, CHARLES & SAYRE, LUVERNA	28 MAR 1897	08:066
GREENLEE, CLABURN & KIMBERLING, MARIA	21 DEC 1881	11:077
GREENLEE, EASOM & STEPHENSON, NANCY J	14 DEC 1865	04:085
GREENLEE, EDWARD & HOLDEWAY, PEGGY	15 AUG 1821	01:005
GREENLEE, EDWARD & HOSCHAR, LUCRITIA G	29 DEC 1897	08:233
GREENLEE, EDWARD & McKINNEY, MARTHA J	10 NOV 1870	07:023
GREENLEE, FRENCH & COLEMAN, DORA	28 FEB 1894	07:056
GREENLEE, GEO W & RIFFLE, ADDA	15 MAY 1892	06:337
GREENLEE, GEORGE A & McDERMITT, RACHEL	08 APR 1868	05:163
GREENLEE, GEORGE B & RUSH, MARY A	05 MAR 1870	06:162
GREENLEE, GEORGE B & NICHOLL, MAGGIE MAY	14 AUG 1899	08:554
GREENLEE, GEORGE L & FORBIS, ADA M	31 JAN 1904	10:468
GREENLEE, GEORGE W & PICKENS, SARAH	26 MAY 1889	05:403
GREENLEE, GEORGE W & BAILEY, MARTHA A	31 AUG 1880	10:293
GREENLEE, GIDEON A & RIFFLE, MARY B	23 JUL 1882	11:178
GREENLEE, GREEN & VANSICKLES, ROSANNA	*15 APR 1859	02:012
GREENLEE, HAMILTON & PREWIT, FRANCES	27 DEC 1827	01:016
GREENLEE, HARRY H & CALDWELL, CAROLINE	19 JUN 1912	13:548
GREENLEE, HENRY & BOOTH, ANGELINA	04 JUN 1849	01:050
GREENLEE, HENRY W & RIFFLE, SARAH E	02 NOV 1882	11:240
GREENLEE, HEZEKIAH & BEARD, SOPHIA C	25 APR 1872	07:216
GREENLEE, HEZEKIAH & RIFFLE, MARY S	15 APR 1869	06:050
GREENLEE, JACOB & SWAN, SARAH C	*20 SEP 1850	02:001
GREENLEE, JACOB & ECKARD, CATHARINE	*20 SEP 1858	02:011
GREENLEE, JACOB & LEWIS, MARY J	01 OCT 1871	07:123
GREENLEE, JACOB N & AMSBARY, ROSETTA C	25 MAR 1874	08:106
GREENLEE, JAMES & HART, EMILY	15 FEB 1827	01:016
GREENLEE, JAMES N & McDERMITT, MINNIE B	11 AUG 1906	11:366
GREENLEE, JOHN & MORRIS, PANTHA	1830	01:024
GREENLEE, JOHN & ALESHIRE, SUSANNA	19 FEB 1809	01:002
GREENLEE, JOHN A & LOVE, ELVA J	27 MAR 1909	12:390
GREENLEE, JOHN D & GREER, IDA	15 MAR 1894	07:062
GREENLEE, JOHN M & SULLIVAN, LURETTA	07 OCT 1869	06:093
GREENLEE, JOHN O & GREENLEE, MARY S	02 JUN 1889	05:405
GREENLEE, JOHN O & TURNER, IDA M	26 FEB 1910	13:016
GREENLEE, JOSEPH & FOGLESONG, MARGARET	20 JAN 1834	01:028
GREENLEE, L A & BUMGARNER, SARAH	21 MAR 1910	13:026
GREENLEE, LEWIS ALLEN & PLANTS, NANCY E	25 SEP 1890	05:618
GREENLEE, MARTIN & BEARD, MARY A	12 SEP 1871	07:120
GREENLEE, MORGAN & GREENLEE, ELIZA JANE	APR 1841	01:034
GREENLEE, MORGAN & LOUDENSLAGER, M A	03 JUL 1884	12:034
GREENLEE, NEELY & KNAP, MARGARET	AUG 1840	01:034
GREENLEE, NEELY & KNAPP, EMELINE	04 MAY 1886	12:323

Names	Date	Ref
GREENLEE, NELEE LUVENES & JENKINS, CORDELIA CATHARINE	30 NOV 1882	11:260
GREENLEE, OTIS C & SELBY, LAURA	04 SEP 1902	10:146
GREENLEE, OTIS O & DUFF, DORA B	26 SEP 1898	08:373
GREENLEE, OTIS E & BURNS, BERTHA	09 APR 1899	08:503
GREENLEE, PERRY M & SMITH, EMELINE M	27 JUL 1882	11:181
GREENLEE, RAY R & NUTTER, LEOTA L	25 DEC 1911	13:352
GREENLEE, ROBERT F & SELBY, ELEANOR	30 AUG 1871	07:115
GREENLEE, SAMUEL A & CASEY, LENA	30 OCT 1902	10:180
GREENLEE, SAMUEL A & GREENLEE, LENA	**21 DEC 1907	12:097
GREENLEE, SAMUEL A & YOUNG, (Mrs) ANNIE	02 APR 1911	13:301
GREENLEE, SYLVESTER W & BARNETT, ESTHER	JAN 1838	01:033
GREENLEE, WILLARD & DUFF, LAURA A	14 JUN 1885	12:184
GREENLEE, WILLARD C, Jr. & BURDETT, ESTELLA M	01 MAR 1908	12:123
GREENLEE, WILLIAM & RIFFLE, CATHARINE	21 JUL 1840	01:033
GREENLEE, WILLIAM C & ELY, EMMA M	27 NOV 1879	10:168
GREENLEE, WILLIAM M & BEALS, ELIZA M	*15 JUN 1872	07:238
GREENLEE, WILLIAM ROBERT & WHITT, AMISHA	25 DEC 1892	06:457
GREENLEE, (Rev) LEWIS L & JOHNSON, FRANCES	*06 OCT 1854	02:006
GREER, CHARLES W & COLEMAN, DELIA M	25 JAN 1893	06:477
GREER, EDGAR CLINTON & TEWKSBURY, MINTIE	25 SEP 1887	05:105
GREER, ELLSWORTH & EDWARD, RESIA J	26 SEP 1894	07:160
GREER, GEORGE W & LONG, ELLA	07 SEP 1908	12:242
GREER, GEORGE WILLIAM & LARUE, FLORENCE	27 MAR 1890	05:532
GREER, JAMES F & STEPHENSON, SARAH C	05 SEP 1872	07:257
GREER, JOHN O & THOMAS, STELLA L	11 NOV 1900	09:236
GREER, JOHN W & LUTTON, REBECCA J	19 JAN 1871	07:046
GREER, JOHN W & GREER, LONA	02 APR 1899	08:492
GREER, JOHN W & GREER, CARRIE	15 JUN 1904	10:537
GREER, LENNIE F & KING, STELLA	03 OCT 1901	09:417
GREER, M E & VAN MATRE, CARRIE C	21 MAY 1913	14:154
GREER, SAMUEL N & GILLESPIE, NORA C	22 NOV 1902	10:194
GREER, SAMUEL P & RICE, LELIA J	*22 APR 1878	09:250
GREER, WILLIAM E & THOMAS, ANNA B	13 NOV 1896	07:613
GREER, WIRT & DAUGHERTY, IVA	28 NOV 1901	09:461
GREGG, CHAS M & DENNIS, ETHEL F	16 SEP 1911	13:378
GREGG, HERBERT H & CURRY, EMMER L	27 DEC 1900	09:269
GREGG, SPENCER W & McNEAL, TABITHA A	17 JUN 1868	05:190
GREGGORY, CALVIN & HOWELL, HANNAH B	14 JAN 1879	10:041
GREGORY, DAVID A & BOGGS, EDITHY V	08 NOV 1868	06:013
GRESHAM, W T & CANTERBERRY, MARGARET J	02 JAN 1866	04:097
GRESS, GEORGE H & SHUMAKER, MARY	15 APR 1883	11:322
GRESS, JOSEPH H & BATTERSON, ANNA	03 JAN 1914	15:107
GRESS, PETER & BATTERSON, ERMINIA D	25 NOV 1885	12:246
GRESS, PETER R & McCARL, KATHRYNE	21 MAY 1901	09:341
GRESS, PHILIP & ROWLEY, ELLA	07 JUN 1893	06:551
GRESS, WILLIAM H & SOMERVILLE, ALTA M	19 AUG 1900	09:175
GREUSER, EDWARD & BOHRAM, VELMA	27 JAN 1908	12:121
GREUSER, HARRY & GRUESER, ETHEL	05 JUL 1909	12:451
GREY, WM H & WARNER, CHARLOTTE	12 MAY 1870	06:189
GRICE, CHARLES I & VEST, LILLIE A	28 SEP 1881	11:025
GRIFFITH, ANDREW & ANSEL, ELIZABETH	23 MAY 1888	05:228
GRIG, SAMUEL & WITHERS, MARTHA	1831	01:024
GRIM, GEORGE WASHINGTON & RICKARD, NANCY CATHARINE	03 NOV 1887	05:128
GRIM, JACOB J & ROLLINS, ELIZABETH C	31 AUG 1865	04:045
GRIM, SYLVESTER J & McDERMITT, LAVINA	12 FEB 1863	03:100
GRIM, WILLIAM & CIRCLE, MARGARET	*23 DEC 1858	02:012
GRIMES, ALEXANDER C & McDADE, SELUDA E	21 JUL 1878	09:288
GRIMES, ALEXANDER C & McCOY, CASIE	**15 MAY 1882	11:149

Name	Date	Ref
GRIMES, ALEXANDER C & FORBES, CHRISTINA	30 OCT 1882	11:239
GRIMES, EARNEST & HOLLINS, MAUD	25 MAY 1909	12:415
GRIMES, JAMES & DOWELL, MAGGIE	07 JUN 1885	12:182
GRIMES, WILSON & HARRIS, SOPHIA	27 NOV 1895	07:441
GRIMM, ADAM & SAYRE, LORA	15 NOV 1896	08:001
GRIMM, ANDREW C & CLARK, DESTA D	24 FEB 1897	08:049
GRIMM, FRANKLIN & SNYDER, CORA	28 MAY 1906	11:329
GRIMM, GEORGE & SAYRE, SARAH H	10 JAN 1891	06:045
GRIMM, JACOB & BUSH, BESSIE	18 AUG 1900	09:174
GRIMM, JACOB M & BROWN, AMANDA	14 JUL 1878	09:286
GRIMM, JAMES ELMER & BOYD, ISABELL	04 APR 1893	06:517
GRIMM, JAMES Mc & ROLLINS, ELIZABETH A	01 JAN 1893	06:458
GRIMM, JNO J & ROUSH, AURILLA	*25 MAY 1857	02:010
GRIMM, JOHN M & CARPENTER, ELLEN	04 MAY 1899	08:525
GRIMM, LEWIS & RICE, ALMEDA	09 JUL 1890	05:589
GRIMM, LEWIS J & GRAHAM, EFFA	30 AUG 1899	08:598
GRIMM, MILO & GIBBS, MARIA EMMA	21 MAY 1890	05:556
GRIMM, OAK & GERLACH, HALLIE B	11 APR 1909	12:397
GRIMM, OTHNIEL E & BROWN, ELLA	20 MAY 1891	06:110
GRIMM, SIMON & O'NAIL, INGARY	16 AUG 1868	05:204
GRIMM, VAN H & WEIGAND, ANNIE	23 JAN 1898	08:250
GRIMM, WARNER W & FRY, STELLA	13 OCT 1894	07:164
GRIMM, WILLIAM McKENDREY M & SATTES, MARY FRANCES	16 OCT 1885	12:237
GRIMM, WILLIAM P & ROUSH, MERTIE C	21 JUL 1894	07:122
GRIMM, WILLIAM W & VICKERS, CARRIE E	31 JUL 1879	10:105
GRIMM, WM & ROUSH, SEREPTA	24 MAR 1910	13:023
GRINSTEAD, HARRY & GIBBS, CARRIE	10 MAR 1909	12:383
GRINSTEAD, JAMES N & VINCENT, MARANDA	23 DEC 1877	09:065
GRINSTEAD, RICHARD A & GRAHAM, HETTIE E	26 JUN 1884	12:032
GRINSTEAD, RICHARD A & ROUSH, SUSAN E	17 NOV 1894	07:192
GRINSTED, SAMUEL PERRY & KAY, ELIZA DOVE	01 JAN 1888	05:174
GRISOM, SAMUEL V & SMITH, LUCY A	22 MAY 1884	12:018
GROVE, AMON D & LYONS, MAGGIE A	08 MAR 1876	08:328
GROVE, JAMES L & LYON, CORDELIA A	01 APR 1886	12:311
GROVE, JEFF P & JARRY, LYDIA	05 SEP 1875	08:269
GROVE, (MD) FRANKLIN & HOBBS, LUELLA	03 SEP 1874	08:156
GROVER, CLARENCE E & JAMES, ETHEL B	**27 JAN 1912	13:476
GROVER, ELMER & MAYES, LAURA	10 APR 1904	10:504
GROVER, EPHRAIM & CHANDLER, MALINDA	11 JUL 1874	08:141
GROVER, JAMES A & ERETT, MARTHA	21 MAY 1882	11:150
GROVER, JOHN A & YEAGER, EDITH E	30 JUL 1910	13:119
GROVER, THOMAS & CHAPMAN, MARY L	05 JUL 1909	12:449
GROVER, THOMAS E W & RIGGS, MINNIE	15 JUL 1880	10:281
GROVER, WALDO VALE & MERCHANT, GARNETTE BELLE	31 DEC 1912	14:078
GROVES, EZRA T & WHEATON, MARY	09 FEB 1910	13:007
GROVES, GEORGE W & HENSON, ELIZABETH	16 JAN 1868	05:138
GROVES, RICHARD & WILEY, GERTIE	24 JUL 1902	10:117
GROVES, RICHARD & MASTERSON, MARTHA	30 JUN 1867	05:064
GROVES, RICHARD T & LOCK, MARGARET J	13 APR 1873	07:342
GROVES, WASHINGTON & DEFFENBAUGH, CATHARINE	25 DEC 1877	09:173
GROVES, WASHINGTON & SANDERS, REBECCA	24 OCT 1882	11:228
GRUESER, ALBERT H & HUNNELL, DURA	28 OCT 1910	13:194
GUESS, JESSE & KLEIN, EMMA	24 DEC 1900	09:262
GUESS, LISTON COLLIN & LaCOLLETT, FRANCES	17 OCT 1900	09:224
GUESS, LISTON C & SHIELDS, (Mrs) CATHARINE	05 NOV 1911	13:409
GULLEY, GEORGE, & WALKER, ROSE O	28 APR 1880	10:251
GULLION, HIRAM F & MARTIN, CAROLINE	23 SEP 1863	03:135
GULLUM, FRANK BARNHART & MITCHELL, EVA LOUISE	31 JUL 1912	13:574

GUTHREY, DAVID QUINN & HENDERSON, ELIZABETH	01 OCT 1846	01:047
GUTHRIE, FRANK A & SMITH, SARAH JANE	26 MAY 1863	03:118
GUTHRIE, G S & COX, SARAH A	*04 JUN 1860	02:014
GUTHRIE, HOWARD H & HAWKINS, JULIA M	17 SEP 1902	10:158
GUTHRIE, JOSEPH E & PEOPLES, ALFRETTA	16 APR 1887	05:011
GUTHRIE, LEWIS VAN GILDER & ENGLISH, MARGARET LYNN	15 JUN 1889	05:413
GUTHRIE, W B & BROWN, MARIAH SELINA	10 NOV 1869	06:114
GUTHRIDGE, JOS R & BUGG, DORA	18 OCT 1912	14:016
GWINN, AHAZ S & JIVEDEN, MARY JANE	20 JUL 1867	05:068
GWINN, ANDY & JOHNSON, ELA	25 AUG 1892	06:394
GWINN, EMANUEL & McCOY, MAGGIE MAY	16 OCT 1901	09:423
GWYNN, ALBERT & ASTON, ELIZABETH	23 OCT 1866	04:161
GYGAX, HANS & MEEK, ELSIE	11 AUG 1907	11:589
GYGAX, PAUL & STONE, BESSIE	19 APR 1910	13:047
HADDON, CHARLES S & HARRAH, MAUDE M	01 APR 1914	15:167
HAER, JOHN C & SMITH, SAMARIA	01 JUN 1909	12:419
HAGAR, EMZA & HANNAN, ADA PEARL	23 NOV 1912	14:032
HAGERMAN, LEONARD & CHEESEBREW, ORA L	13 AUG 1903	10:337
HAGLEY, W C & McCOY, EVA M	03 APR 1909	12:394
HALBERT, REUBEN P & GILLESPIE, SARAH J	25 APR 1880	10:245
HALBLEIB, JOHN N & NEWELL, MARY A	17 FEB 1896	07:499
HALE, BENJAMIN F & TOBIA, ALTHA	30 JUL 1892	06:378
HALE, CLINTON L & RAY, LILLIE B	14 JUL 1897	08:128
HALE, M H & LEWIS, ELIZA S	23 FEB 1848	01:047
HALE, MATTHEW H & GILMORE, ELLEN E	*29 APR 1857	02:010
HALE, PHILIP W & BEALE, MARY M	28 NOV 1839	01:035
HALEY, DAVID & HULL, LILLIE MAY	16 APR 1906	11:292
HALEY, GEORGE W & ROMINE, JULIA A	25 JUL 1906	11:370
HALEY, WILLIAM & STOVER, MALINDA A	14 DEC 1882	11:268
HALFHILL, GEORGE W & ROSE, MIME E	03 NOV 1900	09:233
HALFHILL, JOHN & ROSE, LUCY	11 NOV 1903	10:406
HALFHILL, SAMUEL & TAYLOR, RENA	22 MAY 1893	06:544
HALL, ALLEN & COLWELL, IDOMA	21 SEP 1890	05:615
HALL, ANDREW & DUNCAN, ROSETTA M	07 APR 1900	09:076
HALL, BENJAMIN A & WALLACE, NANCY	16 JUL 1875	08:248
HALL, CHARLES F & MOORE, ROSIE	11 OCT 1907	12:038
HALL, CHARLES T & LOVE, ORA	14 SEP 1902	10:156
HALL, CHAS & PYLES, LOTTIE MAY	13 SEP 1911	13:376
HALL, CLARENCE M & MOORE, HENRIETTA M	08 FEB 1883	11:295
HALL, COLUMBUS & GILLISPIE MARTHA	05 AUG 1886	12:369
HALL, DAVID & HALL, ELIZABETH	13 DEC 1827	01:016
HALL, ERRICK JOHN & NOBLE, AGNES ORA	05 JUN 1905	11:547
HALL, FRANK C & WARNER, LUCY	06 JUL 1902	10:104
HALL, FRANK C & DOWELL, (Mrs) SARAH L	19 MAR 1910	13:025
HALL, GROVER C & PRIDDY, VIRTIE M	21 APR 1906	11:294
HALL, HARRY EVERETT & ARNOLD, NAYOMA	12 JUL 1913	14:194
HALL, IRA A & FINNICUM, FANNY	26 SEP 1871	07:122
HALL, ISAAC & HYDE, DELILA	26 DEC 1823	01:010
HALL, JAMES & CALVERT, ELIZA J	18 APR 1845	01:044
HALL, JAMES D & HUMPHREYS, EVELINE W	13 MAR 1879	10:068
HALL, JASPER A & BECHTLE, VIRGINIA L	23 FEB 1907	11:499
HALL, JESSE W & PLANTS, ANNIE E	11 SEP 1910	13:150
HALL, JOHN & HOGG, OLIVIA	02 DEC 1834	01:029
HALL, NATHAN & JONES, MARY ADDIE	09 AUG 1888	08:254
HALL, OLIVER L & HARDIE, REBECCA	09 DEC 1901	10:203
HALL, OLIVER S & EDMONDS, SYBLE	06 FEB 1873	07:318
HALL, OWEN H & EMBLETON, SARAH	25 JUL 1886	12:364
HALL, RICHARD T & FURTH, FRANCES	22 DEC 1870	07:032

HALL, ROBERT & JOHNSON, EDITH L	03 MAR 1906	11:276
HALL, ROBERT C & YEAGER, BERNETIA	30 APR 1899	08:519
HALL, ROBERT G & STANLEY, MAGGIE B	29 NOV 1893	07:014
HALL, SAMUEL & DEWIT, CHARLOTTE	30 APR 1829	01:018
HALL, SAMUEL J & ECKARD, ANN E	25 DEC 1872	07:299
HALL, SPENCER M & YONKER, FANNIE	31 DEC 1912	14:075
HALL, THOMAS & TURNBULL, MARY J	13 OCT 1879	10:144
HALL, WILLIAM & CHOEN, MARY ANN	21 JUL 1836	01:029
HALL, WILLIAM & McNEALEY, MAGGIE	26 JUL 1897	08:135
HALL, WILLIAM & LANE, LYDIA	1833	01:027
HALL, WILLIAM & CUNNINGHAM, ANNIE	04 JUL 1901	09:367
HALL, WILLIAM & KENNY, MARGARET	24 NOV 1870	07:024
HALL, WILLIAM B & BARNETT, R FANNIE	22 SEP 1892	06:410
HALL, WILLIAM B & BECHTLE, NORA	27 DEC 1899	09:044
HALL, WILLIAM C L & GIBSON, ISABELLA BELL	04 JAN 1862	03:037
HALL, WILLIAM D & DEVOIR, RACHEL J	07 JAN 1879	10:032
HALLIDAY, WILLIAM L & SANDERS, JANNETTE	17 MAY 1866	04:124
HALSEY, WILLIAM H & DOWELL, MIRTIE M	27 JUL 1895	07:351
HALSTEAD, ADAM & GREENLEE, SARAH	24 APR 1823	01:008
HALSTEAD, EARL C & McMILLEN, LUCY B	12 SEP 1914	15:271
HALSTEAD, JACKSON & MALLORY, ELLEN M	13 JUN 1840	01:035
HALSTEAD, JESSE F & BURNS, BISHIE	08 APR 1894	07:069
HALSTEAD, JOHN ALEXANDER & LEWIS, ELIZABETH	*25 DEC 1855	02:007
HALSTEAD, MANN & PALEY, HARRIET	MAY 1840	01:034
HALSTEAD, WILLIAM & EDWARDS, ERCY	1831	01:024
HALSY, ANSEL W & HOLDREN, ALMIRA	25 OCT 1881	11:039
HALTERMAN, DAVID & FREEMAN, ALICE	15 OCT 1904	10:612
HAMBRICK, ALFRED & PRIODE, SOPHIA E	18 NOV 1885	12:253
HAMBRICK, CHAS W & HILL, BLANCH V	06 AUG 1912	13:578
HAMBRICK, GRIFFITH J & WARDEN, ELIZA	07 SEP 1871	07:117
HAMBRICK, IRA ELLIS & WORKMAN, CLARA CATHARINE	27 NOV 1887	05:148
HAMBRICK, JAMES P & WORKMAN, ELIZABETH E	04 SEP 1877	09:126
HAMBRICK, JAMES S & HAYS, ETHEL	24 DEC 1898	08:442
HAMBRICK, LEANDER E & FISHER, JENNIE	08 APR 1895	07:285
HAMILTON, CHARLES W & JORDAN, BESSIE S	30 JUN 1909	12:444
HAMILTON, GEORGE DAVID & HUDSON, ALTA JANE	24 JUN 1888	05:239
HAMILTON, JOHN T & CARTMILL, SARAH M	*26 DEC 1855	02:007
HAMILTON, WILLIAM & JONES, FRANCES	*14 MAY 1856	02:008
HAMILTON, WILLIAM & RHOADES, SARAH A	18 FEB 1882	11:112
HAMILTON, WILLIAM & JONES, ELIZABETH G	*26 MAR 1856	02:008
HAMM, ALBERT G & STRATTON, LUCY M	21 OCT 1907	12:050
HAMM, GUSTAVE & SAYRE, PEARL F	23 JUN 1912	13:552
HAMMONDS, WILLIAM & WILLIAMS, BLANCHE	20 DEC 1897	08:218
HAMPTON, HIRAM L & OLIVER, JANE ANN	11 JUN 1867	05:056
HAMPTON, JAMES M & McCARTY, MARY	14 AUG 1871	07:111
HAMPTON, WADE H & CAMPBELL, EVA M	30 JUL 1910	13:118
HANDLEY, JOSEPH S & BALL, ERIE E	24 DEC 1913	15:105
HANDLY, NELSON & BORAM, LEATHY	11 MAY 1823	01:008
HANES, GEORGE & JONES, MINNIE	18 OCT 1894	07:168
HANES, HENRY & ANDERSON, LUNIA	04 DEC 1874	08:193
HANES, ROBERT & ADDISON, MARGARET	29 DEC 1880	10:361
HANIGAN, SIMEON G & CANTERBURY, BETTIE E	25 SEP 1881	11:023
HANING, EBER & VINCENT, AMANDA V	10 JUN 1882	11:162
HANING, EBER & YAUGER, MARY	23 NOV 1887	05:046
HANING, WILLIAM E & WOOD, MARY	08 NOV 1905	11:200
HANLEY, J C & ADAMS, LEILLIAN E	23 MAY 1909	12:412
HANLEY, THOMAS T & HURST, EDITH	29 OCT 1908	12:294
HANLY, JOHN S & SHIVELY, ORETHA	13 NOV 1865	04:071

Name	Date	Ref
HANLY, SAMUEL C & JORDAN, MARY J	*14 NOV 1857	02:010
HANNA, BRANSON W & STEELE, MARY M	11 JUN 1907	11:550
HANNA, SAMUEL D & BURGESS, ALICE	15 DEC 1867	05:119
HANNAH, ROBERT C & LONG, LUCINDA	23 FEB 1862	03:080
HANNAN, E C & BAKER, ELIZABETH	04 MAY 1885	12:170
HANNAN, EDWARD MONROE & PICK, HARRIET LUCINDA	18 FEB 1902	10:025
HANNAN, ERASTUS D & PRINCE, FRANCES E	28 FEB 1866	04:105
HANNAN, HENRY & HENDERSON, RHODA	07 JUN 1838	01:032
HANNAN, JAMES W & RIGG, GEORGIA F	27 APR 1898	08:296
HANNAN, JESSIE F & MEADOWS, EDITH	10 SEP 1905	11:161
HANNAN, JOHN E & VAN MATRE, ANNIE L	29 APR 1884	12:006
HANNAN, JOSEPH H & WARNER, CLARISSA C	11 SEP 1873	08:022
HANNAN, THOMAS WRIGHT & DIEFENBAUGH, LENORA	14 JUL 1892	06:368
HANNAN, THOMAS E & PAGE, JANE E	*19 MAY 1855	02:006
HANNAN, THOMAS JEFFERSON & WRAY, EMMA ELLA	02 AUG 1888	05:252
HANNIG, ELMER & WELCH, DORA	18 DEC 1809	12:573
HANNING, A & STEEL, ELIZABETH	06 JUL 1884	12:035
HANIS, JAMES C & BEARD, EVA A	01 OCT 1899	08:624
HANNON, HENRY & McMULLEN, CATHARINE	01 FEB 1820	01:005
HANSFORD, JOHN & MORRIS, MARIA E	1831	01:024
HANSHAW, JOSEPH & WIRES, MARY	12 NOV 1822	01:009
HANSHAW, WILLIAM & McCOY, MARY	30 JUN 1845	01:045
HANSHER, CHARLES & THAXTON, MAY	17 FEB 1906	11:269
HANSKINS, J & GREENLEE, (Mrs) MAUDE	19 OCT 1914	15:297
HANSON, JESSE E & HILL, HETTIE E	27 JUN 1896	07:574
HANSON, JESSIE E & STOVER, MINNIE	*03 NOV 1906	11:445
HANSON, JESSY E & STOVER, MINNIE E	28 AUG 1807	11:601
HARBER, NAMAN & WOLFORD, RHODA E	08 APR 1880	10:233
HARBOR, GEROME & BOWEN, LAURA O	03 JUN 1900	09:136
HARBOUR, C W & CAMPBELL, ROSA B	15 SEP 1910	13:159
HARBOUR, EMERY & SIDERS, MARY	14 MAY 1909	12:411
HARBOUR, MADISON JAMES & BATEMAN, LUCY	15 APR 1888	05:207
HARBOUR, PERRY & BATEMAN, ANNIE M	30 DEC 1900	09:271
HARBRECHT, JOSEPH & KILLEEN, THRESA	25 APR 1894	07:077
HARD, HELLER E & STRAUGHN, PEARL M	09 DEC 1910	13:223
HARDEN, CHRISTOPHER C & CHAPMAN, FRANCES S	13 MAY 1882	11:447
HARDEN, WILLIAM & FROST, IDA	14 AUG 1870	08:219
HARDING, GEORGE W & CARTMILL, MARY C	*11 DEC 1856	02:009
HARDMAN, EZRA & MATHENY, ANNIE	16 MAR 1912	13:499
HARDMAN, WESLY & LIVINGSTON, ELIZABETH	24 FEB 1880	10:215
HARDWICK, ROBERT THOMAS & EADS, REBECCA	07 MAR 1888	05:192
HARDWICK, COLUMBUS & NEAL, VERA CRUZ	01 OCT 1882	11:218
HARDWICK, ENOCH H & ROLLINS, VINNIE	10 NOV 1887	05:138
HARDWICK, HENRY C & SPENCER, BESSIE	08 SEP 1909	12:495
HARDWICK, JEREMIAH & BYBEE, ELIZABETH ANN	10 OCT 1836	01:031
HARDWICK, JOHN M & SCHOOLS, LUCINDA C	11 MAR 1875	08:217
HARDWICK, ROBERT T & MEADOWS, ELIZA M	*25 NOV 1858	02:011
HARDWICK, ROBERT T & DAVIS, MARY C	13 APR 1876	08:347
HARDWICK, WILLIAM R & CHATTIN, FLORENCE E	25 DEC 1884	12:106
HARDY, WILLIAM & READ, MARGARET	*31 MAY 1851	02:002
HARFF, ALBERT H & GILLISPIE, CHARLOTTE G	07 APR 1898	08:285
HARKINS, AARON & MARTIN, CAROLINE E	18 SEP 1901	09:409
HARKINS, JAMES THOMAS & DUNN, ALICE MAUD	06 APR 1888	05:203
HARLER, CLYDE C & HUDSON, CARIE M	23 JAN 1904	10:465
HARLER, JESSE A & THOMAS, SARAH A	16 AUG 1900	09:173
HARLESS, HARRY & ELLIS, KATIE	04 MAY 1907	11:523
HARLESS, JUBAL & GOWIN, DORA L	25 DEC 1898	08:437
HARLESS, WM F & DAY, SARAH LUCETTA	10 JUN 1913	15:218

HARMAN, ERASTUS D & WILLIAMS, TABITHA	26 JAN 1875	08:207
HARMON, BAYLUS B & JIVIDEN, GLENN M	20 DEC 1904	11:001
HARMON, JAMES & PIERSON, CATHARINE A	13 DEC 1890	06:019
HARMON, JOHN H & ALINDER, REBECCA	01 JAN 1880	10:187
HARMON, JOSEPH N & BOWEN, ETHEL L	05 MAR 1913	14:104
HARMON, STRAUTHER WALKER & OLIVER, (Mrs) JULIA	30 JAN 1880	11:107
HARMON, THOMAS & CLARK, ETHEL	25 JUN 1909	12:441
HARNSBERGER, GILBERT M & LONG, SARAH H	21 AUG 1901	09:392
HARPER, CINCINNATUS W & BARBEE, MARY B	17 OCT 1877	09:203
HARPER, ELIJAH B W & WILSON, VIRGINIA	27 MAR 1875	08:220
HARPER, HUGH & MARTIN, MARGARET	*27 SEP 1856	02:009
HARPER, JOE L & SINGELTON, ANNA	30 DEC 1891	06:269
HARPER, JOHN S & McGUIRE, SARENA C	03 NOV 1886	12:411
HARPER, JOSEPH & WHEELER, REBECCA	*26 APR 1858	02:011
HARPER, JOSEPH & NIZELY, MAHALA	18 FEB 1872	07:197
HARPER, JOSEPH & McDONALD, MARGARET	23 DEC 1876	09:011
HARPER, ORLAN B & COMSTOCK, LULU G	22 JUL 1903	10:324
HARPER, WILLIAM & CLOCKSTON, ELIZABETH	23 JAN 1868	05:139
HARPER, WILLIAM J & KING, JESSIE A	10 JUN 1900	09:139
HARPER, WILLIAM W & NORRIS, E C	10 SEP 1865	04:049
HARPOLD, CURTIS & PEDEN, CLARA	03 MAY 1874	08:117
HARPOLD, ELIJAH C & WILEY, JULIA W	04 OCT 1871	07:129
HARPOLD, EVERTT M & MORRISON, HANNAH E	08 JAN 1910	12:590
HARPOLD, FRANK H & TAYLOR, MAGGIE	26 AUG 1898	08:324
HARPOLD, HENRY & ROUSH, HESTER	28 FEB 1839	01:031 5
HARPOLD, JOSEPH & CARTMILL, MINNIE	23 AUG 1874	08:153
HARPOLD, LEIGHTON K & BYRNE, MARY R	21 MAR 1877	09:050
HARPOLD, LEMUEL & DONLEY, ROXEY A	28 OCT 1885	12:238
HARPOLE, JOHN & SAYRE, RACHAEL	05 MAR 1811	01:003
HARRAH, MAX E & GIBBS, ROMA E	15 FEB 1911	13:268
HARRIS, ALEXANDER & McCOY, CORA	08 SEP 1813	15:030
HARRIS, ALEXANDER & WEAVER, ETTA	26 AUG 1891	06:170
HARRIS, AMOS & GRAY, ELIZABETH	JUN 1839	01:033
HARRIS, AMOS A & McCOY, CATHARINE	22 JUL 1883	11:377
HARRIS, C E & ROSS, B LILLIAN	13 JUL 1911	13:346
HARRIS, CHARLES & HILL, MARGARET E	19 OCT 1873	08:043
HARRIS, CHARLES JOSEPH & CHAFFIN, MATTIE LEE	03 SEP 1889	05:447
HARRIS, CHARLES J & JOHNSON, CORA E	03 SEP 1899	08:603
HARRIS, CHARLES W & MORTON, BLANCH A	02 APR 1905	11:065
HARRIS, DANIEL & GRAY, NARCISSA	*01 AUG 1860	02:014
HARRIS, DANIEL & HUMPHREYS, MELVIRA ANN	01 JAN 1866	04:088
HARRIS, DANIEL & NEWELL, LELY	30 MAY 1880	10:264
HARRIS, DAVID & HUMPHREYS, LETHA E	21 FEB 1875	08:213
HARRIS, DAVID D & YOUNG, ANNIE	08 NOV 1885	12:247
HARRIS, EDEN & OLDACRE, CELIA	07 APR 1825	01:011
HARRIS, EMERY E & HUGHES, MAZELLA J	02 MAR 1882	11:121
HARRIS, FRANK & McDANIEL, MINA	11 FEB 1906	11:264
HARRIS, JAMES I & O'NAIL, MARY A	18 MAY 1878	09:265
HARRIS, JAMES N & MEADOWS, TELITHA ANN	22 FEB 1866	04:102
HARRIS, JAMES & THORNTON, SALLY	04 AUG 1807	01:001
HARRIS, JOHN & GIBBS, NELLIE	11 OCT 1893	06:624
HARRIS, JOHN FRANKLIN & MUMAW, (Mrs) MARY FLORENCE	20 AUG 1914	15:257
HARRIS, JOHN L & ROLMAN, ELIZABETH J	31 MAR 1877	09:055
HARRIS, JOHN L & ROHNAN, ELIZABETH J	31 MAR 1877	09:055
HARRIS, JOHN P & PERRY, CELIA	25 OCT 1874	08:176
HARRIS, JOHN P & ALLSBURY, SOPHIA	06 APR 1887	05:005
HARRIS, JOSEPH & HALL, MAGGIE MAY	12 OCT 1887	05:117
HARRIS, PRICE F & WRIGHT, NANCY A	20 SEP 1883	11:405

HARRIS, ROBERT N & ROBERTS, FLORELLA M	20 MAY 1880	10:254
HARRIS, ROBERT W & CHAMBERS, LYDA	01 MAR 1905	11:050
HARRIS, SAMUEL & FOWLER, SAMANTHA	30 MAR 1865	04:002
HARRIS, SILAS & LOWE, MARY	24 SEP 1824	01:018
HARRIS, THOMAS D & BUMGARNER, MYRTIE	03 APR 1902	10:044
HARRIS, WARREN & KEARNS, ELLA	22 SEP 1896	07:616
HARRIS, WILBER & SHELINE, MARGARET A	01 OCT 1894	07:162
HARRIS, WILLIAM & BARBER, ETHEL	30 DEC 1912	14:072
HARRIS, WILLIAM L & PECK, SUSAN J	21 DEC 1871	07:159
HARRIS, WILLIAM LEGHTON & BROWN, ELLA EUGENIA	12 SEP 1888	05:269
HARRIS, WILLIAM THOMAS & DONOHEW, SUSIE	14 OCT 1890	05:622
HARRIS, ZACHARIAH & BAKER, MARY FRANCES	*08 JUN 1855	02:007
HARRIS, ZACHARIAH L & JEFFERS, AMY	15 DEC 1887	04:113
HARRIS, ZACHARIAH L & ABSTEN, NANNA A	28 FEB 1911	13:491
HARRISON, DANIEL & KNOPP, KATE	12 APR 1905	11:075
HARRISON, DAVID C & EASTHAM, ANN	22 NOV 1825	01:112
HARRISON, DAVID C & BLACKWELL, MARY	07 MAR 1830	01:019
HARRISON, DAVID C & GEORGE, MARY ELIZABETH	*05 OCT 1853	02:004
HARRISON, EDWARD E & SMELTZER, LAURA GENEVIEVE	15 FEB 1913	14:091
HARRISON, ELIAS & HIRES, ELIZABETH	04 SEP 1829	01:022
HARRISON, FRANCES M & ROADES, MARTHA E	17 SEP 1882	11:209
HARRISON, GEORGE W & LYONS, LUCRETIA	25 FEB 1869	06:036
HARRISON, HENRY & LEWIS, LIZZIE	30 JUN 1886	12:344
HARRISON, JABES & WARNER, POLLY	20 OCT 1828	01:021
HARRISON, JACKSON & SHEARER, LOUISA JANE	*16 JUN 1856	02:008
HARRISON, JOHN & OLDAKERS, FRANCES C	1834	01:039
HARRISON, JOHN & HILL, ANNIE ELIZABETH	26 DEC 1867	05:124
HARRISON, JOHN & OLIVER, VIRGINIA F	26 JUN 1878	09:276
HARRISON, JOHN & ALLIS, ALLISA	14 NOV 1894	07:189
HARRISON, JOHN R & PICKENS, OMA	01 JAN 1893	06:462
HARRISON, JOHN W & KIRKPATRICK, ELIZABETH S	1843	01:041
HARRISON, JOSIAH & HARRIS, FRANCES	1833	01:039
HARRISON, R J A & BRYAN, NANCY	14 DEC 1829	01:022
HARRISON, REUBEN & RANSON, PAULINA A	25 MAR 1864	03:171
HARRISON, THOMAS C & STEPHENS, MARY JANE	*28 DEC 1854	02:006
HARRISON, WILLIAM & ALLEN, ESTHER	21 MAR 1828	01:021
HARRISON, WILLIAM H & HARRIS, CATHARINE	14 FEB 1869	06:034
HARSHAW, FREDERICK & HALL, CATHARINE	31 AUG 1830	01:023
HART, ALLEN & ROUSH, ELIZABETH	21 MAR 1870	06:171
HART, ALONZO & TILLIS, SOPHIA	24 JAN 1828	01:017
HART, ARCH EUGENE & THOMAS, DOLLIE MARIE	18 MAY 1912	13:529
HART, CHARLES & SELBY, ORA	21 OCT 1906	11:434
HART, CHRISTIAN & ROUSH, MARY	24 MAY 1849	01:050
HART, D F O & ROSEBERRY, MARY M	27 AUG 1885	12:215
HART, DANIEL & NEASE, (Mrs) CHRISTINA	*05 MAY 1856	02:008
HART, DAVID F & HANING, ELIZABETH J	05 FEB 1893	06:479
HART, EDWARD & O'HARE, MARY A	20 JUN 1883	11:357
HART, GEORGE & ROUSH, HANNAH	04 NOV 1848	01:048
HART, GILBERT & McDANIEL, ELLEN E	14 DEC 1882	11:266
HART, HENRY & LILLY, MARY	15 MAY 1877	09:077
HART, HENRY MICHAEL & SMITH, ANNIE O	03 FEB 1889	05:346
HART, HENRY S & MINTURN, MARION	11 NOV 1880	10:326
HART, JACOB & BLESSING, ELIZA ANN	04 APR 1844	01:038
HART, JAMES L A & ENTWISTLE, NELLIE	04 JAN 1894	07:032
HART, JESSE & VAIL, CAROLINE	18 OCT 1846	01:046
HART, JESSE G & THORNTON, METTA	28 NOV 1909	12:556
HART, JESSE M & ROSEBERRY, SARAH C	09 DEC 1888	05:317
HART, JOHN & RICKARD, MARY	30 NOV 1848	01:051

HART, JOHN A & CLARKE, KATHARINE R	07 OCT 1914	15:287
HART, JOHN C & TURLEY, ALLIE M	18 MAR 1888	05:196
HART, JONAS & SMITH, MARY E	16 JUL 1885	12:196
HART, JOSEPH & EDWARDS, (Mrs) PERMELIA ANN	*13 JUL 1854	02:005
HART, JOSEPH & MORGAN, MARY JANE	21 SEP 1848	01:049
HART, LINLEY & OLIVER, SARAH VIRGINIA	07 FEB 1889	05:348
HART, LONI & POUNDS, RACHEL EVELENE	20 JAN 1892	06:277
HART, MYRLETO & SMITH, CASSANDRA J	1837	01:040
HART, OSCAR & RICKARD, SEVILLA MARY	22 OCT 1814	15:302
HART, REUBEN & CHILDERS, LUCINDA	02 FEB 1851	02:001
HART, ROBERT & TUCKER, CLARA	27 FEB 1909	12:372
HART, ROBERT S & WARNER, MARY M	06 MAR 1879	10:062
HART, THOMAS & RYAN, JANE	10 SEP 1861	03:020
HART, WILLIAM C & KIMBERLING, ELIZA A	22 MAR 1883	11:310
HART, WILLIAM J & HESSON, MARY A	15 OCT 1899	08:631
HARTENBACH, JACOB S & LEHEW, MABEL G	25 JUN 1913	14:186
HARTER, JUDSON J & CLAXTON, (Mrs) GEORGIA	16 FEB 1911	13:269
HARTINGER, VINT & WALKER, SOPHRONIA	28 FEB 1895	07:262
HARTLEY, EARL R & GIBBS, EVA	17 DEC 1910	13:229
HARTLEY, EVERETT & CLARK, MARGARET	29 NOV 1905	11:212
HARTLEY, J ORVILLE & HARMON, LAURA MAY	19 NOV 1911	13:420
HARTLEY, SAMUEL N & OLIVER, LILLIE B	05 MAR 1910	13:020
HARVEY, EDWARD W & CUMMINGS, LIZZIE	29 MAY 1903	10:294
HARVEY, FRANK SHERMAN & VEITH, LIZZIE MAY	28 DEC 1892	06:460
HARVEY, HENRY & HALE, SALLY	22 JUN 1809	01:002
HARVEY, JAY T & CHASE, KATHLEEN	18 JAN 1905	11:030
HARVEY, JOHN W & RIGG, WILLIE A	20 JUL 1884	12:038
HARVEY, NOAH C & COOPER, FLORENCE A	11 JUL 1906	11:367
HARVEY, ROBERT M & WITHERS, EFFIE	26 SEP 1886	12:392
HASKINS, THOMAS & STEVENS, MAUD	19 NOV 1906	11:450
HASTING, JOHN H & PICKENS, LONA	27 JAN 1891	06:052
HATHAWAY, WM H & EWELL, PRISCILLA	02 DEC 1820	01:007
HAUGHT, LEWIS E & CAMPBELL, STELLA E	31 OCT 1888	05:298
HAUN, HARRY H & LUNSFORD, MABEL J	26 MAR 1910	13:038
HAVERTY, STEPHEN M & SMITH, NIZA	16 APR 1902	10:058
HAWK, NICHOLAS & COOK, MARY	*12 JUL 1853	02:004
HAWKINBERRY, CHARLES W & GASKINS, SEREPTA A	30 AUG 1906	11:399
HAWKINS, ABRAHAM & SPURLOCK, LUNA	20 MAY 1894	07:093
HAWKINS, DAVID H & RHOADES, MYRTLE	16 MAR 1898	08:271
HAWKINS, ENOCH & AMSBERRY, ELLA	16 FEB 1896	07:498
HAWKINS, ENOCH & STEWART, SUSAN	24 SEP 1898	08:370
HAWKINS, JAMES N & MEADOWS, LOTTIE	26 OCT 1892	06:431
HAWKINS, JOHN & WAUGH, AMANDA	*27 APR 1852	02:002
HAWKINS, JOHN I & SEBRELL, BETTIE J	06 JUN 1891	06:124
HAWKINS, JOHN ROBERT & TAYLOR, DORA	18 AUG 1889	05:430
HAWKINS, LEWIS & JOHNSON, SARAH	27 DEC 1877	09:183
HAWKINS, MAXWELL C & FERRELL, FERNIE S	15 MAY 1907	11:533
HAWKINS, PETER FIELDING & STEWART, JULIANN	21 JUN 1849	01:051
HAWKINS, THOMAS & AMSDON, JULIA	07 JUN 1832	01:027
HAWKINS, THOMAS W & TURNER, GRACE P	09 DEC 1899	09:029
HAWKINS, VAUGHN & HALSEY, ELLA	13 OCT 1907	12:040
HAWKINS, WILLIAM & HILL, NANCY J	26 FEB 1896	07:500
HAWKINS, WILLIAM B & SANDERS, MARY J M	*19 DEC 1860	02:015
HAWKINS, WILLIAM J & BAKER, ELIZABETH J	19 JAN 1868	05:137
HAWKINS, WILLIAM R & LEMASTER, LUTITIA	*09 MAR 1857	02:009
HAWLEY, JOSEPH RODGERS & HUMMEL, ELLEN EUGENE	19 AUG 1888	05:260
HAWLEY, STANLEY J & CAIN, (Mrs) JEANETTE	04 JUN 1910	13:085
HAWTHORN, PASCAL B & WAUGH, ELIZABETH S	*26 SEP 1851	02:002

Names	Date	Ref
HAWTHORNE, BOLDEN & WOLF, MARY JANE	01 JAN 1893	06:465
HAWTHORNE, GEORGE WASHINGTON & KING, CYNTHIA ANN	11 MAR 1908	11:174
HAWTHORNE, HOMER A & NOTTINGHAM, LELA M	11 MAR 1908	12:141
HAWTHORNE, JAMES & DEAL, ORETHA	15 DEC 1896	08:018
HAY, MORDECAI D & MEEKS, LILLIE A	25 NOV 1908	12:315
HAYDEN, ALBERT M & BASS, ELIZA J	08 SEP 1878	09:354
HAYDEN, ALBERT M & BASS, ELIZA J	08 SEP 1878	09:314
HAYDEN, HORACE E & BYERS, KATE E	30 NOV 1868	06:012
HAYES, ALBERT & CRUMP, SARAH	07 NOV 1882	11:243
HAYES, ALBERT & HARRIS, ELIZABETH	04 SEP 1888	05:267
HAYES, ALPHA & HOFFMAN, DELIA	19 JAN 1896	07:489
HAYES, BAIRD & MAYES, RETHA ELLEN	08 OCT 1900	09:218
HAYES, BENJAMIN S & WILSON, MINNIE O	19 OCT 1910	13:179
HAYES, CHAUNCY & HUGHES, MAY	10 OCT 1910	13:180
HAYES, FLOYD A & LAMBERT, ETHEL OLEVA	31 JAN 1909	12:360
HAYES, LEVI & PRIDDY, ELLA	21 DEC 1891	05:253
HAYES, R W & LITCHFIELD, SARAH E	05 SEP 1910	13:151
HAYES, STERRETT E & HOLLAND, ELMIRA	24 NOV 1907	12:072
HAYES, WILLIAM & PRIDDY, ELIZABETH C	07 NOV 1871	07:139
HAYMAN, CHARLES H & DONOHUE, MARTHA M	13 JAN 1900	09:058
HAYMAN, DANIEL & LEE, HATTIE	13 NOV 1882	11:252
HAYMAN, DANIEL A & ROUSH, ANN R	10 NOV 1873	08:053
HAYMAN, GEORGE R & NIBERT, MARY H	24 MAY 1898	08:282
HAYMAN, JAMES H & JORDAN, MINNIE R	30 SEP 1890	05:619
HAYMAN, JAMES H & SHELINE, NELLIE	28 NOV 1904	10:649
HAYMAN, JOHN & GILLAND, NANNIE	01 DEC 1881	11:062
HAYMAN, JOHN & STURGEON, AMANDA	28 MAY 1884	12:021
HAYMAN, JOHN H & BLAKE, GERTRUDE	06 OCT 1910	13:177
HAYMAN, ORVIL & RICE, ELLA	06 OCT 1897	08:168
HAYMAN, RICHARD H & WILSON, ANGELINE	02 DEC 1869	06:116
HAYMAN, RICHARD HENRY & GIBBS, ELIZABETH	13 DEC 1913	15:089
HAYMAN, STEPHEN & MATTOX, EMMA	14 JUN 1902	10:090
HAYMAN, STEPHEN E & HULL, NETTIE	06 SEP 1900	09:189
HAYNES, HARRY S & COLEMAN, LIZZIE	31 AUG 1899	08:601
HAYNES, ISAAC N & HUDSON, DASEY	11 MAY 1896	07:547
HAYNES, ISAAC N & HULL, IVA	**26 JUL 1906	11:372
HAYNES, ISAAC N & WOODRUM, CORA A	19 JUN 1910	13:092
HAYNES, ISAAC N & SMITH, LAURA MARGERY	05 JUL 1914	15:230
HAYNES, JOHN & GIBBS, UNIS	11 DEC 1836	01:030
HAYS, BENJAMIN S, Jr & HOPSON, MARY A	23 FEB 1883	11:304
HAYS, CHRISTOPHER B & WOOD, SUSAN	AUG 1840	01:034
HAYS, LEVI & ROUSH, SARAH	JAN 1849	01:049
HAYSE, HENRY F & MITCHELL, ELLA	05 MAR 1882	11:123
HAYSE, LEWIS MILTON & MITCHELL, EMMA	02 DEC 1887	05:152
HAYSHAM, THOMAS & CASSADAY, SARAH	12 MAY 1850	01:049
HAZELETT, ROBT & DUGH, REBECCA	20 FEB 1821	01:007
HAZLETT, JOHN & SHIVELY, MELVINA	27 SEP 1891	06:193
HEARICK, ARTEMUS & PIERCY, ELIZABETH	*18 NOV 1851	02:002
HEATHERINGTON, J PARK & CHAMBERS, KATHARINE D	24 DEC 1894	07:221
HEATON, CASSIUS M & GABBERT, ELLA C	09 SEP 1902	10:152
HEATON, JESSIE O & ADAMS, HELEN M	16 JAN 1903	10:226
HEATON, WILLIAM B & FAIER, EMMA	27 APR 1871	07:078
HEDGE, SADOC & FOWLER, NANCY E	20 SEP 1880	10:301
HEDGE, SADOCK & DUNN, (Mrs) RHODA	20 JUN 1887	05:041
HEDRICK, JACOB & HIGINBOTHAM, MARY	1843	01:041
HEIB, JACOB L & FROST, JESSIE	16 DEC 1913	15:091
HEIGHT, JESSE & CLINE, HANNAH	30 OCT 1826	01:013
HEINER, EDWARD E & GILMORE, CARRIE M	07 JUN 1905	11:105

HEINER, HARRY H & TIPPETT, GEORGIA A	06 JAN 1891	06:044
HEINES, HARRY & DENNIS, BERTHA	03 AUG 1912	13:576
HEINISCH, G H & RABB, LOUISA	29 NOV 1883	11:430
HEINS, LE ROY & DENNIS, KATHARYN	15 JUL 1914	15:240
HELLEMS, WILLIAM MASON & McDERMITT, EMMA	10 NOV 1892	06:439
HELPER, JACOB & LEWIS, NANCY	05 APR 1849	01:050
HEMMINGS, JOHN M & CONGROVE, HATTIE E	05 APR 1894	07:070
HEMPHILL, CHARLES W & BASS, BERTHA MAY	27 NOV 1912	14:036
HEMSLEY, ROBERT & HUGHES, CATHARINE	24 AUG 1872	07:255
HEMSLEY, WILLIAM J & BASS, FLORA A	30 NOV 1873	08:059
HENDERSHOT, GEORGE JACKSON & VAUGHN, MALINDA	24 DEC 1903	10:438
HENDERSHOT, CHARLES W & COOPER, ETHEL	18 OCT 1905	11:190
HENDERSON, CHARLES E & GREENLEE, MARY M	17 FEB 1889	05:352
HENDERSON, HIRAM & RAMSEY, ELIZABETH	24 JUN 1873	08:011
HENDERSON, JAMES S & POFFENBARGER, HATTIE G	23 OCT 1894	07:176
HENDERSON, JOHN FRANKLIN & JONES, MARY	05 MAY 1885	12:171
HENDERSON, JOHN G & STEVENS, ANN E	01 FEB 1826	01:012
HENDERSON, ROBERT & THOMAS, LIZZIE S	19 DEC 1875	08:307
HENDERSON, SAMUEL B & GEORGE, LYDIA L	*05 JAN 1853	02:003
HENESSEY, EDWARD & KLEENE, MAGGIE	20 MAR 1880	10:226
HENGS, ISRAEL C & CROUCH, PAMELIA	22 MAR 1841	01:036
HENIES, ESTIE J & MEYER, FREDA	23 DEC 1910	13:239
HENKEL, CHARLES & SIEGRIST, POLLY	24 MAY 1818	01:003
HENKEL, JOSEPH & WEAVER, LAVINA	*23 FEB 1857	02:009
HENKEL, PHILIP S & SOMERVILLE, SUSAN J	*02 JAN 1854	02:005
HENKLE, BENJAMIN & EDWARDS, DELILA	13 JUN 1844	01:038
HENKLE, IRENEAS N & RUPERT, CAROLINE E	23 OCT 1834	01:029
HENNESSY, NICHOLAS & MARTIN, MARY D	21 NOV 1883	11:425
HENNOSY, PHILIP & McMAHAN, AGNES	13 MAR 1902	10:045
HENOSY, HENRY & RHOADS, MAGGIE	20 DEC 1893	07:023
HENOSY, PHILIP & TUCKER, MINNIE M	24 JAN 1891	06:050
HENRY, B F & EADS, (Mrs) KATIE	14 FEB 1909	12:367
HENRY, CALVIN & PERSINGER, ALTA MAY	24 MAY 1904	10:523
HENRY, EARL & HAYNES, ELLA	08 JAN 1885	12:124
HENRY, EARNEST & EDWARDS, LOTTIE	01 NOV 1897	08:187
HENRY, FRED K & DUNN, RHODA C	25 DEC 1907	12:106
HENRY, GEORGE A & KILE, JANE C	13 SEP 1867	05:083
HENRY, GEORGE L & LEPORT, ADDIE	20 AUG 1906	11:393
HENRY, GEORGES R & BLAIN, MATILDA B	*29 SEP 1856	02:009
HENRY, HIRSHEL W & NIBERT, VERNA M	22 DEC 1910	13:236
HENRY, JAMES & PERSINGER, VIRGINIA F	14 FEB 1884	11:456
HENRY, JAMES A & LANIER, MARTHA N	03 JUN 1885	12:181
HENRY, JAMES A & COON, ELMA	27 OCT 1906	11:440
HENRY, JOHN & WOLF, JANE	11 DEC 1824	01:009
HENRY, JOHN & CAZY, MARY	18 FEB 1827	01:016
HENRY, JOHN F & ROWLEY, MARTHA G	06 AUG 1902	10:125
HENRY, JOSEPH & NIBERT, NANCY	1832	01:026
HENRY, WILLIAM L & COLEMAN, ANNIE	16 JUN 1894	07:105
HENSHAW, GEORGE & McCOY, HADIA E M	02 NOV 1895	07:420
HENSHAW, JOSEPH & CURRY, JANE	27 SEP 1827	01:020
HENSLEY, CHRISTOPHER C & HOWELL, SUSA	17 APR 1878	09:247
HENSLEY, JAMES M & HALL, MAGGIE A	11 DEC 1877	09:166
HENSLEY, JOHN & MOURNING, ELIZA	03 JUN 1883	11:353
HENSLEY, JOHN & BARTRAM, FANNIE	11 SEP 1905	11:167
HENSON, JOHN & CASEY, MARY ANN	06 MAR 1865	03:229
HENSON, JOHN & BRIGHT, MARY	04 JAN 1895	07:230
HENSON, JOHN & BALES, LUSETTA	11 MAR 1908	12:157
HENSON, WILLIAM & NEASE, SABINA S	11 MAY 1848	01:049

HENTHORNE, JOSEPH HARMAN & JOHNSON, SARAH E	12 SEP 1882	11:200
HEPPLEWHITE, JOSEPH & ASTON, DULCEMA	25 NOV 1875	08:302
HERBERT, GEORGE L & RODGERS, VADA G	06 JUN 1913	14:170
HERDLAND, FRANK & FRAZIER, (Mrs) REBECCA	*10 NOV 1858	02:011
HERDMAN, ABE & THOMAS, ELIZABETH	20 OCT 1900	09:227
HERDMAN, ABRAHAM Jr & MATHENY, ELIZABETH	24 DEC 1910	13:242
HERDMAN, CHARLES & McDERMITT, MARY J	07 APR 1897	08:073
HERDMAN, EPHRAIM & STEEL, HETTIE	22 AUG 1900	09:176
HERDMAN, EPHRAIM V & LIVINGSTON, MARY E	18 SEP 1900	09:202
HERDMAN, FOREST & BURCHARD, ELLA F	25 DEC 1895	07:468
HERDMAN, HENRY & BAKER, REBECCA F	18 FEB 1876	08:325
HERDMAN, JAMES & JONES, PERLINA A	31 DEC 1872	07:300
HERDMAN, JOHN W & HYATT, B ELLNORA	03 JUN 1894	07:098
HERDMAN, MICHAEL & BAKER, MARGARET	07 JAN 1877	09:019
HERDMAN, PETER & McDADE, MARTHA E	22 JUN 1874	08:188
HERDMAN, PETER & SAYRE, NANCY D	05 DEC 1896	08:011
HERDMAN, THOMAS W & McCOY, ADELPHIA A	29 JUN 1875	08:252
HEREFORD, BROOK G & HANNAN, MIRIAM	30 OCT 1851	02:002
HEREFORD, JAMES THOMAS & HANLY, VIRGINIA	04 NOV 1891	06:220
HEREFORD, JAMES W & HAYMAN, ELIZABETH J	25 MAR 1869	06:043
HEREFORD, ROBERT E & WITHERS, GRACE	29 APR 1880	10:248
HEREFORD, ROBERT P & GOUDY, MARIAMNE M	20 JUN 1861	03:007
HEREFORD, THOMAS A & WILSON, MARY C	22 JAN 1828	01:017
HEREFORD, VIRGIL E & DABNEY, ROSA M	08 NOV 1903	10:403
HEREFORD, WILLIAM C & SUMMERS, SOPHRONIA	*15 JAN 1855	02:006
HEREFORD, WILLIAM P & GUN, NANCY	01 JUN 1848	01:048
HERMAN, FELIX & GIDDER, AMELIA	*25 JAN 1859	02:012
HERN, JNO A & LEE, MARY D	01 MAR 1874	08:101
HERSHMAN, CHARLES O & DUNN, MARY A	07 MAY 1911	13:316
HERSMAN, CHRISTOPHER H & BRIGHT, BERTHA ELLEN	20 AUG 1913	15:005
HERSMAN, JAMES M & CURRY, LUELLA	15 MAR 1883	11:311
HESLOP, JOHN W C & JARROTT, AURILLA J	28 FEB 1877	09:032
HESS, C EDWIN & TURNBULL, ELIZABETH A	18 JUN 1887	05:043
HESS, CHARLES WARREN & BLAGG, HANNAH JENNIE	15 OCT 1884	12:072
HESS, JNO H & ROUSH, SAMANTHA	*19 NOV 1860	02:014
HESS, NELSON, & CASTO, DELILAH	08 DEC 1901	09:465
HESS, WILLIAM & WHITE, CORA	29 JUL 1900	09:167
HESSEN, CHARLES & GRIMM, AFFIE	25 SEP 1913	15:040
HESSON, DAVID A & POWEL, MARY	*29 DEC 1853	02:005
HESSON, GEORGE & HUGHES, MIRTIE	02 APR 1895	07:275
HESSON, GEORGE & EDWARDS, MARY	23 JAN 1908	12:120
HESSON, GEORGE W & McMILLEN, GARNETTE L	08 JUN 1910	13:087
HESSON, JAMES & HARMON, SARAH JANE	05 FEB 1912	13:479
HESSON, JAMES M & ROUSH, ANNIE	16 AUG 1883	11:369
HESSON, JOHN & HUGHES, MALINDA ROSE ELLEN	23 DEC 1879	10:160
HESSON, JOHN EDWARD & CUNNINGHAM, LYDIA MAE	28 JAN 1899	08:459
HESSON, JOHN W & OLDAKER, IDA M	11 DEC 1895	07:449
HESSON, WILLARD E & MAYES, ZOLA	09 MAR 1904	10:488
HESSON, WILLIAM J & GILL, ANNA B	04 APR 1872	07:208
HESSON, WILLISSON & BURROWS, ANGELINE	16 MAR 1878	09:229
HESTER, SMITH & ROUSH, ROSANNA	09 AUG 1874	08:151
HEWS, JESSE & KING, SARAH	19 DEC 1850	02:001
HICKENBOTTOM, JOS & HARRISON, POLLY	07 SEP 1823	01:008
HICKMAN, GUY & DENNEY, NORA M	23 JAN 1909	12:355
HICKS, PERRY & MOBLEY, NANCY JANE	10 OCT 1889	05:463
HIGGENBOTHAM, ELBERT E & TURLEY, EDNA O	03 JUL 1907	11:569
HIGGENBOTHAM, REUBIN E & CRAIG, LULA J	15 AUG 1907	12:043
HIGGENBOTHAM, ABRAHAM A & RUNION, SOPHA	21 FEB 1902	10:027

HIGGINBOTHAM, AVERD R & KEEFER, ANNIE J	18 JAN 1890	05:510
HIGGINBOTHAM, BENJAMIN F & SAYRE, MIRAM F	24 OCT 1861	03:028
HIGGINBOTHAM, ERNEST & HAYES, LEOTA	10 FEB 1904	10:472
HIGGINBOTHAM, FRANK F & SHANK, VIRGINIA R	03 MAY 1914	15:182
HIGGINBOTHAM, GEORGE & PICKENS, MATTIE	08 APR 1899	08:500
HIGGINBOTHAM, GRADY L & TUCKER, DEARNIE	19 JAN 1900	09:067
HIGGINBOTHAM, JACOB CLARK & SAYRE, ELECTA FLORENCE	07 SEP 1887	05:080
HIGGINBOTHAM, JOHN E & LUCKEY, HAZEL	23 AUG 1911	13:359
HIGGINBOTHAM, JOSEPH & HAYES, ELIZABETH	06 OCT 1881	11:030
HIGGINBOTHAM, LEANDER & HIGGINBOTHAM, EVA I	28 JUL 1902	10:121
HIGGINBOTHAM, M E & MARSHALL, SARAH M	24 DEC 1893	07:028
HIGGINBOTHAM, PERCY FRANCIS & CORFEE, IDA	30 SEP 1886	12:394
HIGGINBOTHAM, PERRY F & BRANNAN, LENA MAY	24 MAY 1913	14:158
HIGGINBOTHAM, WILLIAM RALPH & ROUSH, DORCAS	13 DEC 1914	15:343
HIGGINBOTTHAM, JONATHAN & TUCKER, ARNITIS	11 MAR 1864	03:166
HIGGINBOTTOM, OGLESBERRY & TILLIS, HANNAH	*18 SEP 1860	02:014
HIGGINGBOTTOM, WILLIAM & TILLIS, ANN	*01 SEP 1858	02:011
HIGGINS, ARTHUR I & HYATT, BELLE	17 AUG 1895	07:367
HIGGINS, JAMES R & MEEKS, BETTIE	13 SEP 1900	09:206
HIGGINS, JOHN & RIGGS, MARTHA ANN	*28 NOV 1854	02:006
HIGGINS, JOSEPH L & EDWARDS, ADA M	16 DEC 1912	14:057
HIGGINS, LEROY C & SAYRE, LUCENA	12 JAN 1873	07:306
HIGGINS, WILLIAM RANDOLPH & NEASE, FRANCES ELIZABETH	27 MAR 1914	15:164
HIGH, JOHN W & THORNTON, LUCINDA	03 MAY 1877	09:073
HIGINBOTHAM, JOHN & WHITTEN, ELIZABETH	01 APR 1890	05:537
HILEMAN, JAMES & EYLER, MARY	05 JUL 1891	06:145
HILEWICK, CHARLES A & McCUMBER, JENNIE R	09 AUG 1913	15:009
HILL, ALFRED G & BADGLEY, EFFIE	22 APR 1906	11:296
HILL, ALLEN & CARTRITE, SARAH	25 MAY 1850	01:052
HILL, ANDREW JACKSON & KINARD, CATHARINE VICTORIA	22 JUN 1891	06:138
HILL, BLAINE & STONE, EFFIE	11 FEB 1905	11:042
HILL, CHARLES & NEWLAND, LAURA	19 MAY 1897	08:094
HILL, CHARLES & HARRISON, MANDA A	17 FEB 1900	09:087
HILL, CHARLES CERA & BIRD, FANNIE CATHARINE	29 AUG 1889	05:442
HILL, CHARLES H & REYNOLDS, HATTIE A	09 JUL 1906	11:385
HILL, CHARLES M & KNAPP, SARAH A	*22 MAR 1856	02:008
HILL, CHARLES MELMIRTH & WARNER, HATTIE DEEM	20 OCT 1892	06:429
HILL, CHARLES W & ROLLINS, ETTIE	10 JUL 1909	12:455
HILL, DANIEL & THORNTON, REBECCA	26 MAR 1835	01:029
HILL, DANIEL & HILL, MARTHA R	26 OCT 1901	09:432
HILL, DAVID ELLIS & NEWELL, ELIZABETH	10 JUL 1886	12:351
HILL, EDWARD & DAVIS, NELLIE	17 SEP 1914	15:272
HILL, ELIPHALET MARRION & RAYBURN, LUCINDA	09 OCT 1888	05:287
HILL, ENOCH & KIMBERLING, RACHEL JANE	18 OCT 1866	04:158
HILL, FLEET & BAILS, MAGGIE B	13 SEP 1891	06:179
HILL, GEORGE A & BARNETT, EMILY M	27 MAY 1868	05:183
HILL, GEORGE A & GRAY, RUTH	01 JAN 1896	07:473
HILL, GEORGE H & SULLIVAN, VIRGINIA	12 FEB 1874	08:098
HILL, GEORGE H & WINGET, MINTIE	13 JUN 1897	08:110
HILL, GEORGE WILLIAM & KNAPP, FANNIE	16 JAN 1901	09:278
HILL, H A & HUGHES, OSA L	26 SEP 1914	15:274
HILL, HENRY & PATTERSON, NANCY	05 JUN 1831	01:025
HILL, HENRY & SCHULTZ, MINNIE	26 SEP 1907	12:021
HILL, IRA EDMOND & LYONS, LINNIE L	01 SEP 1889	05:445
HILL, IRA ELLIS & ABSTON, NANCY	31 AUG 1862	03:075
HILL, ISAAC & WADE, MARY C	*10 FEB 1861	02:015
HILL, J F M & VEST, ELLA M	21 MAY 1884	12:016
HILL, JAMES & NEWMAN, MARY CATHARINE	31 DEC 1840	01:035

HILL, JAMES B & HUGHES, IDELLA	13 NOV 1890	06:004
HILL, JAMES E & JIVIDEN, MARY A	19 JAN 1903	10:228
HILL, JARRET & GREENLEE, MARY	MAR 1839	01:033
HILL, JASPER N & LEE, (Mrs) MARY JANE	18 DEC 1911	13:438
HILL, JASPER NEWTON & BAKER, SARAH ELIZABETH	20 MAY 1894	07:156
HILL, JOEL & DUNHAM, MARY E	25 NOV 1894	07:194
HILL, JOHN & SIDERS, JESSIE ATLANTIC	25 NOV 1911	13:124
HILL, JOHN M & McGUFFIN, MARY M	08 FEB 1891	06:059
HILL, JOHN W & JEFFERS, VIRGINIA C	24 NOV 1874	08:183
HILL, JOHN W & LINKINHOGAN, EMMA	08 JUN 1903	10:303
HILL, JOHNATHAN & STEPHENS, MARIA	*21 SEP 1852	02:003
HILL, JOHNATHAN E & MINICH, ELIZABETH	10 SEP 1882	11:196
HILL, LEONIDAS DELENNO & HILL, IDA JANE	06 JUL 1892	06:365
HILL, LEWIS & LEGUE, MURT	16 JUN 1905	11:110
HILL, LINZA & EASTHAM, LUCINDA	06 JAN 1897	08:032
HILL, LORENZO & HENRY, EMILY	*08 SEP 1852	02:003
HILL, NATHAN & JIVIDEN, MINNIE	25 JUL 1896	07:585
HILL, RANKIN & PAGE, EMILY E	*08 DEC 1855	02:007
HILL, RANKIN & POFFENBARGER, SALLIE	22 MAR 1887	12:495
HILL, ROBERT & BIBBEE, FANNIE	23 AUG 1913	15:017
HILL, SAMUEL & WARDEN, AMANDA	17 MAR 1901	09:304
HILL, WALTER S S & PICKENS, DOSHEY	31 DEC 1895	07:466
HILL, WARDEN M & WOLF, MARTHA	09 JAN 1898	08:224
HILL, WILLIAM & HAYS, OLIVIA	22 DEC 1829	01:019
HILL, WILLIAM & JOHNSTON, MARGARET	*25 NOV 1853	02:004
HILL, WILLIAM A & CLICK, LELIA B	26 AUG 1869	06:076
HILL, WILLIAM C & GREENLEE, HATTIE	21 APR 1906	11:297
HILL, WILLIAM S & SIMMONS, SARAH	16 FEB 1872	07:194
HILL, WILLIAM T & ALLEN, JOSIE	27 MAY 1886	12:330
HILLS, JOHN A & CRAIG, LENNIE E	03APR 1884	11:477
HINEMAN, LLOYD M & HASKINS, ZERA M	14 AUG 1914	15:254
HINKLE, BENJAMIN & AUMILLER, CATHARINE	15 AUG 1876	08:375
HINKLE, GIDEON & VANMATRE, PATSY	29 DEC 1836	01:030
HINKLE, JAMES R & EDWARDS, JULIA A	28 AUG 1879	10:115
HINKLE, JOSEPH GIDEON & FRY, MARY PHIDILLA	30 MAR 1892	06:307
HINKLE, LEWIS G & LEWIS, ELIZABETH	*30 MAR 1855	02:006
HINKLE, PHILIP S & BUMGARNER, MARGORE	22 APR 1877	09:066
HINKLE, PLEASANT A & ROUSH, MATTIE V	23 FEB 1910	13:005
HINKLE, TIFF & STATON, ANNA B	10 JUN 1903	08:302
HISCOX, JOSEPH A & KIRKPATRICK, MARY F	02 AUG 1880	10:433
HITE, JONATHAN M & MILLER, LUELLA G	08 NOV 1874	08:179
HIVELY, CURTIS H & CLYSE, LILLIAN F	25 OCT 1913	15:059
HIX, ELI R & FARLEY, MIRTLE E	07 NOV 1907	12:074
HIX, WILLIAM P & COMSTON, CORA E	02 NOV 1899	09:007
HOBBS, ELISHA & FLINT, LAURA E	21 JAN 1904	10:461
HOBBS, HARRY & COLLINS, METTIE	14 OCT 1906	11:430
HOBBS, SAMUEL & JEFFRIES, CORA	05 MAR 1907	11:503
HOBBS, SQUIRE T & GROVES, NANCY	16 MAR 1874	08:108
HOBBS, (Dr) FRANKLIN & WARD, GERTIE	08AUG 1901	09:378
HOBEN, JAMES A & MOORE, ELLEN	24 OCT 1883	11:413
HOCHAR, JOHN WILLIAM & RHOADS, MARTHA ADALINE	28 AUG 1890	05:608
HOCKENBERRY, JOHN W & HELRICH, MARGARET	26 JUL 1913	14:201
HODGE, WILLIAM B & BOGGESS, VILINIA C	22 JAN 1867	05:024
HODGES, STEPHEN & ESTIS, MARY JANE	01 AUG 1847	01:047
HOFF, HENRY OTIS & MAUPIN, AMANDA M	22 SEP 1887	05:101
HOFFMAN, ALBERT & KAYLOR, SARAH	03 JAN 1872	07:178
HOFFMAN, BEN R & GARDNER, EFFIE COLLINS	29 SEP 1910	13:171
HOFFMAN, C N & ZERKEL, L B	29 JUL 1911	13:348

HOFFMAN, CHARLES W & LEWIS, LIZZIE B	14 APR 1897	08:074
HOFFMAN, DAVID & SMITH, VIRGINIA	25 FEB 1864	03:159
HOFFMAN, EDWARD W & CUNNINGHAM, TERISA MAY	27 FEB 1901	09:265
HOFFMAN, ELIAS & CUNNINGHAM, MARTHA L	09:JUL 1865	04:023
HOFFMAN, ERNEST & MATTOX, CORA	29 NOV 1908	12:318
HOFFMAN, EVERETT & STOWERS, VIRGIE MAY	21 FEB 1914	15:144
HOFFMAN, G B & RICKARD, RHODA A	17 OCT 1914	15:295
HOFFMAN, GEORGE & GIBBS, SUSANA	04 AUG 1884	12:043
HOFFMAN, GEORGE & WORK, MARY E	07 JUL 1914	15:235
HOFFMAN, GILLIA F & KEEFER, MINNIE ALICE	09 FEB 1896	07:497
HOFFMAN, HENRY & TURLEY, EMELINE	03 MAR 1867	05:030
HOFFMAN, HENRY & DEWEESE, ANNIE	12 OCT 1875	08:288
HOFFMAN, HENRY & CREASEY, MINERVA JANE	01 MAY 1890	05:554
HOFFMAN, IVON NEWTON & KERWOOD, BERTHA HILDA	20 JUN 1907	11:558
HOFFMAN, J THOMAS & TURNBULL, MAUDE M	23 MAR1913	14:115
HOFFMAN, JAMES & NICHOLS, SIMMERIAN C	06 JUL1876	08:367
HOFFMAN, JAMES R & REED, MARY W	14 FEB 1911	13:267
HOFFMAN, JESSE D & PIERCE, KATE	31 MAY 1902	10:082
HOFFMAN, JOHN & HART, MARY	05 JAN 1850	01:052
HOFFMAN, JOHN & VAN MATRE , MARY M	07 NOV 1865	04:068
HOFFMAN, JOHN & FINICAN, CATHARINE	26 JUL 1874	08:150
HOFFMAN, JONAS & GIBBS, AMANDA E	16 DEC 1884	12:105
HOFFMAN, JOSEPH H & BUFFINGTON, MARY B	23 NOV 1895	07:430
HOFFMAN, LEWIS E & RICKARD, ANNIE	28 JAN 1906	11:251
HOFFMAN, MILFORD & ROUSH, JANE	05 AUG 1895	07:588
HOFFMAN, PERCY L & ZIRKEL, BERTHA	19 SEP 1889	05:455
HOFFMAN, PHILIP & CUNNINGHAM, MARY M	18 SEP 1873	08:027
HOFFMAN, PHILLIP E & ROUSH, SARAH VIRGINIA	21 AUG 1907	11:596
HOFFMAN, R OKEY & RUSSELL, GRACE	13 SEP 1913	15:034
HOFFMAN, ROBERT & HART, CHARLOTTE	17 APR 1873	07:347
HOFFMAN, ROBERT F & POSTON, MARY C	15 DEC 1897	08:210
HOFFMAN, SAMUEL & ROUSH, SALLY	09 OCT 1834	01:029
HOFFMAN, SAMUEL & BURROWS, ANGELINE	09 MAR 1876	08:334
HOFFMAN, SAMUEL & SELBY, ELIZA	*22 FEB 1858	02:010
HOFFMAN, SANFORD ELBERT & VAN MATRE, FANNIE FRANCES	26 SEP 1909	12:437
HOFFMAN, STAR & RISER, ELLA	03 JUL 1898	08:328
HOFFMAN, WALTER & LUTTON, SALLIE	27 APR 1902	10:061
HOFFMAN, WILLIAM E & GLASSBURN, MAGGIE C	22 MAR 1902	10:038
HOFFMAN, WILLIAM G & FISHER, JULIET J	25 DEC 1870	07:030
HOFFMAN, WILLIAM R & SMITH, AUGUSTA E	25 DEC 1898	08:438
HOFFMAN, WILLIAM R & GIBBS, LAURA V	18 FEB 1886	12:295
HOFFMAN, WILLIAM S & BUMGARNER, MILLIE B	13 JUL 1890	05:556
HOFFNER, AUGUST & PEASE, ELIZABETH	20 SEP 1911	13:382
HOGABOOM, WILLARD S & HILL, M MAUD	27 OCT 1896	07:636
HOGAN, JAMES T & CAMDEN, FANNIE E	24 MAY 1891	06:115
HOGAN, PATRICK & McGREERY, CATHARINE	23 FEB 1870	06:153
HOGE, JOHN & CUNNINGHAM, CLARA	26 DEC 1904	11:018
HOGENS, GEORGE W & BOWMAN, WINNIE	13 DEC 1876	09:002
HOGG, ABNEY W & SKEEN, MARY	20 JAN 1842	01:036
HOGG, CAMDEN H & HAWKINS, ALICE	31 DEC 1906	11:487
HOGG, JAMES & HOGG, ELIZABETH	16 JAN 1838	01:032
HOGG, JAMES A & KNIGHT, SUSAN	*12 JAN 1852	02:002
HOGG, JAMES A & WAYBRIGHT, MERLIA F	07 SEP 1907	12:005
HOGSETT, SAMUEL L & KING, ELIZABETH	02 SEP 1872	07:267
HOGSETT, SAMUEL WILLIAM & GUNN, WILLIE MARY	08 SEP 1903	10:350
HOHNES, WOLLIE IRA & JOBE, CORA E	03 APR 1901	09:318
HOLBERT, REUBEN P & McCOY, JANE	27 NOV 1872	07:294
HOLDEN, JOSEPH & LONG, MALINDA	1837	01:040
HOLDREN, BUCK & EDWARDS, AMANDA	12 NOV 1882	11:250

HOLDREN, GEORGE WASHINGTON & MASH, VICTORIA JANE	25 AUG 1887	05:081
HOLDREN, JAMES D & GEARHART, FANNIE	21 MAR 1878	09:234
HOLDREN, MATTHEW S & BEAVER, MINERVA	10 SEP 1882	11:202
HOLESTEIN, FREDERICK B & TILLIS, MARY M	03 AUG 1904	10:567
HOLLAND, ALFRED A & PECK, EMILY M	*28 DEC 1859	02:013
HOLLAND, ALFRED A & PECK, LETITIA H	16 OCT 1872	08:044
HOLLAND, CHARLES N & WEES, MABEL F	13 AUG 1897	08:240
HOLLAND, GEO & RAYBURN, MARTHA A	14 JAN 1861	02:015
HOLLAND, GEORGE & DAVIS, MAHALA	24 NOV 1873	08:064
HOLLAND, WALTER CURTIS & BUMGARNER, ETHEL WINIFRED	26 SEP 1909	12:512
HOLLEY, ANDREW & HOLLEY, ELIZA J	22 MAR 1901	09:309
HOLLEY, BAILEY & BARKER, VIOLA	23 AUG 1913	15:015
HOLLEY, CHARLES & HOLLEY, VERNIE	02 JUN 1914	15:206
HOLLEY, CHARLES R & TACKETT, ROSE E	26 FEB 1893	06:494
HOLLEY, CHARLES W & HALL, ISABELLE	06 MAR 1887	12:487
HOLLEY, CORNELIUS A & HOLLEY, ELIZA J	09 OCT 1898	08:390
HOLLEY, GEORGE E & HAMBRICK, KATE	10 JAN 1906	11:244
HOLLEY, HENDERSON & HOLLEY, EFFIE M	01 MAY 1893	06:535
HOLLEY, JAMES & CHAPMAN, MINNIE	30 JUN 1899	08:565
HOLLEY, JAMES C & BRYANT, BETTIE	04 AUG 1870	06:213
HOLLEY, JAMES H & NOWLIN, RUBY PEARL	25 OCT 1913	15:057
HOLLEY, JAMES M & McWHORTER, NETTIE	09 OCT 1898	08:378
HOLLEY, JEFFERSON & BARNETT, MINNIE	22 DEC 1897	08:220
HOLLEY, JOHN R & HOLLEY, ELCIE	02 JUN 1914	15:205
HOLLEY, JOHN R & CHAPMAN, CORA A	04 JAN 1901	09:272
HOLLEY, JOSEPH & JENKINS, MATILDA A	22 FEB 1890	05:520
HOLLEY, LAFAYETTE & POWELL, SUSAN	04 SEP 1897	08:152
HOLLEY, LIEN ELZIE & CONRAD, ALMEDIA	03 MAR 1901	09:297
HOLLEY, MONROE & FURTH, HENRIETTA	19 SEP 1895	07:384
HOLLEY, MOUNT ETNA & HOLLEY, RETTIE	20 MAR 1898	08:273
HOLLEY, PHILIP & MEADOWS, EVA W	20 JUL 1904	10:562
HOLLEY, ROBERT & SMITH, FANNIE	25 DEC 1882	11:278
HOLLEY, SAMUEL & McMILLIN, (Mrs) REBECCA ANN	*27 AUG 1856	02:008
HOLLEY, SAMUEL & HOLLEY, LEFFLAVER	25 NOV 1902	10:193
HOLLEY, T E & HOGSETT, FANNIE	23 MAY 1894	07:096
HOLLEY, THOMAS L & WATERSON, JENNIE	30 JUN 1901	09:364
HOLLEY, TIMOTHY E & McWHORTER, NORA F	30 AUG 1908	12:241
HOLLEY, VIRGIL & GILLISPIE, ADA	10 OCT 1914	15:291
HOLLEY, W W & CREMEENS, SARAH M	13 NOV 1898	08:404
HOLLEY, WALTER & MILLER, LINDA	10 JUN 1911	13:329
HOLLEY, WILLIAM & TAYLOR, ELIZABETH JANE	*13 FEB 1854	02:005
HOLLEY, WILLIAM ALEXANDER & RUNION, CHARLOTTIE	29 OCT 1893	06:636
HOLLEY, WILLIAM G & GROVES, NANNIE G	19 APR 1882	11:138
HOLLEY, WILLIAM P & BLAKE, MATILDA	13 JUN 1894	07:102
HOLLEY, ZACHARIAH & FORTH, ELLA	20 DEC 1894	07:210
HOLLOWAY, JAMES H & MIDDLECOFF, EMELINE R	22 JUL 1863	03:123
HOLLOWAY, JOSEPH HAYNES & LOGUE, MARY EMMA	03 FEB 1881	10:323 2
HOLLOWAY, PETER G & SCHNEIDER, FLORENCE E M	08 JAN 1879	10:039
HOLLOWAY, ROBERT HINTON & McNEILL, WILLIE R	03 APR 1889	05:378
HOLLOWAY, TIMOTHY H & BROWN, MARIA LOUISA	*21 DEC 1860	02:015
HOLLOWAY, WILLIAM D & GWINN, MINNIE A	21 APR 1906	11:295
HOLLY, A & HOLLY, FANNIE	15 APR 1885	12:162
HOLLY, ALFRED G & HAWTHORN, MARY C	*24 JAN 1860	02:013
HOLLY, BENJAMIN F & DENNY, CAROLINE	09 JAN 1887	12:463
HOLLY, BENJAMIN F & ROY, MINNIE	22 FEB 1893	06:493
HOLLY, CHARLES W & SMITH, FANNIE B	10 DEC 1891	06:244
HOLLY, CORNELIUS & TAYLOR, ANN M H	*10 JAN 1853	02:003
HOLLY, EDMOND & HOLLY, ESTER MAY	25 DEC 1888	05:322

HOLLY, EDWARD & HOLLY, CATHARINE	*04 MAY 1859	02:012
HOLLY, GEORGE & CHAPMAN, LEFAVOR	*26 FEB 1859	02:012
HOLLY, GREENVILLE & CREMEANS, MARY	04 JUN 1862	03:068
HOLLY, HERMAN & SMITH, MARTHA A	03 JAN 1866	04:096
HOLLY, JAMES C & CREMEANS, LUEZA	*03 MAY 1859	02:012
HOLLY, JAMES C & LEWIS, ROSIA A	27 AUG 1885	12:211
HOLLY, JAMES MONROE & CLAGG, MALINDA MIRAM	07 SEP 1889	05:450
HOLLY, JOHN B & CAMP, MARTHA E	22 FEB 1883	11:302
HOLLY, JOHN C & LEWIS, LAVINA F	21 JUN 1877	09:100
HOLLY, JOHN R & LUNSFORD, MALINDA	05 MAR 1883	11:299
HOLLY, JOHN W & IRWIN, NANCY J	02 APR 1885	12:153
HOLLY, JOSEPH T & MEADOWS, CATHARINE ANN	13 NOV 1867	05:117
HOLLY, JULIUS IRA & MILLER, LAURA JOSEPHINE	12 FEB 1893	06:487
HOLLY, L D & ERVEN, JENNIE	15 JUN 1884	12:025
HOLLY, MOSES & BRYAN, EVALINE	*28 DEC 1858	02:012
HOLLY, PHILIP & EDMUNDS, ORACY SIDNEY	*23 MAR 1892	06:311
HOLLY, PHILIP & ASHWORTH, CORA	10 OCT 1895	07:404
HOLLY, R E & MEADOWS, ISABEL	08 MAY 1887	05:019
HOLLY, THEODORE & LEWIS, HULDA CATHARINE	24 JAN 1889	05:343
HOLLY, THOMAS A & HOLLY, DELILA J	25 JUN 1867	05:062
HOLLY, TIMOTHY EDWARD & MILLER, ALICE JORDEN	28 AUG 1889	05:438
HOLLY, WASHINGTON & CREMEANS, HULDY	15 MAR 1831	01:025
HOLLY, WILLIAM FRANKLIN & ERWIN, SARAH	02 FEB 1889	05:345
HOLLY, WILLIAM W & DANIEL, MINER	*27 NOV 1858	02:011
HOLMES, FRANKLIN ELMER & TURLEY, ANNIE	13 SEP 1888	05:278
HOLMES, J B & St CLAIR, ROSE W	25 DEC 1899	09:048
HOLMES, JASPER G & BROWN, ADA B	21 DEC 1881	11:081
HOLMES, JOHN G & FOSTER, CLARA L	11 MAY 1904	10:519
HOLMES, WALTER D & ADKINS, MARY	29 JUL 1873	08:013
HOLMES, WILLIAM A & SMITH, BLANCHE	15 MAR 1898	08:268
HOLT, JAMES & ROBSON, SUSAN	04 FEB 1868	05:149
HOLT, JAMES P & WOODRUM, IDA M	05 APR 1876	08:344
HOLT, RUTTER & BONNETT, LILLIE M	25 JUN 1902	10:097
HOLT, THOMAS G & HALL, LAURA	02 DEC 1914	15:335
HOLT, TOBIAS & SAYRE, HARRIET E	28 DEC 1869	06:130
HOLT, TOBIAS & GABBERT, ELMIRA D	18 FEB 1894	07:047
HOLTER, JOSHUA & CARTWRIGHT, STELLA MAY	14 AUG 1890	05:599
HOLZAPFEL, GEORGE J & HOLCTON, MALINDA	01 JAN 1885	12:119
HONAKER, JOHN & NIBERT, IDA	18 SEP 1904	10:599
HOOD, CLYDE K & HARRIS, CARRIE L	30 NOV 1911	13:433
HOOD, DAVID C & ANDERSON, MARTHA	27 MAY 1871	07:092
HOOD, JAMES W & FRENCH, NANNIE J	30 MAY 1911	13:322
HOOD, JOHN MILTON & HAWKINS, REBECCA FLORENCE	09 DEC 1886	12:436
HOOD, SYLVESTER & KERWOOD, MARY	23 MAY 1871	07:066
HOOD, WILLIAM H & AUFLICK, JANE A	06 NOV 1873	08:063
HOOFF, EDWARD LEE & MILLER, REBECCA	*25 JUN 1856	02:008
HOOFF, JAMES H & MILLER, (Mrs) MARY C	*01 JUN 1853	02:004
HOOK, DAVID & GIBBS, REBECCA	02 JUL 1906	11:355
HOOP, THOMAS H & HOLMES, VERNA C	03 JAN 1900	09:059
HOOPER, JOHN W & TILLIS, WADIE K	13 OCT 1903	10:385
HOOVER, JACOB P & YOUNG, ELIZABETH	08 SEP 1890	05:521
HOOVER, WILLIAM P & MEAD, BETTIE	27 NOV 1903	10:422
HOOVER, WM HARRY & SINGLETON, MAUDE CELESTINA	18 NOV 1811	13:421
HOPE, DANIEL Mc & ROGERS, GRACE	19 DEC 1914	15:346
HOPE, HENRY CLAY & TERRY, LYDDIE	30 DEC 1891	06:268
HOPE, THOMAS R & PAYNE, MARY	01 APR 1845	01:044
HOPKINS, ALFRED B & POLSLEY, AUGUSTA	*13 NOV 1858	02:011
HOPKINS, DAVID A & WINDON, HATTIE M	03 SEP 1878	09:304

Name	Date	Ref
HOPKINS, WILLIAM T & WINDON, NANCY C	05 MAY 1875	08:238
HOPLIGHT, CHARLES & DUNCAN, SUSAN M	10 NOV 1872	07:286
HOPLIGHT, CHARLES F & SIMPKINS, VIRGIE F	29 MAY 1908	12:192
HOPSON, B E & LANIER, MARY	24 APR 1919	12:403
HOPSON, JOHN R & THORNTON, ELIZABETH A	24 AUG 1884	12:049
HORNER, JOHN D & HANNA, KATE V	18 APR 1885	12:160
HORNER, JOHN H & BOYD, JESSIE	28 JUL 1883	11:376
HORNER, ROBERT J & GIBBS, MOLLIE	11 NOV 1901	09:445
HORNIDAY, OTHER E & HARVEY, MISSOURI	10 OCT 1886	12:396
HORSTON, AD & GILMORE, FRANKIE	19 MAR 1894	07:095
HORTON, ROBERT H & MAYES, ELIZABETH J	31 MAR 1865	04:006
HORTON, WINFIELD S & CLONCH, NANCY J	18 DEC 1908	12:334
HOSCHAR, ANDREW G & McCOY, JANNIA	01 JAN 1903	10:219
HOSCHAR, ANDREW K & PLANTS, RHODA E	19 APR 1866	04:117
HOSCHAR, BENJAMIN LEMASTER & VAN MATRE, JENNIE	20 SEP 1888	05:280
HOSCHAR, FREDERICK & OLDFIELD, JEMIMA	26 MAY 1864	03:184
HOSCHAR, FREDERICK GEORGE & SIDERS, SUSAN	01 SEP 1887	05:087
HOSCHAR, JACOB B & UPTON, VIRGINIA M	22 AUG 1901	11:391
HOSCHAR, JOHN P & SPOUNIGAL, MARY	11 NOV 1893	07:002
HOSCHAR, JOHN W & FLOWERS, EMMA	16 APR 1901	09:323
HOSCHAR, ALEXANDER B & RIFFLE, ELIZABETH	*05 JAN 1857	02:009
HOUCK, ALEXANDER & McGUCKIAN, MARY	26 NOV 1879	10:167
HOUCK, ASA E & BELCHER, MARY E	*05 SEP 1911	13:371
HOUCK, CYRUS & SAUNDERS, FLORENCE	02 JAN 1909	12:348
HOUCK, GARET L & SAUNDERS, GARNET	12 NOV 1910	13:204
HOUCK, PLEASANT R & SAUNDERS, JESTIE C	03 JUN 1911	13:325
HOUCK, S HOMER & BAKER, CLARA B	15 SEP 1912	13:600
HOUGHTON, HENRY H & HOOVER, ELIZABETH F	16 DEC 1890	06:017
HOWARD, BRANCH R L & JONES, DELPHIA E	27 MAY 1899	08:541
HOWARD, FRANK McD & THOMPSON, CLYDE E	08 AUG 1894	07:127
HOWARD, HIRAM R & RODGERS, NANNIE A	16 JAN 1866	04:098
HOWARD, JAMES EDWARD & COMSTOCK, MARTHA CAROLINE	01 JAN 1913	14:074
HOWARD, STEPHEN L & RICKARD, ALICE M	22 FEB 1894	07:054
HOWARD, WILLIAM H & ROUSH, IDA F	09 OCT 1878	09:329
HOWEL, ARETUS & COBB, RACHEL I	21 APR 1867	05:043
HOWEL, JOHN F & RHODES, ELIZABETH	31 JAN 1872	07:185
HOWELL, AUGUSTUS & RICHARDS, ADELINE M	*04 FEB 1856	02:007
HOWELL, DELL A & WORK, EMMA A	29 SEP 1908	12:273
HOWELL, E B & CHILDERS, MARTHA	25 AUG 1884	12:062
HOWELL, E C B & MEADOWS, SOPHIA	*12 JUN 1897	08:112
HOWELL, ELIAS B & HIGGINS, MARY C	14 SEP 1879	10:128
HOWELL, FELIX & BOONE, MARY	19 DEC 1886	12:441
HOWELL, FLOYD L & THORNTON, IVA M	25 OCT 1914	15:304
HOWELL, GEORGE L & DEWEES, FLORA A	02 NOV 1897	08:188
HOWELL, HENRY G & CRAIG, ANNIE	27 APR 1879	10:082
HOWELL, JAMES & BRANCH, CORA M	*15 MAY 1906	11:317
HOWELL, JOHN & HALL, (Mrs) ELIZABETH	*17 MAY 1852	02:002
HOWELL, MARCELLOW A & CLARK, LULA A	(no date)	12:007
HOWELL, NATHANIEL B & RIFFLE, SARAH A	08 NOV 1862	03:085
HOWELL, RICHARD & CASTO, RACHEL	17 JAN 1831	01:023
HOWELL, WILLIAM G & COOPER, MARGARET M	20 NOV 1904	10:461
HOWERY, SHERLEY F & HULL, CLARA E	21 APR 1911	13:312
HOY, CHARLES & HENDERSON, JANE	29 APR 1822	01:009
HOY, FRANK D & STERRETT, HELEN V	13 NOV 1878	10:009
HOY, JOHN & PROSSER, MARY H	12 MAY 1818	01:005
HOY, WILL S & TOMLINSON, MAUD	08 NOV 1881	11:049
HOYLMAN, JAMES HAMMOND & PORTER, ANNIE AGNES	21 NOV 1887	05:143
HOYLMAN, WILLIAM EARL & PEAL, MINNIE	18 JUN 1907	11:557

HOYT, ALBERT M & STONE, MARY M	24 DEC 1910	13:246
HOYT, ASEL & BROWN, MARY ANN	*08 OCT 1855	02:007
HOYT, JAMES & MATTHEWS, BIRDIE	23 DEC 1897	08:225
HUDDLESTON, JOHN & RUSSELL, ELVIRA	*25 NOV 1853	02:004
HUDSON, BRADFORD & McCLOUD, ANNA	23 JUL 1881	10:432
HUDSON, CHARLES E & DOWELL, BERTIE	05 APR 1899	08:497
HUDSON, CHARLES E & LEWIS, DELLA D	22 MAY 1914	15:199
HUDSON, DAVID & HUGHES, ANNIE	26 NOV 1903	10:418
HUDSON, EDGAR F & SMITH, HELLEN M	26 MAR 1908	12:149
HUDSON, HARRY & EDWARDS, HELLEN M	19 AUG 1914	15:256
HUDSON, JAMES & WEIGAND, JESSIE	27 MAY 1896	07:538
HUDSON, JOHN & MAYES, SETTIE	19 APR 1903	10:273
HUDSON, JOHN F & TURNER, ELLA MAY	08 APR 1914	15:173
HUDSON, JOHN G & EDWARDS, CORA	01 DEC 1907	12:084
HUDSON, JOHN HANSFORD & ROUSH, CAROLINE A	26 NOV 1891	06:236
HUDSON, LEWIS & LEWIS, MARTHA A	01 JUN 1887	05:032
HUDSON, N C & BAKER, ELLEN E	13 JAN 1912	13:465
HUDSON, NEAL & ROUSH, JENNIE B	19 FEB 1891	06:061
HUDSON, OSCAR & GIBBS, LUCY	*25 MAY 1894	07:097
HUDSON, OSCAR L & GIBBS, LUCY	04 JUL 1894	07:114
HUDSON, OSCAR L & STIMBLE, ELLA	12 AUG 1898	08:343
HUDSON, PRESTON A & ROUSH, SUSAN	17 MAY 1866	04:123
HUDSON, PRESTON A & ROUSH, REBECCA	13 AUG 1868	05:203
HUDSON, RICHARD & HAYES, VIOLA	24 DEC 1910	13:238
HUDSON, WILLIAM DAVID & NOBLE, ROSANA	04 JUN 1892	06:348
HUDSON, WILLIAM H & CHANDLER, SARAH E	25 OCT 1883	11:414
HUDSON, WILLIAM W & HOFFMAN, DORA	18 AUG 1901	09:387
HUFF, JAMES E & KLINE, LAURETTA N	31 MAR 1868	05:160
HUFF, WILLIAM & BLAKE, LIZZIE	28 OCT 1886	12:408
HUFFMAN, DELBERT & LAWRENCE, DARTHULA C	24 DEC 1910	13:231
HUFFMAN, GEORGE W & SLACK, JESSIE P	18 AUG 1911	13:357
HUFFMAN, JOHN & ZIRCLE, CHRISTENA	08 OCT 1835	01:029
HUFFMAN, SAMPSON & ROUSH, BARBARA	20 FEB 1833	01:028
HUFFMAN, WILLIAM & CLAGG, MATILDA	13 MAY 1897	08:093
HUGGART, JOSEPH & BURTON, TACY	18 SEP 1828	01:018
HUGH, TANSY & FRESON, BETSY	26 NOV 1809	01:002
HUGHES, ALBERT C & BELL, JENNIE	28 MAR 1912	13:506
HUGHES, ANDREW L & KNAPPENBERGER, ELIZABETH	26 SEP 1883	11:406
HUGHES, ASHBELL & GRICE, VIOLA C	23 JUN 1870	06:200
HUGHES, ASHBELL & PUSEY, LAURA F	27 AUG 1898	08:351
HUGHES, BENJAMIN F & McCOLLISTER, VIRGINIA S	19 FEB 1872	07:199
HUGHES, CHARLES F & JORDAN, MARY E	16 SEP 1896	07:611
HUGHES, CHARLES W & LIVINGSTON, LOUISA	01 JAN 1901	09:273
HUGHES, DAVID & COTTERELL, FLORA	08 MAR 1900	09:092
HUGHES, DAVID E & WRAY, MARY F	04 JUL 1905	11:123
HUGHES, DAVID M & WALKER, ANGIE	22 DEC 1906	11:473
HUGHES, EDWARD & FLETCHER, HATTIE	13 NOV 1897	08:196
HUGHES, FELIX & OHLINGER, LYDIA	20 DEC 1900	09:253
HUGHES, FRANCIS M & WALLIS, MARY J	15 FEB 1872	07:196
HUGHES, GEORGE D & SAYRE, MINERVA J	09 MAY 1903	10:289
HUGHES, GEORGE M & ROBISON, MARY	20 OCT 1902	10:174
HUGHES, GEORGE M & CREMEENS, EFFIE	16 SEP 1904	10:596
HUGHES, HANSOME S & NEWELL, MARTHA F	08 OCT 1886	12:395
HUGHES, JAMES N & DAVIS, MARGARET J	13 JUN 1878	09:272
HUGHES, JAMES R & HUGHES, SARAH A	30 APR 1894	07:081
HUGHES, JAMES R & FRAKES, BERTHA	14 OCT 1911	13:368
HUGHES, JOHN H & FRY, SUSAN C	20 JAN 1881	10:370
HUGHES, JOHN R & CANTOR, NONA	28 NOV 1906	11:462

HUGHES, JOHN W & WALLIS, MARTHA A	10 NOV 1869	06:095
HUGHES, JOHN W & WAUGH, NANCY E	22 JUL 1891	06:150
HUGHES, JOSEPH & GRIMM, OSIE F	20 JUN 1886	12:339
HUGHES, JOSEPH H & STANLEY, JENNIE M	22 AUG 1894	07:142
HUGHES, LEANDER & CASEY, NANCY	27 FEB 1870	06:157
HUGHES, LEANDER & FROIDVEAUX, MARY	18 OCT 1908	12:280
HUGHES, MILES B & CRAIG, GERTIE	01 OCT 1911	13:385
HUGHES, THOMAS & JOHNSON, ROSETTA	21 OCT 1871	07:134
HUGHES, THOMAS & WEIRS, JEMIMA	19 JUL 1883	11:373
HUGHES, WILL D & BRUESTLE, LILLIE F	01 SEP 1902	10:143
HUGHES, WILLIAM & PICKENS, ELLEN	27 JUN 1881	10:425
HUGHES, WILLIAM M & FRANKLIN, MARY C	24 NOV 1880	10:337
HUGHES, WILLIAM M & KNAPP, BETTIE	08 AUG 1883	11:385
HUGHES, WILLIAM P & HURDMAN, MARY MARGARET	21 APR 1867	05:044
HUGHES, WILLIAM P & ROSEBERRY, MAGGIE M	26 APR 1908	12:170
HUGHEY, JAMES C & GARTON, JUDY B	1843	01:041
HUGHS, CHARLES & STEELE, ELIZABETH J	05:SEP 1897	08:151
HUGHS, DAVID & POSTLETHWAIT, ELIZA	25 FEB 1877	09:034
HUGHS, FRANCIS M & WALLIS, JANE A	15 NOV 1880	10:324
HUGHS, HENRY & NICHOLAS, MARIAH	16 DEC 1824	01:010
HUGHS, JAMES & HAMILTON, MARY	19 JAN 1826	01:014
HUGHS, JAMES & McCOY, IBELIZA	09 OCT 1845	01:045
HUGHS, JAMES & PORE, SARAH	01 OCT 1874	08:168
HUGHS, JEREMIAH & STARCHER, ANNA	*03 JAN 1860	02:013
HUGHS, JEREMIAH & MASON, MARIA	08 APR 1877	09:060
HUGHS, JESSE & ROBINSON, ELIZA A	03 OCT 1865	04:059
HUGHS, JOSEPH R & LEE, MARY E	08 NOV 1876	08:408
HUGHS, WILLIAM & MACKLEY, BARBARA	26 JUN 1823	01:010
HULBERT, GUY L & WARNER, CLEO P	09 MAR 1913	14:103
HULBERT, TRUMAN GUTHRIE & LOOMIS, CLARA M	30 APR 1891	06:100
HULL, ALVA DOE & PHELPS, FLOSSIE LENORA	29 JUN 1907	11:563
HULL, EDWARD & RIFFLE, ALICE	20 DEC 1900	09:254
HULL, GEORGE W & LOVE, IVA I	13 NOV 1903	10:405
HULL, HENRY C & CLICK, MARY M	19 MAY 1906	11:320
HULL, JOHN Q A & KNAPP, MARTHA L	19 AUG 1894	07:136
HULL, ROBERT J F & LANE, ROSETTA	31 SEP 1898	08:387
HULL, SAMPSON & LOWERY, ALLIE U	17 OCT 1890	05:625
HUL, (Parson) G W & LOVE, IVY	22 OCT 1904	10:617
HULL, (Parson) G W & BOSTIC, LILLIE M	16 OCT 1906	11:432
HULL, (P G) W H & McDADE, EVELINE	19 JUN 1897	08:113
HUMPHREY, EDWARD G & BYRD, GARNETTE W	23 AUG 1908	12:232
HUMPHREY, ELIAS & CHESLEY, LOUISA	24 NOV 1825	01:012
HUMPHREY, WILLIAM M & BOYLES, CAROLINE	27 DEC 1877	09:182
HUMPHREYS, FLAVIUS J & ZERKEL, JENNIE	16 JUN 1872	07:237
HUMPHREYS, JAMES E & HUNTER, ELIZABETH	27 JUN 1875	08:251
HUMPHREYS, JAMES E & BOYCE, EMMA	08 MAR 1881	10:380
HUNNEL, JNO M & YEAGER, ANNA	19 NOV 1879	10:165
HUNT, ABIJAH & HUGHS, MARY	13 JUN 1828	01:021
HUNT, FRANK & NEWELL, BERTHA	12 NOV 1895	07:425
HUNT, JAMES M & CARSEY, CAROLINE	05 DEC 1878	10:013
HUNT, WILLIAM & MOORE, RHODA JANE	22 MAR 1888	05:197
HUNTER, ED & GILLIS, LIZZIE G	26 MAR 1891	06:087
HUNTER, JOHN E & HAWTHORNE, KATIE	10 MAY 1894	07:091
HURLEY, JAMES H & SMITH, MALISSA	14 MAY 1881	10:412
HURLEY, JOSEPH P & BOWEN, EDNA B	11 JAN 1913	14:082
HURLOW, CHARLES WILLIAM & FOWLER, DORA ETHEL	30 JUN 1900	09:151
HURLOW, JAMES & ROBERTS, FLORENCE	20 JAN 1895	07:237
HURLOW, JAMES & PARSONS, INA MAY	25 AUG 1900	09:180

Names	Date	Ref
HURSHEY, WILLIAM T & LEWIS, ELIZA J	16 MAY 1869	06:054
HUSHER, JOHN V & VANMATRE, ZELPHA	03 JAN 1843	01:037
HUSS, JACOB & BOYD, ELEANOR	25 APR 1821	01:008
HUSSELL, THEODORE J & PEARSON, LELA A	19 MAY 1910	13:070
HUSTON, DUDLEY & ROE, ALICE	07 SEP 1908	12:253
HUSTON, WILLIAM BRIGHT & TIPPETT, EDITH BLAIR	13 FEB 1893	06:489
HUTCHESON, THOMAS B & SAYRE, LIZZABETH J	19 MAR 1913	14:109
HUTCHINSON, CHARLES A & CHARLES, EVA	19 SEP 1882	11:210
HUTCHINSON, JAS & BALL, MARGT E	*15 MAR 1853	02:004
HUTCHINSON, JOHN L & HENDERSON, MARY E	*28 MAY 1855	02:006
HUTCHISON, WILLIAM B & LYKENS, MIRIAM	15 AUG 1889	05:428
HUTSON, SAMUEL & MOULDING, LUCY M	*04 APR 1878	09:241
HUTTON, CHARLES I & DENNY, FRANCES	26 JUN 1905	11:118
HUTTON, WILLIAM A & WALKER, CARRIE I	18 JUL 1896	07:581
HYATT, ALBERT & JIBEAUT, EVALINE	19 AUG 1870	06:215
HYATT, HEZEKIAH & CRIG, PRUDY E	06 JUL 1877	09:107
HYATT, ISAIAH & BARNETT, ELLEN J	06 OCT 1861	03:024
HYATT, J A & SHEPPARD, VERNA LOUISE	21 DEC 1913	15:092
HYDE, JOHN & FLESHER, NANCY	08 FEB 1827	01:020
HYLTON, ARCHIE B & McMILLIN, BERTHA	18 JAN 1899	08:454
HYLTON, IRA & MELTON, ELIZABETH	06 FEB 1862	03:046
HYSELL, AZEL & LEE, SARAH	09 SEP 1876	08:385
HYSELL, CURTIS & SMITH, PLEASANT W	20 NOV 1884	12:096
HYSELL, DANIEL A & WOODALL, JENNIE	18 JAN 1885	12:129
HYSELL, DAYTON & PLANTS, DONA	30 NOV 1906	11:463
HYSELL, EARL C & JEFFERSON, MARIE	23 SEP 1896	07:618
HYSELL, ED R & McCUMBER, LYDIA	10 DEC 1910	13:224
HYSELL, GEORGE & ORD, MARY	07 OCT 1882	11:219
HYSELL, HAL & BUTCHER, VIRGINIA	04 JUL 1888	05:244
HYSELL, HARVEY & RUSSELL, ELMIRA J	*15 MAR 1881	10:336
HYSELL, SHIRLEY S & BENEDICT, OLLIE P	08 JUL 1912	13:562
HYSELL, THEODORE & McDOWELL, MARIE A	*13 MAR 1907	11:505
ICENHOWER, ALLEN A & KEITH, LUCETTA	16 SEP 1866	04:147
ICENHOWER, JACOB M & DONERY, EMILY	17 JAN 1875	08:204
ICENHOWER, JOHN F & MARTINE, GEORGIA L	07 MAY 1901	09:333
ICENHOWER, JOHN W & TAYLOR, SARAH	29 AUG 1872	07:256
ICENHOWER, JOSEPHUS & LONG, AMANDA	09 DEC 1869	06:128
IHLE, CHARLES H & SIEGRIST, SERENA L	09 NOV 1884	12:092
IHLE, MICHAEL WILLIAM & ROUSH, MARTHA SUSAN	04 MAR 1885	12:148
IHLE, ORLANDO GRAY & FOGLESONG, MINNIE JANE	19 OCT 1892	06:430
ILDERTON, JOHN & WHEATLEY, MARY	08 SEP 1872	07:259
ILDERTON, ROBERT & DAVIS, MARY A	14 FEB 1871	07:053
IMAN, WILLIAM H & WOOD, JEANIE D	11 MAR 1891	06:077
INGLES, CHARLES LESLIE & STEWART, BERTHA I	24 MAY 1914	15:201
INGELS, CLYDE C & MOCK, EMMA	15 JAN 1910	12:592
INGELS, JOHN & WEAVER, FRANCES EVELINE	15 JUN 1846	01:045
INMAN, WILLIAM J & WILSON, CYNTHIA R	21 JAN 1876	08:321
IRVIN, ANDREW & WEST, CLARA	06 APR 1884	12:002
IRVIN, EZRA J & RUSSELL, BERTHA H	18 APR 1889	08:506
IRVIN, ROBERT & WILEY, JENNIE	28 DEC 1815	01:004
IRVIN, SAMUEL & JORDAN, ELIZABETH E	18 MAR 1877	09:040
IRWIN, JOSEPHUS & MILLER, MARTHA E	23 NOV 1880	10:332
ISAAC, HENRY & LEWIS, SARAH	13 MAY 1890	05:557
ISENBURG, JAMES H & TIDROW, LYDIA A	15 OCT 1907	12:044
ISENHAUER, JOSEPH & CAYLOR, LYDIA	MAY 1842	01:043
JACKSON, ANDREW & MUNDELL, MALINDA	29 JAN 1909	12:359
JACKSON, BENJAMIN H & SMITH, EDITH M	27 DEC 1904	11:021
JACKSON, CHARLES W & MARTIN, VERNIE L	07 DEC 1907	12:091

Name	Date	Ref
JACKSON, DANIEL W & NEASE, MELVINA	09 MAY 1878	09:257
JACKSON, ELMER C & CHAPMAN, MAUD M	02 DEC 1907	12:081
JACKSON, HARRY & LANIER, LETHA M	23 FEB 1910	13:015
JACKSON, JOHN & MACKLEY, POLLY	20 DEC 1819	01:006
JACKSON, JOHN & MOORE, ANN	22 APR 1866	04:118
JACKSON, JOHN R & GORDON, GOLDIE	10 DEC 1903	10:427
JACKSON, ORRIS EUGENE & ROUSH, JULIA E	20 JAN 1889	05:340
JACKSON, ROBERT E & MARKHAM, MAUD M	19 NOV 1899	09:020
JACKSON, THOMAS & VAZEY, MARY	*17 OCT 1851	02:003
JACKSON, WILLIAM ARTHUR & CANTERBURY, MAYE	09 JUN 1900	09:140
JACKSON, WILLIAM I & FOSTER, MATILDA G	18 JUE 1892	06:352
JACKSON, WILLIAM W & ROUSH, MARY C	04 JUN 1868	05:185
JACOBS, HENRY & LAWSON, JESSIE L	28 OCT 1903	10:394
JACOBS, ISAAC & KIMBERLING, PRUDENCE	22 APR 1892	06:329
JACOBS, JOHN & CAIN, LETITIA	04 MAR 1875	08:216
JACOBS, JOHN & MARTIN, LULA	02 JUN 1910	13:082
JACOBS, LABAN C & HARRIS, SARAH E	30 MAR 1902	10:037
JACOBS, LABEN & KIMBERLING, VICTORIA B	26 MAY 1897	08:097
JACOBS, LEVI & MASTERS, MARY E	12 FEB 1885	12:133
JACOBS, LEVI & GALBREATH, AGNES S	02 JAN 1873	07:302
JACOBS, WILLIAM & COLWELL, CATHARINE	17 JUL 1884	12:037
JACOBS, WILLIAM F & MASON, (Mrs) MARY	24 MAY 1910	13:071
JAMES, AARON E & AMOS, MARY	28 DEC 1841	01:036
JAMES, HEBER & WEAVER, ELLEN	24 DEC 1912	14:067
JAMES, ISAAC & DAIGH, ALICE	20 AUG 1894	07:139
JAMES, SAMUEL K & GRAHAM, MALINDA	13 OCT 1872	07:274
JAMISON, A R M & COOPER, RHODA E	15 OCT 1899	08:629
JAMISON, CHARLES F & McMILLIN, MILDRED E	12 DEC 1900	09:248
JAMISON, CHARLES W & FOWLER, MARY E	04 APR 1871	07:071
JAMISON, MOSES P & WOODWARD, MARY JANE	12 AUG 1863	03:126
JAMISON, ROBERT GRAHAM & WATTS, MARY E	09 MAY 1914	15:190
JACHINS, RICHARD F & WHARFF, STELLA FAYE	30 MAY 1907	11:543
JANNEY, MICHAEL & McCOLLISTER, MARY J	24 MAR 1878	09:236
JAQUES, FRANK F & McKINEY, ANNA B	01 JUL 18996	07:578
JAQUES, JOHN & BURDETT, DANIE M	04 MAR 1902	10:032
JAQUES, JOHN GEHIEL & JOHNSON, MALISA JANE	09 MAR 1879	10:065
JAQUES, MAT S & COOPER, ELMIRA	22 MAR 1877	09:044
JARRETT, GUTHRIE RAYMOND & SKINNER, GRACE G	04 MAR 1914	15:151
JARROTT, JAMES W & ADAMS, EMMA	03 OCT 1895	07:399
JEFFERDS, OLIVER W & LEWIS, MARY C J	01 FEB 1842	01:036
JEFFERS, ART & BONECUTTER, MINNIE	20 FEB 1895	07:257
JEFFERS, CALVIN & NEWELL, EMILY J	10 JUN 1869	06:056
JEFFERS, CHARLES & CLONCH, NANCY J	07 SEP 1886	12:384
JEFFERS, CHARLES & McCOY, SALLIE	27 OCT 1906	11:439
JEFFERS, CHARLES & LITCHFIELD, SADIE	29 JUN 1913	14:187
JEFFERS, CHARLES M & WAMSLEY, HATTIE	06 FEB 1912	13:480
JEFFERS, ELIAS & BATEMAN, BETTIE	10 NOV 1901	09:444
JEFFERS, ENOCH & McGUIRE, MARY	02 DEC 1850	01:052
JEFFERS, ENOCH & PUTNEY, SARAH C	05 SEP 1861	03:017
JEFFERS, ENOCH J & BOLES, ELVA M	20 DEC 1908	12:335
JEFFERS, FELIX & RHODES, RACHEL	*01 DEC 1859	02:013
JEFFERS, FELIX & MATHENY, MARY A	06 AUG 1884	12:045
JEFFERS, FLOYD & WAMSLEY, NOLEY M	25 DEC 1912	14:066
JEFFERS, GEORGE L & SANDS, MATTIE L	01 JAN 1896	07:479
JEFFERS, GEORGE P & HALL, IVA B	11 DEC 1904	10:654
JEFFERS, HAMILTON & JEFFERS, MARY JANE	*01 SEP 1855	02:007
JEFFERS, HARRY A & FLOWERS, HATTIE A	24 SEP 1912	14:008
JEFFERS, HENRY & FERGUSON, MYRTLE	29 AUG 1914	15:262

Name	Date	Ref
JEFFERS, HERMAN & FOWLER, VIOLA	04 MAY 1992	06:333
JEFFERS, HOMER & NEAL, KATIE MARGARET	16 MAY 1913	14:150
JEFFERS, JAMES & HANES, CATHARINE	09 MAY 1824	01:010
JEFFERS, JAMES & McCOY, CATHARINE	15 SEP 1825	01:014
JEFFERS, JAMES & McGUIRE, ELIZABETH	20 NOV 1826	01:013
JEFFERS, JAMES & MILLER, AGENORA	01 FEB 1875	08:210
JEFFERS, JAMES FELIX & GRANDSTAFF, EDDETH ELDONA	27 OCT 1889	05:469
JEFFERS, JOHN & HARRIS, VIOLETTA	24 DEC 1894	07:219
JEFFERS, LAFE & SALMONS, ROENA	08 AUG 1914	15:251
JEFFERS, MORRIS & HAYES, SARAH C	01 AUG 1904	10:565
JEFFERS, PRESTON & DECKER, LIZZIE A	20 DEC 1899	09:050
JEFFERS, PRESTON & CHILDERS, REBECCA	08 FEB 1891	06:058
JEFFERS, ROBERT & SAXTON, WILLIE	30 APR 1894	07:083
JEFFERS, ROBERT & CARPENTER, VICTORIA	27 JUL 1912	13:541
JEFFERS, SAMUEL B & FORREST, ETHEL M	10 MAR 1889	05:363
JEFFERS, WILLIAM & JEFFERS, RACHEL	05 NOV 1831	01:025
JEFFERS, WILLIAM B & HALL, VERNIA	21 SEP 1902	10:159
JEFFERSON, HAMILTON & SAYRE, SARAH	15 FEB 1815	01:004
JEFFRESS, ELI & JORDAN, SARAH MARGARET	13 FEB 1851	02:001
JEFFRESS, ELIAS & GRIM, CATHARINE	1834	01:040
JEFFRESS, JAMES & McCOY, ELIZA A	18 JAN 1844	01:042
JEFFRESS, JOHN Jr & McCOY, MALINDA	1834	01:039
JEFFRESS, WILLIAM & FULLER, SARAH	06 APR 1837	01:031
JEFFRIES, ROBERT & HUDSON, LAVINIA E	29 JAN 1880	10:202
JENKINS, ANDERSON & DANIELS, ELIZA	20 DEC 1838	01:031 5
JENKINS, ANDREW B & NOBLE, SARAH E	27 MAY 1899	08:515
JENKINS, AUGUSTUS LEMUEL & HOLLY, CORA FRANCES	27 JUN 1895	07:326
JENKINS, BRIANT & ERWIN, NANCY	06 JAN 1848	01:048
JENKINS, CALVIN & ALEXANDER, JULIAN	24 FEB 1833	01:028
JENKINS, CALVIN & CLAGG, NANCY	25 NOV 1840	01:032 5
JENKINS, CHARLES & SMITH, LELA	03 JUL 1895	07:329
JENKINS, CHARLES W & SUTTON, MELISSA ANN	27 SEP 1867	05:095
JENKINS, COLONEL & FORTH, DELLA	27 AUG 1908	12:236
JENKINS, COLONEL A & ASHWORTH, OKEY	20 MAR 1902	10:035
JENKINS, GEORGE BOOTEN & WOLF, JULIA CATHARINE	07 JUN 1893	06:550
JENKINS, H BEN & MILLER, SARAH E	14 SEP 1870	07:064
JENKINS, HENRY & TURNBULL, LARAHAN	23 MAR 1895	07:272
JENKINS, HENRY J & MEADOWS, MARY A F	13 OCT 1883	03:136
JENKINS, J J & CONRAD, VENA	08 SEP 1813	15:028
JENKINS, JAMES H & CREMEENS, MATILDA	18 DEC 1895	07:453
JENKINS, JAMES V & LYKINS, ROSETTA	16 APR 1905	11:076
JENKINS, JEFFERSON & MEADOWS, ELCIE	21 SEP 1899	08:615
JENKINS, JOHN & MEADOWS, ROSA M	05 MAY 1887	05:018
JENKINS, JOHN J & HOLLEY, ELIZABETH	17 JUN 1875	08:249
JENKINS, JOSEPH E & LINSCOTT, EMMA E	30 MAY 1904	10:525
JENKINS, MONROE R & FORREST, M MARY	24 JAN 1802	10:012
JENKINS, MORGAN, Jr. & CHAPMAN, BERTHA P	15 JUL 1896	07:579
JENKINS, MOUNERVILLE MONROE & CHAPMAN, ELIZABETH MARGT	19 FEB 1880	10:209
JENKINS, PHILIP & MITCH, EDDA	12 MAR 1904	10:487
JENKINS, RICHARD & REESE, MARGARET	11 MAY 1867	05:049
JENKINS, ROWLEY & JOHNSON, MAUD	06 DEC 1905	11:219
JENKINS, THOMAS J & COTTRELL, PHOEBE A	11 MAY 1887	05:023
JENKINS, WILLIAM & EDWARDS, CORDELIA	01 JUN 1875	08:244
JENKINS, WILLIAM A & ROTHGEB, TENA	29 AUG 1886	12:382
JENKINS, WILLIAM W & ALESTOCK, MARY	26 MAR 1871	07:069
JENKS, WILLIAM R & AMSBERRY, MARGARET E	26 SEP 1871	07:170
JENNINGS, FRANK & DEEM, LETTIE L	04 AUG 1910	13:124
JESSE, WILLIAM R & GARDNER, JANE	02 APR 1907	11:512

Name	Date	Ref
JETER, TINSLEY W & WHITE, MATILDA J	28 MAY 1873	07:354
JETT, CHARLES C & BRYAN, MARY E	05 NOV 1878	10:006
JEWELL, JAMES HENRY & HOFFMAN, VENA	19 OCT 1914	15:293
JEWELL, JESSE E & IHLE, CORA M	04 MAY 1910	13:056
JEWELL, MATHIAS & BOWEN, (Mrs) RACHEL A	09 FEB 1914	15:138
JEWELL, WILLIAM & ROUSH, MARY A	20 APR 1887	05:014
JIBBEAUT, EMMA & WHITTINGTON, BESS	28 MAY 1902	10:081
JILES, BENJAMIN & HANES, LILLIE	30 MAR 1893	06:510
JINKENS, H BEN & MILLER, SARAH E	14 SEP 1870	06:225
JIVIDEN, AARON & BAILEY, SARAH IDA	21 MAY 1893	06:542
JIVIDEN, EZEKIEL & BARNETT, ELIZA JANE	*21 FEB 1860	02:013
JIVIDEN, EZEKIEL & BENNETT, JOAN	22 AUG 1901	09:390
JIVIDEN, EZEKIEL M & HILL, RINNA M	18 AUG 1901	09:366
JIVIDEN, EZEKIEL V & SMITH, LINNIE	20 JAN 1902	10:009
JIVIDEN, GEORGE & HUGHES, LIZZIE	02 OCT 1903	10:379
JIVIDEN, HORACE & LITTLE, FREDA	15 NOV 1913	15:069
JIVIDEN, JOHN & BUCK, OLETHA	03 MAR 1870	06:161
JIVIDEN, JOHN & CHAPMAN, MARY	29 SEP 1890	05:620
JIVIDEN, JOHN & RICHIE, DANIE	08 JAN 1903	10:223
JIVIDEN, JOHN D & WAUGH, VIRGINIA B	28 OCT 1888	05:297
JIVIDEN, JONATHAN & CRAIG, MARY	29 OCT 1907	12:057
JIVIDEN, JONATHAN & SEARLS, M J	*29 MAR 1861	02:015
JIVIDEN, JONATHAN & CRAIG, MARY A	19 MAY 1904	10:522
JIVIDEN, JONATHAN & WARNER, BELLE	09 SEP 1907	12:006
JIVIDEN, JONATHAN & CRAIG, ORA	*26 AUG 1910	13:145
JIVIDEN, O L & FORBUS, VIOLA	13 JUN 1909	12:425
JIVIDEN, R C & McCOY, ORA	21 APR 1910	13:048
JIVIDEN, ROSCOE & LITTLE, ELVA	19 SEP 1908	12:264
JIVIDEN, RUTHERFORD & BAILEY, ALICE P	25 NOV 1895	07:437
JIVIDEN, WADE & LUH, IDA	31 MAR 1898	08:275
JIVIDEN, WILLIAM & HILL, HETTIE E	09 JAN 1905	11:028
JOACHIM, J P & PRICE, STELLA	17 JUL 1912	13:566
JOHNS, FRANK S & BARNETT, LOTTIE	27 AUG 1909	12:490
JOHNSON, ALBERT W & SWANN, ANNIE G	22 NOV 1905	11:209
JOHNSON, ALEXANDER & BOOTH, SARAH J	05 NOV 1882	11:241
JOHNSON, ANDREW & EDWARDS, MARIA E	10 APR 1887	05:002
JOHNSON, ASA S & EDWARDS, HENRIETTA	24 OCT 1864	03:203
JOHNSON, CHARLES & MOURNING, ORA E	07 OCT 1914	15:288
JOHNSON, CHARLES AUGUSTUS & JONES, MINNIE	14 APR 1892	06:324
JOHNSON, CHARLES H & CROOKHAM, MAUD M	03 JUL 1893	06:564
JOHNSON, CLYDE & STEENBERGEN, FRANCES	16 AUR 1906	11:391
JOHNSON, DAVID & MULFORD, JANE	APR 1845	01:049
JOHNSON, DAVID L & SPROUSE, NANCY E	29 DEC 1898	08:258
JOHNSON, DAVID LEWIS & JOHNSON, IDA MAY	02 SEP 1880	10:297
JOHNSON, DAVID M & COOPER, LUCY M	21 JAN 1890	05:514
JOHNSON, EDGAR & HESSON, CLARA	03 NOV 1913	15:062
JOHNSON, ELI & YEAGER, CATHARINE	23 NOV 1843	01:038
JOHNSON, ELMORE & BURK, MARY C	17 JAN 1876	11:209
JOHNSON, FERDINAND D & HELLEMS, MARGARET	14 JUN 1893	06:553
JOHNSON, GEORGE & COLEMAN, MARGARET	28 DEC 1871	07:165
JOHNSON, GEORGE & RUNNION, BETSY	30 MAR 1868	05:158
JOHNSON, GEORGE FRANKLIN & YEAGER, MAGGIE LEE	09 MAR 1992	06:303
JOHNSON, GEORGE W & KNAPP, ROENA	25 JUL 1900	09:160
JOHNSON, H R & SHAIN, IDA	22 AUG 1886	12:377
JOHNSON, HARVEY & STEWARD, NANNIE E	29 SEP 1907	12:023
JOHNSON, HENRY & ZERCKEL, HANNAH MARY	20 FEB 1851	02:001
JOHNSON, HENRY & BROWN, MARY C	27 FEB 1870	06:160
JOHNSON, HENRY & LEE, IDA	20 JUN 1882	11:164

Name	Date	Ref
JOHNSON, HENRY A & FURTH, MARTHA	23 JAN 1878	09:198
JOHNSON, J HAMILTON & CLENDINEN, SARAH U	24 FEB 1870	06:155
JOHNSON, JACK & PENCE, MARTHA E	05 AUG 1900	09:170
JOHNSON, JACOB W & CHAPMAN, MARY K	30 JAN 1879	10:047
JOHNSON, JAMES & HARPER, FRANCES	25 JAN 1872	07:184
JOHNSON, JAMES & JOHNSON, ELLEN	09 FEB 1885	12:136
JOHNSON, JAMES A & MARTIN, ANNIE L	06 APR 1887	05:006
JOHNSON, JAMES E & HALFHILL, MINNIE	21 NOV 1903	10:412
JOHNSON, JAMES P & HART, SARAH E	04 OCT 1881	11:029
JOHNSON, JOHN & HARDIN, MARTHA JANE	*19 AUG 1850	02:001
JOHNSON, JOHN & CIRCLE, LUTITIA	19 APR 1878	09:248
JOHNSON, JOHN & WASHINGTON, MINA M	20 OCT 1880	10:314
JOHNSON, JOHN & HUNDLEY, MARTHA S	29 APR 1883	11:329
JOHNSON, JOHN & MIDDLETON, ELIZABETH	21 JAN 1885	12:131
JOHNSON, JOHN C & SMITH, CLEMANTHA J	27 AUG 1908	12:240
JOHNSON, JOHN E & LEWIS, PLENORA S	05 SEP 1878	09:309
JOHNSON, JOHN E & ADKINS, MARY	29 SEP 1879	10:135
JOHNSON, JOHN W & KERWOOD, MARY A	*27 APR 1858	02:011
JOHNSON, JOHN W & PARKER, LAURA M	01 SEP 1861	03:018
JOHNSON, JOHN W & HARRIS, ANNA M	25 DEC 1880	10:349
JOHNSON, LEVI & DIVERS, LELIA	15 JUN 1883	11:356
JOHNSON, LEWIS & BARROWS, AUGUSTA E	20 JUN 1869	06:661
JOHNSON, LEWIS W & JORDAN, GEORGIANNA	20 MAY 1891	06:099
JOHNSON, LORENZO A & SAYRE, (Mrs) ORILLA R	*12 JUN 1854	02:005
JOHNSON, LYNCH & FROST, PATSY	08 JUN 1807	01:002
JOHNSON, MARTIN & EDWARDS, LAURA	29 DEC 1892	06:461
JOHNSON, MARTIN & OLIVER, MAY	16 MAR 1903	10:255
JOHNSON, MARTIN EDWARD ALEXANDER & BYRNE, BETTIE HILL	14 MAY 1896	07:548
JOHNSON, MORRIS H & VAN MATRE, EDNEY F	20 MAY 1905	11:093
JOHNSON, NOAH & ROACH, SOPHIA V	03 NOV 1872	07:285
JOHNSON, OKEY L & ZERKEL, LANORA	20 MAR 1912	13:502
JOHNSON, OLAND & ZERKEL, LUELLA	31 DEC 1902	10:220
JOHNSON, OMER & WRIGHT, DAMIE J	02 MAY 1903	10:280
JOHNSON, OSCAR & HALL, ALMA F	02 AUG 1893	06:582
JOHNSON, OSCAR & VAN MATRE, NORA E	20 JUN 1901	09:358
JOHNSON, PATRICK & SEARLS, SARAH C	10 JUL 1879	10:099
JOHNSON, PHILIP & ROBSON, ELIZABETH	05 SEP 1867	05:076
JOHNSON, RAY & PERRY, GRACE	17 APR 1913	14:122
JOHNSON, REUBEN & WILLIAMS, PATSY	16 DEC 1871	07:154
JOHNSON, RICHARD & ROUSH, MILLIE	04 JUL 1907	11:567
JOHNSON, RICHARD D & PRICE, MINTORA	27 JUN 1878	09:278
JOHNSON, RICHARD JAMES & WILLIAMS, MARY M	02 JUL 1884	12:033
JOHNSON, ROBERT & LINCOLN, JESSIE D	14 DEC 1913	15:087
JOHNSON, ROBERT A & WHALEY, NELLIE F	26 DEC 1911	13:449
JOHNSON, ROMEY R & KENT, URMA E	04 JUL 1910	13:107
JOHNSON, TAYLOR & SMITH, JESSIE	16 JAN 1901	09:277
JOHNSON, THOMAS & ALEXANDER, LOUISA	25 DEC 1845	01:045
JOHNSON, THOMAS & CROSS, MARTHA	29 DEC 1877	09:181
JOHNSON, THOMAS & McCLELLAN, BERT	04 APR 1878	09:240
JOHNSON, THOMAS A & ALLIN, MARTHA	*09 AUG 1858	02:011
JOHNSON, VAN D & VANMETRE, ANNIE M	29 MAR 1888	05:198
JOHNSON, WESLEY & BECHTLE, ELIZA S	02 OCT 1895	07:397
JOHNSON, WILLIAM & STOKELY, ISABEL	18 JAN 1877	09:022
JOHNSON, WILLIAM & ARMSTEAD, EMMA BELLE	28 MAY 1909	12:418
JOHNSON, WILLIAM E & WINKLEY, ADA O	30 NOV 1879	10:170
JOHNSON, WILLIAM E & GUARD, JULIA A	02 JAN 1883	11:289
JOHNSON, WILLIAM E & GIBBS, HANNAH E	24 MAY 1899	08:537
JOHNSON, WILLIAM JAMES & PICKENS, DELLA PEARL	13 APR 1902	10:054

JOHNSON, WILLIAM M & PIERCE, FANNIE	25 MAR 1906	11:283
JOHNSON, WILLIAM W & WHITT, SARAH A	10 OCT 1892	06:422
JOHNSON, WILLIAM H & GRAHAM, DELPHA R	05 MAY 1905	11:088
JOHNSTON, H E & TEETERS, ANNA G	03 MAY 1884	12:012
JOHNSTON, JAMES & VANMATRE, MARGARET	08 APR 1830	01:022
JOHNSTON, JAMES & FIELDER, ELIZABETH	15 APR 1847	01:047
JOHNSTON, JAMES A & GREGORY, SARAH M	14 MAY 1882	11:145
JOHNSTON, JAMES M & LONG, SARAH C	27 JUL 1869	06:067
JOHNSTON, JOSEPH A & GERMAN, MARY	11 MAR 1891	06:075
JOHNSTON, ROBERT C & McMILLEN, ELMA	03 OCT 1899	08:626
JOLLEY, GEORGE W & WATTERSON, LIZZIE	11 JUL 1899	08:571
JOLLY, CHARLES & WILLIAMS, MARY M	22 JUN 1885	12:185
JOLLY, THOMAS E & HANLY, DORA	08 FEB 1893	06:483
JONES, ALFRED P & MOSLEY, MAGGIE	24 SEP 1874	08:160
JONES, ALLEN THURMAN & FRASHIER, EDITH	22 MAR 1908	12:148
JONES, ALONZO & BRIGHT, MARY	22 MAY 1892	06:340
JONES, ANDREW & TROUBAUGH, MARY	25 FEB 1825	01:011
JONES, BENJAMIN & HENSON, SUSANAH	23 NOV 1846	01:046
JONES, BENJAMIN F & ROSEBERRY, MARY MARGARET	26 APR 1848	01:048
JONES, BENJAMIN P & SAYRE, MAY	05 FEB 1873	07:311
JONES, CADWALDER, Jr & McCARTY, JULIA	11 AUG 1886	08:372
JONES, CHARLES & WRIGHT, RHODA	29 NOV 1829	01:022
JONES, CHARLES & SAYRE, ANNIE BELLE	15 JUL 1890	05:591
JONES, CHARLES & CAUFLE, ANNIE	10 NOV 1893	07:004
JONES, CHARLES & SHAFFER, EMMA F	24 JUN 1905	11:117
JONES, CHARLES A & MINTURN, JANE	19 OCT 1848	01:049
JONES, CHARLES A & THORNTON, ODA A	05 SEP 1909	12:493
JONES, CHARLES C & MAYES, SALLIE C	29 JUN 1890	05:578
JONES, CHARLES E & SMITH, FLORA A	*17 AUG 1852	02:003
JONES, CHARLES HENRY & WILES, AMELIA FRANCES	05 JAN 1890	05:508
JONES, CLEVELAND & GREENLEE, IDA E	04 JUL 1907	11:572
JONES, DANIEL & THOMAS, MARGARET	18 MAY 1871	07:087
JONES, DAVID & BYRAM, MARTHA A	20 OCT 1846	01:046
JONES, DAVID & BECK, EMILY	28 NOV 1866	05:006
JONES, DAVID M & KAYLOR, MARY	*17 DEC 1860	02:014
JONES, DAVID WALLACE & NEWELL, MARY	17 NOV 1895	07:427
JONES, EDWARD & HUNTER, CATHARINE	07 FEB 1879	10:053
JONES, EDWARD B & EASTHAM, ALICE L	25 NOV 1891	06:231
JONES, EDWARD R & LANE, ANN ELIZA	28 DEC 1826	01:014
JONES, ERNEST V & MOORE, IVY A	02 DEC 1899	09:026
JONES, GARFIELD & THEVENIN, EDITH A	24 DEC 1899	09:045
JONES, GEORGE & ECKARD, MARTHA MATILDA	*04 NOV 1856	02:009
JONES, GEORGE & PAYNE, LUCINDA	19 OCT 1872	07:279
JONES, GEORGE W & WASHINGTON, EMMA	26 APR 1879	10:083
JONES, GEORGE W & STRIBLING, IDA V	17 JUN 1901	09:355
JONES, GEORGE WILLIAM & WILLIAMS, ELLA MARIA	01 JUN 1887	05:034
JONES, HARRY & CONNER, HAZEL	27 APR 1910	13:053
JONES, IRA C & SMITH, MAMIE E	28 NOV 1907	12:080
JONES, J P & MINTURN, LENA J	24 NOV 1910	13:210
JONES, JAMES & TOLES, JANE	18 NOV 1896	08:002
JONES, JAMES & GILMORE, REBECCA	(no date)	07:301
JONES, JESSIE & GREENLEE, CLARA B	17 OCT 1908	12:288
JONES, JINK & JEFFERS, IMAGENE	28 AUG 1901	09:394
JONES, JOHN & McCALLISTER, ANN	28 APR 1819	01:006
JONES, JOHN & FINICAL, ISIBEL	*21 MAR 1855	02:006
JONES, JOHN & HALL, LUCY	05 APR 1882	11:134
JONES, JOHN H & PARSONS, PEARL	12 MAR 1914	15:155
JONES, JOHN L & ROSEBERRY, FLORA A	18 MAY 1883	11:338

JONES, JOHN N & JONES, AGNES	22 APR 1889	05:389
JONES, JOSEPH H & FOWLER, HARRIET B	*16 OCT 1860	02:014
JONES, L D & HERDMAN, NANNIE J	27 FEB 1897	08:048
JONES, LEWIS & SAYRE, REBECCA	28 AUG 1834	01:028
JONES, MASON & BLESSING JULIANN M	15 FEB 1849	01:051
JONES, MILTON A & SAYRE, ELIZABETH	19 MAR 1846	01:044
JONES, MOSES & SHANG, PRILLA	28 FEB 1841	01:044
JONES, PETER & JAMES, AMANDA	18 SEP 1870	06:229
JONES, PHILIP & ROUSH, EXEVERIA	08 OCT 1874	08:169
JONES, ROBERT & WHITTINGTON, SARAH	11 JUL 1889	05:425
JONES, ROBERT H & ROLAND, MARTHA A	27 JAN 1878	09:205
JONES, SILAS VERNON & SAYRE, LOUISE MARIE	25 AUG 1912	13:587
JONES, THOMAS & TEMPLETON, ELIZABETH	26 FEB 1845	01:044
JONES, THOMAS & ALEXANDER, MARGARET	01 FEB 1846	01:045
JONES, THOMAS & TILLIS, ELLEN	08 SEP 1895	07:381
JONES, THOMAS B & GARDNER, HENRIETTA G	28 JUN 1880	10:273
JONES, W L & DEEM, MARY E	25 DEC 1866	05:016
JONES, WILLIAM & McALLISTER, BETSY	01 SEP 1825	01:011
JONES, WILLIAM & BARNETT, CAROLINE	24 FEB 1892	06:293
JONES, WILLIAM H & NEAL, SARAH ANN	09 APR 1851	02:001
JONES, WILLIAM J & WETZEL, MARGUERITE	24 JAN 1898	08:255
JONES, WILLIAM J D & SHORT, MARY A F	03 AUG 1881	10:435
JONES, WILLIAM ROBERT & CASON, JANE LUCY	10 JAN 1889	05:338
JONES, WILLIAM S & LAYNE, ELLEN F	05 NOV 1884	12:087
JONES, WILLIAM SIMINGTON & RUSSELL, LUELLA	08 SEP 1887	05:089
JONES, WILLIAM THOMAS & POWERS, BARBARA CATHARINE	09 AUG 1888	05:255
JORDAN, ABSOLOM & NEWMAN, MARY C	(no date)	02:012
JORDAN, ALBERT & ELAM, MAGGIE	11 DEC 1895	07:451
JORDAN, ANDREW M & McCOY, MARY	*03 MAR 1856	02:008
JORDAN, ANDREW V & WALLIS, NANCY J	*30 MAR 1856	02:008
JORDAN, ATTISON E & WHITT, HETTIE G	02 AUG 1911	13:350
JORDAN, CHARLES L & BROMFIELD, MAGGIE	06 JUL 1904	10:557
JORDAN, CHARLES W & SLACK, NANCY	15 APR 1894	07:062
JORDAN, CHARLES W & LEWIS, ELVIRA	25 DEC 1896	08:023
JORDAN, CHRISTOPHER C & SHANK, MARY J	13 OCT 1867	05:100
JORDAN, EDWARD CLARK & DAIGH, ANNIE	20 MAR 1895	07:271
JORDAN, EDWARD E & MELTON, SARAH E	26 SEP 1870	07:015
JORDAN, ELI NORRIS & FETTY, EMMA	24 DEC 1914	15:357
JORDAN, F M & BYUS, SIRENEA J	10 MAY 1885	12:172
JORDAN, FINLEY L & SWISHER, LUELLA	02 APR 1904	10:500
JORDAN, GEORGE H & McCARNY, ELLEN	21 DEC 1871	07:161
JORDAN, GEORGE R & NEAL, ALICE	11 APR 1875	08:230
JORDAN, GEORGE S & JONES, JETTIE	22 DEC 1898	08:441
JORDAN, GEORGE S & JOHNSON, LIZZIE	10 OCT 1910	13:181
JORDAN, HARVEY A & POWELL, ROXY A	13 MAY 1900	09:125
JORDAN, J W & SAXTON, BERTHA F	08 SEP 1910	13:153
JORDAN, JAMES A & WAUGH, ALICE	07 NOV 1907	12:062
JORDAN, JAMES B & DAVIS, LAURA B	30 MAR 1897	08:067
JORDAN, JAMES M & HOSKINS, AURILLIA	05 DEC 1910	13:222
JORDAN, JOHN & WOOTEN, MARY MARGARET	22 FEB 1893	06:492
JORDAN, JOHN & RARDON, CARRIE	07 JUL 1900	09:154
JORDAN, JOHN L & McCOY, CATHARINE MARGARET	*04 APR 1853	02:004
JORDAN, JOHN W & SAUNDERS, ELIZABETH F	22 DEC 1870	07:033
JORDAN, JOHN W & GEORGE, ANNIE E	09 MAR 1905	11:057
JORDAN, JOHN W & NIBERT, KITTIE	15 JUL 1905	11:132
JORDAN, JOSEPH & MAYZE, REBECCA	21 MAR 1824	01:010
JORDAN, JOSEPH G & ARNOLD, CLEO	06 SEP 1913	15:027
JORDAN, ORIS V & ROSE, ANNA M	16 SEP 1908	12:262

JORDAN, OSCAR & FISHER, JOSIE	09 OCT 1909	12:524
JORDAN, SAMUEL J & McCOY, JANE ANN	*18 SEP 1856	02:008
JORDAN, SAMUEL L & IRVIN, ELIZA	06 SEP 1883	11:399
JORDAN, SAMUEL W W & JORDAN, EMAZETTA M	23 DEC 1903	10:434
JORDAN, STANDLEY & JEFFRIES, MAHALIA	(no date)	01:027
JORDAN, STANLY & JEFFRESS, MAHALIA	1833	01:039
JORDAN, WELLINGTON H & CARROLL, KATHARINE M	25 DEC 1902	10:217
JORDAN, WILLARD C & CHAMBERS, SALLIE	12 JUN 1906	11:337
JORDAN, WILLIAM & MARTIN, NORA	22 OCT 1911	13:400
JORDAN, WILLIAM A W & McWHORTER, JENNIE	03 MAR 1880	10:219
JORDAN, WILLIAM JASPER & SNYDER, FLOSSIE MAY	25 JAN 1914	15:130
JORDAN, WILLIAM M & TAYLOR, MARY F	13 FEB 1870	06:150
JORDAN, WILLIAM N & AMOSS, DELILA	16 APR 1850	01:051
JORDAN, WINSTON & WOODALL, SARAH	26 MAR 1863	03:111
JORDAN, ANDREW L & FARGO, EMILY C	*19 SEP 1859	02:013
JORDAN, ANDREW V & McCOY, NANCY	*16 MAR 1852	02:002
JORDAN, FOUNTAIN F & MIDDLETON, SARAH E	13 APR 1873	07:342
JORDAN, JAMES J & WRAY, LUCY J	26 DEC 1875	08:310
JORDAN, JOHN & AMES, SARAH	*24 JAN 1856	02:007
JORDAN, JOHN & RIDGEWAY, SUSAN	18 JAN 1879	10:042
JORDAN, JOSEPH & SLACK, MARY	*02 JAN 1856	02:007
JORDAN, NORRIS & TUCKER, ELIZABETH	11 SEP 1873	08:025
JORDAN, THOS V & McCOY, ELIZA F	*01 AUG 1860	02:014
JUDSON, AUSTIN & SMITH, CORA	05 DEC 1914	15:338
JUDSON, CHARLES W & HINKLE, CARRIE	30 AUG 1914	15:263
JUDSON, WILLIAM A & HARRIS, SUSAN M	08 FEB 1881	10:374
JUDSON, WILLIAM Jr & RHODES, CARRIE	22 SEP 1913	15:036
JUDY, FRANK & VOLLERT, SOPHIA B	13 OCT 1886	12:399
JUDY, LUTHER A & STONE, MARY J	07 JUL 1874	08:146
JUHLING, HUGO & HESLOP, MARTHA	19 SEP 1900	09:205
JUHLING, JULIUS HUGO & SHANK, ELIZABETH	26 JUL 1863	03:125
JUHLING, WILLIAM & SHAEFER, ANNIE C	02 FEB 1882	11:105
JURDAN, JAMES & ERWEN, ELIZABETH	20 NOV 1826	01:015
JURDAN, JONATHAN & ERWEN, MARGARET	04 JAN 1827	01:016
JUSTIS, MAJOR M & HUDSON, MARY OLEVIA	19 AUG 1912	13:586
KAIN, DAVID F & KING, MARTHA	06 JUN 1910	13:084
KAIN, WILLIAM & MORRISON, DORA J	08 MAY 1910	13:058
KAIVEN, JNO & McMILLEN, JANE	*04 JUN 1860	02:014
KALLONOWSKI, HARRY & CLARK, LORA	19 OCT 1908	12:290
KANARD, CHARLES E & BAIRD, SARAH J	21 DEC 1901	09:474
KANARD, JOHN H & ROBISON, FLORA I	23 JUN 1895	07:321
KANIFAX, JAMES A & DABNEY, MARY E	03 MAR 1877	09:036
KANTZ, JACOB C & KRANSZ, BARBARA	24 SEP 1876	08:393
KAPP, ISAAC & HARTLEY, MABEL	11 SEP 1912	13:597
KAPP, JAMES O & BAKER, MARY M	20 JUN 1897	08:115
KAPP, JOHN GEORGE & BAKER, MARY E	11 MAR 1879	10:069
KAPP, OSCAR & LIVINGSTON, MINLINDA	25 MAY 1907	11:537
KARNES, RUFUS H & CULP, P LAURA	09 APR 1902	10:041
KARNES, THOMAS & RUCKER, MARY J	03 DEC 1874	08:192
KARR, JOHN M & MURRY, SARAH A	16 NOV 1886	12:424
KASPER, NORMAN A & EAKIN, FANNIE E	27 AUG 1908	12:239
KATES, WILEY & COPAS, ALTA O	24 AUG 1909	12:487
KAUF, JOHN & ROUSH, SARAH E	06 AUG 1865	04:036
KAUFF, GEORGE & MILLS, ANNA	26 DEC 1876	09:013
KAUFF, JOHN & BOWLEN, LEVISA	04 APR 1885	12:157
KAUFF, JOHN & WILSON, JENNIE	21 JUN 1891	06:134
KAUFF, WILLIAM & MILLS, JENNIE	17 DEC 1881	11:070
KAUFMAN, JOHN THOMAS & WHITEHEAD, COLUMBIA JANE	*29 DEC 1856	02:009

KAY, ABLE S & BARR, CHRISTENA	22 MAR 1883	11:312
KAY, CHARLES M & MASON, LENORA	22 JAN 1884	11:451
KAY, ELOY J & LANE, ELIZA	*11 SEP 1858	02:011
KAY, JAMES H & GRIMM, ELIZA JO	*01 SEP 1856	02:008
KAY, JAMES C & McCLAINE, EMMA F	01 AUG 1886	12:367
KAY, JOSEPH A & FRY, MAGGIE L	16 SEP 1900	09:200
KAY, JULIUS & BOYCE, HANNAH	*07 JAN 1861	02:015
KAY, STEPHEN D & GRIM, SARAH J	16 MAR 1879	10:066
KAY, WILLIAM R & FRINLEY, MAGGIE	23 SEP 1903	10:369
KAYLER, JOHN O & GRIMM, FANNIE	24 DEC 1888	05:329
KAYSER, GEORGE E & ADKINS, ROSA A	12 JAN 1883	11:292
KEADLE, WALTER BRADLEY & MILLER, MARY D	14 MAY 1907	11:532
KEARNS, ASA H & SANDS, GEORGIA E	16 FEB 1907	11:496
KEARNS, FREDRICK J & BALL, ORPHA E	16 APR 1902	10:053
KEARNS, GEORGE T & SANDS, AGNES	*09 NOV 1901	09:443
KEARNS, GEORGE T & SANDS, AGNESS	24 SEP 1903	10:371
KEARNS, JESSE & GEE, PHEBE ANN	*24 SEP 1853	02:004
KEARNS, JESSE & PRITCHETT, PHEBE	25 MAR 1835	01:029
KEARNS, JESSE & STEWART, MARTHA M	07 NOV 1871	07:145
KEARNS, JOHN & JOHNSON, NORA	08 OCT 1903	10:378
KEARNS, JOHN T & HOFFMAN, MARGARET	12 JUL 1866	04:139
KEARNS, RICHARD W & HALL, GRACE	24 DEC 1907	12:102
KEARNS, THOMAS JEFFERSON & NICHOLSON, JAINIE DANEAL	26 APR 1893	06:530
KEARNS, WILLIAM & RICE, MARY E	27 SEP 1899	08:623
KEATHLEY, ABRAM O & BOWEN, BETTIE	15 OCT 1871	07:133
KEEFER, BENJAMIN F & WILLIAMS, ALBERT CHRISTENIA	26 MAR 1868	05:156
KEEFER, BURT & ROUSH, CARRIE E	15 AUG 1896	07:590
KEEFER, DANIEL T & KING, REWAMA	01 OCT 1871	07:124
KEEFER, EPHRAIM F & ABSTON, MAGGIE	14 JUL 1907	11:578
KEEFER, JOHN T & KEEFER, ISABELLA	21 MAY 1903	10:292
KEEFER, JOSEPH & STEWART, CLARISSA J	24 AUG 1871	07:113
KEEP, ALONZO J & CLARK, ISABELLA J	09 SEP 1873	08:024
KEESEY, EMMETT & SHAW, BLANCHE	02 JAN 1902	10:001
KEFER, HARRY & ROLLINS, VICTORIA F	02 JUL 1905	11:120
KEFER, HENRY M & CASTO, MARTHA J	30 AUG 1903	10:344
KEIFER, BENJAMIN FRANKLIN & STEWART, ZILPHA	16 DEC 1890	06:020
KEISEL, HENRY & HEIN, JOSEPHINE A	29 APR 1888	05:218
KEISTER, CLAY & McCOY, MYRTLE	*05 DEC 1914	15:339
KEISTER, J WORTHY & HEREFORD, M MARGARET	29 JUN 1904	10:555
KEISTER, WILLIAM J & COBB, LAVINA	07 JUN 1864	03:186
KEISZLING, ANDREW & PICKENS, LAURA	29 OCT 1881	11:041
KEITH, A W & TATE, LUCY O	06 AUG 1883	11:382
KELL, JOHN G & ROLLISON, ANNIE	24 MAY 1883	11:339
KELL, JOHNSON, Jr & HUNTER, ANN	16 AUG 1888	05:258
KELL, SPENCER & KAYLOR, MINNIE	12 MAY 1896	07:545
KELLER, JACOB & THOMPSON, HARRIET	04 MAR 1877	09:037
KELLEY, JACOB & KNIGHT, (Mrs) OAKLEY	24 MAY 1913	14:157
KELLEY, LEWIS J & McCLOUD, VERNA	30 APR 1899	08:518
KELLEY, MARTIN & JAMES, CATHARINE	17 SEP 1869	06:089
KELLING, WALTER G & ROUSH, ANN E	10 SEP 1911	13:372
KELLY, DANIEL & PATTERSON, JENNIE	28 NOV 1886	12:427
KELLY, GEORGE F & NEWMAN, FRANCES	13 APR 1882	11:136
KELLY, JAMES S & STEWART, MARY M	*30 MAY 1855	02:006
KELLY, JOHN W & BROOKS, MARY ELIZABETH	09 AUG 1886	12:374
KELLY, S J & QUICKEL, (Mrs) MARY J	13 NOV 1912	14:028
KELLY, THOMAS & WARD, MARY	22 DEC 1881	11:083
KELSO, ALEXANDER & CLENDENIN, IRIS	21 OCT 1910	12:266
KEMPER, P A C & HARVEY, MARTHA A	24 JAN 1837	01:031

KENDRICK, JOHN F & WALKER, JENNIE	25 DEC 1900	09:263
KENNARD, RICHARD G & VARIAN, MABEL L	30 SEP 1903	10:376
KENNEDY, JOHN & DAVIS, AMANDA J	28 MAY 1871	07:089
KENNEDY, WILLIAM & EDWARDS, OLIVIA	25 MAR 1890	05:553
KENNEDY, WILLIAM R & HESSON, ELIZABETH	22 MAR 1864	03:169
KENNELL, JAMES & McCARTY, MARY A	01 NOV 1878	09:343
KENSLER, BENJAMIN & BALL, MINNIE E	23 NOV 1913	15:071
KENSLER, BENJAMIN FRANKLIN & HALE, CYNTHIA ANN	19 JAN 1910	12:593
KENSLER, WILLIAM A & CHRIST, NANCY J	07 JAN 1880	10:194
KENT, OSCAR A & SANFORD, FLORA E	14 MAR 1894	07:058
KENZEL, GOTTLEB & SHAFER, MARGARET	14 APR 1861	03:002
KENZEL, JOHN G & YAUGER, NANCY J	21 FEB 1884	11:458
KERBY, WILLIAM R & HALL, ETTA	18 DEC 1885	12:266
KERNS, CURTIS E & DUNN, BERTHA	04 DEC 1912	14:037
KERNS, FRANCIS R & HOIT, MARY M	21 DEC 1865	04:087
KERNS, G JOHN & HANLY, ORETHA	24 FEB 1897	08:053
KERNS, JAMES & HARRISON, HARRIET	25 JUN 1840	01:032 5
KERNS, WILLIAM & OLIVER, MARY	17 JUN 1866	04:132
KERR, WILLIAM D & LOCKE, MARTHA M	14 APR 1878	09:245
KERR, WILLIAM H & PIERSOL, ANNIE B	17 AUG 1884	12:042
KERSEY, WALTER & CANTRELL, GERTRUDE	20 DEC 1909	12:574
KERWOOD, CHARLES F & KOSTER, MARY	25 JAN 1876	08:322
KERWOOD, CURTIS & FRANCES, MARTHA	27 JAN 1881	10:371
KERWOOD, E E & McDANIEL, LILLIE B	28 OCT 1883	11:418
KERWOOD, EARLIE W & THOMAS, MAGGIE A	29 MAY 1901	09:348
KERWOOD, EDWARD E & ANDERSON, (Mrs) ELIZABETH	20 NOV 1914	15:323
KERWOOD, ELIJAH KELLEY & SMITH, KATE	12 MAR 1896	07:506
KERWOOD, FRED H & JOHNSON, RUBY	14 OCT 1901	09:422
KERWOOD, GEORGE W & STAATS, CYNTHIA	14 JUL 1872	07:245
KERWOOD, JAMES K & KERWOOD, MARGARET I	*17 APR 1858	02:011
KERWOOD, JOHN & NEWELL, OLEVIA	31 JAN 1909	12:361
KERWOOD, PERRY M & THOMPSON, LOUISETTA	27 DEC 1866	05:014
KERWOOD, RICHARD & TAYLOR, LAURA	27 MAR 1905	11:063
KESSEL, JACOB & JACOBS, LUTITIA	21 JUL 1891	06:149
KESSEL, K VAUGHT & SMITH, MAY	21 SEP 1902	10:157
KESSEL, WILLIAM L & WOODALL, CORA	27 MAY 1896	07:552
KESSELL, JACOB & BOWLES, FRANCES	11 MAR 1830	01:022
KESSELL, JOHN & CASTO, DELILA	23 MAR 1826	01:015
KIBBLE, FREDRICK & WEAVER, CLARA T	26 APR 1905	11:083
KIBLER, ROSCOE R & GLENN, IDA	28 JAN 1902	10:015
KIDDER, WILLIAM B & ROBBINS, HARRIET A	23 NOV 1907	12:073
KIDWELL, EDGAR & VAN SICKLE, NANCY E	12 JUN 1891	06:127
KIEFER, GEORGE W & GRIMES, RHODA A	09 JUL 1894	07:120
KIGER, EVERRETT & HEATHERINGTON, MABEL	08 AUG 1894	07:130
KIGER, ROBERT & WINKLEY, HARRIET B	23 MAY 1866	04:126
KILLINGSWORTH, RICHARD & FIELDER, MAMMIE	29 JUN 1901	09:366
KIMBERLIN, ELIJAH & REYNOLDS, LOUISA ANN	01 JAN 1825	01:011
KIMBERLING, EDGAR & GREENLEE, LUCETTA	30 NOV 1884	12:099
KIMBERLING, ELISHA & HANDLEY, SARAH	03 APR 1845	01:044
KIMBERLING, JAMES & MUSGRAVE, MARY E	25 AUG 1886	12:378
KIMBERLING, JOHN & JACOBS, LIZZIE	28 OCT 1888	05:294
KIMBERLING, JOHN & DOUGLAS, ALICE	22 FEB 1893	06:485
KIMBERLING, JOSEPH & JORDAN, ELIZABETH	18 APR 1867	04:042
KIMBERLING, JOSEPH N & MILLER, RACHEL E	26 SEP 1886	12:391
KIMBERLING, JOSEPH N, Jr & SNYDER, EMMA B	30 DEC 1911	13:457
KIMBERLING, KENNARD & KNAPP, ETHEL	29 NOV 1914	15:331
KIMBERLING, MARCUS & SWON, OLIVIA	22 NOV 1849	01:051
KIMBERLING, MORRIS & BARNETT, MARY	08 OCT 1847	01:047

KIMBERLING, NATHANIEL & CRAIG, MIRIAM	1838	01:041
KIMBERLING, NATHANIEL & BRANNON, MAGGIE L	30 SEP 1893	06:612
KIMBERLING, NATHANIEL & CLENDENIN, MARGARET LUELLA	05 MAY 1903	10:288
KIMBERLING, WILLIAM & HART, RHODA	1836	01:040
KIMBERLING, WILLIAM & DAYLONG, MARANDA	DEC 1840	01:034
KIMBERLING, WILLIAM & FRENCH, ADALINE L	10 DEC 1912	14:047
KIMBERLING, WILLIAM & MAYS, MARY	29 FEB 1848	01:000
KINARD, CHARLES A & ARY, JULIA A	13 APR 1873	07:344
KINCADE, ANDREW J & RAYBURN, CAROLINE	10 FEB 1876	08:323
KINCADE, ANDREW JACKSON & BROWN, CARRIE A	18 FEB 1883	11:298
KINCADE, J C & CULLEN, ARTA	24 DEC 1910	13:245
KINCADE, JOHN G & LEMASTER, LUTITIA	16 OCT 1879	10:147
KINCADE, JOHN G & CLENDENIN, SARAH F	30 NOV 1898	08:420
KINCADE, JUNIUS & HARRIS, CATHARINE	20 NOV 1862	03:090
KINCADE, ROBERT O & LEMASTER, CORNELIA F	24 SEP 1879	10:133
KINCADE, ROY & McCOY, JESSIE	25 DEC 1904	11:010
KINCADE, ANDREW & ECKARD, MARY	15 DEC 1836	01:031
KINCAID, ARTHUR O & HUNTER, ANNA J	27 MAY 1809	12:417
KINCAID, EARL W & STOVER, (Mrs) EMMA JANE	19 DEC 1912	14:046
KINCER, EDWARD & KEYS, LIZZIE	07 JUL 1906	11:364
KINDLE, JOHN F & MATTHEWSON, LEONA M	25 JAN 1906	11:253
KINE, JOHN & OTER, ELIZABETH	07 DEC 1893	07:019
KING, ADAM & JONES, ARLA	05 JUN 1912	13:534
KING, ALBERT F & BATEMAN, SOPHIAH E	20 JUL 1902	10:109
KING, ALBERT Z & HARDWICK, LURANEY C	16 NOV 1865	04:075
KING, ALFRED & EADS, LAVINIA	14 NOV 1878	10:010
KING, ALLEN & MULLEN, ARTIE	13 JUN 1899	08:553
KING, BENJAMIN E & BRANNON, SARAH E	17 AUG 1894	07:134
KING, BENJAMIN FRANKLIN & ADKINS, MARY ANN	09 JUN 1866	12:133
KING, BENJAMIN H & CAIN, DELILAH	05 FEB 1893	06:480
KING, BERTRUM ALONZO & PICKENS, BERTHA ALICE	24 MAR 1901	09:310
KING, CHARLES & STEWART, LENA E	28 MAY 1914	15:203
KING, CHARLES H & MILLER, MYRTLE	05 APR 1905	11:070
KING, CHARLES N & HILL, LOUISA J	12 MAY 1881	10:411
KING, CHARLES T & ZERKEL, AMANDA M	28 OCT 1888	05:296
KING, CHARLES W & SPEARS, VICIE B	10 MAR 1913	14:105
KING, CHARLES W & LEACH, MARY E	18 JUN 1905	11:112
KING, CHAS H & CHEESBREW, CORA MAY	04 AUG 1914	15:249
KING, EARNEST C & PICKENS, CLARA B	09 SEP 1910	13:154
KING, EDIE & SISSELL, ELLA	26 OCT 1903	10:393
KING, ELIJAH & CRUZAN, SUSANNAH	31 DEC 1822	01:009
KING, ELIJAH H & FISHER, LILLIE D	24 SEP 1879	10:131
KING, FRANCIS M & CLEMMES, CATHERINE	28 JUL 1880	10:283
KING, GEO H & CAIN, LULA	16 AUG 1914	15:255
KING, GEORGE H & HICKS, MARY J	18 AUG 1905	11:149
KING, MARLEY & ARCHER, HAZLE	22 JUL 1908	12:218
KING, HARRY J & ROACH, MABEL M	14 SEP 1908	12:280
KING, HENRY & BRICKLES, CYLASKIE	03 FEB 1902	10:016
KING, HENRY J & LANIER, LOVENIA	26 JAN 1881	10:369
KING, HOWARD & CHILDERS, SUSIE	*29 APR 1907	11:521
KING, IRESDELL & HUGHS, NANCY	15 OCT 1829	01:022
KING, ISAAC & GIBBEAUT, CELIA	27 MAY 1877	09:080
KING, J W & STEWART, SARAH E	06 MAY 1909	12:407
KING, JAMES & ROUSH, MAUD M	26 NOV 1873	08:062
KING, JAMES BOOKER & FADELEY, KATE MISSOURI	11 AUG 1887	05:071
KING, JAMES K & ROUSH, NANCY	06 DEC 1866	05:007
KING, JAMES L & VAN SICKLES, KATIE M	11 APR 1896	07:526
KING, JEPSY & BAKER, CLARA	27 JUN 1903	10:311

KING, JOHN & CURRY, DELPHA	31 DEC 1911	13:458
KING, JOHN E & BOYER, IDA M	16 JUL 1899	08:579
KING, JOHN P & FADELEY, JESSIE A	03 SEP 1885	12:218
KING, JOHN T & STOVER, OLLIE M	04 MAR 1892	06:296
KING, JOSEPH & CRAWFORD, MARY	01 OCT 1904	10:608
KING, JOSEPH A & WRAY, ARAMANTHA F	29 AUG 1880	10:291
KING, LEONARD & HUGHS, ELIZABETH	12 SEP 1826	01:015
KING, MORDICAI V & KING, NANCY J	24 OCT 1876	08:404
KING, NEWELL & ROUSH, ELECTA A	26 MAY 1869	06:055
KING, OREN F & McNEILL, BESSIE A	22 JUN 1904	10:541
KING, QUINCY L C & GRAHAM, STELLA M	17 FEB 1897	08:045
KING, ROY & GRAHAM, ADDA A	27 SEP 1914	15:282
KING, SAMUEL W & FENIMORE, HANNAH E	20 APR 1884	12:005
KING, WILLIAM & McCOY, OMA	22 JAN 1905	11:034
KING, WILLIAM ALEXANDER & KING, ELLA F	27 SEP 1885	12:223
KING, WILLIAM E & WRAY, NANCY V	23 DEC 1878	10:024
KING, WILLIAM H & GREENLEE, EMMA F	21 SEP 1873	08:030
KING, WILLIAM L & WALLIS, CYNTHIA ANN	12 MAY 1870	06:191
KINGARY, ABRAHAM & SKEEN, POLLY	03 MAY 1908	01:002
KINNEY, LAWRENCE & BURGESS, ANNE O	29 NOV 1869	06:110
KINSER, MICHAEL & JEFFERS, MARY E	30 AUG 1865	04:447
KINZEL, EDWARD & WALKER, FANNIE	25 JAN 1891	06:051
KINZEL, PHILIP & MERRITT, MATILDA M	15 FEB 1914	15:140
KIRBY, FLAVIUS J & RINGS, LIZZIE	02 SEP 1891	06:176
KIRBY, GEORGE L & RIGGS, MINNIE R	03 JUL 1909	12:447
KIRK, THOMAS & COLWELL, ABBY R	*02 JUN 1851	02:002
KIRK, WILLIAM S & WALLIS, MARGARET J	29 JAN 1890	05:516
KIRKER, JOSEPH E & SMITH, DIMMA S	24 DEC 1906	11:476
KIRKMAN, JERRY & KNAPP, ALICE	16 APR 1908	12:160
KIRKPATRICK, BENJAMIN FRANKLIN & THOMPSON, ALBERTA	04 JUL 1893	06:567
KIRKPATRICK, HIRAM & MORRIS, SUSAN	20 OCT 1894	07:113
KIRWOOD, WILLIAM H & WHITE, DEMARRIS L	24 MAY 1868	05:181
KISAR, JACOB & HOLT, LILLIE	09 OCT 1909	12:526
KISAR, JOHN W & FUGETT, MARY A	10 DEC 1896	08:014
KITE, JAMES P & FRAZIER, MARY E	05 APR 1864	03:173
KITTERMAN, ISAAC & STATTS, ELIZABETH	08 JUN 1820	01:007
KIZER, CHARLES & HART, ELLA	16 JUL 1896	07:580
KLAAS, THOMAS F & ROY, MARY A	24 DEC 1891	06:260
KLINE, WILLIAM M & QUINBY, FANNIE	05 JUN 1878	09:270
KLINGENSMITH, WILLIAM PERCY & MILLER, MARY M	20 JUN 1889	05:415
KLINZING, JOHN E & MILLER, CAROLINE H W	02 AUG 1883	11:380
KNAPP, A L & FORBUS, ORA	06 AUG 1910	13:125
KNAPP, ALBERT W & OLIVER, LELIA V	19 MAY 1881	10:413
KNAPP, BENJAMIN F & GIBSON, MARY J	22 AUG 1894	07:140
KNAPP, BENJAMIN THOMAS & EDMONDS, SALLIE	04 JUL 1900	09:156
KNAPP, CHARLES E & McDANIEL, BIRDIE	09 DEC 1897	08:211
KNAPP, CLARK C & WOODALL, MARY E	21 FEB 1878	09:210
KNAPP, JACOB & HAWKINS, JANE T	12 NOV 1835	01:031
KNAPP, JAMES & NIECE, EMILY VIRGINIA	*01 NOV 1852	02:003
KNAPP, JAMES & GIBBS, ORA M	26 OCT 1904	10:620
KNAPP, JAMES B & WHITTINGTON, ELLA	01 JUN 1907	11:540
KNAPP, JAMES T & GRAY, IDA A	27 DEC 1891	06:262
KNAPP, JESSIE & WHITTINGTON, MAMIE	01 SEP 1905	11:159
KNAPP, JOHN & MAYES, ELIZA Y	19 MAY 1840	01:035
KNAPP, JOHN & CARTRITE, ELIZABETH	21 MAR 1847	02:047
KNAPP, JOHN H & HALL, LEOTTIE	30 APR 1902	10:065
KNAPP, LEE & RICE, MAGGIE M	24 SEP 1905	11:179
KNAPP, LONNIE & McKINEY, DESSIE M	06:SEP 1908	12:246

Name	Date	Ref
KNAPP, M F & EDINGTON, EVA	25 FEB 1884	11:462
KNAPP, MOSES & SMITH, SAMANTHA	24 NOV 1864	03:210
KNAPP, OLIVER A & LAMBERT, DELIA	31 JAN 1884	11:454
KNAPP, PETER & CALDWELL, ANN	26 JAN 1834	01:028
KNAPP, PETER H & JOHNSON, NETTIE	06 SEP 1900	09:191
KNAPP, PHILIP & PECK, CAROLINE	07 FEB 1833	01:028
KNAPP, REUBEN & McDANIEL, SARAH	28 JUL 1842	01:037
KNAPP, ROBERT A & FOWLER, LETTIE M	01 JUL 1891	06:144
KNAPP, SAMUEL & SMITH, RACHAEL	*06 FEB 1858	02:010
KNAPP, SAMUEL L & DEWEESE, IDA C	19 JAN 1896	07:488
KNAPP, SANFORD A & MILLER, MAGGIE	24 AUG 1881	11:003
KNAPP, SQUIRE T & McGARVEY, ELIZA	*02 JUN 1854	02:005
KNAPP, WALTER & MATTOX, NANCY UNORA	21 MAY 1913	14:153
KNAPP, WILLIAM & HERSMAN, LUCINDA	14 APR 1869	06:047
KNAPP, WILLIAM & KNAPP, LUCY	11 MAY 1895	07:300
KNAPP, WILLIAM & DEWEESE, CLARA	31 DEC 1895	07:478
KNAPP, WILLIAM H & SMITH, ANNIE	01 JAN 1897	08:030
KNAPP, WILLIAM H & SHINN, CLARA J	06 JUN 1897	08:108
KNAPP, WILLIAM L & ROUSH, (Mrs) BERTHA E	02 MAR 1914	15:149
KNAPP, WILLIAM SHERMAN & DEWEESE, LUELLA ABIGAL	11 MAR 1888	05:195
KNAPP, WILLIAM W & SMITH, MARY A	*05 DEC 1854	02:006
KNAPPENBERGER, MATTHIAS M & SIGMAN, MALISSA	08 OCT 1892	06:420
KNAPPENBERGER, WILLIAM S & HYATT, CELIA	18 JUL 1889	05:426
KNIGHT, A L & WILLIS, SUSAN F	*03 DEC 1855	02:007
KNIGHT, AUGUST & HUMMELL, MARY A	26 JUN 1876	08:364
KNIGHT, EDWARD P & WILKINSON, ELIZA	01 AUG 1867	05:077
KNIGHT, ELSON & ROSS, ANNA A	24 DEC 1884	12:107
KNIGHT, FREDERICK & SWAIN, GOLDEN	15 DEC 1902	10:208
KNIGHT, GEORGE W & TAYLOR, AMANDA	10 OCT 1872	07:273
KNIGHT, JACOB & COMBS, SALLIE	*02 NOV 1873	08:052
KNIGHT, JAMES L & SWON, LOUISA	*16 FEB 1857	02:009
KNIGHT, ODIE & MEEKS, SADIE	30 NOV 1898	08:422
KNIGHT, ROBERT FREEMAN & HOLT, BARBARA	23 SEP 1891	06:186
KNIGHT, THOMAS H & HARRIS, NELLIE J	20 MAY 1895	07:305
KNIGHT, WALLACE T & HEPPLEWHITE, ANNIE	22 APR 1893	06:526
KNOPP, CHARLES S & LEWIS, ROSE E	13 AUG 1895	07:362
KNOPP, EARNEST G & WHITE, RUTH L	21 JUN 1914	15:222
KNOPP, GEORGE W & WISEMAN, NANCY L	30 MAY 1867	05:052
KNOPP, JACOB & WINDON, ELIZABETH A	11 DEC 1886	03:091
KNOPP, JACOB C & SANDERS, LIZZIE E	12 OCT 1873	08:039
KNOPP, MICHAEL P & CLENDENIN, MAGGIE E	28 FEB 1871	07:058
KNOPP, PETER M & SOMERVILLE, VIRGINIA B	17 MAY 1893	06:540
KNOPP, THOMAS H & LAMBERT, SARAH J	06 MAR 1873	07:328
KNOTT, GEORGE & JOUMELL, (Mrs) MARSHALINE	*24 AUG 1855	02:007
KNOWLES, J F & GWYNN, ELLA BELLE	29 DEC 1910	12:584
KOBLENTZ, HENRY & JENKINS, MAGGIE ELLEN	23 SEP 1882	11:213
KOESTER, WILLIAM H & HUDLIN, FRANCES H	13 JUN 1904	10:536
KOHL, ANDREW & WHITE, MAUD	27 MAY 1897	08:098
KOONS, CARL A & O'NEILL, ALICE	11 OCT 1913	15:048
KOONTZ, HARVEY & STONE, FRANCES	22 AUG 1844	01:042
KOONTZ, JOHN J & THORNTON, ADALINE	02 DEC 1900	09:245
KOUKOSKIA, JNO & ADAMS, MARY M	08 MAY 1875	08:240
KOUNS, GEORGE M & PROSSER, ELIZABETH	05 FEB 1827	01:016
KOUNTZ, HENRY & HOOVER, BETTIE	17 JUL 1883	11:375
KRAFT, CHARLES P & HUNTER, JULIA	19 APR 1904	10:503
KREBBS, DANIEL W & WORRELL, MINNIE J	19 MAR 1902	10:036
KREBS, CHARLES & STEWART, SARAH JANE	*12 SEP 1857	02:010
KREBS, HARRY L & GREENLEE, MARY ETHEL	03 MAY 1913	14:138

Names	Date	Ref
KREBS, SAMUEL & SMITH, LONA	25 MAR 1891	06:084
KREBS, VALENTINE & HERDMAN, MARY J	03 APR 1905	11:068
KREPS, JOSHUA & TAYLOR, MATILDA E	14 JAN 1877	06:021
KRIEG, MARCELLUS K & FRAZIER, HARRIET S	17 MAR 1804	10:493
KUHN, JACOB C & FRANKLIN, FANNIE L	09 DEC 1874	08:194
KUNTZ, CHRISTIAN & FRANZ, MARY	03 JUN 1873	08:002
KUPPINGER, CHRIS & WILLIAMS, MARTHA J	09 MAR 1881	10:384
KUPPINGER, GEORGE H & KEARNS, NETTIE E	30 JUN 1878	09:277
LAFERTY, ARTHUR H M & SNIFF, MARY	22 JUL 1888	05:250
LAIDLEY, MADISON M & SMITH, FANNIE M	27 SEP 1881	11:026
LAINE, NATHAN & BOOTH, ANN	23 NOV 1891	06:230
LAKIN, FINNEY LEE & TYLER, CHARLOTTE BEVERLEY	11 JUN 1914	15:213
LALANCE, JOHN & SHERWOOD, SARAH	10 JUN 1830	01:022
LALLANCE, PETER & BOGGESS, MARGARET A	01 MAY 1834	01:028
LALLANCE, SAML & PARK, MARY A	*01 SEP 1857	02:010
LAMASTER, BENJAMIN & GREER, JANE	19 APR 1826	01:013
LAMB, JOSEPH & GILLIS, MARY ANN	18 OCT 1884	03:201
LAMBERT, ANDY & GARDNER, EVA	06 MAR 1911	13:497
LAMBERT, CHARLES C & BARNETT, SARAH	11 DEC 1886	12:438
LAMBERT, DENNIS B & STONE, FRANCES J	27 JUN 1903	10:307
LAMBERT, EDWARD & LONG, LIZZIE	15 AUG 1898	08:344
LAMBERT, J F & MEADOWS, BERTHA	01 OCT 1910	13:173
LAMBERT, JASPER & FRAZIER, CARRIE	22 JUN 1904	10:544
LAMBERT, JOHN HENRY & NIBERT, TINA LURE	23 APR 1913	14:129
LAMBERT, JOHN L & WILSON, ALLIE	29 APR 1908	12:172
LAMBERT, PLEASANT & HOLLY, M ELIZABETH	*22 APR 1889	05:388
LAMBERT, THOMAS LEE & SINES, MARY ELIZABETH	22 JUN 1890	05:575
LAMBERT, WALTER & NIBERT, GRACIE	23 APR 1913	14:130
LAMBOY, ADAM & RUTSCHMIER, MARY A	25 JAN 1869	06:029
LAMITY, WILLIAM G & POST, LAURA E	22 JUL 1908	12:219
LANDFIELD, HENRY & GARLACH, ELIZABETH	*20 DEC 1876	09:007
LANDRES, ELISHA & SMITH, CATHERINE	12 FEB 1865	03:222
LANE, ALFRED & CALDWELL, LAURA	19 NOV 1896	08:004
LANE, CHESTER H & CREMEANS, MARY E	*26 DEC 1857	02:010
LANE, EARNEST W & KERR, SADIE M	22 OCT 1906	11:437
LANE, JACOB & DAUGHERTY, MARY	10 APR 1828	01:021
LANE, JAMES P & WEAVER, ELIZA	*09 AUG 1854	02:005
LANE, JOHN & BAITY, EMILY	06 OCT 1825	01:014
LANE, JOHN F & LANE, ELIZABETH	06 FEB 1895	07:247
LANE, LEWIS F & NOBLE, RACHEL A	28 JAN 1866	12:266
LANE, MARREL & EDWARDS, LEAH	01 SEP 1881	11:013
LANE, PLEASANT G & WEAVER, ELIZABETH	16 MAR 1865	04:001
LANE, WILLIAM & GREEN, MARY A	09 OCT 1874	08:177
LANE, WILLIAM & RIFFLE, MARTHA F	17 SEP 1905	11:172
LANGLEY, HARRIE M & BLACK, OLLIE M	24 NOV 1907	12:075
LANHAM, GEORGE W & SUMMERS, SAMANTHA	24 MAY 1891	06:114
LANHAM, HARRY C & BROWN, JENNIE S	12 JUN 1894	07:103
LANHAM, JAMES W & MARTIN, IVA M	09 OCT 1907	12:034
LANHAM, RICHARD A & SMITH, MOLLIE	28 DEC 1890	06:026
LANHAM, ROBERT H & SPEARS, MATILDA	30 DEC 1897	08:235
LANIER, BENJAMIN O & GROVES, BELLE	19 DEC 1895	07:459
LANIER, FRANCIS M & SIM, ROSA V	04 MAY 1899	08:527
LANIER, GEORGE M & EDWARDS, MARGARET	23 DEC 1907	12:087
LANIER, HARRY F & PEARSON, FLORENCE	22 DEC 1910	13:233
LANIER, ISAAC N & LEWIS, SARAH L	21 SEP 1886	12:389
LANIER, JAMES L & KING, JUDY	24 DEC 1876	09:005
LANIER, JOHN A D & BUSH, MARY JANE	20 FEB 1862	03:048
LANIER, JOHN P & BLACK, MARY	*03 JUN 1910	13:083

LANIER, JOHN R & DUNCAN, MATILDA J	27 AUG 1885	12:210
LANIER, LEWIS E & KIMBERLING, NANCY	*30 DEC 1850	02:001
LANIER, RICHARD H & ECKARD, MARY ELIZABETH	26 OCT 1889	05:470
LANIER, SHIRLEY B & GORDON, BERTHA	24 AUG 1895	07:370
LANIER, WILLIAM A & GLASSBURN, LULU M	05 AUG 1894	07:129
LAPORT, JAMES & NEALE, LUELLA	05 MAR 1903	10:267
LARIMER, ISAAC C & GREGGORY, EMMA B	25 OCT 1882	11:229
LARIMER, OLIVER C & ASTON, MARIA	09 JUN 1886	12:335
LARK, EDWARD & CHANCY, POLLY	22 AUG 1865	04:044
LARUE, FRANCIS L & BOYCE, ESTELLE JANE	25 MAY 1907	12:535
LARUE, ISAIAH W & COLEMAN, CORDELIA E	04 JUL 1892	06:363
LARUE, JOSHUA R & OLIVER, HARRIET	30 OCT 1879	10:154
LARUE, LEWIS & GIBBS, BLANCH	27 OCT 1901	09:427
LASLEY, HARVEY ANSEL & CARROLL, NELLIE	14 OCT 1893	06:625
LATHAM, CHARLES T & RODGERS, ALMIRA E	19 MAR 1882	11:129
LATHAM, WILLIAM AMOS & STEWART, MAY BELLE	01 DEC 1889	05:489
LATHEY, JOHN TAYLOR & HARRIS, SUSAN JANE	22 AUG 1889	05:434
LATHEY, NORMAN L & REED, RUBY E	16 MAY 1914	15:196
LATHEY, RAYMOND A & HYSELL, MARY E	25 DEC 1906	11:480
LAUDERMILT, WALTER & SMITH, LEATHA ANN	13 MAY 1913	14:146
LAUGHLIN, WILLIAM & BAREMORE, MARY E	26 MAR 1882	11:131
LAUTENSCHLAGER, JOHN & LYER, BARBARA	08 OCT 1872	07:271
LAUTERMILK, ROBERT & HUDSON, HESTER A	*25 SEP 1885	12:226
LAVENDER, FRANK & KEARNS, LIZZIE M	22 APR 1896	07:530
LAVENDER, JOSEPH & MOORE, MARTHA	16 AUG 1904	10:574
LAVENDER, PETER & ERVIN, IDA	14 DEC 1901	09:469
LAVENDER, WILLIAM H & GIBBS, SUSAN A	04 JAN 1869	06:025
LAWHORN, PATRICK H & HENDERSON, MINNIE	25 NOV 1895	07:438
LAWRENCE, CAIN & WEARS, (Mrs) LILLIE	08 OCT 1910	13:178
LAWRENCE, GEORGE & MORROW, JEANETTE	05 DEC 1891	06:240
LAWRENCE, JAMES W & SLACK, SARAH A	09 AUG 1877	09:116
LAWSON, ANDREW P & PULLINS, SARAH A	25 MAR 1875	08:221
LAWSON, GEORGE A & SMART, LAVINIA	01 SEP 1881	11:009
LAWSON, HENRY & HANING, LYDIA J	07 OCT 1879	10:138
LAWSON, J DELBERT & EGGENSCHWILLER, LIZZIE	27 OCT 1897	08:183
LAWSON, JAMES & JONES, JANE	14 JAN 1836	01:029
LAWSON, JOHN H & HENDERSON, HULDAH T	*25 JUN 1858	02:011
LAWSON, LEVI & SPENCER, CATHARINE	07 MAR 1876	08:352
LAWSON, WALTER & ECKARD, MALINDA	29 DEC 1881	11:089
LAWSON, WESLEY LEROY & MUGRIDGE, MINNIE MAY	31 OCT 1893	06:638
LAWSON, WILLIAM & KINCADE, ELIZABETH	21 APR 1870	06:181
LAWSON, WILLIAM & LOVE, EMMA C	21 AUG 1904	10:583
LAWSON, WILLIAM H & VINCENT, EMILY C	26 SEP 1869	06:081
LAWYER, FRANK & COCHRAN, MARY	18 FEB 1882	11:111
LAYNE, ALLEN L & CAPEHART, MAGGIE P	21 MAR 1894	07:063
LAYNE, JESSE & ROUSH, ANNA	01 AUG 1867	05:069
LAYNE, JOHN G & RIGGS, LULA F	28 JUN 1893	06:563
LAYNE, JOSEPH ANDREW & CHESTER, EVA DELIA	14 JAN 1900	09:064
LAYWELL, WILLIAM & COAL, ELIZABETH	*20 JUL 1860	02:014
LEACH, F N & NIBERT, ELIZA J	29 DEC 1886	12:457
LEACH, LAUREN L & KIRKENDALL, SADIE A	05 JUL 1909	12:452
LEACH, OTIS A & GRESHAM, VIRGINIA	05 JUL 1904	10:558
LEACH, WILLIAM H & MULLIN, BERTHA	24 JUN 1912	13:553
LEADMON, WILLIAM T & MILLER, MARGARET E	01 OCT 1882	11:214
LEAGUE, WILLIAM & MARTIN, CATHARINE	1837	01:040
LEAKE, CHARLES P & CLARKSON, MARY E	03 JAN 1886	12:275
LEAKE, ROBERT L & BOWMAN, MATTILDA	24 MAY 1891	06:117
LEAR, EDMAN H & ELKINS, (Mrs) EFFIE M	11 OCT 1912	14:015

Name	Date	Ref
LEBHARDT, C F & REOECH, CATHARINE	31 MAY 1885	12:180
LEDMON, JOHN & ROUSE, BERTHA M	13 OCT 1898	08:385
LEE, AARON & ROBERTS, IDA	05 SEP 1875	08:270
LEE, ALBERT W & MEES, BERTHA S	30 JUN 1904	10:548
LEE, ANDREW P & CHEESBREW, NANCY E	23 FEB 1871	07:056
LEE, BENJAMIN E & PLANTS, MARY F	24 APR 1893	06:527
LEE, CHARLES F & JEFFERS, VIRGIE	08 OCT1900	09:219
LEE, CHARLES W & DAVIS, FRANCES J	21 APR 1870	06:182
LEE, CURTIS & GIBBS, CATHARINE	26 DEC 1905	11:233
LEE, DUDLEY & VAN MATRE, SARAH AMANDA	05 MAY 1867	05:048
LEE, DUDLEY & STAATS, REBECCA C	19 AUG 1873	08:018
LEE, ELIAS F & HERN, MAY	22 SEP 1901	09:411
LEE, ELLSWORTH & CAPEHART, MINNIE	21 SEP 1892	06:412
LEE, FELIX M & WOODS, MARY JANE	22 FEB 1863	03:103
LEE, FELIX & BAKER, ELZENE	01 OCT 1893	06:613
LEE, FELIX & GARBY, LARINDA	16 APR 1902	10:057
LEE, GEORGE FRANKLIN & JONES, ANNIE	24 JUN 1886	12:341
LEE, GEORGE S & STEWART, JULIA A	08 MAR 1866	04:110
LEE, GEORGE S & DAVIS, JULIA	02 NOV 1875	08:292
LEE, GEORGE W & ARMSTEAD, LETITIA	28 SEP 1871	07:125
LEE, GEORGE WASHINGTON & BENNETT, ELLEN	15 OCT 1879	10:146
LEE, JAMES ANDERSON & RHODES, MINERVA	17 SEP 1840	01:032.5
LEE, JAMES R & KERWOOD, EFFIE	03 NOV 1901	09:438
LEE, JOHN & SPROUSE, SUSIE	02 AUG 1896	07:587
LEE, SHULL M & MARY, ELIZA	MAR 1838	01:033
LEE, TAYLOR G & CHAFFIN, CASSEY	07 MAY 1887	05:021
LEE, THEODORE & MONK, ELIZABETH	02 JUL 1897	08:122
LEE, THOMAS & CLARK, MARY ELIZABETH	03 DEC 1887	05:154
LEE, WILLIAM & GARDNER, NANCY ANN	*23 FEB 1856	02:008
LEE, WILLIAM FELIX & SCHOOLS, ANNIE BELL	25 AUG 1892	06:392
LEG, JOHN & HAYS, SARAH	*15 APR 1859	02:012
LEGG, ALFRED & TILLIS, KIZZIE	23 OCT 1897	08:179
LEGG, CLARK & JONES, INA	23 SEP 1905	11:176
LEGG, DAVID & BALL, MARY JANE	*25 APR 1855	02:006
LEGG, ENOCH & McCOY, IDA	17 DEC 1906	11:470
LEGG, ERWIN & KAUFLEY, ROSEY	04 DEC 1898	08:425
LEGG, FLOID & TILLIS, ELZINA	22 DEC 1899	09:040
LEGG, JACOB W & RAYBURN, MATTIE B	24 JUN 1901	09:361
LEGG, LEANDER & RUNION, CHARLOTTE	31 MAR 1897	08:069
LEGG, RICHARD & CLARK, SARAH M	07 JUL 1809	12:453
LEGG, WILLIAM & McCOY, SARAH	23 DEC 1827	01:016
LEGUE, GEORGE S & BOARDMAN, EVA	04 JUL 1906	11:361
LEGUE, JNO & JEFFRIES, POLLY	(no date)	01:027
LEGUE, JOHN & JEFFRESS, MARY	1832	01:039
LEGUE, JOHN WILLIAM & McCOY, BETSEY ANN	14 SEP 1870	06:226
LEGUE, JOHN WILLIAM & McCOY, BETZY ANN	14 SEP 1870	07:002
LEGUE, JOSIAH & ECKARD, JOSEPHINE	18 DEC 1895	07:457
LEGUE, NEWTON & HALL, MARY	20 DEC 1888	05:325
LEGUE, SIMPSON M & STURGEON, MARTHA	20 JAN 1870	06:143
LEGUE, WILLIAM F & COLWELL, LIDDE	18 DEC 1894	07:209
LEGUE, WILLIAM F & SELBY, ROXY	08 OCT 1898	08:381
LEITNER, SAMUEL N & WARD, FLAVIA O	19 APR 1914	15:177
LEKE, ABRAHAM & GUILD, EUPHEMIA	14 DEC 1817	01:003
LEMASTER, ANDREW & ASTON, ELIZABETH	1831	01:026
LEMASTER, ARTHUR J & FIELDER, GERTRUDE	22 NOV 1808	12:308
LEMASTER, BEN & McMAHON, KIZZAIAH	02 NOV 1835	01:029
LEMASTER, CHARLES E & CREE, JERUSHA	21 JAN 1847	01:046
LEMASTER, CHARLES E & McDANIEL, HANNAH	02 DEC 1880	10:340
LEMASTER, FERD H & BOARDMAN, JULIA	01 JUN 1883	11:349

Name	Date	Ref
LEMASTER, GEORGE R & SHEPHERD, MARGARET	*15 DEC 1858	02:011
LEMASTER, H A M & McDERMITT, ANNIE R	10 FEB 1887	12:481
LEMASTER, ISAAC & BUCKALOO, REBECCA A	13 DEC 1871	07:153
LEMASTER, ISAAC, Jr & CRUMP, REBECCA JANE	10 JAN 1864	03:152
LEMASTER, JAMES & MASH, NETTIE	14 JUN 1886	12:232
LEMASTER, JAMES & GIBSON, MARY	01 JUL 1907	11:562
LEMASTER, JAMES B & SLACK, MARY M	21 SEP 1907	12:017
LEMASTER, JAMES G & THOMAS, MARY	*05 JUL 1856	02:008
LEMASTER, JASPER & McDANIEL, CYNTHIA	05 APR 1880	10:232
LEMASTER, JNO D & RHODES, MARY A	*10 JAN 1859	02:012
LEMASTER, JOHN & HAYES, MARY	05 NOV 1911	13:410
LEMASTER, JOHN C & MAYFIELD, OLIVE B	22 DEC 1864	03:213
LEMASTER, JOHN C & KINCADE, VIRGINIA	11 MAY 1869	06:053
LEMASTER, JOHN R & EADS, NANCY C	09 DEC 1896	08:013
LEMASTER, JOHN S & BALLENGER, SALLIE A	18 SEP 1909	12:510
LEMASTER, JOHN T & McCOMBS, ELIZABETH M	28 FEB 1884	11:463
LEMASTER, LEE W & KINCADE, LENA	31 AUG 1898	08:356
LEMASTER, M F & ALEXANDER, (Mrs) RUBY E	23 FEB 1911	13:276
LEMASTER, O L & CRUMP, MARY	NOV 1909	12:557
LEMASTER, PERRY & MEEK, NANCY	*27 JAN 1852	02:002
LEMASTER, RICHARD & NEWELL, BARBARY	1840	01:041
LEMASTER, WILLIAM & LOVE, PERMELIA	*06 DEC 1854	02:006
LEMASTER, WILLIAM & MASH, BETTIE I	19 JUN 1891	06:132
LEMLEY, ANDREW S & ALLEN, LUELLA	19 AUG 1898	08:347
LEMON, DeWITT V & O'LEARY, ANNA C	10 APR 1912	13:511
LENERE, JOSEPH B & HIGGENBOTHAM, ELIZABETH	27 AUG 1873	08:020
LEONARD, CLAUD D & REES, ANNIE B	13 NOV 1905	11:203
LEONARD, HENRY & WALTER, ENOLA	27 OCT 1880	10:319
LEONARD, WILLIAM & GANO, PERMELIA	31 DEC 1891	06:273
LEOPARD, CYRUS & RHODES, MARINDA	02 NOV 1871	07:144
LEPORT, ISAAC & HOPLITE, BERTHA E	30 JUL 1912	13:571
LEPORT, JOHN L M & WISE, MAUD	10 SEP 1903	10:351
LEPORT, THOMAS & JEFFERS, JENNEVA	18 APR 1909	12:400
LERNER, BARNEY J & GINTHER, CAROLINE	23 SEP 1880	10:303
LERNER, WILLIAM F & DAINS, LIZZIE M	30 JUL 1892	06:380
LEWELLYN, GEORGE F & REEVES, HARRIET L	26 MAR 1892	06:312
LEWES, WILLIAM & CLENDENEN, LUCENA	09 MAR 1808	01:001
LEWES, WILLIAM & LANE, PENELOPE	19 FEB 1819	01:004
LEWIS, A H & SHELINE, ROSABELL	27 DEC 1881	11:088
LEWIS, ALLEN & RUSSELL, LOUISA	07 APR 1864	03:175
LEWIS, ANDERSON & DODSON, MARY I	*11 JUN 1860	02:014
LEWIS, B CARL & CORNWELL, NORA B	28 AUG 1905	11:154
LEWIS, BEN T & EDWARDS, NANCY V	22 AUG 1886	12:376
LEWIS, BENJAMIN & STEEL, JANE C	*22 OCT 1860	02:014
LEWIS, C C & ROUSH, MAHALA	*01 AUG 1859	02:012
LEWIS, CAMDEN & EDWARDS, JANE A	02 JUN 1870	06:195
LEWIS, CHARLES A & VILLARS, MARY A	28 NOV 1895	07:434
LEWIS, CHARLES C & STEENBERGEN, ELIZA	07 MAR 1826	01:012
LEWIS, CHARLES C & NEALE, CATHARINE M	11 DEC 1901	09:467
LEWIS, CHARLES E & AMOS, DELILA	03 JAN 1828	01:017
LEWIS, CHARLES E & BOARD, FANNIE	05 SEP 1897	08:154
LEWIS, CHAS E & MAUPIN, EVELYN L	30 JAN 1915	14:089
LEWIS, DAVID H & ADAMS, ANNIE E	11 MAY 1887	05:022
LEWIS, DAVID H & BUCKLE, ALVIRA	25 NOV 1888	05:309
LEWIS, ED & ROBERTS, MARY E	04 APR 1881	10:393
LEWIS, EDWARD & GLASSBURN, EMMA D	30 MAR 1899	08:491
LEWIS, EDWARD L & BANKS, MAHALA FRANCES	26 NOV 1891	06:234

Names	Date	Ref
LEWIS, ELI & LAW, CATHARINE	*06 JUL 1854	02:005
LEWIS, FLEMMING, Jr & AILER, AMERICA	27 DEC 1881	11:090
LEWIS, FRANCIS & SOMERVILLE, JULIA A	25 SEP 1873	08:029
LEWIS, FRANCIS CLAYTON & BUMGARNER, MYRTLE	30 MAY 1809	12:413
LEWIS, FRANKLIN & ECKARD, MARY	24 DEC 1903	10:440
LEWIS, FREDRICK & HOLLEY, MARY JANE	*03 MAR 1857	02:009
LEWIS, FREDRICK W & HOLLY, IDA A	26 APR 1888	05:214
LEWIS, GEORGE & PULLINS, ANN	27 JAN 1831	01:023
LEWIS, GEORGE & SETTLES, GERTRUDE	02 JUN 1910	13:081
LEWIS, GEORGE A & GRAY, MARY E	30 DEC 1885	12:274
LEWIS, GEORGE E & GIBBS, MOLLIE D	21 JUL 1894	07:123
LEWIS, GEORGE H & VANSICKLE, BESSIE	24 NOV 1904	10:643
LEWIS, GEORGE W & EDWARDS, LUCY	20 AUG 1846	01:046
LEWIS, GEORGE W & CORNWELL, NANCY M	24 MAR 1904	10:495
LEWIS, HARRY F & GIBBS, LULA C	22 JAN 1914	14:129
LEWIS, HENRY E & EDWARDS, SULLA	22 JUL 1899	08:583
LEWIS, HOWEL & BURCH, EMILY	1831	01:024
LEWIS, ISAAC & STANFORD, MARGARET	10 JUL 1836	01:030
LEWIS, ISAAC & ROUSH, ROSANNA	*14 OCT 1850	02:001
LEWIS, ISAAC A & FURGUSON, SARAH J	20 FEB 1868	05:144
LEWIS, ISAAC E & HARRIS, CATHARINE	14 MAY 1831	01:023
LEWIS, ISAAC J & WETZEL, ELIZABETH	04 JUL 1877	09:104
LEWIS, J T & RICE, LIDA	11 JAN 1885	12:123
LEWIS, JAMES & YOUNG, (Mrs) MARGARET	*19 JUN 1857	02:010
LEWIS, JAMES A & CONSOLL, IDA	02 SEP 1881	11:011
LEWIS, JAMES C & GREER, ONIE	22 FEB 1883	11:303
LEWIS, JAMES C & HALL, OLLIE W	12 JAN 1896	07:485
LEWIS, JAMES H & McCULLOCH, MARTHA OLIVIA	*12 JUN 1851	02:002
LEWIS, JAMES T & PRIDDY, ANNIE E	09 NOV 1882	11:244
LEWIS, JAMES W & WORKMAN, ELIZABETH J	18 JAN 1880	10:196
LEWIS, JESSE & DOWNS, HANNAH	07 MAY 1896	07:541
LEWIS, JOHN & EDWARDS, BETSY	22 DEC 1829	01:022
LEWIS, JOHN & FORD, ELDA	20 JUL 1909	12:461
LEWIS, JOHN B & CROWE, ELIVIRA	*28 AUG 1854	02:005
LEWIS, JOHN E & RAYBURN, CATHARINE	01 APR 1830	01:022
LEWIS, JOHN H & JONES, CHRISTINA	11 MAR 1907	11:504
LEWIS, JOHN MORGAN & HILL, ALLIE	26 JUN 1889	05:418
LEWIS, JONATHAN & WILLIAMS, MALINDA S	14 OCT 1869	06:097
LEWIS, JOSEPH CLARENCE & SOMERVILLE, CORDELIA	27 FEB 1887	12:484
LEWIS, LEANDER JOSEPH & CREMEANS, ELZA MINTA	20 OCT 1889	05:467
LEWIS, LEOTUS E & KNAPP, SARAH E	06 APR 1902	10:050
LEWIS, LEVI & VANMATRE, MARGARET ANN	21 AUG 1862	03:073
LEWIS, LINN G & SHIVELEY, LEONA B	06 MAR 1889	05:362
LEWIS, LOUIS THOMAS & WEBBER, ORA E	03 APR 1913	14:117
LEWIS, MILES C & BRANNAN, NAOMI	01 SEP 1895	07:374
LEWIS, PETER S & McCULLOCH, MARGARET P	08 AUG 1872	07:251
LEWIS, RILEY W & SMITH, FANNIE S	28 AUG 1879	10:117
LEWIS, ROBERT & BROWN, FANNY	03 MAR 1872	07:202
LEWIS, STEPHEN ALLEN & ROLLINS, LAVINA CATHARINE	06 FEB 1889	05:349
LEWIS, THOMAS J & GWYNN, MARY A	21 APR 1897	08:077
LEWIS, VAN & CART, ELLEN J	30 JAN 1870	06:147
LEWIS, VIRGIL A & STONE, LIZZIE	31 OCT 1886	12:409
LEWIS, WESTON & OSBORN, SUSANNA	*21 JUN 1856	02:008
LEWIS, WILLIAM & WARTH, ELIZA	11 MAY 1826	01:015
LEWIS, WILLIAM & NEICE, LOUISA	21 JAN 1880	10:200
LEWIS, WILLIAM E & HOLLY, MAUD A	10 JUN 1904	10:535
LEWIS, WILLIAM H & MORRISTON, MELISSA	06 APR 1873	07:341
LIETWILER, JOHN J & HAGERMAN, EVA S	10 MAY 1907	11:526

LIETWILLER, ADAM & NEASE, SARAH E	03 JUL 1870	06:204
LIEVING, ALFRED Y & FISHER, BETTIE L	11 JAN 1883	11:288
LIEVING, ELWOOD J & OHLINGER, LUELLA B	20 OCT 1901	09:425
LIEVING, FRANK V & HART, LORENA C	15 MAR 1897	08:058
LIEVING, WALTER E & THOMPSON, ELMA L	03 DEC 1902	10:199
LIGHTER, JASPER T & PULLIN, SELMMA L	23 MAY 1906	11:322
LIGHTER, JOSEPH B & SHIELDS, ADDIE	01 FEB 1891	06:055
LIGHTER, JOSEPH B & RUSK, OLLIE E	28 SEP 1891	06:196
LIGHTNER, WILLIAM & NEEDHAM, ELIZABETH	19 FEB 1804	11:457
LIGON, WILLIAM C & PROSSER, ELIZABETH J	15 NOV 1938	01:032 5
LIKINS, HERBERT E & MOORE, ROSA	24 APR 1905	11:071
LILLICH, JOHN & EDWARDS, CARRIE	23 DEC 1881	11:084
LILLICH, LEWIS & ROBINSON, FANNIE G	28 AUG 1878	09:302
LILLY, CHARLES & LYRE, MAGGIE	18 SEP 1878	09:303
LINCH, ROBERT & THOMAS, MALINDA	16 JUN 1884	12:026
LINCOLN, JAMES C & BATES, ELSIE M	18 JUN 1903	10:322
LINCOLN, JOSEPH & CRAIG, MARIA	07 OCT 1878	09:328
LINCOLN, WALTER RODMAN & CAPEHART, ALICE ELLA	03 JUN 1909	12:422
LINDSAY, JAMES A & WINDLE, SARAH	27 NOV 1892	06:448
LINDSEY, IRA & AYRES, LYDIA M	1833	01:026
LINDSEY, JAMES A & DUNCAN, SARAH	17 DEC 1908	12:325
LINDSEY, JOHN & PILES, MARY	15 OCT 1885	12:235
LINDSEY, JOSEPH & GILMORE, EFFIE	16 MAY 1908	12:179
LINEBAU, JAMES & McCRONEY, SARAH	08 AUG 1886	12:366
LINKFIELD, FRANCIS R & ELMORE, MARY	28 MAY 1846	01:047
LINKFIELD, FRANK & WALLIS, ELLEN	04 FEB 1891	06:056
LINKFIELD, JAMES WALTER & GROVER, SUSAN MALINDA ELLEN	05 NOV 1900	09:234
LINKFIELD, SHELBY L & FRANCE, IDA E	07 MAR 1908	12:139
LINKFIELD, WILLIAM & EDEN, MINNIE	19 DEC 1903	10:431
LINKFIELD, GEORGE Jr & RHODES, MINNIE C	25 NOV 1891	06:232
LINKHART, HENRY FRANKLIN & RAMSEY, MAY	08 NOV 1909	12:540
LINKHART, JOHN C & EDWARDS, SALLY A	23 OCT 1881	11:035
LINNIHAN, MURTY & GUESS, ELLEN	19 OCT 1870	07:016
LINSCOTT, JOHN C & ROUSH, ANNA R	26 MAY 1882	11:154
LISLE, JOHN R & EGGENSCHWILLER, ANNA M	06 DEC 1893	07:018
LISTON, WILSON L & STARKEY, SUSIE	25 SEP 1890	05:617
LITCHFIELD, ALLEN E & SMITH, ESTELLA E	23 DEC 1908	12:336
LITCHFIELD, CHARLES F & CUMPSTON, CORA	15 SEP 1901	09:046
LITCHFIELD, ELISHA & HOWEL, FRANCES E	01 OCT 1871	07:126
LITCHFIELD, ELZA M & TERRY, ELIZA C	24 FEB 1909	12:369
LITCHFIELD, JAMES E & MEADOWS, MINNIESOTA	20 APR 1899	08:512
LITCHFIELD, J E & HONAKER, ADA L	24 NOV 1913	15:075
LITCHFIELD, J H & BALL, ROSIE C	02 OCT 1884	12:066
LITCHFIELD, JAMES L & HUGHES, JEMIMA R	10 AUG 1874	08:172
LITCHFIELD, JOHN M & DONALLY, LETHA	11 OCT 1905	11:188
LITCHFIELD, LAWRENCE & SPEARS, NORA	04 JUL 1914	15:234
LITCHFIELD, LUTHER & FOLDEN, E F	16 DEC 1889	05:493
LITCHFIELD, W EMORY & JEFFERS, LILLIE MAY	31 MAY 1914	15:165
LITCHFIELD, WILLIAM H & SINES, SARAH M	01 AUG 1895	07:354
LITLER, JOSEPH B & LEWIS, ALICE M	23 DEC 1880	10:351
LITTEN, SILAS U & KIDDER, (Mrs) HARRIET A	09 DEC 1912	14:048
LITTLE, DAVID & STATTS, SARAH	16 APR 1818	01:005
LITTLE, DELLA FLOYD & WARNER, ETHEL	28 MAR 1904	10:499
LITTLE, ISAAC & CUNNINGHAM, ELIZABETH	01 SEP 1881	11:012
LITTLE, JAMES W & BOSTIC, ELMA C	20 FEB 1902	10:026
LITTLE, JONAS & CRUZAN, CATHARINE	19 DEC 1822	01:009
LITTLE, LEVERETTE & BENNETT, LOTTIE	25 AUG 1909	12:448
LITTLE, OFA B & WARNER, EMMA	16 JAN 1902	10:005

Names	Date	Reference
LITTLE, OLEY H & HARMON, SEIGOUS A	13 JUL 1902	10:110
LITTLE, REUBEN G & JIVIDEN, LIZZIE	17 FEB 1902	10:024
LITTLE, WESLEY L & BUTCHER, BERTHA H	02 MAR 1907	11:502
LITTLE, WILLIAM H & HUGHS, GRACE	09 FEB 1830	01:022
LITTRELL, JAMES W & DAVAULT, CATHARINE J	24 OCT 1867	05:116
LITTRELL, WILLIAM & SPENGLER, ELIZABETH H	07 APR 1868	05:166
LIVEZEY, JOSEPH & HARBOUR, MARY C	08 MAR 1911	13:286
LIVEZEY, REUBEN A & STALDER, MYRTLE	26 SEP 1899	08:621
LIVING, GEORGE FRANKLIN & ROUSH, SARAH	14 JUL 1892	06:369
LIVING, HENRY & YONKER, SARAH F S	*24 SEP 1859	02:013
LIVINGSTON, ADOLPHUS & HAMBRICK, EMILY S	06 DEC 1877	09:164
LIVINGSTON, ADRA & JORDAN, RILLA	20 FEB 1910	13:013
LIVINGSTON, EBER & HANNIS, KATHERINE D	*11 JUN 1907	11:549
LIVINGSTON, HENRY & KING, ELIZABETH	27 AUG 1871	07:114
LIVINGSTON, WILLIAM & JOHNSON, MARGARET	29 DEC 1872	07:301
LLOYD, JAMES & SMITH, MARGARET	28 APR 1880	10:249
LLOYD, WARREN ERNEST & SHIFLET, ELVERETTA FRANCES	25 DEC 1907	12:108
LOCK, WILLIAM G & TAYLOR, (Mrs) ELZAMINTA	29 SEP 1853	02:004
LOCKART, JOHN & POTTS, MARY	10 MAR 1827	01:016
LOCKE, JAMES H & KENT, MALINDA A	02 SEP 1874	08:157
LOCKE, WILLIAM ANDREW & YOUNG, ARTIE MISHA	29 DEC 1891	06:265
LOCKET, GEORGE & QUINBY, JANE	26 OCT 1871	07:138
LOCKETT, F M & COMPSON, CLARA	24 DEC 1910	13:243
LOCKETT, JAMES & ROSS, VIRGINIA	22 APR 1908	12:164
LOCKETT, JOHN & McCLOUD, ETHA	26 NOV 1898	08:415
LOCKETT, JOHN W & ASTON, MARY A	09 MAY 1876	08:353
LOCKHART, EUGENE & BOWEN, VIRGIE	15 MAY 1902	10:072
LOCKHART, HEIBERT D & ROSE, LUCY	26 SEP 1899	08:620
LOCKHART, JOHN WILLIAM & McGUIRE, ELIZA A	18 JUN 1887	05:044
LOCKHART, ROBERT S & HAMAKER, KATE D	07 JUL 1895	07:336
LOCKOT, FRANK & LEWIS, DAISY L	24 DEC 1899	09:046
LOCKWOOD, R S & MANNING, LILLIAN D	02 JAN 1914	15:115
LOGAN, WILLIAM & PATTERSON, PARTHENA	03 MAR 1901	09:300
LOGGINS, JOSEPH & MUNDELL, RACHEL	*30 DEC 1891	06:271
LONDON, JOSEPH & QUILLEN, MOLLEY	25 NOV 1903	10:414
LONG, BENJAMIN & JOHNSTON, MARY	04 NOV 1819	01:005
LONG, BENJAMIN & EVANS, LYDIA	23 AUG 1827	01:020
LONG, BENJAMIN & HARRIS, SARAH ANN	12 JAN 1853	02:003
LONG, BENJAMIN F & McCLOUD, MALINDA J	15 OCT 1873	08:042
LONG, BRIGHAM & CARROLL, ELLA	27 JUN 1887	05:240
LONG, CHARLES & RAYBURN, CAROLINE	22 AUG 1844	01:045
LONG, CHARLES & HANSON, MINNIE	18 MAR 1887	12:492
LONG, CHARLES D & HOLLIE, MARY	18 AUG 1909	12:483
LONG, CHARLES E & ANGELL, EDNA E	12 AUG 1903	10:336
LONG, CHARLES N & McNEALY, RHUA	23 FEB 1899	08:470
LONG, CHARLES V & CONNOLLY, MAUD M	16 FEB 1900	09:084
LONG, COLUMBUS & BURGESS, NETTIE	31 JAN 1903	10:232
LONG, DAVID & HOLLY, NANCY	05 MAR 1840	01:032.5
LONG, EDMOND & BROWN, REBECCA	*03 NOV 1851	02:002
LONG, FRANK & BRIGHT, LUVINIA S	18 NOV 1902	10:188
LONG, FREDERICK & PIERCE, ALLIE	12 SEP 1899	08:610
LONG, GEORGE W & WITHERS, MARY C	*21 NOV 1859	02:013
LONG, GIDEON & DUDLEY, NANCY	15 JAN 1841	01:033
LONG, HOWARD A & FRUTH, KATHARINE	21 NOV 1914	15:325
LONG, ISAAC & GEORGE, MARGARET ANN	DEC 1840	01:034
LONG, JACKSON & SOMERVILLE, JANE ANN	*20 FEB 1854	02:005
LONG, JAMES & CLEMMENS, ELIZABETH	08 AUG 1886	12:371
LONG, JAMES M & DARNELL, AMERICA S	17 OCT 1867	05:097

LONG, JAMES M & HOGG, MARY F	03 APR 1877	09:057
LONG, JAMES R & SEWELL, CARRIE E	27 NOV 1900	09:241
LONG, JAMES S & KING, LILLIE F	31 DEC 1911	13:459
LONG, JOHN & PATTERSON, BARBARA A	25 JUN 1871	07:098
LONG, JOHN T & SMITH, LIZZIE MAY	02 NOV 1904	10:628
LONG, JONAS & CONRAD, ELIZA A	05 APR 1903	10:265
LONG, JOSEPH & KRAUTER, BARBARA	04 MAY 1905	11:087
LONG, MARTIN & LONG, ANN ELIZA	*22 DEC 1856	02:009
LONG, MATHEW & WALLIS, ALMA	09 FEB 1906	11:259
LONG, PHERSTER & KING, MARY	25 DEC 1910	13:241
LONG, R L & FETTY, GOLDIE E	29 JAN 1914	15:134
LONG, REUBEN L & SIZEMORE, ROSA A	02 OCT 1902	10:166
LONG, ROBERT FRANKLIN & LUTTON, MARY ELEANOR	14 JAN 1886	12:280
LONG, STRAWDER & BRINKER, CAROLINE	30 SEP 1849	01:050
LONG, STRAWDER M & GORDON, MYRTIE L	04 JAN 1909	12:349
LONG, WALTER & COMPSTON, BERTHA	03 FEB 1904	10:470
LONG, WILLIAM A & AYRES, SAVENA	*04 MAY 1858	02:011
LONG, WILLIAM G & SCOTT, MARY B	09 DEC 1881	11:065
LONG, WILLIAM H & JOHNSON, ELLEN	31 AUG 1862	03:076
LONGANECKER, BENJAMIN & NEWELL, MARGARET	05 JUL 1825	01:011
LOOKADOO, RICHARD & COX, MARY E	06 JUL 1883	11:370
LOOKADUE, THOMAS & GARDNER, OLIVIA J	25 DEC 1882	11:280
LOOMIS, JOSEPH V & FRUTH, NORA MAY	01 FEB 1914	15:135
LOOMIS, WILLIAM E & HUMPHREYS, LOUISA	27 DEC 1866	05:012
LOON, WILBERT & GILLESPIE, NORA	01 OCT 1911	13:386
LORING, WILLIAM H & PUTNEY, MINNIE E	24 JUL 1892	06:374
LOTT, HARRISON L & LEMASTERS, ANNA	28 MAY 1914	15:204
LOTT, LUTHER J & SAYRE, EVA	19 JUN 1887	05:045
LOTTERMILK, HERBERT F & SNOW, SALLY	09 MAY 1907	11:527
LOUDENSLAGER, JOHN A & WELLS, MAY G	31 OCT 1880	10:320
LODERMILT, ANDREW & GIBBS, SARAH	01 JAN 1885	12:118
LOUKS, GILBERT N & GILPIN, BLANCH	13 JUN 1895	07:317
LOVE, ARTHUR & GREER, OLLIE	08 SEP 1901	09:401
LOVE, CHARLES FRANKLIN & McGUFFIN, EMMA J	04 NOV 1886	12:415
LOVE, CHARLES FRANKLIN & GREER, NANNIE M	27 JAN 1892	06:281
LOVE, CHRISTOPHER C & ROLLINS, REBECCA	04 JAN 1863	03:096
LOVE, GEORGE & HARRIS, ELIZABETH	*02 MAY 1859	02:012
LOVE, GEORGE & BAKER, DELPHINE	23 APR 1873	07:348
LOVE, GEORGE & ALLENDER, MARIE L	29 JUN 1914	15:227
LOVE, HARRY G & WOLFE, LUELLA MABEL	17 AUG 1910	13:133
LOVE, HENRY & ROUSCH, SARAH	18 JUN 1833	01:027
LOVE, HENRY & WEIGAND, EUNICE	09 APR 1899	08:499
LOVE, HENRY & PICKENS, MARGARET	28 APR 1912	13:519
LOVE, JAMES B & HAWKINS, MAGGIE H	04 APR 1878	09:227
LOVE, JAMES H & KNIGHT, ARTIE M	08 OCT 1892	06:421
LOVE, JAMES S & OLIVER, MARY C	04 JAN 1871	07:038
LOVE, JNO T & RAYBURN, MARY E	*26 FEB 1861	02:015
LOVE, JOHN W & RAYBURN, HATTIE M	02 NOV 1882	11:236
LOVE, LEWIS ALLEN & RAYBURN, DIANA	*28 FEB 1856	02:008
LOVE, LEWIS S & EASTHAM, EMILY	AUG 1838	01:133
LOVE, MORGAN SMITH & ECKARD, LILLIAN	01 DEC 1901	09:463
LOVE, ROBERT J & BURGOYNE, REBECCA J	06 JAN 1870	06:140
LOVE, ROBERT J & ESHFIELD, MARY	03 APR 1881	10:391
LOVE, ROBERT & SAYRE, FLORA	17 JUL 1881	10:429
LOVE, SAMUEL C & BOGGESS, OLIVIA D	23 JUL 1863	03:122
LOVE, WILLIAM & BOGGESS, MARTHA	25 JAN 1830	01:019
LOVE, WILLIAM P & PROFFITT, MARY E F	24 NOV 1864	03:206
LOVE, WILLIAM P & DAUGHERTY, CORA B	16 SEP 1906	11:408

LOVE, WILSON & SINES, CASSIE	06 DEC 1888	05:316
LOVE, (Dr) WILLIAM PRESTON & HAWKINS, JULIA E	22 APR 1886	12:318
LOVEGROVE, GEORGE W & HENRY, MARY	04 JAN 1880	10:188
LOVELLE, JOSEPH & FEENY, MARY A	07 AUG 1877	09:117
LOVELY, THOMAS L & HAWKINS, ALICE N	17 APR 1900	09:111
LOVETT, JOSEPH C & EDWARDS, DRUZILLA	25 DEC 1874	08:198
LOW, SAMUEL & EVERETTE, JANE	19 APR 1826	01:013
LOWDENSLAGER, DANIEL & GEHO, FRANCES A	02 JUL 1883	11:366
LOWE, LORINZO NEWTON & PULLIN, MINNIE ELLEN	24 OCT 1893	06:627
LOWE, WILLIAM & ROLLINS, MARY	09 MAR 1888	05:193
LOWERY, PEARL R & HOWELL, BERTHA V	14 AUG 1896	07:589
LOWRIE, LEWIS W & KNAPP, LORA L	04 MAY 1897	08:089
LOWTHER, ARTHUR WIRT & EMBLETON, JENNIE	21 AUG 1889	05:429
LOYD, JOSEPH & HUGHES, MELINDA	23 JUN 1825	01:014
LOYD, WILBUR & BAILEY, CATHARINE	15 OCT 1904	10:611
LOYER, JOHN & SCHWARTZ, BARBARA	08 APR 1890	05:540
LOZIER, ALBERT & HOLLY, BETTIE J	09 JUN 1877	09:095
LOZIER, ALBERT & CREMEANS, MARY E	09 AUG 1883	11:387
LOZIER, ONA & MEADOWS, LONA MAY	13 JUL 1914	15:238
LOZIER, WILLIAM & KING, CORA E	28 JUL 1905	11:138
LUCAS, JUNIE & BALL, MEARLIE E	01 JUL 1912	13:557
LUCAS, RICHARD & STANLEY, BRIDGET	03 JAN 1819	01:005
LUCAS, WALTER CHARLES & PERRY, LULA MAY	01 JAN 1912	13:462
LUCE, ALGERNON & HART, RHODA E	28 DEC 1871	07:171
LUCKDOO, ELLA & PRICE, KATIE	16 MAY 1906	11:318
LUE, PHILIP & STOVER, IVA MAY	25 SEP 1892	06:413
LUH, BALSER & HILL, LOUISA	15 AUG 1863	03:127
LUH, JASPER & FORREST, MINNIE SABRIE	25 DEC 1887	05:163
LUH, JOHN & HART, JANE	28 DEC 1897	08:231
LUNCEFORD, WILLIAM & GREENLEE, JANE	14 FEB 1825	01:011
LUNSFORD, A FRANK & MOTTS, GERTRUDE	14 SEP 1898	08:365
LUNSFORD, GEORGE & BALL, MOLLIE	14 AUG 1909	12:479
LUNSFORD, JOHN H & McCAULEY, FANNIE M	10 DEC 1873	08:069
LURTON, THOMAS & STEPHENS, JANE	11 JAN 1831	01:025
LUSK, MARVIN E & BARROWS, SARAH E	22 DEC 1878	10:022
LUTE, DANIEL & HAUCK, MAGGIE	19 JAN 1890	05:512
LUTE, MICHAEL & HOWELL, DOROTHY E	11 DEC 1898	08:429
LUTTON, CHARLES & BOILES, DELIA MAY	25 JUN 1910	13:103
LUTTON, FRANK & BURRIS, MARY LEVENIA	17 APR 1899	08:511
LUTTON, MATTHEW & SMITH, MARY MARGARET	28 MAR 1867	05:040
LUTTON, POLLOCK & GREER, MARGARET I	10 SEP 1891	06:180
LUTTON, PRESTON L & EDWARDS, NANCY A	22 NOV 1883	11:426
LUTTON, ROBERT & THOMAS, MARGARET	*26 MAR 1857	02:009
LUTTON, SAMUEL FRANKLIN & SELBY, ELLA	24 MAR 1890	05:601
LUTTON, WILLIAM J & McCANY, MARY E	28 JUL 1872	07:250
LUTTON, WILLIAM J & NEALY, REBECCA	25 JUN 1882	11:167
LYCAN, THOMAS J & LOZIER, MELVINA M	03 DEC 1882	11:264
LYLE, GEORGE T & MENAGER, MARIA L	13 MAY 1879	10:087
LYMAN, ALVIN & McGEE, MARGARET	09 APR 1846	01:045
LYMAN, JAMES N & ASKEW, MARY J	26 SEP 1874	08:164
LYNCH, CARL E & GASKINS, RUBY M	27 APR 1914	15:181
LYNCH, JOHN T & ROBINETTE, MAUDE G	23 APR 1910	13:051
LYNCH, SAMUEL & LYONS, LUANA	25 JAN 1893	06:475
LYNCH, SEWARD & HARSCHBARGER, MINNIE	*09 DEC 1903	10:426
LYNCH, WILLIAM S & HARSHBARGER, NANNIE E	09 DEC 1903	10:433
LYNN, MARSHALL L & McGILL, VIRGINIA LEE	04 NOV 1914	15:316
LYON, ABLE & HILL, SALLY	09 SEP 1830	01:023
LYON, ANDREW JACKSON & HANN, BELLE	15 FEB 1885	12:139

LYONS, DANIEL & ROUSH, ALMA	23 NOV 1902	10:095
LYONS, ENOS BENJAMIN & LAWSON, MARY LEVINIA	11 AUG 1892	06:386
LYONS, GEORGE W & QUICKLE, KEARLIE	03 NOV 1901	09:439
LYONS, HART D & DAVIS, EVA	05 FEB 1897	08:041
LYONS, HENRY Mc & INMAN, URNA F	23 AUG 1894	07:143
LYONS, HIRAM & GILL, HARRIET A	04 JAN 1878	09:191
LYONS, JAMES & KNAPP, MARY M	29 APR 1891	06:101
LYONS, JOHN B & PICKENS, MELISSA M	20 SEP 1882	11:212
LYONS, JOHN B & MILLER, MARY	15 JUN 1907	11:553
LYONS, JOHN W & WILSON, MARGARET E	07 SEP 1865	04:050
LYONS, ROBERT & OHLINGER, EMMA	11 JUL 1894	07:121
LYONS, SAMUEL & THORNTON, MISSOURI	26 SEP 1886	12:393
LYONS, THOMAS & CUNNINGHAM, MINA	31 MAY 1902	10:083
LYONS, WILLIAM & MAYS, NANCY	06 SEP 1838	01:031 5
MacDANIEL, EZEKIEL & HICKMAN, ELEANOR R	10 SEP 1840	01:035
MACE, ROBERT L & GRINSTEAD, JULIA	05 AUG 1875	08:259
MACER, LEWIS & ATKESON, VELLA	31 JAN 1909	12:358
MACER, WILLIAM & SAYRE, OLA	10 NOV 1908	12:303
MACHIR, FRANK & VAN MATRE, ANNIE I	31 DEC 1895	07:477
MACHIR, HARRY & EDWARDS, CYRENA F	05 MAY 1910	13:060
MACHIR, JOHN A & RIFFLE, SARAH E	23 DEC 1880	10:353
MACHIR, JOHN A & McDANIEL, ETTA	27 OCT 1898	08:396
MACHIR, JOSEPH S & BONNETT, HARIET	04 MAR 1847	01:047
MACHIR, PHILIP W & FOWLER, WILLIE G	30 NOV 1893	07:016
MACHIR, WILLIAM H & MACHIR, LAURA V	13 NOV 1862	03:089
MACHIR, WILLIAM H & MACHIR, FANNIE S	23 SEP 1880	10:304
MACK, WILLIAM & NEFF, HATTIE R	14 NOV 1877	09:130
MACKLEY, JAMES W & REYNOLDS, FLORENCE B	03 JUL 1897	08:123
MACKLEY, NEWTON & NEWELL, ELIZABETH	13 JAN 1870	06:141
MACKLEY, STEPHEN L & AICKER, EMMA B	28 DEC 1905	11:238
MADDEY, WILLIAM L & SHAW, MARIA S	*08 DEC 1858	02:011
MADDIN, ALEXANDER & STEPHENS, REBECCA ANN	*23 APR 1853	02:004
MADDOX, HIRAM L & MORRISON, LOUISA	04 OCT 1893	06:618
MADDY, JAMES C & YOUNG, VIRGINIA K	22 SEP 1906	11:418
MADDY, LEWIS L & TYLER, MARGARET LEE	18 MAY 1912	13:530
MADDY, WILLIAM W & REYNOLDS, CORA L	10 JAN 1902	10:002
MAERZ, DANE J & YOUNG, JESSIE	30 OCT 1902	10:181
MAGEE, WILLIAM & FOUGHT, REBECCA	28 MAY 1809	01:002
MAGILL, WILLIAM & JENKINS, GWINNIE	21 SEP 1867	04:099
MAGUET, S S & WITHERS, ELIZA F	27 JUL 1885	12:200
MAHONEY, GRAFTON & PRIDDY, LANA L	05 MAR 1909	12:379
MAIGS, FRANCIS J E & DIDGUS, EMMA A	04 FEB 1905	11:040
MALLORY, BENJAMIN B & HAYMAN, NANCY E	19 JUL 1874	08:148
MALLORY, BENJAMIN BOON & SINES, CATHARINE L	01 MAR 1885	12:135
MALONE, BLUFORD J & McDANIEL, MARY J	28 NOV 1873	08:065
MALONE, BLUFORD JOSEPH & PIERCE, MARY JANE	23 FEB 1885	12:145
MALONE, SAMUEL H & NICHOLSON, SARAH A	09 AUG 1887	05:070
MALONE, THOMAS WOOD & KENNEDY, ANTOINETTE OSBORNE	15 NOV 1894	07:181
MALONE, WILLIAM R & ALEXANDER, SARAH E	14 SEP 1865	04:053
MALONEY, MARTIN & MORARITY, BIDDIE	31 OCT 1883	11:411
MAN, JNO & McDADE, SEANY	11 APR 1821	01:008
MANKIN, THOMAS & VICKERS, (Mrs) LOUISA	*19 JUL 1855	02:007
MANLEY, CLEMENT VANLANDINGHAM & LAVENDER, SARAH	25 MAY 1892	06:343
MANLEY, HARVEY & BUTCHER, ELLEN	19 MAY 1880	10:262
MANLEY, JASPER N & THOMAS, HANNAH M	13 NOV 1894	07:188
MANLEY, VIRGIL S & AUMILLER, LILLIAN M	19 SEP 1910	13:149
MANLY, WILLIAM B & FIELDS, MARGARET A	09 NOV 1904	10:632
MANNING, ADDISON & WHITTINGTON, MARTHA JANE	26 DEC 1846	01:045

Name	Date	Ref
MANNING, DENNIS & MOSGROVE, ANNA	13 AUG 1869	06:069
MANSFIELD, WILLIAM D & SENTERS, JOSEPHINE M	29 MAR 1866	04:113
MANUEL, E L & LAMBERT, LAURA C	20 OCT 1909	12:553
MAPLE, DAVID R & ARNOLD, EFFIE M	21 OCT 1904	10:616
MARCUM, JESSE B & HARMON, CLARA HELEN	17 JUN 1909	12:431
MARION, ELIJAH & SPENCER, JANE	24 AUG 1848	01:050
MARKHAM, CHARLES T & HARBOUR, BERTHA L	04 JUL 1905	11:127
MARKHAM, CLARENCE G & WHITT, ALMA L	17 JUN 1908	12:198
MARKHAM, JOHN E & BIRD, EMILY	22 MAY 1876	08:355
MARKS, PERRY FRENCH & BIRD, JOSIE BELLE	17 JUL 1907	11:581
MARR, CHARLES SHERIDAN & BLESSING, IDA MALINDA	12 JUL 1893	06:572
MARR, ELMER R & SMITH, MALISSA	03 JUL 1905	11:121
MARR, FRANCIS B & BURRIS, SARAH C	02 SEP 1880	10:296
MARR, JOHN W & EDEN, FOREST	22 MAR 1914	15:159
MARR, JONAS & GIBBS, HANNAH L	09 JUL 1902	10:107
MARR, REUBEN F & ROUSH, PHEBE	*22 NOV 1856	02:009
MARSH, JAMES E & ECKARD, MINNIE M	07 APR 1906	11:288
MARSHALL, CHESTER V & RICHEY, RUBY B	24 DEC 1911	13:441
MARSHALL, ERNEST E & WOLFE, RUBY B	04 MAY 1912	13:524
MARSHALL, FENDOLPH & BOZWELL, SUSAN	1843	01:042
MARSHALL, FRED W & GROGAN, MABEL L	10 SEP 1914	15:270
MARSHALL, J WILLIAM & FLAIG, EMMA	17 MAY 1888	05:226
MARSHALL, JOHN B & HALSY, MARY M	22 JUN 1882	11:165
MARSHALL, RADFORD E & McDERMITT, SARAH L	17 JUN 1906	11:343
MARSHALL, THOMAS H & SEBRELL, BLANCHE PRESTON	13 NOV 1888	05:302
MARSHALL, WALTER S & NORVELL, ANNIE	13 MAR 1902	10:034
MARSHALL, WILLIAM ATWILL & McGUFFIN, IDA M	22 JAN 1889	05:342
MARSHALL, WILLIE & JONES, (Mrs) IDA V	26 NOV 1914	15:330
MARTENA, PERRY & AUSTIN, ELCIE	13 APR 1898	08:290
MARTIN, ALBERT ROSS & THOMAS, SARAH MARGARET	28 OCT 1893	06:631
MARTIN, ALFRED & HALBLEIB, MITTIE	30 DEC 1913	15:111
MARTIN, AUGUSTUS L & HAYMAN, FLORA R	*21 APR 1894	07:075
MARTIN, AUGUSTUS L & HAYMAN, FLORA	13 FEB 1895	07:252
MARTIN, CHARLES ADDISON & PADEN, EMMA	06 FEB 1892	06:286
MARTIN, CHARLES E & PATTERSON, POLLEY A	06 AUG 1905	11:141
MARTIN, CHARLES R & FRIDLEY, BARBARA E	29 JUN 1865	04:021
MARTIN, EDWARD D & RAYBURN, SARAH E	19 FEB 1885	12:141
MARTIN, ELMER C & ELIAS, JENNIE	12 JAN 1911	13:259
MARTIN, EMMITT L & HICKS, ETHEL H	07 JAN 1911	13:258
MARTIN, EMORY E & VANSICKLE, MAGGIE E	01 JAN 1905	11:024
MARTIN, FRANCIS A & ADAMS, LUCY E	22 AUG 1865	04:042
MARTIN, GEORGE W & MACE, MARTHA J	20 JAN 1878	09:204
MARTIN, HARRY A & SIMPKINS, LEATHA	09 JUL 1914	15:237
MARTIN, JAMES & GILPIN, MARGARET	13 FEB 1905	11:044
MARTIN, JOHN & HOFFMAN, OLIVIA	1832	01:026
MARTIN, JOHN & CIRCLE, CHARLOTTE M	12 APR 1861	03:001
MARTIN, JOHN & BULMER, ANN	17 JUN 1865	04:020
MARTIN, JOHN DRYDEN & JONES, EDITH MAY	22 SEP 1891	06:188
MARTIN, LINDSAY C & WARD, ORETHA	09 APR 1904	10:509
MARTIN, LUTHER WILLIAM & JORDEN, ELIZA EMILY	21 MAR 1880	10:224
MARTIN, MACK & BADGLEY, NELLIE	14 NOV 1911	13:416
MARTIN, MOSES R & MOORE, (Mrs) NANCY ANN	*28 MAR 1854	02:005
MARTIN, ORVILL & NOWLIN, GARNETT	16 OCT 1907	12:045
MARTIN, PRESTON & WITHERS, SARAH J	04 NOV 1900	09:235
MARTIN, RILEY & HUFFMAN, NANCY	04 FEB 1830	01:019
MARTIN, ROBERT A & HENRY, CORA	11 NOV 1899	09:016
MARTIN, ROBERT T & ALEXANDER, MAMIE C	29 JUL 1885	12:201
MARTIN, SHANNON & CONKLE, SARAH	17 MAR 1908	12:144

MARTIN, THOMAS W & FENIMORE, KATE	28 MAY 1883	11:346
MARTIN, VAN & CAMPBELL, SARENA A	09 APR 1865	04:007
MARTIN, WILLIAM & McCAULEY, MARTHA J	24 JUL 1878	09:290
MARTIN, WILLIAM A & FLORA, THENORA	26 NOV 1893	07:011
MARTIN, WILLIAM ALEXANDER & SOMERVILLE, ELIZABETH BLANCH	26 DEC 1889	05:505
MARTIN, WILLIAM J & GREENLEE, ALICE	10 JUL 1886	12:355
MARTIN, WILLIAM W & LEWIS, LILLY E	24 OCT 1891	06:215
MARTIN, WOODSON & WARNER, SUSAN	29 FEB 1844	01:042
MARTINDILL, MILLARD L & KEISTER, LIZZIE F	26 DEC 1894	07:224
MARTZ, HENRY & WORRELL, SABRE	12 DEC 1904	10:653
MASER, CHARLES & SULLIVAN, REBECCA	06 APR 1902	10:049
MASER, CONRAD & MARTIN, MARY	22 MAR 1903	10:260
MASH, CHARLES & BREWER, TINNIE	04 DEC 1909	12:562
MASH, GEORGE WASHINGTON & FIELDER, ANGELINE JOSEPHINE	13 AUG 1891	06:160
MASH, JACOB & FORDE, AMANDA CATHARINE	24 JAN 1882	06:280
MASH, JAMES & CRUMP, HARRIET E	27 JUL 1884	12:039
MASH, JAMES & WHITTINGTON, DAISY	20 AUG 1910	13:139
MASH, JOSEPH & LEMASTER, FANNIE	29 NOV 1894	07:198
MASH, WILLIAM H & BROFFERD, CATHERINE E	11 OCT 1885	12:231
MASON, CHARLES H & McBRIDE, AMANDA M	22 JUN 1876	08:363
MASON, CHARLES W & FULTZ, MARIA H	24 JUN 1869	06:062
MASON, EDWARD TWINING & SAYRE, MIRIAM VICTORIA	28 JUN 1892	06:356
MASON, ISAAC J & TURNER, ELIZA M	28 SEP 1873	08:034
MASON, JOHN & STRIMBACK, MATILDA	*22 OCT 1860	02:014
MASON, JOHN & LEE, JENNETTE	22 JUL 1878	09:289
MASON, JOHN L & MARTIN, LULIE	03 JUL 1883	11:368
MASON, JOSEPH & ROBINSON, FRANCES A	18 APR 1868	05:171
MASON, LEWIS & EDWARDS, NARCISSA	11 JAN 1849	01:049
MASON, MARCELLOUS C & BRINKER, LUCIE V	24 NOV 1892	06:442
MASON, PHILIP HENRY SHERIDAN & FRANCIS, EMMA	24 DEC 1888	05:328
MASON, THOMAS H & BRYAN, SOPHIA	22 MAR 1819	01:004
MASON, THOMAS H & KNOPP, JESSIE E	27 NOV 1898	08:419
MASON, WILLIAM E & FUNK, CYNTHIA	17 JUL 1881	10:426
MASSIE, FRANCIS M & POOL, EMMA	04 DEC 1894	07:204
MASSIE, OLLIE & DARST, NANNIE MAY	25 NOV 1914	15:328
MATHENEY, DANIEL H & THOMAS, EMMA	24 APR 1906	11:298
MATHENY, J H & PARMER, (Mrs) ELLA	02 NOV 1910	13:197
MATHENY, JERRY A & BAILEY, JULIA O	10 FEB 1890	05:522
MATHENY, JOSEPH H & WALLACE, NORRIS L	29 NOV 1883	11:431
MATHENY, JOSEPH HARVEY & CENTERS, (Mrs) LINNIE	17 FEB 1887	12:482
MATHENY, SEMORE J & COOPER, EFFIE	16 AUG 1899	08:595
MATHENY, SIMON & POSTLEWEIGHT, LUCINDA	13 APR 1876	08:345
MATHEWS, EDWARD P & PARK, (Mrs) MALINDA A	05 JUL 1911	13:341
MATHEWS, GEORGE WASHINGTON & PERRY, MARY ELIZABETH	25 JUL 1887	05:062
MATHEWS, J E & WARNER, VERNA A	17 JUL 1910	13:112
MATHEWS, J R & MURPHY, NORA	15 APR 1912	13:515
MATHEWS, VIRGIL & WARNER, IVA	14 FEB 1909	12:365
MATTHEWS, GEORGE & FRANCIS, MARY	23 JUN 1861	03:008
MATTHEWS, JOHN W & KELL, ANNIE	09 OCT 1884	12:071
MATTHEWS, PHILIP & SHELINE, CATHARINE E	02 MAY 1894	07:086
MATTOCK, TOBIAS & CRUZAN, HARRIET	08 JUL 1830	01:023
MATTOX, ALBERT OTIS & JONES, GENEVA SUSAN	29 JUL 1911	13:336
MATTOX, ALEXANDER L & GREENLEE, SUSAN	23 DEC 1880	10:350
MATTOX, CHAS H & ELLIOTT, CORA	03 JUL 1912	13:560
MATTOX, GEORGE A & OLIVER, AMANDA M	25 MAR 1903	10:261
MATTOX, GIDEON OLIVER & STEELE, HATTIE	02 MAR 1902	10:031
MATTOX, JAMES R & OLIVER, EVA B	27 JUN 1908	12:202
MATTOX, JOSIAH W & VANCE, SUSAN EMILY	*07 JAN 1857	02:009

MATTOX, MATHEW JOSEPH & PLANTS, NANCY JANE	25 OCT 1891	06:213
MATTOX, ROBERT J & HULL, FRANCES C	25 DEC 1898	08:444
MATTOX, T W & PLANTS, MARY J	27 DEC 1883	11:443
MAUPIN, CHAPMAN W & HOPE, MATILDA F	17 JAN 1845	01:044
MAUPIN, COLLIS P H & SULLIVAN, FLORENCE E	21 MAY 1902	10:078
MAUPIN, LINDSAY & AMSDEN, ELVIRA	20 FEB 1849	01:051
MAUPIN, SAMUEL & GILMORE, ELIZABETH	02 NOV 1820	01:007
MAUPIN, SAMUEL MASON AYRES & HOLLOWAY, ANNIE M	04 NOV 1891	06:221
MAVNEY, AMOS & HATHAWAY, LUCY	22 FEB 1821	01:007
MAXON, HIRAM & LONG, NANCY	23 MAR 1838	01:031
MAXWELL, ALRED B & RAYBOULD, MARY M	11 SEP 1881	11:017
MAXWELL, CHARLES L & DABNEY, NORA	18 MAY 1899	08:535
MAXWELL, SAMUEL F & PICKENS, ELIZA A	24 DEC 1879	10:176
MAXWELL, THOMAS P & WHITTEN, FRANCES	12 SEP 1822	01:008
MAXWELL, WILLIAM C & STRIMBACK, MARY M	11 JAN 1877	09:020
MAY, WILLIAM HENRY & WOODS, VIOLA KATHARINE	25 SEP 1887	05:099
MAYS, ALBERT L & HUGHES, MARY F	*03 DEC 1904	10:652
MAYES, CHARLES I & GILMORE, SHIRLEY M	27 DEC 1909	12:585
MAYES, CHARLES WESLEY & SANDS, FRANCES B	23 DEC 1880	10:355
MAYES, GEORGE R & AUSTIN, KATHARYNE L	12 MAY 1909	12:409
MAYES, GEORGE W & NEEDHAM, LILLIE	22 JUL 1898	08:339
MAYES, ISAAC & JAMES, MARY E	09 APR 1904	10:502
MAYES, ISAAC MONROE & LANIER, MARY S	14 FEB 1889	05:350
MAYES, JAMES & CHAPMAN, RHODA	17 MAR 1906	11:282
MAYES, JAMES W & LOCKE, SILOTA B	21 MAY 1882	11:152
MAYES, JOHN WILLIAM & BOUDER, MARY	04 AUG 1887	05:068
MAYES, JOSEPH & RAINEY, OLLIE	22 NOV 1885	12:257
MAYES, LEMUEL & BEARD, DELLA	23 JAN 1900	09:071
MAYES, MATHISON & FLETCHER, JUNE ADA	20 MAR 1899	08:483
MAYES, NICHOLAS & GREEN, MITTIE	24 DEC 1900	09:264
MAYES, ROBERT & TAYLOR, ANNIE L	20 JAN 1912	13:466
MAYES, RUSSELL B & BOOTH, LULA	14 FEB 1912	13:484
MAYES, THOMAS N & HARBER, JANE	09 JAN 1895	07:235
MAYES, W A & ECKARD, NAOMA	04 MAR 1913	14:101
MAYES, WORTHY & WEEKLY, RUBY	31 JUL 1909	12:470
MAYFIELD, WILLIAM & MIDDLECOFF, MARY JANE	20 OCT 1836	01:031
MAYNARD, P B & WEBSTER, GEORGE ANNA	06 APR 1912	13:509
MAYS, CHARLES & MAYS, ELIZABETH J	19 JAN 1848	01:048
MAYS, DAVID & BAUMAN, MARY	16 MAY 1878	09:260
MAYS, GEORGE Jr & EADS, NANCY	12 AUG 1847	01:048
MAYS, GEORGE W & SPENCER, SARAH C	05 JUN 1884	12:022
MAYS, GEORGE W & LAVENDER, ELLEN J	18 MAR 1886	12:305
MAYS, JOHN M & MATHEWS, ELIZABETH M A	*24 FEB 1855	02:006
MAYS, JOSEPH J & HAWTHORN, NANCY E	02 MAY 1875	08:236
MAYS, PHILIP S & LINKFIELD, ALICE	28 DEC 1871	07:174
MAYS, SAMUEL H & HAWTHORN, MARY	02 FEB 1872	07:187
MAYS, THOMAS F & WAUGH, VIRGINIA G	03 JUL 1879	10:098
MAYS, THOMAS F & CALL, MARY L	21 MAR 1901	09:301
MAYSE, BENJAMIN & HAWTHORN, ELIZABETH	11 AUG 1878	09:296
MAYSE, GEORGE W & DOSS, FLORENCE	13 JUL 1908	12:206
MAYSE, PETER S & HUGHS, MARGARET E	12 SEP 1867	05:080
MAYSE, THOMAS & ALEXANDER, FRANCES	1836	01:032
MAYSE, THOMAS & TYLER, MARY F	14 JUN 1846	01:045
MAYSE, WILLIAM W & McDANIEL, NANCY	20 APR 1841	01:035
MAZE, ISAAC & WILSON, BETSY	14 JAN 1812	01:003
MAZE, ISAAC & BATEMAN, SUSANNA	30 SEP 1819	01:004
McADKINS, WILLIAM & EVANS, LORENA	25 SEP 1866	04:153
McALISTER, WILLIAM T & McCOY, EVELINE	1842	01:041

McALLISTER, ARCHIBALD & SIMMONS, LONA MAUD	19 JAN 1911	13:260
McALLISTER, GARRETT & McGRADY, ELIZABETH	02 FEB 1826	01:012
McALLISTER, HUGH & LONG, EVALENE	03 JAN 1917	11:489
McANALLY, JOHN & MOORE, MARY	22 APR 1880	10:240
McARDLE, ARTHUR & STANLEY, LEONA	23 FEB 1909	12:370
McBRIDE, ANDREW & ADKINS, SARAH F	24 DEC 1871	07:157
McBRIDE, AUGUSTUS & HACKET, MARY F	24 DEC 1871	07:156
McBRIDE, CHARLES H & BELL, DELLA	02 JUN 1913	14:165
McBRIDE, HALLECK & ROLLER, EVA C	06 JAN 1895	07:232
McBRIDE, JACOB & WATKINS, ELIZABETH	05 SEP 1878	09:312
McBRIDE, MILTON & HORNER, MARY W	12 NOV 1902	10:186
McCALISTER, PERRY D & GOODALL, SARAH A	09 NOV 1886	12:419
McCALL, ALLEN J & TUCKER, OLIVE J	14 JAN 1893	06:468
McCALL, J S & McCALL, MAGGIE MAY	29 JUL 1909	12:468
McCALLISTER, A HARRISON & BATEMAN, SARAH	03 JUN 1897	08:107
McCALLISTER, ANDREW D & DUNCAN, ELIZABETH L	*30 OCT 1852	02:003
McCALLISTER, ANDREW J & MEADOWS, OLIVIA	26 SEP 1889	05:460
McCALLISTER, C A & CHAPMAN, SARAH E	17 JAN 1906	11:249
McCALLISTER, CALVIN A & SHANK, EMMA E	25 DEC 1893	07:026
McCALLISTER, CALVIN A & DAILY, ELDA E	02 SEP 1908	12:245
McCALLISTER, GEORGE W & ROSE, ALICE J	24 FEB 1887	12:483
McCALLISTER, JOHN & ERVIN, MARIA	22 DEC 1842	01:037
McCALLISTER, JOHN W & SOMERVILLE, REBECCA	06 FEB 1862	03:047
McCALLISTER, NATHAN & HANNAN, JENNIE	04 DEC 1879	10:173
McCALLISTER, ROBERT & BATEMAN, MARY L	08 JAN 1896	07:483
McCALLISTER, THOMAS & McGRADY, MARGARET	13 JAN 1820	01:006
McCALLISTER, WILLIAM J & WHITTINGTON, MARIA	26 DEC 1878	10:027
McCANAHAY, DAN & AUBERRY, (Mrs) ELLA	06 OCT 1909	12:522
McCARDLE, PATRICK F & MULLEN, KATIE A	21 JUN 1891	06:135
McCARL, JAMES & STEELE, ALICE	26 JUL 1890	05:592
McCARLEY, J M & PHILIPS, CYNTHIA ALICE	22 MAY 1913	14:155
McCARTER, GEORGE & YOUNG, DERTHA R	26 NOV 1898	08:416
McCARTY, CHARLES E & CREW, GUSTA	11 NOV 1907	12:069
McCARTY, ELMER E & MEADOWS, OLLIE	26 AUG 1904	10:584
McCARTY, GEORGE NICHOLAS & GORDAN, JESSIE	05 JUN 1889	05:408
McCARTY, JAMES & WHEELER, IVA	26 OCT 1913	15:056
McCARTY, MARTIN EDGAR & DIXON, HANNAH B	23 JUN 1909	12:438
McCARTY, RILEY & ALMAN, KATHARINE	12 FEB 1878	09:213
McCARTY, ROBERT A & HALL, EMMA	04 DEC 1909	12:559
McCARTY, WALTER E & ROGERS, SALLIE S	22 APR 1897	08:082
McCAULEY, WILLIAM B & SELBY, SARAH JANE	*20 JUN 1853	02:004
McCAULEY, WILLIAM HENRY & JONES, BETTIE	11 OCT 1885	12:232
McCLAIN, JOHN & ROUSH, MARGARET	13 MAY 1880	10:256
McCLANACHAN, JOHN R & MAUPIN, ELIZABETH	06 NOV 1828	01:018
McCLANE, MILTON & BROWN, MARY	1832	01:026
McCLANE, U G & JEFFERS, KATIE	14 MAY 1905	11:092
McCLASKEY, C BRYCE & RUSSELL, SAMMA DALE	05 AUG 1913	15:004
McCLASKEY, GROVER & HAWTHORNE, ELIZABETH	17 SEP 1909	12:504
McCLASKIE, JOHN W & HARBOR, LESTA	22 NOV 1910	13:213
McCLASKY, THOMAS A & HENRY, EMMA	28 FEB 1895	07:261
McCLINTICK, REUBEN B & McCLOUD, MARY C	10 AUG 1875	08:264
McCLINTOCK, FRANK B & SAYRE, VETRICE	04 OCT 1909	12:519
McCLOUD, BENJAMIN F & HALL, MARY ANN	18 JUN 1867	05:058
McCLOUD, CURTIS & OLINGER, SUSANNAH	28 APR 1888	05:220
McCLOUD, DAVID & HUDSON, CATHARINE	29 JUN 1867	05:063
McCLOUD, JOHN & ALLEN, JENNIE	03 MAR 1875	08:215
McCLOUD, MADISON & BURROWS, AURILLA	24 SEP 1884	12:063
McCLOUD, PATTERSON & WEBSTER, JENNIE B	20 FEB 1881	10:376

McCLOUD, RADFORD & BARNETT, NANCY J	31 DEC 1868	06:023
McCLOUD, WILLIAM & MARTIN, MARGARET A	12 NOV 1871	07:147
McCLOUD, WILLIAM & NUCKLES, MARTHA	20 OCT 1874	08:175
McCLURE, A L & CAIN, CHRISTENA	28 NOV 1909	12:555
McCLURE, ADAM & BEATTY, MARGARET	16 MAR 1872	07:200
McCLURE, ADAM L & KNAPP, MAKE	21 SEP 1902	10:160
McCLURE, ALEXANDER & SMITH, MANERVA	17 JUN 1893	06:555
McCLURE, JAMES & STEWART, OLLIE	21 OCT 1900	09:226
McCLURE, JAMES H & CAIN, ADALINE	24 AUG 1910	13:141
McCLURE, JOHN & STEWART, SARAH C	23 NOV 1882	11:256
McCLURE, ROBERT E & WOOD, ROSA V	04 AUG 1877	09:115
McCLURE, SAMUEL & McDADE, DORA A	11 JAN 1895	07:236
McCLURG, ANDREW & ANSEL, MAUD W	20 APR 1909	12:401
McCOLLISTER, ISAAC & ERVIN, REBECCA	03 DEC 1835	01:030
McCOLLISTER, JACKSON & CHAPMAN, MINERVA F	31 AUG 1865	04:046
McCOLLISTER, JNO & McGRADY, HETTY	01 JAN 1820	01:007
McCOLLOUGH, FRED P & McNEAR, LINA E	13 NOV 1890	06:005
McCOLLUM, ISAAC J & MORRISON, VELLA M	17 SEP 1903	10:357
McCOMAS, B F & McWHORTER, AMANDA	18 MAR 1874	08:096
McCOMAS, JOHN & SPURLOCK, LOLA	26 DEC 1908	12:340
McCOMB, THOMAS & AMSBARY, JANE	15 JAN 1867	05:020
McCONIHAY, HOWARD E & BRIGHT, EDITH E	27 NOV 1898	08:418
McCONLEY, FRANKLIN P & GIBSON, EFFIE	31 MAR 1901	09:315
McCONNELLY, JAMES & TOLDS, ELIZABETH	20 APR 1875	08:232
McCORD, HORACE MINOR & NEASE, NANNIE LOUISE	22 OCT 1906	11:436
McCORD, WILLIAM & HARPER, CATHARINE	25 OCT 1884	12:081
McCOWN, WILLIAM & WILSON, JERUSHA	1832	01:026
McCOWN, GILBERT & FLESHER, LIDIA	10 MAY 1819	01:006
McCOWN, JOSEPH & HUGHS, PARMELIA	25 SEP 1828	01:018
McCOY, ABNER & STARKEY, ELIABETH	20 NOV 1873	08:056
McCOY, CHRISTOPHER C & FORREST, ORENI	24 DEC 1868	06:022
McCOY, CLAYTON I & SAYRE, HARRIET E	10 JAN 1904	10:459
McCOY, DAVID & NICHOLS, JANE	1831	01:024
McCOY, DAVID Jr & FINNEY, ELIZABETH	FEB 1841	01:034
McCOY, EDWARD & HESSON, MINNIE F	10 JUN 1904	10:534
McCOY, GEORGE & STRAIT, MARY	10 MAY 1878	09:254
McCOY, GEORGE & HERMAN, MURL	02 FEB 1904	10:471
McCOY, GEORGE W & SAYRE, LOUISE	10 MAY 1903	10:284
McCOY, GIDEON F & ROBINSON, LIZZIE	14 MAY 1893	06:537
McCOY, HENRY W & BROWN, ANNIE C	03 AUG 1903	10:331
McCOY, IRVIN & HARDY, EMATELL	1836	01:040
McCOY, ISIAH & McGUIRE, (Mrs) JANE	*28 NOV 1854	02:006
McCOY, JAMES & KING, MARIAH	03 NOV 1881	11:046
McCOY, JAMES B & GIBBS, MARY C	*28 APR 1857	02:009
McCOY, JAMES HERBERT & YOUNG, LILLIE OLIE	21 FEB 1903	10:244
McCOY, JAMES Jr & McDADE, MARY M	16 JAN 1876	08:319
McCOY, JAMES W & WILLIAMS, REBECCA	01 MAY 1875	08:235
McCOY, JOHN & CRAIG, MATILDA	28 AUG 1878	09:300
McCOY, JOHN C & MOORE, SALLIE E	12 SEP 1908	12:257
McCOY, LEWIS & MARTIN, THIRSEY	11 FEB 1830	01:019
McCOY, LEWIS W & YOUNG, MINNIE T	03 JUN 1899	08:545
McCOY, NOAH L & STEWART, BLANCH E	07 APR 1905	11:072
McCOY, R HOLLEY & RAYBURN, LILLIAN ANN	01 APR 1914	15:166
McCOY, SAMUEL & CHANDLER, MARY J	18 NOV 1881	10:331
McCOY, SAMUEL A & COLLIER, NANCY E	17 FEB 1870	06:148
McCOY, SYLVESTIS A & CASTO, UFANNIE B	06 NOV 1907	12:061
McCOY, THOMAS & BLAKE, EMILY	1836	01:040
McCOY, THOMAS J & YOUNG, SUSAN J	18 JUN 1904	10:538

McCOY, WILBER V & WHEATON, MAUD	01 MAR 1899	08:475
McCOY, WILLIAM & SNELL, MARTHA ANN	OCT 1839	01:034
McCOY, WILLIAM & CANADA, MARY	1840	01:041
McCOY, WILLIAM P & STOVER, NETTIE	24 MAR 1881	10:388
McCOY, WM & LEG, RUTH	07 AUG 1820	01:007
McCOY, ZACH & HUGHS, ELIZABETH	19 APR 1847	01:047
McCRACKEN, ISAAC V & WOODRUM, EVA L	04 APR 1994	07:067
McCRAY, JAMES W & PILLOW, LAURA	02 DEC 1914	15:337
McREADY, ALEXANDER & COOPER, MARY PRISCILLA	16 SEP 1849	01:049
McCREERY, WILLIAM H & CLICK, LILLIE	20 AUG 1906	11:394
McCULLOCH, ALEXANDER & STEENBERGEN, MARY E	17 AUG 1834	01:028
McCULLOCH, CHARLES E & CHAPMAN, EMMA	17 DEC 1884	12:100
McCULLOCH, CHARLES E & COUCH, MARGUERITE	07 DEC 1912	14:044
McCULLOCH, CHARLES RUSSEL & BOWYER, NEIDA CHANCELLOR	26 SEP 1906	11:419
McCULLOCH, JAMES A & SOMERVILLE, (Mrs) CATHARINE	*03 OCT 1853	02:004
McCULLOCH, JOHN & BRYAN, MARY	25 JUL 1839	01:031 5
McCULLOCH, JOHN A & BYERS, CORDELIA A	29 OCT 1873	08:048
McCULLOCH, JOHN A & BARBEE, KATE L	03 OCT 1877	09:136
McCULLOCH, JOHN D & LEWIS, SARAH A	25 APR 1866	04:119
McCULLOCH, JOHN S & CLENDENEN, ELIZABETH E	25 DEC 1890	06:026
McCULLOCH, R H & KINCADE, BLANCHE	09 OCT 1909	12:520
McCULLOCH, ROBERT & SAYRE, DELILA	13 MAY 1833	01:027
McCULLOCH, SAMUEL & CREECH, MARTHA ANN	21 APR 1829	01:019
McCULLOCH, SAMUEL S & BIRD, ELIZABETH	14 JAN 1906	11:248
McCULLOM, WADE A & BARNETT, MALISSA	28 SEP 1910	13:168
McCUMBERS, ELIJAH & COTTEREL, MARY	04 JUN 1820	01:006
McCUNE, DANIEL & PIERCE, BETTIE	20 DEC 1899	09:034
McCURDY, HARRY A & KING, VIRGINIA L	27 AUG 1912	13:590
McCUTCHEON, ELISHA C & WILSON, HELLEN P	*25 FEB 1857	02:009
McCUTCHEON, WILLIAM T & BYUS, KATIE	19 AUG 1907	11:594
McDADE, A J & WATSON, DORA A	17 JUN 1891	06:131
McDADE, ALBERT J & SMITH, LUSETTA	04 OCT 1898	08:377
McDADE, BARNEY, Jr & RHOADS, MARY S	17 FEB 1877	09:031
McDADE, FRANK & EDWARDS, GERTIE M	18 FEB 1900	09:086
McDADE, GEORGE & SIMPSON, NANCY E	10 DEC 1865	04:084
McDADE, GEORGE & ROUSH, ROSA	23 JUL 1898	08:338
McDADE, GEORGE B & MATTOX, BARBARA	*09 OCT 1891	06:198
McDADE, GEORGE W B M & KNAPP, CARRIE ESTELLA	25 FEB 1893	06:497
McDADE, JACKSON & ROLLINS, ELIZABETH	*01 SEP 1855	02:007
McDADE, JAMES & STUART, MARGARET	17 MAR 1825	01:012
McDADE, JAMES W & STOVER, LUVENIA	26 APR 1894	07:074
McDADE, JESSE & CASTO, SARAH	03 NOV 1825	01:014
McDADE, SAMUEL & STUART, MARY	18 DEC 1828	01:021
McDADE, SAMUEL C & RHOADS, EMELINE	21 OCT 1894	07:175
McDADE, WILLIAM & OLDAKER, JANE	22 APR 1863	03:113
McDANIEL, ALEXANDER & MARAN, MARY	11 AUG 1842	01:043
McDANIEL, ALEXANDER & EADS, SARAH E	09 JUL 1874	08:147
McDANIEL, ALEXANDER & HIGINBOTHAM, SARAH ELIZABETH	21 MAY 1890	05:561
McDANIEL, AMOS C & WATSON, CORA E	06 FEB 1808	12:127
McDANIEL, ELMER S & FOGLESONG, VIRGIE L	01 AUG 1904	10:598
McDANIEL, GEORGE & FISHER, CATHARINE	03 SEP 1855	02:007
McDANIEL, GEORGE & FRIDLEY, REBECCA J	10 OCT 1867	05:092
McDANIEL, GEORGE C & MOODY, JESSIE	16 MAY 1886	12:327
McDANIEL, GEORGE H & BURRIS, MARY L	17 SEP 1903	10:358
McDANIEL, GEORGE M & JONES, LUCY	31 OCT 1865	04:065
McDANIEL, GEORGE W & KNUCKLES, ROSA	25 DEC 1914	15:358
McDANIEL, HENRY & CALDWELL, SAMANTHA R	*27 MAR 1852	02:002
McDANIEL, JAMES & HULL, MARGARET JANE KYLE	05 DEC 1839	01:034

Name	Date	Ref
McDANIEL, JAMES & GARDNER, MARTHA	23 MAY 1872	07:225
McDANIEL, JAMES & BETTS, BERTHA R	09 JUL 1891	06:148
McDANIEL, JAMES & LEMASTERS, RHODA	20 FEB 1913	14:092
McDANIEL, JAMES HENRY & BARRETT, LILLIE ALMA	21 APR 1899	08:514
McDANIEL, JAMES S & CARTMILL, IDA L	28 MAR 1886	12:310
McDANIEL, JEREMIAH & JOHNSON, MARY A	*09 MAR 1861	02:015
McDANIEL, JEREMIAH & GASKINS, JUDA R	23 MAR 1862	03:054
McDANIEL, JEREMIAH Jr & WOOD, SARAH JANE	10 JUN 1852	02:005
McDANIEL, JOHN & ANDERSON, FLORELLA H	04 MAY 1848	01:050
McDANIEL, JOHN & WOODWARD, ALMIRA CAROLINE	*11 MAR 1854	02:005
McDANIEL, JOHN W & BLESSING, SARAH S	03 NOV 1895	07:421
McDANIEL, JOHN W & FORESHEE, MARY CATHARINE	22 OCT 1899	08:635
McDANIEL, LEONARD & WEST, BESSIE	06 OCT 1900	09:209
McDANIEL, LEWIS & GERMAN, LILLIE	28 SEP 1907	12:014
McDANIEL, O F & McCAULEY, ELLA B	02 APR 1879	10:072
McDANIEL, REUBEN & PROFFITT, FRANCES	28 MAR 1893	06:511
McDANIEL, REUBEN, Jr & HOFFMAN, CLARA E	14 FEB 1894	07:048
McDANIEL, SAMUEL W & DOOLITTLE, MARY C	28 OCT 1883	11:417
McDANIEL, VAN D & BALL, FRANCES E	*21 FEB 1859	02:012
McDANIEL, WILLIAM & MILLER, ANN E	19 JUL 1839	01:033
McDANIEL, WILLIAM & STEEL, CATHARINE	07 JUL 1846	01:045
McDANIEL, WILLIAM & STEWART, ELIZABETH	19 DEC 1861	03:338
McDANIEL, WILLIAM & BENNETT, MARGARET	26 APR 1913	14:134
McDANIEL, WILLIAM C & McDANIEL, GRACE L	15 APR 1883	11:324
McDANIEL, WILLIAM CLAYTON & JONES, MARTHA ANN	22 MAR 1891	06:082
McDANIEL, WILLIAM E & ELLIOTT, MARY E	30 NOV 1881	11:061
McDANIEL, WILLIAM EDGAR & CHAFFIN, MALISA JANE	*28 AUG 1881	11:006
McDERMIT, CHARLES & RAYBURN, MARTHA J	12 JAN 1871	07:043
McDERMIT, JOHN & McCAULEY, ELLA B	02 APR 1879	01:043
McDERMITT, ADAM & RAYBURN, HANNAH	03 DEC 1860	02:014
McDERMITT, ALBERT W & CHAPMAN, NANNIE M	24 AUG 1892	06:389
McDERMITT, ANDREW JOHNSON & STONE, SARAH MINERVA	29 NOV 1891	06:237
McDERMITT, ANDREW P & SHIRLEY, MARY R	*30 DEC 1852	02:003
McDERMITT, C A & LANE, MARY F	26 AUG 1911	13:364
McDERMITT, CALVIN & MARSHALL, MARY A	05 SEP 1867	05:073
McDERMITT, CHARLES E & WINDELS, BERTHA	19 AUG 1901	09:389
McDERMITT, CICERO AMOS & SIMPKINS, LAVENIA	13 SEP 1892	06:407
McDERMITT, GEORGE & COTHERN, NORA	05 AUG 1905	11:140
McDERMITT, GEORGE ERWIN & DEWEES, RUTH	11 FEB 1886	12:292
McDERMITT, GREENBERRY & SMITH, JOSEPHINE C	22 NOV 1866	04:171
McDERMITT, HARRY F & WHITMORE, MINNIE	29 DEC 1906	11:485
McDERMITT, HENRY & STEEL, SARAH A	15 SEP 1881	11:019
McDERMITT, HENRY & STEEL, ELIZABETH	*26 NOV 1855	02:007
McDERMITT, HIRAM & PULLIN, JANE A	04 MAY 1865	04:011
McDERMITT, JAMES M & POWEL, CAROLINE	02 APR 1846	01:046
McDERMITT, JAMES O & CARSON, MOLLIE R	14 APR 1892	06:323
McDERMITT, JAMES S & NICKLE, JANE	25 MAR 1869	06:043
McDERMITT, JEREMIAH & GLOVER, ROSINA	*17 DEC 1851	02:001
McDERMITT, JOHN & ROBINSON, CLARISSA A	08 MAY 1862	03:061
McDERMITT, JOHN & LOVE, MARTHA JANE	03 SEP 1863	03:132
McDERMITT, JOHN & FURGUSON, REBECCA	21 DEC 1876	09:006
McDERMITT, JOHN H & BENNETT, JENNIE A	01 SEP 1881	11:014
McDERMITT, JOHN H & CASEY, STELLA	17 OCT 1908	12:289
McDERMITT, JOHN L & OLIVER, MAUDE E	18 NOV 1911	13:419
McDERMITT, JOHN THOMAS & LOVE, ELLA	28 JAN 1892	06:282
McDERMITT, ODUS & KIRNES, SHALLIE	01 APR 1895	07:272
McDERMITT, ROBERT ORIE & CAIRENS, JESSIE ELLEN	02 MAY 1900	09:121
McDERMITT, SAMUEL & MINICK, JANE ANN	*22 OCT 1855	02:007

McDERMITT, SAMUEL & RAYBURN, SUSAN	15 DEC 1870	07:031
McDERMITT, SAMUEL & FINICON, CLARA	18 MAY 1879	10:089
McDERMITT, SAMUEL & PILCHARD, ANNIE	12 SEP 1882	11:203
McDERMITT, SCOTT & STANLEY, DAISEY	22 MAY 1905	11:095
McDERMITT, SHERMAN M & ROUSH, MARY E	17 JUN 1914	15:216
McDERMITT, SHERMAN T & ROUSH, LAURA A	08 DEC 1886	12:434
McDERMITT, SIMPSON & MILLER, MONIE	13 DEC 1903	10:428
McDERMITT, VALENTINE & SOMMER, MARY CATHARINE	16 AUG 1898	08:345
McDERMITT, VALENTINE H & KINCADE, ADA FRANCES	26 JUN 1910	13:102
McDERMITT, WILLIAM & STONE, ALICE M	04 AUG 1895	07:356
McDERMOTT, GEORGE W & DURST, CORA A	31 DEC 1902	10:221
McDONALD, ELIJAH B & POUNDS, SUSANA	20 JUL 1882	11:177
McDONALD, FRANK B & VAN MATRE, (Mrs) ANNA E	21 JUN 1910	13:096
McDONALD, NEWTON J & ROUSH, SARAH M	11 DEC 1893	07:020
McDONOUGH, WM C & OHLINGER, RUBY J	25 DEC 1912	14:064
McDOWELL, JAMES & HALL, SOPHIA	14 JAN 1819	01:004
McELHANEY, HENRY & HALLEY, BLANCH	31 MAY 1904	10:526
McELHINIRY, HOWARD & GANDY, JESSIE	13 MAR 1909	12:385
McFADDEN, MATHEW THOMAS & JOHNSON, ELLA	29 MAY 1879	10:092
McFARLAND, ANDREW & JONES, LUCETTA	01 MAY 1899	08:523
McFARLAND, DAVID WITH & SCARBERRY, REBECCA	25 APR 1890	05:546
McFARLAND, JOHN & GROVER, MITTIE	29 APR 1889	05:393
McFETTERS, ARTHUR & GREEN, MARY	14 NOV 1898	08:406
McGARVY, GEORGE & SMITH, NANCY	16 APR 1826	01:015
McGEE, SAMPSON & CRAIG, ALICE	26 JUN 1904	10:552
McGHEE, ELZA & DYER, SUSAN	20 AUG 1896	07:596
McGHEE, SAMUEL & WILLIAMS, MARY	06 JUN 1883	11:351
McGLAUGHLIN, HENRY & PARSINGER, JANE	21 AUG 1909	01:002
McGLAUTHLIN, JOHN & YOUNG, FLORA ELLEN	05 MAY 1881	10:323 3
McGLOTHLIN, LEWIS C & KNAPP, MARY J	*20 MAY 1852	02:003
McGRATH, CYRUS D & STEINMETZ, EMMA	29 APR 1901	09:327
McGRAW, ARVIL A & BLAIN, VIRGIE	27 JUL 1913	14:198
McGRAW, GEORGE A & HEDRICK, MARIA J	31 MAR 1870	06:174
McGRAW, J EVERETT & AMOS, HALLIE	18 OCT 1910	13:186
McGRAW, JASPER & HILL, DIANA	30 MAR 1865	04:004
McGRAW, JOHN & CABLE, BLANCH	29 NOV 1899	09:025
McGRAW, OTIS & GRIMM, OSA	20 MAY 1910	13:069
McGREW, EMMETT & CASTO, LYDIA L	06 SEP 1902	10:150
McGREW, JOHN A & BATEMAN, MARY M	09 AUG 1886	12:372
McGREW, JOHN P & SHANK, EUGENE M	05 SEP 1869	06:087
McGREW, LEMUEL B & BRANNAN, MARY M	26 MAY 1877	09:083
McGREW, REUBEN & GILLILAND, SARAH J	*12 SEP 1859	02:013
McGREW, SAMUEL B & MASON, VIRGINIA	25 DEC 1866	05:013
McGRUE, JOHN W & BEARD, ORA G	08 NOV 1896	07:638
McGUCKEN, THOMAS & WHALEY, FANNIE	25 OCT 1893	06:626
McGUFFIN, BRUCE & BROWN, ZENA	19 JUL 1909	12:460
McGUFFIN, FREDRICK C & WHALEY, MARY L	20 DEC 1904	11:003
McGUFFIN, JOHN A & HOGG, MARIA	17 JUN 1873	08:005
McGUFFIN, JOHN F & RAIRDEN, MARY E	21 AUG 1884	12:046
McGUFFIN, JOSEPH E & ECKARD, MATTIE B	15 JUN 1899	08:555
McGUFFIN, ROBERT F & FOWLER, INNEZ L	15 OCT 1914	15:294
McGUFFIN, THOMAS & BUSH, FLOYA	18 FEB 1906	11:270
McGUFFIN, THOMAS V & BUSH, MADGE	22 DEC 1910	13:235
McGUFFIN, WILLIAM B & VICKERS, ANNIE FLORENCE	10 JUL 1889	05:406
McGUIRE, CHARLES & DUFFER, SUSAN JANE	*06 JAN 1855	02:006
McGUIRE, JOHN & MACKLEY, NELLY	08 NOV 1806	01:001
McGUIRE, JOHN & MEHONE, ELIZA ANN	12 FEB 1835	01:029
McGUIRE, JOHN & JONES, EMILY	19 FEB 1841	01:033

McGUIRE, JOHN & DAVIS, MAHALIA	13 AUG 1843	01:042
McGUIRE, JOHN & BLADEN, MARY JANE	01 FEB 1846	01:045
McGUIRE, LEWIS A & WALLACE, EMEZETTA	04 AUG 1880	10:284
McGUIRE, LEWIS ALLEN & WALLACE, BETTIE	27 MAY 1885	12:177
McGUIRE, SAMUEL & CANTERBERRY, SUSANA	10 FEB 1828	01:017
McGUIRE, SAMUEL M & LOCKE, VIOLA S S	26 FEB 1863	03:104
McGUIRE, THOMAS C & COLLIER, LAURA	26 AUG 1875	08:268
McHAFFIE, JOHN A & PULLIN, LENORA M	15 MAR 1886	12:301
McHAFFIE, R E & PULLIN, MARGARET B	02 MAY 1913	14:137
McHALE, JOHN & WARD, BINA	15 JAN 1884	11:446
McHENRY, HENRY W & NORTHUP, VIVIAN L	21 SEP 1914	15:275
McINTOSH, CHANNING & BARRINGER, LAURA L	13 SEP 1877	09:128
McINTOSH, GEORGE & DUFFY, ELLA	28 DEC 1914	15:360
McINTOSH, JAMES R & CAMPBELL, ELIZABETH	28 MAR 1878	09:233
McINTOSH, JOHN & EDWARDS, AMA W	04 JUL 1866	04:137
McINTOSH, ROBERT C & CARTWRIGHT, GRACE M	20 DEC 1905	11:224
McINTOSH, THOMAS J & ROSS, ELIZABETH J	28 APR 1886	12:321
McINTOSH, WILLIAM C & LONG, ISABELL	03 JUL 1878	09:284
McINTYRE, WALTER L & ZIRKLE, SUSIE	27 DEC 1905	11:235
McKAY, F M & MOODESPAUGH, ELIZABETH	09 SEP 1909	12:494
McKAY, SPENCER & DOUGLAS, SAMANTHA E	26 APR 1871	07:083
McKEE, ALBERT & BURNS, MAYME BELLE	01 JAN 1914	15:115
McKEE, JOHN J & STONE, LINNIE M	20 JAN 1891	06:047
McKEE, JOSEPH C & ALLEN, ANNA	29 MAR 1887	12:496
McKEEVER, YANCEY M & SMITH, LODICIE A	07 NOV 1904	10:633
McKENNEY, JAMES & BROWN, MARY	11 AUG 1895	07:364
McKESSON, WILLIAM & HARRISON, JENNIE	24 DEC 1873	08:078
McKIBBEN, NATHANIEL E & WALLACE, MARGARET E	09 MAR 1898	08:267
McKINEY, ANDREW & LOVE, NORA L	24 DEC 1911	13:444
McKINEY, ELIAS & SMITH, ANNIE M	11 MAR 1897	08:059
McKINEY, JAMES & HAINEY, MARY	18 AUG 1901	09:388
McKINEY, JOHN W & SPURLOCK, LILLIE M	24 AUR 1902	10:139
McKINNEY, CHARLES & CASTO, LILLIE	24 DEC 1913	15:093
McKINNEY, EARLY H & SAYRE, VIRGIE F	05 AUG 1909	12:474
McKINNEY, EDDIE E & BAKER, MALISSA	26 JUN 1909	12:433
McKINNEY, SAMUEL & HART, BLANCHE	08 OCT 1907	12:028
McKINNEY, SAMUEL P & SANTEE, ELIZA	01 JAN 1912	13:461
McKINNEY, WILSON & HOSCHAR, MARTHA F	01 SEP 1887	05:086
McKINNISS, WARREN & HALTERMAN, MAUD	20 JUL 1904	10:563
McKINNISS, WILLIAM & FREEMAN, MIDE	12 MAY 1902	10:074
McKINNY, ELIAS & SCARBERRY, HANNAH E	28 SEP 1878	09:326
McKINNY, ELIJAH & DUNCAN, SARAH A	07 AUG 1873	08:017
McKINNY, G & SMITH, RACHEL	12 AUG 1885	12:207
McKINNY, GARRISON & RIDDLE, SARAH A	31 AUG 1879	10:121
McKINNY, JAMES & RIARSON, ELIZABETH	30 MAY 1875	08:243
McKINNY, WILSON & SHIELDS, OLIVIA	22 OCT 1874	08:174
McKINSTRY, KENNETH T & GABBERT, NANNIE M	20 JUN 1906	11:344
McKINSTRY, KOSSUTH T & ENGLISH, EUNICE	30 OCT 1901	09:435
McKINSY, JOHN H & BARNETT, LILLIE F	03 JUN 1904	10:530
McKNIGHT, CHARLES F & DICKS, CORA M	17 OCT 1907	12:047
McKNIGHT, CLYDE A & ARMSTRONG, EVE E	24 DEC 1907	12:099
McKNIGHT, ELLSWORTH & DALTON, SALLIE A	08 AUG 1907	11:588
McKNIGHT, FRANK L & PIERCE, BESSIE MAUD	02 SEP 1906	11:385
McKNIGHT, GEORGE & FULTZ, MATTIE	24 APR 1890	05:539
McKNIGHT, GEORGE & WETZEL, SOPHRONIA B	10 SEP 1891	06:177
McKNIGHT, SAMUEL E & SHANK, OCTAVIA V	23 DEC 1875	08:309
McKNIGHT, TOBIAS M & HALL, CLARA	04 JUL 1901	09:368
McKNIGHT, WILLIE & WINES, NELLIE	17 NOV 1907	12:068

McKOWN, JAMES HARRY & CRAWFORD, VERDA ODESSA	22 JUN 1910	13:098
McLAIN, BENJAMIN W & COOPER, MARGARET J	05 DEC 1865	04:079
McLAUGHLIN, JOSEPH A & PAINTER, VIRGIE L	*05 DEC 1906	11:466
McLEAN, ARTHUR & NEWLON, LUCY A	15 APR 1898	08:270
McLOUD, SAMUEL & BAKER, MINNIE FRANCES	05 SEP 1908	12:247
McMANN, JAMES D & MASH, MATILDA	31 MAY 1878	09:267
McMILLEN, CLINTON R & MORROW, DOLLIE A	04 NOV 1908	12:298
McMILLEN, FRANKLIN PIERCE & ROUSH, GEORGETTIE	*22 JAN 1896	07:493
McMILLEN, GILBERT & ROUSH, LYDIA	03 NOV 1868	06:011
McMILLEN, HUGH S & SWON, MATTIE L	12 OCT 1910	13:182
McMILLIN, CAMPBELL & RICKARD, ELIZABETH A	*25 OCT 1852	02:003
McMILLIN, JOHN & ANGEL, SALLY	1832	01:026
McMILLIN, JOSEPH E & PETTY, ALICE L	27 NOV 1884	12:089
McMILLIN, JOSEPHAS & RICKARD, NANCY	10 DEC 1863	03:147
McMILLIN, LEWIS A & SOMERVILLE, MARY L	21 NOV 1897	08:201
McMILLIN, LEWIS E & HART, VESTA	17 JAN 1892	06:275
McMIRLIN, JOSHUA D & HOLMES, VERNA	20 JAN 1904	10:463
McMULLEN, MADISON & OLDAKER, JEMIMA	04 MAR 1830	01:022
McMULLIN, ANDREW J & STRIBLING, SALLIE A	05 NOV 1867	05:107
McMULLIN, MADISON & LANGTRY, CATHARINE M	1835	01:040
McNEAL, GEORGE E & ALLINDER, BLANCHE	27 NOV 1913	15:076
McNEAL, JOHN A & CHILDERS, JULIAN	*03 OCT 1874	08:167
McNEAL, SAMUEL & WESSEN, PAULINA B	09 APR 1844	01:038
McNEALEY, C G & ERWIN, NORA	05 JAN 1911	13:253
McNEALEY, JOHN C & FADELEY, MITTIE A	19 JUN 1900	09:163
McNEIL, SAMUEL H & GUNN, NANCY	*19 NOV 1856	02:009
McNEILL, ASAHEL WESSON & HEREFORD, SARAH SANSON	02 NOV 1880	10:322
McNEILL, JOHN M & TULLY, LUCY	11 APR 1896	07:527
McNEILL, SAMUEL H & KEISTER, LILLIE J	18 NOV 1886	12:423
McNEILL, SAMUEL H & PAULIN, LILLIE M	28 JUL 1901	09:374
McNICKLE, WM F & FRY, MATTIE E	03 AUG 1912	13:577
McTHENA, CHARLIE E & BELL, LINNIE J	02 JUN 1908	12:193
McTHENY, MANSFIELD & McDANIEL, ELLA	01 SEP 1880	10:292
McTHENY, WM & GIPSON, MARY	1836	01:032 5
McWHORTER, JACOB F & HOLLY, LOUISA F	03 OCT 1872	07:269
McWHORTER, JOHN H & TRISLER, SARAH	12 SEP 1882	11:199
McWHORTER, JOHN O V & BUSH, ELIZABETH M	16 MAY 1880	10:257
McWHORTER, WILLIAM H & FETTY, MALINDA	01 JAN 1879	10:035
McWILLIAMS, CHRISTIAN & ROUSH, ADALINE B	08 DEC 1867	05:106
MEAD, LYMAN & FARLEY, EASTER	*11 MAY 1878	09:263
MEADOWS, A K & SIDERS, ANNA	**16 OCT 1913	15:050
MEADOWS, ALBERT F & MAYES, LOTTIE M	13 DEC 1911	13:436
MEADOWS, ALBERT GALLATIN & CHANDLER, ELIZA MARGARET	23 MAY 1883	11:340
MEADOWS, ALLEN & CHANDLER, MARY E	13 APR 1877	09:063
MEADOWS, ALONZO & WARD, VIRGINIA F	18 JUN 1885	12:183
MEADOWS, ANDREW & TAYLOR, ELIZABETH F	27 SEP 1867	05:096
MEADOWS, ANDREW S & CAMP, LELIE A	02 JUN 1889	08:316
MEADOWS, ANTHONY CANE & BERGER, LAURA C	01 OCT 1885	12:228
MEADOWS, AUSTIN & HOLLY, MATILDA	*07 JUN 1852	02:003
MEADOWS, BENTON L & McCALLISTER, VIRGINIA	28 JAN 1887	12:473
MEADOWS, CHARLES F & BARBER, SADIE	07 JAN 1914	15:121
MEADOWS, CHARLES MERVIN & GILLESPIE, ESSIE	24 OCT 1914	15:303
MEADOWS, CHARLES S & CHAPMAN, SARAH	*24 SEP 1909	12:515
MEADOWS, DANIEL R & JENKINS, IRENE E	14 MAR 1893	06:501
MEADOWS, DAVID & RIGG, IDA A	20 MAR 1889	05:371
MEADOWS, EDMOND & HOLLY, MALISSA ANN	*14 MAR 1855	02:006
MEADOWS, EDMOND & CHAPMAN, ANNIE	16 JUN 1901	09:353
MEADOWS, EDMOND P & FETTY, ELIZABETH A	13 JUN 1879	10:096

Name	Date	Ref
MEADOWS, EDMOND PIERCE & TAYLOR, MARY ELLA	31 JAN 1889	05:339
MEADOWS, EDWARD P R & HOLLY, MATILDA C	25 AUG 1881	11:002
MEADOWS, ELY & MEADOWS, MILLIE P	25 DEC 1900	09:250
MEADOWS, EMERY W & CHAPMAN, LOUISIANA	10 SEP 1913	15:029
MEADOWS, ESTELLE LOUIS & SMITH, NELLIE DELANCY	24 MAY 1909	12:414
MEADOWS, EVERETT E & STEVENSON, STELLA	25 FEB 1911	13:280
MEADOWS, FRANK M & DOUTT, ROSALIE	23 JAN 1895	07:238
MEADOWS, FURNEAU L & HOLLY, SUSAN	29 NOV 1877	09:159
MEADOWS, GALLITIN AUSTIN & McCOY, MARY ELLA	14 SEP 1892	06:403
MEADOWS, GALLITON A & WHEATON, HATTIE E	19 OCT 1898	08:389
MEADOWS, GASPER J & WORRELL, CARRIE E	31 MAY 1901	09:350
MEADOWS, GEORGE M & SMITH, IDA	24 SEP 1892	06:409
MEADOWS, GILBERT A & HOLLEY, ADDIE A	28 SEP 1898	08:366
MEADOWS, HENRY ALBERT & HOLLEY, HULDAH JANE	26 JAN 1888	05:179
MEADOWS, ISAAC & CARPENTER, REBECCA	20 APR 1864	03:179
MEADOWS, JACOB & CLAGG, DELITHA	*24 SEP 1853	02:004
MEADOWS, JACOB & NEMMO, MARY E	30 MAY 1882	11:155
MEADOWS, JACOB C & HOLLY, MALINDA	19 APR 1883	11:326
MEADOWS, JACOB E & YOUNG, MINNESOTA	03 NOV 1881	11:047
MEADOWS, JOHN & CREMEENS, MALINDA	04 MAR 1841	01:036
MEADOWS, JOHN B & CHRIST, CORDELIA	30 JUN 1894	07:109
MEADOWS, JOHN J & MYERS, MATILDA	26 AUG 1863	03:130
MEADOWS, JOHN R & EDMUNDS, CLARINDA	14 DEC 1876	08:418
MEADOWS, JOSHUA & JENKINS, AROLLA	05 MAR 1895	07:264
MEADOWS, LAFAYETTE & WITHERS, ELIZABETH A	NOV 1878	10:008
MEADOWS, LARRY C & SMITH, ADA	12 FEB 1905	11:043
MEADOWS, LEWIS E & VAUGHN, LUDA	25 JUL 1902	10:116
MEADOWS, LEWIS P & HUGHES, NANCY A	07 APR 1895	07:280
MEADOWS, LORENZO D & HANNAN, JENNIE B	*15 OCT 1881	11:032
MEADOWS, MILLARD & SIMPSON, ELLA	19 SEP 1909	12:503
MEADOWS, OLIVER & MEADOWS, MINNIE C	12 DEC 1906	11:461
MEADOWS, PETER & TAYLOR, SUSANAH	09 DEC 1868	06:019
MEADOWS, ROBERT K & LYKENS, EMMA	08 DEC 1904	10:651
MEADOWS, S A & BARGAR, IRENA C	23 DEC 1886	12:444
MEADOWS, S O & EDMUNDS, LUCY E	06 JAN 1887	12:452
MEADOWS, S W & HOLLEY, MYRTIE M	24 AUG 1902	10:137
MEADOWS, S W & MEADOWS, SOPHIA M	18 DEC 1909	12:569
MEADOWS, SAMUEL & JENKINS, ROSA MAY	05 JUL 1890	05:579
MEADOWS, SAMUEL & GIBSON, MARTHA VIRGINIA	22 FEB 1911	13:275
MEADOWS, SAMUEL W & BLAKE, VIRGINIA L	02 FEB 1888	05:181
MEADOWS, THEODORE & JENKINS, PRUCILLA	23 MAR 1904	10:494
MEADOWS, THOMAS & HOLLY, OULTA E	29 JUN 1871	07:100
MEADOWS, URIAS & LITCHFIELD, NANCY	28 SEP 1902	10:162
MEADOWS, WADE H & HOLLEY, ODA E	01 SEP 1898	08:355
MEADOWS, WADE H & MEADOWS, (Mrs) IDELLA	06 JUN 1914	15:211
MEADOWS, WALTER W & NEEDHAM, VIRGIE M	28 NOV 1914	15:332
MEADOWS, WILLIAM & HOLLY, SALLY	1836	01:032
MEADOWS, WILLIAM & SMITH, MARGARET	15 JAN 1874	08:090
MEADOWS, WILLIAM D & GASKINS, MARIA J	16 AUG 1865	04:041
MEADOWS, WILLIAM E & HOLLY, ARIZONA	02 JAN 1874	08:088
MEADOWS, WILLIAM J & HOLLEY, HENRIETTA	06 DEC 1882	11:258
MEADOWS, WILLIAM M & HOLLY, MARTHA JANE	04 APR 1865	04:005
MEADOWS, WILLIAM RUFUS & MEADOWS, ADIE	29 APR 1900	09:118
MEADOWS, WILLIAM, Sr & JENKINS, (Mrs) NANCY	*19 NOV 1855	02:007
MEANS, ANNANIAS & SAYRE, LIZZIE JANE	16 OCT 1894	07:166
MEANS, IRA & LINDSAY, IDA	22 MAR 1899	08:488
MEANS, MICHAEL & SHAY, MARGARET	*08 OCT 1874	08:173
MEARS, THOMAS & MENAGER, HENERIETTA B	*19 OCT 1857	02:010

Name	Date	Ref
MEDLEY, CHARLES A & BOYLES, WILLIE E	25 JUL 1899	08:585
MEDLEY, JAMES & LEMASTER, EMMA	07 JAN 1885	12:122
MEDLEY, JOHN C & LEMASTER, MARTHA A	27 AUG 1891	06:174
MEDLEY, WILLIAM H & CLONCH, DORA	29 JUL 1884	12:041
MEDORS, ARTHUR B & ROBINSON, GRACIE	24 NOV 1911	13:427
MEDORS, J BENTON & SAYRE, ESTHER J	17 APR 1910	13:045
MEEK, ALBERT L C & JENKINS, LUCY M	02 OCT 1891	06:199
MEEK, BAZALEEL & SELBY, EMILY MARIA	*20 MAR 1858	02:011
MEEK, HENRY A & McDANIEL, THENA H	09 DEC 1868	06:018
MEEK, JAMES R & KNIGHT, SARAH L	*01 OCT 1860	02:014
MEEK, JASPER N & LAWRENCE, SARAH E	12 DEC 1876	08:419
MEEKLY, DAVID & BETHOULT, LEAH	30 NOV 1865	04:078
MEEKS, CHARLES E & PECK, CARENA C	*20 DEC 1859	02:013
MEEKS, CHARLES K & SELBY, ARIE E	30 APR 1896	07:540
MEEKS, HORACE C & PONTZLER, ALMIRA	17 MAR 1872	07:205
MEEKS, JAMES & JOHNSON, ELIZABETH F	07 NOV 1875	08:294
MEEKS, RICHARD W & SHANK, LELIA M	20 AUG 1862	03:074
MEEKS, ROBERT FELIX & CARTWRIGHT, EVA RUTH	24 DEC 1889	05:500
MEES, A WILLIAM & LOOMIS, ELLA M	02 FEB 1903	10:234
MEES, ARTHUR J & GINTHER, JENNIE L	18 FEB 1911	13:272
MEES, CHARLES & YOUNG, ANNA BLANCHE	20 NOV 1902	10:190
MEES, GEORGE & REUTHER, ANNIE M	05 OCT 1902	10:164
MEINHARDT, HENRY & KUPPINGER, BARBARA	25 JUL 1900	09:150
MEINHART, FRED & BOYLES, CORA	14 FEB 1912	13:487
MELLOTT, STEPHEN H & FARMER, MARY	12 SEP 1912	13:599
MELTON, ALBIN GRANT & TURLEY, HESTER JANE	26 AUG 1890	05:602
MELTON, CHARLES A & WRIGHT, ELIZABETH A	20 DEC 1865	04:089
MELTON, JAMES W & OAKS, JULIA E D	23 APR 1879	10:080
MELTON, JEREMIAH & SANDERS, MARY	14 OCT 1874	08:171
MELTON, JOSEPH & HOWELL, MARTHA A	08 DEC 1864	03:211
MELTON, WILLIAM B P & MEADOWS, CLARINDA J	02 JUL 1877	09:102
MELTON, WILLIAM R & MORRISTON, NANCY E C	*08 NOV 1899	09:013
MELTON, WILLIAM T & BALL, NANCY	16 AUG 1861	03:013
MENAGER, JAMES BOBIN & POMEROY, FANNIE SEHON	14 JUN 1886	12:336
MENAGER, LEWIS B & STEENBERGEN, CAROLINE	20 APR 1837	01:031
MENGE, EDWARD & ROBSON, ELLA R	08 JUL 1898	08:329
MENIFEE, JOHN J & BURCH, ELOSHA	27 NOV 1828	01:018
MERCER, DAVID & McDERMITT, SUSAN	13 JUN 1877	09:098
MERCER, DAVID R & FROST, FLORA A	08 JAN 1905	11:027
MERIT, WILLIAM & MINKS, MARY ALICE	18 OCT 1891	06:204
MERRITT, MARTIN & VINCENT, RUTH	21 OCT 1894	07:171
MESSICK, ERNEST H & CANTERBERRY, LOUISA	19 DEC 1899	09:033
METCALF, MARIAN & HALL, MERAL	05 SEP 1897	08:153
METCALF, WILLIAM B & PIERCE, ELIZA	28 AUG 1897	08:149
METHENY, JOHN W & HERDMAN, DORA	08 JUL 1899	08:572
MEYER, ROBERT S & ROSEBERRY, LENA LORENA	23 OCT 1894	07:178
MIDCAP, BERNARD & WARNER, MARY A	22 AUG 1891	06:168
MIDDLECOFF, EDWARD BENJAMIN & NEWBRAUGH, ADDIE R	22 JUN 1895	07:320
MIDDLECOFF, JAMES S & LEMASTERS, JANE CATHARINE	*03 FEB 1855	02:006
MIDDLESWART, ESBERRY J & SOMERVILLE, MATILDA R	27 DEC 1875	08:312
MIDDLETON, WILLIAM E & KREPPS, MALINDA JANE	31 JAN 1893	06:476
MILES, JOHN W & MARTIN, LENA A	18 OCT 1911	13:399
MILLER, ANDREW & ROBINSON, JULIA FRANCES	27 SEP 1891	06:192
MILLER, ANDREW & HOFFMAN, JENNIE F	20 FEB 1894	07:050
MILLER, CHARLES A & FULLMER, ELLA	14 AUG 1881	10:441
MILLER, CHARLES C & CANTRELL, ELLEN J	01 DEC 1832	01:025

MILLER, CORNELIUS & ALESHIRE, BETSY	09 APR 1808	01:001
MILLER, EARNEST & SAYRE, FANNY	08 SEP 1914	15:266
MILLER, FRANK MARION & STONE, EMMA ALMIRA	25 FEB 1892	06:292
MILLER, FRANKLIN P & BUXTON, ELECTA LODISA	31 MAY 1877	09:089
MILLER, FRED S & BENNETT, JOANNA	06 MAR 1895	07:263
MILLER, GEORGE & BROWN, MARY	13 SEP 1884	12:058
MILLER, GEORGE & CHAPMAN, ELVA	27 JAN 1902	10:013
MILLER, GEORGE EDGAR & BENNETT, MARTHA RACHEL	20 MAY 1900	09:131
MILLER, GEORGE E & THOMAS, EDNA	07 NOV 1908	12:301
MILLER, HENRY & THOMAS, AMELIA	02 JUL 1890	05:582
MILLER, H F & CAIN, ELZINA	27 APR 1913	14:123
MILLER, IRA & WOOD, SUSAN	NOV 1843	01:043
MILLER, J M & STRAIT, (Mrs) LILLIE	21 JUN 1913	14:184
MILLER, JACOB & ADAM, SARAH	11 APR 1839	01:031 5
MILLER, JACOB & MITCHELL, MARY M	15 APR 1885	12:161
MILLER, JAMES & HAINES, MARY J	01 MAY 1882	11:144
MILLER, JAMES & BIRCHFIELD, REBECCA J	24 JUN 1894	07:107
MILLER, JAMES C & BLAZER, ADA G	08 MAY 1898	08:300
MILLER, JAMES M & KNAPP, ROSA J	20 DEC 1877	09:171
MILLER, JAMES M & ESTEP, AMANDA E	22 OCT 1896	07:633
MILLER, JAMES T & PAGE, MILDRED A	23 DEC 1869	06:131
MILLER, JOHN & HENDERSON, SALLY	16 OCT 1823	01:012
MILLER, JOHN CULBERSON & PICKENS, MAGGIE	05 MAR 1893	06:500
MILLER, JOHN F & LEWIS, UNA Z	14 JUN 1913	14:179
MILLER, JOHN G & NEVILLE, NORA B	22 SEP 1907	12:018
MILLER, JOHN H & MILLER, HANNAH JANE	21 MAR 1867	05:035
MILLER, JOHN HENRY & BALL, LEOTI C	01 MAY 1889	05:392
MILLER, JOHN M & SHEPPARD, BLANCH	19 JUN 1895	07:319
MILLER, JOHN MILLIGAN & BARR, ELZINA	28 MAR 1890	05:535
MILLER, JOSEPH & DILL, JULIA	*10 MAY 1856	02:008
MILLER, JOSEPH & LEE, ELIZABETH A	27 JUN 1900	09:147
MILLER, JOSEPH & SHEETS, ANNA M	04 APR 1906	11:285
MILLER, JOSEPH HENRY & RUSSELL, EVE MAY	04 JUL 1906	11:357
MILLER, JOSEPH S & SHAW, MATTIE J	11 JAN 1872	07:180
MILLER, LEVI L & EDENS, MARY C	02 JAN 1890	05:507
MILLER, LEWIS M & POWELL, LYDIA	17 JUN 1834	01:028
MILLER, LEWIS MONTGOMERY & SAYRE, ALLIE BELLE	15 FEB 1893	06:488
MILLER, LUTHER & BOARD, LANORA	31 DEC 1883	11:444
MILLER, OKEY & DUNHAM, IONA	25 OCT 1899	08:639
MILLER, OWEN & MINIS, MINNIE	02 NOV 1907	12:060
MILLER, P H & LUCAS, CAROLINE	30 OCT 1884	12:083
MILLER, ROBERT D & CROOKHAM, ANNIE L	23 NOV 1873	08:061
MILLER, ROY E & WEDGE, NANNIE	05 MAR 1913	14:099
MILLER, ROZALVO & GREATHOUSE, AMANDA	21 MAR 1907	11:506
MILLER, WARREN & FORBUS, OLA	10 SEP 1903	10:349
MILLER, WESLEY & SMITH, JESSIE MAY	06 OCT 1913	15:044
MILLER, WILLIAM A & McGUIRE, ELIZABETH J	23 OCT 1866	04:156
MILLER, WILLIAM A & JOHNSON, CAROLINE V	14 MAY 1870	06:184
MILLER, WILLIAM A & BALL, ALICE O	09 AUG 1885	12:206
MILLER, WILLIAM M & LEIGHTON, NANCY A R	24 NOV 1898	08:414
MILLER, WILLIAM SCOTT & JENKINS, SUSAN MALINDA	03 JUL 1889	05:420
MILLER, WILLIAM T & SHIVELY, ANGELINE	28 OCT 1882	07:282
MILLER, WILSON & TRIPP, LINNA	11 SEP 1904	10:593
MILLION, ELZA & BONECUTTER, ZONA	14 AUG 1901	09:382
MILLIRONS, MILLBERN & JARVIS, IDA M	13 MAY 1896	07:550
MILLS, GEORGE & JOHNSON, JANE	01 AUG 1845	01:044
MILLS, HENRY & ASTON, MARY E	14 MAY 1882	11:146
MILLS, HENRY & HUTCHINSON, ELLA	04 MAY 1892	06:334

MILLS, J WILLIAM & WHITE, CORA BELLE	16 JAN 1913	14:180
MILLS, JAMES & JOHNSON, MARY	09 DEC 1882	11:265
MILLS, JOHN N & SHARON, MAY	31 DEC 1912	14:077
MILLS, SAMUEL & KINCAID, ELIZABETH	AUG 1843	01:043
MINICK, PHILIP & McNICHOLE, CYNTHIA	*24 JAN 1853	02:003
MINIS, PATRICK & ROBINSON, KATIE	18 SEP 1909	12:508
MINK, GEORGE E & LEACH, LILLIE D	04 JUL 1894	07:116
MINK, JAMES E & WITHERS, MARY C	05 JAN 1876	08:318
MINKS, ADOLPHUS M & KRAUSE, CATHARINE	15 MAR 1892	06:306
MINKS, JAMES E & NEVILLE, HANNAH M	30 SEP 1877	09:134
MINNICK, PHILIP & BAILEY, ANNE	*09 SEP 1856	02:008
MINTURN, GEORGE C & MORGAN, EMMA K	05 JUN 1895	07:313
MINTURN, ISAAC & ROSEBERRY, JANE	*19 JUN 1857	02:010
MINTURN, LORRIN T & KNAPP, CATHARINE	07 APR 1842	01:036
MISENER, SAMUEL N & LANDSTUFFER, NANCY	08 APR 1881	10:392
MITCHELL, ANSEL & KNAPP, MILLIE BERTHA	15 JUN 1889	05:413
MITCHELL, BERT & QUICKLE, WILLIE	30 SEP 1900	09:214
MITCHELL, CLARENCE O & DAVIS, GEORGIA M	06 SEP 1909	12:492
MITCHELL, CLAUDIUS J & JOHNSON, KATE E	30 OCT 1890	05:631
MITCHELL, ELLIS EDGAR & FRAZIER, ARLI GERTRUDE	06 SEP 1900	09:188
MITCHELL, ISAAC FRANKLIN & McDERMITT, MARY SUSAN	27 MAY 1894	07:099
MITCHELL, JAMES A & LOVE, DELLA	27 SEP 1908	12:269
MITCHELL, JAMES FRANKLIN & JOLLY, ANGELINE B	24 AUG 1882	11:189
MITCHELL, JAMES W & PULLINS, JENNIE M	12 AUG 1902	10:128
MITCHELL, JEFFERSON & KEEVER, ELIZA J	20 NOV 1873	08:060
MITCHELL, JOHN & WAGGENER, HANNAH L	30 NOV 1843	01:038
MITCHELL, JOHN THOMAS & PERDUM, DAISY M	19 JUN 1902	10:192
MITCHELL, LEWIS & WISEMAN, MARY J	03 FEB 1887	12:475
MITCHELL, LEWIS & CHILDS, FANNIE	08 JUN 1890	05:569
MITCHELL, LEWIS & HALL, ALLIE	01 AUG 1897	08:136
MITCHELL, PHILIP & COLEMAN, MARY ANN	21 APR 1864	03:178
MITCHELL, THOMAS & SOMERVILLE, BARBARA	24 NOV 1842	01:038
MITCHELL, WILLIAM & HYATT, ELLEN J	17 FEB 1873	07:323
MITCHELL, WILLIAM & WILSON, VIRGIE	23 JUN 1900	09:145
MOCK, JACOB & AMSDON, LUCY	22 MAY 1835	01:029
MOFFET, ISAAC & WADE, SARAH JANE	*05 AUG 1854	02:005
MOHR, JOHN A & THORN, CLARA M	28 MAY 1891	06:118
MOHR, JOHN A & ALFORD, MARY	27 JAN 1909	12:354
MOLDEN, BENJAMIN F & BRANCH, MELVINA	25 MAY 1878	09:258
MOLDEN, BENJAMIN FRANKLIN & HUGHES, MARY ELLEN	07 MAY 1890	05:553
MOLDEN, FRANK & BASS, (Mrs) FANNIE	21 AUG 1910	13:137
MOLDEN, JAMES H & FRANCIS, KATIE	28 OCT 1883	11:416
MOLDEN, JOHN R & HALL, CLARA	23 MAY 1883	11:343
MOLER, HENRY G & TURLEY, MARY	23 SEP 1893	06:609
MOLZ, EDWARD J & McDADE, MARGARET	17 JUL 1898	08:336
MONK, ABNER & CARTMILL, ELIZABETH	*07 OCT 1854	02:006
MONOHAN, ARTHUR B & OUSLEY, ANNA L	04 APR 1894	07:068
MONROE, GEORGE W & HEREFORD, VIRGINIA	*13 AUG 1850	02:001
MONROE, GEORGE W & CARTER, MATILDA A	11 NOV 1874	08:178
MONROE, JAMES H & MULLAN, NETTIE C	31 OCT 1900	09:231
MONROE, JOHN & NEWAL, DRUSILLA	1832	01:026
MONTGOMERY, CHARLES E & WRIGHT, DEBBIE E	11 JUN 1912	13:544
MONTGOMERY, LOMA & GREENLEE, MARY	04 MAR 1896	07:504
MONTGOMERY, MILO EVERET & WAUGH, MARY LEVINA	29 DEC 1891	06:267
MOODESPAUGH, DANIEL & GLASPIE, OLIVIA	24 JUL 1879	10:103
MOODESPAUGH, RUFUS & PLANTS, EFFIE	22 AUG 1902	10:138
MOODY, J M & HART, FANNIE	04 JUN 1911	13:327
MOODY, JOHN & FRANKLIN, CELIA	04 AUG 1882	11:185

MOODY, WALTER & GILMORE, FLORENCE C	04 JUN 1891	06:122
MOONEY, FRANKLIN & THOMPSON, CORA E	15 FEB 1906	11:266
MOORE, ABNER & MAYES, LILLIE E	25 NOV 1903	10:416
MOORE, ALFRED L & BAKER, MARY JANE	01 NOV 1866	04:166
MOORE, ANDERSON & PAGE, SARAH E	07 MAR 1886	12:298
MOORE, C F & TATE, EDNA M	26 OCT 1910	13:192
MOORE, CHARLES A & HILL, MINNIE C	27 MAR 1899	08:490
MOORE, CHARLES A & GARDNER, SEVIE	26 NOV 1906	11:451
MOORE, CHARLES T B & McCULLOCH, MARY E	09 NOV 1870	07:065
MOORE, EDWARD & GREER, ESSIE	08 JUN 1897	08:111
MOORE, EDWARD M & PEYTON, MARY E	21 NOV 1877	09:158
MOORE, ELMER J & LOVE, LILLIE	27 MAY 1899	08:540
MOORE, FRED F & McLEOD, MATTIE	27 MAR 1901	09:311
MOORE, GEORGE A D & McCOY, ANNIE C	13 AUG 1905	11:147
MOORE, HOWARD & MINK, GERTIE	05 DEC 1906	11:465
MOORE, ISAAC D & MARTIN, HELEN H	20 MAY 1891	06:113
MOORE, J LEWIS & BOWMAN, HATTIE	19 NOV 1899	09:019
MOORE, JAMES F & ORONIGS, IDA V	05 FEB 1880	10:206
MOORE, JOHN & ANDERSON, NANCY	04 SEP 1873	08:021
MOORE, JOHN A & MENAGER, MARY E	05 DEC 1850	01:052
MOORE, JOSEPH T & KIMBERLING, ANYTIS	17 SEP 1873	08:028
MOORE, LEI M & CASEY, MINNIE	26 DEC 1899	09:054
MOORE, MARCUS L & BASS, CLARA	17 SEP 1903	10:360
MOORE, MORGAN & MILLER, ATLANTIC O	21 JUL 1863	03:121
MOORE, MORRIS & SCHMIDT, LOUISA T	05 JUN 1879	10:094
MOORE, ROME & CASTO, FANNIE	08 AUG 1903	10:333
MOORE, ROY DONALD & DYKE, LUCILE ESTHER	23 MAR 1910	13:029
MOORE, SCOTT & STONE, MARY ELIZABETH	08 SEP 1889	05:451
MOORE, SCOTT & THOMAS, MARY	03 JAN 1906	11:242
MOORE, SHEPARD WILLS & MOORE, MARY MARGARET	29 OCT 1889	05:471
MOORE, THOMAS & HOWLES, ANN	*21 MAY 1856	02:008
MOORE, THOMAS & GOODNITE, ELIZABETH	25 SEP 1912	14:006
MOORE, VIRGIL P & HADDOX, ROSALIE	16 SEP 1883	11:401
MOORE, WILBERT & BASS, EVA	06 JAN 1904	10:457
MOORE, WILLIAM J & GIBBS, SARAH A	26 JUN 1881	10:424
MOORE, WILLIAM L & BURNELL, ELIZABETH E	09 MAY 1899	08:529
MOORE, WILLIAM T & SMITH, BETHA	22 MAY 1898	08:307
MOORE, WILLIAM T & SMITH, NORA B	11 DEC 1904	10:655
MOOREHEAD, NATHANIEL & RICHARD, MARY	02 DEC 1822	01:009
MOREHEAD, WILLIAM A & MARTIN, MATILDA A	22 APR 1875	08:225
MOREHOUSE, PERIL G & SCOTT, LUCY	*24 JUL 1886	12:363
MORGAN, BENJAMIN & EDWARDS, MARY	07 JUL 1871	07:101
MORGAN, CHARLES RAYMOND & GREENLEE, NELLIE ERMA BLANCHE	11 MAY 1907	11:524
MORGAN, D H & NELSON, NORA	29 APR 1909	12:405
MORGAN, DAVID M & DAVIS, ELIZABETH	07 JUL 1868	05:196
MORGAN, HARRY & HENNOSY, MARY ELSIE	21 JUN 1911	13:330
MORGAN, HARVEY W & EDWARDS, CORA	20 SEP 1911	13:379
MORGAN, JAMES B & LONG, SARAH E	27 NOV 1867	05:110
MORGAN, JAMES HARVEY WATSON & SMITH, MARY	07 JUL 1887	05:056
MORGAN, JAMES H W & PIERSON, RACHEL	19 MAR 1896	07:516
MORGAN, JAMES L & ROLLINS, WILLIA VERNENA	30 NOV 1913	15:077
MORGAN, JEREMIAH & EDWARDS, MARTHA	07 MAY 1868	06:177
MORGAN, JOHN C & BOWEN, EMMA B	24 NOV 1881	11:059
MORGAN, JOHN HOWARD & MITCHELL, SOPHIA JANE	25 AUG 1887	05:079
MORGAN, JOHN THOMAS & HANNAN, NELLIE ELLEN	12 OCT 1911	13:394
MORGAN, MOSES & JARROT, MATTIE L	29 SEP 1875	08:276
MORGAN, SAMUEL & DARST, LYDIA M	29 NOV 1863	03:143
MORGAN, SOLOMON & CALWELL, RACHEL W	13 FEB 1845	01:045

MORGAN, WILLIAM A & DARST, ELIZABETH	05 JUN 1862	03:067
MORGAN, WILLIAM S & HANLY, MARY E	20 APR 1898	08:294
MORIARITY, MICHAEL & SHANNAN, ANNIE	17 OCT 1881	11:033
MORIARTY, JOHN & FITSGERALD, ELLEN	18 APR 1866	04:115
MORIARTY, MICHAEL & KIRBY, ELIZABETH	11 JAN 1871	07:042
MORNING, JAMES H & RICE, SARAH F	18 NOV 1875	08:299
MORNING, JAMES P & SPENCER, NANCY	*18 AUG 1852	02:003
MORRIS, ALBERT J & KIMBERLING, SARAH HARRIET	*29 DEC 1853	02:005
MORRIS, BENJAMIN FRANKLIN & SHORT, ELIZABETH A	01 MAR 1891	06:070
MORRIS, CHARLES E & DARST, MARGARET L	11 APR 1901	09:321
MORRIS, EDWARD G & COBB, MARY	04 APR 1878	09:239
MORRIS, JAMES E & ROSEBERRY, MARY J	18 APR 1875	08:231
MORRIS, JOHN & GREEN, JANIE	14 SEP 1899	08:611
MORRIS, JOHN A & LIKENS, EMILY D	01 JAN 1883	11:283
MORRIS, JOHN M & CARTWRIGHT, CLARA F	03 SEP 1879	10:124
MORRIS, JOHN M & KING, CYNTHA J	30 DEC 1886	12:455
MORRIS, JOHN W & McCOY, HARRIET	*21 JAN 1856	02:007
MORRIS, JOHN W & LEPORT, SALLIE	06 MAR 1899	08:477
MORRIS, JOSEPH & McDADE, JANE	*12 JUL 1859	02:012
MORRIS, JOSEPH E & TUCKER, ALCEY A	11 JUN 1891	06:126
MORRIS, ROY McKINLEY & RAYBURN, GOLDIE O	26 SEP 1914	15:278
MORRIS, WILLIAM H & CHAMBERLAIN, CATHARINE	16 JUL 1865	04:026
MORRISON, ANDREW B & FORBIS, FANNIE	15 MAY 1898	08:305
MORRISON, BERT & HILL, MEGGIE	08 MAY 1906	11:310
MORRISON, CARDER L & CAIN, MARY	05 SEP 1906	11:401
MORRISON, F A & WARNER, LUCY B	28 AUG 1902	10:140
MORRISON, FRANK & GROVER, VESTA	14 FEB 1899	08:464
MORRISON, FRANK & LINKFIELD, ALICE	07 NOV 1904	10:635
MORRISON, GEORGE DELMER & JACOBS, DELIA	02 FEB 1896	07:495
MORRISON, HENRY & HALL, SARAH J	14 SEP 1883	11:402
MORRISON, HOLLY V & STONE, MYRTLE B	05 FEB 1902	10:017
MORRISON, JAMES & HILL, OLIVE	16 OCT 1826	01:014
MORRISON, JAMES & BRADLEY, MARY	13 OCT 1841	01:037
MORRISON, JESSE & CAIN, VIOLA	21 AUG 1910	13:135
MORRISON, JOHN F & BARNETT, ALZINA J	22 MAR 1870	06:169
MORRISON, PERRY W & BARNETT, PERMELIA F	25 APR 1880	10:239
MORRISON, ROBERT H & GRINSTEAD, MARY G	10 DEC 1881	11:067
MORRISON, ROBERT W & McDANIEL, ALICE R	16 SEP 1875	08:274
MORRISON, VIRGIL S & BURDETT, ETHEL S	03 JUL 1906	11:358
MORRISON, WESLEY A & BARR, MALINDA	04 SEP 1876	08:383
MORRISTON, ALONZO T & WAMSLEY, REBECCA ANN	16 OCT 1866	04:157
MORRISTON, FRANK & ROBBINS, FLORENCE	19 MAR 1905	11:059
MORRISTON, HEZEKIAH C & WAMSLEY, NANCY M	21 JUN 1870	06:199
MORROW, CHARLES & ROBERTS, CLARINDA	*22 JUL 1852	02:003
MORROW, CHARLES HENRY & ALLEN, EMMA	05 JUN 1900	09:138
MORROW, EDWARD & MILLER, STELLA M	25 DEC 1904	11:014
MORROW, GEORGE R & WATSON, JULIA	02 NOV 1893	06:639
MORROW, IVA & SCOTT, MINNIE	23 SEP 1905	11:177
MORROW, JAMES & DANNER, CARRIE	24 DEC 1900	09:259
MORROW, JOHN W & WINDON, ANNIE R	25 NOV 1891	06:235
MORROW, PEARL R & SHELINE, MINNIE	01 AUG 1906	11:377
MORROW, ROBERT R & DUNN, CORDELIA A	04 JUL 1877	09:103
MOSES, CHARLES B & HOLLY, ELIZABETH R	25 SEP 1881	11:022
MOSS, ANDREW J & BROWN, CYNTHIA C	*23 MAR 1861	02:015
MOSSMAN, ELMORE J & McDANIEL, MARY E	13 APR 1879	10:078
MOSSMAN, SAMUEL A & JORDAN, ELIZABETH	*22 NOV 1853	02:004
MOURNEN, WILLIAM H & STEWART, SARAH C	16 NOV 1865	04:076
MOURNING, A J L & RAINEY, LIZZIE S	09 MAY 1885	12:173

MOURNING, ANDREW J & CHEESEBREW, EMILY JANE	20 SEP 1866	04:151
MOURNING, ANDREW J S & HESSON, MARY	10 SEP 1891	06:181
MOURNING, EDWARD C & BIRD, ALMA F	07 SEP 1908	12:252
MOURNING, GEORGE W & GISE, ELIZA J	10 APR 1872	07:209
MOURNING, JOHN WILLIAM & RICKARD, SAVANAH FRANCES	25 DEC 1887	05:160
MUGGRIDGE, DANIEL J & TURLEY, SARAH M	04 DEC 1870	07:027
MUGRIDGE, CHARLES & GIBBS, DAISEY	11 MAY 1907	11:531
MULFORD, ABRAHAM & DAYWALT, SARAH ANN	24 MAY 1849	01:051
MULFORD, ARTHUR & WATKINS, HATTIE	26 APR 1908	12:169
MULFORD, CHESTER A & NOTTER, NETTIE E	28 NOV 1907	12:082
MULFORD, ENOS & VANMATRE, ZEBA ANN	*07 FEB 1852	02:002
MULFORD, GEORGE T & HOPE, AURILLA J	*04 AUG 1875	08:261
MULFORD, WILLIAM H H & FLOWERS, FANNIE	12 MAR 1908	12:136
MULLANS, GEORGE FREEMAN & FILSON, MYRTIE ROSS	18 APR 1900	09:112
MULLEN, ERNEST & GIBBONS, IDA K	24 DEC 1894	07:217
MULLEN, HENRY E & TROSCHKE, MATTIE E	07 DEC 1908	12:322
MULLEN, WILLIAM F & JEFFERS, MARY M	01 OCT 1905	11:180
MULLENS, MITCHEL & ELLSNICK, LILLIE	28 OCT 1905	11:193
MULLFORD, ABRAHAM & SLACK, NANCY	1831	01:024
MUMAW, JACOB & CLAGG, MARY	08 MAR 1867	05:034
MUNROW, SAMUEL & FRY, ELIZABETH	26 NOV 1840	01:043
MURDOCK, JAMES C & BEALE, CATHARINE M	25 NOV 1846	01:044
MURPHY, ARTHUR J H & McDANIEL, (Mrs) MARY	09 OCT 1911	13:391
MURPHY, JOHN & O'DONEL, BRIDGET	26 NOV 1878	10:012
MURPHY, OLIVER & KIRK, MILLIE M	02 JUN 1904	10:527
MURPHY, THOMAS & POWER, BRIDGET	06 NOV 1861	03:032
MURPHY, WILLIAM E & KERWOOD, PEARL E	11 SEP 1901	09:405
MURRAY, CHARLES H & SMITH, MINTIE L	30 SEP 1895	07:398
MURRAY, JOHN & LAWSON, ELIZA ANN	01 JUL 1866	04:135
MURRAY, JOHN & SCOLLARD, ROSA	11 APR 1880	10:237
MUSGRAVE, ADAM & YEAGER, POLLY	10 SEP 1829	01:018
MUSGRAVE, ASA & VANMATRE, PRISCILLA ANN	01 APR 1852	02:002
MUSGRAVE, CHARLES G & YAUGER, EVA	01 APR 1900	09:102
MUSGRAVE, E E & LOVE, MAGGIE L	27 MAR 1884	11:474
MUSGRAVE, ELIJAH G & ROSEBERRY, EMMA C	*11 FEB 1857	02:009
MUSSO, MICHAEL & ROUSE, SARAH ANN	11 MAY 1887	05:024
MYERS, ABRAM & BARNETT, NANCY A	10 AUG 1876	08:365
MYERS, ANDREW J & EDWARDS, EMILY	21 JUL 1872	07:248
MYERS, ARTHUR G & WILLIAMSON, MAUD B	06 SEP 1903	10:346
MYERS, BUREN & WHITTINGTON, CLARISSA	28 FEB 1909	12:374
MYERS, EDWARD B & BRANDY, ANNIE	04 DEC 1878	10:014
MYERS, GEORGE B & BARNETT, SARAH	27 JUL 1865	04:032
MYERS, JOHN H & BATTERSON, ESTELLA	13 MAY 1889	05:398
MYERS, JOHN N & FULTZ, RHEA PEARL	26 AUG 1914	15:259
MYERS, OKEY & MARTIN, LIZZIE L	09 SEP 1904	10:592
MYERS, OKEY & STOVER, MARY L	23 APR 1908	12:168
MYERS, ROY C & SULLIVAN, BESSIE L	23 AUG 1906	11:397
MYERS, WILLIAM & ZERKLE, IDA	22 JUL 1880	05:249
NAGLE, CHARLES J & HAYMAN, (Mrs) MINNIE R	11 AUG 1909	12:477
NAIL, DAVID & COTTRILL, MARY C	16 NOV 1880	10:268
NAPPER, ELMER & FREEMAN, LUCY	23 OCT 1902	10:177
NARET, EDWARD & PITRAT, HARRIETTE BENOITE	1843	01:042
NASH, HENRY & DAWALT, ELIZABETH	27 MAR 1840	01:043
NATROSS, MARTIN & WADDEL, MARY	31 JUL 1864	03:190
NEAL, WILLIAM H & SPURLOCK, MARIAH	31 MAR 1898	08:280
NEALE, CARLE & BATES, CARRIE O	08 JUL 1911	13:343
NEALE, CHARLES & ULRICH, ANGELINA	11 JUL 1903	10:319
NEALE, CHARLES K & GARDNER, FRANCIS	09 OCT 1873	08:038
NEALE, CLYDE & CRAFT, IRENE	20 JUN 1914	15:224

NEALE, DANIEL C & FARLEY, GRACE	30 NOV 1879	10:169
NEALE, DAVID L & HOLLEY, LOTTIE B	03 SEP 1907	12:002
NEALE, EDWIN L & WAGGENER, ATTARAH B	10 NOV 1870	07:020
NEALE, FRANK O & CHRISTY, AMANDA	15 AUG 1880	10:285
NEALE, FREDRICK & WITHERS, BERTHA	17 MAY 1906	11:319
NEALE, GORDON F & REED, LIZZIE	20 JUN 1906	11:345
NEALE, HORACE GREELY & MORROW, MARY J	14 JUN 1900	09:143
NEALE, JOHN HARDY & SMITH, MARY T	15 FEB 1905	11:045
NEALE, JOHN W & ANDERSON, EMMA S	*29 SEP 1852	02:003
NEALE, JOHN W & CUTCHALL, FLURRY	18 FEB 1895	07:256
NEALE, JOSEPH D & TAYLOR, MARY	04 JAN 1905	11:025
NEALE, JOSEPH L & MILES, LULIE J	25 JUL 1866	04:143
NEALE, SAMUEL & SPEARS, BETTIE	03 APR 1995	07:278
NEALE, WILLIAM H H & CONDIFF, RHODA C	25 SEP 1867	05:088
NEALE, WILLIAM J & BLAKE, HESTER A	07 SEP 1901	09:396
NEALE, WILLIAM P & WAGGENER, HELEN V	11 DEC 1873	08:070
NEALE, WILLIAM P L & STEENBERGEN, CATHARINE	27 FEB 1838	01:032
NEASE, BRADFORD L & CARPENTER, SARAH E	29 NOV 1893	07:012
NEASE, EDDIE O & ZIRKLE, ESTA E	05 DEC 1903	10:437
NEASE, EDGAR A & BUMGARNER, JOSIE N	04 APR 1905	11:067
NEASE, EMMETT L & LEWIS, ROSA B	19 FEB 1908	12:131
NEASE, GEORGE E & FRY, ROSA M	15 AUG 1906	11:389
NEASE, GEORGE M & LIVING, MARY E	02 MAR 1882	11:119
NEASE, GEORGE W & DODSON, OLLIE A	30 SEP 1908	12:271
NEASE, GROVER C & HARRIS, PEARL L	27 MAY 1913	14:161
NEASE, HENRY & SMITH, ELIZABETH	*19 AUG 1859	02:013
NEASE, HENRY B & GIBBS, BESSIE	18 DEC 1910	13:228
NEASE, HENRY F & McDANIEL, REBECCA	*12 JAN 1854	02:005
NEASE, HOSEA G & SOMERVILLE, REBECCA J	19 OCT 1875	08:290
NEASE, JACOB & ZERKEL, NANCY	JUL 1845	01:049
NEASE, JACOB L & ZERKEL, CHRISTINA	*14 FEB 1852	02:002
NEASE, JAMES W & YONKER, LAURA E	JUN 1874	08:137
NEASE, JOSEPH H & HAWK, MARY JANE	*02 JUL 1853	02:004
NEASE, LESTER C & VARIAN, CARRIE M	07 SEP 1904	10:591
NEASE, LEVI A & OHLINGER, ANN B	09 NOV 1865	04:067
NEASE, LEWIS & FRY, CHRISTENA	01 MAY 1834	01:028
NEASE, LEWIS H & ROUSH, MARY L	*19 APR 1856	02:008
NEASE, LEWIS J & LOVE, MARTHA J	13 APR 1877	09:062
NEASE, LINCOLN & CAPEHART, MATTIE A	21 OCT 1885	12:241
NEASE, MADISON & ROGERS, MARY JANE	*07 FEB 1851	02:001
NEASE, MARION E & KIRBY, ODESSA M	17 NOV 1895	07:428
NEASE, WINFIELD SCOTT & VICKERS, LUCY M	04 OCT 1892	06:619
NEASE, WINFRED S & WETZEL, EUPHRASIA A	08 APR 1875	08:228
NEEDHAM, AARON E & ADKINS, ANNIE E	25 DEC 1891	06:259
NEEDHAM, JAMES & LONG, MARTHA J	06 FEB 1879	10:051
NEEDHAM, JAMES & CASEY, LILLIE J	27 APR 1899	08:516
NEEDHAM, JOSEPH T & BROWN, CORA S	07 APR 1885	12:155
NEEDHAM, WILLIAM K & SNYDER, (Mrs) EMMA	11 NOV 1911	13:417
NEFF, CLINTON & HANNA, MILDRED NORRIS	20 JUN 1900	09:142
NEIGHBORS, ELISHA G & WATKINS, ELIZABETH	03 JUL 1878	09:281
NEIGLAR, RALPH F & ROUSH, JESSIE C	**14 MAY 1914	15:195
NELLIS, ROBERT B & PIATT, CATHARINE	23 DEC 1876	09:009
NELSON, ALEXANDER & MATSON, MARY J	03 OCT 1869	06:082
NELSON, ARBUCKLE & GREENLEE, JENNY	1830	01:024
NELSON, CHARLES F & HANNA, ANNIE	23 APR 1908	12:166
NELSON, DAVIS G & GREENLEE, JANE	1834	01:040
NELSON, FREEMAN & GRIMM, CORDELIA A	20 JUN 1886	12:338
NELSON, HENRY & PHILLIPS, RACHEL LORINDA	01 JAN 1892	06:274

NELSON, JOHN F & GILMORE, DORA B	27 MAY 1911	13:321
NELSON, LAWRENCE A & MONROE, ETTA M	22 NOV 1911	13:425
NEUMAN, JOHN W & ROLLINS, MAGGIE E	18 JUN 1902	10:092
NEVILLE, AUSTIN & LEMASTER, NANCY ANN	23 JUL 1863	03:124
NEVILLE, BENJAMIN FRANKLIN & KINDER, MAUD LULU	*30 MAY 1893	06:548
NEVILLE, ELIJAH M & TIPTON, PERLIE A	14 SEP 1896	07:608
NEVILLE, GEORGE E & WRAY, LENA M	18 SEP 1903	10:363
NEVILLE, H M & SHAHAN, ZENNA E	15 SEP 1910	13:158
NEVILLE, JOHN R & BURNS, MARY E	23 OCT 1894	07:177
NEVILLE, WALTER H & GLOVER, AUDLEY	28 APR 1906	11:302
NEVILLE, WILLIAM & BRIGHT, LOUISA	17 JUN 1899	08:558
NEWBERRY, JOSEPH & GIBBS, ELIZABETH	*30 JUL 1855	02:007
NEWBERRY, MARION D & CUTSHAW, SENA	03 NOV 1898	08:398
NEWBRAUGH, DANIEL W & ROSE, MARY	14 APR 1902	10:055
NEWEL, HOMER & McCLOUD, DELIA	22 NOV 1898	08:411
NEWEL, JOHN W & ABBOTT, REBECCA E	26 JAN 1871	07:048
NEWEL, PRESTON & PARSONS, REBECCA	*11 DEC 1854	02:006
NEWELL, DENIS & CLUFT, HATTIE	05 APR 1911	13:305
NEWELL, DENNIS & BARBER, VINIA	30 APR 1903	10:282
NEWELL, ELIJAH F & MORRISON, SARAH ANN	*23 DEC 1851	02:001
NEWELL, ERASTUS J & McGLOUGHLIN, OLIVE J	23 JAN 1874	08:092
NEWELL, GEORGE C & JOHNSON, LETHA J	23 SEP 1899	08:617
NEWELL, GEORGE WILLIAM & BARBER, ELIZABETH ELLEN	03 SEP 1900	09:186
NEWELL, HOMER & EDWARDS, ALICE	10 FEB 1907	11:494
NEWELL, J P & KNAPPENBERGER, FLORENCE	25 SEP 1884	12:064
NEWELL, JACOB & JACKSON, MARY	28 SEP 1819	01:006
NEWELL, JAMES & BARBER, FANNY	25 DEC 1905	11:228
NEWELL, JOHN T & CONKLE, DORKIEST L	04 SEP 1905	11:160
NEWELL, MILLARD & FLOWERS, MARY E	26 FEB 1892	06:294
MEWELL, MILLARD & BUCK, MILLIE	04 JUL 1895	07:332
NEWELL, STEPHEN E & MILLER, MINERVA G	21 JAN 1875	08:206
NEWELL, W A & LANIER, CHARLOTTE	06 AUG 1910	13:126
NEWLAND, EDWARD B & STUMP, MARGARET J	10 NOV 1868	06:009
NEWLAND, EDWARD B & FOSTER, FANNIE A	02 JAN 1896	07:480
NEWMAN, CHARLES & SULLIVAN, MARY JANE	*24 DEC 1853	02:005
NEWMAN, CHARLES & KING, FRANCES E	23 FEB 1882	11:115
NEWMAN, JAMES L & KIMBERLING, PENELOPE	05 DEC 1846	01:046
NEWMAN, LEROY & ATKINSON, ELIZABETH A	09 APR 1845	01:044
NEWMAN, R & SPRAWLS, ETHEL	18 JUL 1910	13:115
NEWSOME, WILLIAM & WRIGHT, LOU	22 MAY 1893	06:543
NEWTON, DOUGLAS E & MOREDOCK, JENNIE S	18 OCT 1864	03:302
NIBERT, BERT & HUDSON, DELLA	14 FEB 1909	12:366
NIBERT, CARL & LANIER, DELLA	17 DEC 1913	15:090
NIBERT, CHARLES & LANIER, VIRGINIA C	03 DEC 1879	10:172
NIBERT, GEORGE & SPEARS, KATE	23 OCT 1904	10:615
NIBERT, GEORGE R & WARD, EMMA	10 JAN 1885	12:125
NIBERT, JOHN W & FLORA, MARY A	*06 AUG 1878	09:295
NIBERT, JOSEPH & GIFT, CATHARINE	04 FEB 1847	01:047
NIBERT, PETER & FIFE, ELIZABETH	21 JAN 1887	12:470
NIBERT, PETER & HOWELL, MARY B	27 MAR 1896	07:520
NIBERT, SEBASTIN & DUFOUR, NETTIE	25 DEC 1889	05:499
NICELEY, NORDA & CAMP, ATTIE	12 MAR 1902	10:033
NICHOLL, ANDREW & SMITH, SUSAN	15 APR 1892	06:322
NICHOLS, ALFRED D & CRAIG, IDA MAY	11 JUL 1902	10:108
NICHOLS, CHARLES A E & RUSSELL, ETTA	06 MAY 1888	05:224
NICHOLS, FRANCIS MARRION & McDERMITT, BLANCH	*21 JAN 1892	06:278
NICHOLS, GEORGE W & MOORE, SARAH M B	24 AUG 1885	12:212
NICHOLS, HENRY W H & CASTO, MARGARET E	13 OCT 1878	09:331

NICHOLS, NATHAN & LEGUE, LELA	03 MAR 1888	05:191
NICHOLS, THOMAS & LEE, BETSY	1832	01:027
NICHOLS, THOMAS & LEE, ELIZABETH	1833	01:039
NICHOLS, WM EMIT & JACKSON, E ETHEL	29 AUG 1911	13:367
NICHOLSON, JOHN W & RUTTER, MARY E	09 MAR 1911	13:288
NICKLEN, DAVID E & ROBSON, MARIETTA	13 JUL 1889	05:424
NIDAY, ERCEL E & KANOUS, ELLIE E	24 MAR 1910	13:030
NIDAY, HUBERT C & CARTER, BESSIE J	14 AUR 1909	12:480
NIDAY, LUTHER McKINLEY & KLICKER, ELLA	28 OCT 1914	15:307
NIPPS, JAMES W & ROUSH, ADA M	31 MAR 1909	12:392
NISSE, EMMANUEL & AUMILLER, CATHARINE	14 DEC 1817	01:003
NOBLE, ANSON & DICKEN, MARY	07 JAN 1869	06:028
NOBLE, ANSON ALBERT & GLEASON, BARBARA ELIZABETH	03 JUN 1913	14:166
NOBLE, ELI & STEWART, DIEMMA	27 NOV 1887	05:150
NOBLE, ERASTUS & LEWIS, ELIZA JANE	21 JUL 1862	03:071
NOBLE, HARRY W & JONES, ELSIE J	26 NOV 1906	11:459
NOBLE, ISAIAH & WEAVER, ROXANA	11 NOV 1908	12:304
NOBLE, JAMES & BASS, EVA	08 SEP 1892	06:401
NOBLE, JAMES R & BROOKS, LIZZIE	21 MAY 1898	08:312
NOBLE, JOHN T & DOW, NANNIE J	19 OCT 1884	12:076
NOBLE, JOHN WILLIAM & PILES, ANNIE	30 SEP 1891	06:194
NOBLE, LEWIS A & THORNTON, JULIA CAROLINE FRANCES	03 JUL 1890	05:584
NOBLE, MARCUS D & THOMPSON, ANNA	16 SEP 1875	08:272
NOBLE, MARCUS D & SAULSER, LUCINDA	*24 DEC 1858	02:012
NOBLE, RUSSELL & DAVIS, CYNTHIA	20 APR 1879	10:077
NOBLE, WILLIAM THURMAN & MOURNING, LAURA ELLEN	04 JUN 1889	05:407
NOGAN, ORAN & PIERCE, MARY F	23 DEC 1877	09:176
NORRIS, JOHN & BARKER, HARRIET A	13 OCT 1907	12:039
NORRIS, JOHN L & KNAPP, NEVA A	19 DEC 1914	15:347
NORRIS, PHILSON & WRIGHT, LYDIA A	06 JUN 1875	08:295
NORSE, WILLIAM & HENRY, ELIZABETH	28 DEC 1837	01:032
NORTH, ANDREW & WALLIS, NANCY E	29 MAR 1883	11:333
NORTH, COLUMBUS & SHOWALTERS, ROSA	31 JAN 1887	12:474
NORTH, WILLIAM E & FLETCHER, LILLIE M	14 AUG 1897	08:141
NORTH, WILLIAM E & WRIGHT, BESSIE MAY	23 DEC 1909	12:577
NORTON, HARRY J & REDMAN, OLIVIA A	03 NOV 1886	12:413
NORTON, JULIAN H & WORK, GRACE A	22 DEC 1899	09:039
NORVELL, BENJAMIN J & LAW, MARY JANE	1837	01:040
NORVELL, CARY WINDON & JEFFERS, ELIZABETH	18 OCT 1827	01:020
NORVELL, JAMES & CRAIG, VIRGINIA	28 DEC 1882	11:281
NORVELL, JOSIAH & SHILTS, JANIE	28 NOV 1887	05:151
NORVELL, THOMAS & FARGO, DELILA	1831	01:024
NORVELL, WILLIAM & KAUFMAN, MARTHA ANN	*19 MAR 1851	02:001
NORVELL, WILLIAM G & KNAPP, LILLIE	01 SEP 1892	06:397
NORVELL, WILLIS S & HIGENBOTHAM, NANCY	1843	01:041
NOTT, CHARLES & TAYLOR, LAURA	12 MAR 1896	07:508
NOTT, CLAUDE E & LONG, CAROLINE	10 JUL 1909	12:456
NOTT, EBER E & WITHERS, NELLIE B	04 JUL 1906	11:363
NOTTINGHAM, FRANK & FLETCHER, MATTIE	11 OCT 1908	12:283
NOTTINGHAM, JAMES C & McCALLISTER, OLIVIA	30 DEC 1892	06:494
NOTTINGHAM, WILLIAM & BLACK, MALINDA	23 MAY 1831	01:025
NOURSE, ALVIN L B & HOWARD, AUGUSTA E	03 NOV 1897	08:190
NOWLIN, ELLIS & WRAY, JANE	29 MAR 1872	07:206
NOWLIN, JAMES A & McCALLISTER, EVA	02 NOV 1907	12:058
NOWLIN, JOSEPH WILSON & LEGGE, EMMA	29 NOV 1892	06:449
NUCKLE, SAMUEL F & FURGET, NANCY C	23 MAR 1905	11:060
NUCKLES, DENNIS R & BUFFINGTON, ANNA M	19 AUG 1914	15:258
NUCKLES, JAMES W & SMITH, ELIZA J	14 MAR 1894	07:061

NUCKLES, JOHN E & CAVET, CLARA	11 DEC 1879	10:174
NUCKLES, JOHN E & HERDMAN, MARTHA E	27 MAY 1908	12:186
NULL, HENRY & WHITE, MINTIE	23 DEC 1911	13:446
NULSEN, WILLIAM K & STEWART, EDNA	30 AUG 1908	12:243
NUTTER, BINAS & YOUNG, AGNES C	27 JUN 1903	10:310
NUTTER, CURTIS M & BIRCHFIELD, LETIE A	16 MAY 1882	11:151
NUTTER, CURTIS MATHEW & THARP, BELLE	28 NOV 1888	05:314
NUTTER, JAMES E & SWALLOW, MARY E	15 JUN 1880	10:267
NUTTER, ROBERT E & GIBSON, MISELLANA	30 APR 1885	12:168
NUTTER, SAMUEL P & YEAGER, EMELINE	*01 MAR 1854	02:005
NYBERT, GEORGE & MAYES, ANN E	14 MAR 1838	01:032 5
NYE, GEORGE B & FOWLER, GERTRUDE	10 OCT 1908	12:282
NYE, SAMPSON S & HIGGINS, LAURA S	24 MAY 1877	09:084
O'BRIEN, WILLIAM J & VOLLERT, LOUISE C	16 OCT 1894	07:169
O'DANIEL, WILLIAM & BURNS, KATIE	01 JUN 1904	10:529
O'DELL, THOMAS H & GAMBLE, CLARA E	14 DEC 1910	13:226
O'DONNELL, PATRICK & GRESS, (Mrs) ATLINE	26 FEB 1865	03:226
O'HARA, JOHN & BARCUS, MARTHA MAY	02 MAR 1910	13:019
O'NAIL, SOLOMON & ROSEBERRY, MINNIE	27 AUG 1887	05:077
O'NEAL, WILLIAM & HUDSON, LINNIE	05 APR 1893	06:519
ONEIL, JOHN & HOLMES, EDNA B	24 MAY 1905	11:097
OAKES, JAMES W & HAWKINS, ELVIRA J	*01 DEC 1860	02:014
OGDEN, NELSON GREEN & POLSLEY, HARRIET S	28 APR 1879	10:076
OHLINGER, ABRAHAM & ROUSH, DOLLY	27 OCT 1869	06:107
OHLINGER, CHARLES T & PECK, ELLA	07 MAR 1903	10:252
OHLINGER, CLIFFORD L & BORHAM, EVA L	11 DEC 1909	12:566
OHLINGER, FREDRICK T & ZERCKLE, FRANCES V	07 APR 1901	09:320
OHLINGER, FRED T & ROUSH, FANNIE E	22 FEB 1911	13:270
OHLINGER, GEORGE L & EDWARDS, HELEN J	29 NOV 1885	12:259
OHLINGER, HENRY & ROUSH, SARAH ANN	26 DEC 1867	05:123
OHLINGER, HENRY D & ROUSH, IDA F	26 OCT 1902	10:179
OHLINGER, JESSE N & RICKARD, HATTIE M	12 JUL 1911	13:344
OHLINGER, JNO & ROUSH, MARY	*04 MAR 1861	02:015
OHLINGER, JOHN & ALTICE, ANNA	*07 JAN 1861	02:015
OHLINGER, JOHN & ROUSH, LOUISA C	26 MAY 1870	06:192
OHLINGER, JOHN L & FISHER, CLARA A	25 DEC 1894	07:220
OHLINGER, JOSEPH H & ROUSH, MILLIE S	23 NOV 1904	10:640
OHLINGER, JOSEPH R & McDANIEL, CORA BELLE	18 AUG 1895	07:361
OHLINGER, LAFAYETTE & LIONS, NANCY JANE	28 AUG 1889	05:435
OHLINGER, ROBERT T & VICKERS, LOUISANA	27 MAR 1889	05:376
OHLINGER, SIMON P & TUCKER, NANCY	05 JUN 1873	08:110
OHLINGER, W H & LIEVING, FREDRIECA	23 JUN 1914	15:225
OHLINGER, WESLEY PETER & COX, STELLA TENNESSEE	19 FEB 1903	10:243
OHLINGER, WILLIAM & SMITH, SARAH C	*02 APR 1860	02:014
OHLINGER, WILLIAM V & BROWN, ANNIE	10 APR 1895	07:284
OLDAKER, BIRT C & NIBERT, MARY	06 JAN 1908	12:116
OLDAKER, GEORGE ALLEN & VOLENTINE, LUCY ELIZABETH	12 SEP 1892	06:405
OLDAKER, JAMES W & HALL, MARIAM	02 AUG 1867	05:070
OLDAKER, JOSEPH & SAUNDERS, JANE A	04 OCT 1878	09:325
OLDAKER, JOSEPH & JEFFERS, RUBY	(no date)	11:571
OLDAKER, LEWIS & CRAIG, MARY	19 FEB 1893	06:491
OLDAKER, BENJAMIN & KIRKPATRICK, MARTHA	23 MAY 1844	01:042
OLDAKER, PASCHAL & KIRKPATRICK, MARY JANE	26 DEC 1844	01:042
OLDAKER, WASHINGTON & BUTCHER, LULA	13 MAY 1895	07:302
OLDAKER, WILLIAM & PRIDDY, MARY	22 FEB 1831	01:025
OLIPHINT, THOMAS J & KIMBERLING, EVA B	31 JUL 1878	09:291
OLIVER, ANDREW & RICKART, MALINDA	*24 DEC 1851	02:001
OLIVER, CHARLES H & DURST, LULA M	22 JUN 1901	09:362

Name	Date	Ref
OLIVER, CHARLES J & MORIARITY, KATIE	21 FEB 1882	11:114
OLIVER, CHARLES W & LEMASTER, LULA	08 AUG 1908	12:223
OLIVER, DANIEL & DOWNES, MARY ANN	03 SEP 1848	01:050
OLIVER, DANIEL C & FISHER, SARAH	*15 NOV 1854	02:006
OLIVER, ELI & BARR, MARY ELLEN	26 NOV 1863	03:144
OLIVER, ELI & BRANNAN, MATILDA C	26 DEC 1886	12:445
OLIVER, ELSWORTH P & GILSON, POLLY	26 FEB 1882	11:117
OLIVER, ESLA MARION & ROLLINS, VIRGINIA	11 AUG 1888	05:256
OLIVER, FRANCIS M & STEPHENSON, JULIA	19 DEC 1861	03:040
OLIVER, GEORGE & VANMATRE, HARRIET	14 JUN 1829	01:018
OLIVER, GEORGE N & KNAPP, EMMA F	22 JAN 1893	06:472
OLIVER, GEORGE W & RUSSELL, HATTIE B	07 APR 1880	10:230
OLIVER, GEORGE W & CLARK, LENA	03 JUL 1895	07:328
OLIVER, JOHN & MEHEN, MARGARET J	25 NOV 1875	08:301
OLIVER, JOHN & CLARK, ELLA	18 AUG 1897	08:143
OLIVER, JOHN C & CHEESEBREW, BARBARA A	05 APR 1870	06:177
OLIVER, LEWIS D & POTTS, BELLE	11 MAY 1880	10:253
OLIVER, LEWIS W & McMARRY, MARGARET	22 AUG 1908	12:230
OLIVER, MIER & KNAPP, CHARLOTTE M	26 DEC 1869	06:129
OLIVER, OAFFA & KNAPP, IDA	05 APR 1896	07:522
OLIVER, SAMUEL & GREENLEE, HANNAH C	27 JAN 1865	03:218
OLIVER, SAMUEL & EDWARDS, MARY E	18 SEP 1904	10:600
OLIVER, THOMAS D & MONROE, MARTHA W	10 NOV 1872	07:287
OLIVER, WILLIAM & EVERETT, LUCY	08 JAN 1840	01:033
OLIVER, WILLIAM HENRY & BARNETT, ALTA	24 MAY 1814	15:200
OLMSTEAD, CHARLES A & JONES, LUELLA	20 SEP 1896	07:612
ORD, ARTHUR & ROUSH, MARY FRANCES	10 DEC 1913	15:084
ORD, ELSDON & CHESTER, ELLEN A	08 JUN 1871	07:095
ORD, GEORGE E & PRITCHARD, SARAH E	24 DEC 1893	07:027
ORD, JOHN W & GRINSTEAD, SARAH	23 FEB 1879	10:058
ORMSTON, JAMES WILLIAM & PECK, ETTA MAY	06 JUN 1900	09:137
ORR, EDWARD F & HARRISON, MAGGIE	27 NOV 1884	12:095
ORR, ROBERT F & LOVE, LUTITIA	11 SEP 1879	10:127
ORR, WILLIAM H & WILSON, CATHARINE	19 NOV 1881	11:056
OSBORN, JOHN E & SCHOONOVER, ADDA I	03 AUG 1904	10:566
OSBORNE, HARVEY & CLENDINEN, OZELLA	05 DEC 1865	04:080
OSBURN, CHAMPEON L & YEAGER, MARY	26 JUN 1838	01:031
OSHEL, VICTOR S & MAUPIN, ELIZABETH J	23 OCT 1895	07:410
OTT, STEPHEN S & GREER, SYLVIA L	*02 APR 1907	11:520
OURS, CHARLES E & McGUIRE, NANCY M A	22 APR 1886	12:320
OURS, JOHN & BONNET, MARY	29 APR 1821	01:007
OVERMIRE, EARL L & DYER, ELMA G	08 AUG 1905	11:133
OVERSHINER, ABRAHAM & McDANIEL, SARAH	*22 JOCT 1850	02:001
OVERSHINER, MARTIN & MINNICK, SARAH	23 NOV 1845	01:045
OWEN, ROBERT & STANSBERRY, SALLIE V	05 FEB 1894	07:043
OWENS, JOHN H & RILEY, LELA A	11 APR 1908	12:158
OWENS, JOHN L & ROUSH, JEMIMA	23 MAY 1899	08:539
OWENS, OKEY J & HERLOW, BERTHA	07 JAN 1900	09:061
OWENS, WILLIAM & CREMEANS, JULIA A	18 JUL 1878	09:287
OWENS, WILLIAM T & GASKINS, NANCY	18 AUG 1844	03:193
OZMINT, YARBURN N & HICKS, SUSAN	06 FEB 1848	01:046
PAGE, HENRY W & FETTY, LUCINDA J	03 JUN 1877	09:092
PAGE, JOHN W & SNELL, ELVIRA	31 DEC 1840	01:034
PAINTER, JAMES & LEWIS, ELIZABETH	03 SEP 1846	01:046
PALMER, ISAAC & PATTERSON, HULDA	09 MAY 1892	06:335
PALMER, ISAAC & TERRY, SARAH C	23 FEB 1904	10:479
PANNILL, JACKSON L & WILEY, VIRGINIA W	03 NOV 1903	10:402
PARENT, ROBERT & WHITE, LOTA MAY	24 MAY 1913	14:159

PARISH, JASPER & GOULDING, MARY A	25 APR 1871	07:080
PARK, SIMON NELSON & WILEY, MALINDA ANN	17 NOV 1887	05:140
PARKER, EDWARD E & MULFORD, VERNA MAY	25 JUN 1910	13:099
PARKER, HUGH & NEWEL, SARAH	*23 APR 1855	02:006
PARKER, MARTIN L & LEGG, ANNIE LAURA	05 MAY 1900	09:123
PARKER, SAMUEL & LEVISAY, FANNIE	10 SEP 1863	03:133
PARKINS, NATHAN & CAMPBELL, ISABELLA	20 OCT 1847	01:047
PARR, HAMILTON A & ROSEBERRY, CORA L	27 FEB 1893	06:498
PARROTT, WILLIAM & KEEFER, JANE	15 FEB 1871	07:051
PARRY, CHARLES & CONRAD, STELLA	06 MAR 1908	12:135
PARSINGER, ALEXANDER & MAZE, PATSY	04 JUN 1821	01:009
PARSON, WILLIAM & BONNETT, SUSANNA	12 NOV 1826	01:015
PARSONS, CALVIN W & BUMGARNER, SARAH	*01 APR 1861	02:015
PARSONS, CHARLES & TAYLOR, EVA L	06 SEP 1884	12:054
PARSONS, CHARLES A & COLEMAN, DICIA	19 MAR 1903	10:259
PARSONS, CLARENCE E & PRICE, LEAH K	04 NOV 1908	12:285
PARSONS, DAVID & ROUSH, ELIZABETH	*18 FEB 1856	02:008
PARSONS, DELLA J & PARSONS, ROSA L	28 DEC 1903	10:450
PARSONS, ELBERT W & MITCHELL, EDNA	23 JUN 1912	13:549
PARSONS, GEORGE & WOODRUFF, FANNY	01 MAR 1827	01:020
PARSONS, GEORGE F & HUDSON, MARY A	26 JUL 1884	12:040
PARSONS, GEORGE W & ROLLER, MINA M	20 FEB 1889	05:355
PARSONS, GEORGE W & WORELL, ELLA	31 DEC 1903	10:454
PARSONS, HENRY & TURNER, LEVINA	05 JUN 1823	01:010
PARSONS, JAMES & McDANIEL, ADALINE	18 FEB 1895	07:249
PARSONS, JAMES M & SCHLARB, EMMA R L	09 DEC 1880	10:335
PARSONS, JOHN & MILLER, SALLY	09 JAN 1820	01:006
PARSONS, JOHN & SAYRES, R	19 JUN 1823	01:010
PARSONS, JOHN A & MILLER, ELIZABETH PEARL	16 OCT 1913	15:051
PARSONS, JOHN N & BARNETT, EMILY	*01 JAN 1855	02:006
PARSONS, LEMON & McDERMITT, OSA	16 DEC 1874	08:195
PARSONS, LEMAN & MATTOX, SUSAN	22 FEB 1913	14:093
PARSONS, LOYD & SKEENS, ESTELLA	03 OCT 1903	10:380
PARSONS, MEREDITH & CLONCH, ELIZABETH	06 FEB 1825	01:011
PARSONS, PERRY F & HOWELL, LORA B	15 SEP 1912	14:002
PARSONS, THORNTON A & ROSEBERRY, MAUDE	23 DEC 1912	14:062
PARSONS, TRAVIS & HESS, POLLY	06 MAY 1830	01:023
PARSONS, WILLIAM S & ALLEMONG, ALICE B	10 APR 1898	08:266
PARTLOW, ADAM & LEE, SUSIE	17 AUG 1913	15:012
PASCOE, JOHN A & ROUSH, MINNIE V	22 AUG 1894	07:141
PATEN, WILKES & PASIN, CATHARINE	02 MAR 1880	10:220
PATTERSON, DONALD & ADKINS, SARAH A	06 AUG 1904	10:569
PATTERSON, HEZEKIAH S & LEPORT, EUNICE J	03 MAR 1881	10:378
PATTERSON, HEZEKIAH & PATTERSON, NANCY	26 JUN 1882	11:168
PATTERSON, JACOB & SHELINE, HULDAH	07 OCT 1873	08:037
PATTERSON, JACOB & BOSTER, COREVA	07 FEB 1909	12:364
PATTERSON, JACOB ALEXANDER & DAYVALT, MARY FRANCES	02 OCT 1892	06:418
PATTERSON, JAMES WM & DOSS, LAVINA ANN	16 JUL 1863	03:120
PATTERSON, JOHN & MOBLEY, AUGUSTA	16 NOV 1889	05:482
PATTERSON, JOHN L & RULEN, LUCINDA	27 APR 1902	10:060
PATTERSON, OBEDIAH & CLONCH, EMILY MARGARET	24 JAN 1900	09:072
PATTERSON, ROBERT J & KNIGHT, LAURA S	07 SEP 1892	06:402
PATTERSON, ROBERT W & PECK, GEORGIA	11 AUG 1903	10:335
PATTON, GEORGE W & BALL, ANNIE	14 FEB 1900	09:082
PAULEY, CALAHAN & MARLIN, HARRIET E	25 AUG 1874	08:154
PAULEY, CORNELIUS & HOOPS, MARY	16 NOV 1868	06:006
PAULEY, THOMAS A & WESTFALL, IVA	22 SEP 1909	12:513
PAULINE, JOHN E & McCOLLISTER, AMANDA E	*14 SEP 1860	02:014

PAXTON, WILLIAM & WEAVER, MARTHA E	30 APR 1874	08:115
PAYNE, JAMES A & OLDAKER, URENIA	09 NOV 1826	01:013
PAYNE, JOHN & CARTER, CLARA	04 MAY 1871	07:085
PAYNE, JOSEPH & VIRCA, ELIZABETH	26 DEC 1880	10:362
PAYNE, SOTHI & WATSON, BESSIE	05 APR 1910	13:037
PEARCE, CHARLES & PERSINGER, VIRGINIA	20 APR 1879	10:077
PEARCE, THOMAS & KELL, ELIZABETH	19 JUN 1870	06:202
PEARCE, ELIJAH & GARTON, PATSY	(no date)	01:027
PEARSON, GRANVILLE & ELLIOTT, NANCY E	24 NOV 1906	11:454
PEARSON, HENRY FREDERICK & ROBERTS, EFFIE E	19 DEC 1901	09:472
PEARSON, JAMES W & SHELINE, CATHARINE E	24 AUG 1869	06:084
PEARSON, JOSEPH & VAN SICKLE, DELLE	02 AUG 1912	13:579
PEARSON, WILLIAM & DUNCAN, LURAY J	25 AUG 1898	08:353
PEARSON, WILLIAM H & ROGERS, STELLA	06 JUL 1904	10:650
PECK, ALEXANDER & BARBER, MARTHA	11 JAN 1898	08:245
PECK, ANDREW J & RIGGS, SUSAN E	28 DEC 1865	04:093
PECK, BENJAMIN F & LANHAM, MATTIE B	12 OCT 1880	10:310
PECK, E D & KNICKLES, MANDY	30 DEC 1911	13:460
PECK, ED & FULLERTON, FLOSSIE	30 JAN 1899	08:460
PECK, FRANK E & WOOD, ALLIE L	15 JAN 1908	12:119
PECK, HENRY V & GARDNER, ANN	16 MAR 1852	02:002
PECK, ROBERT M & RYAN,	*04 JUN 1856	02:008
PECK, SILAS & THOMAS, MARY J	24 OCT 1897	08:176
PECK, WILBER W & SPAUN, WINNIE MAY	16 FEB 1890	05:523
PEGRAM, WILLIAM E & DURST, RILLA J	01 SEP 1895	07:375
PENCE, MARION & EDWARDS, MARGARET	28 DEC 1871	07:164
PENNICK, WILLIAM B & WADDELL, KATIE	16 NOV 1880	10:329
PENNIE, CHARLES A & CONNARD, SARAH A	02 AUG 1887	05:067
PENNINGTON, JOHN A & MORRIS, SUSAN M	25 JAN 1877	09:029
PEREGO, JOHN E & BUSH, ELIZABETH R	17 APR 1884	12:008
PERKINS, MARION F & DARST, MARY MAGDALENE	20 MAR 1909	12:388
PERKINS, WELLINGTON COLBY & CLARKE, NANNIE MARIE	09 NOV 1914	15:311
PERRY, ABNER L K & CROWDER, LENORA	28 APR 1899	08:521
PERRY, ADDISON & ROUSH, MARTHA	03 DEC 1868	06:015
PERRY, CHARLES A & KRAUTTER, ANNIE	23 JUL 1899	08:580
PERRY, CURTIS & NESSELLROOD, BERTHA	23 JUL 1899	08:581
PERRY, DAVID & RODGERS, ELIZABETH	04 SEP 1887	05:078
PERRY, GEORGE & MORROW, NANCY F	19 AUG 1873	08:019
PERRY, HENRY R & MASH, LUCY L	29 OCT 1863	03:140
PERRY, JESSIE & FOWLER, ADA	28 JAN 1908	12:122
PERRY, JOHN & BALL, MARTHA	14 APR 1877	09:065
PERRY, NELSON F & HERTJE, BARBARA	21 NOV 1906	11:454
PERRY, OLIVER H & SPENCER, MARY A	28 JAN 1893	06:478
PERRY, THOMAS E & FAUDREE, IDA R	01 JUN 1896	07:559
PERRY, WILLIAM & McCOY, MINNIE	23 SEP 1896	07:615
PERSINGER, ALEXANDER & CHAPMAN, MARY	*30 JAN 1860	02:013
PERSINGER, CHARLES LEE & HUMPREY, MARY E	04 APR 1866	04:115
PERSINGER, CHARLES REUBEN & BARTRAM, FRANCES	02 MAR 1888	05:190
PERSINGER, CHARLES S & SIMPKINS, VIRGINIA S	30 APR 1872	07;219
PERSINGER, IRA & STOVER, IDA M	26 AUG 1891	06:171
PERSINGER, THOMAS & SIDERS, FANNIE	18 JAN 1892	06:276
PERSINGER, THOMAS J & CONRAD, VIRGINIA	28 AUG 1884	12:050
PETERS, CHARLES W & YOUSE, ANNIE A	15 OCT 1904	10:613
PETERS, LEWIS EDWARD & CHAPMAN, MARGARET L	25 APR 1882	11:142
PETREL, PETER & McGREW, ISABEL	15 OCT 1865	04:061
PETTY, CHARLES W & BROWN, NETTIE A	29 JAN 1896	07:494
PETTY, WILLIAM H & GREGORY, ALTHEA S	27 JUL 1893	06:581
PEYATT, JOHN S & SNIDER, MARY C	18 SEP 1864	03:196

PEYATT, WILLIAM H & SNYDER, LUCINDA	29 MAR 1868	05:157
PEYTON, JOHN W & JONES, NANCY	15 JUL 1869	06:066
PEYTON, V B HORTON & PHILLIPS, EMILY J	22 FEB 1888	05:186
PFOST, GEORGE W & RICKARD, ANGALINA	*09 AUG 1854	02:005
PFOST, LEWIS A & ROUSH, ROXA	10 DEC 1888	05:319
PHELPS, JAMES & COLWELL, LULA	20 SEP 1885	12:222
PHELPS, JAMES, & COLWELL, LENA	22 FEB 1891	06:066
PHELPS, OLIVER & McBRIEN, WILHELMINA	01 MAY 1870	06:186
PHELPS, OLIVER & JONES, BIRDIE	27 MAR 1889	05:375
PHELPS, THORNTON L & HOBBS, HENRIETTA	22 MAY 1879	10:091
PHILIPS, E N & STAATS, MARY L	20 OCT 1878	09:338
PHILIPS, RUEL ELVA & TAYLOR, MARY	24 DEC 1902	10:215
PHILLIPS, JOHN P & WEIRS, MARY J	*27 APR 1858	02:011
PHILLIPS, MARION S & POTTS, ANNA	21 AUG 1893	06:588
PHILLIPS, WILLIAM A & STORTZ, MARY	05 DEC 1876	08:417
PHILLIPS, WILLIAM J & RAPP, DORA	29 NOV 1905	11:215
PHILLIPS, WILLIAM N & JEFFERS, MARY E	27 NOV 1874	08:190
PHILLIPS, ZACHARIAH & HALL, CATHARINE	05 JUL 1885	12:190
PIATT, ANDREW & ROUSH, MARTHA J	12 DEC 1873	08:071
PIATT, BENJAMIN F & HARSHEY, NANCY J	24 JUL 1865	04:030
PIATT, CHARLES Z & HARSHA, MATTIE	03 APR 1886	12:314
PIATT, WILLIAM & BLAKE, EVA M	14 JUN 1910	13:088
PICKENS, ALBERT S & FISHER, NINA M	11 SEP 1894	07:150
PICKENS, ANDREW & DERINBERGER, RUTH	23 AUG 1838	01:032
PICKENS, ANDREW O & DEWEES, REBECCA E	06 DEC 1898	08:426
PICKENS, ABIAL A & BURRIS, LOUISA	18 JUN 1880	10:270
PICKENS, ARTIMUS & NUCKLES, MARY L	18 FEB 1900	09:085
PICKENS, CALVIN ELA & MEDLEY, MARY ELLEN	12 OCT 1887	05:119
PICKENS, DAVID S & JEFFERS, HARRIET E	29 APR 1870	06:185
PICKENS, EZRA & CARNES, SARAH L	23 JAN 1886	12:284
PICKENS, FLOYD & RIFFLE, ANNIE	26 DEC 1900	09:268
PICKENS, FRED & ARTHUR, MARY A	23 OCT 1884	12:079
PICKENS, GEORGE W & HALBLEIB, MAGGIE	29 JUN 1906	11:352
PICKENS, HENRY & KLINGENSMITH, ELIZABETH J	22 JUN 1865	04:017
PICKENS, HENRY C & WILSON, SARAH J	06 MAY 1883	11:335
PICKENS, HOMER A & CAIN, DEBORAH	05 AUG 1905	11:135
PICKENS, JAMES P & RICKARD, MARY C	10 MAY 1866	04:120
PICKENS, JOHN & BERTHAL, MARTHA	10 FEB 1863	03:098
PICKENS, JOSEPH A & THOMAS, BLANCHE	22 JAN 1902	10:010
PICKENS, MINER & JIVIDEN, IDA	17 FEB 1899	08:467
PICKENS, OKEY MILTON & BLESSING, ALTA AUGUSTA	25 OCT 1913	15:058
PICKENS, PHILIP & COSSIN, ELLA M	04 OCT 1904	10:609
PICKENS, RICHARDSON & TAYLOR, JULIA ANN	*22 NOV 1854	02:006
PICKENS, ROBERT & ROUSH, CAROLINE	06 JAN 1870	06:139
PICKENS, ROY E & YONKER, MABLE BONNER	05 JUN 1912	13:537
PICKENS, SPENCER & KNAPP, MARGARET ANN	*04 AUG 1852	02:003
PICKENS, WILLIAM E & ROUSH, DELLA F	23 JAN 1896	07:492
PICKENS, WILLIAM R & RILEY, CORA P	30 JUL 1904	10:554
PIERCE, CHAS A & BEBEE, ROSA L	26 AUG 1890	05:603
PIERCE, GEORGE F & WHITT, FRANCES	22 JUN 1891	06:137
PIERCE, GEORGE W & HOLLEY, EVA	22 FEB 1905	11:047
PIERCE, HOMER W & SPRADLING, BESSIE J	08 AUG 1814	15:252
PIERCE, ISAAC F & ANDERSON, MARY S	11 JAN 1879	10:054
PIERCE, JAMES P & CLARK, VIRGINIA	11 JAN 1878	09:196
PIERCE, JOSEPH & LOVE, CAROLINE	27 SEP 1882	11:215
PIERCE, JOSEPH & SNIDER, BERTHA L	01 MAR 1892	06:298
PIERCE, LAFAYETTE & PARKS, ELIZABETH	16 JUN 1893	06:556
PIERCE, LAWSON E & WEETHEE, ROSABELL	26 MAR 1901	09:308

Names	Date	Ref
PIERCE, SHERMAN & WOGAN, (Mrs) EMMA	06 OCT 1911	13:389
PIERCE, WILLIAM H & HUDSON, ELIZABETH	03 FEB 1882	11:106
PIERCE, WILLIAM H & GEHO, SARAH M	15 DEC 1898	08:433
PIERCE, ELIJAH & GARTON, PATSY	1833	01:039
PIERCE, JAMES P & CARTWRIGHT, MARY SABRA	*30 JUL 1853	02:004
PIERCY, WILLLIAM & PRIDDY, LUCY	02 JAN 1831	01:025
PIERSON, BERRIMAN B & ROBERTS, LILLIE M	24 DEC 1900	09:258
PIERSON, JAMES & HAYMAN, LETTIE A C	28 FEB 1914	15:150
PIERSON, JOHN & YAUGER, RACHEL	13 FEB 1877	09:030
PIERSON, WILLIAM & ELLIOTT, ALNORAH	03 JUN 1906	11:331
PIKE, JAMES A & CASEY, EMMA F	13 MAR 1896	07:509
PIKE, JAMES & BLAKE, (Mrs) JESSIE	12 APR 1910	13:040
PILCHARD, LEONIDAS T & YOUNG, LINNA DROWN	29 MAY 1890	05:563
PILCHARD, WILLIAM H & BROWN, FRANCES J	17 OCT 1877	09:141
PILES, ELI & JOHNSON, LAURA	25 OCT 1899	08:636
PILES, JOSHUA & WOODYARD, LOTTIE	29 AUG 1889	05:444
PILLOW, JAMES R & DOWELL, SUSAN M	06 MAY 1903	10:287
PILLOW, WILLIAM J & GARDNER, LUCY	12 NOV 1868	06:002
PILLOWS, WILLIAM T & BOARDMAN, HATTIE	03 MAY 1906	11:308
PINE, JAMES & PARKER, CHARLIE ANNA	09 AUG 1866	04:145
PINICK, JOHN T & SINES, ELIZABETH	19 JAN 1865	03:217
PINNELL, PERRY C & PUMPHREY, MARY EMMA	*03 FEB 1853	02:004
PINNICK, HENRY C & TURNBULL, HANNAH	23 DEC 1891	06:252
PLACE, HARRY & KOBLENTZ, ANNIE	20 DEC 1893	07:025
PLANTS, CHRISTIAN & LAWSON, ISABELLA	01 MAR 1866	04:106
PLANTS, CHRISTIAN B & KNAPP, CARRIE	02 MAY 1901	09:332
PLANTS, CHRISTOPHER C & ROUSH, SARAH M	16 OCT 1896	07:630
PLANTS, CHRISTOPHER C & PLANTS, ELLA	10 MAR 1901	09:303
PLANTS, ESQUIRE A & CRUMP, SARAH	25 JAN 1882	11:101
PLANTS, FRANCIS MARION & MURRY, MARY	14 FEB 1892	06:288
PLANTS, G L & DeWITT, E GRACE	25 FEB 1912	13:488
PLANTS, GEORGE THOMAS & POWELL, AMANDA	21 MAY 1889	05:402
PLANTS, GEORGE W & HARRIS, SARAH	20 JUN 1867	05:060
PLANTS, GEORGE W & WAMSLEY, ELIZABETH	29 MAY 1895	07:310
PLANTS, ISAAC G & WHITTINGTON, MARY B	19 MAR 1896	07:517
PLANTS, J H & CLONCH, ROMA	14 APR 1913	14:125
PLANTS, JACOB & GRIM, LYDIA MARGARET	23 FEB 1890	05:525
PLANTS, JACOB Jr & THOMAS, ANN	*23 JAN 1861	02:015
PLANTS, JAMES LAWSON & KNAPP, DRUSILLA	29 MAY 1892	06:344
PLANTS, JEROME & STEELE, ANNA M	25 DEC 1901	09:478
PLANTS, JOHN & SMITH, MARY MARIA	*25 MAY 1853	02:004
PLANTS, JOHN & HOSCHAR, JANE C	08 MAR 1866	04:109
PLANTS, JOHN & MORRIS, EMILY	25 MAR 1883	11:313
PLANTS, JOHN H & NEVILLE, SARAH	*16 DEC 1905	11:225
PLANTS, JOSEPH F & HOSCHAR, ELIZABETH	27 JUL 1865	04:031
PLANTS, JOSEPH F & WINDON, ROSA D	21 JAN 1896	07:490
PLANTS, LEONARD & CALDWELL, OLIVIA FRANCES	*01 MAR 1858	02:010
PLANTS, LEWIS L & GREG, NANNIE S	05 MAR 1904	10:486
PLANTS, ROBERT & SIDERS, REBECCA S	13 AUG 1885	12:208
PLANTS, THEODORE H & McKINEY, MARY	*29 SEP 1894	07:161
PLATT, GEORGE & BRANCH, BEATRICE	03 NOV 1890	05:638
PLATT, LOUIS A & ARTHUR, LENA	06 SEP 1913	15:026
PLUNKETT, JESSE THOMAS & BEARD, SARAH E	11 JAN 1891	06:042
POAG, ROBERT & HAWKINS, ELIZABETH	10 DEC 1819	01:004
POFFENBARGER, ANDREW WOLF & SEAL, IDA P	23 SEP 1885	12:225
POFFENBARGER, CLINTON & LEWIS, SARAH	*15 FEB 1853	02:004
POFFENBARGER, GEORGE & SIMPSON, LIVIA N	10 MAY 1894	07:092
POFFENBARGER, HENRY & GILLIAN, LYDIA	30 NOV 1830	01:023

Names	Date	Ref
POFFENBARGER, HENRY & MARTIN, MARY ANN	*15 JUL 1853	02:004
POFFENBARGER, HENRY & MORRIS, ELLEN S	11 AUG 1878	09:297
POFFENBARGER, MONROE & BEARD, MAGGIE	23 FEB 1895	07:259
POFFENBARGER, THOMAS H & HALL, OLA L	24 DEC 1899	09:051
POFFENBARGER, WILLIAM H & MAUPIN, MILDRED V	18 SEP 1861	03:022
POLAN, FRANK & FRIEDMAN, PRUDENCE	*24 SEP 1910	13:166
POLSLEY, EDGAR A & SAYRE, AUGUSTA A	16 OCT 1873	08:041
POLSLEY, EDGAR A & HALE, GRACE S	01 JUN 1905	11:103
POLSLEY, GEORGE J & BRINKER, FLORIDA	30 DEC 1897	08:232
POMEROY, CHARLES R & SEHON, FANNIE	*26 FEB 1856	02:008
POMEROY, LEWIS S & VOLLERT, PAULINE C	29 SEP 1897	08:161
PONTSLER, SERICK & WALKER, ANGELINE	17 DEC 1868	06:016
PONTZLER, JOSEPH W & WALKER, MARTHA J	*23 SEP 1857	02:010
POOR, JOHN THOMAS & SYDENSTRICKER, CLEMMA	24 NOV 1913	15:074
POOR, WILLIAM & GEORGE, NANCY	*25 JUL 1851	02:002
POPE, ALBERT L & MALONE, NELLIE L	25 SEP 1901	09:413
PORTER, H H & HARRISON, ALTA E	21 DEC 1912	14:061
PORTER, HOWARD & HARRISON, MARY	19 APR 1913	14:128
PORTER, JAMES & REYBURN, ELIZABETH	29 OCT 1835	01:030
PORTER, JAMES B & ROUSH, MILLIE E	13 DEC 1898	08:432
PORTER, JAMES L & FORRESTER, JOANNA	19 APR 1864	03:181
PORTER, JOHN & TURNER, M F	28 SEP 1895	07:396
PORTER, LEWIS & HENSLEY, PARSENA	11 MAY 1889	05:396
PORTER, WILLIAM & ROBINSON, CATHARINE	03 APR 1897	08:072
PORTER, WYMAN E & PLYMALE, BEATRICE	18 SEP 1912	14:003
POSEY, NELSON & BAKER, JANE	21 JAN 1872	07:181
POSTLE, GEORGE T & HUNTER, LAKIE M	01 MAY 1914	15:185
POSTLEWEIGHT, ALBERT & STARCHER, CATHARINE	*17 DEC 1876	09:004
POSTON, GEORGE W & BLAIN, LUELLA	09 JUN 1878	09:271
POSTON, OTHO C & JENKS, ETHEL	09 FEB 1902	10:020
POTEET, JOHN CALVIN & LUSK, MARY E	13 DEC 1888	05:320
POTTS, AQUILLA & WITHERS, CATHARINE	10 JAN 1828	01:016
POTTS, CALVIN & POTTS, SOPHRONIA	*13 OCT 1852	02:003
POTTS, GEORGE & SCURLOCK, IDA MAY	22 OCT 1900	09:228
POTTS, HENRY & WINSHIP, HANNAH	*30 DEC 1853	02:005
POTTS, JAMES HENRY & PENCE, RACHEL	16 MAR 1887	12:491
POTTS, THOMAS & BATEMAN, ELIZABETH	24 APR 1829	01:019
POTTS, THOMAS & TATE, ALCINA C	05 SEP 1878	09:313
POTTS, WILLIAM & VAN MATRE, MILLIE	06 JUL 1889	05:422
POTTS, WILLIAM & THOMAS, MABEL G	01 NOV 1902	10:183
POUNDS, JOHN & WEAVER, CHRISTENA	*16 OCT 1860	02:014
POUNDS, JOSEPH & ROUSH, LYDIA	08 SEP 1870	06:223
POUNDS, JOSEPH M & VICKERS, SUSAN A	05 OCT 1885	12:250
POWEL, HENRY & HOLLEY, MARGARET	13 MAR 1841	01:035
POWELL, ALFRED & PLANTS, ADA	28 AUG 1890	05:605
POWELL, CHARLES & GRAHAM, IDA	17 JUN 1897	08:114
POWELL. EDWARD & HOLLEY, DELLER	25 JAN 1912	13:473
POWELL, FREDERICK & DILCHER, JOSEPHINE	27 FEB 1868	05:214
POWELL, J W & BUCKLE, (Mrs) MARY	18 DEC 1912	14:058
POWELL, JAMES W & HYSEL, DINAH	26 DEC 1877	09:174
POWELL, JOHN & ANDERSON, ELIZA B	01 OCT 1865	04:056
POWELL, JOHN & FURTH, MARY	05 MAR 1877	09:049
POWELL, OSCAR E & HOLLEY, SARAH ANN	02 JUN 1901	09:349
POWELL, SOMERFIELD & OLIVER, MARY A	12 MAR 1877	09:043
POWELL, WESLEY P & MAIGE, DAISEY	07 JUN 1896	07:561
POWELL, WILLIAM & WHITE, ELIZABETH	11 OCT 1866	04:154
POWELL, WILLIAM & BUMGARNER, OLEVA	31 DEC 1893	07:031
POWELL, WILLIAM H & GREATHOUSE, EMELINE	31 AUG 1865	04:048

POWELL, WILLIAM H & MEADOWS, MARY E	17 MAY 1872	07:224
POWELL, WM R & WASHINGTON, VIRGINIA S	23 NOV 1892	06:443
POWELL, ZED & GRAHAM, JESSIE	22 FEB 1908	12:130
POWERS, CALVARY J & BIDGOOD, EMILY A	12 SEP 1876	08:388
POWERS, EDWARD ANDERSON & BENNETT, ANNIE GORDON	06 MAY 1890	05:555
POWERS, JOHN W & ECKARD, BARBARA C	16 JUL 1881	10:427
PREECE, BURTON & ALLISON, MARY	12 DEC 1894	07:207
PRESTON, CHARLES H & EWINGS, CORAH	22 SEP 1873	08:031
PREWET, OBADIAH & TINGLE, NANCY	01 FEB 1822	01:005
PREWIT, GRANVILLE & SHELTON, LUCY ANN	05 MAR 1829	01:019
PRIBBLE, ULYSSES & SMITH, MARIA L	25 MAR 1862	03:055
PRICE, CHARLES JUNE & RADER, SUSAN	18 JUL 1887	05:060
PRICE, CHARLES W & CANTERBERRY, ALTA A	29 MAY 1897	08:101
PRICE, FRED J & RIFE, MILLIE	19 APR 1913	14:127
PRICE, GEORGE A & FLETCHER, MYRTIE	11 JUN 1891	06:125
PRICE, MARK ELMER & SMITH, MARY VIRGINIA	18 MAR 1890	05:530
PRIDDY, B I & LANGLEY, (Mrs) F P	16 DEC 1909	12:568
PRIDDY, BENJAMIN I & SMITH, FRANCES A	16 FEB 1879	10:056
PRIDDY, BENJAMIN I & HOLLEY, MARY F	22 MAY 1901	09:345
PRIDDY, JOHN & WHITTINGTON, MARTHA A	21 OCT 1878	09:336
PRIDDY, JOHN EDGAR & MYERS, MATILDA A	19 NOV 1893	07:001
PRIDDY, JONATHAN & OLDAKER, LAVINIA	1833	01:039
PRIDDY, SAMUEL C & TUCKER, SARAH E	15 APR 1880	10:238
PRIDDY, WASHINGTON G & RIPLEY, MARY ANN	1841	01:041
PRIDDY, WILLIAM H & McCLURE, SARAH J	16 OCT 1872	07:275
PRIESTLY, JAMES C & STERRITT, MARY E	*12 JAN 1857	02:009
PRINCE, HENRY & HEREFORD, LAVINIA E	17 MAR 1870	06:165
PRINCE, JAMES M & DUNCAN, NANCY C	21 FEB 1864	03:164
PRINCE, WILLIAM C & RADFORD, SUSAN C	03 MAY 1867	05:047
PRINDLE, MYRON B & HENSLEY, ADELAIDE	26 NOV 1903	10:420
PRINGLE, RUFUS & STONE, LUCY	01 APR 1900	09:101
PRIODE, DANIEL W & LIVINGSTON, EDITH L	01 MAR 1899	08:473
PRITCHARD, GEORGE & PIKE, LUCINDA	16 JUL 1897	08:126
PRITCHARD, HENRY & WAMSLEY, VIETTA	23 MAR 1899	08:489
PRITCHARD, DUCKET & REYNOLDS, VIRGINIA E	*28 DEC 1852	02:003
PRITT, ALEXANDER & HILL, REBECCA J	03 MAR 1878	09:222
PRITT, GEORGE H & WARNER, ELLA	30 MAY 1908	12:190
PROBST, CHARLES O & KNIGHT, EVA L	28 SEP 1881	11:027
PROCTOR, CHARLES S & STONE, BLANCHE C	14 SEP 1903	12:012
PROCTOR, THOMAS W & SIMPKINS, MAGGIE	*12 OCT 1889	05:464
PROFFITT, EMORY WILSON & CHATTEN, JULIA MARGARET	08 SEP 1888	05:271
PROFFITT, JAS W R & ROUSH, MATILDA	*10 OCT 1859	02:013
PROFFITT, JOHN FULKISON & JONES, FRANCES	20 DEC 1883	11:436
PROFFITT, JOSEPH H & VINCENT, MARY	14 SEP 1882	11:396
PROFFITT, LATON & LATHEY, LEOLA	21 AUG 1892	06:387
PROFFITT, WILLIAM H & CLENDENEN, LAURA C	10 NOV 1881	11:048
PROSE, CHARLES G & COURTWRIGHT, MARY F	13 JUL 1914	15:239
PROWS, SAMUEL & MESUSAN, LYDIA	FEB 1822	01:005
PRUETT, GEORGE W & HOLLY, ELIZABETH S	26 DEC 1871	07:166
PRUNTY, DARIUS H & BYER, OMA B	24 DEC 1908	12:337
PRYOR, ALLEN & NEWMAN, FRANCIS	15 JAN 1848	01:048
PRYOR, CHARLES K & BROWN, JENNIE	01 NOV 1884	12:088
PUGH, JAMES & PHILIPS, MARGARET	17 OCT 1868	05:221
PULLIAM, JOHN A & BOGGESS, NORA L	04 SEP 1895	07:379
PULLIN, ALLEN T & SMITH, RACHEL	23 APR 1896	07:534
PULLIN, CHARLES H & COSSEN, ALMIRA	12 APR 1868	05:165
PULLIN, ENATHLESS & EDWARDS, JANE	MAR 1644	01:043
PULLIN, G F C & LEMASTER, JULIA	13 JUL 1886	12:356

Name	Date	Ref
PULLIN, GEORGE W & MIDDLECOFF, CORNELIA A	01 DEC 1869	06:118
PULLIN, JAMES & CAMDEN, EMMER M	03 JAN 1878	09:188
PULLIN, JAMES WILLIAM & GREER, SARAH C	30 MAY 1888	05:230
PULLIN, JAMES Y & ROLLINS, MARY M	03 AUG 1892	06:383
PULLIN, JOHN & LEWIS, REBECCA	10 SEP 1837	01:030
PULLIN, JOHN THOMAS & LEMASTER, SOPHIA	22 MAR 1888	05:199
PULLIN, JONATHAN & CLENDENEN, ELLEN M	20 DEC 1871	07:158
PULLIN, ORN & COTTRELL, CAROLINE	18 JAN 1898	08:252
PULLIN, S V & SHELINE, MARY J	30 APR 1885	12:167
PULLIN, SAMUEL & TILLA, HANNAH	03 JAN 1871	07:039
PULLIN, TAYLOR E & CHEESBREW, AUGUSTA L	20 JUN 1910	13:094
PULLINS, ALBAN WALLACE & ECKARD, ORA ETHEL	02 SEP 1911	13:368
PULLINS, ALLEN THOMAS & STOVER, EMILY J	23 JUN 1892	06:354
PULLINS, ASA ROSCOE & PHILLIPS, CORA MAY	01 AUG 1913	15:001
PULLINS, CHARLES J & McKINNEY, EMMA	18 NOV 1903	10:411
PULLINS, JAMES & COOPER, MARY	15 FEB 1826	01:014
PULLINS, JOSEPH & McDERMITT, SARAH	20 JUN 1891	06:136
PULLINS, SAMUEL & LEWIS, SUSANNA	31 OCT 1837	01:032
PURCELL, ERNEST C & MOORE, BIRD	18 JAN 1898	08:254
PURCY, JAMES & JEFFERS, MARY	31 JUL 1828	01:018
PURDUM, HARRY H & SHANK, MARY E	01 APR 1908	12:150
PURDUM, JOHN M & MOODY, MAGGIE M	30 JAN 1884	11:453
PURDY, ALEXANDER & FRENCH, MARY CATHARINE	25 JUL 1892	06:375
PURDY, LEWIS D & WOLFE, AMERICA	10 AUG 1899	08:593
PURDY, SAMUEL T & SAYRE, ANNA	17 AUG 1876	08:377
PURSER, ARTHUR C & ELLISON, EDNA E	21 MAR 1908	12:147
PUTNEY, ANDREW W & SAXTON, CLARA	25 APR 1897	08:083
PUTNEY, CHARLES D & SAXTON, SALLIE	24 DEC 1904	11:011
PUTNEY, EDWARD & BOWEN, ROXIE	23 JUN 1903	10:309
PUTNEY, KENNIE & BATEMAN, BEATRICE	24 DEC 1911	13:442
PUTNEY, RICHARD & COLEMAN, NORA	30 JUL 1910	13:121
PUTNEY, ROBERT W & FULKERSON, MARTHA W	08 FEB 1866	04:101
PUTNEY, WILLIAM H & JEFFERS, ANNIE E	23 JUN 1903	10:305
PYLES, CHARLES & PEARSON, MINNIE	24 JAN 1903	10:231
PYLES, LEWIS & STEVENS, WILLIE B	03 MAY 1899	08:526
PYLES, ROBERT LEE & HOFFMAN, ALICE	08 NOV 1888	05:303
QUICK, J U S GRANT & ROLLINS, HATTIE A	22 OCT 1897	08:178
QUICKLE, FRANK L & JACOBS, NESSIE R	28 NOV 1913	15:078
QUICKLE, JOHN M & SMITH, (Mrs) EMILY A	29 NOV 1911	13:141
QUICKLE, KNIGHT & COLEMAN, FLORENCE C	29 MAY 1902	10:080
QUICKLE, LUTHER & COSSIN, MOLLIE	13 JAN 1897	08:034
QUICKLE, NATHAN & YAUGER, DOROTHY	09 JUL 1893	06:573
QUIGLEY, OWEN & MARTIN, ELIZABETH	*07 JAN 1859	02:012
QUIGLEY, JOHN & PARSONS, HANNAH	07 MAY 1822	01:011
QUILLEN, ALEXANDER & WATERS, ELIZABETH	20 OCT 1895	07:408
QUILLEN, GEORGE W & DONOVAN, BRIDGET	11 SEP 1894	07:152
QUILLEN, HEZEKIAH & SLACK, BELLE B	10 APR 1889	05:380
QUILLEN, NATHAN WEBSTER & ZERKLE, ALMIRA S	24 NOV 1886	12:426
QUILLEN, SAMUEL J & HALL, MARY	30 SEP 1893	06:614
QUILLIN, CLARENCE H & JOHNSON, LIZZIE K	17 MAY 1906	11:313
QUILLIN, GEORGE EMERSON & ALLINDER, FRIEDA MARIE	25 MAR 1911	13:505
QUILLIN, O'NEAL F & FIELDS, LILLIAN R	29 AUG 1914	15:264
QUILLIN, WILLIAM SHERMAN & HALL, LENNA	13 MAR 1893	06:503
QUINN, HUGH & GILLASPIE, MARTHA	13 DEC 1844	01:044
QUINN, JEROME & SMITH, ARRIENA	29 DEC 1881	11:091
RABURN, JNO & LEE, LUCINDA	25 NOV 1847	01:048
RADCLIFF, I F & CASTER, NANNIE M	18 OCT 1911	13:398
RADER, MADISON C & McINTOSH, LOUISA M	17 FEB 1876	08:326

RADFORD, FRANCIS & GALLAGHER, FANNIE	24 JAN 1877	09:025
RAIKE, WILLIAM & TOTTEN, GOLDIE	03 NOV 1914	15:313
RAINEY, ALBERT Z & EADES, SARAH F	*23 JAN 1851	02:001
RAINEY, ALONZO E & VAN SICKLES, NANNIE F	14 OCT 1897	08:173
RAINEY, CHARLES F & EADS, MARY J	13 OCT 1871	07:132
RAINEY, CHARLES F & VAN SICKLE, MARTHA S	27 OCT 1892	06:433
RAINEY, COLUMBUS, W & GASKINS, EFFIE A	16 OCT 1898	08:386
RAINEY, GEORGE D & KLINGENSMITH, LOUISA	28 MAY 1890	05:560
RAINEY, JAMES T & McDANIEL, MINNIE J	13 JUL 1879	10:107
RAINEY, JOHN EDWIN & PECK, SARAH HAMILTON	23 AUG 1893	06:590
RAINEY, PEACHY FRANKLIN & RICE, SARAH LILLIE	12 NOV 1891	06:224
RAIRDEN, FELIX & YOHO, MARGARET	31 MAY 1886	12:331
RAIRDEN, HARVEY C & McDANIEL, RACHEL	04 MAR 1880	10:221
RAIRDEN, JOHN W & KNAPP, STELLA A	24 JUN 1906	11:347
RAIRDEN, MARRION & HILL, ADDIE	10 NOV 1889	05:476
RAIRDEN, STEPHEN W & BUTRICKS, MARY M	30 DEC 1880	10:364
RAIRDON, JAMES H & PARSONS, ESTHER L	08 MAY 1910	13:061
RAKE, WILLIAM & JEFFERS, JESTA	31 MAY 1911	13:324
RAMBOW, WM HENRY FRANZ-THEO & POLSLEY, EMMA GERTRUDE	28 SEP 1887	05:108
RAMSEY, GEORGE W & VIA, MIRANDA	23 OCT 1902	10:178
RAMSEY, WILLIAM & MOBLEY, BERTHA A	18 NOV 1897	08:197
RANDALL, JOHN & RUSSELL, ELIZA	11 MAR 1880	10:222
RASP, CONRAD E & MASON, FANNIE L	02 DEC 1906	11:455
RATHBURN, MARVIN C & WILES, MOLLIE	27 SEP 1896	07:614
RAUSCH, LEWIS & RICKARD, SUSAN	02 MAR 1829	01:021
RAWSON, CHARLES C & BATEMAN, EMILY C	08 DEC 1869	06:123
RAWSON, CHARLES C & BATEMAN, MARY A	11 SEP 1894	07:151
RAWSON, JOS V & PINE, MARY A	*25 DEC 1860	02:015
RAWSON, ONEY E & BLAND, BETHLEHEM	15 DEC 1909	12:567
RAWSON, VALMER H & CLENDENIN, LILLIE	20 SEP 1900	09:215
RAWSON, WILLIAM F & COSBY, MARY ANN	06 AUG 1865	04:035
RAWSON, (Dr) DEWITT & VARNEY, BERTHA	29 DEC 1904	11:023
RAY, RUPERT R & KIMBERLING, FANNIE M	07 FEB 1910	13:004
RAY, WILLIAM & WRIGHT, RUTH	18 APR 1826	01:015
RAY, WILLIAM & DUN, JANE	03 JUN 1847	01:048
RAYBOLD, B F & YOUNG, MAUDE	03 JUL 1911	13:339
RAYBOULD, EDWARD & O'LEARY, CATHERINE	24 AUG 1907	11:597
RAYBOULD, EDWARD & CARLETON, LIZZIE G	09 JUL 1911	13:342
RAYBURN, ALONZO H & FOGLESONG, SARAH F	05 SEP 1878	09:307
RAYBURN, ANDREW & SAYRE, HANNAH	02 OCT 1887	05:111
RAYBURN, CHARLES & TRANOR, GRACE	17 SEP 1903	10:361
RAYBURN, CHARLES E & KINCADE, DELLA M	04 FEB 1903	10:235
RAYBURN, CHARLES T & ZUSPAN, CARIE L	03 NOV 1892	06:435
RAYBURN, CURTIS & GIBBS, ZELMA LEE	06 OCT 1912	14:012
RAYBURN, FRANCIS W & HOPKINS, JOSIE V	18 DEC 1901	09:470
RAYBURN, FRDRICK E & MILLER, FLORENCE	03 FEB 1907	11:493
RAYBURN, GEORGE B & THORNTON, RHODA B	30 APR 1896	07:539
RAYBURN, GEORGE O & HILL, SARAH E	02 SEP 1877	09:123
RAYBURN, GILBERT & WEAVER, CASSY	26 APR 1842	01:036
RAYBURN, GRANVILLE & BALL, OLIVE J	19 SEP 1878	09:315
RAYBURN, GRANVILLE & SEBRELL, JOSIE	11 FEB 1903	10:238
RAYBURN, GRIFFIN & MOREHEAD, MARY	*26 JUN 1858	02:011
RAYBURN, HENRY & BARNETT, BETSEY	23 DEC 1824	01:010
RAYBURN, HENRY H & RAYBURN, NANCY	29 AUG 1853	02:004
RAYBURN, JAMES & RADER, POLLY	10 MAY 1807	01:001
RAYBURN, JAMES & LEE, NANCY	1838	01:040
RAYBURN, JAMES & BALL, MARY A	08 FEB 1842	01:036
RAYBURN, JAMES A & FISHER, MARY ANN	*23 MAY 1859	02:012

Name	Date	Ref
RAYBURN, JAMES C & CALDWELL, ANNIE	24 DEC 1906	11:479
RAYBURN, JAMES P & HOWARD, CASSIE	25 DEC 1898	08:443
RAYBURN, JOHN & FRAZIER, SARAH F	*18 APR 1860	02:014
RAYBURN, JOHN & LOVE, SARAH JANE	10 MAY 1866	04:121
RAYBURN, JOHN & HAWKINS, BLANCH	05 JAN 1898	08:240
RAYBURN, JOHN FRANKLIN & RIFFLE, JENNIE FRANCES	20 DEC 1888	05:353
RAYBURN, JOHN F & RIFFLE, EMMA	02 OCT 1898	08:376
RAYBURN, JOHN F & HOWARD, MARTHA J	30 NOV 1905	11:214
RAYBURN, JOHN L & STATON, JULIA M	25 DEC 1884	12:108
RAYBURN, JOHN R & CABLE, MARY E	04 FEB 1891	06:057
RAYBURN, LEWIS N & RAYBURN, JENNIE V	26 AUG 1894	07:145
RAYBURN, MAXWELL & WINDON, MARY JANE	*15 DEC 1853	02:005
RAYBURN, ROBERT & HAWKINS, LILY J	24 MAR 1881	10:390
RAYBURN, ROBERT EDWARD & SCARBERRY, ELLA FRANCES	05 JUN 1889	05:409
RAYBURN, ROBERT H & FOGLESONG, ALICE C	25 DEC 1884	12:113
RAYBURN, S S & ZERCKEL, REBECCA	08 AUG 1883	11:386
RAYBURN, SAMUEL G & BOLES, CARRIE	13 JUL 1808	12:213
RAYBURN, TAYLOR NORTH & WINDON, ADA DAY	25 DEC 1901	09:476
RAYBURN, THOMAS & VARIAN, REBECCA J	*26 SEP 1853	02:004
RAYBURN, THOMAS & GRAY, SARAH J	30 DEC 1875	08:311
RAYBURN, WASHINGTON & McDERMITT, RACHAEL	*18 OCT 1856	02:009
RAYBURN, WILLIAM E & LAMBERT, MARY S	06 MAR 1873	07:329
RAYBURN, WILLIAM E & McCOY, BESSIE	27 NOV 1904	10:645
RAYBURN, WILLIAM M & CRAWFORD, OCTAVIA G	20 APR 1865	04:008
REA, JAMES H & SAYRE, BERTHA E	10 MAR 1911	13:291
REA, ROBERT & ROSE, PRISCILLA	28 SEP 1897	08:160
REA, ROBERT Jr & ROUSH, VINA E	31 DEC 1913	15:113
REASE, GEORGE W & JORDAN, VIRGINIA P	14 JAN 1841	01:035
REBLING, CHARLES & SHAWN, MATILDA	30 APR 1846	01:047
RECKTERWALD, EDWARD & ENGLISH, MARY S	26 APR 1887	05:016
RECTANUS, WILLIAM & McGUCKIN, ELLA	09 NOV 1882	11:249
REDMAN, FOY A & BOARD, KATE	02 FEB 1905	11:038
REDMIRE, JOHN H & FINDLEY, ALICE	23 OCT 1890	05:629
REDMOND, BENJAMIN J & HALL, ELIZABETH J	25 FEB 1862	03:051
REDMOND, JOHN ANDREW & RICE, JESSIE H	30 MAY 1889	05:404
REDMOND, JOHN O & ADKINS, EMMA F	02 APR 1901	09:311
REECE, JOSEPH K & LONG, STELLA	16 FEB 1914	15:141
REECE, M HARRY & BOSO, MARIE EDNA	03 JUL 1914	15:233
REECE, THOMAS U & DEFOE, MARTHA ANN	MAY 1839	01:033
REED, ELIAS & TAYLOR, MARY E	22 JAN 1887	12:471
REED, FRANK & JORDAN, IDA	25 MAY 1876	08:357
REED, FRANKLIN PORTER & PULLIN, MARY E	01 JUN 1887	05:035
REED, GEORGE L & SAYRE, MAUDE E	31 JAN 1914	15:136
REED, JAMES F & LAVENDER, MINA	27 AUG 1912	13:591
REED, JAMES H & ZAPF, MARY	10 APR 1882	11:137
REED, JEFFERSON J & YONKER, HATTIE G	10 JUN 1913	15:217
REED, JOHN E & HICKMAN, EMILY J	13 APR 1912	13:513
REED, LISSIE J & McCOY, LORENA	16 FEB 1908	12:129
REED, MARION & ROUSH, SARAH	26 JUN 1873	08:006
REED, MORDECAI & NEWELL, SARAH ELIZABETH	22 SEP 1887	05:102
REEDER, JOHN & PRICKETT, PATSY	20 OCT 1807	01:001
REEDER, JOSEPH W & HILDEBRAND, CLARA	22 OCT 1890	05:628
REEL, SOL H & BUTCHER, NELLIE L	15 MAY 1890	05:558
REES, JOSEPH & GASKIL, ANNIE M	13 MAY 1874	08:120
REES, THOMAS W & WENDELAND, CATHARINE	17 DEC 1905	11:223
REESE, JOHN H & PIATT, SARAH	*23 AUG 1875	08:267
REEVES, JAMES PERRY & GOODIN, MARY DELLA	31 OCT 1888	05:300
REILLY, PETER & ELLIOT, ANNIE V	23 DEC 1886	12:447

Names	Date	Reference
REINWALD, A C & AUSTIN, LELIA O	06 MAR 1909	12:378
REISINGER, JOHN CAMPBELL & LONG, ELLA	20 APR 1889	05:386
REITMIER, HENRY & HUDSON, MAGGIE	27 APR 1896	07:537
REITMIER, GOTTLIP & PRICE, CARRIE G	13 MAY 1899	08:532
REITMIRE, HENRY & FINDLEY, BESSIE	25 SEP 1899	08:619
RENDOERFER, LAWRENCE F & BILLINGSLEY, REBECCA E	19 JAN 1898	08:253
REUTHER, JOHN & COLEMAN, MILDRED	27 JAN 1904	10:466
REUTHER, LEONARD & CUMMINGS, ROSA	09 MAY 1900	09:122
REYBURN, JOSEPH & PORTER, MARTHA	21 OCT 1832	01:025
REYNOLDS, CHARLES & McKIAG, ALICE	30 APR 1899	08:522
REYNOLDS, HARVEY & GREENLEE, ELIZABETH	22 JAN 1829	01:018
REYNOLDS, J W & SHORTER, JENNIE	03 MAR 1909	12:377
REYNOLDS, JOHN & KIMBERLIN, RUTH	12 JAN 1826	01:012
REYNOLDS, JOHN & POUNDS, ANN	*28 DEC 1852	02:003
REYNOLDS, JOHN P & MALONE, TERESA	06 FEB 1899	08:463
REYNOLDS, JOHN R & KREPPS, EDITH M	29 JUN 1904	10:542
REYNOLDS, PEARL A & POWERS, MARGARET A	11 MAY 1910	13:067
REYNOLDS, RANDOLPH & COFFMAN, REBECCA	1832	01:026
REYNOLDS, SILAS & MORRIS, MINERVA	01 OCT 1821	01:005
REYNOLDS, THOMAS & BOWYER, MAGGIE	17 MAR 1884	11:469
REYNOLDS, THOMAS M & WATERSON, LIZZIE M	17 APR 1895	07:288
REYNOLDS, WILLIAMS G & ROBINSON, MAY O	15 MAR 1886	12:302
RHEA, FRANK H & BROWN, MARY I	30 JUN 1890	05:581
RHOADES, CHARLES L & ROWLEY, (Mrs) LULA MAUDE	02 DEC 1914	15:336
RHOADES, DANIEL B & COFFMAN, MARY M	04 JUL 1877	09:106
RHOADES, LEONIDAS M & SISSON, OLIVE H	30 DEC 1875	08:317
RHOADES, THOMAS V & BAXTER, ELIZABETH	31 JUL 1907	11585
RHOADES, WILLIAM & PRITCHARD, LIZZIE	29 MAR 1893	06:512
RHOADES, WILLIAM L & GESS, ALMIRA	02 OCT 1891	06:201
RHOADS, BURRELL L & TUCKER, SARAH E	24 DEC 1882	11:275
RHOADS, GEORGE & MATTOX, BARBARA ELIZABETH	25 OCT 1891	06:214
RHOADS, GEORGE A & SPENCER, HARRIET M	12 APR 1881	10:395
RHOADS, JAMES R & CAMPBELL, MATTIE	05 NOV 1895	07:422
RHOADS, NORBERT R & HARPOLD, ELECTA E	28 APR 1881	10:408
RHOADS, THOMAS V & SMITH, CATHARINE	01 JAN 1891	06:040
RHODES, ALVIN L & SCHOMEHL, EMILY	03 AUG 1809	12:469
RHODES, BAZILLA M & McCOY, CHRISTENA F	20 AUG 1876	08:378
RHODES, BENJAMIN & SMITH, HATTIE	29 MAY 1882	11:156
RHODES, BENJAMIN B & LEMASTER, LUCETTA	*12 APR 1859	02:012
RHODES, BENJAMIN R & BOGGESS, RHODA	*06 SEP 1859	02:013
RHODES, GEORGE & HOLSEY, HATTIE	05 MAR 1911	13:285
RHODES, GEORGE A & BATES, MARY ANN	04 MAY 1870	06:187
RHODES, GEORGE WILLIAM & BARR, ELZA JANE	29 DEC 1882	11:282
RHODES, J W & LEWIS, CASSIE	10 MAY 1885	12:175
RHODES, JOHN & SHORT, ELIZA J	06 FEB 1894	07:044
RHODES, JOHN P & COMPSON, MARY E	15 FEB 1883	11:300
RHODES, JOHN P & THRASH, VERA	12 MAY 1906	11:312
RHODES, SAMUEL & LEMASTER, DRUZILLA C	26 JAN 1870	06:146
RICE, CHARLES E & EDWARDS, MARY M	25 MAY 1877	09:081
RICE, CHARLES E & ZIRKEL, EMMA B	11 FFEB 1900	09:077
RICE, CLARK & JINKINS, JENNIE	25 DEC 1889	05:502
RICE, DANIEL & WILLARD, ELIZABETH	23 NOV 1827	01:020
RICE, DANIEL & AMSBERRY, MARIETTA	(no date)	01:027
RICE, EUCLID E & NUCKLES, MARY R	26 JUN 1904	10:549
RICE, GEORGE H & EADES, BERTHA J	02 APR 1891	06:092
RICE, GEORGE T & FOGLESONG, MARTHA E	28 AUG 1895	07:372
RICE, GEORGE W & HARDWICK, LEONER E	*19 MAR 1857	02:009
RICE, GEORGE W & CHATTIN, MARY	27 MAR 1884	11:476

Names	Date	Ref
RICE, HARRISON & HARDWICK, MARY JANE	18 OCT 1866	04:159
RICE, JAMES D & STEWART, DELLA	31 DEC 1896	08:029
RICE, JAMES G & MOORE, KATIE	06 SEP 1900	09:195
RICE, JAMES H & GREENLEE, ELIZABETH	*19 DEC 1850	02:001
RICE, JAMES LAWRENCE & BALL, MARTHA JANE	04 JAN 1870	06:138
RICE, JAMES N & GREENLEE, ELIZABETH	28 DEC 1850	01:052
RICE, JAMES C & LONG, (Mrs) MARGARET A	*04 DEC 1855	02:007
RICE, JOHN H & FOWLER, DAISY L	26 JUN 1901	09:365
RICE, JOHN H & RIFFLE, LINNIE V	25 DEC 1907	12:098
RICE, JOHN H & BOTTRILL, BEATRICE V	02 FEB 1910	13:001
RICE, JOHN Q & LOTTRIDGE, MERLE E	17 OCT 1911	13:397
RICE, JOHN RICHARD & ROLLINS, MARY VIANA	21 AUG 1889	05:433
RICE, LEWIS B & FISHER, ADIE E	03 FEB 1904	10:469
RICE, LEWIS BALL & McDANIEL, CORNELIA	20 AUG 1896	07:595
RICE, MARCELLUS GRANT & GRINSTEAD, NANCY JANE	03 JUL 1885	12:191
RICE, MARCELLUS G & ROSS, (Mrs) LIZZIE	07 AUG 1911	13:352
RICE, NELSON O & GREENLEE, MARTHA JANE	*21 JUL 1857	02:010
RICE, ROBERT L & HILL, CORA M	01 MAY 1894	07:085
RICE, ROBERT L & GREENLEE, ELLEN F	11 OCT 1896	07:628
RICE, ROBERT LEE & BASS, MAGGIE	23 SEP 1888	05:282
RICE, SAMUEL J T & SAYRE, ADALIZA M	02 JUN 1897	08:106
RICE, THEODORE S & LONG, MINNIE	28 OCT 1905	11:192
RICE, THEODORE S & PLANTS, VICTORIA	28 MAY 1911	13:320
RICE, THOMAS & EMANUEL, ANNA B	17 NOV 1879	10:330
RICE, VINCENT D & LEE, JEMIMA C	*05 NOV 1856	02:009
RICE, VINCENT D & CHATTIN, ALMEDIA S	MAY 1877	09:088
RICE, VINCENT D & GRIMM, ALMEDIA	17 SEP 1908	12:263
RICE, VINCENT E & SWISHER, BELLE F	08 JUN 1901	09:351
RICE, VINCENT ELLSWORTH & NOBLE, ANN ELIZA	20 SEP 1888	05:281
RICE, WADE H & CARSEY, (Mrs) JANE	03 JUL 1912	13:559
RICE, WILLIAM & KEARNS, JENNIE SCOTT	22 APR 1889	05:383
RICE, WILLIAM & SNYDER, HETTIE	31 DEC 1891	06:272
RICE, WILLIAM T & LEE, ELLEN O	22 MAR 1863	03:109
RICHARD, JOHN & FRY, LOUISA	*16 AUG 1858	02:011
RICHARD, JONAS & KLINGENSMITH, LEAH ANN	25 MAR 1863	03:107
RICHARD, WILLIAM R & FRY, LENA L	30 NOV 1882	11:257
RICHARDS, JAMES W & MITCHELL, FLORENCE V	18 OCT 1877	09:142
RICHARDS, JOSEPH W & BROWN, NANCY E	27 OCT 1896	07:635
RICHARDS, WILLIAM B F & HIBBARD, ADA	01 MAR 1882	11:120
RICHARDSON, H S & RINE, ANNA	13 OCT 1870	07:012
RICHARDSON, JOHN F & THORNTON, MARY E	20 AUG 1904	10:579
RICHARDSON, LEWIS M & JOHNSTONE, MAGGIE M	05 DEC 1911	13:435
RICHARDSON, RICHARD A & LINKFIELD, MARY	*29 SEP 1859	02:013
RICHARDSON, VERNON & PRICE, GARNET	30 DEC 1914	15:362
RICHARDSON, WORTHY & HARBOUR, GRACE	11 FEB 1906	11:262
RICHEY, FLEMING & HILL, FLORA	11 JAN 1887	12:464
RICHTER, JOHN F W & GISE, REBECCA C	21 MAY 1877	09:078
RICKARD, ADAM & ROUSH, LOUISA	26 MAR 1861	07:068
RICKARD, ANTHONY & McKEEVER, GEORGIANA	24 NOV 1878	10:011
RICKARD, C B & RILEY, ELLA	24 FEB 1911	13:279
RICKARD, CAMPBELL M & KLINGINGSMITH, KATE	18 SEP 1895	07:385
RICKARD, DORSEY LEE & QUILLIN, BIRDIE LELIA	09 AUG 1899	08:590
RICKARD, E R & NOBLE, BERTHA M	06 MAR 1912	13:494
RICKARD, FRANKLIN & PICKENS, SEVILLEY A	16 MAR 1876	08:339
RICKARD, GEORGE M & ROUSH, MYRTLE A	19 MAR 1904	10:492
RICKARD, GEORGE W & JACKSON, SARAH M	27 DEC 1906	11:483
RICKARD, HENRY & ROUSH, LAURA A	21 DEC 1882	11:269
RICKARD, HENRY C & ROUSH, DRUSILLA	*06 FEB 1879	10:052

Name	Date	Ref
RICKARD, JACOB & HURLOW, MARGARET ANN	19 FEB 1893	06:490
RICKARD, JOHN & BLESSING, CHRISTINA M	21 NOV 1872	07:291
RICKARD, JONAS & FOGLESONG, ELIZABETH	25 SEP 1884	12:061
RICKARD, JOSEPH & FRY, SARAH S	03 NOV 1872	07:281
RICKARD, JOSEPH M & MOURNING, NANCY J	19 APR 1885	12:163
RICKARD, LEWIS & McMILLIN, ELIZABETH	*22 MAR 1859	02:012
RICKARD, MICHAEL & KARNES, SARAH	04 FEB 1869	06:031
RICKARD, OTMER & STOKLEY, MABEL M	24 FEB 1907	11:498
RICKARD, P M & THOMPSON, IDA	21 JUL 1912	13:564
RICKARD, PERRY L & HOFFMAN, LAURA B	09 NOV 1898	08:400
RICKARD, REUBIN & HOFFMAN, ARTIE M	11 MAY 1898	08:302
RICKARD, SAMUEL & HART, MARIA	04 MAY 1848	01:049
RICKARD, SAMUEL A & FRY, LAURA L	05 APR 1883	11:317
RICKARD, WILLARD H & FRY, CLARA	29 OCT 1914	15:308
RICKART, ADAM & GOODFELLOW, EMELINE	19 AUG 1832	01:025
RICKART, ADAM & WOODARD, AMANDA	07 OCT 1838	01:031.5
RICKART, GEORGE & GIBBS, REBECCA ANN	*03 DEC 1850	02:001
RICKART, JOSEPH & ROUSH, SALLY	09 JAN 1834	01:028
RIDDLE, JOHN & MATTOX, HANNAH	*01 SEP 1856	02:008
RIDDLE, MOSES & GASTON, ANN	28 FEB 1868	05:142
RIDDLE, MOSES A & BRADFORD, MARY A	*28 AUG 1858	02:011
RIDDLE, MUEHURST S & BUMGARNER, CAROLINE	25 SEP 1873	08:032
RIDDLE, WILLIAM & GLEASON, (Mrs) KATIE	23 NOV 1912	14:035
RIDDLE, WILLIAM E & RAYBURN, ANNIE	25 JUL 1901	09:372
RIDENOUR, HAWLEY ERNEST & SHIRLEY, BESSIE	24 DEC 1899	09:038
RIDINGER, ALEXANDER H & GERLICH, MARGARET	30 MAR 1878	09:235
RIFE, GEORGE SAMUEL & OWENS, MARY ELIZABETH	04 SEP 1888	05:270
RIFFLE, ALEXANDER & FOGLESONG, ELIZABETH J	28 AUG 1879	10:114
RIFFLE, ALEXANDER & FIELDER, STELLA	10 APR 1906	11:289
RIFFLE, AMIDEE C & CUNNINGHAM, CORA C	15 OCT 1911	13:362
RIFFLE, ANDREW & HYATT, REBECCA J	22 DEC 1881	11:075
RIFFLE, ANDREW A & BIRCHFIELD, VIOLA O	23 DEC 1902	10:213
RIFFLE, ANDREW F & GREENLEE, SARAH M	26 SEP 1872	07:265
RIFFLE, ANDREW JOHNSON & KINCADE, ANNIE AGNESS	14 FEB 1889	05:353
RIFFLE, ANDREW WILLIAM & STEWART, IDA	27 OCT 1895	07:415
RIFFLE, BENSON & SULLIVAN, CLARA	17 AUG 1902	10:130
RIFFLE, CHARLES & STEWART, ELIZABETH	29 DEC 1861	03:041
RIFFLE, CLINTON B & BAKER, TABITHA E	10 MAY 1913	14:141
RIFFLE, CONRAD & CALDWELL, JANE B	29 MAR 1832	01:025
RIFFLE, DAVID & VAN KIRK, LYDIA	25 JUN 1868	05:194
RIFFLE, DAVID B & GRAY, LINNIE A	19 MAY 1913	14:152
RIFFLE, DAVID HAMILTON & SCHOOLS, REBECCA BLANCH	11 AUG 1892	06:384
RIFFLE, EARLY S & DUFF, CASSIE R	28 OCT 1903	10:398
RIFFLE, EDWARD & ECDARD, ALICE	07 JAN 1906	11:245
RIFFLE, FRANCIS & LANE, MARY	11 NOV 1878	10:007
RIFFLE, FRANCIS H & KAPP, ANNIE L	22 APR 1903	10:274
RIFFLE, GEORGE & BROWN, NANCY	24 JUN 1937	01:003
RIFFLE, GEORGE & SAYRE, ALICE	18 APR 1897	08:080
RIFFLE, GEORGE W & SMITH HARRIET	*02 MAR 1861	02:015
RIFFLE, GEORGE WILLIAM & CLENDENIN, FRANCIS MARGARET	08 SEP 1887	05:090
RIFFLE, GUSTAVUS & RIFFLE, CATHARINE JANE	*26 AUG 1850	02:001
RIFFLE, HENRY JESSE & SAYRE, LUCY LUELLA	01 JAN 1913	14:073
RIFFLE, IRA T & LOVE, MAGGIE E	30 DEC 1886	12:454
RIFFLE, ISAAC M & DECKER, ROSA L	15 JAN 1899	08:452
RIFFLE, ISAAC N & WORRELL, LOUISA	18 MAY 1879	10:090
RIFFLE, J W & FOGLESONG, M MARGARET	29 MAR 1911	13:298
RIFFLE, JACOB & FOGLESONG, SARAH	08 APR 1830	01:020

Name	Date	Ref
RIFFLE, JACOB & BORING, CATHARINE L	06 NOV 1879	10:159
RIFFLE, JAMES & ECKARD, LUCY	29 MAR 1858	02:011
RIFFLE, JAMES & PROFFITT, MARTHA J	13 OCT 1864	03:199
RIFFLE, JAMES E & SCHOOLS, SADIE L	19 APR 1896	07:531
RIFFLE, JAMES G & ARMSTRONG, SUSAN J	27 MAY 1883	11:345
RIFFLE, JAMES G & HARRIS, MAGGIE E	25 FEB 1913	14:097
RIFFLE, JASPER N & STEVENS, MALINDA	12 NOV 1903	10:407
RIFFLE, JESSE B & RIFFLE, NANCY R	*10 APR 1859	02:012
RIFFLE, JOHN & HILL, CHRISTENA	07 AUG 1904	10:571
RIFFLE, JOHN C & DECKER, MINNIE M	04 SEP 1892	06:399
RIFFLE, JOHN C & SHIELDS, VIOLA	24 OCT 1897	08:186
RIFFLE, JOHN HENRY & THORNTON, NANCY F	12 MAR 1892	06:302
RIFFLE, JOHN M & HILL, MARTHA J	12 OCT 1879	10:142
RIFFLE, JOHN V & FISHER, MARTHA ANN	28 NOV 1861	03:034
RIFFLE, JONATHAN & STEEL, NANCY S	13 MAR 1863	03:106
RIFFLE, JOSEPH & WOODS, MARY	13 NOV 1845	01:044
RIFFLE, JOSEPH & ROLLINS, SARAH M	16 SEP 1880	10:302
RIFFLE, JOSEPH C & FOGLESONG, MARY J	30 OCT 1890	05:632
RIFFLE, JOSEPH S & GREENLEE, VIRGINIA B	09 SEP 1894	07:149
RIFFLE, JUNIUS & BOGGESS, VIRGINIA C	17 OCT 1872	07:277
RIFFLE, MILLARD & GIBBS, ROSA	20 APR 1902	10:059
RIFFLE, NATHANIEL & ECKARD, MARY ANN	23 APR 1844	01:038
RIFFLE, NORMAN R & ROUSH, CORA	17 MAY 1902	10:076
RIFFLE, RICHARD & RIFFLE, JANE	*05 OCT 1857	02:010
RIFFLE, ROBERT & PROFFITT, SOPHIA A	19 DEC 1867	05:114
RIFFLE, ROBERT & ECKARD, MARY E	08 AUG 1872	07:252
RIFFLE, ROBERT J & HOSCHAR, MARGARET A	08 NOV 1898	08:402
RIFFLE, SAMUEL & GREENLEE, ELIZABETH	30 OCT 1873	08:049
RIFFLE, SAMUEL J & CHILDERS, ELIZABETH	03 NOV 1895	07:419
RIFFLE, TITUS VESTFASHON & STEWART, LONA	25 AUG 1892	06:393
RIFFLE, TITUS V & PICKENS, DELINDA	11 MAR 1897	08:057
RIFFLE, WILLIAM & ECKARD, JANE	25 SEP 1836	01:030
RIFFLE, WILLIAM & LOVET, (Mrs) MARY ANN	*02 JAN 1857	02:009
RIFFLE, WILLIAM H & McKINDLEY, ORA L L	31 OCT 1891	06:217
RIFFLE, WILLIAM J & SHIELDS, MARGARET	04 MAY 1884	12:010
RIFFLE, WILLIAM JASPER & RICE, RHODA MARGARET	28 AUG 1879	10:113
RIGG, ESAU & TEMPLETON, LUCINDA	07 JUL 1837	01:032
RIGGS, BAZEL J & ROUSH, ELLA	01 JAN 1883	11:285
RIGGS, CHARLES E & CAMPBELL, NANCY E	*31 JUL 1851	02:002
RIGGS, EASTHAM H & CARROLL, NANCY	05 MAR 1865	03:227
RIGGS, HARVEY B & WEAVER, BELLVINA	15 APR 1906	11:284
RIGGS, JAMES M & KARNES, ROSA	16 MAR 1895	07:270
RIGGS, JOHN R & KEARNS, MALINDA C	16 DEC 1895	07:454
RIGGS, THOMAS & HUGHS, CELIA	1832	01:026
RIGGS, THOMAS M & McINTOSH, NONA A	06 APR 1902	10:048
RIGGS, WILLIAM A & FINDLEY, STELLA	11 DEC 1897	08:212
RILEY, FRANCIS M & HARRIS, VIRGINIA	27 JAN 1884	11:452
RILEY, JOHN & KING, KITTY	04 JAN 1831	01:023
RILEY, JOHN & HARRISON, JANE	10 MAY 1868	05:178
RILEY, ROBERT F & HILL, OMA O	15 DEC 1906	11:469
RILEY, ROY & STEWART, LAURA	**24 DEC 1912	14:065
RILEY, THOS & DENKENS, SUSAN	26 OCT 1822	01:007
RIMMEY, GEORGE W & BAKER, EMMA	23 DEC 1897	08:223
RIMMEY, GEORGE WASHINGTON & HICKS, SUSAN A	13 OCT 1885	12:233
RINE, JOSEPH L & SHIRLY, EMILY J	22 NOV 1867	05:103
RINE, JOSEPH L & SAYRE, PAMELA	25 FEB 1877	09:035
RINE, MICHAEL & ROUSH, REBECCA ANN	*19 NOV 1850	02:001
RINE, MICHAEL B & McDERMITT, MATILDA	*29 MAR 1858	02:011

Names	Date	Ref
RINGS, CHARLES A & CUNNINGHAM, MATTIE	25 DEC 1911	13:448
RIPLEY, ENOCH & PICKENS, MARY	22 OCT 1826	01:015
RIPLEY, JOHN & HARRIS, POLLY	23 MAR 1830	01:022
RIPLEY, JOHN & PECK, MALINDA A	*03 OCT 1853	02:004
RIPLEY, JOHN & ZAPF, ELIZABETH	04 AUG 1881	10:436
RIPLEY, JOSHUA & PIERCY, DELILA	1837	01:040
RISER, JOSHUA H & CHAPMAN, MARTHA V	19 AUG 1870	06:217
RISK, FRANK BELL & COBB, ELIZABETH MAY	07 MAY 1893	06:532
RISOR, THOMAS & McMILLEN, MATILDA	20 DEC 1866	05:011
RITCHIE, WILLIAM L & RAYBURN, OLIVIA J	25 FEB 1875	08:214
RIZER, JOSHUA H & NEALE, FLURY	27 APR 1901	09:236
ROACH, HENRY T & EDWARDS, FLOSSIE J	02 APR 1903	10:264
ROACH, JACOB & FREED, HARRIET	MAR 1844	01:043
ROACH, JEREMIAH & AUSTIN, LYDIA	04 JUL 1891	06:147
ROACH, JOHN & AUMILLER, AMANDA M	19 SEP 1872	07:263
ROACH, MILTON E & ROGERS, NANCY E	08 APR 1894	07:071
ROACH, NOAH W & EDWARDS, ADA	01 JAN 1896	07:474
ROACH, OSCAR & DRUMMOND, ALICE	15 NOV 1875	08:298
ROACH, RHUDA M & GIBBS, ANNIE A	04 FEB 1905	11:041
ROACH, SAMUEL J & GIBBS, OLIVIA J	16 APR 1904	10:505
ROACH, WILLIAM & CARNEY, DELILAH	02 DEC 1819	01:007
ROADS, JOSHUA & CUMPSTON, MARGARET	01 FEB 1826	01:014
ROBBINS, WILLIAM JACKSON & FARLEY, MALINDA JANE	20 JAN 1889	05:334
ROBERTS, ALFRED & TOLES, MARY	28 FEB 1878	09:220
ROBERTS, BRADFORD & DEFENBACH, ELIZABETH	09 SEP 1874	08:158
ROBERTS, CALVIN & EDWARDS, ELIZABETH	*17 SEP 1850	02:001
ROBERTS, CHARLES & ROBERTS, MINNIE	18 JAN 1902	10:008
ROBERTS, CHARLES M & BRIGHT, FLORA M	19 APR 1905	11:077
ROBERTS, DAVID & HICKMAN, MARY E	06 SEP 1877	09:125
ROBERTS, DAVID A & DIEHL, EMMA McCLAIN	15 JUL 1900	09:162
ROBERTS, FLEMING & HARE, CATHARINE	18 JUL 1903	10:323
ROBERTS, HARRY MELVILLE & SHIRLEY, LUANA	30 SEP 1908	12:274
ROBERTS, JAMES ANDREW & WINDON, HARRIET JANE	28 AUG 1887	05:083
ROBERTS, JOHN J & CASEY, BESSIE	21 JUL 1910	13:116
ROBERTS, JOHN T & GEARHART, CLARA A	21 APR 1880	10:242
ROBERTS, JOHN W & SHELINE, ANNA	28 JUL 1887	05:066
ROBERTS, OLIVER P & SHELINE, CATHARINE	07 DEC 1865	04:081
ROBERTS, SAMUEL & JONES, MARTHA JANE	03 SEP 1846	01:046
ROBERTS, THOMAS & WEAVER, ELIZABETH	26 FEB 1837	01:031
ROBERTS, THOMAS A Jr & NEAL, MARY SUSAN	02 NOV 1904	10:629
ROBERTS, TOBIAS J & CONNER, MARY O	03 JUL 1878	09:279
ROBERTS, WILBER & CHILDERS, (Mrs) ADA	28 DEC 1910	13:248
ROBERTS, WILLIAM & CAMPBELL, FANNY	29 MAR 1877	09:048
ROBERTS, WILLIAM & RIFFLE, BARBARA	20 DEC 1808	01:002
ROBERTS, WILLIAM & LOVE, REBECCA A	12 MAY 1872	07:223
ROBERTS, WILLIAM R & THOMPSON, JENNIE V	27 AUG 1884	12:052
ROBEY, HOWARD L & WINDON, KATHRYN L	04 DEC 1907	12:086
ROBINSON, ALBERT & ZIMMER, MARGARET	14 SEP 1911	13:374
ROBINSON, ASA & DAVIS, (Mrs) MARGARET E	*27 SEP 1860	02:014
ROBINSON, CHARLES I & TAYLOR, AUGUSTA	18 APR 1890	05:543
ROBINSON, CUTHBERT & FIELD, BLANCHE	18 NOV 1901	09:451
ROBINSON, FRANCIS M & HUTTON, MADALINE R	07 NOV 1905	11:199
ROBINSON, GEORGE & PIKE, EMMA	24 MAY 1914	15:194
ROBINSON, GEORGE D & DEFORD, HANNAH ANN	18 JUL 1866	04:141
ROBINSON, GEORGE E & OVERHOLTS, MARY D	10 APR 1895	07:287
ROBINSON, HENRY & CHASE, MALINDA	31 MAY 1847	01:046
ROBINSON, JNO & DEWET, LYDIA	03 APR 1820	01:007
ROBINSON, KINSY, Jr & GODLEY, LAVINIA L	08 FEB 1869	06:033

ROBINSON, ROBERT & ROUSH, SUSANNAH	26 SEP 1861	03:023
ROBINSON, THOMAS H & GROSS, MYRTLE	12 AUG 1910	13:128
ROBINSON, WILLIAM & HELPER, CLARISSA ANN	*28 OCT 1852	02:003
ROBISON, ELZA CLAYTON & DEWITT, NORMA C	17 JUN 1900	09:144
ROBISSON, BENJAMIN AARON & BENNETT, ELLEN	28 OCT 1910	13:170
ROBSON, CUTHBERT & SOULSBY, JANE	01 JUN 1874	08:126
ROBSON, CUTHBERT WILLIAM & BASS, LIZZIE	08 OCT 1893	06:621
ROBSON, THOMAS & BOWDEN, JANE	02 SEP 1870	06:222
ROCK, JOHN L & STEPHENSON, MINNIE	31 AUG 1898	08:368
ROCKHOLD, BENJAMIN & WRIGHT, SARAH	23 JUL 1827	01:020
RODGERS, CHARLES F & BUMGARNER, REBECCA JANE	*14 JUL 1856	02:008
RODGERS, CHARLES H & RAINEY, MARGARET V	21 SEP 1907	12:016
RODGERS, CHARLES W & EDWARDS, MYRTLE M	18 MAR 1906	11:281
RODGERS, COLUMBUS & GRIMES, BESSIE	09 AUG 1905	11:144
RODGERS, GEORGE D & ARMSTRONG, ORA L	22 MAY 1901	09:346
RODGERS, IRA S & YOUNG, MINNIE M	24 NOV 1904	10:644
RODGERS, JESSE S & HARDWICK, BETTIE B	24 NOV 1897	08:203
RODGERS, LEMUEL F & GILLESPIE, EFFIE	19 SEP 1878	09:317
ROE, CHARLES & WERNER, MOLLIE	20 JUL 1895	07:344
ROE, ROY E & THOMAS, DELLA MAY	25 AUG 1914	15:260
ROECK, HENRY & FENIMORE, HARRIET	30 JUL 1882	11:183
ROECK, JACOB, Jr & ZIRKEL, SARAH E	06 SEP 1881	11:008
ROGER, E W & SMITH, ISABELLA A	10 MAR 1884	11:467
ROGERS, ADDISON & SMITH, CORNELIA	30 OCT 1873	08:050
ROGERS, CLIFFORD F & BURTON, HORTENSE	16 JUN 1904	10:539
ROGERS, EDWARD ALLEN & GILLISPIE, OLLIE MAY	04 SEP 1892	06:400
ROGERS, FORST & SULLIVAN, MAGGIE	26 AUG 1908	12:237
ROGERS, FRANCIS G & AUSTIN, PEARL	14 NOV 1908	12:305
ROGERS, GALEN O & DABNEY, MARY V	09 MAR 1895	07:267
ROGERS, GEORGE C H & RANEY, MARY E	31 AUG 1871	07:116
ROGERS, J O & McMANAWAY, MAY	19 FEB 1910	13:014
ROGERS, J W & RAINEY, VINA F	24 MAR 1910	13:031
ROGERS, NEHEMIAH & CAPEHART, SALLY	08 JAN 1828	01:017
ROGERS, PERRY A & JONES, ANNIE E	09 DEC 1886	12:437
ROGERS, SAML H & ROWLEY, ELIZABETH	*04 DEC 1858	02:011
ROGERS, WILLIAM T & JOHNSON, VIRGINA A	19 DEC 1877	09:170
ROHRBAUGH, JAMES WEBSTER & SNYDER, EFFIE S	16 OCT 1892	06:427
ROLISON, ISAAC & VICKERS, HELEN Z	27 MAR 1884	11:471
ROLLER, JAS & ROUSH, ANGELINE M	*13 MAR 1860	02:013
ROLLINS, ADONIJAH W & BAKER, NANCY JANE	*22 APR 1854	02:005
ROLLINS, ASA E & KNAPP, ELLORA V	24 DEC 1913	15:102
ROLLINS, AUTTIE L & DEVAULT, SERENA ORA ETHEL	12 DEC 1914	15:344
ROLLINS, BARNEY J & VINCENT, MINNIE	10 APR 1887	05:008
ROLLINS, BEN F & SIEGRIST, SARAH A	25 JUN 1871	07:097
ROLLINS, BENJAMIN ARTHUR & CHILDERS, NELLIE	*07 MAY 1907	11:525
ROLLINS, BYRD & EDWARDS, ELIZABETH	23 JUN 1912	13:551
ROLLINS, CHARLES & LEWIS, LUCINDA	31 JAN 1828	01:017
ROLLINS, CHARLES WESLEY & JOHNSON, ANNIE G	03 DEC 1889	05:490
ROLLINS, CYRUS & ROUSH, SARAH	03 FEB 1848	01:048
ROLLINS, CYRUS N & ROADES, MIRRAM	07 OCT 1882	11:220
ROLLINS, E J & SINES, MARY C	31 DEC 1882	11:284
ROLLINS, ELISHA E & SINES, LYDIA M	28 FEB 1878	09:221
ROLLINS, FLOYD & MEADOWS, IVA M	20 AUG 1913	15:014
ROLLINS, GEORGE W & KING, MARY A D	14 FEB 1886	12:294
ROLLINS, GEORGE WASHINGTON & HIGH, LUCINDA	*26 JUL 1888	05:251
ROLLINS, GIDEON D & BAKER, MARTHELA MARGARET	*01 SEP 1855	02:007
ROLLINS, JEREMIAH & WILSON, ROSELLE	24 AUG 1837	01:031
ROLLINS, JOHN & HUFFMAN, MARY	20 MAY 1829	01:021

ROLLINS, JOHN & DUFF, SARAH J	27 NOV 1887	05:142
ROLLINS, JOHN W & WILSON, NANCY	*08 FEB 1854	02:005
ROLLINS, JOS L & MERITT, GOLDA	27 JUL 1913	14:199
ROLLINS, T S & VINCENT, MARY	10 APR 1887	05:007
ROLLINS, THOMAS W & DURST, ALICE H	04 JUL 1900	09:155
ROLLINS, WILLIAM HENRY & DUFF, ROSA L	23 AUG 1891	06:164
ROLLINS, WILLIAM J & SMITH, ELIZABETH R	22 OCT 1908	12:287
ROLLINS, WILLIAM J B & BOLDEN, MARY E	27 FEB 1873	07:327
ROLLINS, WILLIAM M & PARSONS, FRANKIE	04 OCT 1893	06:615
ROLLINS, Z W & GLENN, ANNIE E	25 APR 1875	08:234
ROLLINS, ZACHARIAH W & GRIM, ANGELINE	12 SEP 1861	03:021
ROLLISON, JACOB A & KAY, EMMA JENNINGS	06 NOV 1887	05:136
ROMINE, JOHN & JORDAN, FLORA	01 NOV 1888	08:299
ROMINE, JOHN L & DENNY, JESSIE FAY	06 OCT 1914	15:289
ROOT, DAVID & ANDERSON, MARY	28 OCT 1830	01:022
ROSE, CLEMENT L & LANHAM, ANNIE	01 JAN 1895	07:226
ROSE, EDGAR L & SOMERVILLE, ELSIE C	11 OCT 1893	06:622
ROSE, ELSWORTH H & KEMPER, CARRIE L	05 OCT 1907	12:030
ROSE, GEORGE A & YEAGER, MARY M	08 APR 1885	12:156
ROSE, JOHN H & GIBBS, ZUBY ANN	*02 APR 1855	02:006
ROSE, JOHN P R B & JENNINGS, VERNA LILLIAN	28 FEB 1814	15:146
ROSE, JOSEPH W & NEWMAN, SUSAN M	22 MAY 1866	04:125
ROSE, LUMAN & HOFFMAN, BARBARA	16 NOV 1904	10:639
ROSE, M WILBER & CASH, WILLIE M	20 JUN 1908	12:201
ROSE, MYRON W & HARBOR, EFFIE G	*20 SEP 1905	11:174
ROSE, REUBEN B & BEAVER, LORAINE M	26 DEC 1895	07:472
ROSE, THOMAS & GIBEAUT, SARAH	08 DEC 1868	06:017
ROSEBERRY, ANDREW HORTON & BEALE, JULIA LEWIS	15 NOV 1899	09:017
ROSEBERRY, ANDREW M & LAMBERT, EMILY B	27 MAY 1877	09:085
ROSEBERRY, ASA M & KEARNS, NANNIE A	17 SEP 1910	13:163
ROSEBERRY, E W & MITCHELL, ALTHA	13 JUN 1914	15:221
ROSEBERRY, EDMOND F & ROUSH, MARY ELLEN	19 MAR 1867	05:038
ROSEBERRY, ELIJAH & McDERMITT, CLARISSA ANN	*29 DEC 1856	02:009
ROSEBERRY, GEORGE W & ADKINS, ELIZABETH	19 JUN 1877	09:093
ROSEBERRY, HERNANDO C & LERNER, ANNA M	18 MAY 1899	08:534
ROSEBERRY, HOMER L & HUGHES, DORA	28 OCT 1903	10:392
ROSEBERRY, JAMES L & THORNTON, EFFIE	*31 JUL 1891	06:154
ROSEBERRY, JOHN & AMOS, HENNY	01 APR 1827	01:017
ROSEBERRY, JOHN PETER & HAWKINS, MARTHA J	25 SEP 1870	07:007
ROSEBERRY, M F & STEEL, JOSEPHINE	05 OCT 1884	12:069
ROSEBERRY, MICHAEL & KNOP, LUCINDA	20 OCT 1827	01:017
ROSEBERRY, PETER & BROWN, MARY I	*24 JOCT 1859	02:013
ROSEBERRY, ROBERT BRUCE & ROBERTS, VIRGINIA E	31 OCT 1886	12:410
ROSEBERRY, WILLIAM A & ALLEN, HARRIET L	28 JUN 1891	06:141
ROSENBERGER, ARTHUR R & LONG, EVA K	26 APR 1883	11:330
ROSENBERRY, ROBERT A & WETZEL, MARY JANE	19 FEB 1864	03:161
ROSS, ABSOLOM & TULLY, VIRGINIA E	04 JUL 1891	06:146
ROSS, GEORGE W & BOOTH, MAGGIE E	17 OCT 1886	12:402
ROSS, HOWARD & HYSELL, JENNIE	24 DEC 1900	09:261
ROSS, HUGH S C & GALE, SUE A	11 OCT 1882	11:188
ROSS, JAMES & FARGO, AMANDA	1831	01:024
ROSSER, ISAIAH & PARKER, MARY	11 APR 1863	03:112
ROTH, WALTER A & PRIODE, IDA M	22 JUL 1897	08:130
ROTHGEB, ROY DERMONT & EWING, NINA FAYE	17 MAR 1814	15:160
ROUP, F M & HOGSETT, ROSABELL	30 NOV 1863	03:145
ROUSCH, DANIEL & YEAGER, CATHARINE	02 JAN 1810	01:002
ROUSCH, GEORGE & FIFE, BETSY	11 JAN 1831	01:023
ROUSCH, JOHN & ROUSCH, REGINA	18 MAY 1808	01:002

ROUSCH, JNO & RICKART, MARGARET	APR 1817	01:003
ROUSCH, LEWIS & ECKART, BARBARA	26 MAR 1818	01:003
ROUSCH, LEWIS & RICKART, SUSAN	02 MAR 1829	01:021
ROUSCH, MICHAEL & OLIVER, ELIZABETH	04 NOV 1817	01:003
ROUSH, ABEL & VAN MATRE, MARGARET ANN	23 MAY 1850	01:049
ROUSH, ABRAM & LOVE, DORA E	04 DEC 1887	05:153
ROUSH, ACQUILLA & KNAPP, ANNIE S	04 DEC 1890	06:015
ROUSH, ACQUILLA & NEASE, LORETTA C	28 MAY 1904	10:521
ROUSH, ADAM & GRIMM, ISABELLE	13 FEB 1899	08:466
ROUSH, ADAM & ZERKLE, ELIZABETH	*21 APR 1851	02:002
ROUSH, ADAM & FRANCIS, SARAH	25 APR 1900	09:107
ROUSH, ADAM, Jr & SCHOLL, SARAH E	12 OCT 1879	10:139
ROUSH, ALBERT & HUDSON, MARTHA JANE	22 AUG 1888	05:264
ROUSH, ALBERT & HARRIS, JENNIE	01 NOV 1890	05:636
ROUSH, ALBERT & STALNAKER, FANNIE	25 FEB 1901	09:296
ROUSH, ALLEN & WILCOXEN, SALIMA	*02 JAN 1857	02:009
ROUSH, ALLEN S & FRY, OLIVE	03 DEC 1874	08:191
ROUSH, ALONZO H & PICKENS, LUCY E	03 APR 1895	07:277
ROUSH, AMBROSE & ARMSTRONG, MARGARET S	05 MAR 1868	05;152
ROUSH, ANDREW & RIGGS, HARRIET D	02 OCT 1873	08:035
ROUSH, ANDREW J & FRY, ALMIRA	*27 OCT 1856	02:009
ROUSH, ANTHONY & HOFFMAN, CATHARINE	11 JAN 1837	01:030
ROUSH, ANTHONY & POUNDS, LYDIA	21 MAR 1841	01:043
ROUSH, ANTHONY & SHIPLEY, FRANCES	03 FEB 1874	08:097
ROUSH, ARTHUR E & LAWSON, SADIE MAY	21 AUR 1909	12:484
ROUSH, ASBERRY B & BLESSING, SARAH C	01 JUN 1882	11:157
ROUSH, AUSTIN E & BLAIR, CHARLOTTA	11 JUL 1895	07:340
ROUSH, BERT & PATTERSON, (Mrs) EMMA	19 JUL 1913	14:196
ROUSH, CALVIN & CLICK, LOUISA BELL	18 AUG 1888	05:259
ROUSH, CALVIN L & ROUSH, SUSAN J	27 NOV 1866	05:004
ROUSH, CHARLES & SAYRE, ELZINA	07 AUG 1873	08:016
ROUSH, CHARLES B & FRY, MILLIE	10 SEP 1899	08:609
ROUSH, CHARLES M & CHAPMAN, SARAH L	25 JAN 1877	09:027
ROUSH, CHARLES W & QUILLEN, VINNIE	24 DEC 1893	07:029
ROUSH, CLAUD & CUNNINGHAM, JOSIE	14 OCT 1901	09:419
ROUSH, CLYDE E & THOMAS, DELLA B	17 OCT 1906	11:433
ROUSH, CURTIS E & BURNS, EDITH M	15 JUN 1902	10:088
ROUSH, DAVID & POUND, RACHEL	27 OCT 1846	01:046
ROUSH, DAVID & HART, CHARLOTTE	*05 NOV 1853	02:004
ROUSH, DAVID & ROUSH, _____	*23 OCT 1855	02:007
ROUSH, EARNEY E & HART, OLGA	20 AUG 1907	11:595
ROUSH, EDGAR & ROBINSON, WILLIE	13 AUG 1891	06:163
ROUSH, EDMOND & MELTON, LAURA	01 JUL 1869	06:063
ROUSH, EDWARD E & FRY, IDA F	08 NOV 1899	09:011
ROUSH, EDWARD L & FIELDS, FLORENCE M	18 SEP 1903	10:362
ROUSH, ELDIA LATON & BOARD, ANNA L	14 FEB 1901	09:291
ROUSH, ELIAS & GIBBS, MARY CAROLINE	*27 FEB 1854	02:005
ROUSH, ELLIS P & BASS, LAURA	25 JAN 1900	09:073
ROUSH, ELMER WILSON & FOWLER, LENA FRANCES	15 AUG 1891	06:158
ROUSH, ELMORE & QUILLIN, OLIVIA	09 JUL 1885	12:193
ROUSH, EMERY C & OHLINGER, VESTA M	28 DEC 1904	11:015
ROUSH, EMORY & HESSON, JESSIE	24 AUG 1906	11:398
ROUSH, EMORY B & HILL, MARY F	09 MAR 1879	10:063
ROUSH, ENOS & ZERKEL, BARBARA	26 NOV 1839	01:043
ROUSH, ERNEST & PICKARD, MARY L	21 DEC 1909	12:575
ROUSH, ERNEST M & QUILLEN, EVA G	08 DEC 1895	07:442
ROUSH, ERVIN & CLICK, JENNIE	16 OCT 1882	11:222
ROUSH, EVERRETT N & LEITWILER, MARY M	15 JUN 1897	08:109

ROUSH, EZRA & WEAVER, MARGARET E	07 APR 1870	06:174
ROUSH, FRANCIS M & PICKENS, KIZZIAR	21 DEC 1882	11:270
ROUSH, FRED M & VAN MATRE, IDA L	29 JUN 1907	11:565
ROUSH, GEORGE & RISER, JOSEPHINE	12 APR 1877	09:061
ROUSH, GEORGE & ROUSH, SUSAN	JAN 1844	01:043
ROUSH, GEORGE H & BASS, MARY A	18 JAN 1882	11:100
ROUSH, GEORGE LEIGHTON & ENIZE, ANNA	27 SEP 1891	06:191
ROUSH, GEORGE M & ROUSH, SAREPTA	08 DEC 1891	06:241
ROUSH, GEORGE MARION & CUNDIFF, AMANDA V	19 FEB 1893	06:484
ROUSH, GEORGE W & ADAMS, MIRTIE M	15 AUG 1886	12:375
ROUSH, GEORGE W & WOOLFINGBARGER, LAURA B	24 DEC 1902	10:214
ROUSH, GIDEON E & WOLFE, ELIZABETH A	21 JAN 1883	11:293
ROUSH, GROVER C & ROUSH, LIZZIE	05 AUG 1906	11:379
ROUSH, HARLEY B & LOVE, OSCEOLA	18 JUN 1911	13:332
ROUSH, HARRY & BASS, FLORA	04 MAR 1909	12:376
ROUSH, HARRY A & ROOD, BLANCHE A	16 NOV 1913	15:068
ROUSH, HARVEY P & OHLINGER, MARY V	20 NOV 1898	08:408
ROUSH, HENRY & POUNDS, LYDIA	18 SEP 1845	01:045
ROUSH, HENRY & STOKELY, MARY	14 DEC 1876	09:001
ROUSH, HENRY C & RICKARD, CLARINDA	01 NOV 1883	11:419
ROUSH, HENRY C & McMILLEN, ANGIE	15 JAN 1908	12:111
ROUSH, HENRY C & HARRIGAN, NORA	21 MAY 1899	08:536
ROUSH, HENRY L & ROUSH, CATHARINE	21 NOV 1867	05:118
ROUSH, HENRY L & WEAVER, VERINITIA	27 SEP 1888	05:284
ROUSH, HENRY N & SPENCER, LESTA A	23 JUL 1902	10:118
ROUSH, HENRY P & SAYRE, DELLA	01 JAN 1891	06:039
ROUSH, HENRY PARK & ROUSH, ETTA	14 NOV 1896	07:640
ROUSH, HOMER & FISHER, ELLA	21 APR 1906	11:293
ROUSH, HOMER N & SURGEON, BLANCH	25 DEC 1901	09:479
ROUSH, ISAAC NELSON & GRAY, HETTIE ANN	14 OCT 1888	05:289
ROUSH, IVAN & HALL, MABLE	21 FEB 1914	15:145
ROUSH, J J & McGLOTHLIN, LAURA	07 FEB 1884	11:455
ROUSH, JACKSON & WRIGHT, SARAH	25 JUN 1896	07:572
ROUSH, JACOB & HOFFMAN, ELIZABETH	11 MAR 1832	01:025
ROUSH, JACOB & NEASE, CATHARINE	14 MAY 1839	01:042
ROUSH, JACOB & BURROWS, EDITH	10 APR 1851	02:001
ROUSH, JACOB & BIRTHISEL, FRANCES J	*29 DEC 1859	02:013
ROUSH, JAMES & GRIM, SARAH	*13 SEP 1853	02:004
ROUSH, JAMES & HOFFMAN, IDA	25 JAN 1885	12:120
ROUSH, JAMES R & POUNDS, SARAH E	13 DEC 1893	07:021
ROUSH, JASPER N & STATTS, CLARA	14 NOV 1908	12:306
ROUSH, JEREMIAH & GRIMM, MARTHA ROSE	08 NOV 1891	06:216
ROUSH, JEROME A & TURNBULL, JESSE B F	28 OCT 1882	11:234
ROUSH, JESSE & HARTINGER, EDITH	11 JUL 1900	09:159
ROUSH, JOHN & SERGEANT, (Mrs) CATHARINE	21 JUN 1849	01:049
ROUSH, JOHN & BLESSING, SAREPTA A	11 AUG 1849	01:051
ROUSH, JOHN & NEASE, BERTHA E	24 FEB 1897	08:050
ROUSH, JOHN HENSON & KEMPER, ORMA	28 APR 1907	11:520
ROUSH, JOHN H & ESTEP, GERTRUDE	04 SEP 1914	15:265
ROUSH, JOHN J & ROUSH, MARGARET	31 DEC 1876	09:017
ROUSH, JOHN S & SIEGRIST, MARGARET	13 JUN 1876	08:360
ROUSH, JOHN S & BOGGESS, BEATRICE	14 DEC 1896	08:017
ROUSH, JOHN W & ROUSH, REBECCA	01 NOV 1866	04:165
ROUSH, JONAS & HUFFMAN, LUCINDA	*05 DEC 1859	02:013
ROUSH, JONAS & YONKER, ELIZABETH ANN	31 OCT 1866	04:164
ROUSH, JONAS & TAYLOR, MARGARET	06 MAR 1884	11:466
ROUSH, JONATHAN E L & SOMERVILLE, VINNIE M	16 OCT 1898	08:375
ROUSH, JOSEPH & GRIM, CAROLINE	09 MAY 1867	05:050

ROUSH, JOSEPH & WEAVER, ANGELINE	31 JAN 1880	10:295
ROUSH, JOSEPH ALBERT & ROUSH, MARGARET	07 DEC 1848	01:051
ROUSH, JOSEPH E & YEAGER, REBECCA	03 NOV 1878	10:004
ROUSH, JOSEPH E & YEAGER, SARAH M	17 NOV 1890	06:009
ROUSH, JOSEPH F & EVANS, MARY J	01 DEC 1881	11:063
ROUSH, JOSEPH M & SHIRLEY, MATILDA	13 NOV 1866	04:170
ROUSH, JOSEPH M & McDANIEL, FRANCES C	21 DEC 1882	11:271
ROUSH, LAFAYETTE & RHODES, JENNIE D	28 DEC 1871	07:162
ROUSH, LEE R & KIRBY, NAOMI	02 JAN 1911	13:254
ROUSH, LEONARD R & BURRIS, SUSAN J	02 OCT 1902	10:165
ROUSH, LEVI & NEASE, MARY A	01 OCT 1846	01:046
ROUSH, LEVI & RANDALL, ALICE	*02 JAN 1857	02:009
ROUSH, LEVI J & GIBBS, GENORA C	30 DEC 1885	12:273
ROUSH, LEWIS M & GRIMM, MARY C	15 JUL 1880	10:280
ROUSH, LEWIS M & POUNDS, ARLETTA	01 FEB 1894	07:042
ROUSH, LEWIS W & WEAVER, LYDIA	26 AUG 1880	10:289
ROUSH, LINLEY & DAVIDSON, MARY	30 JUL 1912	13:572
ROUSH, LORENZO & VAN MATRE, ANNIE E	04 APR 1888	05:201
ROUSH, LUTHER S & FISHER, MARY C	27 OCT 1804	10:618
ROUSH, MARK & VANMATRE, MARY	29 DEC 1836	01:030
ROUSH, McKENDRIE C & HOFFMAN, CAROLINE	16 JUN 1874	08:133
ROUSH, McKENDRIE C & HOFFMAN, MILLIE B	07 OCT 1896	07:627
ROUSH, MICHAEL & ROUSH, MARY	12 SEP 1839	01:043
ROUSH, MICHAEL & SPROUT, SARAH	13 APR 1841	01:043
ROUSH, MICHAEL & ROUSH, MARY	19 DEC 1867	05:120
ROUSH, MILLARD & LIEVING, RETTA V	22 DEC 1904	11:004
ROUSH, MORGAN & LYONS, LAURA	27 NOV 1887	05:147
ROUSH, MORGAN L & SAYRE, CELIA A	24 FEB 1884	11:461
ROUSH, MOSES & ROUSH, LYDIA	30 SEP 1883	11:392
ROUSH, MOSES & SAYRE, EMMA	02 NOV 1907	12:076
ROUSH, MOSES & SAYRE, ELLA	28 MAY 1908	12:187
ROUSH, MOSES B & KEARNS, (Mrs) MARGARET	29 MAY 1910	13:073
ROUSH, MOSES B & ELLIOTT, (Mrs) MARGARET A	28 DEC 1911	13:454
ROUSH, MOSES G & TULLER, ANN M	08 NOV 1848	01:051
ROUSH, NICHOLAS B & HART, HAZEL H	26 JUL 1913	14:200
ROUSH, NOAH & GRIM, LYDIA	*28 NOV 1853	02:005
ROUSH, OKEY & PICKENS, ALMA	09 FEB 1899	08:461
ROUSH, OKEY ALLEN & LIETWILER, MILLIE	25 OCT 1888	05:293
ROUSH, ORIS C & RAYBURN, DELLA P	24 SEP 1911	13:381
ROUSH, ORVAL D & THORNTON, LUCY M	27 FEB 1905	11:051
ROUSH, OSCAR H & BUSH, NELLIE	30 NOV 1911	13:432
ROUSH, OSCAR TAYLOR & SOMERVILLE, EMMA LORENA	24 JAN 1912	13:470
ROUSH, OTHA MARFORD & RIFFLE, LUCY LUELLA	26 APR 1903	10:275
ROUSH, OTMER & ROUSH, KATHERINE M	26 NOV 1912	14:034
ROUSH, OTTIS C & OHLINGER, LYDA M	24 DEC 1907	12:095
ROUSH, PARK LEE & SMART, AURILLA	01 SEP 1889	05:446
ROUSH, PEARL & CUNNINGHAM, BERTHA	30 MAY 1908	12:191
ROUSH, PERRY S & SAYRE, HATTIE	07 APR 1906	11:287
ROUSH, PETER C & ARMSTRONG, MARY A	02 SEP 1869	06:086
ROUSH, PETER EARLY & WEAVER, MINA E	27 OCT 1887	05:127
ROUSH, PHILIP & SKEIN, MAHALIA	04 SEP 1834	01:028
ROUSH, PROBE E & FOREMAN, LAURA M	27 DEC 1905	11:230
ROUSH, REUBEN & ROUSH, ELLA M	29 JUN 1895	07:324
ROUSH, ROBERT & RICKARD, OMA L	22 FEB 1899	08:472
ROUSH, ROBERT W & PICKENS, LUCINDA E	12 FEB 1882	11:110
ROUSH, RUDU R & ROLLINS, ADDA VIRGINIA	22 AUG 1891	06:169
ROUSH, RUFUS E & GLENN, SARAH E	27 SEP 1913	15:041
ROUSH, SAMUEL C & LEWIS, OLGA	01 NOV 1900	09:230

ROUSH, SAMUEL, Jr & SNYDER, ELIZABETH	03 MAY 1842	01:036
ROUSH, SAMUEL N & RAYBURN, MARGARET	12 MAY 1881	10:323 1
ROUSH, SOLOMON & MUSGRAVE, MARY C	*27 JAN 1857	02:009
ROUSH, SOLOMON A & ADAMS, JENNIE M	10 NOV 1897	08:195
ROUSH, SPENCER & GRAY, MARY A	05 MAR 1885	12:147
ROUSH, STAUDER & ZIRKEL, SUSANNAH	*05 NOV 1860	02:014
ROUSH, TAYLOR B & WORLEY, LUCY M	04 JAN 1905	11:006
ROUSH, THOMAS B & FRY, MARY M	17 FEB 1897	08:044
ROUSH, THOMAS E & BALL, MARY L	20 JAN 1886	12:283
ROUSH, THOMAS J & RICKARD, MARGARET A	09 MAR 1882	11:124
ROUSH, VERN L & CAPEHART, KELSIE F	29 JUN 1907	11:564
ROUSH, WADE H & VAN MATRE, LILLIE	11 JAN 1899	08:449
ROUSH, WALAS & ROUSH, JOSIE	20 AUG 1908	12:221
ROUSH, WALLAS & ROUSH, (Mrs) JOSIE	29 OCT 1910	13:195
ROUSH, WALTER D & BOSTON, EDNA MAY	02 JUN 1907	11:546
ROUSH, WANDA E & EADS, DICIE ELLEN	25 DEC 1913	15:099
ROUSH, WILLARD H & LEWIS, LUELLA	01 DEC 1901	09:462
ROUSH, WILLARD J & NEASE, EFFIE L	24 DEC 1895	07:463
ROUSH, WILLIAM & ZERCKLE, REBECCA J	30 DEC 1875	08:313
ROUSH, WILLIAM & BURROWS, MARTHA ELLEN	24 SEP 1887	05:104
ROUSH, WILLIAM H & WAYLAND, MARY W	28 APR 1870	06:183
ROUSH, WILLIAM HENRY & BLESSING, MARY ALICE	02 MAY 1889	05:394
ROUSH, WILLIAM R & BLESSING, VIRGINIA A	28 APR 1881	10:407
ROUSH, WILLIAM V & FRY, DELPHA	13 JUL 1899	08:573
ROUSH, WILLIE P & QUILLEN, SADIE N	20 OCT 1882	11:230
ROUSH, WILLIE P & QUILLEN, ANNA	22 JUL 1895	07:347
ROUSH, WINFIELD & WEAVER, ROSETTA	12 NOV 1903	10:410
ROUSH, WYATT F & BUMGARNER, MINNIE	30 NOV 1901	09:450
ROWAN, EDWARD & KING, MARY	25 SEP 1898	08:367
ROWE, FRANK & ELLIOTT, MAUDE	03 JUL 1910	13:108
ROWLEY, EDGAR E & GREENLEE, NANCY M	09 MAY 1885	12:174
ROWLEY, GEORGE W & CHAPMAN, OLLIE M	04 DEC 1900	09:246
ROWLEY, HARVEY D & ESTEP, BESSIE L	13 SEP 1913	15:032
ROWLEY, WARREN SEYMOUR & SPURLOCK, MARY ELIZABETH	10 AUG 1910	13:127
ROWLEY, WILLIAM S & SHULER, NANNIE G	29 APR 1909	12:406
ROWSEY, JAMES H & WATTERSON, SARAH E	10 DEC 1895	07:445
ROWSEY, WILLIAM H & STURGEON, MARGARET	26 MAR 1876	08:340
ROWSEY, WILLIAM H & BALL, (Mrs) JULIA A	11 NOV 1866	04:163
ROY, GEORGE & HALL, MATTIE	07 MAY 1901	09:334
ROY, HOMER E & BABER, EMMA C	11 JUN 1913	14:172
ROY, JOHN & YAUGER, LETTIE	13 OCT 1897	08:172
ROY, WILLIAM T & WOLF, FLORENCE	01 MAY 1879	10:084
ROYER, GEORGE W & McMURRAY, RACHEL	25 AUG 1898	08:346
RUCKER, ISAAC M & BALL, SUSANNAH	*12 JUN 1854	02:005
RUCKER, W T & RUCKER, FRANCES E	24 AUG 1870	06:218
RUFFNER, JOHN N & BOYLES, SARAH	02 APR 1840	01:034
RUFFNER, WILLIAM L & SHAW, JUDITH E	27 OCT 1864	03:204
RULON, JOSEPH F & McNAUGHTON, HANNAH L	26 MAY 1868	05:182
RUNION, JAMES F & STEWART, NETTIE L	25 SEP 1885	12:227
RUNION, JOSEPH & JENKINS, MARTHA J	03 APR 1893	06:515
RUNNEON, HENRY & KING, SARAH	23 APR 1818	01:005
RUNNEON, JOHN & CARPENTER, DEBORAH	30 SEP 1820	01:006
RUNNER, ELIJAH & BENNETT, MARY	06 MAY 1823	01:010
RUNNION, FRANCIS J & CUNNINGHAM, BETSY ANN	*13 AUG 1851	02:002
RUSCHEL, JOHN & HIGINBOTHAM, LENIA	16 APR 1890	05:544
RUSH, JAMES & SIMMS, LOUISA H	20 AUG 1871	07:112
RUSSELL, A L & NORRIS, CARRIE D	06 JUL 1886	12:352
RUSSELL, ALBERT G & MOORE, OLIVIA M	18 FEB 1868	05:145

RUSSELL, ALLEN J & NEWTON, MARY F	17 SEP 1869	06:090
RUSSELL, BONNIE & LOCKETT, ANNIE	03 SEP 1900	09:185
RUSSELL, CLEVELAND & HYSELL, GARNETT	12 APR 1913	14:121
RUSSELL, DANA M & RIGGS, LULA B	25 JUL 1909	12:467
RUSSELL, DANIEL & LANE, LUCY	16 APR 1829	01:019
RUSSELL, DANIEL & THOMPSON, LUELLA MARGARET	02 OCT 1887	05:110
RUSSELL, DANIEL & MINK, ALICE	26 JUL 1893	06:580
RUSSELL, EDWARD & SAXTON, MARY	08 JUN 1889	05:410
RUSSELL, EMANUEL & MONTGOMERY, GRACE	24 MAY 1902	10:070
RUSSELL, GEORGE W & STEVENS, CAROLINE	02 NOV 1876	08:407
RUSSELL, HARRY & WITHERS, LULA	16 DEC 1905	11:222
RUSSELL, HARRY V & WARD, RENA	24 JUN 1899	08:563
RUSSELL, HARRY V & DWYER, (Mrs) MARY A	13 JUN 1910	13:090
RUSSELL, HARVEY S & HANNAH, MAGGIE G	21 MAY 1908	12:178
RUSSELL, HENRY & DAVIS, MARY	01 JUN 1887	05:031
RUSSELL, HIRAM & McCLOUD, MARY	04 SEP 1878	09:306
RUSSELL, HIRAM & VANMATRE, MARY	*04 APR 1855	02:006
RUSSELL, HOMER V & KERNS, MAE E	08 JUN 1910	13:089
RUSSELL, HOWARD BUDD & GLOECKNER, HAZEL CLEO	11 APR 1914	15:176
RUSSELL, HOWARD C & WOODARD, BERTHA SELL	13 JUN 1907	11:551
RUSSELL, JAMES & PHILLIPS, MINNIE L	19 AUG 1899	08:596
RUSSELL, JESSE & GREENLEE, MARTHA	23 APR 1900	09:115
RUSSELL, JESSE & MONTGOMERY, ELLA	15 MAY 1906	11:315
RUSSELL, JOHN NELSON & MATTHEWS, CLARA INDIA	16 SEP 1886	12:387
RUSSELL, LEWIS & LEWIS, ELIZA ANN	*28 MAY 1852	02:003
RUSSELL, LEWIS & JONES, JANE	*23 JAN 1858	02:010
RUSSELL, MARLOW & LAWSON, EDNA	02 JUL 1903	10:312
RUSSELL, MARSHALL & STEWART, GEORGIA A	06 AUG 1883	11:384
RUSSELL, NAPOLEON B & TURNER, ANNIE	19 JUL 1868	05:198
RUSSELL, OSCAR E & BERRIDGE, OSA M	26 JUN 1912	13:555
RUSSELL, OWEN & MARTIN, HATTIE L	10 JUN 1914	05:219
RUSSELL, PAUL D & RATHBURN, SARAH	19 NOV 1914	15:324
RUSSELL, RALSTON & LINDSEY, HELEN BROWN	02 APR 1907	11:509
RUSSELL, RAYMOND C & RUSSELL, JETTA L	21 MAR 1912	13:504
RUSSELL, RENNIE & VAN MATRE, DESSIE	18 APR 1908	12:162
RUSSELL, SHEFFIELD & STEADMAN, (Mrs) MARTHA J	**28 SEP 1910	13:169
RUSSELL, SHERMAN & RICE, FANNY	15 MAY 1887	05:020
RUSSELL, WILLIAM G & SHIVELEY, NANNIE	28 APR 1897	08:084
RUSSELL, WILLIAM R & FRENCH, HATTIE	19 JUN 1890	05:574
RUSSILL, DAVID & BENNET, JULIA	06 SEP 1819	01:007
RUTH, EDWARD S & BAILEY, MARY J	12 NOV 1895	07:426
RUTTENCUTTER, L J & GOLD, MARY MAGDALENE	19 OCT 1913	15:052
RUTTENCUTTER, WILLIAM EDWIN & JARROTT, SADIE FRANCES	04 MAR 1885	12:149
RYAN, C E & McGRAW, BETTIE	11 JUL 1909	12:457
RYAN, CLAUD J & COSTELO, MARGARET	04 OCT 1906	11:255
RYAN, JAMES & FRANKLIN, ELIZA	30 DEC 1835	01:029
RYAN, JOHN E & CANTER, SARAH	27 JUL 1877	09:112
RYAN, JOHN HENRY & TAYLOR, EFFIE	17 NOV 1892	06:440
RYAN, PATRICK FRANCIS & JONES, ANNIE ELIZABETH	12 OCT 1892	06:419
RYAN, THOMAS & McCRONEY, MARY	26 APR 1865	04:009
RYDER, JULIUS H & CAMPBELL, MYRTLE	14 NOV 1898	08:403
RYSON, ERNEST & ROBINSON, ESTELLA	08 JUL 1909	12:454
St CLAIR, ALFRED & St CLAIR, MARGARET S	24 FEB 1898	08:264
St CLAIR, CARL & JONES, SARAH E	14 FEB 1894	07:046
St CLAIR, GEORGE & HANDSHAW, VICTORIA	24 OCT 1895	07:414
St CLAIR, HUGH & FLOWERS, SARAH	24 APR 1823	01:008
St CLAIR, THOMAS & HARRIS, ERSULA	*09 MAR 1853	02:004
St JOHN, RALPH & MINTURN, ELLEN A	04 OCT 1843	01:038

Name	Date	Ref
SAFFORD, ROBERT F & HARRISON, ANN	01 OCT 1818	01:004
SAMPLE, FRANK & SMALL, HARRIET	23 JUN 1887	05:050
SAMPLES, AGRIPPA & HALEY, MILDRED	18 SEP 1865	04:051
SAMPSON, THOMAS J & WARDEN, CUMA	11 DEC 1902	10:204
SANDERS, CLARINTON D & BURCH, ELIZABETH G	27 MAY 1847	01:047
SANDERS, CLAY M & CLARK, GLADYS E	05 JUL 1902	10:103
SANDERS, EDWARD & BLAIN, MISSOURI	02 DEC 1896	08:010
SANDERS, EMERSON & WATKINS, VIRGINIA C	25 JUN 1874	08:138
SANDERS, HARRY B & THOMPSON, CARRIE W	19 NOV 1902	10:191
SANDERS, HARRY MARION & HOOFF, JENNIE MOORE	29 MAY 1890	05:564
SANDERS, JAMES ALLEN & JOHNSON, MAGGIE	10 FEB 1885	12:137
SANDERS, JOHN A & NEIGHBORS, NANCY M	11 DEC 1872	07:295
SANDERS, JOHN B & KNOPP, AMANDA	23 JUL 1872	07:249
SANDERS, ROBERT & COLLINS, BERTHA	04 APR 1897	08:071
SANDERS, SOLOMON D & WARNER, MARIETTA D	19 FEB 1885	12:142
SANDERS, THOMAS F P & YEAGER, SARAH C	10 AUG 1871	07:107
SANDFORD, GEORGE W & HARPOLD, DRUZILLA	21 OCT 1869	06:099
SANDS, ELMER E & WHALEY, ESTELLA M	05 DEC 1886	12:433
SANDS, JAMES & PRITCHARD, MARY	24 DEC 1894	07:218
SANDS, JOSEPH A & CHEESEBREW, CICELY D	28 OCT 1880	10:318
SANDS, JOSEPH B & KASTER, ADDA L	18 JUL 1896	07:582
SANDS, S A & JOHNSON, IDA	09 AUG 1913	15:008
SANDS, WILLIAM L & McDERMITT, MAUDE E	26 APR 1913	14:135
SANFORD, JAMES W & HAWK, LIZZIE M	05 JUL 1894	07:119
SANNS, GEORGE W & VAN SICKLES, SARAH E	08 NOV 1862	03:086
SANSBURY, DAVID L & MURREY, MARGARET M	23 AUG 1913	15:021
SANTEE, SAMUEL M & BURDETT, JESSIE	18 JUN 1911	13:331
SAPP, ALBERT & ROUSH, ELVIRA	29 SEP 1868	05:211
SAPP, E R & PURVIANCE, ALTA MAY	17 MAY 1912	13:528
SARGENT, HARRY H & LEE, MARTHA F	12 JAN 1898	08:247
SARGENT, WILLIAM H & McDANIEL, IDA	03 APR 1867	05:041
SATTIS, JOHN F & CHAPMAN, URSULA J	03 MAR 1868	05:151
SAUL, ISAAC & HUMPHRIES, LUCY M	21 FEB 1864	03:162
SAULSBURY, JAMES & THORNTON, RACHEL J	17 JUL 1870	06:206
SAUNDERS, ALBERT G & PREWETT, EMILY	FEB 1838	01:033
SAUNDERS, ALEXANDER N & DAYLONG, SUSAN	1833	01:027
SAUNDERS, JASPER T & TAYLOR, NEVADA	28 JAN 1911	13:263
SAUVAGE, VALENTINE & JOACHIM, ELIZABETH	22 SEP 1913	15:038
SAVINE, JOSEPH T & GREEN, SARAH A	08 JUN 1873	08:001
SAVINE, LORENZO D & AUMILLER, HANNAH	24 MAY 1866	04:127
SAWYER, JAMES I & RIFFLE, HATTIE M	23 OCT 1901	09:328
SAWYERS, ALBERT W & MEADOWS, MARY A	27 JUN 1874	08:139
SAXTON, C D & TAYLOR, (Mrs) M J	02 NOV 1911	13:406
SAXTON, CHARLES & EDWARDS, MARY C	22 MAR 1884	11:470
SAXTON, CHARLES & NEWELL, MYRTLE B	23 JUL 1905	11:136
SAXTON, HARVEY & ENGLE, ROSE	28 SEP 1891	06:190
SAXTON, JAMES & ROUSH, LAURA	27 FEB 1888	05:188
SAXTON, JOHN R & GILPON, GRACE	29 AUG 1901	09:395
SAXTON, PRINT & DICKEN, MARY L	28 SEP 1901	09:416
SAXTON, THURMAN & ROSEBERRY, FLORA	23 AUG 1893	06:591
SAYRE, ALONZO C & TILLIS, OLIVE B	*10 OCT 1859	02:013
SAYRE, ANDREW & JACOBS, SARAH J	05 FEB 1878	09:207
SAYRE, ANDREW J & HOPE, ELLEN	27 APR 1872	07:218
SAYRE, ARCHIE E & HYLTON, JESSIE C	17 OCT 1900	09:221
SAYRE, ARTHUR & RODGERS, LINA	10 MAY 1910	13:064
SAYRE, BENJAMIN & HUGHS, DELILAH	06 JAN 1828	01:021
SAYRE, BERT E & THOMAS, MYRTLE	24 AUG 1898	08:348
SAYRE, CALVIN C & RINE, NANCY M	24 DEC 1873	08:080

SAYRE, CHARLES & McDERMITT, MALINDA	*26 FEB 1855	02:006
SAYRE, CHARLES & DAVIS, SARAH E	01 APR 1883	11:316
SAYRE, CHARLES E & HARRIS, LOUISA	08 JUL 1887	05:055
SAYRE, CLAUD & RICE, LUCY H	03 MAY 1894	07:087
SAYRE, DANIEL & McMILLEN, MARY S	10 MAY 1870	06:190
SAYRE, DANIEL & WILLIAMS, NELLIE	07 DEC 1902	10:198
SAYRE, DANIEL B & STEPHENSON, MARY	03 OCT 1844	01:044
SAYRE, DANIEL B & SLAUGHTER, RUTH	13 DEC 1896	08:016
SAYRE, DANIEL FRANCIS & MORRIS, LAURA	29 AUG 1879	10:118
SAYRE, DANIEL J & ROLLAR, CATHERINE	26 APR 1864	03:182
SAYRE, DANIEL R & KING, NANCY	31 OCT 1877	09:151
SAYRE, DANIEL W & BUFFINGTON, MARTHA J	10 APR 1883	11:320
SAYRE, DAVID & STEPHENSON, MARY J	18 JUL 1872	07:246
SAYRE, DAVID & SCANTLING, NANCY	27 JUL 1876	08:371
SAYRE, DAVID & TOTH, ALMIRA	24 FEB 1878	09:217
SAYRE, DAVID ABSOLOM & FERGUSON, MINNIE	25 DEC 1887	05:164
SAYRE, DAVID B & CAIN, MARY M	01 JAN 1912	13:456
SAYRE, E S & GLENN, MAUDE E	29 JAN 1913	14:087
SAYRE, EDWARD ARMSTRONG & GIST, ELLA B	23 OCT 1888	05:292
SAYRE, EMORY S & OLIVER, LULU	17 DEC 1902	10:207
SAYRE, EPHRAIM & CHILDERS, MATILDA C	24 NOV 1898	08:412
SAYRE, ERNEST & WARNER, NORA	19 AUG 1908	12:227
SAYRE, ERNEST & HESSON, EVA	27 MAR 1911	13:293
SAYRE, EUGENE F & VAN MATRE, ANNIE J	20 NOV 1881	11:057
SAYRE, EZEKIEL & BARR, SUSAN S	14 MAR 1889	05:369
SAYRE, FISHER & LITTLE, IDA	14 JUL 1898	08:335
SAYRE, FISHER L & LIEVING, CLARA	27 AUG 1892	06:395
SAYRE, GEORGE B & COLE, LILLIE B	14 FEB 1883	11:297
SAYRE, GEORGE W & VARIAN, HANNAH ELIZA	01 SEP 1861	03:016
SAYRE, GEORGE W & JIVIDEN, BERTHA	25 DEC 1895	07:465
SAYRE, GEORGE W & MINTURN, FRANCES	03 FEB 1900	09:075
SAYRE, GROVER C & COSSIN, BETHA M	20 APR 1911	13:311
SAYRE, HENRY & LAMBERT, JENNIE	04 SEP 1876	08:381
SAYRE, HIRAM C & BAKER, ELLA L	24 AUG 1892	06:388
SAYRE, ICHABOD B V & LEE, MINERVA	17 DEC 1845	01:045
SAYRE, ISAAC N & BAILEY, EMMA A	26 FEB 1888	05:189
SAYRE, JACOB & STANLEY, EDY	02 JAN 1828	01:021
SAYRE, JAMES & CHILDERS, ELLEN	25 MAY 1889	05:401
SAYRE, JAMES HARPER & CLARKE, ELLA	01 JUN 1887	05:036
SAYRE, JAMES M & SAUNDERS, LUCINDA	12 JUN 1913	14:174
SAYRE, JOBE & RECE, MILLIE	27 AUG 1829	01:022
SAYRE, JOHN EDWARD & SMITH, RACHEL ELLEN	13 SEP 1891	06:183
SAYRE, JOHN H & LINNELL, EMOGENE J	23 JUN 1904	10:547
SAYRE, JOHN L & STONE, LUCRETIA F	11 JUN 1914	15:214
SAYRE, JOHN W & VANCE, MARY S	03 DEC 1894	07:202
SAYRE, JONAS & VARIAN, MATILDA	*17 FEB 1851	02:001
SAYRE, JOSEPH & STATTS, MELINDA	20 JUN 1830	01:022
SAYRE, JOSIAH C & JONES, EMILY B	01 FEB 1871	07:049
SAYRE, KELLY & CASEY, VIRGIE	27 APR 1900	09:117
SAYRE, LEANDER WOODBURN & LIEVING, FANNIE EMELINE	05 JAN 1887	12:461
SAYRE, LEWIS & CASTO, JANE	21 JUN 1884	12:030
SAYRE, LEWIS MILTON & THORNTON, BELLE	31 DEC 1891	06:270
SAYRE, MARK & VARIAN, IVA	21 MAY 1874	08:123
SAYRE, MARK G, Jr & SMITH, LELIA NYE	13 JUL 1898	08:334
SAYRE, NOAH R & McGRAW, MAGGIE MAY	01 JAN 1912	13:463
SAYRE, OLSON O & ZERKLE, LUNIA V	28 NOV 1914	15:334
SAYRE, PERRY A & RAIRDEN, IDA M	31 OCT 1906	11:442
SAYRE, PETER & VOLKERT, SARAH	08 MAR 1882	11:308

SAYRE, RALEIGH & MATHENY, DORA F	12 NOV 1910	13:202
SAYRE, RELAFORD & BATTRELL, CARRIE	28 APR 1912	13:520
SAYRE, ROBERT F, Jr & SURRATT, GEORGIA	09 MAY 1886	12:324
SAYRE, SABON & BARR, MARY CATHARINE	30 MAY 1872	07:226
SAYRE, SAMUEL F & CANTER, ALICE	28 OCT 1911	13:403
SAYRE, SULLIVAN S & BENTZ, BERTHA M	04 APR 1911	13:303
SAYRE, THOMAS & HARPER, AGNES	MAR 1844	01:043
SAYRE, W S & NEWBERRY, (Mrs) IDA	17 MAR 1910	13:021
SAYRE, WILBER ELSWORTH & RICE, CLARA H	31 DEC 1894	07:228
SAYRE, WILLIS C & JONES, RACHEL E	(no date)	07:017
SAYRE, WILLMON A & RICKARD, BERTHA K	11 JUN 1912	13:543
SAYRE, WILSON & CREIG, AMERICA	26 DEC 1886	12:450
SAYRES, ABSALOM & FLAHARTY, RACHEL	1832	01:026
SAYRES, DANIEL & PRICHARD, JANE	01 OCT 1868	05:215
SAYRES, WESLEY & HILL, OLIVIA	16 APR 1849	01:050
SCANLAN, F E & BARNES, (Mrs) PEARL	29 OCT 1912	14:020
SCANTLING, ALBERT ROSS & SAYRE, MARY ANN	10 NOV 1891	06:222
SCANTLING, HANIBAL & HUGHES, MARIETTA C	18 APR 1881	10:401
SCANTLING, JOHN & JEFFERS, ANALIZA	06 MAY 1869	06:052
SCARBARY, JOHN G & CREMEANS, PARTHENA	12 JUL 1885	12:194
SCARBERRY, DAVID & CASTO, EDNA	02 AUG 1912	13:563
SCARBERRY, ELEMANDER & CAMP, (Mrs) ELIZA JANE	02 NOV 1911	13:408
SCARBERRY, ELEMANDER J & LIKENS, NANCY A	24 FEB 1889	05:357
SCARBERRY, GEORGE & SNYDER, CARRIE	19 FEB 1910	13:012
SCARBERRY, GEORGE & HERREN, MARTHA M	02 DEC 1913	15:081
SCARBERRY, ISAAC & BALL, MARY E	12 SEP 1893	06:600
SCARBERRY, JOHN WILLIAM & McFARLAND, SUSAN I	29 AUG 1889	05:443
SCHAEFER, ERNEST E & ELLENBACH, CAROLINE	13 JUN 1894	07:104
SCHARF, GEORGE & TROEGER, JULIA	09 NOV 1893	07:003
SCHEIVLEY, JACOB & BICKEL, ANN ELIZA	01 SEP 1887	05:088
SCHERZHEL, NICHOLAS & YOUNG, MARGUIRETTA	20 APR 1882	11:128
SCHINTAG, GEORGE G & GINTHER, ELIZABETH MARY	15 DEC 1887	05:157
SCHLAEGEL, MOSES P & STOVER, JULIA A	19 FEB 1898	08:262
SCHLARB, ANDREW & ZAPF, BARBARA	18 OCT 1896	07:631
SCHLOSSER, GEORGE & AUMILLER, AMA S	05 SEP 1861	03:019
SCHMOOTZ, JNO & SCHMITH, MARIANN	25 JUL 1875	08:256
SCHNEIDER, HARRY L & STILES, GARNETTE L	12 AUG 1912	13:581
SCHOLL, JACOB E & GRIM, MARY F	09 JUN 1887	05:040
SCHOOLS, JAMES E & RICE, MARGARET L	24 JUN 1906	11:346
SCHOOLS, JOHN DENNIS & McDANIEL, ANN ELIZA	26 FEB 1888	05:187
SCHOOLS, PAUL & BERGEN, MARY	*06 DEC 1858	02:011
SCHOOLS, PAUL & KING, LURANY C	27 FEB 1873	07:325
SCHOOLS, PAUL O & LEWIS, HANNAH	14 SEP 1893	06:604
SCHRAY, JOSEPH S & DEAMS, VIOLA E	04 MAY 1881	10:410
SCHREINER, JOHN & KRAUTTER, LAURA	21 APR 1897	08:078
SCHRIKERT, GEORGE W & STOVER, ELLA E	25 AUG 1908	12:231
SCHUL, WILLIAM & BADGLEY, SAMARIA C	13 MAR 1887	12:489
SCHULER, DANIEL & CHAPMAN, RUTHA J	21 NOV 1907	12:070
SCHULTZ, CAMERON & DUNCAN, NORA	07 NOV 1914	15:319
SCHULTZ, CHARLES WILLIAM & JIVIDEN, CORA A	12 JUN 1895	07:315
SCHULTZE, AUGUST F & CAIN, MARIAH	25 JUL 1883	11:378
SCHULTZE, CHARLES W & KERWOOD, KATE	04 APR 1899	08:495
SCHULTZE, CHARLES W & McDERMITT, ALTA MAY	21 DEC 1913	15:094
SCHUMACHER, WILLIAM & LASHER, ELIZABETH SUSAN	27 NOV 1907	12:077
SCHWARTZ, BENJAMIN F & BUSH, DAISY T	03 MAY 1908	12:174
SCHWARTZ, PAUL H & COLLINS, CLARA M	11 JAN 1899	08:451
SCHWARTZ, RHEINNOLD & KRAUTHER, ELLEN	28 JUN 1902	10:100
SCHWARZ, HERMAN R & McCLURE, LIZZIE E	31 OCT 1901	09:436

Name	Date	Ref
SCHWARZ, LEWIS & SHIRLEY, JOSIE J	23 DEC 1897	08:221
SCHWARZ, LEWIS & THORNTON, EDDIE	02 JUN 1898	08:318
SCHWARZ, SIMON & TUCKER, WYNONA B	11 AUG 1905	11:148
SCHWARZWALDER, JOSEPH & COLLET, PHEBE	05 JUN 1875	08:245
SCOTT, COLUMBUS & SMITH, MINERVA J	16 OCT 1867	05:109
SCOTT, EVERETT N & COUGHENOUR, TILLIE	11 JUL 1910	13:110
SCOTT, FRANCIS & WINGO, GILLEY FRANCES	21 NOV 1867	05:130
SCOTT, JOHN C & KNIGHT, MAGGIE	23 FEB 1892	06:291
SCOTT, N B & HOLLEY, GOLDIE S	19 NOV 1913	15:066
SEAHORN, JNO L & LEWIS, AGNES	18 SEP 1823	01:009
SEALY, ELGAN & CHEVALIAR, LILLIAN	31 JAN 1906	11:260
SEARLES, JOHN F & HILL, SARAH M	29 MAY 1898	08:315
SEARLS, JACOB H & JIVIDEN, JOSEPHINE	24 AUG 1860	02:014
SEATON, WARREN & BLADES, MARGARET	06 OCT 1864	03:198
SEBRELL, FRANK G & DUNN, EMOGENE	28 DEC 1904	11:019
SEBRELL, GEORGE L & WILSON, ISABELLA	14 SEP 1905	11:169
SEBRELL, JAMES R & HAWKINS, JOSIE	24 MAR 1877	12:497
SEBRELL, JOHN P & McCONIHAY, MARY S	27 MAY 1865	04:013
SEBRILL, GEORGE & LOVE, POLLY	02 FEB 1820	01:005
SEE, GEORGE & BEATTIE, MARY M	23 APR 1885	12:166
SEE, MICHAEL & GREENLEE, NANCY	29 JUN 1808	01:002
SEE, ROBERT & BUCKALEW, CLARA E	12 AUG 1897	08:139
SEE, STRAWTHER & PICKENS, CHRISTENA	01 OCT 1893	06:611
SEE, STRAWTHER & FRY, VINNIE R	22 NOV 1908	12:312
SEEDS, JAMES M & WEAVER, ANGELINE	13 MAY 1877	09:047
SEHEW, PETER A & HESLOP, SARAH E	13 OCT 1870	07:013
SEHON, COLUMBUS & LEWIS, AGNES S	14 JUN 1876	08:361
SEHON, JAMES & HALE, SUSAN	17 JAN 1833	01:027
SEHUN, DAVID & BASS, VIRGINIA BELLE	07 JUN 1870	06:196
SELBE, JOHN R & BICKEL, MARY F	18 SEP 1866	04:148
SELBY, CHARLES H & QUILLON, ELLENOR	26 MAR 1868	05:155
SELBY, CHARLES W & KNAPP, MYRTIE E	17 MAR 1897	08:063
SELBY, ENOS & HERZMAN, EDITH	07 DEC 1880	10:336
SELBY, GRANT & GAINES, MARY FRANCES	20 AUG 1888	05:262
SELBY, HUBBERT T & FOLEY, PRECILLA DUNLAP	*04 FEB 1857	02:009
SELBY, JOHN & POWELL, REGINA	01 OCT 1846	01:046
SELBY, JOHN B & MORGAN, OLIVE	15 NOV 1905	11:204
SELBY, JOSEPH S & GROVER, VIOLA	01 MAR 1899	08:474
SELBY, MILTON & McGUFFIN, ANNIE L	†23 JUN 1899	08:560
SELBY, THOMAS E & RICE, MINNIE B	25 JAN 1911	13:262
SELBY, WILLIAM E & COLEMAN, WINONA E	24 AUG 1893	06:593
SELLERS, EZRA M & TWYFORD, ADDA Z	04 JUL 1898	08:331
SETTLES, CHARLES W & SAUNDERS, MARY E	02 MAR 1894	07:040
SETTLES, JACOB T & BELL, MARY	07 NOV 1883	11:262
SHABBODY, ALEXIS & WATKINS, MARY	23 DEC 1873	08:076
SHABDEW, CHARLES & CRAIG, EUGENIA	06 APR 1878	09:242
SHAFER, LINESS & MANNON, LAURA	28 FEB 1903	10:248
SHAFFE, SAMUEL H & RIFFLE, OLIVIA	26 DEC 1866	12:446
SHAFFER, D R S & HILL, MARGARET A	21 SEP 1884	12:060
SHAFFER, JOHN & HUFF, EMMA	06 JUN 1872	07:231
SHAFFER, WATSON F & WILSON, ELIZABETH	02 JUL 1874	08:142
SHAMBLIN, EZEKIEL & REYNOLDS, IDA M	13 JAN 1898	08:248
SHAMBLIN, JESSE & PARSONS, MARGARET	17 JAN 1822	01:009
SHAMBLIN, JOHN & TURNER, MARY	09 DEC 1827	01:020
SHAMBLIN, JOHN W & COLLINS, ANNIE R	07 FEB 1882	11:108
SHANK, ALVIN ADAM & BARNETT, ELIZABETH JANE	02 DEC 1891	06:238
SHANK, CHARLES C & SOMERVILLE, MARTHA S	14 JAN 1875	08:203
SHANK, CHARLES S & McCOLLISTER, MARY A	12 SEP 1883	11:400

SHANK, CHARLES W & SOULSBY, BESSIE	19 JUL 1913	14:197
SHANK, CHAS E & CARPENTER, LAVINIA	15 NOV 1868	06:003
SHANK, EDGAR D & HINKLE, MARY S	28 OCT 1866	04:162
SHANK, GARLAND F & GRELLE, LEFA L	01 JUL 1908	12:203
SHANK, GEORGE C & PUGH, LULU	*30 AUG 1879	10:123
SHANK, GEORGE M & BARNETT, VIRGINIA F	18 FEB 1891	06:662
SHANK, GEORGE W & VAN MATRE, ALFRETTY	25 JUL 1903	10:321
SHANK, ISAAC & THORNTON, ELIZABTH	04 JUN 1844	01:038
SHANK, JAMES & HALL, MARY VIRGINIA	08 SEP 1886	12:383
SHANK, JOHN H & BOWEN, ELIZABETH	*22 OCT 1860	02:014
SHANK, MARTIN C & HUGHES, CALLIE M	06 SEP 1904	10:590
SHANK, ROBERT ANDERSON & FOWLER, MARIA VIRGINIA	25 DEC 1888	05:327
SHANK, WALTER BROOKS & SOMERVILLE, ADA ROSE	05 NOV 1911	13:411
SHANK, WILLIAM EDWARD & O'NEAL, FLORENCE	**11 NOV 1909	12:242
SHANK, WILLIAM J & FOWLER, WINNIE M	29 JAN 1898	08:257
SHANNON, FRANK & STEWART, ELLA J	25 NOV 1874	08:187
SHANNON, THEODORE S & KOELER, MARY H	09 JAN 1906	11:246
SHARP, CHARLES & MAYES, ROSA B	11 AUG 1886	12:368
SHARP, CHARLES & YOUNG, MAGGIE	22 MAR 1910	13:028
SHARP, CHARLES, Jr & BOOTH, IVA M	04 JUN 1913	14:168
SHARP, EDWARD RAM & NORTH, MARY ELIZABETH	12 SEP 1893	06:599
SHARP, JOHN G & HOLLY, EMMA C	30 DEC 1890	06:035
SHARP, THOMAS W & WALLIS, EMMA	02 FEB 1879	10:049
SHARP, WILLIAM & HOLLEY, RENA	27 NOV 1901	09:458
SHARPE, THOMAS A & PFADT, LIZZIE	05 AUG 1885	12:204
SHATTUCK, ADELBERT E & STEVENSON, ALICE L	18 NOV 1891	06:227
SHAVER, JOHN & SHAVER, MATILDA	10 JUN 1831	01:024
SHAW, CHARLES EDWARD & HUSTON, MARY ELIZABETH	18 OCT 1887	05:123
SHAW, ENOCH & WARD, GINSY	22 FEB 1826	01:013
SHAW, JAMES & HAYMAN, GEORGIA A	16 JAN 1887	12:467
SHAW, SAMUEL C & BLAKE, ONEY E	30 MAY 1906	11:330
SHAW, SAMUEL G & THOMAS, ELIZABETH N B	12 MAR 1833	01:028
SHAW, SILAS R & CAMPBELL, EMMA F	29 APR 1883	11:331
SHEA, JAMES & O'CONNOR, JOSIE	27 NOV 1889	05:486
SHEETS, H C & LANIER, ROMA G	12 SEP 1911	13:373
SHEETS, JACOB E & GARLIC, MATTIE E	14 OCT 1906	11:424
SHEETS, JOHN H & SEWELL, IDA E	14 NOV 1899	09:012
SHEETS, RENO V & HERN, LULU B	16 MAR 1912	13:501
SHEFF, DANIEL H & RIGG, NANCY J	24 MAR 1869	06:044
SHELBY, WM D & DAVIS, BESSIE M	05 AUG 1911	13:351
SHELINE, ANDREW J & CHAMBERLIN, MARY F	09 JUN 1902	10:086
SHELINE, ANDREW J & WAMSLEY, SOPHRONIA	29 AUG 1895	07:373
SHELINE, CHARLES W & SMITH, CORA BELL	23 OCT 1895	07:412
SHELINE, GEORGE W & WORKMAN, EFFIE	10 SEP 1901	09:403
SHELINE, J W & FULLER, EMMA M	16 JUL 1910	13:114
SHELINE, JESSE B & RODGERS, EFFIE	14 JUN 1891	06:130
SHELINE, JNO & PEARSON, SARAH C	*19 JAN 1860	02:013
SHELINE, JOHN M & AUSTIN, MYRTIE L	02 JUN 1894	07:100
SHELINE, JOHN R & MARTIN, MARY J	29 MAR 1888	05:200
SHELINE, JOSEPH & HEREFORD, ELIZABETH CATHARINE	31 DEC 1851	02:001
SHELINE, JOSEPH & HARDWICK, (Mrs) REBECCA A	23 DEC 1912	14:060
SHELINE, JOSEPH, Jr & JORDAN, FRANCES	29 DEC 1876	09:016
SHELINE, MICHAEL & CLONCH, MARY	22 NOV 1906	11:452
SHELINE, SAMUEL & KIMBERLING, FRANCIS J	*22 JAN 1859	02:012
SHELINE, WM P & SOMERS, VIRGINIA	04 JUL 1892	06:362
SHELL, RICHARD & TATE, ELIZABETH	07 NOV 1869	06:102
SHELL, WILLIAM & BOOTH, MAYME	24 DEC 1903	10:444
SHELTON, ALBERT H & BALL, CATHARINE	30 MAR 1826	01:013

SHELTON, BLAKE & FORTUNE, FRANCES N	1842	01:041
SHELTON, GRANVILLE & GREENLEE, HARRIET E	28 DEC 1843	01:038
SHELTON, RICHARD E & SEE, ELIZABETH	1832	01:026
SHELTON, THOMAS H & LONG, ANN E	15 SEP 1868	05:212
SHEPARD, JOHN T & MILLER, VICTORIA V	14 SEP 1876	08:369
SHEPHARD, ANDREW J & MOSS, CYNTHIA	15 APR 1869	06:048
SHEPPARD, ELIHU & CHANNEL, N ESTELLA	01 NOV 1912	14:022
SHEPPARD, MELVIN E & CHAPMAN, MARY E	09 SEP 1908	12:255
SHEPPARD, SAMUEL & HUGHES, EMMA	24 MAY 1900	09:133
SHEPPARD, WILLIAM A J & MULLEN, ETTA	31 MAY 1910	13:076
SHERMAN, CURTIS & FORBES, CATHARINE	10 MAR 1867	05:032
SHERMAN, S LEROY & YOUNG, SADIE S	03 APR 1907	11:511
SHERMAN, WILLIAM & DAVIS, (Mrs) NANCY ANN	12 JAN 1914	15:125
SHERRETT, AARON A & MORROW, SARAH	23 MAY 1908	12:184
SHIBLER, JOHN W & EDWARDS, ALICE	26 JAN 1910	12:597
SHIELDS, ARTHUR & PARSONS, DELPHA	14 SEP 1904	10:595
SHIELDS, FRED A & CANTER, MYRTLE	15 OCT 1913	15:049
SHIELDS, GEO M & HANING, CORA M	10 AUG 1890	05:598
SHIELDS, GEORGE & TERRY, SARAH E	22 MAR 1871	07:067
SHIELDS, HENRY S & WALKER, EMMA R	09 DEC 1888	05:318
SHIELDS, HIRAM M & RIFFLE, SARAH A	08 APR 1877	09:056
SHIELDS, JAMES & GREENLEE, RACHEL	25 AUG 1836	01:030
SHIELDS, JAMES & McKINDLEY, ADA B	01 JUL 1883	11:365
SHIELDS, JOHN & MESUSAN, CATHARINE	19 MAR 1929	01:019
SHIELDS, LEWIS & GREER, SARAH M	26 FEB 1880	10:217
SHIELDS, NOAH & MERRITT, DELLA B	22 MAR 1896	07:518
SHIELDS, PHIL S & LYONS, MYRTLE	07 SEP 1902	10:148
SHIELDS, WILLIAM H & GRIMM, MAY	28 MAY 1906	11:328
SHIELDS, WILLIAM M & LYONS, LILLIE M	01 NOV 1903	10:401
SHIFLET, JOHN & NEALE, IDA	21 OCT 1906	11:435
SHIFLETT, LEMUEL & AUSTIN, EVA A	27 JUL 1870	06:211
SHILTS, ELISHA B & HUGHES, MARY E	24 FEB 1878	09:219
SHILTS, JOHN J & CARPENTER, NANCY	23 JAN 1882	11:098
SHILTS, PEARLIE D & LOUDEN, FLOSSIE A	03 FEB 1910	13:003
SHINDEL, GEORGE K & CROOKHAM, LUCINDA G	07 OCT 1900	09:217
SHINDLE, SAMUEL J & HALL, ELLEN V	22 DEC 1872	07:298
SHINN, GEORGE & SAYRE, (Mrs) ELIZABETH	*05 APR 1855	02:004
SHINN, GLENN A & JIVIDEN, AUDREY A	20 SEP 1908	12:265
SHINN, IRA V & HARPER, WILLIE B	25 NOV 1896	08:005
SHINN, J O & KREBS, MARY E	04 AUG 1881	10:437
SHINN, JOSHUA & SAYRE, ELZINA	*06 FEB 1860	02:013
SHINN, NEHEMIAH L & KNAPP, HANNAH	*22 MAR 1856	02:008
SHINN, NEHEMIAH SMITH & PURDY, ANNIE	07 APR 1895	07:283
SHINN, SAMUEL & CARNEY, AROLE	05 APR 1829	01:021
SHINN, STANLEY & McDERMITT, MAE	19 DEC 1912	14:050
SHINN, WILLIAM H & BUTTRIX, SARAH E	10 MAR 1881	10:382
SHIPLEY, JOSEPH & GORSUCH, EDITH	25 DEC 1909	12:581
SHIPLEY, S A D & BROWN, DORA	01 AUG 1885	12:202
SHIPMAN, HARRY A & BUCKNER, (Mrs) JULIA	05 NOV 1910	13:198
SHIRLEY, ANDREW J & ROUSH, MATILDA	*24 AUG 1855	02:007
SHIRLEY, ANDREW J & PILCHARD, NANCY E	28 JAN 1864	03:155
SHIRLEY, ANDREW J & SAYRE, PHILENA	14 JUN 1868	05:188
SHIRLEY, ANDREW J & BROWN, SUSAN M	19 DEC 1870	07:029
SHIRLEY, ANDREW J & ROUSH, KATIE	06 NOV 1907	12:056
SHIRLEY, ANDREW Z & BALL, ARABELL R	21 DEC 1874	08:197
SHIRLEY, BENSON & SAYRE, LIZZIE	04 JUL 1886	12:346
SHIRLEY, FLOYD O & VARIAN, FREDA	02 AUG 1914	15:248
SHIRLEY, NORMAN & SNYDER, LOUELLA	06 NOV 1906	11:444

SHIRLEY, OSCAR R & SAYRE, EMMA	17 NOV 1886	12:422
SHIVELY, ANDREW & FOLDING, NANCY J	13 JAN 1880	10:197
SHIVELY, VARNER & BURDETT, ARMINA	30 APR 1877	09:071
SHIVLEY, JOSEPH L & JOHNSON, AURILLA R	*27 DEC 1858	02:012
SHOBE, ANDREW B & SAYRE, SARAH A	14 MAY 1867	05:051
SHOE, FRANKLIN H & ENTSMINGER, MARGARET E	10 APR 1881	10:394
SHOEMAKER, GEORGE WASHINGTON & WILLIAMS, L DORAH ANN	14 MAY 1879	10:088
SHOEMAKER, WILLIAM & SWISHER, ROSA	15 MAR 1909	12:386
SHOOK, BERT B & SMITH, OLIVIA E	01 JUN 1910	13:079
SHORE, ALBERT & STUMP, MARY ANN	21 JUN 1868	05:192
SHORT, JOHN W & GROVES, MARY M	01 OCT 1898	08:359
SHORT, WILLIAM & CLEEK, CHRISTIANE	17 JUL 1828	01:017
SHOTT, NICHOLAS & CUNNINGHAM, ANNA	19 SEP 1877	09:127
SHOTT, WILLIAM E & HART, CATHERINE F	12 OCT 1880	10:307
SHOWEN, L E & KIRKER, (Mrs) LENA M	12 NOV 1913	15:067
SHREWSBURY, JOHN H & HEARN, MURL W	10 MAY 1894	07:090
SHUE, FRANK & CHILDERS, MARY A	20 JUL 1879	10:100
SHUE, JOHN C & DUNN, MAGLINE	03 SEP 1896	07:603
SHULER, EDWARD JAMES & BARTON, NEVA	04 APR 1888	05:202
SHUMAKER, LEMUEL SARGENT & MALONE, ELIZABETH	22 FEB 1892	06:290
SHUMATE, T J & GILBERT, CLARE	09 MAY 1910	13:063
SIBERG, ABRAHAM & KING, MARIAH	1836	01:032
SIDEBOTTOM, JOHN & SANDS, LOUISA	*06 JUL 1853	02:004
SIDENSTRICKER, JACOB H & PETERSON, MARY	13 DEC 1888	05:315
SIDERS, ANDREW & NIBERT, MARY E	20 MAR 1893	06:505
SIDERS, CHARLES & BOWEN, ELLA	26 NOV 1890	06:011
SIDERS, EARL H & SHELINE, EFFIE	05 FEB 1911	13:264
SIDERS, GEORGE A & ALDERMAN, OLLIE C	*25 NOV 1902	10:196
SIDERS, JAMES WILLIAM & ROBERTS, HATTIE BELLE	*28 AUG 1890	05:609
SIDERS, JAS W & BARTRUM, (Mrs) ISADORA	25 DEC 1909	12:582
SIDERS, JOHN HENRY & DARST, MARY AMANDA	13 MAR 1889	05:364
SIDERS, SIMON & JOHNSON, DORA F	02 SEP 1876	08:382
SIDERS, WILLIAM H & HIVELY, LYDIA L	02 SEP 1906	11:400
SIDERS, WILLIAM S & THOMAS, ESTHER C	03 APR 1891	06:093
SIEGRIST, EMORY E & LAYNE, SARAH A	04 JUL 1880	10:275
SIEGRIST, JAMES MONROE & BURRIS, EDA	30 APR 1893	06:533
SIEGRIST, JOHN & FRY, ELIZABETH	31 OCT 1822	01:005
SIEGRIST, JOSEPH & WEAVER, MARGARET	*15 NOV 1852	02:003
SIEGRIST, PHILIP S & ROUSCH, CATHARINE	23 FEB 1831	01:023
SIEGRIST, RILEY & CUNDIFF, LOTTIE	25 OCT 1896	07:632
SIEGRIST, SAMUEL PHILIP & COLWELL, CORA LONG	04 JAN 1888	05:170
SIEGRIST, WASHINGTON & HOFFMAN, CATHARINE	*16 AUG 1857	02:010
SIGMAN, JILES E & HARLESS, SARAH A	24 DEC 1899	09:042
SILBY, BALLARD P & WILLIAMS, REWHAMA J	02 FEB 1871	07:050
SILLARS, JONATHAN & REDMAN, POSEY	08 MAR 1827	01:020
SILMAN, ROBERT EMMET & VAN MATRE, MIRIAM JANE	16 OCT 1907	12:046
SIMMONDS, JOSEPH & HALL, MARGARET	11 OCT 1868	05:220
SIMMONS, ANDREW J & CLARK, MARY	16 JUN 1908	12:199
SIMMONS, DAVID J & BARNETT, EMMA S	25 AUG 1895	07:369
SIMMONS, OSWY G & CASTO, CLARA E	21 AUG 1906	11:392
SIMMONS, WALKER & MORROW, LILLY	*02 JUN 1896	07:560
SIMMS, DUDLEY LEE & DAY, ELIZABETH	25 JUN 1891	06:140
SIMMS, ISAAC D & LEWIS, SARAH	20 APR 1851	02:002
SIMMS, JOHN & BENNETT, LYDIA	29 NOV 1827	01:020
SIMMS, RICHARD & BLAKE, LOUISA	02 JUN 1864	03:185
SIMMS, WILLIAM F & PAGE, SARAH F	12 JUL 1874	08:149
SIMPKINS, C P & BLAINE, (Mrs) WILLIE E	04 JUL 1911	13:340
SIMPKINS, CARL CLAY & FETTY, VERNA ELIZABETH	16 NOV 1910	13:207

Names	Date	Ref
SIMPKINS, CHARLES C & JORDAN, MARY M	27 MAR 1902	10:043
SIMPKINS, CHARLES THOMAS & SCHRAY, MARY	*06 AUG 1881	10:438
SIMPKINS, DAVID JACKSON & BUTLER, ANNIE MAY	08 JAN 1888	05:177
SIMPKINS, JAMES JEREMIAH & ROHRABAUGH, MARY	29 AUG 1887	05:085
SIMPKINS, JAMES L & CLICK, MARIA S	07 JAN 1877	09:018
SIMPKINS, WILLIAM F & ASBERRY, SARAH E	31 DEC 1871	07:176
SIMPSON, GEORGE M & McGRAW, HENRIETTA	29 JUN 1897	08:118
SIMPSON, GEORGE R & CAPEHART, MARY M	20 OCT 1898	08:392
SIMPSON, HENRY E & KIGER, ARABELLA	02 APR 1896	07:523
SIMPSON, JOHN G & FULLER, CLARA B	20 SEP 1911	13:383
SIMS, EARNEST C & WRIGHT, ETHEL G	04 FEB 1914	15:137
SIMS, HARRY C & BARNET, GOLDIA G	13 JUN 1909	12:427
SINCLAIR, ALFRED & GASKINS, MARGARET S	03 MAY 1873	07:350
SINCLAIR, BENJAMIN H & HENTHORN, MAHALA	07 APR 1870	06:179
SINCLAIR, EDWARD S & YEAGER, FLORA C	17 FEB 1897	08:046
SINCLEAR, ALFRED & SHIELDS, SUSAN	*03 DEC 1860	02:014
SINE, HENRY J & SAYRE, SARAH ANN	*27 JUN 1855	02:077
SINES, HENRY & COOPER, NANCY	23 MAR 1882	11:130
SINES, HENRY & SHAMBLIN, MARGARET	27 APR 1871	07:081
SINES, HENRY W & STOVER, DOSHA O	20 NOV 1902	10:189
SINES, JACOB C & BAXTER, LIZZIE	22 NOV 1890	06:012
SINES, JAMES & STOVER, ANNIE A	26 AUG 1883	11:391
SINES, JOHN & JOHNSON, MARY E	01 DEC 1870	07:026
SINES, JOHN & YAUGER, SOPHIA	22 JAN 1896	07:487
SINES, JOHN D & GARNES, ALICE M	29 NOV 1908	12:317
SINES, JOSIAH & BARR, SARAH M	20 SEP 1866	04:149
SINES, LEWIS & FISHER, REBECCA	*10 JAN 1859	02:012
SINES, PETER & CULVER, MARIA	22 JUL 1881	10:431
SINES, RIGOR ALFRED & SKILES, ELLA MARGARET	*10 OCT 1879	10:141
SINES, THOMAS A & YAUGER, LEUCRETIA E	09 NOV 1896	07:639
SINES, WILLIAM & MITCHELL, CATHARINE M	*24 MAR 1858	02:011
SINES, WILLIAM H & PARSONS, ADELPHIA M	18 JUN 1899	08:557
SINES, WILLIAM LEWIS & SMITH, SARAH B	31 MAY 1892	06:347
SISSON, E A & HYSELL, SYLVIA	04 MAY 1912	13:526
SISSON, GILES JAMES & BALL, LURA M	13 SEP 1888	05:274
SISSON, HENRY W & BUTIN, MAGGIE L	25 DEC 1885	12:271
SISSON, NATHAN & EVANS, ANNA ETHEL	31 MAY 1907	11:544
SISSON, ROBERT N & WEARS, MINERVA J	07 OCT 1877	09:139
SISSON, WILLIAM B & HUGHES, HARRIET	06 AUG 1883	11:383
SKELTON, THOMAS J & SCHLAGLE, ROSINA B	23 FEB 1903	10:245
SKIDMORE, OTIE O & ROWSEY, MARGARET	27 DEC 1903	10:449
SKINNER, CYRUS MELVIN & ROSE, MINNIE DAY	03 NOV 1895	07:416
SKINNER, GEORGE E & POSTON, AUGUSTA E	01 JAN 1885	12:114
SLACK, A F & BAKER, ISABEL	*14 MAY 1875	08:242
SLACK, CHARLES J & DEWEESE, LUCINDA J	13 FEB 1879	10:055
SLACK, CORNELIUS & McGUIRE, MARY	1831	01:024
SLACK, ELIJAH & FLESHER, GRACE	29 JAN 1829	01:021
SLACK, JOHN W & WOODRUM, SARAH ELIZABETH	*03 DEC 1855	02:007
SLACK, THOMAS ABRAHAM & WALKER, MARY E	28 APR 1888	05:221
SLAUGHTER, ABRAHAM & STATTS, NANCY	11 FEB 1820	01:006
SLAUGHTER, CALVIN M & GEE, MARY M	04 DEC 1863	03:150
SLAUGHTER, EMMET J & FRIEND, AMANDA J	08 NOV 1871	07:146
SLAUGHTER, GEORGE E & ESKEW, HESTER	28 AUG 1908	12:238
SLAUGHTER, JACOB B & BAKER, NANCY J	01 NOV 1865	04:066
SLAUGHTER, JAMES C & SLAUGHTER, LEVERNIA T	24 APR 1890	05:549
SLAUGHTER, ROBERT & GILSON, ANN E	27 NOV 1875	08:304
SLAUGHTER, SYLVESTER & GEHO, ANNIE C	22 MAR 1899	08:485
SLAYTON, CYRUS & DOWELL, MARTHA E	11 JAN 1885	12:127

Name	Date	Ref
SLAYTON, CYRUS E & HANSLEY, NANNIE	19 FEB 1894	07:052
SLAYTON, CYRUS E & HUGHES, ISABELLE	10 NOV 1911	13:415
SLAYTON, G R & DENNY, ROSA	06 AUG 1910	13:123
SLAYTON, GEORGE A & COX, SARAH E	28 APR 1881	10:406
SLAYTON, GEORGE A & WAMSLEY, MITTIE	13 DEC 1908	12:327
SLAYTON, JACOB THADDEUS & SANDS, MARY	15 JUN 1890	05:572
SLAYTON, JAMES W & DUNCAN, MARTHA	26 SEP 1867	05:087
SLAYTON, JAMES WILLIAM & MEDLEY, MARY	*10 OCT 1887	05:116
SLAYTON, JOHN ROBERT & FARLEY, REBECCA	24 AUG 1913	15:016
SLAYTON, JOHN S & GRAHAM, HANNAH	18 AUG 1911	13:356
SLAYTON, SAMUEL V & WAUGH, MANDA	18 SEP 1901	09:408
SLY, GEORGE & BROWN, JINCY	14 SEP 1823	01:010
SLY, JOSEPH & HOY, CATHARINE	06 JAN 1824	01:010
SMALLEY, BENJAMIN F & MOSIER, JULIA E	30 MAY 1888	05:229
SMELTZER, JOSEPH WILLIAM & MATTHEWS, EVA MAE	20 NOV 1913	15:072
SMELTZER, LEWIS & HUMPHRIES, LOUISA	23 SEP 1900	09:211
SMITH, AARON & TANNER, JEMIMA	1843	01:042
SMITH, AARON & BARNETT, ELIZABETH	02 AUG 1883	11:381
SMITH, ALBERT R & BLAIR, MARTHA	14 AUG 1906	11:388
SMITH, ALEXANDER & SEE, MAGGIE	12 MAY 1907	11:529
SMITH, ALONZO P & SHELINE, CLARA B	21 JAN 1905	11:035
SMITH, ANDREW & GLOVER, ARTINSA	22 SEP 1875	08:275
SMITH, ANDY & KEEFER, DORA ELLEN	21 SEP 1910	13:164
SMITH, ARTHUR & MILLER, DORA	05 JAN 1908	12:115
SMITH, AUGUST V & OHLINGER, FLORENCE MAY	27 JAN 1910	12:594
SMITH, BARTON & STATEN, HENRIETTA	17 SEP 1867	05:094
SMITH, BENJAMIN F & WILEY, CHARITY ANN	*17 OCT 1854	02:006
SMITH, BURTON & STATON, ADALINE	11 MAR 1877	09:042
SMITH, BURWELL S, Jr & RIFFLE, MAGGIE	21 MAR 1894	07:065
SMITH, CALLIE & SMITH, CARRIE B	28 AUG 1903	10:342
SMITH, CASSIUS LESLEY & OLINGER, BARBARA ANN	15 MAY 1887	05:026
SMITH, CHARLES A & REA, MARTHA A	18 OCT 1903	10:365
SMITH, CHARLES M & DAY, FRANCES M	*29 OCT 1877	09:148
SMITH, CHARLES M & RAYBURN, ALICE C	30 JUL 1896	07:586
SMITH, CHARLES W & KING, NELLIE	*30 JAN 1903	10:233
SMITH, CHARLES W S & SPENCER, EDITH F	30 SEP 1896	07:623
SMITH, CHARLES B & JONES, LUELLA	17 JUN 1888	08:238
SMITH, CLARKSON EZEKIEL & HARRIS, ELLEN	02 MAR 1887	12:485
SMITH, D V & ROUSH, JOSEPHINE	28 SEP 1902	10:163
SMITH, DANIEL & SMITH, MARY M	10 NOV 1908	12:299
SMITH, DAVID & McDADE, GRACY	*12 APR 1859	02:012
SMITH, DAVID & GEORGE, ELIZABETH W	*14 JUN 1859	02:012
SMITH, DAVID & McGRAW, LUCRETIA A	17 FEB 1864	03:160
SMITH, DAVID & NEIGHBORGALL, ANNIE	15 DEC 1891	06:239
SMITH, DAVID L & CONNOLLY, MARTHA R	24 JUL 1902	10:119
SMITH, DAVID MARION & VAN MATRE, IDA	03 JUL 1890	05:585
SMITH, DAVID W & HAYMAN, MARY J	13 DEC 1898	08:431
SMITH, EDWARD J & SMITH, FREDA	08 NOV 1908	12:300
SMITH, ELIAS H & SAYRE, MATILDA	12 SEP 1886	12:386
SMITH, EMORY & SHANK, KATIE	30 JUN 1892	06:359
SMITH, ESLEY & BAILEY, MARY EVA	13 JUL 1893	06:574
SMITH, ESLEY & HILL, MINNIE	03 SEP 1903	10:345
SMITH, EZEKIEL & COOK, MARY M	02 FEB 1895	07:246
SMITH, FRANK & DAVIS, LUCINDA	26 MAR 1892	06:308
SMITH, FRANK SEIG & MOCK, BLANCHE I	22 MAR 1913	14:113
SMITH, FRANKLIN HARVEY & EDWARDS, MINNIE	20 APR 1892	06:327
SMITH, FREDRICK & GLOECKNER, MAGGIE	27 JAN 1906	11:257
SMITH, G S & SMITH, LUCY	06 MAR 1912	13:494

SMITH, GEORGE & BAKER, MARY	12 APR 1876	08:346
SMITH, GEORGE & ROUSH, INEZ	22 NOV 1895	07:431
SMITH, GEORGE & RIFFLE, PEARL	02 NOV 1914	15:312
SMITH, GEORGE H & OHLINGER, DOLLY	08 MAY 1894	07:089
SMITH, GEORGE O & STEWART, MADLEN	29 OCT 1893	06:635
SMITH, GEORGE S & HART, MARION FRANCIS	28 FEB 1909	12:373
SMITH, GEORGE SCOTT & PARSONS, HAZEL	19 JUN 1909	12:434
SMITH, GEORGE W & SISSON, MARTHA R	*28 APR 1857	02:010
SMITH, GEORGE W & HENSLEY, ELIZABETH F	10 JAN 1883	11:290
SMITH, GIDEON O & THOMAS, MARTHA J	28 JUL 1882	11:180
SMITH, HARRY G D & SAYRE, NANCY B	30 MAY 1911	13:323
SMITH, HARRY L & MOORE, MARY S	06 APR 1898	08:284
SMITH, HARVEY & WINTER, DENA	31 OCT 1905	11:195
SMITH, HENRY F & HILL, RHODA V	17 JAN 1878	09:189
SMITH, HENRY F & STEWART, ROEANNA	06 APR 1899	08:496
SMITH, HENRY I & McCAULEY, PLEASANT U	31 MAR 1875	08:223
SMITH, HOMER H & CROOKS, AMY L	19 JAN 1911	13:261
SMITH, IRVING & LYNCH, JUANITA	20 SEP 1911	13:380
SMITH, ISAAC & McGUIRE, RACHEL	07 FEB 1828	01:021
SMITH, ISAAC & COSSIN, MARY E	01 APR 1898	08:279
SMITH, ISAAC V & WHITAKER, FLORENCE	31 AUG 1901	09:397
SMITH, JACKSON & HOWELL, CASANDA	01 FEB 1838	01:031.5
SMITH, JACKSON & DUFFER, MARGARET	09 DEC 1869	06:125
SMITH, JACOB T & RAYBURN, ROXY	05 JUN 1890	05:567
SMITH, JAMES & SEE, MALVINA	07 MAY 1835	01:029
SMITH, JAMES & DICKINSON, BELLE	*07 JUN 1884	12:023
SMITH, JAMES B & HOLLY, HULDAH A	14 FEB 1878	09:212
SMITH, JAMES E & KERWOOD, SARAH E	07 AUG 1879	10:108
SMITH, JAMES E & McCOY, HATTIE M	22 DEC 1880	10:352
SMITH, JAMES E & WOLF, IDA	15 NOV 1882	11:253
SMITH, JAMES E & SAYER, SELIA	29 MAR 1899	08:493
SMITH, JAMES E & SMITH, BETTIE W	09 OCT 1909	12:529
SMITH, JAMES H & NICKLE, MARY	24 NOV 1874	08:186
SMITH, JAMES H & O'LEARY, NORA	01 JAN 1887	12:460
SMITH, JAMES H & ROWSEY, ISADORE B	18 OCT 1894	07:165
SMITH, JAMES M & YEAGER, LUCINDA	02 FEB 1862	03:045
SMITH, JAMES O & HYATT, ANNA B	13 JUL 1899	08:574
SMITH, JAMES T & ZEARLY, FRANCES J	06 JUN 1877	09:094
SMITH, JAMES T & CHAPMAN, ANNIE	*27 MAY 1897	08:099
SMITH, JASPER & MEDORS, BLANCHE	01 JUN 1910	13:075
SMITH, JOHN & FLOWERS, DELIA	13 OCT 1898	08:383
SMITH, JOHN A & HOFFMAN, GERTRUDE B	30 NOV 1899	09:024
SMITH, JOHN E & RULEN, FANNIE	11 MAY 1902	10:071
SMITH, JOHN F & NICKLE, MARY R	17 JAN 1867	05:022
SMITH, JOHN M & GIBSON, LILLIE L	28 NOV 1894	07:199
SMITH, JOHN McD & KING, OMA N	18 SEP 1912	14:004
SMITH, JOHN P & GRAY, FLORA B	25 DEC 1905	11:236
SMITH, JOHN P & JEFFERS, MODJESKA	01 MAR 1911	13:283
SMITH, JOHN T & HYLTON, HENRIETTA	05 FEB 1896	07:496
SMITH, JOHN W & THOMAS, MARY P	26 AUG 1893	06:589
SMITH, JOHN W & GREENLEE, NANCY	24 DEC 1894	07:216
SMITH, JOHN W & GODFREY, HELEN LOUISE	28 DEC 1912	14:071
SMITH, JOHN WILLIAM & ROBINSON, CHARLOTTE O'DELL	27 FEB 1889	05:360
SMITH, JOHN PETER ROMANS BURIAN & THOMAS, MARIA L	10 MAY 1865	03:230
SMITH, JOSEPH & CONRAD, BETTIE	08 AUG 1871	07:109
SMITH, JOSEPH W & MARTENESS, EMMA E	06 JUN 1867	05:053
SMITH, JULIUS M & STEWART, LIZZIE	06 SEP 1900	09:190
SMITH, LABON A & PIERCE, EMMA	11 NOV 1879	10:162

SMITH, LON & HOLT, MARY E	26 APR 1896	07:533
SMITH, LONDUS D & SAYRE, CYNTHIA	21 SEP 1910	13:165
SMITH, MARTIN & WESBAY, SARAH C	*12 AUG 1858	02:011
SMITH, MILTON & WHITE, (Mrs) ELIZABETH D	20 SEP 1909	12:511
SMITH, MORRIS H & EDWARDS, FLORILLA	26 AUG 1891	06:172
SMITH, MOSES & JOHNSON, SARAH MARGARET	06 SEP 1881	11:016
SMITH, NATHAN & ROSEBERRY, ANN	24 DEC 1826	01:014
SMITH, NATHAN & TILLIS, HARRIET	*24 JAN 1852	02:002
SMITH, NEHEMIAH & WETZEL, RACHAEL	22 MAY 1828	01:018
SMITH, ORVILL & BADGLEY, SAMARIA	05 MAR 1899	08:476
SMITH, PEARL M & SINES, LONA	13 SEP 1904	10:594
SMITH, PHILIP & DANIELS, LENA M	21 SEP 1907	12:015
SMITH, PLEASANT SUMMERS & JIVIDEN, ROXY	30 MAR 1901	09:313
SMITH, REUBEN & THORNTON, LUELLA	19 MAR 1887	12:493
SMITH, SAMUEL & HARRISON, OLETHA	12 JAN 1849	01:050
SMITH, SAMUEL & JOHNSON, LUTITIA	06 FEB 1898	08:260
SMITH, SAMUEL A & LONG, ELLEN V	21 APR 1880	10:243
SMITH, SAMUEL D & HARRIS, MARY	30 AUG 1902	10:141
SMITH, SAMUEL M & PARSONS, ELIZABETH	*07 JUN 1856	02:008
SMITH, SCOTT & ZEARLEY, MINERVA	09 DEC 1869	06:124
SMITH, SCOTT & WARNER, HARRIET	12 OCT 1876	08:396
SMITH, SCOTT & KIMBERLING, LUCETTA	15 NOV 1899	09:018
SMITH, THOMAS & POWELL, EMELINE	MAY 1845	01:049
SMITH, THOMAS G & SMITH, ROSA A	01 MAY 1892	06:332
SMITH, THOMAS H & SAYRE, EMMA R	15 MAR 1909	12:387
SMITH, THOMAS L & VAN MATRE, KATE	20 NOV 1899	09:021
SMITH, VAN B & HART, LOUISA	OCT 1839	01:034
SMITH, VIRGIL L & McDANIEL, IDA MAY	25 DEC 1879	10:181
SMITH, VIRGIL O & PICKENS, LOAH A	02 OCT 1902	10:167
SMITH, WALLACE A & MOORE, FLORENCE V	31 JUL 1913	14:204
SMITH, WALTER & SCARBERRY, EFFIE	01 DEC 1904	10:650
SMITH, WALTER A & KING, BESSIE P	21 AUG 1899	08:599
SMITH, WILEY W & PARK, CAROLINE	*07 JAN 1898	08:243
SMITH, WILLIAM & CAPEHART, OLIVIA J	14 SEP 1848	01:050
SMITH, WILLIAM & STRIBLING, NANCY T	*24 APR 1853	02:004
SMITH, WILLIAM & POLSLEY, HARRIET B	03 JUN 1869	06:060
SMITH, WILLIAM & GRAY, CHARLOTTE	04 JUL 1883	11:369
SMITH, WILLIAM & HENRY, BARBARA ANN	21 JUL 1857	05:058
SMITH, WILLIAM & LOWE, MARY A	08 DEC 1898	08:424
SMITH, WILLIAM A & COOK, CHARLOTTE	22 NOV 1890	06:010
SMITH, WILLIAM A & KNAPP, ALMIRA	24 FEB 1904	10:482
SMITH, WILLIAM B & PETTY, GLADYS	09 MAY 1914	15:192
SMITH, WILLIAM C & SMITH, NANCY J	25 APR 1861	03:003
SMITH, WILLIAM F & SHIRLEY, BERTIE	01 MAY 1914	15:186
SMITH, WILLIAM FINLEY & DEEM, SUSAN	13 AUG 1891	06:165
SMITH, WILLIAM H & VANMATRE, MARY E	14 AUG 1864	03:192
SMITH, WILLIAM HENRY & WHEELER, ELLERDEYER	27 JUN 1892	06:357
SMITH, WILLIAM J & FURGUSON, MARY C	22 AUG 1869	06:075
SMITH, WILLIAM MILROY & TILLIS, CARRIE ALICE	31 JAN 1886	12:288
SMITH, WILLIAM P & GREENLEE, MARTHA F	05 OCT 1871	07:127
SMITH, WILLIAM W & WARNER, MARY A	12 MAY 1870	06:188
SMITH, WILLIAM W & SCANTLING, MARY A	26 NOV 1895	07:439
SMITH, WILLIAM WILEY & THARP, MARY	30 JUN 1887	05:053
SMITH, WM R & BLAGG, BELVA L	31 OCT 1914	15:310
SMOOT, WILLIAM & CASEY, MISOURI	24 NOV 1861	03:033
SMOUT, BARTHOLOMEW & OVERSHINER, SARAH	05 MAY 1833	01:028
SNIDER, JOB & RIFFLE, CHRISTENA	05 JUN 1866	04:129
SNIDER, JOHN & BLESSING, PENELOPE	02 JAN 1870	06:134

SNIDER, RUSSELL E & SHELINE, RONA	06 MAY 1902	10:068
SNODGRASS, M E & SPEARS, OLLIE	05 AUG 1909	12:473
SNODGRASS, THEODORE & WALLACE, OTI	14 AUG 1906	11:390
SNOW, JAMES & SNYDER, SARAH	*12 NOV 1879	10:163
SNOWDEN, EARL RAYMON & FOLDEN, HILDAH MAY	08 DEC 1914	15:342
SNYDER, DAVID S & HALL, MATTIE A	08 FEB 1882	11:109
SNYDER, FRANK W & HENNOSSY, KATE	23 OCT 1897	08:180
SNYDER, GEORGE & RIFFLE, MARY E	07 FEB 1889	05:351
SNYDER, HENRY & STOVER, ADALINE	15 JAN 1887	12:466
SNYDER, JAMES & BOOTH, SUSAN	30 JUN 1883	11:364
SNYDER, JAMES A & CLENDENEN, EMILY	*18 DEC 1854	02:006
SNYDER, NEWTON & SHIELDS, EMMA	25 DEC 1907	12:103
SNYDER, ORAN M & THORNTON, DESSIE L	26 FEB 1913	14:094
SNYDER, THOMAS & DEWEES, ELVIRA	11 APR 1880	10:236
SOHN, GEORGE W & ELY, MINNIE A	23 SEP 1896	07:617
SOLADEAN, SCOTT & DARST, PEARL	05 APR 1901	09:317
SOLES, LESTER G & QUICKLE, NELLIE M	22 NOV 1910	13:214
SOMERVILLE, ANDREW & LONG, MARY J	02 NOV 1848	01:051
SOMERVILLE, ANDREW A & LEWIS, LAURA S	18 OCT 1876	08:399
SOMERVILLE, B E & CLENDENIN, ADA M,	05 JAN 1910	12:588
SOMERVILLE, CALVIN & HOGG, MARTHA M	22 MAR 1836	01:031
SOMERVILLE, CHARLES W & MILLER, MARY	29 SEP 1879	10:134
SOMERVILLE, DAVID & PICKENS, MAHALA J	25 DEC 1862	03:094
SOMERVILLE, EDWARD G & BALE, SARAH L	06 JAN 1869	06:027
SOMERVILLE, EDWARD J & KISAR, MAUD	29 APR 1911	13:315
SOMERVILLE, EDWARD R & EADES, ETHEL C	25 SEP 1901	09:414
SOMERVILLE, GEORGE W & GRAY, VIRGIE E	01 JAN 1904	10:455
SOMERVILLE, GORA T & YEAGER, STELLA E	08 DEC 1907	12:088
SOMERVILLE, JAMES & McDANIEL, FANNIE	30 MAR 1865	04:003
SOMERVILLE, JAMES T & TULLY, CATHARINE	02 DEC 1885	12:261
SOMERVILLE, JOHN & MITCHELL, NANCY	20 APR 1837	01:031
SOMERVILLE, JOHN R & SOMERVILLE, ELLA B	02 DEC 1880	10:338
SOMERVILLE, JOHN T & LOVE, IDA F	14 SEP 1884	12:056
SOMERVILLE, JOHN T & LOVE, LUCINDA	05 DEC 1895	07:444
SOMERVILLE, LEONIDAS & POWELL, EMMA J	05 NOV 1879	10:152
SOMERVILLE, LEWIS EDGAR & ARMSTRONG, SARAH ALICE	19 JUL 1893	06:575
SOMERVILLE, ROBERT V & LAWSON, MAGGIE	10 FEB 1892	06:284
SOMERVILLE, ROBERT W & BOGGESS, JANE C	15 NOV 1866	04:169
SOMERVILLE, SAMUEL P & KNOPP, SARAH ELIZABETH	13 NOV 1862	03:088
SOMERVILLE, SAMUEL P & WASHINGTON, JUDITH R	05 APR 1877	09:059
SOMERVILLE, VAN B & ROSEBERRY, EFFIE F	22 JUN 1890	05:573
SOMERVILLE, WESTON D & ROSEBERRY, MARGARET JANE	30 OCT 1862	03:083
SOMERVILLE, WILLIAM & BOGGESS, MARY	1832	01:026
SOMERVILLE, WILLIAM & WOMELSDORFF, HENRIETTA	*10 NOV 1851	02:002
SOMERVILLE, WILLIAM R & WINDON, MARY E	10 NOV 1870	07:022
SOMMERVILLE, EUGENE W & GRAY, LYDIA M	11 FEB 1904	10:474
SOMMERVILLE, SAMUEL J & CHAMBERLAIN, MARY P	19 DEC 1839	01:035
SOMMERVILLE, SAMUEL W & BALL, MARY MATILDA	*25 OCT 1854	02:006
SOUASH, JAMES FREDERICK & JORDEN, ELIZABETH JANE	07 MAR 1879	10:064
SOULSBY, EDWARD & HOLT, JANE	23 JUN 1869	06:058
SOULSBY, MATTHEW & ASKEW, HARRIET	04 JAN 1866	04:095
SOULSBY, ROBERT & GILPIN, HARRIET S	28 JUL 1870	06:212
SOWARDS, WILLIAM HENRY & MILLER, ANNIE	20 AUG 1888	05:263
SPANGLER, L & PROSSER, DORTHY	21 JUN 1820	01:007
SPANN, SAMUEL & MARTIN, LOU	11 FEB 1894	07:045
SPAUN, SAMUEL & MILLER, (Mrs) MARY C	28 APR 1913	14:136
SPEAR, ELZA & STERLING, EDITH M	07 MAY 1905	11:089
SPEAR, LEE & LEPORT, JENNIE B	*30 APR 1904	10:512

SPEARS, ADAM & FLORAY, EFFIE LUCINDA	11 OCT 1912	14:014
SPEARS, ALLEN & ROACH, SARAH	25 MAR 1913	14:116
SPEARS, ARCH & SHELTON, MARY	25 JAN 1886	12:285
SPEARS, ERVIN & KING, DORA E	06 NOV 1904	10:631
SPEARS, GEORGE H & FLOWERS, ELECTA A	13 NOV 1906	11:448
SPEARS, HARRISON & HALL, ETTA	11 NOV 1907	12:067
SPEARS, ISAAC WEBSTER & FLOWERS, (Mrs) VIRGINIA G	23 SEP 1914	15:276
SPEARS, JOHN P & PEARSON, KATIE	17 JAN 1901	09:279
SPEARS, JOHN P & KING, BESSIE M	06 NOV 1904	10:630
SPEARS, W E & PARSONS, JENNIE M	25 DEC 1914	15:356
SPEARS, WILLIAM A & HALL, ELIZABETH	09 OCT 1907	12:035
SPENCE, ESAU & BYUS, ETTA	31 JUL 1906	11:375
SPENCE, JOHN W & ROUSH, SARAH M	15 JAN 1885	12:128
SPENCE, ROY L & THOMAS, ADER MAY	30 JUL 1912	13:573
SPENCE, TYRA D & CARTWRIGHT, (Mrs) SABRA	*01 APR 1858	02:011
SPENCER, ANDREW & BYBEE, MARY ANN	29 AUG 1839	01:032 5
SPENCER, ANDREW K & MOBLEY, LUCY A	01 NOV 1891	06:218
SPENCER, CECIL C & OHLINGER, ADDIE E	16 SEP 1896	07:610
SPENCER, CLARDY C & HAY, VERA M	22 NOV 1905	11:210
SPENCER, EUGENE R & DURST, ZILLIAN E	02 JUN 1912	13:540
SPENCER, GEORGE DAILY & FOWLER, HARRIET E	22 OCT 1891	06:210
SPENCER, HARVEY & IRNES, MARY E	18 JAN 1905	11:032
SPENCER, HARVEY M & ROUSH, NANNIE R	04 MAR 1891	06:073
SPENCER, HERALD B & SMITH, EDITH M	01 DEC 1910	13:220
SPENCER, JOHN & RICE, MARIA	*16 NOV 1852	02:003
SPENCER, JOHN H & HOFFMAN, CAROLINE	10 SEP 1868	05:210
SPENCER, JOHN SAMUEL & McCULLOCH, KATE LOUISE	26 JUL 1887	05:063
SPENCER, JOHN T & ADKINS, ANNIE	14 JUL 1883	11:374
SPENCER, JOSEPH & STEENBERGEN, SUSAN V	04 OCT 1847	01:047
SPENCER, JOSHUA MELTON & OLIVER, SARAH LOUISA	04 JAN 1888	05:175
SPENCER, MARTIN & CRUMP, JENNIE	20 JUL 1895	07:346
SPENCER, MOSES & KIRKWOOD, SARAH JANE	31 DEC 1851	02:001
SPENCER, PERRY F & HOPE, ELIZABETH M	21 DEC 1881	11:079
SPENCER, ROSCOE ODELL & GROVER, PEARL SOPHIA	24 DEC 1899	09:036
SPENCER, SIMON & AMOS, ADALINE	11 SEP 1912	13:598
SPENCER, WILLIAM HENRY T & JAMES, MARY MAGDALEN	23 DEC 1880	10:358
SPENCER, WILLIAM P & SANDS, CORDELIA C	10 MAY 1878	09:256
SPENCER, WILLIAM T & POSEY, KATY	07 OCT 1874	08:172
SPENCER, WILLIAM THOMAS & EADS, MINNIE ALICE	18 AUG 1888	05:261
SPENGLER, GEORGE P & WINDON, ROSANA	01 AUG 1850	02:002
SPINDLE, H H & LONG, ELIZABETH E	25 OCT 1876	08:405
SPONACHER, JACOB & SHOEMAKER, MARTHA E	22 JUN 1881	10:423
SPRAGG, J WORTH & CARROLL, LILLIE J	17 JAN 1901	09:276
SPRAY, JOHN & AUMILLER, MARY M	*19 JUN 1851	02:002
SPROUSE, ARTHUR E & SNOW, LILLIE	24 DEC 1903	10:447
SPROUSE, CHARLES & CHEESEBREW, BLANCHE	21 APR 1912	13:577
SPROUSE, JACOB & SNYDER, AMANDA J	06 SEP 1877	09:124
SPURLOCK, ALBERT & HAGER, MATILDA	30 JUL 1895	07:353
SPURLOCK, ALLEN & DAVIS, ROSA	12 JUL 1899	08:575
SPURLOCK, HARVEY & CAMPBELL, ELIZABETH	23 JUL 1840	01:036
SPURLOCK, LEANDER & HAYES, ANNIE B	17 JAN 1894	07:038
SPURLOCK, LEE & CRAIG, ORA	07 APR 1911	13:297
SPURLOCK, NORMAN H & HARMAN, CYNTHA	21 MAY 1905	11:100
SPURLOCK, SHERMAN & JORDAN, HATTIE N	22 MAR 1911	13:294
SPURLOCK, THOMAS & HANNON, MINERVA	29 JUL 1831	01:025
SPURLOCK, WILLIAM & MILLER, ELLA	06 MAR 1892	06:301
SPURLOCK, WIRT & RAMSEY, IDA B	16 OCT 1895	97:409
SQUIRES, GEORGE & BANNISTER, ADACADE	18 JUL 1826	01:013

STAATS, A B & HART, CATHARINE	04 NOV 1906	11:443
STAATS, ALBERT W & MYERS, ELIZABETH	23 FEB 1873	07:315
STAATS, ISAAC & WELCH, IDA	26 SEP 1910	13:167
STAATS, J DR & FISHER, MARY B	*12 DEC 1856	02:009
STAATS, JOHN H & DASHNER, MARY L	29 OCT 1861	03:030
STAATS, JOSHUA HAMILTON & FURNELL, LIZZIE	07 MAY 1883	11:325
STAATS, LEWIS & FISHER, CATHARINE E	*28 JUL 1853	02:004
STAATS, PHILIP & CUTSHAW, REBECCA	22 NOV 1885	12:252
STAATS, PHILIP & TAYLOR, (Mrs) RACHEL	06 JAN 1914	15:120
STAATS, WILLIAM R & JORDAN, LORA	30 SEP 1914	15:284
STAATS, WILLIAM SHERMAN & CLARK, SARAH ALICE	27 NOV 1887	05:149
STAATS, WILLIAM Y & HARRIS, ELIZABETH J	*26 DEC 1860	02:015
STAFFORD, SAMUEL T & HARMON, OMA	12 MAY 1913	14:145
STAHL, JAMES E & HUGGINS, RETTA MABEL	17 JUL 1914	15:245
STALDER, CHARLES & WOLF, EVA	18 JUL 1899	08:582
STALDER, WILLIAM F & ROSE, LORETTA J	28 AUG 1878	09:301
STALNAKER, CALVIN S & HOLT, JENNIE	05 NOV 1886	12:418
STANLEY, ALFRED O & WILSON, GOLDIE	18 JUL 1914	15:247
STANLEY, CHARLES & NESSELROAD, MARGARET L	28 MAY 1895	07:309
STANLEY, DAVID & RICHARDS, HANNAH	12 MAY 1825	01:014
STANLEY, FORREST & BURGER, LULA	28 DEC 1887	05:169
STANLEY, GRANDVILLE ELIJAH & LYDA, MARTHA LAVINIA	15 OCT 1891	06:206
STANLEY, JAMES & CLAGG, MAGGIE	07 MAY 1893	06:536
STANLEY, JOHN B & MILLS, ELLA	10 MAY 1883	11:337
STANLEY, THOMAS & STANLEY, ELIZA	30 APR 1829	01:021
STANLEY, W C & NETROSS, ELLENOR T	20 OCT 1884	12:077
STANLEY, WARNER & MOORE, NANNIE	25 DEC 1914	15:110
STANLEY, WILLIAM & BELLEE, SARAH	17 AUG 1826	01:015
STANLEY, WILLIAM B & FORREST, LILLIE	04 JUL 1994	07:117
STANLEY, WILLIAM CASTLE & OLIVER, GEORGIA ANGELINE	25 NOV 1888	05:311
STANLY, COLUMBUS & EDWARDS, ALICE	02 JUL 1872	07:243
STANLY, WILLIAM & MINK, HANNAH	04 OCT 1893	06:620
STANLY, WILLIAM F & McGRAIL, SARAH J	02 JUL 1872	07:242
STANSBERRY, ISRAEL & SHOEMAKER, ADALINE	07 FEB 1876	08:324
STANSBURY, WILLIAM E & SHUMAKER, SARAH V	25 DEC 1878	10:018
STARCHER, JACOB & WOODRUFF, RACHEL	11 FEB 1823	01:008
STARCHER, JOHN & LYONS, CHARITY	25 FEB 1820	01:006
STARCHER, JOHN H & KING, WAVIE J	30 MAY 1900	09:135
STARCHER, WILLIAM & HANSHAW, MARY	22 SEP 1821	01:009
STARCHER, WILLIAM & EVANS, SALLY	11 OCT 1827	01:020
STARK, THOMAS & DONNALLY, POLLY	23 AUG 1906	01:001
STARKEY, EDGAR & HOLLEY, ONA	23 NOV 1912	14:033
STARKEY, GEORGE W & FETTY, ROSALIE	16 NOV 1899	09:015
STARKEY, JOHN W & BUTLER, FLORA B	15 MAY 1887	05:025
STARKEY, OWEN & REED, MAGGIE	18 OCT 1891	06:207
STARKEY, WILLIAM W & CREMEANS, NANCY	28 APR 1872	07:215
STARKEY, WILLIAM W & GREASER, SARAH	09 SEP 1905	11:158
STATEN, JAMES D & FRAZER, MARGARET ANN	NOV 1839	01:034
STATS, JOSEPH & CUMINGS, SARAH	05 JAN 1826	01:014
STATTON, ISAAC K & WALLAHAN, ESTER JANE	*01 JAN 1855	02:006
STATTON, (Rev) JOHN F & YEAGER, ANN ELIZA	*27 JAN 1855	02:006
STATTS, CORNELIUS & CARNEY, ANNA	26 SEP 1812	01:003
STATTS, ELIJAH & EVANS, ANN	16 DEC 1829	01:022
STATTS, ELIJAH M & POSTLEWEIGHT, RHODA J	01 DEC 1870	07:028
STATTS, JOHN & McGRAW, SARAH	02 SEP 1881	11:015
STEARNS, LEONARD E & HUFFMAN, LILLIE	20 JUL 1912	13:568
STEED, JOHN & HENSHAW, ELIZABETH	11 MAR 1827	01:020
STEEL, A M & LAMBERT, IDA M	16 OCT 1884	12:073

STEEL, GEORGE & MAYES, LUTITIA ELLEN	14 DEC 1865	04:086
STEEL, JOHN & EADS, NANCY	*24 SEP 1856	02:008
STEEL, JOHN A & McKINEY, NANCY J	25 DEC 1896	08:026
STEEL, SAMUEL V & HART, MAY	25 SEP 1904	10:606
STEEL, THOMAS & McDERMITT, ROSE ANN	*06 JAN 1858	02:010
STEEL, WILLIAM P & KNAPP, CHARLOTTE A	03 APR 1879	10:073
STEELE, AUGUSTUS M & HULL, NETTIE	01 JUN 1903	10:297
STEELE, AUGUSTUS M & HAYMAN, ANNA	03 MAR 1904	10:485
STEELE, AUGUSTUS MARRION & SMITH, LOUISA	12 SEP 1891	06:184
STEELE, JOHN L & MILLER, ELLOURIA	25 MAR 1885	12:151
STEELE, JOHN W & PRIDDY, LAVINIA F	22 FEB 1870	06:152
STEELE, LEWIS & MEADOWS, ESSIE A	01 APR 1911	13:299
STEELE, ROBERT & KNAPPENBERGER, EFFIE E	18 AUG 1895	07:365
STEELE, WELCH D & KNAPPENBERGER, DORA	18 AUR 1895	07:366
STEELE, WILLIAM E & RHOADS, MARGARET	31 JUL 1900	09:169
STEELE, WILLIAM F & LONG, IDA	15 MAY 1899	08:533
STEELE, WILLIAM T & CLENDENIN, SARAH	16 SEP 1869	06:088
STEEN, CHARLES & SELBY, ORILLA	09 MAR 1876	08:335
STEENBERGEN, WILLIAM & McCULLOCH, CHARLOTTE BYERS	29 DEC 1904	11:022
STEENBURGEN, PETER HIGGINS & McCULLOCH, SALLIE LEWIS	25 JUN 1902	10:098
STEIF, ANDREW & KRIEG, (Mrs) EVA	01 DEC 1910	13:217
STEIN, THOMAS & KIRKPATRICK, CHARLOTTE	03 SEP 1846	01:046
STEINBACH, WILLIAM & MINICH, SOPHA	29 OCT 1882	11:231
STEPHAN, EMIL & BUMGARNER, ADA	31 MAY 1897	08:103
STEPHENS, AARON & McGARVEY, MARY	11 SEP 1848	01:048
STEPHENS, BENJAMIN R & MILLER, EDITH C	23 SEP 1885	12:224
STEPHENS, BRAZIL M & McDERMITT, MARY M	19 DEC 1878	10:016
STEPHENS, CHARLES E & DURST, WILLIA H	26 JUN 1910	13:100
STEPHENS, GEORGE EVERETT & MOORE, SARAH E	23 DEC 1903	10:435
STEPHENS, J J & SOVINE, ELLEN O	24 DEC 1884	12:111
STEPHENS, JOHN A & SAYRE, ROSA	24 OCT 1903	10:389
STEPHENS, JOHN W & MEAD, NANNIE L	20 DEC 1899	09:037
STEPHENS, NELSON & WASHINGTON, MARGARET	01 APR 1882	11:133
STEPHENS, SAMUEL HARTFORD & BAKER, MINNIE F	02 APR 1903	10:263
STEPHENS, SAMUEL M & BYERS, HATTIE	21 NOV 1867	05:108
STEPHENS, SHERMAN & KEARNS, NANNIE	08 AUG 1899	08:594
STEPHENS, THOMAS W & GATES, CLARA	01 JUL 1899	08:566
STEPHENS, WASHINGTON & THORNTON, LETITIA	*18 AUG 1860	02:014
STEPHENS, WM & REDMAN, NANNIE	*09 NOV 1857	02:010
STEPHENSON, BENJAMIN & ROACH, SARAH	18 JUN 1829	01:019
STEPHENSON, CHARLES & STEPHENSON, NANCY	01 OCT 1855	02:007
STEPHENSON, CHARLES V & JONES, MARY JANE	*13 OCT 1851	02:002
STEPHENSON, CHARLES WALLACE & ROLLINS, ORA	21 JUL 1912	13:567
STEPHENSON, CLENDINEN & LEWIS, EVELINE	30 MAY 1850	01:052
STEPHENSON, ENOS & BEBEE, MARY ANN	27 APR 1848	01:048
STEPHENSON, ENOS R & HESS, SARAH C	08 MAR 1882	11:126
STEPHENSON, ENOS R & GLOVER, VIRGINIA	05 DEC 1895	07:443
STEPHENSON, GEORGE C & GREER, MARY M	13 JUN 1867	05:057
STEPHENSON, GEORGE W & SEELY, BLANCHE	27 SEP 1895	07:393
STEPHENSON, HENRY & BARNETT, MARGARET	*19 DEC 1857	02:010
STEPHENSON, HIRAM & GREER, ADELIA	27 MAR 1862	03:057
STEPHENSON, JACOB V & CLENDENEN, JULIA	18 DEC 1862	03:092
STEPHENSON, JAMES & BARNETT, MARY	05 MAY 1824	01:010
STEPHENSON, JAMES & OLIVER, JANE	14 JAN 1840	01:033
STEPHENSON, JAMES M & FOWLER, MARY A	*25 NOV 1857	02:010
STEPHENSON, JOHN A & STEWART, CLARA	01 MAR 1909	12:375
STEPHENSON, OSCAR C & HUDSON, RILLA	05 SEP 1914	15:268
STEPHENSON, ROBERT & THOMPSON, ELIZA L	09 APR 1885	12:159

Names	Date	Ref
STEPHENSON, ROBERT P & CLENDINEN, MARY ANN	07 NOV 1861	03:031
STEPHENSON, ROBERT P & CLENDENEN, ANN ELIZA	*09 APR 1855	02:006
STEPHENSON, THEODORE & POWEL, CAROLINE	04 SEP 1842	01:037
STEPHENSON, WILLIAM G & LEWIS, MARY	*05 DEC 1853	02:005
STEPHENSON, WILLIAM T & GLOVER, FANNIE M	20 MAY 1833	11:341
STEPHENSON, WILLIAM THOMAS & SMITH, EVA VAN VATRE	19 MAR 1890	05:531
STEPHENSON, WILLIAM WARDEN & McDADE, MARY MARTHA	19 OCT 1888	05:290
STEPHENSON, WILLIAM WILEY & ROLLINS, MARY MALINDA	15 DEC 1891	06:248
STERLING, WILLIAM F & MARTIN, LILLIE A	22 MAR 1882	11:113
STERNE, GEORGE E & CARSON, E LILLIAN	01 AUG 1906	11:376
STERNE, HARRY G & DAUGHERTY, MARY ZELDA	12 FEB 1912	13:483
STERNE, WILLIAM O & SAYRE, MARY	02 JUL 1896	07:577
STERRETT, BENJAMIN & ALEXANDER, CATHARINE	11 JUN 18356	01:031
STERRETT, CHARLES W & PULLIN, DAISY	16 MAY 1900	09:126
STERRETT, GEORGE WM & SWON, JEANNET	21 OCT 1891	06:209
STERRETT, GEORGE WILLIAM & MOORE, FRANCES HANNAH	*19 FEB 1856	02:008
STERRETT, JAMES & STERRETT, EVELINA M	10 APR 1828	01:018
STERRETT, JAMES B & ALEXANDER, FRANCES C	13 OCT 1864	03:200
STERRETT, JAMES B & STEPHENS, FANNIE	27 AUG 1884	12:051
STERRETT, WASHINGTON & LONG, ELIZABETH	01 APR 1830	01:020
STERRETT, WILLIAM S & MILLER, MARY JANE	07 MAY 1850	01:052
STERRETT, WILLIAM S & MILLER, MARY ELLEN	*07 DEC 1853	02:005
STEVENS, BENJAMIN & JACKSON, MAMIE	05 MAR 1908	12:128
STEVENS, BENJAMIN E & PEARSON, IRS	10 MAY 1904	10:517
STEVENS, EDWIN B & KNIGHT, REBECCA	09 APR 1880	10:235
STEVENS, H M & KRAUS, DELLA E	29 DEC 1913	15:097
STEVENS, JOHN B & CLINDENEN, RACHEL S	*21 APR 1856	02:008
STEVENS, JOHN B & FADELY, MARY	05 APR 1866	04:114
STEVENS, PERL C & INMAN, ADA D	08 DEC 1914	15:341
STEVENSON, BENJAMIN F & PORTER, ESTHER	24 MAY 1849	01:051
STEVENSON, JAMES HERMAN & NEWELL, SADDIE	10 NOV 1892	06:437
STEVENSON, SAMUEL C & SHOEMAKER, JOANA B	14 OCT 1873	08:040
STEWARD, JOSEPH A & WATSON, JENNIE L	17 DEC 1890	06:021
STEWART, ADAM & SMITH, ELENOR JANE	*21 MAY 1853	02:004
STEWART, ALBERT O & GREENLEE, SARAH	07 JUL 1898	08:332
STEWART, ALEXANDER & STEPHENS, MARY C	16 JUL 1906	11:368
STEWART, AMIDEE R & FISHER, RUTHA B	27 OCT 1903	10:397
STEWART, ANDREW & EDWARDS, MARY CAROLINE	05 JUL 1893	06:570
STEWART, ANDREW R & FURGUSON, LIZZIE	15 JAN 1898	08:246
STEWART, BALLARD P & HALL, EMILY	05 OCT 1871	07:130
STEWART, BURWELL & RIFFLE, FLORA C	03 SEP 1893	06:595
STEWART, CHARLES & SMITH, PAULINA CATHARINE	*22 DEC 1858	02:011
STEWART, CHARLES P & SHELL, EMILY MAY	17 MAY 1893	06:538
STEWART, CLYDE & KEARNS, MATTIE N	11 JUN 1902	10:087
STEWART, CLYDE & FOX, EMMA	09 NOV 1910	13:200
STEWART, COLUMBUS & SAYRE, MARY M	03 OCT 1869	06:113
STEWART, DAVID D & LEWIS, ELLA L	30 JUN 1886	12:347
STEWART, ELIHUE & WINEBRENER, FLORENCE	27 SEP 1903	10:374
STEWART, F H & WORKMAN, CORA	17 AUG 1912	13:584
STEWART, FRANK & FORBES, ETHEL	19 JUL 1909	12:459
STEWART, GEORGE & KESSEL, LUTITIA	09 SEP 1899	08:607
STEWART, GEORGE T & RICKARD, ROSA	31 AUG 1905	11:157
STEWART, GEORGE W & CHAFIN, LIDA	03 JAN 1898	08:237
STEWART, HARRISON & JOHNSON, NANCY	31 DEC 1910	13:252
STEWART, HENRY E & THOMPSON, EVA L	26 SEP 1906	11:421
STEWART, HENRY T & HILL, AMERICA	09 JAN 1878	09:193
STEWART, HENRY W & McDANIEL, DEBORAH	15 SEP 1882	03:078
STEWART, J V & DENBEL, E E	30 NOV 1910	13:196

STEWART, JAMES & LATHEY, MAUD	05 SEP 1896	07:604
STEWART, JAMES H & STEWART, MARY E	29 JUN 1897	08:117
STEWART, JAMES L & McDADE, HARRIET I	03 AUG 1900	09:171
STEWART, JAMES O & CARDER, MAMIE M	28 JAN 1914	15:133
STEWART, JAMES R & VANMATRE, AGNESS E	11 NOV 1868	05:226
STEWART, JAMES W & CANTERBERRY, ABIGAIL	05 JUL 1892	06:364
STEWART, JESSE & HARSHBARGER, LILLIE	21 JUL 1900	09:164
STEWART, JESSE WASHINGTON & LEWIS, CASANDER	19 JAN 1882	11:096
STEWART, JOHN & BUCK, ROENA	20 MAR 1864	03:168
STEWART, JOHN & KNAPP, CHRISTINA	29 MAY 1884	12:019
STEWART, JOHN B & RAINER, ANNA	28 SEP 1870	06:221
STEWART, JOHN H & CHAPMAN, HELLEN	02 JAN 1911	13:255
STEWART, JOHN M & LEWIS, DORA	18 OCT 1899	08:633
STEWART, JOHN M & VAN METRE, LIZZIE	25 APR 1908	12:168
STEWART, JOHN R & RIFFLE, MAHALA E	12 NOV 1879	10:161
STEWART, JOHN T & EDWARDS, CHRISTINA M	30 DEC 1896	08:027
STEWART, JOSEPH N & JOHNSON, MARGARET A	29 SEP 1870	07:008
STEWART, LEWIS & COOPER, ELIZABETH	08 JAN 1874	08:089
STEWART, MILLARD F & ABSTEN, CORA	15 MAR 1908	12:142
STEWART, MORRIS B & WHITESIDE, MARTHA ELIZABETH	25 JUN 1914	15:228
STEWART, REUBEN & BARNETT, ADA O	14 JUL 1892	06:366
STEWART, SAMUEL & PICKENS, AURILLA	03 OCT 1887	05:113
STEWART, SYLVESTER & JONES, MAGGIE	14 OCT 1886	12:400
STEWART, VIRGIL & PARK, ALICE	28 MAR 1878	09:232
STEWART, WILBERT CRAYTON & FRENCH, ALICE	28 NOV 1914	15:332
STEWART, WILLIAM & FRANCIS, MARY A	18 OCT 1876	08:401
STEWART, WILLIAM C & CAIN, ALMA	19 JUL 1914	15:244
STEWART, WILLIAM F & McDANIEL, MADALINE	01 DEC 1879	10:171
STEWART, WILLIAM, Jr & RICE, NANCY	31 JUL 1845	01:044
STEWART, WILLIAM MACK & RIFFLE, SARAH	23 JUN 1892	06:355
STEWART, WILLIAM R & YOUNG, ARDENA A	27 SEP 1882	11:216
STEWART, WILLIE C & KINCADE, JOSIE E	25 DEC 1904	11:013
STILES, DELL S & WILL, JENNIE M	20 DEC 1913	15:096
STILES, DELMER F & SCHNEIDER, ANNE M	07 DEC 1912	15:045
STILES, RAYMOND V & HUGHES, MAYMIE V	18 JUL 1913	14:181
STILES, W H & TURLEY, DELIA	23 APR 1901	09:325
STITT, SAMUEL H & YOUNG, STELLA	20 DEC 1886	12:443
STIVERS, CHARLES H & GRUESER, NEIDA M	07 MAY 1910	13:062
STOBERT, JOHN & MOORE, (Mrs) ANN	*19 APR 1856	02:008
STOCKHOFF, CLIFFORD C & WALKER, LULA B	27 SEP 1903	10:372
STOKELEY, WOODMAN & SCOTT, FLARA ETTA	04 JUL 1890	05:587
STOKELY, WILLIAM H & ROUSH, MARTHA A	04 JUL 1878	09:282
STOKLEY, JACOB & LAWSON, SARAH JANE	*19 APR 1852	02:002
STONAKER, LON & WILSON, DORA	01 OCT 1908	12:275
STONE, ANDREW L & BARR, SYNTHIA A	04 AUG 1877	09:114
STONE, CHARLES & WILLIAMSON, INEZ	24 FEB 1912	13:489
STONE, CHARLES C & REYNOLDS, BESSIE M	19 JUN 1914	15:223
STONE, CHARLES DEEM & HENTHORNE, ANNIE E	14 JUN 1888	05:236
STONE, GEORGE & BROWN, MARY	11 AUG 1897	08:138
STONE, HARRY K & STERNE, GUSTA O	05 OCT 1910	13:174
STONE, JACOB & JOSEPH, NETTIE	01 SEP 1895	07:377
STONE, JACOB & WALTERS, LIZZIE	23 AUG 1900	09:179
STONE, JOHN & PRATT, LUCRETIA	22 JUN 1862	03:069
STONE, JOHN & MITCHELL, ANNA LAURA	19 JUL 1894	07:157
STONE, JOHN L & BOWLEY, NANNIE	25 DEC 1895	07:464
STONE, JOHN T & RIDER, MARY D	17 SEP 1885	12:221
STONE, MADISON H & CHAPMAN, LUCINDA	09 NOV 1843	01:042
STONE, MINOR & MYERS, ELIZA M	26 FEB 1902	10:029

Name	Date	Ref
STONE, NICHOLAS K & PECK, DEBORAH J	27 NOV 1889	05:485
STONE, PRESLEY & GLENN, MARY ELLEN	18 APR 1862	03:058
STONE, REUBEN & DUNHAM, ANTHE	01 JAN 1895	07:227
STONE, RICHARD I & STONE, (Mrs) ANN ELIZA	*19 JUL 1859	02:012
STONE, RICHARD T & TIBBS, VIRGINIA L	12 FEB 1895	07:250
STORMONT, ANDREW L & WALTER, LOTTIE L	12 MAR 1904	10:490
STORTS, EVERETT F & PRIDDY, MONA G	19 OCT 1907	12:049
STORTZ, FRANK ALBERT & MUNFORD, FLORENCE MAE	08 JAN 1896	07:484
STORTZ, JOHN C & BETTINGER, LOUISA	18 OCT 1894	07:172
STORTZ, SIMON & STONE, MARY J	24 DEC 1878	10:021
STORTZ, WILLIAM C & SAWYER, JENNIE	06 AUG 1899	08:592
STORY, JACOB JOHN & BAUER, KATE	08 JUN 1886	12:334
STOVER, ANDREW G & SULLIVAN, MINA D	25 MAR 1891	06:083
STOVER, ASBERRY & GRAY, EMMA	27 APR 1895	07:294
STOVER, CHARLES & LAMBERT, EDITH GOLDIE	30 JUN 1906	11:345
STOVER, CHARLES C & IRWIN, ANNIE J	22 MAR 1899	08:481
STOVER, DANIEL & DAVIS, ANNIE E	19 DEC 1895	07:456
STOVER, DAVID H & RHODES, MARY A	03 JUL 1873	08:007
STOVER, EMERY & DUNCAN, CORA E	08 JUN 1896	07:563
STOVER, EZRA V & BURNSIDE, LUCY	14 AUG 1909	12:478
STOVER, GEORGE W & POSTTLEWEIGHT, SARAH E	27 JUL 1865	04:028
STOVER, GEORGE W & COCHRAN, FLORA E	14 FEB 1886	12:282
STOVER, HENRY H & KING, ALICE M	10 MAR 1895	07:286
STOVER, HOLLY & VAUGHN, BERTHA	03 JUL 1909	12:448
STOVER, IRA & RIMMEY, PEARL R	30 JUN 1896	07:575
STOVER, JAMES L & BAKER, CHRISTENA C	28 JUL 1864	03:189
STOVER, JAMES R & ROGERS, LULU J	02 JAN 1898	08:238
STOVER, JASPER & KING, JEMIMA MAY	28 NOV 1911	13:430
STOVER, JOHN A & KREBS, MAGGIE	17 MAR 1886	12:304
STOVER, JOHN A & MEADOWS, MARTHA H	29 MAY 1899	08:542
STOVER, JOHN W & FLESHER, (Mrs) CATHARINE	*28 MAY 1913	14:163
STOVER, JOHN W & ANDERSON, SARAH J	*26 SEP 1857	02:010
STOVER, JUBEL H & IRVIN, LORA E	25 DEC 1898	08:436
STOVER, M E & PRICE, GOLDIE M	07 JUN 1912	13:542
STOVER, MADISON & PRITT, DOLLIE	07 MAY 1910	13:062
STOVER, OLIVER & SHUMATE, VIRGINIA C	03 FEB 1881	10:373
STOVER, SAMUEL L & BOLES, NELLIE	19 AUG 1907	11:591
STOVER, SAMUEL P & HILL, ELIZA JANE	*27 OCT 1856	02:009
STOVER, SYLVANUS H & HUGHS, HARRIET A	20 FEB 1862	03:049
STOVER, ULYSSES G & PRITT, ORA E	14 MAR 1903	10:256
STOVER, WILLIAM PARSON & EDWARDS, MILLIE	07 NOV 1886	12:416
STOWERS, MANNA & HOFFMAN, CORA	06 AUG 1911	13:349
STRAIGHT, ALMA C & CAIN, WILLIE A	27 SEP 1914	15:280
STRAIT, JESSE & PEARSON, LILLIE	03 APR 1895	07:276
STRAWDERMAN, JOHN ANTHONY & McDERMITT, ANNIE LAURA	11 JUL 1888	05:246
STRIBLING, BENJAMIN & SMITH, CLARA	20 JUN 1901	09:359
STRIBLING, GEORGE W & NEAL, MARY N	10 APR 1828	01:017
STRIBLING, GEORGE W & LONG, ANNETTE K	17 JUN 1896	07:565
STRIBLING, JOHN P R B & BATES, HORTENSE	23 MAR 1904	10:496
STRIBLING, J P R B & BREWEN, LAURA	05 AUG 1907	11:587
STRIBLING, JOSEPH A & BLACKWELL, ADA	30 JAN 1895	07:245
STRIBLING, MATHEW W & HEREFORD, ELIZABETH P	23 JAN 1828	01:017
STRIBLING, MATTHEW W & HUNTER, MARY M	29 DEC 1896	08:028
STRIBLING, OTIS T & NEALE, JENNIE C	09 NOV 1869	06:103
STRIBLING, TALIAFERRO & WORK, MARGARET E	25 AUG 1904	10:586
STRICKLEN, CHARLES E & GILPIN, GRACE	25 MAR 1905	11:062
STRICKLEN, DAVID L & DAVIS, EMILY J	22 FEB 1880	10:212
STRICKLEN, GEORGE W & BURNS, LEW ALICE	09 SEP 1900	09:199

Names	Date	Ref
STRIETELMIER, HENRY & BEAN, KATIE	09 OCT 1888	05:288
STRIMBACK, A D & PARKER, (Mrs) MATILDA	*08 JAN 1853	02:003
STROMIDER, THOMAS L & BEBEE, SARAH M	03 NOV 1881	11:045
STRONG, GEORGE W & SIDEBOTTOM, MARY E	*01 DEC 1856	02:009
STRONG, JARED L & MOORE, LUCRETIA H	*05 NOV 1851	02:002
STRONG, PETER & TUCKER, MARY	27 JAN 1850	01:052
STUART, THOMAS F & McCONIHAY, ELLA	05 NOV 1879	10:157
STUART, WILLIAM & PARSONS, MARY	26 MAR 1829	01:021
STURGEON, CLARK & RHODES, ELIZABETH	17 MAR 1897	08:064
STURGEON, GEORGE & DAIGH, NANCY	19 DEC 1894	07:211
STURGEON, HARVEY & REECE, ETHEL	20 JAN 1913	14:084
STURGEON, HENRY & WHEATON, LOUESA	22 MAR 1911	13:295
STURGEON, JAMES & TERRY, MARY E	19 OCT 1868	05:222
STURGEON, JAMES A & EWELL, MARY JANE	10 DEC 1867	05:104
STURGEON, JAMES S & KINSER, NANCY	06 DEC 1890	06:016
STURGEON, JOHN & WALLIS, SIDENA	26 MAR 1902	10:040
STURGEON, JOHN R & SISSON, MARTHA	09 NOV 1911	13:413
STURGEON, MARTIN & MEADOWS, MINERVA	27 JAN 1905	11:037
STURGEON, NAPOLON & STEELE, BESSIE	30 MAY 1906	11:326
STURGEON, OWEN & SHARP, JENNIE	12 OCT 1895	07:406
STURGEON, PETER & BEARD, ETHEL M	13 SEP 1907	12:008
STURGEON, PETER & BEARD, ETHEL M	28 NOV 1907	12:083
STURGEON, ROBERT & ERRETT, JOSEPHINE	01 JAN 1878	09:185
STURGEON, ROBERT & EVRETT, JOSEPHINE	01 JAN 1878	09:285
STURGEON, ROSCO & YOUNG, CARRIE	10 NOV 1906	11:446
STURGEON, SAMUEL & JORDEN, MARY N	*13 FEB 1855	02:006
STURGEON, SAMUEL & BEARD, SOPHRONA	09 MAR 1890	05:527
STURGEON, WALTER E & SMITH, ANNIE E	02 SEP 1904	10:589
STURGEON, WILLIAM & GROVES, RUTH A	27 JAN 1870	06:144
STUTLER, GEORGE & STOVER, MARY M	22 JUL 1886	12:360
STUTLER, JOHN LAMBERT & STRAIT, MARY BLANCHE	01 JAN 1910	12:586
STUTLER, LABAN & JIVIDEN, INA	12 SEP 1902	10:161
STUTLER, SPENCER & WILDMAN, LIZZIE	03 JUL 1909	12:450
STUTLER, SPENCER & HIGGINBOTHAM, EDITH L	17 JUN 1913	14:178
STYLES, RAYMOND F & HUGHES, MAMIE V	18 JUN 1913	14:181
SUBLETT, JOSEPH HENRY & BOOTEN, MINNIE A	11 AUG 1887	05:072
SULLIVAN, ALFRED T & GREENLEE, NANCY C	03 MAR 1869	06:039
SULLIVAN, ALFRED T & PETTY, SARAH J	18 OCT 1897	08:174
SULLIVAN, DANIEL M & SCOTT, ELIZA JANE	20 AUG 1868	05:205
SULLIVAN, DAVID W & KESSEL, PEARL	20 JAN 1912	13:469
SULLIVAN, FRED ALVA & DUNN, MARTHA REGINA	26 DEC 1903	10:432
SULLIVAN, G W & STROSNIDER, MAGGIE	20 FEB 1883	11:459
SULLIVAN, GUILFORD D & BURNS, CATHARINE R	24 DEC 1861	03:039
SULLIVAN, JAMES A & SNYDER, ZONA	15 JAN 1907	11:491
SULLIVAN, JOHN & NELSON, ELIZA JANE	24 JUL 1828	01:017
SULLIVAN, JOSEPH & WALKER, MARIA	13 JUL 1865	04:022
SULLIVAN, LAUNCEFORD & GREENLEE, MELVINA	25 OCT 1826	01:013
SULLIVAN, MILTON E & CLARK, ROSETTA C	19 AUG 1882	11:190
SULLIVAN, PATRICK & DOWER, MARY ELIZABETH	25 NOV 1908	12:314
SULLIVAN, RICHARD & MARTIN, BRIDGET	29 MAY 1873	07:358
SULLIVAN, W D & MARTIN, JANE	09 MAY 1886	12:326
SULLIVAN, WILLIAM & THORNTON, RACHEL F	*05 NOV 1850	02:001
SULLIVAN, WILLIAM H & GREENLEE, FLORA	29 FEB 1872	07:201
SUMMERS, ALBERT S & BLAKE, MARY ANN	1840	01:041
SUMMERS, HARVEY & DUNFIELD, ELIZABETH B	09 JUL 1846	01:046
SUMMERS, HENRY & THORNTON, JANE	06 AUG 1876	08:374
SUMMERS, JACOB M & OLIVER, MARY	27 APR 1834	01:028
SUMMERS, SAMUEL B & FORD, ELIZA	17 MAY 1827	01:016

Name	Date	Reference
SUMMERS, WEBSTER NOAH & HAMBRICK, LOUISE M	25 JAN 1895	07:240
SUMERS, WILLIAM & PAIN, MARY	05 JUN 1828	01:017
SUPPLE, ROBERT G & GOULD, CARRIE	16 DEC 1897	08:215
SURATT, JOHN A & SHIRLEY, CAROLINE E	07 JUL 1862	03:070
SURGEON, JOHN W & ALLEN, SARAH ELIZABETH	24 DEC 1889	05:497
SUSPON, CHARLES J & HUFFMAN, ELIZABETH	*06 JAN 1854	02:005
SUTTON, JAMES A & DILL, CLARA M	19 MAY 1910	13:049
SWAGGER, WILLIAM N & HOLEY, MATIE	20 JAN 1900	09:069
SWAN, THOMAS E & GIBBONS, LUCY A	12 APR 1898	08:289
SWANCY, JOSEPH & SYRUS, CATHARINE	13 SEP 1895	07:383
SWANGER, JOHN & RISLEY, EMMA	13 AUG 1910	13:129
SWANN, RICHARD & STATON, ELIZA C	01 MAY 1879	10:081
SWARTZ, JOHN GEORGE & DONOHUE, MARY LETTIE	13 FEB 1893	06:486
SWARZ, DANIEL E & FAUVER, ALTIE J	14 DEC 1893	07:022
SWAYNE, CALVESTER & FRY, MIRIAM A	09 DEC 1880	10:341
SWETT, GEORGE G & BAKER, MARTHA	24 AUG 1908	12:235
SWINDLER, JOHN D & CHILDS, LIZZIE	13 DEC 1889	05:492
SWISHER, BAILEY & CARTMILL, JULIA M	21 NOV 1888	05:308
SWISHER, FRANKLIN A & TERRY, ANNIE L	25 APR 1908	12:165
SWISHER, IRA Z & LANIER, JESSIE P	06 SEP 1902	10:151
SWISHER, JACOB & POWERS, MABEL	26 MAY 1909	12:416
SWISHER, JOHN & SCOTT, EFFIE E	07 AUG 1878	09:298
SWISHER, JOHN S & BAIRD, DOLLIE	01 MAY 1904	10:513
SWISHER, NELSON & JOHNSON, MARY	01 DEC 1900	09:244
SWISHER, PEARL M & PULLIN, DORA M	15 DEC 1904	10:668
SWISHER, WILLIAM H & ROSEBERRY, JENNIE	17 SEP 1903	10:366
SWON, EDWARD EVERETT & CIRCLE, ROSA CATHARINE	13 NOV 1889	05:477
SWON, JAMES A & SOMERVILLE, MARY MARGARET	*11 JAN 1859	02:012
SYDENSTRICKER, FLOYD & MURRAY, ALICE	26 SEP 1895	07:392
SYDENSTRICKER, JAMES W & MADDY, ORILLA	25 DEC 1900	09:267
SYGMON, PETER & SULLIVAN, DELILA L	02 SEP 1863	03:131
SYRUS, JAMES R & McCLARA, LAURA	31 OCT 1904	10:627
TABIT, JOHN A & HEREFORD, ELLA E	12 AUG 1908	12:226
TACKETT, WILLIAM P & GROVER, SARAH C	18 MAR 1903	10:258
TALIFERO, GEORGE EMERY & HUGHES, MAHALA	29 JAN 1895	07:241
TALIFERO, THOMAS A & CHRIST, JOSEPHINE	26 FEB 1896	07:502
TALLMAN, B Z & BOARD, MABLE	22 AUG 1909	12:486
TANNER, WM S & PARRISH, ROSA E	05 MAR 1913	14:098
TATE, ELI & DYKE, LYDIA M	18 NOV 1877	09:157
TATE, GROVER C & ROWLEY, FRANCES E	23 MAY 1908	12:182
TATE, JAMES A & VAN MATRE, EMMA C	23 DEC 1880	10:354
TATE, JAMES A & RICE, CATHARINE	17 DEC 1872	07:297
TATE, JOHN C & CORDONIA, ALEXENIA	22 DEC 1870	07:034
TATE, JOHN F & ROBERTS, FANNIE F	13 OCT 1878	09:330
TATE, JOSEPH N & BARKER, ALICE M	31 AUG 1836	08:380
TATE, ROBERT L & VAN MATRE, RUTH V	02 NOV 1885	12:244
TATE, WILLIAM & TATE, ARABELLA A	05 SEP 1878	09:311
TATE, WILLIAM & BAREMORE, ANN	25 OCT 1884	12:082
TATE, WILLIAM & STEWARD, M CATHARINE	27 MAR 1913	14:188
TAYLOR, ADAM & RICKARD, ELIZABETH	*19 FEB 1856	02:008
TAYLOR, ADAM & VENNOY, RACHEL	71 DEC 1873	08:085
TAYLOR, ALBERT & MEADOWS, JENNIE	19 APR 1894	07:073
TAYLOR, ALBERT W & STEWART, AURILLA F	10 NOV 1897	08:193
TAYLOR, ANDREW & McBRIDE, CAROLNE	02 JUN 1867	05:054
TAYLOR, BEVERLY J & WOODY, LUCY J	26 FEB 1873	07:321
TAYLOR, CHARLES & SIDENSTRICKER, MARY H	21 JUL 1888	05:248
TAYLOR, CHARLES & GIBBEAUT, ANNIE	31 AUG 1896	07:597
TAYLOR, CHARLES L & BURRIS, ROSA B	28 NOV 1904	10:648

TAYLOR, CHESTER & BROWN, VICTORIA	08 NOV 1869	06:109
TAYLOR, CHRISTY & KIRKENDALL, EVA	05 MAY 1880	10:252
TAYLOR, ELZEY & SYDENSTRICKER, NANCY E	02 JAN 1888	05:172
TAYLOR, EMMITT A & STONE, MARY G	21 FEB 1906	11:274
TAYLOR, FOSTER & TULLY, RUBY MAY	23 JUL 1899	08:588
TAYLOR, FRANCIS T & WILSON, ELSIE	31 MAY 1903	10:293
TAYLOR, FRANK & GREENLEE, MYRTIE	06 AUG 1893	06:583
TAYLOR, FRED M & SMITH, HANNAH J	25 DEC 1901	09:481
TAYLOR, HARVEY W & CHAPMAN, GEORGIA A	22 MAR 1893	06:507
TAYLOR, J E & SLAYTON, OLA	08 OCT 1910	13:176
TAYLOR, JACOB & GARD, MARY	27 MAR 1882	11:127
TAYLOR, JAMES & WILLIAMS, MARY JANE	15 JUN 1842	01:037
TAYLOR, JAMES & NEEDHAM, MATILDA J	14 SEP 1862	03:079
TAYLOR, JAMES B & KELLY, SAMANTHA J	31 JAN 1886	12:290
TAYLOR, JAMES B & SAXTON, ELLA	04 SEP 1901	09:399
TAYLOR, JAMES F & TODOFF, LOUISA	12 AUG 1866	04:144
TAYLOR, JAMES H & TAYLOR, ELIZABETH J	17 JUN 1885	12:186
TAYLOR, JAMES L & MILAM, SARAH	15 JAN 1870	06:142
TAYLOR, JAMES W & LEE, ELLA	15 APR 1899	08:508
TAYLOR, JAMES WEBSTER & BURNS, (Mrs) FRANCES	12 MAR 1914	15:154
TAYLOR, JESSIE B & HOFFMAN, OSIE	31 AUG 1905	11:155
TAYLOR, JOHN & HARDEN, LUZETTA	14 AUG 1867	05:098
TAYLOR, JOHN & TAYLOR, MARTHA A E	19 DEC 1887	05:115
TAYLOR, JOHN & GREER, JULIA	04 SEP 1895	07:378
TAYLOR, JOHN M & COOPER, SARAH E	17 OCT 1876	08:402
TAYLOR, JOHN M & POUR, ELIZA A	20 OCT 1882	11:224
TAYLOR, JOSIAH & JORDEN, LEAH MARGARET	24 SEP 1846	01:047
TAYLOR, MARTIN & POWEL, ARIMINTY	09 DEC 1846	01:046
TAYLOR, MARTIN I & WOODYARD, MINERVA S	*09 APR 1859	02:012
TAYLOR, MELTON & MEADOWS, LORNA	22 MAR 1914	15:161
TAYLOR, MORTIMER D & WILSON, EVA L	04 FEB 1902	10:018
TAYLOR, SAMUEL A & SWISHER, CARRIE	27 MAY 1906	11:327
TAYLOR, SAMUEL J & WITHERS, IDA	21 FEB 1886	12:293
TAYLOR, THOMAS & JORDAN, AMERICA	13 APR 1843	01:038
TAYLOR, THOMAS & MOTT, SARAH	21 MAR 1886	12:306
TAYLOR, TOLIVER E & FOWLER, MAY B	03 JUN 1914	15:209
TAYLOR, WESLEY B & STURGEON, ELIZABETH	10 JAN 1867	05:019
TAYLOR, WESLEY BALL & BALL, MARY ELIZABETH	12 JUN 1888	05:235
TAYLOR, WILLIAM & TAYLOR, REBECCA	27 JUL 1891	06:153
TAYLOR, WILLIS & BOARD, FANNIE B	29 MAR 1891	06:088
TAYLOR, WILSON & GORDON, LOUISA	28 MAY 1893	06:547
TEAFORD, JAMES & COMMONS, AUGUSTA B	21 JUL 1888	05:247
TEAFORD, THOMAS & McGRAW, LILLIE	17 MAR 1891	06:080
TELLY, FRANCIS & ENGEL, EDITH	13 SEP 1910	13:157
TEMPLETON, EDWARD & FORREST, MARY	1838	01:032
TEMPLETON, ISAAC & PARRISH, VIRGINIA	25 DEC 1845	01:044
TEMPLETON, ISAAC M & BATEMAN, MARY A	(no date)	09:208
TERREL, HARRY & BARKER, FLORIDA MAY	25 MAY 1912	13:535
TERRY, CHARLES & TURNER, BELLE	29 JUN 1875	08:253
TERRY, EDWARDS & GATES, MARY ANN	07 JAN 1867	05:090
TERRY, ISAAC R & FINDLEY, MARTHA L	25 SEP 1878	09:322
TERRY, JAMES & PLANTS, ROSA	*14 JUN 1906	11:338
TERRY, JAMES & PLANTS, ROSA B	22 AUG 1906	11:396
TERRY, JOHN & CHRISTY, MARY A	13 OCT 1878	09:322
TERRY, WILLIAM H & BUSH, SOPHIA E	18 JUL 1861	03:010
TEWKSBURY, AARON & JACKSON, JENNIE	07 NOV 1912	14:025
THARP, CHARLES E & HONSHELL, ANNIE	23 FEB 1895	07:260
THARP, GEORGE T & HUTTON, VIOLA	31 JAN 1886	12:289

Name	Date	Ref
THAXTON, BERT & SWICK, BLANCHE	04 DEC 1912	14:042
THAXTON, DAVID L & CONRAD, LELIA F	25 DEC 1879	10:185
THAXTON, HOMER & LAMBERT, EDNA	. 21 AUG 1904	10:581
THEISS, ALBERT HENRY & AUMILLER, ANNA MATILDA	13 MAY 1900	09:126
THERIN, ERNEST & McDERMITT, REBECCA J	07 APR 1912	13:510
THOMAS, ALBERT H & STOVER, CATHARINE J	23 DEC 1906	11:474
THOMAS, ALLEN WASHINGTON & FOWLER, ANNIE L	29 JUN 1892	06:562
THOMAS, BENJAMIN & HOLLAND, LELA	10 OCT 1889	05:462
THOMAS, BENJAMIN A & CRAIGLOW, MARY A	28 OCT 1897	08:185
THOMAS, BENJAMIN H & SMITH, LOVIE	22 JUN 1904	10:543
THOMAS, BERT & JORDAN, RODIE	24 APR 1900	09:116
THOMAS, CHANCY & PEARSON, HERMA	31 AUG 1897	08:150
THOMAS, CHARLES F & WEIGAND, KATIE M	22 AUG 1897	08:145
THOMAS, CLIFTON W & GLUESENCAMP, ANNIE	21 MAY 1902	10:075
THOMAS, CLYDE E & JOHNSON, EDNA O	22 JUL 1908	12:217
THOMAS, CORNELLIS & REDMOND, MARY LIZZIE	22 APR 1900	09:114
THOMAS, D A & MEEKS, ADDIE M	15 SEP 1884	12:057
THOMAS, DANIEL & BARNETT, MARIA	19 OCT 1865	04:062
THOMAS, EARL & HOWARD, NELLIE	24 MAY 1896	07:554
THOMAS, EDMUND & HEMSLEY, ELIZABETH F	21 OCT 1865	04:060
THOMAS, ENOS & DINGEY, RACHEL A	27 APR 1882	11:143
THOMAS, ENOS & BURKLEY, EVELENA	13 JAN 1903	10:024
THOMAS, FRANK & GREER, FLORA	27 OCT 1904	10:624
THOMAS, FRANKLIN & THORNTON, SUSANNAH F	08 APR 1864	03:172
THOMAS, GEORGE & JORDAN, JESSIE	30 JUN 1907	11:566
THOMAS, GEORGE P & HOFFMAN, MATILDA	11 AUG 1867	05:074
THOMAS, GEORGE W & BLACKWELL, MINERVA	02 MAR 1882	11:122
THOMAS, HARLEY ALBERT & GIBBS, MARY LOUISE	16 APR 1903	10:270
THOMAS, HERBERT W & MACKLEY, VIRGINIA M	21 JAN 1894	07:041
THOMAS, HOY & DURST, MAE L	25 MAR 1914	15:158
THOMAS, ISAAC C & ROLLINS, ROSA E	03 NOV 1878	10:003
THOMAS, ISAIAH V Z & MAYS, RUTHY ANN	05 DEC 1850	01:052
THOMAS, ISAIAH V Z & MAYES, RUTHY ANN	*05 DEC 1850	02:001
THOMAS, JAMES & WILLIAMS, LELIA	*21 APR 1892	06:328
THOMAS, JOAL B & RIFFLE, HESTER	*20 FEB 1856	02:008
THOMAS, JOHN & GREER, LENA LEOTI	17 SEP 1890	05:612
THOMAS, JOHN & WALLACE, EVA	11 NOV 1899	09:014
THOMAS, JOHN & PULLIN, NELLIE L	19 APR 1908	12:161
THOMAS, JOHN C & ATKINSON, ROXY A	09 NOV 1869	06:104
THOMAS, JOHN C & EMBLETON, MARY E	11 FEB 1891	06:060
THOMAS, JOHN H & DAUGHERTY, EMMA B	28 DEC 1882	11:279
THOMAS, JOHN H & MATHENY, CORA	24 DEC 1914	15:351
THOMAS, JOHN L & BADGLEY, CATHARINE E	22 JUN 1911	13:333
THOMAS, JOHN M & HOLLEY, BESSIE	16 MAR 1903	10:257
THOMAS, JOHN W & KNOPP, FANNIE S	03 OCT 1865	04:057
THOMAS, JOSEPH & MORRISON, MOLLIE	29 APR 1899	08:517
THOMAS, LEVI & SELBY, MARTHA	*22 NOV 1855	02:007
THOMAS, LEVI & CUNDIFF, RHODA M	02 NOV 1890	05:634
THOMAS, NICHOLAS & OLIVER, HANNAH M	08 JUN 1874	08:127
THOMAS, OKEY & CLEEK, NANNIE	25 SEP 1908	12:268
THOMAS, ORVILLE & PIERSON, BLANCHE	23 JUN 1901	09:357
THOMAS, PETER V & CARNEY, MALINDA	11 NOV 1830	01:023
THOMAS, PHILIP & THORNTON, CATHARINE M	*18 JAN 1858	02:010
THOMAS, RAY & PRIDDY, ADDIE	09 DEC 1908	12:320
THOMAS, ROBERT & BLESSING, SEREPTA	10 FEB 1870	06:149
THOMAS, ROBERT M & HUDSON, SARAH A	06 FEB 1890	05:519
THOMAS, SAMUEL & CAVIT, MARGARET A	10 SEP 1865	04:052
THOMAS, SAMUEL & McDERMITT, JOSEPHINE C	28 APR 1888	05:222

Name	Date	Ref
THOMAS, SAMUEL & LEMASTER, ANNIE R	02 JUN 1895	07:311
THOMAS, THOMAS H & CHARLES, JENNIE	05 JUL 1882	11:172
THOMAS, WARDEN F & CANTER, BIRDIE	15 MAR 1896	07:510
THOMAS, WILEY & JOHNSON, BERTHA E	02 JUL 1910	13:106
THOMAS, WILLIAM & WILSON, LOUISA	22 JAN 1871	07:045
THOMAS, WILLIAM & EDWARDS, ARAMINTA JENNIE	19 AUG 1993	06:587
THOMAS, WILLIAM & ROLLINS, MOLLIE	08 MAY 1895	07:299
THOMAS, WILLIAM F & SMITH, JULIA M	04 JUN 1913	14:167
THOMAS, WILLIAM M & CHANDLER, MELISSA	17 JAN 1878	09:202
THOMASON, CHARLES L & BRIGHT, MARY B	22 DEC 1898	08:440
THOMPSON, ALONZO & HOFFMAN, HANNAH	02 APR 1902	10:047
THOMPSON, BENJAMIN & BRIGHT, MANDY V	07 MAY 1903	10:286
THOMPSON, BENJAMIN S & LEWIS, ELIZABETH	01 JUL 1841	01:036
THOMPSON, CHARLES E & KING, VIOLA F	24 OCT 1893	06:629
THOMPSON, ERMAN E & ENTWHISTLE, MAGGIE M	17 APR 1898	08:291
THOMPSON, FINLEY O & SIMS, MABEL A	12 AUG 1913	15:010
THOMPSON, FRANCIS & BAKER, LIZZIE	02 JUL 1876	08:366
THOMPSON, HARRY & ROUSH, ADA F	05 APR 1908	12:151
THOMPSON, HENRY & GREEN, MINNIE B	17 JUN 1907	11:554
THOMPSON, JAMES E & RICKARD, EMMA F	31 JUL 1901	09:375
THOMPSON, JAMES THOMAS & LYONS, JENNIE	28 AUG 1889	05:440
THOMPSON, JOHN & DAVIS, RUTH E	02 DEC 1867	05:131
THOMPSON, JOHN W & FAUDREE, SALLIE M	22 NOV 1896	08:006
THOMPSON, LAWSON & AMSDEN, SARAH A	30 AUG 1849	01:051
THOMPSON, LAWSON G & CROOKHAM, SARAH	29 MAY 1881	10:396
THOMPSON, LEWIS W & PARSONS, MARIA	18 APR 1868	05:172
THOMPSON, MELVIN & RUNION, MYRTLE S	10 JAN 1900	09:062
THOMPSON, PHILIP & RISK, MARY JANE	09 SEP 1847	01:047
THOMPSON, RILEY & CLONCH, RHODA F	24 OCT 1893	06:628
THOMPSON, ROBERT L & BOARD, EMMA	24 FEB 1913	14:096
THOMPSON, SALATHIEL H & DEEM, NANCY	10 OCT 1869	06:094
THOMPSON, SAMUEL E & SMITH, PHEBE I	28 DEC 1907	12:109
THOMPSON, VOLNEY G & GIBBS, MARY M	23 SEP 1869	06:080
THOMPSON, WILLIAM H & JACKSON, MARY E	17 JUN 1901	09:356
THORN, CLARENCE L & STEWART, ALBERTA	25 JUL 1900	09:165
THORNBURG, BENJAMIN F & CROPLEY, MARY	01 JUL 1880	10:276
THORNBURGH, GEORGE & HALL, MARY A	24 DEC 1881	11:086
THORNILAY, W CREAVER & BLAZER, SONORA M	29 DEC 1909	12:583
THORNTON, A L & SHARP, (Mrs) EMMA	08 NOV 1910	13:199
THORNTON, ALBERT & RIFFLE, MAHALA	03 JUL 1902	10:105
THORNTON, ALBERT E & LYONS, EVA L	10 SEP 1905	11:166
THORNTON, ALLEN & OLDAKERS, VIANA V	13 AUG 1846	01:046
THORNTON, ALLEN W & COALMAN, ELLEN	22 FEB 1866	04:103
THORNTON, CHARLES & BYERS, JANE	*23 MAY 1859	02:012
THORNTON, CHARLES N & LIVINGSTONE, CHLOE	24 DEC 1911	13:443
THORNTON, CLARENCE A & RIFFLE, LIZZIE	07 AUG 1906	11:382
THORNTON, FRANCIS & THOMAS, MARY	17 AUG 1862	03:072
THORNTON, GEORGE & KNAPP, HANNAH	1835	01:040
THORNTON, GEORGE T & PILLOWS, OLEVIA J	29 AUG 1887	05:084
THORNTON, GILBERT & KING, DORA	01 MAY 1903	10:281
THORNTON, HENRY & VARIAN, URENA CLACK	*15 MAR 1852	02:002
THORNTON, HENRY & BLACKBURN, ELIZA M	*18 JAN 1856	02:007
THORNTON, HIRAM & MORGAN, MARGARET T	08 NOV 1863	03:142
THORNTON, ISAAC & SMITH, MARY	13 APR 1837	01:031
THORNTON, JESSE & EDMONDS, REGINA	27 APR 1871	07:077
THORNTON, JNO & SNOW, INGRY	02 JUN 1882	11:158
THORNTON, JOHN & UTERS, ALICE	05 JUN 1893	06:549
THORNTON, JOHN & KNOTT, EMMA	25 DEC 1903	10:448

THORNTON, JOHN P & KING, MARY C	20 OCT 1870	07:017
THORNTON, LLOYD E & MILLER, HELEN E	21 MAY 1902	10:077
THORNTON, McCLELLAN & COLEMAN, ROSE B	12 AUG 1886	12:373
THORNTON, ORVAL & HAWKINS, ORTHA	02 SEP 1908	12:244
THORNTON, SAMUEL & EDMONDS, SUSANNA MARY MARGT THEOD'A	02 JAN 1867	05:018
THORNTON, SIMEON N & JEFFERS, ARTIE	(no date)	08:285
THORNTON, SYLVESTER G & PIERSON, BERTHA	23 NOV 1893	07:010
TILLIS, CALEB & WALLACE, ABIGAIL	1841	01:041
TILLIS, CALEB & MACRIA, ELIZA	*01 MAY 1854	02:005
TILLIS, CLARK & PONTZLER, ELLEN	*05 MAR 1860	02:013
TILLIS, CLARK & PREDY, MARY M	27 JUL 1883	11:379
TILLIS, CLARK & ELLIS, MARY F	04 MAY 1891	06:103
TILLIS, ELIAS & DEWEESE, ELLA A	20 NOV 1887	05:141
TILLIS, JESSE & DAVIS, ANN	*17 OCT 1859	02:013
TILLIS, JOHN C & MILLER, ALMA G	26 JUN 1894	10:551
TILLIS, JOSHUA & CARTRITE, NANCY	JUN 1839	01:034
TILLIS, JOSHUA & PRIDDY, MARTHA	14 SEP 1849	01:050
TILLIS, LEWIS G & SAYRE, EMILY J	22 FEB 1883	11:301
TILLIS, MILES & KIMBERLING, NANCY	*24 DEC 1852	02:003
TILLIS, PETER & GARD, VIOLA	03 SEP 1877	09:122
TILLIS, RICHARD & SMITH, ELIZABETH	12 SEP 1829	01:022
TILLIS, SAMUEL P & KELLY, LAURA E	22 SEP 1892	06:408
TILLIS, SMITH & KING, MARY A D	05 AUG 1897	08:137
TILTON, LORENZO D & ALEXANDER, CARRIE	25 JUN 1905	11:116
TIMBERS, JAMES AMBROSE & STRIBLING, SARAH MALINDA	01 JUN 1887	05:033
TIMMONS, ASA & PICKENS, ELIZABETH B	25 SEP 1895	07:394
TIMMS, JOHN E & KIMBERLING, GERTRUDE	16 JUN 1868	05:189
TIPPETT, CLIFF C & HESS, FRIEDA M	04 NOV 1897	08:191
TIPPETT, GEORGE W & RISK, SARAH ELIZABETH	*11 SEP 1856	02:008
TIPPETT, HARRY EMERSON & BOWLING, HATTIE E	30 JUN 1887	05:054
TIPPETT, JAMES B & DAY, LIDIA B	29 OCT 1879	10:153
TIPPETT, JAMES BELL & CAMPBELL, CORNELIA D	03 DEC 1901	09:464
TIPPETT, WILLIAM R & PARSONS, BIRDIE	13 DEC 1881	11:069
TODD, JOSHUA & ROUSH, AMANDA E	27 OCT 1877	09:143
TOLES, JAMES & CRAIG, BLANCHE	05 JAN 1897	08:031
TOLLEY, JOHN & RHODES, ANNA	29 SEP 1903	10:375
TOLLIVER, OLLIE EDGAR & BLAKE, EMMA OLA	31 MAY 1913	14:164
TOMLINSON, WILLIAM H & BARNETT, ELLEN	*20 JUN 1855	02:007
TOMPKINS, JOSEPH G & LEWIS, NONA	23 DEC 1896	08:022
TONAN, JESSE & CARPENTER, POLLY	14 AUG 1820	01:006
TONEY, EVERETT V & HOFFMAN, KATIE D	18 DEC 1906	11:412
TOPE, BEACH & GILES, LYDA K	16 AUG 1912	13:585
TOWNSEND, C W & LARWOOD, (Mrs) ANNA L	13 AUG 1910	13:131
TRACY, JAMES & MULFORD, LUCINDA	20 FEB 1840	01:035
TRACY, MICHAEL EDWARD & FRANKLIN, LULU BLANCHE	02 JUN 1891	06:121
TRACY, THOMAS T & HOLT, MERREL	09 SEP 1891	06:178
TRANTMAN, HENRY L & SHANK, OLIVETTI F	04 SEP 1899	08:604
TRIBBETT, W A & ESKEW, JULIA	26 JUL 1809	12:164
TRIBBLE, GEORGE WASHINGTON & PEARSON, IDA	16 APR 1893	06:524
TRIBBLE, SCHUYLER WASHINGTON & FERGUSON, ELLA ELIZABETH	10 NOV 1895	07:424
TRIPP, ALVIN E & LEWIS, NORA	15 MAY 1909	12:410
TRIPP, ROBERT M & CUNNINGHAM, MARTHA F	25 OCT 1883	11:415
TRIPPETT, FRANKLIN A & LOOMIS, MARY A	17 JUN 1874	08:132
TROBRIDGE, WESLEY & GRIMM, MAGGIE	18 JUL 1897	08:129
TROEGER, EARNEST & HARNSPACHER, SEVILLE	14 DEC 1871	07:152
TROEGER, JOHN & HOGG, SARAH JANE	17 JUL 1865	04:027
TROSCHKE, JOHN FREDRICK & WINDON, LELIA EDITH	30 SEP 1908	12:272
TROTTER, VIRGIL A & ROADIAMOUR, EMILY C	28 AUG 1913	15:022

Name	Date	Ref
TRUTZSCHLER, AUGUST & YOUNG, ELIZABETH	25 DEC 1883	11:439
TRYON, WILLIAM C & POLLOCK, MINNIE	17 APR 1900	09:105
TUCK, ANDREW M & ROBERTS, ELIZA	10 OCT 1878	10:334
TUCKER, ALBEY & HAYES, ELLEN	01 APR 1911	13:296
TUCKER, ARTHUR C & ZERKLE, CORA B	17 SEP 1905	11:170
TUCKER, CLIFTON C & ROUSH, SARAH V	20 JUN 1877	09:068
TUCKER, COLUMBUS & ENTSMINGER, ELIZA	*24 SEP 1859	02:013
TUCKER, DANIEL & McCALL, MURTIE	**22 DEC 1903	10:441
TUCKER, EDWARD & MARSHALL, SAMANTHA M	28 MAR 1894	07:066
TUCKER, GEORGE & WHITTINGTON, MINNIE O	10 JUL 1901	09:370
TUCKER, GEORGE & TUCKER, CYNTHIA J	23 JUL 1868	05:200
TUCKER, JAMES WILLIAM & HART, MARIA F	17 SEP 1893	06:605
TUCKER, JOHN M & McCOY, ELIZABETH	1835	01:040
TUCKER, JOHN W, Jr & JORDEN, AURRILLA	12 MAR 1863	03:108
TUCKER, L & ALSBERRY, SARAH	14 JUN 1821	01:007
TUCKER, MELONI C & HILL, CLARA MAY	28 FEB 1910	13:018
TUCKER, MONROE & LEGG, ERNA	06 DEC 1909	12:563
TUCKER, PERRY & SUMMERS, MARY M	1843	01:041
TUCKER, PERRY & LEGG, ANNIE L	24 MAY 1881	10:416
TUCKER, SAMUEL & WHITTINGTON, ALICE	06 SEP 1900	09:139
TUCKER, SHERMAN & TILLIS, REBECCA	18 JUN 1893	06:558
TUCKER, WILLIAM H & WHITE, CLARA H	18 DEC 1877	09:169
TUCKER, WILLIAM T & WALKER, MARY	*10 SEP 1860	02:014
TUCKER, ZEBADEE & HAYES, MINNIE	30 JUL 1903	10:329
TUDOR, CLARK & BUCK, MARY	10 FEB 1910	13:008
TULLAS, VALENCOURT & JONES, SARAH W	APR 1841	01:034
TULLEY, GEORGE & LIONS, ANNA	24 DEC 1901	09:480
TULLY, HENRY & HESS, LUCY L	*01 NOV 1902	10:184
TULLY, W D & HAMBLEY, SUSAN P	25 DEC 1882	11:276
TUNING, GEORGE FRANKLIN & KAULBERCH, CHRISTENA	11 NOV 1894	07:185
TURLEY, ALBERT T & FIELDS, FRANCES	24 DEC 1894	07:208
TURLEY, ELWOOD L & KOBLENTZ, ELIZABETH	04 AUG 1891	06:159
TURLEY, GEORGE C & ROBINSON, LIZZIE	23 DEC 1900	09:257
TURLEY, GEORGE F & JORDAN, ARIZONA E	23 SEP 1891	06:189
TURLEY, HOWARD T & ROBSON, MARGARET	29 AUG 1891	06:175
TURLEY, JAMES & ZIRCLE, MARGARET E	05 DEC 1869	06:119
TURLEY, JOHN A & STEVENSON, LUCY	05 DEC 1881	11:064
TURLEY, THEODORE & KNIGHT, SUSIE	03 AUG 1902	10:122
TURLEY, WILLIAM P & TURNBULL, ELLEN	23 FEB 1871	07:054
TURNBULL, G L & SLACK, SARAH ELIZABETH	14 OCT 1885	12:230
TURNBULL, JOHN J & SINES, ARAMINTA	06 JUN 1890	05:568
TURNBULL, JOHN R & TURLEY, NANNIE F	14 SEP 1893	06:601
TURNBULL, RICHARD & RIFFLE, CARRY F	06 JUN 1906	11:334
TURNBULL, THOMAS & RISER, SAMANTHA	17 AUG 1865	04:038
TURNBULL, THOMAS F & WINTER, ANNA M	25 OCT 1898	08:395
TURNBULL, WILLIAM H & RICKARD, VERNISHIA	20 SEP 1883	11:403
TURNER, AARON H & FETTY, SARAH F	24 MAR 1873	07:316
TURNER, CHARLES S & WAUGH, VINA C	14 NOV 1897	08:192
TURNER, DEWITT C & McDONALD, ALEXY	31 JAN 1865	03:219
TURNER, EDWARD & MIDDLECOFF, MARGARET S	07 MAR 1883	11:309
TURNER, GEORGE & McDERMITT, KATIE M	22 MAY 1904	10:520
TURNER, HENRY COTTON & GYGAX, CAROLINE	24 JAN 1912	13:472
TURNER, JAMES & MAYES, ROZETTA	11 NOV 1898	08:405
TURNER, JOHN & PARSONS, HANNAH	07 MAY 1822	01:009
TURNER, JOHN W & RAYBURN, IDA	20 AUG 1904	10:582
TURNER, JOHN WILLIAM & WALLIS, ELIZA	25 MAR 1891	06:085
TURNER, OBADIAH C & ROBERTS, MARY L	04 MAR 1900	09:090
TURNER, OSCAR C & CLENDENIN, RUBY LEE	26 OCT 1914	15:306

TURNER, RICHARD T & COOPER, ELIZABETH E	06 MAY 1871	07:084
TURNER, ROBERT & BROWN, MARY A	21 FEB 1871	07:057
TURNER, SIMON V & RAYBURN, ANNIE B	01 MAR 1913	14:100
TURNER, THEODORE & FLOWERS, FANNIE	24 JUN 1890	05:576
TURNER, VAN C & MOORE, MARY L	17 OCT 1880	10:313
TWEEDY, JAMES B & CRAIG, SUSAN	19 OCT 1887	05:125
TYLER, GEORGE R & FRAZIER, CLEMMIE	24 DEC 1907	12:105
ULING, JACOB & JULICK, MARY ANN	03 FEB 1874	08:095
ULRICH, GEORGE W & HOFFMAN, ANNIE	*19 NOV 1898	08:410
ULRICH, GEORGE W & DUNLAP, ANGELINE	27 NOV 1898	08:417
UMPHREY, WILLIAM M & STEPHENSON, SARAH	20 DEC 1881	11:076
UNDERWOOD, JORDAN SOLOMON & RAYBURN, ELLA FRANCES	07 JUN 1888	05:233
UNDERWOOD, JORDEN S & BALL, CAROLINE	28 APR 1877	09:070
UNSMINGER, ADOLPH & FRUTH, ANNIE	01 OCT 1903	10:377
UPTON, WATSON E & KEEFER, LIZZIE MAY	14 DEC 1912	14:055
URTON, HARRY & TAYLOR, FANNIE M	26 JUL 1909	12:465
UTT, ANDREW & CAZAD, CATHARINE	18 MAR 1827	01:020
UTT, ENOCH & JACKSON, EDA E	25 JAN 1877	09:028
VAIL, JAMES & DUNN, ELIZABETH	12 JUN 1849	01:049
VALE, FERN A & BRATTON, AMY A	08 DEC 1905	11:221
VALENTINE, GEORGE & MICHAEL, MARY JANE	*12 SEP 1854	02:006
VALENTINE, JAMES & STONE, FANNIE	09 MAY 1883	11:336
VAN MATRE, ABSOLOM T & CARLIND, SARAH J	15 DEC 1881	11:068
VAN MATRE, ANDREW J & McLANE, LOUISA A	02 JAN 1866	04:094
VAN MATRE, CHARLES H & BUTCHER, MARY	19 NOV 1895	12:254
VAN MATRE, CHARLES W & HAYNES, ELLA B	30 AUG 1910	13:134
VAN MATRE, D F & ROSEBERRY, MARTHA J	09 DEC 1883	11:432
VAN MATRE, DANIEL W & YEAGER, ELIZA J	20 JUN 1872	07:239
VAN MATRE, DAVID & LEWIS, HARRIET R	25 APR 1875	08:233
VAN MATRE, DAVID S & HOVER, NETTIE M	10 FEB 1878	09:209
VAN MATRE, EDWARD V & BASS, CLARA M	28 JUL 1906	11:373
VAN MATRE, FRANCIS & ROUSH, ELIZABETH	*05 DEC 1859	02:013
VAN MATRE, FRANK & RUSSELL, MAY	24 DEC 1910	13:244
VAN MATRE, GEORGE & FOWLER, ADDIE	22 APR 1888	05:213
VAN MATRE, GEORGE E & GIBBS, LILLIE	04 JUL 1895	07:334
VAN MATRE, GEORGE W & SNIDER, CHARLOTTE E	13 JAN 1881	10:366
VAN MATRE, GEORGE W & McKINEY, MYRTIE	18 SEP 1904	10:601
VAN MATRE, HARRY A & STEWART, MAUDE B	25 DEC 1907	12:104
VAN MATRE, HARRY B & KERWOOD, GRACE B	31 OCT 1913	15:160
VAN MATRE, HARRY H & MILLER, NELLIE	24 MAY 1906	11:323
VAN MATRE, HARRY W & ROWLEY, ANNIE	03 DEC 1905	11:216
VAN MATRE, HARRY W & CARTER, JENNIE	**12 DEC 1912	14:053
VAN MATRE, HERMAN E & HARRIS, AURELLIA	21 JUN 1896	07:569
VAN MATRE, JACOB & LEWIS, SUSAN	17 SEP 1865	04:055
VAN MATRE, JAMES & WOODS, ELANORA	27 OCT 1880	10:317
VAN MATRE, JAMES R & FISHER, MATTIE	20 FEB 1894	07:053
VAN MATRE, JOHN & CART, LYDIA	01 APR 1877	09:053
VAN MATRE, JOHN & LEE, SALLIE ELIZABETH	03 SEP 1893	06:596
VAN MATRE, JOHN E & ZERKLE, EDNA E	21 SEP 1903	10:364
VAN MATRE, JOHN W & EDWARDS, MARY M	*18 MAR 1878	09:231
VAN MATRE, JOHN W & ROSEBERRY, ELIZABETH	08 APR 1883	11:319
VAN MATRE, JUSTICE JONAS & ROUSH, MARY	05 JUN 1881	10:420
VAN MATRE, LEWIS & CART, HARRIET C	26 OCT 1871	07:135
VAN MATRE, NORMAN G & JOHNSON, CORA B	01 JUN 1912	13:538
VAN MATRE, OLIVER H P & STEWART, MARY M	01 JAN 1874	08:086
VAN MATRE, OLLIE & VARIAN, CLARA M	10 SEP 1910	13:155
VAN MATRE, OTTO & HOGG, OLLIE	19 FEB 1899	08:469
VAN MATRE, PERRY & GRIM, DELILA	10 DEC 1865	04:082

VAN MATRE, ROBERT & NICHOLS, EVA	01 JAN 1911	13:250
VAN MATRE, ROBERT H & ADKINS, ELIZABETH	15 AUG 1880	10:287
VAN MATRE, RODOCWA & EDWARDS, HANNAH	30 NOV 1865	04:077
VAN MATRE, WALTER & ROWLEY, NELLIE	26 OCT 1907	12:053
VAN MATRE, WILLIAM T & FISHER, ROSE B	25 FEB 1880	10:211
VAN MATRE, WILLIAM T & CANSOL, VICTORIA	29 OCT 1884	12:084
VAN MATRE, WINFIELD S & RUSSELL, MAGGIE	18 AUG 1879	12:112
VAN METER, GEORGE E & GASKINS, JESSIE	22 OCT 1898	08:393
VAN METER, HARRY & CHAPMAN, MAY	20 MAY 1898	08:309
VAN METRE, EDWIN HARNESS & BEALE, ELEANOR MOORE	10 DEC 1885	12:263
VAN METRE, HOWARD & STEWART, JULIA H	26 AUG 1905	11:152
VAN METRE, JOHN W & WARD, MARY	11 SEP 1905	11:165
VAN METRE, LATEN & CHAFFIN, BLANCH	07 OCT 1905	11:187
VAN SICKLE, ALEXANDER & BARTRAM, GERTIE	26 JUL 1899	08:584
VAN SICKLE, ELI J & FOGLESONG, FANNIE	07 NOV 1894	07:183
VAN SICKLE, ELI W & ECKARD, MARY M	02 JUL 1895	07:330
VAN SICKLE, FRANK & FLINT, MARY	08 JAN 1906	11:243
VAN SICKLE, GEORGE & LATHEY, MARY	17 OCT 1902	10:173
VAN SICKLE, WILLIAM & LUTTON, VIRGINIA	15 MAY 1901	09:337
VAN SICKLE, WILLIAM & HAYES, LAURA M	04 JUL 1903	10:317
VAN SICKLE, WILLIAM & CHEESEBREW, ARDELLA B	06 NOV 1897	08:194
VAN SICKLE, ZACHARIAH & MOURNING, SARAH C M	09 MAY 1877	09:075
VAN SICKLES, DANIEL C & ROBERTS, MARY M	08 FEB 1872	07:190
VAN SICKLES, GEORGE & FISHER, LUCY ANN	22 AUG 1889	05:432
VANCE, JACOB & HOSCHAR, CATHARINE	25 JAN 1838	01:032
VANCE, SILAS N & MORRIS, MARY S	04 JUL 1877	09:105
VANDALE, R D & BURKE, MARGARET M	04 APR 1914	15:171
VANKIRK, HENRY M & SCOTT, ALLENA L	16 JUL 1886	12:358
VANMATER, ANTHONY B & PARSONS, LETHA ANN	*23 MAR 1857	02:009
VANMATER, TAYLOR & JENNINGS, MYRTLE M	26 NOV 1913	15:073
VANMATRE, JOHN & SHARP, ELITHA	02 DEC 1832	01:025
VANMATRE, JOHN HENRY & STEEL, REBECCA	20 DEC 1849	01:049
VANMATRE, MARK & COOPER, ELIZA	14 JUL 1831	01:024
VANMATRE, MARK B & VARNER, MALINDA	27 DEC 1864	03:214
VANMATRE, OLIVER P H & SAYRES, MIRIAM	01 APR 1838	01:031 5
VANMATRE, WILLIAM & LEWIS, DELILAH	*15 MAR 1853	02:004
VANMATRE, WILLIAM C & BUMGARNER, MATILDA	02 JAN 1870	06:136
VANMETRE, LEONARD & EDWARDS, ELIZABETH	*16 JAN 1854	02:005
VANNESS, WILBER BURTON & BARNHEART, MARY JANE	27 APR 1903	10:279
VANOY, EPHRAIM & MOORE, JENNIE	16 NOV 1876	08:412
VANPELT, JOHN F & MILLER, ELIZABETH	31 AUG 1847	01:048
VANSICKLE, ABRAHAM & RIFFLE, POLLY	07 JAN 1830	11:019
VANSICKLE, GILBERT & STEWART, SARAH J	06 FEB 1868	05:140
VANSICKLE, JOSEPH & HENKEL, MARY M	26 DEC 1833	01:028
VANSICKLE, JOSEPH & RICKART, SARAH	29 DEC 1836	01:030
VANSICKLE, SAMUEL & BIRCHFIELD, REBECCA	16 APR 1868	05:168
VANSICKLE, SAMUEL & ECKARD, SUSAN	23 JAN 1834	01:028
VANSICKLES, ANTHONY & RIFFLE, ANN MAGDELENA	*10 FEB 1854	02:005
VARIAN, CHARLES H & STONE, EDITH J	30 MAY 1877	09:090
VARIAN, CHARLES H & SHAW, ANN A	04 JUN 1902	10:084
VARIAN, DANIEL H & BUTCHER, CLARA	07 APR 1914	15:172
VARIAN, ELMER E & EVANS, RACHEL L	15 JAN 1884	11:448
VARIAN, ELMER E & GIBBS, LUCINDA B	30 APR 1906	11:305
VARIAN, ENOS & FRY, MARTHA J	14 AUG 1877	09:120
VARIAN, ENOS & JONES, BIRDIE	10 MAR 1885	12:150
VARIAN, FRANK H & LEE, GERTRUDE	29 NOV 1912	14:040
VARIAN, FREEMAN & SAYRE, CORDELIA E	27 MAY 1873	07:356
VARIAN, FREEMAN & FISHER, SARAH L	27 MAY 1897	08:104

VARIAN, HOMER & HAYMAN, ADA	16 APR 1879	10:075
VARIAN, JOSEPH & HUSTON, IDA M	17 DEC 1884	12:104
VARIAN, WILLIAM & SELBY, ADALINE	18 NOV 1847	01:047
VARIAN, WILLIAM R & CURRY, CASSEY M	13 NOV 1901	09:448
VAUGHAN, TUCKER & FROST, MAUD	13 DEC 1908	12:326
VAUGHN, CLARENCE & LITTLE, LONA	03 OCT 1908	12:277
VAUGHN, EDGAR B & McGLOTHLIN, SABINA J	10 OCT 1872	07:272
VAUGHN, J & ASHWORTH, MELVINA	24 SEP 1895	07:388
VAUGHN, RUSSELL E & AUSTIN, ALICE A	19 MAR 1913	14:110
VAUGHN, W B & FOX, MARY	24 SEP 1884	12:065
VAUGHN, WILLIAM W & MEADOWS, CYNTHA A	16 MAY 1880	10:260
VAUGHT, WILLIAM H & HOGG, ORA	11 DEC 1895	07:450
VAUGHT, (Rev) STEPHEN K & MILLER, NANCY L	*07 SEP 1852	02:003
VEITH, WILLIAM & MYERS, BELLE V	12 OCT 1905	11:189
VENOY, ANTHONY & HARRIS, JOSEPHINE	18 APR 1888	05:211
VERIGAN, FRANK & GREGORY, ROSETTA	23 JUL 1906	11:359
VERIGAN, GARRET E & VALE, LEONA DARE	10 JUN 1914	15:220
VERIGAN, JAMES K & PHILLIPS, MINNIE A	27 NOV 1907	12:079
VEST, JOHN R, Jr & SHANK, SARAH E	*25 NOV 1891	06:233
VEST, JOHN R, Jr & PILLOW, ANNIE M	04 JAN 1893	06:467
VEST, THOMAS L & BUTCHER, LENA L	04 NOV 1900	09:232
VICKERS, C H & GRAHAM, HANNAH E	26 MAR 1884	11:472
VICKERS, JOHN F & SULLIVAN, HANNAH	24 DEC 1907	12:107
VICKERS, WILLIAM T & CHAPMAN, LIZZIE J	26 MAY 1871	07:091
VICKERS, WM T & GALLEHUE, LOUISE G	21 DEC 1911	13:459
VIERS, AARON & MADDY, OLIVE ELIZABETH	24 SEP 1890	05:616
VIERS, CHANCY H & DAVIDSON, LOUISE A	01 JAN 1896	07:475
VIERS, JOHN & WARD, MARGARET SUSAN	03 AUG 1892	06:382
VIERS, MOSES JAMES & CHAPMAN, VIRGINIA SOPHIA	19 NOV 1889	05:483
VIERS, MOSES JAMES & NEWELL, RHODA	19 NOV 1892	06:353
VIERS, SAMUEL CINCLAIR & DANNIER, ALICE SAMANTHA	11 NOV 1884	12:093
VILLARS, GEORGE W & HOLLY, CHARLOTTE M	09 SEP 1882	11:197
VILLARS, THOMAS A & FETTY, KATIE	01 AUG 1895	07:352
VILLERS, GRANT & BLAND, BIRDIE	21 MAR 1887	12:494
VILLERS, PEARL V & FETTY, CLAUDIE M	06 NOV 1909	12:539
VINCENT, ALMON H & THORNTON, CORA	29 JUN 1895	07:327
WACKENHUTH, CHARLES L & RODGERS, LENNA	15 SEP 1908	12:258
WADDELL, JOHN & MORIARTY, ELLEN	30 SEP 1875	08:277
WADE, JOHN H & STEPHENS, EDITH M	26 FEB 1907	11:500
WADE, JOHN P & FOWLER, MARY ELIZABETH	*17 JUN 1856	02:008
WADKINS, McCLURG & CHAVIS, PEARL A	05 AUG 1901	09:377
WAGGENER, ANDREW C & STRIBLING, MATILDA J	29 APR 1862	03:059
WAGGENER, CHARLES B & LEWIS, MARGARET S	02 FEB 1836	01:031
WAGGENER, CHARLES B & MURDOCK, CATHARINE M	26 AUG 1869	06:085
WAGGENER, CHARLES B & MAUPIN, MARY M	23 OCT 1879	10:151
WAGGENER, EDMOND & ADAMS, MARY ANN	07 MAY 1850	01:052
WAGGENER, GRAHAM B & WINDON, CLARA E	27 SEP 1893	06:610
WAGGENER, HANSON & MacDANIEL, CATHARINE	11 NOV 1841	01:037
WAGGENER, WILLIAM H & ARNOLD, MINNIE B	13 JUL 1908	12:214
WAGGONER, WILLIAM & PRIOR, ELIZA	07 DEC 1820	01:006
WAITS, C K & TAYLOR, MARY E	(no date)	13:355
WALDEN, SHERMAN E & ROBERTS, JULIA C	14 OCT 1900	09:222
WALDEN, SIGAL & HILL, RACHEL M	11 JUL 1902	10:111
WALDEN, THOMAS & MEADOWS, ALICE	05 JUL 1893	06:568
WALDEN, HENRY F & GRANT, LOTTIE	14 MAR 1899	08:482
WALDEN, PETER & GIBBS, MARGARET	03 MAY 1842	01:043
WALKER, ARCH H & PARKER, VIRGINIA	12 AUG 1875	08:260
WALKER, CHARLES & SAYRE, MARY	01 MAR 1832	01:027

WALKER, CHARLES & HENRY, IVA	15 DEC 1898	08:434
WALKER, DAVID J & MARTIN, MARY CATHARINE	21 NOV 1912	14:031
WALKER, ELMORE & HILL, KEZIA	23 JAN 1825	01:011
WALKER, GEORGE & EDWARDS, (Mrs) ELIZABETH	*05 JUL 1850	02:001
WALKER, GEORGE W & CHANDLER, FLORENCE	17 JUL 1905	11:133
WALKER, IRA & AUSTIN, LAURA	26 MAY 1891	06:116
WALKER, JACKSON & STEEL, MARY ANN	26 MAY 1848	01:046
WALKER, JESSE & MORROW, REBECCA	12 FEB 1904	10:475
WALKER, JESSE J, Jr & HARRIS, MARY	19 OCT 1895	07:407
WALKER, JOSEPH W & VANSICKLE, CHRISTENA	13 MAR 1831	01:023
WALKER, LEWIS & HENRY, IDA	17 JUN 1899	08:556
WALKER, MARCUS G & FROST, MARY M	16 JAN 1905	11:031
WALKER, ROBERT F & GARRISON, NANCY J	*04 FEB 1861	02:015
WALKER, ROSCOE D & GIBSON, LEVAGA E	12 MAR 1914	15:157
WALKER, WALKER & MORROW, MELINDA	21 MAR 1825	01:011
WALKUP, JAMES & MADDOCK, HANNAH	*19 JUN 1857	02:011
WALKUP, JOHN SAMUEL & YEAGER, MARGARET MERTILLA	26 JUL 1887	05:061
WALKUP, JOSEPH & JOHNSON, SUSAN	*19 APR 1852	02:002
WALL, CARL M & MAYES, MARGARET	07 AUG 1903	10:334
WALL, WILLIAM G & OLDAKER, LILLIE B	27 MAY 1907	11:539
WALLACE, A L & ALFORD, ELIZABETH	29 NOV 1883	11:429
WALLACE, ALBERT O & WADE, RUTH E	30 APR 1912	13:522
WALLACE, AUGUSTUS D & WEARS, MALVINA	12 DEC 1846	01:046
WALLACE, CHARLES C & ALFORD, MARY C	25 DEC 1877	09:177
WALLACE, EDGAR & CLAYPOOL, MARY ELIZABETH	24 DEC 1901	09:485
WALLACE, FREDERICK & DABNEY, ELIZABETH	22 MAY 1828	01:017
WALLACE, GEORGE ALLEN & WITHERS, VIRGINIA	18 MAY 1893	06:541
WALLACE, HIBERT & EVANS, ONETA D	21 JUL 1903	10:313
WALLACE, IRA M & MEADOWS, ELLA	08 MAY 1897	08:091
WALLACE, ISAAC & BOWMAN, ELIZABETH	22 APR 1897	08:074
WALLACE, ISAAC M & WALLACE, NANCY	1834	01:040
WALLACE, JAMES & ALEXANDER, MARY JANE	02 SEP 1847	01:046
WALLACE, JAMES & CREMEENS, AMANDA	20 FEB 1899	08:468
WALLACE, JOHN A & HAWTHORN, ROSA M,	28 JUN 1891	06:142
WALLACE, JOHN M & MARTIN, OLIVIA	1838	01:040
WALLACE, JOHN W & McCOMB, VIOLA P	24 FEB 1897	08:051
WALLACE, JOSEPH & WATTERSON, EDITH A	21 FEB 1901	09:293
WALLACE, LEVI & WEERS, ABIGAIL	14 JUN 1844	01:042
WALLACE, LOVE C & LOCK, DELILAH E	12 NOV 1868	05:224
WALLACE, Mt ETNA & LINKFIELD, IDA	28 DEC 1871	07:173
WALLACE, OSCAR & HOLLY, ADA	02 FEB 1910	13:002
WALLACE, THOMAS & WITHERS, SARAH	20 DEC 1827	01:016
WALLACE, THOMAS A & DAVIS, ANNIE V	19 MAY 1886	12:329
WALLACE, W M & BALL, ELIZABETH T	14 MAY 1885	12:176
WALLACE, WALTER E & McKIBBEN, WILD R	24 DEC 1902	10:211
WALLACE, WILLIAM & OLDACRE, CYNTHIA	24 MAR 1824	01:010
WALLACE, WILLIAM & DAVIS, MARY ANN	18 DEC 1904	10:670
WALLIS, ABRAHAM E & BALL, ELSIE P	09 OCT 1907	12:031
WALLIS, ABRAM & BOWMAN, NANCY	27 JUN 1871	07:099
WALLIS, ALONZO & CRUM, HATTIE E	08 AUG 1896	07:591
WALLIS, ALVIN M & BLESSING, MAMIE A	25 DEC 1895	07:470
WALLIS, ANDREW, Jr & HAWTHORN, SUSAN	04 MAR 1841	01:036
WALLIS, EDMUND & MATTHIS, MARY	21 MAY 1846	01:045
WALLIS, EMMET & WAUGH, ROSA	01 MAY 1901	09:329
WALLIS, FRANK & NICHOLS, SALLIE	02 MAR 1898	08:265
WALLIS, FREDERICK & AMOS, JEMIMA	11 AUG 1842	01:038
WALLIS, FREDRICK S & HEREFORD, JULIET E	*29 APR 1854	02:005
WALLIS, GEORGE ALLEN & WARDEN, LILLIE MAY	27 MAY 1893	06:546

WALLIS, GEORGE W & TAYLOR, ELIZABETH F	15 JUN 1843	01:038
WALLIS, GEORGE W & CLENDENIN, SOPHRONIA ELIZABETH	06 APR 1892	06:321
WALLIS, HIRAM HENRY & PRICE, ROSSETTA	20 MAR 1889	05:372
WALLIS, ISAAC M & WAUGH, MAHALA	20 SEP 1846	01:046
WALLIS, ISAAC N & LITTERELL, EMILY C	*13 APR 1860	02:014
WALLIS, JAMES H & HALL, GLENIA	23 OCT 1904	10:619
WALLIS, JESSE A & HENRY, MARTHA F	08 FEB 1903	10:236
WALLIS, JOHN R & WAUGH, MARTHA	*16 OCT 1858	02:011
WALLIS, JOSEPH H & CONRAD, ELVIRA S	11 DEC 1895	07:448
WALLIS, ROBERT W & GUNN, HARRIET A	28 NOV 1855	02:007
WALLIS, THOMAS & WITHERS, ELIZA	07 AUG 1845	01:045
WALLIS, WILLIAM A & MORRISON, LULU	17 MAY 1896	07:551
WALLIS, WILLIAM H & GISE, EMILY M	*30 OCT 1856	02:009
WALLIS, WILLIAM H & HOLLEY, MARY A	26 OCT 1882	11:226
WALLIS, WILLIAM T & WAUGH, MARTHA	22 MAR 1873	07:335
WALLIS, WILLIAM T & THOMAS, LUCRETIA J	28 FEB 1876	08:239
WALLS, GEORGE W & JEFFERS, FLORA J	25 DEC 1863	03:151
WALTERS, CHARLES CHESTER & BRALEY, MORA ELIZABETH	23 DEC 1903	10:442
WALTERS, JAMES & McGLAUGHLIN, NARSISSES	02 SEP 1879	10:122
WALTERS, JOHN & McCUMBER, LIZZIE	28 JAN 1904	10:464
WAMSLEY, ABNER D & PATTERSON, AMANDA C	24 DEC 1868	06:021 5
WAMSLEY, BENJAMIN F & MORROW, SOPHRONIA J	05 MAR 1881	10:363
WAMSLEY, CHARLES & HARRIS, MITTIE	30 JUL 1900	09:168
WAMSLEY, CHARLES F & FROST, VEVA E	04 JUL 1907	11:570
WAMSLEY, JOHN L & HARRIS, SARAH C	10 JUL 1895	07:339
WAMSLEY, ROBERT D & LEPORT, FRANCES	16 OCT 1910	13:185
WAMSLEY, WILLIAM E & SMITH, MOLLIE	09 JUN 1906	11:336
WAMSLEY, WILLIAM I & WOODS, MARY A	*03 MAR 1858	02:010
WANDLING, HENRY S & JIVIDEN, MARGARET J	23 JUL 1905	11:137
WARD, ANDREW & McFANN, (Mrs) LIZZIE	11 APR 1914	15:175
WARD, CHARLES F & DAVIS, CLOE V	30 NOV 1909	12:558
WARD, DAVIS C & LEWIS, SARAH C	12 MAR 1878	09:225
WARD, FLOYD A & CHERRINGTON, LULU	30 AUG 1907	11:602
WARD, GEORGE & MUNSELL, CLARINDA	14 MAR 1811	01:003
WARD, GEORGE H & ZIRKEL, SARAH F	01 JAN 1862	03:042
WARD, HENRY D & HANNAN, FRANCES A	03 MAY 1885	12:169
WARD, HORACE H & EMBLETON, IDA	25 JUL 1894	07:124
WARD, HUGH & HUGHES, SARAH	06 JAN 1891	06:041
WARD, JACOB BACHTEL & HODGES, EMMA J	28 NOV 1895	07:440
WARD, JAMES & WOOD, SUSAN	01 APR 1841	01:035
WARD, JAMES A & SNYDER, AGNES N	11 JUN 1908	12:197
WARD, JAMES W & KERWOOD, LAURA G	07 APR 1886	12:316
WARD, JOHN & BURRELL, LUCRETIA	11 APR 1827	01:016
WARD, JOHN & MIDDLECOFF, ADELINE	03 SEP 1837	01:032
WARD, JOHN & CORNELL, ANNIE	05 MAY 1908	12:175
WARD, JOHN W & CASEY, LUCY J	04 APR 1878	09:237
WARD, LAVENDAR & MEADOWS, SALLIE	20 JUL 1902	10:115
WARD, LLOYD HAMILTON & ATEN, LIZZIE JANE	28 APR 1890	05:551
WARD, MARNIE O & BUTLER, ELLA C	03 APR 1877	09:051
WARD, MARTIN LECURGUS & CLENDENIN, CELINA	27 SEP 1888	05:283
WARD, PHILIP E & THOMPSON, CORA E	29 JUL 1905	11:139
WARD, THEODORE F & GRIMM, IDA M	19 JAN 1908	12:118
WARD, WILLIAM W & STEPHENSON, SALLIE	14 APR 1857	02:009
WARD, WILLIAM W & SEBRELL, SARAH ANN	30 DEC 1847	01:047
WARD, WILSON & RICE, LUCETTA C	01 OCT 1891	06:200
WARDEN, GEORGE M & CREMEANS, CUMA	*01 MAR 1877	09:038
WARDEN, JAS M & HEREFORD, MARTHA	29 NOV 1838	01:031 5
WARDEN, SEBERT & NEWMAN, MARY E	26 APR 1877	09:072

WARDEN, WILLIAM & HULL, SARAH F	11 NOV 1868	05:223
WARES, MOSES & SHANK, GRACE E	09 APR 1880	10:234
WARNER, AUGHTICE & BIRCHFIELD, FLORA	05 NOV 1908	12:297
WARNER, BOUDIDGE & RAYBURN, RUTH	11 DEC 1845	01:045
WARNER, BURWELL S & VIRON, MARY L	01 JAN 1868	05:128
WARNER, CHARLES L & STEPHENS, CLARA B	27 AUG 1882	11:193
WARNER, DANIEL M & DAVIS, MARY A	30 AUG 1868	05:208
WARNER, EDGAR ESLEY & JIVIDEN, ANNIE	16 APR 1891	06:047
WARNER, ERKEY D & CASTO, CLARA A	04 DEC 1909	12:560
WARNER, IRA W & KNOPP, LENA M	07 JAN 1899	08:448
WARNER, JAMES A & STOVER, LIVY	14 AUG 1901	09:384
WARNER, JAMES T & WAUGH, SARAH A	11 SEP 1873	08:023
WARNER, JASPER N & CARNEY, MARY F	21 FEB 1878	09:211
WARNER, JASPER N & TRIBBLE, MARY E	02 OCT 1908	12:278
WARNER, JOHN C & HULBERT, MARY E	08 APR 1885	12:158
WARNER, PERRY M & MOREHEAD, ANNIE E	19 MAR 1874	08:103
WARNER, ROBERT & CARTWRIGHT, MARIA A	14 JUN 1873	08:003
WARNER, THOMAS & COOKE, CELINDA	22 JUN 1849	01:050
WARNER, WILBER J & SAYRE, CORA A	11 OCT 1906	11:425
WARNER, WILLIAM & ATKINSON, MARY F	11 JAN 1844	01:042
WARNER, WILLIAM & LEGG, JANE ANN	17 APR 1879	10:076
WARNER, WILLIAM P & DUNDESS, ROSIE L	17 APR 1901	09:324
WARNER, WILLIAM & HUDSON, ANN GEMIMA	18 OCT 1849	01:050
WARREN, PERCIVAL PERKINS & BURDETT, LELA E	17 OCT 1886	12:401
WARTENBERG, ALEXANDER & DARST, HANNAH C	*23 JUL 1859	02:012
WARTENBERG, DANIEL T & SINES, EVA M	14 SEP 1888	05:275
WARTENBERG, PETER W & DONOHEW, LYDIA	30 OCT 1887	05:131
WARTENBERG, FRED A & MONROE, FRANCES	26 JUL 1909	12:466
WARTH, CHARLES SHIPMAN & HARDEN, LOUISA ISABELLE	14 NOV 1869	06:106
WARTH, ROBERT WILLIAM & DUNN, STELLA MAE	19 JUL 1893	06:576
WASHINGTON, CHAMP & JOHNSON, MATTIE	01 SEP 1886	13:381
WASHINGTON, COLUMBUS & WILLIAMS, ROSA	23 DEC 1897	08:224
WASHINGTON, EDWARD & SCHRUGG, ANNIE	24 OCT 1910	13:191
WASHINGTON, FRANCIS A & GARTON, MALVINA M	20 FEB 1843	01:037
WASHINGTON, GEORGE F & GARTON, FRANCES A	1843	01:042
WASHINGTON, JESSE & YERTY, MARTHA ELIZABETH	**01 JAN 1889	05:336
WASHINGTON, ROBERT CUSTIS & ZIRKLE, MARY ELLEN	04 SEP 1890	06:604
WASHINGTON, SAMUEL T & CHAMBERLAIN, MARTHA E	23 AUG 1899	08:600
WASHINGTON, STEPTOE A & ALEXANDER, HATTIE C	20 NOV 1901	09:453
WASHINGTON, WILLIAM M & SOMERVILLE, MARTHA ANN	*08 SEP 1856	02:008
WATERS, JOHN C & HESLOP, SUE D	24 JAN 1906	11:252
WATKINS, ALEXANDER & LARIMER, ROSE	17 MAY 1877	09:074
WATKINS, DRYDEN & VANMATRE, NANCY	26 MAR 1840	01:043
WATKINS, HENDERSON & CAPEHART, ROSANE	18 NOV 1828	01:018
WATKINS, JAMES & HUCHINSON, ELIZABETH A	31 MAY 1877	09:091
WATKINS, JOHN H & NEIGHBORS, ELIZABETH	25 FEB 1873	07:324
WATKINS, LEWIS & MILLER, LIZZIE	19 DEC 1886	12:442
WATKINS, THOMAS J & HENDERSON, MARIA E	16 NOV 1881	11:053
WATSON, ALONZO PRESTON & PERRY, MAY	29 SEP 1914	15:284
WATSON, ANDREW & KELL, MAGGIE	15 APR 1890	05:542
WATSON, ANDREW & BERKLEY, MARY M	21 NOV 1909	12:550
WATSON, BOYD & ELLWANGER, FLORENCE	19 AUG 1904	10:580
WATSON, CHARLES & FRY, ELIZABETH C	07 AUG 1895	07:359
WATSON, CHARLES F & WILSON, CORA	04 MAY 1903	10:285
WATSON, GEORGE & BARTROM, JENNIE	22 MAY 1905	11:096
WATSON, JOHN W & ARTHUR, NORA B	19 DEC 1905	11:227
WATSON, THOMAS A & SNYDER, ETHEL O	03 SEP 1912	13:594
WATSON, THOMAS L & NEASE, LAURA L	14 APR 1891	06:096

Names	Date	Ref
WATSON, WILLIAM & DUNCAN, HANNAH	27 NOV 1875	08:305
WATSON, WILLIAM & BENNINGTON, CATHARINE	14 SEP 1882	11:204
WATTERSON, JOHN A & COVERSTON, MARIA	14 APR 1872	07:210
WATTERSON, JOHN H & FARLEY, LAURA	02 JUN 1901	09:339
WATTS, ALBERT B & HUGHES, ADDIE	23 AUG 1910	13:140
WATTS, D R & MORGAN, KATHRYN JANE	28 OCT 1911	13:405
WATTS, J F & DAY, (Mrs) J F	24 MAR 1910	13:027
WAUGH, ALEXANDER & LEE, FRANCES	JAN 1838	01:033
WAUGH, ANDREW & KELLY, SARAH E	25 MAY 1884	12:017
WAUGH, ANDREW & JOHNSON, JULIAN	07 JAN 1836	01:029
WAUGH, EDWARD & CHICK, JESSIE	26 DEC 1904	11:016
WAUGH, GORIE & POWELL, ABIGAIL	30 AUG 1870	06:220
WAUGH, HENRY W & HARNESS, ELZINA J	11 APR 1891	06:095
WAUGH, JOHN G & POWELL, MALINDA	28 OCT 1893	06:632
WAUGH, JOHN G & WATTERSON, LAURA M	14 JUN 1908	12:196
WAUGH, JOHN T & ADAMS, EUDELIE ANN	13 FEB 1867	05:027
WAUGH, PARLEY & ERWIN, VIOLA	27 FEB 1904	10:483
WAUGH, PERRY A & SANDERS, MARIETTA	21 FEB 1895	07:258
WAUGH, PHILIP S & LANIER, MARY A	13 SEP 1888	05:276
WAUGH, ROBERSON & HANNAN, SARAH	*31 JUL 1852	02:003
WAUGH, RODRICK & HAWKINS, ELIZABETH	*19 JAN 1852	02:002
WAUGH, WILLIAM & HAWKINS, MARY JANE	*01 NOV 1852	02:003
WAUGH, WILLIAM & HUGHES, MALINDA	19 MAY 1898	08:308
WAUGH, JAMES & TALAFERO, ANNIE MAY	29 JUL 1897	08:134
WAYLAND, IRA E & McKITRICK, CAMMIE A	19 OCT 1910	13:188
WAYLAND, SHELDON L & CHAPMAN, LUCY L	19 FEB 1879	10:057
WEARES, FRANK & COLEMAN, IVA	27 AUG 1892	06:396
WEARS, ADOLPHUS & DOWELL, MINERVA	26 SEP 1907	12:024
WEARS, EDWARD D & WAMACK, LUCINDA B	17 MAR 1890	05:529
WEARS, FRANK A & LEGUE, NORA	27 SEP 1899	08:618
WEARS, IRA W & LEGUE, NANNIE Z	16 AUG 1893	07:137
WEARS, JOHN F & WHITTINGTON, IDA	27 AUG 1885	12:214
WEARS, ROBERT & PIERCE, EMMA L	13 FEB 1900	09:083
WEARS, THOMAS & CURRY, SARAH A	28 MAR 1866	04:111
WEARS, VAN W & KING, LIEARENA	04 OCT 1890	05:621
WEARS, VAN W & DOWELL, SARAH	11 FEB 1903	10:240
WEARS, WALTER & CURRY, LILLIE B	28 FEB 1897	08:054
WEAVER, ABRAHAM & JEWELL, MARY C	24 OCT 1878	09:340
WEAVER, ADAM H & STEPHENSON, VIOLA T	09 MAR 1879	10:067
WEAVER, ADLEY & SAYRE, SARAH	18 NOV 1830	01:023
WEAVER, ANDREW J & FRY, SHARON	28 OCT 1877	09:144
WEAVER, DECATE & ROUSH, MAHALA	*16 MAY 1859	02:012
WEAVER, DECATUR & RIPLEY, GERTRUDE	13 OCT 1868	05:217
WEAVER, ELMER L & FIELDS, MARY E	24 DEC 1907	12:100
WEAVER, HAMILTON & SHIPLEY, MARY JANE	22 FEB 1866	04:104
WEAVER, HENRY & DAVIS, ANN REBECCA	21 AUG 1838	01:031.5
WEAVER, HENRY & STARCHER, MARGARET	26 MAR 1863	03:115
WEAVER, HENRY & STOUT, LUCINDA C	04 NOV 1869	06:120
WEAVER, JAHEU & ROUSH, MARY F	24 DEC 1890	06:027
WEAVER, JAMES B & CUNNINGHAM, VIRGINIA B	17 NOV 1884	12:094
WEAVER, JOHN, Jr & McFARLAND, ANNA MARIA	11 DEC 1851	02:001
WEAVER, JOHN K & McDANIEL, VIRGINIA	*10 SEP 1854	02:005
WEAVER, JOHN W & SOMERVILLE, LUADA E	01 JUN 1910	13:077
WEAVER, JOSEPH W & ROUSH, MARY E	24 JAN 1884	11:450
WEAVER, LEROY E & CUNDIFF, MELVINA C	04 APR 1887	05:004
WEAVER, MARK W & ROUSH, ARLETTA	01 JUL 1911	13:338
WEAVER, MARK W & FINDLEY, ORILLA	30 APR 1885	12:165
WEAVER, MONROE & POWELL, CASSIE	29 NOV 1893	07:015

WEAVER, NICHOLAS, Jr & ROUSH, ELIZABETH	25 FEB 1869	06:035
WEAVER, OBEDIAH & WERNER, OLEVIA	15 JUL 1899	08:577
WEAVER, PEARL R & BURROWS, SUSIE	27 MAY 1905	11:099
WEAVER, WADE H & RICKARD, BERTHA	07 OCT 1902	10:171
WEAVER, WILBERT & JOHNSON, EDNA	30 NOV 1912	14:038
WEAVER, WILLIAM & JENKINS, MAGGIE	02 MAR 1879	10:060
WEAVER, WILLIAM M & WOODS, ELIZA	24 FEB 1894	07:055
WEBB, E W & MABE, CYNTHIA M	16 NOV 1909	12:547
WEBB, LEWIS W & KINDER, LUARY	25 SEP 1873	08:033
WEBSTER, GEORGE W & THORNTON, LUCINDA	24 DEC 1868	06:020
WEBSTER, JOSIAH & ALLISON, MARIA	04 MAY 1876	08:350
WEBSTER, ROEZELVOE M & SCHWARZ, JOSIE A	03 JUL 1899	08:568
WEDGE, DENCIL & GERLOCK, DORATHY E	11 JUL 1908	12:207
WEEKLY, CHARLES & DAVIS, OLLIE	05 AUG 1903	10:332
WEEKLY, OATH & JONES, ALICE	07 APR 1870	06:178
WEESE, CHRIS & HENESEY, MARGARET	20 MAY 1873	07:352
WEGENER, HARRY F & SIMMONS, KATE F	15 APR 1896	07:528
WEIGAND, EDWARD & THOMPSON, NAOMA	25 DEC 1904	11:007
WEIGAND, FREDK & HAYMAN, IVABEL	14 MAY 1876	08:354
WEIGAND, HENRY & HOOVER, DORA	04 NOV 1875	08:293
WEIGAND, OSCAR & THORNTON, DELLA	23 APR 1899	08:513
WEIGAND, PHILIP & SHIRLEY, ABBIE E	19 APR 1899	08:509
WEIK, OSCAR F & GRESS, LENA C	26 DEC 1914	15:348
WEIN, NORMAN O & STONE, BLANCHE L	27 NOV 1912	14:039
WEINS, ADAM & FREEMAN, MARY S	29 MAY 1909	12:420
WEISEMAN, NICHOLAS & HART, ANNA C	28 JUN 1911	13:335
WEISS, CHRISTOPHER & GRESS, ANNIE M	21 JUN 1885	12:187
WEISS, CHRISTOPHER & BAUMGARTNER, BARBARA	30 AUG 1903	10:343
WEISS, JOHN & TROEGER, LORENA	29 APR 1902	10:066
WEISS, NICK & KNIGHT, CLARA	05 NOV 1909	12:527
WELCH, HARRY & LEMLEY, MINNIE	31 MAR 1909	12:393
WELCH, HARRY & RUSK, ETTIE	24 MAY 1897	08:096
WELCH, HARRY & UHRIG, LOTTIE M	03 JUL 1905	11:124
WELCH, JOHN & BEHAN, JANE	03 MAR 1867	05:033
WELCH, LONZO L & CHAPMAN, FLORENCE M	16 JUL 1910	13:111
WELCH, MARTIN & MURRY, MARY A	*27 APR 1858	02:011
WELKER, ELMER OAKLEY & PLANTZ, MAGGIE	21 JAN 1909	12:353
WELKER, O M & HOWARD, BERTHA M	12 APR 1911	13:307
WELLMAN, WM T P & MASON, BIRTA D	25 DEC 1911	13:445
WELLS, CURRELUS & MOODY, CELIA	16 MAY 1889	05:400
WELLS, HARRY R & BURKS, BONNIE B	06 JUN 1906	11:333
WELLS, HOWARD B & SAUNDERS, EMELIA	07 JAN 1901	09:284
WELLS, JAMES S & CLARKE, MARY ALICE	04 MAY 1898	08:299
WELLS, WILLIAM O B & BUFFINGTON, ORPHALINA	13 APR 1869	06:046
WELTON, CHARLES H & KENNEDY, MAGGIE L	23 SEP 1874	08:160
WERNER, JOHN A & SAYRE, ANNIE	16 DEC 1903	10:430
WESLEY, WILLIAM & SHIVELY, HENRIETTA	12 MAR 1889	05:367
WESSON, BRYAN A & FRAZIER, LUELLA	17 APR 1895	07:289
WESSON, WALTER & MUMAW, LYDIA	12 NOV 1874	08:055
WEST, WILLIAM C & PARKER, KATE A	13 APR 1871	07:075
WESTFALL, JOHN McKEE & COMSTOCK, KATHRYN VINCENT	22 JUN 1909	12:436
WESTFALL, NOAH & McKEE, MARGARET	29 JUL 1871	07:104
WESTFALL, STEPHEN & MORRISON, BETSY	18 JUL 1818	01:005
WESTFALL, WILSON & MARVEN, CATHARINE	12 NOV 1826	01:015
WETHEE, JEFF & PEARSON, SOPHIA R	18 FEB 1872	07:193
WETHERHOLT, ARBY & JEFFERS, OTTIE M	04 OCT 1903	10:381
WETSEL, WILLIAM & McCOY, SARAH	09 AUG 1810	01:003
WETZEL, ALBERT R L & HENSLEY, MARY J S	19 JAN 1871	07:044

Names	Date	Ref
WETZEL, EZEKIEL C & DAVIS, MALINDA	05 OCT 1865	04:058
WETZEL, FRANCIS M & SHOWALTER, ELIZABETH	12 OCT 1870	07:010
WETZEL, PERRY & OVERSHINER, ELISA A	07 MAY 1840	01:035
WETZEL, RICHARD D & FRY, SUSAN E	14 JUN 1881	10:421
WETZEL, WILLIAM E & MILLER, FANNY E	*10 DEC 1851	02:001
WEYGAND, CARL & ROCK, ALMA	19 DEC 1897	08:216
WHALEY, CHARLES M & DUVALL, ANNIE	10 SEP 1893	06:598
WHALEY, FULTON M & DOTSON, SARAH J	14 NOV 1880	10:328
WHALEY, HARLAN L & KARRICK, JENNIE M	07 JUN 1877	09:097
WHARF, THOMAS L & PROSE, JENNIE	06 OCT 1908	12;281
WHEALDON, DANA & BURFORD, EVA LUCINDA	09 DEC 1908	12:323
WHEATLEY, CHARLES WILLIAM & HUMPHREY, NORA	01 JUN 1907	11:541
WHEATLEY, HENRY & GABBERT, ELLA C	21 MAY 1874	08:122
WHEATLEY, LEWIS OTMER FLEET & REED, IDA FRANCES	23 NOV 1905	11:208
WHEATLEY, THOMAS & ROUSH, HANNAH	13 AUG 1868	05:201
WHEATON, EDGAR H & STARKEY, ANNIE M	21 DEC 1898	08:439
WHEATON, HERSCHEL E & SCHWARZ, MARTHA JOSEPHINE	26 JAN 1914	15:131
WHEATON, JOHN F & STURGEON, MARY	23 DEC 1903	10:439
WHEELDON, WILLIAM BURTON & LIVINGSTON, ESTER	17 AUG 1909	12:481
WHEELER, CHARLES C & YAUGER, MARY FLORENCE	15 NOV 1891	06:226
WHEELER, CICERO J & METHENA, ELSIE	01 APR 1908	12:152
WHEELER, DELLA & BARNETT, BERTHA	04 NOV 1890	05:637
WHEELER, GEORGE D & HUMPHREYS, (Mrs) ORA	27 MAY 1914	15:202
WHEELER, JOSEPH & McNAUGHTON, SARAH V	30 MAR 1870	06:173
WHEELER, ROBERT & TATE, ADDIE	07 DEC 1906	11:467
WHEELER, SAMUEL & CARTRIGHT, IRENE V	15 OCT 1907	12:042
WHEELER, SHERMAN A & HANNAN, ALLIE	14 SEP 1907	12:009
WHEELER, THOMAS J & KENNEDY, ELIZABETH R	02 APR 1871	07:070
WHEELER, WILLIAM R & RAYBURN, MARY	20 AUG 1865	04:043
WHEELER, WILLIAM V L & BEATTY, MELISSA	*25 FEB 1855	02:006
WHEELER, WILLIAM V L & ROLLINS, NANCY	10 DEC 1863	03:148
WHETZEL, MARTIN M & McDANIEL, MARGARET E	30 MAR 1893	06:513
WHIPKEY, JOHN & CARROLL, MERTY MELISSA	24 JUL 1887	05:057
WHIPKEY, JOHN & WOOTEN, LUCRETIA	21 DEC 1891	06:254
WHITE, C W & STEWART, ZILPHA R	05 NOV 1863	03:141
WHITE, CHARLES & COX, ERNESTINE	05 NOV 1902	10:185
WHITE, EVERETT E & VENOY, ELECTA	30 DEC 1902	10:222
WHITE, EVERET E & DAULTON, ELZANA	06:APR 1907	11:514
WHITE, FARBANN C & BAHR, DESSIE D	15 AUG 1904	10:575
WHITE, FREDRICK St ELMO & PORTER, MAYME	20 MAR 1901	09:307
WHITE, HENDERSON & DAVIS, ROSANNA	*21 DEC 1850	02:001
WHITE, HENRY C & SCHOOLS, LULA E	30 OCT 1904	10:625
WHITE, HENRY M & SNELL, NANNIE	09 MAR 1870	06:159
WHITE, JAMES H & TAYLOR, FRANCES	12 MAR 1874	08:104
WHITE, JNO J & PEASE, ELIZABETH	*01 JAN 1858	02:010
WHITE, JOHN H & BURNETT, L PEARL	30 DEC 1897	08:227
WHITE, JOSEPH & CLONCH, BETSY J	14 DEC 1899	09:031
WHITE, LATEN A & TAYLOR, SELENA L E	09 JAN 1895	07:233
WHITE, LEONARD & GUY, (Mrs) MARTHA	07 JUN 1913	14:147
WHITE, LINDLEY R & McCOLLISTER, ELLEN	07 NOV 1877	09:153
WHITE, NICHOLAS LEONARD & LIVEZEY, FANNIE M	31 AUG 1892	06:391
WHITE, OVERTON C & McADAMS, CHRISTINA M	29 MAY 1890	05:565
WHITE, R W & ALEXANDER, MAMIE L	11 OCT 1900	09:220
WHITE, ROSS & RUTHERFORD, MAUDE	02 MAY 1910	13:055
WHITE, WILLIAM & DEBOLT, CHARITY A	08 JUN 1865	04:015
WHITE, WILLIAM W & KOPP, KATIE	01 MAY 1887	05:017
WHITECOTTON, JAMES & CASTO, SARAH	10 MAR 1831	01:023
WHITENTON, WILLIAM & TILLIS, MELINDA	01 NOV 1827	01:015

Names	Date	Ref
WHITING, TRACY R & VINEY, AUGUSTA	09 JUN 1898	08:319
WHITMORE, MARTIN & BRYSON, PATSY	26 MAR 1829	01:019
WHITNEY, GEORGE W & TAYLOR, ELIZABETH	05 APR 1884	12:001
WHITT, BOYD & LEPORT, POLLY	04 OCT 1905	11:182
WHITT, JOHN C & MASON, HANNAH	15 APR 1912	13:514
WHITT, WILLIAM A & HUGHES, BETTIE	07 JUN 1892	06:349
WHITTEN, JOHN LAMAR & GWINN, MARY RACHEL	18 APR 1888	05:210
WHITTEN, JOHN W & CAMPBELL, MELINDA A	*16 DEC 1859	02:013
WHITTICO, C T & ALEXANDER, IDA E	29 NOV 1913	15:080
WHITTINGTON, ALBERT & TUCKER, MAHALA ELIZABETH	11 APR 1888	05:206
WHITTINGTON, ALBERT & TAYLOR, (Mrs) MOLLIE	30 AUG 1909	12:489
WHITTINGTON, ALFRED & COLEMAN, SARAH ELIZABETH	30 SEP 1887	05:109
WHITTINGTON, ALFRED & DOWELL, ALICE	04 AUG 1894	07:128
WHITTINGTON, CHARLES M & TUCKER, ALTA	02 MAY 1906	11:307
WHITTINGTON, GEORGE W & SANDERS, GERTIE B	15 AUG 1902	10:129
WHITTINGTON, HENRY C & TUCKER, MARY	18 NOV 1900	09:239
WHITTINGTON, HILLIARY & McCALL, LAURA	31 JUL 1892	06:381
WHITTINGTON, JAMES R & EADS, DELLA	12 MAR 1896	07:511
WHITTINGTON, JAMES R & McDERMITT, LOTTIE	08 SEP 1896	07:606
WHITTINGTON, JOHN & COLEMAN, VIRGIE	19 MAR 1901	09:306
WHITTINGTON, JOHN W & RIFFLE, LYDIA	11 JUN 1865	04:016
WHITTINGTON, JOHN W & KINCADE, LOUISA	16 JAN 1890	05:511
WHITTINGTON, JOSHUA & HOOVER, MARY	14 SEP 1896	07:609
WHITTINGTON, LAWRENCE L & JONES, RETHA A	25 OCT 1911	13:401
WHITTINGTON, MATTHEW A & RIFFLE, EVELINE	19 FEB 1863	03:102
WHITTINGTON, RICHARD & LEGG, SARAH F	24 MAY 1881	10:417
WHITTINGTON, RICHARD & LEGUE, ELNORA C	04 JUN 1895	07:314
WHITTINGTON, WILLIAM & BEASLEY, ELIZA	1840	01:041
WHITTINGTON, WILLIAM & McCOY, ELIZABETH	23 FEB 1871	07:063
WHITTINGTON, WILLIAM F & BUCKNER, SUSAN C	06 FEB 1863	03:099
WHITZGALL, CHRISTOPHER & DEAL, CATHARINE	23 NOV 1867	05:061
WIANT, FRENCH & HARTLESS, LIDE	24 MAR 1892	06:310
WIANT, JOHN & CONRAD, NANCY	12 MAY 1839	01:032 5
WIATT, JOHN W & ROSEBERRY, FLORA A	*10 MAY 1852	02:002
WIATT, SAMUEL T & BLACKWELL, CATHARINE A	13 NOV 1839	01:033
WICKLINE, EDWIN F & GWINN, MARTINA	16 NOV 1904	10:638
WIGHTMAN, FRANCIS A & BUTLER, CORDELIA E	16 APR 1882	11:139
WILBERT, HARRY & RHOADES, FANNIE	24 JUN 1906	11:349
WILCOXEN, ANTHONY & McCLURE, EMILY J	01 DEC 1870	07:025
WILCOXEN, FRANK & DURST, ALTA	18 NOV 1883	11:424
WILCOXON, ALPHA D & SELBY, MINNIE	24 JUN 1902	10:095
WILCOXON, JOHN S & SINES, ABIGAIL	26 JAN 1864	03:156
WILCOXON, MOLBY & WEDGE, MEARLA	24 MAR 1907	11:507
WILDING, GEORGE C & HALL, MARY JANE	19 NOV 1868	05:227
WILDMAN, HIRAM & SAVINE, HANNAH	26 JUL 1870	06:210
WILDMAN, REES & KING, ANN E	15 DEC 1880	10:339
WILEY, ABRAHAM & WILLIS, MARY ANN	22 AUG 1867	05:072
WILEY, MATTHEW A & WOODALL, REBECCA J	12 JAN 1878	09:192
WILEY, ORIN M & MESSICK, ELIZABETH C	20 DEC 1866	05:010
WILEY, RANKIN, Jr & MILLER, BLANCHE C	17 SEP 1879	10:129
WILEY, ROBERT & McCALLISTER, MARY	25 MAY 1826	01:013
WILEY, WILLIAM T & HARROLD, MARY E	13 OCT 1875	08:287
WILEY, WILLIAM THOMAS & BALL, MILLIE CATHARINE	24 OCT 1893	06:630
WILHELM, RAYMOND HERMAN & SMITH, BESSIE RUTH	26 DEC 1926	15:354
WILKES, OWEN LESLIE & SHUMARD, VIRGINIA MARGARET	16 SEP 1914	15:273
WILKINS, MAJOR & FISHER, SARAH	18 APR 1881	10:400
WILKINSON, JAMES E & KELLY, IDA E	25 NOV 1874	08:189
WILL, HOMER H & DIEHL, LONA M	16 DEC 1908	12:331

WILLARD, JAMES M & DRAKE, MARY E	11 MAR 1880	10:223
WILLIAMS, A J & WALKER, EMILY	*05 DEC 1859	02:013
WILLIAMS, AARON & BOOKER, MARGARET	31 JAN 1897	08:040
WILLIAMS, ALLEN & TICE, WILLIE	13 DEC 1875	08:306
WILLIAMS, ARCHIBALD & McINTIRE, MARY	28 JAN 1836	01:030
WILLIAMS, ARTHUR J & SAYRE, MARY	14 APR 1910	13:043
WILLIAMS, AUGUSTUS B & SNYDER, SARAH B	06 OCT 1870	07:009
WILLIAMS, BALLARD P & CASTO, SARAH B	20 JAN 1897	08:033
WILLIAMS, BOYD & BURGIN, LAVINIA	03 JUL 1867	05:065
WILLIAMS, CASWELL & PAINE, SOPHA	14 SEP 1870	06:227
WILLIAMS, CASWELL & PAINE, SOPHIA	14 SEP 1870	07:005
WILLIAMS, CHARLES C & HAYNES, LULU	17 AUG 1894	07:138
WILLIAMS, CHARLES GREENLEE & WEBB, MARY MELISSA	20 OCT 1881	11:034
WILLIAMS, CHARLES M & DAVIS, ELLA	06 DEC 1898	08:427
WILLIAMS, CHRISTOPHER & HARPER, JANIE	25 OCT 1899	09:001
WILLIAMS, CLARENCE & GOWER, LIZZIE	28 JUL 1903	10:328
WILLIAMS, CLARENCE A & STEWART, MYRTLE M	11 NOV 1914	15:321
WILLIAMS, FIELDING & HARRIS, REBECCA	01 DEC 1898	08:421
WILLIAMS, GENERAL E & THORNTON, NORA	08 OCT 1905	11:186
WILLIAMS, GENERAL W & KIMBERLING, NANCY	02 APR 1879	10:071
WILLIAMS, GEORGE G & DOLMAN, ELLA	28 OCT 1885	12:245
WILLIAMS, GEORGE S & SAYRE, CORA D	02 APR 1892	06:319
WILLIAMS, HARRY J & McKNIGHT, MARY E	18 AUG 1904	10:578
WILLIAMS, HENRY & HALE, MARY	24 OCT 1909	12:545
WILLIAMS, HUGH E & GEBHART, EVA NORMA	19 OCT 1910	13:187
WILLIAMS, IRA & FORBUS, MARY M	29 APR 1880	10:250
WILLIAMS, JAMES & SANDERS, MARY	27 NOV 1890	06:014
WILLIAMS, JAMES H & BARNETT, HANNAH	25 JUL 1839	01:034
WILLIAMS, JAMES IRA & BALL, SARAH ELIZABETH	24 DEC 1891	06:249
WILLIAMS, JEFFERSON & KIMBERLING, SARAH F	18 AUG 1863	03:128
WILLIAMS, JOHN & BUMGARNER, MARGARET	31 DEC 1835	01:030
WILLIAMS, JOHN & MORGAN, ELIZABETH	*30 OCT 1857	02:010
WILLIAMS, JOHN & RIGGS, MARY J	*02 JUL 1875	08:254
WILLIAMS, JOHN & BUMGARNER, EMILY S	10 OCT 1877	09:138
WILLIAMS, JOHN & PIERSON, HANNAH	25 FEB 1880	10:214
WILLIAMS, JOHN F & MILLER, ALICE	27 FEB 1876	08:327
WILLIAMS, JOHN F & TILLIS, ALICE	27 DEC 1903	10:446
WILLIAMS, JOHN L & MORRISON, REBECCA L	29 OCT 1903	10:395
WILLIAMS, JOHN R & LANIER, SUSAN F	*03 NOV 1851	02:002
WILLIAMS, JOHN WILLIAM & WOODYARD, SARAH	*22 DEC 1856	02:009
WILLIAMS, JOHN WILLIAM & JOHNSON, PHOEBE ANNIE	13 NOV 1889	05:479
WILLIAMS, JOHN Z & NUCKLES, MARTHA	07 APR 1889	05:377
WILLIAMS, LASLEY & LUTTON, MARY	25 JAN 1887	12:472
WILLIAMS, LEWIS O & KESSEL, LUCY	*27 JAN 1910	12:598
WILLIAMS, LEWIS V & ECKARD, LUCY J	06 NOV 1886	12:417
WILLIAMS, LLEWELLYN & FOWLER, LILA	04 FEB 1906	11:254
WILLIAMS, MARTIN W & McCOY, CHRISTENIA F	09 NOV 1879	10:160
WILLIAMS, MASSINIA BIRD & WILLIAMS, MARY	06 OCT 1887	05:115
WILLIAMS, ROY M A & DEWITT, EDITH C	27 NOV 1901	09:459
WILLIAMS, RUFUS W & DIVES, LELIE	07 JUN 1896	07:562
WILLIAMS, SAMUEL & SHIELDS, ELLA	31 DEC 1888	05:333
WILLIAMS, THOMAS & AYLER, SARAH	11 SEP 1895	07:380
WILLIAMS, THOMAS R & WOLF, DOROTHY	01 DEC 1861	03:335
WILLIAMS, THOMAS Z & SAYRE, ELLEN	04 FEB 1886	12:291
WILLIAMS, WILLIAM & CLONCH, SARAH	04 JAN 1832	01:025
WILLIAMS, WILLIAM & WHITTEN, SARAH M	14 MAR 1843	01:038
WILLIAMS, WILLIAM A & DEWEESE, DIANAH	01 MAR 1891	06:669
WILLIAMS, WILLIAM AUGUSTUS & HOWARD, NANNIE HELEN	20 SEP 1906	11:416

WILLIAMS, WILLIAM P & DIEFENBACH, ANNA M	25 APR 1883	11:328
WILLIAMS, WILLIAM R & EVANS, ELIZABETH	26 MAY 1877	09:082
WILLIAMS, WILLIAM T & GILES, MAGGIE	25 NOV 1897	08:206
WILLIAMS, WILLIAM T & BANKS, HATTIE	17 DEC 1905	11:226
WILLIAMS, WILLIAM THOMAS & WILLIAMS, ROSA	17 JUL 1887	05:559
WILLIAMS, WILLIS & STEPHENS, AMANDA	01 MAR 1892	06:300
WILLIAMS, WILLIS & PAGE, HARRIET	07 OCT 1897	08:170
WILLIAMSON, AARON H & MARTIN, LYDIA J	06 OCT 1888	05:286
WILLIAMSON, CHARLES & COLE, (Mrs) LUCINDA	*13 DEC 1854	02:006
WILLIAMSON, H C, Jr & HOFFMAN, IDA MAE	01 JUN 1912	13:536
WILLIAMSON, JAMES & WOYAN, BARBARA	27 JUL 1895	07:350
WILLIAMSON, L A & DENNY, LEONA M	07 AUG 1911	13:353
WILLIAMSON, ROBERT F & HAMILTON, MARGARET	01 OCT 1868	05:216
WILLIS, BENJAMIN M & ROUSH, ELIZABETH	25 JUL 1844	01;045
WILLIS, EARL & SMITH, MARGARET	23 NOV 1914	15:329
WILSON, ALEXANDER & BROWN, MARGARET E	01 AUG 1865	04:033
WILSON, CHARLES JOSEPH & VARIAN, MARY LEOTA	24 JUL 1912	13:570
WILSON, CHARLES Mc & CAVETT, ADA	28 AUG 1881	11:004
WILSON, CHARLES W & McDADE, MIRAM	17 SEP 1899	08:613
WILSON, DAVID & COBB, SARAH	22 SEP 1867	05:084
WILSON, EVERETT & KEEFER, MENERVA LOUIZA	02 MAY 1912	13:525
WILSON, EVERETT & PECK, VIRGIE	23 DEC 1913	15:100
WILSON, EZEKIEL H & BARNITT, MARY A	*31 JAN 1853	02:004
WILSON, FLOYD & RICE, CARRIE	30 APR 1906	11:303
WILSON, GEORGE W & ROLLINGS, ALCINDA	04 JUL 1844	01:042
WILSON, GEORGE W & CAVET, SARAH	24 DEC 1879	10:179
WILSON, GEORGE W & SPURLOCK, MARY	28 MAY 1897	08:102
WILSON, JAMES & TUCKER, EMILY ELIZABETH	*13 DEC 1855	02:007
WILSON, JAMES & DYER, ANN	02 DEC 1869	06:111
WILSON, JAMES E & RINE, ADDIE	29 JAN 1885	12:132
WILSON, JAMES E & TURLEY, NANNIE	24 DEC 1891	06:255
WILSON, JOHN & SANDERS, NANCY	11 SEP 1871	07:118
WILSON, JOHN R & FLORAY, JANNA J	03 JAN 1891	06:037
WILSON, JOHN R & ARMSTRONG, ISABELLE	02 MAR 1892	06:299
WILSON, JOHN S & ADAMS, BERTHA	20 JUN 1907	11:559
WILSON, JOHN W & ROUSH, IDA F	24 DEC 1878	10:029
WILSON, JOSEPH A & HENDERSON, ANNA E	27 OCT 1880	10:321
WILSON, LESTER & SHOLL, ELLEN	25 MAY 1912	13:533
WILSON, LINDEN R & SOMMER, VIOLA	25 NOV 1909	12:459
WILSON, LORENZO D & THOMPSON, ELIZABETH	13 MAR 1875	08:218
WILSON, N C & BROWN, LAURA J	17 MAR 1884	11:468
WILSON, NATHAN & ROLLINS, MINNIE F	23 NOV 1895	07:342
WILSON, PAT M & PULLIN, GRETCHEN	19 APR 1905	11:078
WILSON, PHILIP & MINTURN, ROXA	29 OCT 1888	05:295
WILSON, PHILIP & CHAPMAN, ANNIE	06 MAY 1900	09:124
WILSON, ROBERT & VANMATRE, MARY MAHALA	*14 MAY 1856	02:008
WILSON, ROBERT & CORBETT, BETTIE	17 AUG 1882	11:187
WILSON, ROBERT C & AUSTIN, LOTTIE C	22 FEB 1902	10:288
WILSON, SAMUEL T & JOHNSON, VIRGINIA	19 MAR 1868	04:159
WILSON, WALKER F & JONES, OLLIE	*09 MAY 1891	06:105
WILSON, WALTER & HILL, ORILLA	08 NOV 1896	07:637
WILSON, WILLIAM & POFFENBARGER, VIRGINIA	*06 FEB 1851	02:001
WILSON, WILLIAM & LOVE, MARY A	23 JUN 1872	07:241
WILSON, WILLIAM H & SISSON, ELLEN L	*18 MAR 1860	02:014
WILSON, WILLIAM H & WHITE, MARGRETTIE T	08 FEB 1902	10:021
WILSON, WILLIAM R & McKINNY, MIRANDA	02 JUL 1874	08:143
WILSON, WILLIAM S & MIDDLECOFF, SARAH E	30 SEP 1847	01:047
WILT, CHARLES & SHOEMAKER, HATTIE	13 DEC 1910	13:225

Name	Date	Ref
WILT, JOHN P & RUSSELL, OLLIE H	23 AUG 1913	15:020
WINCHELL, CHARLES E & SAYLOR, CATHARINE A	30 MAY 1883	11:348
WINDLE, DANIEL & WORKMAN, FANNIE	24 JUL 1898	08:340
WINDLE, GEORGE W & SUMMERS, VIRGINIA	19 JUL 1870	06:207
WINDLE, JOHN H & WINDLE, REBECCA	02 SEP 1896	07:602
WINDON, ALBERT & CLONCH, ELIZABETH	19 APR 1860	02:014
WINDON, ALFRED & VANMATRE, MARIA JANE	*06 JAN 1852	02:002
WINDON, FRANCIS H & HENKLE, CAROLINE H	12 NOV 1844	01:044
WINDON, FRANCIS H & HOGG, ELIZABETH	26 MAY 1856	02:008
WINDON, GORA B & KEARNS, MAGGIE	04 AUG 1913	15:003
WINDON, HENRY & WATKINS, JANE	24 MAY 1821	01:009
WINDON, HENRY & MITCHELL, MARGARET	18 JUL 1829	01:019
WINDON, JAMES & ADAMS, MARGARY	11 NOV 1841	01:037
WINDON, JAMES W & WINDON, MATTIE J	07 JAN 1869	06:026
WINDON, JAMES & MORROW, OLIVE	20 JUN 1889	05:417
WINDON, JOHN W & HOGG, MARY LUCY	*26 OCT 1857	02:010
WINDON, JOHN W & CLENDINEN, JANE	18 NOV 1869	06:117
WINDON, JOSEPH & MITCHELL, SUSAN	20 NOV 1828	01:018
WINDON, JOSEPH H & WINDON, RHODA J	19 APR 1865	04:116
WINDON, JOSEPH H & LEWIS, DELILAH S	31 DEC 1882	11:287
WINDON, JOSEPH S & SHIRLEY, LORENA	30 DEC 1908	12:344
WINDON, SAMUEL & HOGG, ARABELLA J	13 JAN 1840	01:035
WINDON, THOMAS & HOGG, PATSEY	30 JAN 1862	03:044
WINDON, WILLIAM J & TERRY, MARY B	19 JAN 1893	06:471
WINDON, WILLIAM J & CRAWFORD, HARRIET M	27 JUL 1902	10:120
WINDSOR, WILLIAM B & WILEY, AMERICA J	08 DEC 1865	04:083
WINE, ADAM & CHESTER, ADDIE F	24 DEC 1884	12:101
WINE, JAMES & BUSH, SARAH A	27 SEP 1838	01:031.5
WINE, JAMES & FOWLER, MARGARET	SEP 1840	01:034
WINE, JOHN F & OLINGER, CAROLINE	29 AUG 1879	10:120
WINE, PRESLEY & SPIRES, ANNA	22 FEB 1869	06:037
WINEBRENER, JOHN MONROE & SMITH, MINNIE BELLE	23 DEC 1891	06:256
WINEBRENNER, ALEXANDER H & BOLES, ISABELLA	09 APR 1868	05:167
WINEBRENNER, JOHN W & GRIMM, MARY J	04 APR 1897	08:070
WINES, JAMES W & HESS, LUCY L	08 SEP 1906	11:405
WINES, WILLIAM V & WARD, MARY E	20 AUG 1884	12:047
WINGER, SAMUEL C & RIFFLE, MARY JANE	20 FEB 1868	05:143
WINGER, WILLIAM W & MACHIR, CARRIE F	21 FEB 1894	07:051
WINGET, ALVIN A & GRAY, JANE	14 SEP 1908	12:261
WINGET, CHARLES F & BOLES, MARY B	05 MAR 1899	08:480
WINGO, ALKANA G & KINGRY, NANCY ELIZABETH	02 JUL 1867	05:066
WINKLER, ASHER J & McCARTHY, MARGARET E	08 NOV 1905	11:201
WINKLER, PEARL J & EDINGTON, BELLE	16 SEP 1909	12:505
WINTER, HENRY & REITMIRE, ANNA	13 APR 1893	06:523
WINTERS, RICHARD & HOPKINS, NANNIE	23 NOV 1881	11:060
WINTERS, WILLIAM H & PAGE, MARGARET	11 AUG 1872	07:253
WIRES, JAMES W & HESS, LUCY L	08 SEP 1906	11:405
WIRT, CALEB T & BOOTH, BETHLEHAM	10 JUL 1876	08:368
WIRTH, WILLIAM & HORTON, ELIZABETH	08 JUN 1867	05:055
WISE, D W & MIDDLECOFF, ANNETTA B	28 AUG 1911	13:365
WISE, DAVID BAILEY & HOLLEY, MARY E	30 OCT 1885	12:243
WISE, GILBERT V & DUFFY, LILLIE B	07 JUN 1913	14:171
WISE, HAMILTON & PRIDDY, ALLSONA M	16 NOV 1881	11:052
WISE, JAMES A & CARROL, PARTHENA	28 MAR 1875	08:222
WISE, JOHN & GARLAND, ADA C	31 JAN 1897	08:038
WISECARVER, FRANCIS P & KEISER, ANTOINETTE	07 FEB 1906	11:261
WISEMAN, JOHN & RAYBURN, ELLA	24 DEC 1882	11:274
WISEMAN, JOHN & MITCHELL, MARY E	21 OCT 1884	12:078

WITHEE, MORRIS E & KENNEY, MARY L	01 JAN 1899	08:447
WITHERS, A L & BUDGET, MILDRED V	*26 MAR 1884	11:475
WITHERS, BENJAMIN F & BARKER, EMILY	*15 OCT 1860	02:014
WITHERS, CHARLES A & WALLACE, SARAH ANN	15 JUL 1866	04:140
WITHERS, COLUMBUS & MORRIS, SARAH JANE	05 JAN 1865	03:215
WITHERS, EDGAR D & CROSSLEY, SARAH	19 DEC 1889	05:495
WITHERS, EDWARD A & BEHAN, MARY F	05 AUG 1867	05:071
WITHERS, EDWIN LAFAYETTE & HEREFORD, MARY EVELINE	*21 APR 1887	05:212
WITHERS, ESOM & MORRISON, MAY	06 SEP 1887	05:091
WITHERS, GABRIEL WILLIAM & LOCKHARD, MARY ANN	11 JAN 1887	12:459
WITHERS, JACOB & NEIGHBERT, NANCY	14 APR 1818	01:004
WITHERS, JACOB W & WOOTEN, MATILDA	12 MAR 1876	08:337
WITHERS, JAMES & LOCKHART, DORIS	25 DEC 1889	05:503
WITHERS, JEFF & MORRISON, SALLIE	23 JUL 1899	08:586
WITHERS, JOHN M & GEORGE, SARAH ANN	*26 JAN 1858	02:010
WITHERS, JOHN M & JACKSON, LILLIE M	23 SEP 1914	15:279
WITHERS, JOSEPH F & HILL, NANCY G	02 AUG 1877	09:113
WITHERS, ROBERT EDGAR & YOUNG, MARY DORCAS	12 DEC 1891	06:245
WITHERS, SPENCER G & LONG, MARY E	07 AUG 1890	05:596
WITHERS, W F & McCALLISTER, ANNA E	04 DEC 1889	05:488
WITHERS, WALTER J & KIESTER, WILLA E	09 NOV 1907	12:063
WITHROW, E H & McGRAW, IVY	18 DEC 1883	11:437
WITT, ANDREW J & PAULIN, MARY J	27 SEP 1877	09:133
WOGAN, WILLIAM & CLAGG, HOLLIE ANN	07 MAR 1897	08:056
WOLF, ALLEN & KRIBS, CLARA B	02 OCT 1902	10:168
WOLF, ANDERSON & WALLER, SARAH	1838	01:032
WOLF, ARTHUR E & CLENDENIN, JENNIE	16 JAN 1909	12:352
WOLF, CHARLES & JORDAN, MAGGIE	27 AUG 1889	05:436
WOLF, CHARLES & MITCHELL, DORA	02 OCT 1898	08:374
WOLF, CHARLES & GENHEIMER, ADA	15 SEP 1905	11:171
WOLF, CHARLES MASON & JIVIDEN, ETHEL MABEL	10 JAN 1900	09:060
WOLF, DANIEL W & BENNETT, LAURA D	05 MAY 1898	07:296
WOLF, DAVID & DEWEESE, ABIGAIL	*28 DEC 1860	02:015
WOLF, F M & ROUSH, V J	23 DEC 1886	12:448
WOLF, GEORGE & CRITES, ELIZABETH	26 FEB 1830	01:022
WOLF, GEORGE & VARIAN, MARTHA MALINDA	13 MAR 1838	01:031 5
WOLF, HENRY & WAUGH, CATHARINE	20 MAR 1873	07:334
WOLF, HENRY & OLINGER, MARY C	15 SEP 1880	10:300
WOLF, HENRY S & SULLIVAN, GEORGEANNA	29 MAR 1891	06:090
WOLF, ISRAEL & COULTER, MARY J	20 MAY 1995	07:307
WOLF, JESSE & PARSON, CATHARINE	06 JAN 1825	01:012
WOLF, JOHN & WOLF, BARBARA	24 FEB 1814	01:004
WOLF, JOHN H & HILL, LIZZIE	17 APR 1895	07:282
WOLF, JOHN PERRY & ROUSH, ADA Z	26 AUG 1886	12:379
WOLF, JOHN W & BRIGHT, ELLA B	27 DEC 1881	11:087
WOLF, JONAS & VARIAN, JOANNA	12 MAY 1836	01:030
WOLF, MALLORY & HILL, MARY M	23 FEB 1865	03:224
WOLF, MILLARD & RIFFLE, MOLLIE A	07 MAR 1894	07:057
WOLF, MORGAN & PARSONS, JESSIE	05 JUL 1894	07:113
WOLF, NOAH L & ESKEW, VIRGIE L	08 AUG 1900	09:172
WOLF, PETER & BOWLES, MATILDA	28 OCT 1871	07:136
WOLF, ROBERT ANDERSON & MORRIS, ELVIRA	24 AUG 1887	05:078
WOLF, ROBERT K & ADAMS, IVA M	22 AUG 1895	07:368
WOLF, STEPHEN W & WARDEN, VIRGINIA E	20 DEC 1876	09:003
WOLF, WILLIAM & RICE, ELLA	27 JUL 1871	07:102
WOLF, WILLIAM & STEWART, RACHEL A	02 DEC 1877	09:162
WOLFE, ANDREW J & CHICK, GERTRUDE M	19 SEP 1907	12:013
WOLFE, CHARLES M & CROOKHAM, LUCY	23 MAY 1908	12:180

WOLFE, CHARLES RAY & GERLACH, LONA LEONORA	17 SEP 1910	13:161
WOLFE, EARLIE & PICKENS, MINNIE	23 DEC 1900	09:255
WOLFE, GEORGE M & BEATTIE, LAURA M	05 NOV 1913	15:064
WOLFE, IRA & ORD, ADDIE F	17 DEC 1910	13:227
WOLFE, JOHN & SOWERS, (Mrs) VINA	05 MAY 1910	13:059
WOLFE, JOHN & KING, CLARA MABEL	22 DEC 1911	13:440
WOLFE, L E & ROLLINS, INA	05 APR 1910	13:039
WOLFE, WILBERT WESLEY & CAMPBELL, MARIETTA	11 NOV 1888	05:304
WOLFE, WILLIAM ALEXANDER & ROUSH, GENORA	04 JUL 1889	05:423
WOLFE, WM C & MULFORD, AMY I	21 DEC 1910	13:232
WOLFORD, DAVID & ASHWORTH, EARIE	05 NOV 1899	09:005
WOLFORD, GEORGE & CREMEENS, JENNIE F	30 JAN 1895	07:243
WOLFORD, GEORGE WILLIAM & MEADOWS, MALINDA SUSAN	22 SEP 1889	05:457
WOLFORD, JAMES W & VILLARS, ONA A	07 APR 1901	09:319
WOLFORD, JAMES WESLEY & HALL, FRANCES	18 MAY 1890	05:559
WOLFORD, JOHN & POWELL, NORA	12 JUL 1899	08:576
WOLFORD, PHILIP & BLAKE, CORA B	30 NOV 1910	13:218
WOLFORD, SYLVESTER & HUPP, REBECCA	25 MAR 1883	11:314
WOLFORD, WILLIAM & TAYLOR, SARAH	10 JUL 1884	12:036
WOMELDORFF, HOWARD R & SWINK, AUGUSTA V	05 AUG 1886	12:370
WOMELSDORFF, JAMES W & HARDWICK, WILLIA A	14 FEB 1875	08:212
WOMICK, THOMAS & ASHER, MARY	07 NOV 1882	11:247
WOOD, ELZA J & MARTIN, BESSIE A	27 JUN 1901	09:363
WOOD, FOUNTAIN & EADS, MARY A	01 FEB 1849	01:051
WOOD, HENRY M & EDMONDS, ROXIE	25 MAR 1901	09:312
WOOD, HERBERT & MARTIN, KATE	25 DEC 1894	07:223
WOOD, HOWARD D & DeWITT, DAISE	10 MAR 1914	15:153
WOOD, JAMES W & GREENLEE, ANNA C	09 MAR 1871	07:074
WOOD, JOHN & BOLES, REBECCA	21 NOV 1886	12:425
WOOD, JOHN P & McDANIEL, MARY ANN	27 FEB 1866	04:107
WOOD, JOSEPH & HORNBY, MANERVA	14 NOV 1912	14:027
WOOD, LEWIS A & SIDERS, JESSIE A	15 JAN 1899	08:453
WOOD, MASON ELSWORTH & BRANNON, MARY	21 SEP 1891	06:185
WOOD, WALTER A & WHITTINGTON, FLORA M	26 SEP 1907	12:022
WOOD, WILLIAM A & FIELDS, ADIE F	28 JUN 1883	11:360
WOOD, WILLIAM HOMER & RINE, LINNIE MAY	21 AUG 1887	05:074
WOODAL, JAMES & YEAGER, MARY	09 FEB 1837	01:031
WOODRUFF, ALBERT & HOPKINS, LAURENA	*02 OCT 1860	02:014
WOODRUFF, ALBERT & LONG, MARGARET M	12 APR 1864	03:174
WOODRUFF, WILLIAM J & WILSON, ELIZA F	06 NOV 1876	08:416
WOODRUM, ARCHIBALD & DAVIS, SARAH JANE	16 DEC 1866	05:009
WOODRUM, ARTHUR B & RAYBOULD, LUCY J	10 NOV 1901	09:442
WOODRUM, ISAAC & GARDNER, MARY M	*07 MAR 1859	02:012
WOODRUM, JOSEPH E & SMITH, ALICE M	17 NOV 1894	07:193
WOODRUM, RICHARD & RUSSELL, ELIZA	*24 JAN 1855	02:006
WOODRUM, RICHARD & WILSON, SARAH A	02 NOV 1871	07:141
WOODRUM, THOMAS & DRAKE, ZENIA	23 DEC 1889	05:498
WOODRUM, WILLIAM & RUNNION, MARY A	09 MAY 1874	08:121
WOODRUM, WILLIAM & COLLINS, NEELY	30 OCT 1881	11:042
WOODS, ABRAHAM & KINCADE, JANE	11 DEC 1840	01:035
WOODS, CHARLES A & BATEMAN, MAGGIE B	10 MAR 1895	07:265
WOODS, CHARLES E & LANIER, SARAH A	15 AUG 1894	07:133
WOODS, JAMES A & CIRCLE, FRANCES	27 JUN 1864	03:189
WOODS, JAMES A & CORN, ANNA CAROLINE	01 JAN 1868	05:133
WOODS, JAMES I & WINDLE, BERTHA	*14 MAY 1895	07:303
WOODS, JOHN E & LEWIS, LAURA	23 JUL 1881	10:430
WOODS, JOHN W & WALLIS, MARGARET J	18 OCT 1852	02:006
WOODS, JOSEPH W & YOHO, MARY E	28 JUN 1880	10:269

WOODS, OTTO H & KNAPP, NEVA A	25 DEC 1912	14:070
WOODS, ROBERT & RIPLEY, MARTHA J	05 AUG 1841	01:035
WOODS, WILLIAM & RAY, SARAH ANN	*04 DEC 1852	02:003
WOODS, WILLIAM F & LEMASTER, ELIZABETH	*19 AUG 1857	02:010
WOODS, WILLIAM R & HILL, ELIZA J	15 JAN 1880	10:199
WOODS, WINFIELD S & McKEOWN, MARY E	03 SEP 1882	11:196
WOODS, WM & ELLIOTT, (Mrs) MANDA	31 OCT 1912	14:021
WOODY, HENRY F & EGGENSCHWILLER, MARY	22 JUN 1898	08:323
WOODY, JOHN N & SIMMS, KATIE E	09 MAY 1894	07:088
WOODY, WILLIAM F & McGUIRE, ARMEDA A	06 SEP 1883	11:398
WOODY, WILLIAM G & SPURLOCK, MARY C	22 AUG 1875	08:258
WOODY, WILLIAM T & LEWIS, MEDORAH	13 JUN 1875	08:247
WOODYARD, JAMES I & BYUS, SALLIE M	14 MAR 1894	07:060
WOODYARD, SAUNDERS B & HEIB, CLARA A	04 JUL 1913	13:561
WOODYARD, WILLIAM C & ARTHUR, TELITHA F	11 MAY 1865	04:012
WOODYARD, WILLIAM HENRY & CHERRINGTON, ANNIE ELIZA	19 MAR 1893	06:504
WOOLFENBARGER, ANTONE & EDEN, DORA MAY	06 APR 1903	10:266
WOLLFINGBARGER, ANTONA & FLOWERS, VIOLA	10 MAR 1906	11:279
WOOLWEAVER, ALONZO & JOHNSON, LUCY	12 DEC 1908	12:324
WOOMER, BENJAMIN & OLIVER, MAMIE	14 OCT 1908	12:530
WOOTEN, ANDERSON & NIBERT, LUCRETIA	20 SEP 1873	07:262
WORK, ALBERT & GREEN, MINNIE	25 DEC 1890	06:033
WORKMAN, CHARLES & ROGERS, ANNA LEE	23 FEB 1911	13:277
WORKMAN, EBENEZER L & HILL, ELIZABETH I	*29 MAR 1859	02:012
WORKMAN, GEORGE & MARTIN, LAURA	20 AUG 1891	06:167
WORKMAN, MARION M & SUMMERS, (Mrs) L M	11 FEB 1910	13:009
WORKMAN, THOMAS R & HILL, NANCY A	20 APR 1893	06:525
WORLEY, JACOB H & KEARNS, ORA ELLEN	11 SEP 1909	12:501
WORLEY, JOHN P & ALESHIRE, MARY B	15 MAY 1862	03:062
WORLEY, ROBERT JOSEPH & NEALE, FLORENCE	16 OCT 1892	06:428
WORLEY, WILLIAM & HOGG, FLORA	08 APR 1875	08:229
WORRELL, JAMES M & DAVIS, SALVE	27 AUG 1874	08:155
WORTENBERG, GEORGE McCLELLAN & GILL, VICTORIA	16 OCT 1880	10:312
WORTHINGTON, CHARLES A & THOMAS, SARAH	01 MAY 1905	11:086
WORTHINGTON, FRANKLIN & CAMPBELL, LUCY A	*10 NOV 1860	02:014
WOSTER, CHARLES E & DOUGLAS, MARY A	16 DEC 1873	08:073
WOYAN, EDWARD & CRUMP, BLANCH	25 FEB 1814	15:147
WRAY, ALFORD W & CAIN, LINDA	21 JUN 1904	10:540
WRAY, ASA & JORDAN, CAROLINE	*26 DEC 1856	02:009
WRAY, CHARLES F & JORDAN, EDITH M	26 DEC 1911	13:453
WRAY, CREED F & WAUGH, MARY M	*05 DEC 1854	02:006
WRAY, FRANK & HUGHES, CORA	26 APR 1906	11:300
WRAY, GEORGE & WRIGHT, BERTHA	23 MAY 1905	11:094
WRAY, ISAAC M & BLAKE, ARAMINTA	24 OCT 1863	03:134
WRAY, JAMES D & PORE, CYNTHIA A	23 DEC 1883	11:440
WRAY, JAMES D & HOBBS, ELIZABETH	15 MAR 1896	07:512
WRAY, JAMES MONROE & WAUGH, ROWANNA	20 MAY 1879	10:093
WRAY, JOHN H & WAUGH, ELIZABETH	*27 OCT 1851	02:002
WRAY, JOHN H & CAISEY, JULIA E	16 NOV 1891	06:225
WRAY, JOHN W & PILLOWS, SALLIE S	23 DEC 1896	08:019
WRAY, TILMAN & HEREFORD, SARAH C	30 JAN 1850	01:051
WRAY, W T & CAIN, JULIA	22 SEP 1905	11:173
WRAY, WILLIAM & DUNCAN, MARY J	27 FEB 1880	10:218
WRAY, WILLIAM C & WAUGH, ELIZA	*17 SEP 1856	02:008
WRAY, WILLIAM E & CREMEENS, BESSIE L	10 MAR 1905	11:058
WRAY, WILLIAM ELLIS & DONALLY, ABBY	20 SEP 1899	08:614
WRIGHT, BENJAMIN & FLOWERS, MIRIAM	07 JUN 1827	01:020
WRIGHT, BENJAMIN & SMITH, LOVICA JANE	25 DEC 1889	05:504

WRIGHT, BRYANT & KING, CHARITY	05 FEB 1827	01:016
WRIGHT, CHARLES B & CASEY, BERTHA	07 AUG 1905	11:142
WRIGHT, CHARLES N & LANIER, LOUISA E	04 JUL 1895	07:333
WRIGHT, DANIEL & BLATCHLEY, MARY	18 JAN 1825	01:012
WRIGHT, DANIEL & BLATCHLEY, MARY	18 JAN 1825	01:014
WRIGHT, DAVID G & JEFFERSON, CORA	02 SEP 1900	09:183
WRIGHT, FRANK L & HART, ISABELLA R	17 OCT 1907	12:048
WRIGHT, FRED P & WRIGHT, EMMA	**24 MAY 1912	13:532
WRIGHT, GAD & SEBRIEL, BETSEY	01 NOV 1821	01:009
WRIGHT, GAD & SMITH, SARAH E	02 OCT 1862	03:082
WRIGHT, HENRY & KNAPP, BETSEY	(no date)	01:027
WRIGHT, HENRY & KNAPP, BETSY	1832	01:039
WRIGHT, JAMES B & WINKLEY, BEDA A	14 JAN 1880	10:198
WRIGHT, JAMES WESLEY & WALLACE, EMMAZETTA	22 FEB 1903	10:242
WRIGHT, JOHN & MONTGOMERY, NAOME	20 JAN 1825	01:011
WRIGHT, JOHN F & McCUNE, RACHAEL	21 NOV 1821	01:009
WRIGHT, JOSEPH & SETTLES, BESSIE E L	18 DEC 1901	09:471
WRIGHT, JOSEPH & MORRISON, CLEE O	*18 NOV 1908	12:310
WRIGHT, SAMUEL ROBERT WYATT & WOODS, MARY ANN	29 NOV 1888	05:312
WRIGHT, WILTON & HARMON, CORA A	20 NOV 1898	08:200
WRIGHT, WILTON & McCOY, DELIA	17 JAN 1914	15:127
WYATT, JOHN R & BUMGARNER, EMMA	16 OCT 1882	11:225
WYATT, JOSEPH W & WILSON, MARY A	20 MAY 1874	08:124
WYNE, JAMES DANIEL & WARNER, MAGGIE	23 FEB 1889	05:359
YARDLEY, CHARLES & INGHAM, ROMIE R	30 JUN 1886	12:348
YAUGER, ARTISAN & SINES, ALMEDA	30 JAN 1883	11:294
YAUGER, BAZALEEL & FULLNER, MARY	01 JAN 1872	07:175
YAUGER, HENRY & DARST, _____	*25 OCT 1852	02:003
YAUGER, JACKSON & GIBAUT, (Mrs) ELIZABETH	*24 SEP 1855	02:007
YAUGER, JEREMIAH, Jr & KINTZEL, ELMIRA	24 MAY 1893	06:539
YAUGER, PHILIP & LUTTON, SOPHIA	*10 AUG 1854	02:005
YEAGER, ALBERT & ECKARD, MARGARET ANN	30 SEP 1851	02:002
YEAGER, CHARLES A & ROUSH, ORILLA C	01 MAR 1883	11:306
YEAGER, DONNELLY H & CARDER, LAURA A	**09 DEC 1913	15:085
YEAGER, EDGAR B & EADS, MARY F	27 OCT 1897	08:182
YEAGER, GEORGE & KNAPP, PALMYRA	*08 MAR 1852	02:002
YEAGER, GEORGE NEWTON & WASHINGTON, MARY LOUISE	20 JUN 1888	05:237
YEAGER, ISAAC LINCOLN & BUMGARNER, JULIA ELIZABETH	28 DEC 1892	06:459
YEAGER, JACOB & BROWN, SALLY	10 APR 1834	01:028
YEAGER, JAMES S & FISHER, MARY L	14 NOV 1882	11:251
YEAGER, JAMES W & ROSEBERRY, HANNAH D	27 OCT 1870	07:018
YEAGER, JASPER B & McKOUN, ANNIE J	18 JUN 1874	08:130
YEAGER, JOSEPH & KINCADE, ISABELLA	12 DEC 1839	01:035
YEAGER, JOSEPH & CLENDENEN, DELILAH O	*14 DEC 1857	02:010
YEAGER, JOSEPH, Jr & ECKARD, BARBARA	12 FEB 1850	01:052
YEAGER, JOSEPH OSCAR & SEBRELL, MARGARET	12 APR 1888	05:205
YEAGER, LORENZO & RIFFLE, MARGARET ANN	*17 APR 1854	02:005
YEAGER, OWEN V & RAYBURN, ANNIE J	19 OCT 1898	08:391
YEAGER, PETER & WHITE, SUSAN F	03 JUL 1866	04:136
YEAGER, REED & BAKER, ADDIE	25 DEC 1878	10:023
YEAGER, ROBERT MILROY & QUILLEN, HARRIET LURA	29 MAR 1893	06:508
YEAGER, SOLOMON & FISHER, SUSANNA	06 JUL 1820	01:007
YEAGER, WILLIAM E & KIRKER, JESSIE	17 JUL 1907	11:580
YEAGER, WILLIAM E & SWON, CLAUDIA V	18 MAY 1910	13:068
YOCOM, RAY E & WILSON, GOLDIE L	29 DEC 1910	13:249
YONELL, JAMES & POTTS, MARGARET ANN	31 DEC 1865	04:092
YONKER, A H & DUNCAN, FANNIE	28 FEB 1904	10:481
YONKER, ABRAM, Jr & PHILLIPS, MARY W	18 JAN 1885	12:130

Name	Date	Ref
YONKER, CHARLEY & CUNDIFF, JESSIE	05 NOV 1914	15:314
YONKER, ED H & ROBINSON, IDA F	01 JAN 1885	12:116
YONKER, GEORGE M & McWILLIAMS, EXEVERIA	27 NOV 1886	12:428
YONKER, SAMUEL W & NEASE, SARAH F	13 MAR 1877	09:041
YONKER, W H & YONKER, LOVINA	07 MAR 1809	12:380
YONKER, WILLIAM HENRY & GOSSETT, LAVINIA FRANCES	14 FEB 1888	05:185
YOUNG, ADAM & LONGLUTZ, BARBARA	02 NOV 1882	11:237
YOUNG, ALBERT G & McGUIRE, DIMMIE	07 APR 1887	05:003
YOUNG, ALVA A & SMITH, SARAH A	20 OCT 1901	09:426
YOUNG, ANDREW G & MORRIS, MARY	*01 AUG 1857	02:010
YOUNG, ANDREW N & NANCE, LANEY A	27 MAR 1873	07:337
YOUNG, AUGUSTUS & WISE, REBECCA J	03 DEC 1868	06:010
YOUNG, AUGUSTUS & AUXIER, CARRIE	21 JAN 1891	06:048
YOUNG, BUD & HOFFMAN, OLIVIA NORTON	24 DEC 1903	10:445
YOUNG, CHARLES & LINKHART, CATHARINE	22 DEC 1913	15:103
YOUNG, CHARLES M & GIBSON, SYLVIA MAY	24 DEC 1913	15:103
YOUNG, CHARLES W & WILEY, MARGARETTA	15 MAY 1878	09:262
YOUNG, FLETCHER & CLARK, AURILLA J	21 MAR 1877	09:045
YOUNG, FRANK F & SPIES, CARRIE M	27 OCT 1909	12:585
YOUNG, FRED BRADBERRY & DUNN, LUTTIA BETTIE	14 NOV 1894	07:186
YOUNG, GEORGE & EDMONDS, NEVADA	06 MAY 1904	10:514
YOUNG, GEORGE D & BOOTH, DORA E	24 DEC 1900	09:260
YOUNG, GEORGE F & BARNETT, HADIE	29 OCT 1903	10:400
YOUNG, H B & GEARHART, ANNA	25 AUG 1910	13:142
YOUNG, JAMES CHARLES & SMITH, LAURA JANE	13 MAY 1900	09:128
YOUNG, JAMES M & CLAGG, CORA B	18 MAR 1896	07:515
YOUNG, JOHN & PARSONS, MARTHA	28 JAN 1888	05:180
YOUNG, JOHN ALBERT & BURGGESS, STELLA C	20 APR 1886	12:317
YOUNG, JOHN C & WISEMAN, MARY	03 OCT 1883	11:407
YOUNG, JOHN G & HAZLETT, LIZZIE	24 DEC 1905	11:231
YOUNG, JOHN H & CAMPBELL, VIRGINIA A	24 DEC 1882	11:277
YOUNG, JOHN S & BITGOOD, RUTH E	06 NOV 1878	10:002
YOUNG, JOHN W & McCOLLISTER, MARY J	*29 SEP 1859	02:013
YOUNG, JOSEPH F & LUTZ, MARY A	10 OCT 1907	12:036
YOUNG, LORENZO DOW & HIGINBOTHAM, LIZZIE	28 AUG 1889	05:439
YOUNG, PETER & JOCHIM, BETTIE	03 NOV 1881	11:038
YOUNG, ROBERT H & STEELE, NANCY E	10 AUG 1892	06:385
YOUNG, ROBERT MITCHELL & HALL, MARTHA ELIZABETH	11 JUL 1885	12:194
YOUNG, SIMEON & PEDEN, ALICE	*07 OCT 1876	08:395
YOUNG, SIMON & PADEN, ALICE	16 MAY 1880	10:259
YOUNG, THOMAS & McCALLISTER, SARAH M	08 FEB 1880	10:208
YOUNG, THURMAN O & KNAPP, FLORENCE	17 SEP 1910	13:162
YOUNG, WILLIAM & HOFFMAN, ROSETTA M	23 MAY 1908	12:183
YOUNGER, CHARLES & JOHNSON, CLARISSA J	09 APR 1864	03;177
ZEARLEY, ADONIRAM JUDSON & GEHO, IDA IRENE	17 DEC 1895	07:452
ZEIHER, HENRY & ZIRCKLE, DORCAS M	25 DEC 1899	09:043
ZEIHER, PETER & COLEMAN, HATTIE	13 SEP 1889	05:452
ZEIHER, PETER & COLEMAN, GEORGIA	03 FEB 1892	06:285
ZERCKEL, JOSEPH & NEASE, SUSANNA	29 MAY 1851	02:002
ZERCKEL, MICHAEL & CHAPMAN, MILLIE C	19 FEB 1875	08:211
ZERCKEL, WILLIAM S & CUNNINGHAM, CAROLINE	23 JUL 1876	08:370
ZERCKLE, HARVEY & GOODNIGHT, LYDIA	30 APR 1881	10:409
ZERKEL, HERMAN A & DODSON, SARAH F	28 DEC 1910	13:247
ZERKEL, LEWIS & ROUSH, FRANCES E	04 NOV 1889	06:101
ZERKEL, FRANK & CUNDIFF, DAISY	02 JUL 1913	14:191
ZERKLE, JAMES R & McMILLON, SARAH M	12 DEC 1883	11:433
ZERKLE, NEWTON & ROLLINS, ISA DORA	01 JUL 1900	09:152
ZERKLE, SAMUEL & YONKER, ELLEN J	16 JAN 1880	10:193

Names	Date	Ref
ZERKLE, THOMAS L & SAYRE, PEARL	23 SEP 1905	11:178
ZERKLE, W S & BUMGARNER, (Mrs) EMMA C	23 MAR 1913	14:112
ZERKLE, WILLIAM & EDWARDS, JOSIE	31 JUL 1879	10:104
ZERKLE, WILLIAM J & HOFFMAN, EMALIZA	02 JUN 1872	07:229
ZETIKE, JOSEPH & HARPOLD, ALICE V	20 SEP 1882	11:207
ZIEHER, FRANK & NICHOLSON, BESSIE	18 FEB 1906	11:268
ZIPPERICH, ZENO A & WESSON, EMMA B	05 JAN 1896	07:482
ZIRCKEL, EMERY H & ROLLER, MARY C	27 JUN 1883	11:363
ZIRCKEL, JAMES & NEASE, (Mrs) MARTHA MATILDA	*17 JUL 1853	02:004
ZIRCKEL, NOAH & BUMGARNER, NANCY	19 MAR 1840	01:043
ZIRCKEL, SAMUEL & TURNBULL, MARY A	09 SEP 1875	08:271
ZIRCKEL, HENRY & PARRY, HANNAH	28 DEC 1887	05:161
ZIRCKLE, WILLIAM & MEEKS, SOPHIA	13 NOV 1873	08:054
ZIRCLE, JOHN & HART, ELIZABETH	JAN 1843	01:037
ZIRCLE, JOSEPH & AUMILLER, SUSANNAH	27 MAY 1832	01:025
ZIRKEL, JOHN & HUTSON, PERMELIA	20 NOV 1864	03:208
ZIRKEL, MILLARD F & VAN MATRE, IDA MAY	06 JUL 1899	08:569
ZIRKEL, SHERMAN & CARTMILL, OTA B	16 SEP 1903	10:353
ZIRKLE, CURTIS & WINTER, EMMA	31 MAR 1902	10:046
ZIRZKALL, HENRY & MITCHELTREE, SARAH F	*17 OCT 1854	02:006
ZUSPAN, CHARLEY B & SOMERVILLE, ANNIE L	19 OCT 1882	11:227
ZUSPAN, EZRA J & HYLTON, BERTHA E	08 DEC 1892	06:452
ZUSPAN, FILLIE O & McMILLEN, ANNIE	01 JAN 1904	10:452
ZUSPAN, GEORGE W & HARRIS, FRANCES M	14 AUG 1881	11:001
ZUSPAN, GEORGE W & MARTIN, EMMA F	08 MAR 1906	11:278
ZUSPAN, HENRY A & HYLTON, MARY D	27 FEB 1885	12:143
ZWEIFEL, WILLIAM F C & STIVERS, EMMA	18 JUL 1906	11:369

Brides' Index for Mason County, West Virginia Marriages, 1806 – 1915

Name	Page		Name	Page
ABBOTT, REBECCA E	124		MAMIE C	106
ABRAMS, LIZZIE	44		MAMIE L	182
ABSTEN, CORA	165		MARGARET	89
NANNA A	70		MARY JANE	177
ORPHA	52		SARAH E	105
ABSTON, MAGGIE	91		ALFORD, ELIZABETH	177
NANCY	75		MARY	119
SUSAN T	24		MARY C	177
ACKLEY, EVA L	38		ALHANDS, BETTIE	60
ADAM, SARAH	118		ALINDER, REBECCA	69
ADAMS, ANNIE E	99		ALLEMONG, ALICE B	128
BERTHA	185		ALLEN, ANN E	49
EMMA	84		ANNA	114
ESTA	3		ANNIE	53
ESTHER	1		BERTHA E	25
EUDELIE ANN	180		BETSY	7
GERTRUDE J	21		EMMA	121
HELEN M	72		EMMA E	2
HESTER G	46		EMMA J	49
IVA M	187		ESTHER	70
JENNIE M	147		HARRIET L	143
LEILLIAN E	67		JENNIE	109
LOUISA	26		JOSIE	76
LUCY E	106		LUELLA	99
MARGARY	186		MINNIE M	8
MARY ANN	176		SARAH ELIZABETH	168
MARY J	40		ALLENDER, MARIE L	103
MARY M	95		ALLIN, MARTHA	87
MIRTIE M	145		ALLINDER, BLANCHE	115
ADDISON, MARGARET	67		FRIEDA MARIE	134
SALLIE	42		ALLIS, ALLISA	70
ADKINS, ANNIE	161		NELLIE	40
ANNIE E	123		ALLISON, MARIA	181
ELIZABETH	143		MARY	133
ELIZABETH	175		ALLSBURY, SOPHIA	69
ELOSHA E	31		ALMAN, KATHARINE	109
EMMA F	136		ALSBERRY, SARAH	173
GENERVA	2		ALTICE, ANNA	126
JANE F	21		AMSDEN, FANNIE E	77
MARY	79		AMES, RACHAEL	61
MARY	87		SARAH	90
MARY ANN	93		AMOS, ADALINE	161
NORA	7		ADELLA	16
ROSA A	91		DELILA	99
SARAH A	128		ELIZABETH	12
SARAH F	109		HALLIE	113
AICKER, EMMA B	105		HENNY	143
AILER, AMERICA	100		JEMIMA	177
ALDERMAN, LETHA A	26		MARY	84
OLLIE C	155		ROSIE	36
ALESHIRE, BETSY	118		AMOSS, DELILA	90
MARY B	189		JANE	10
SUSANNA	63		AMSBARRY, SARAH F	10
ALESTOCK, MARY	85		AMSBARY, AMELIA M	26
ALEXANDER, (Mrs) RUBY E	99		JANE	110
CARRIE	172		ROSETTA C	63
CATHARINE	164		RUTH	15
FRANCES	108		AMSBERRY, ELLA	71
FRANCES C	164		LAVINA	18
HATTIE C	179		MARGARET E	85
IDA E	183		MARIETTA	137
JULIAN	85		AMSDEN, ELVIRA	108
LILLIE B	29		SARAH A	171
LOUISA	87		AMSDON, JULIA	71

Name	Page
LUCY	119
ANDERSON, (Mrs) ELIZABETH	92
ANN	10
ELIZA B	132
EMMA S	123
FLORELLA H	112
ISABELLE	9
ISABELLE J	54
LUNIA	67
MARTHA	23
MARTHA	79
MARY	143
MARY S	130
NANCY	120
SARAH J	166
ANGEL, ALICE	25
LOUISA S	49
SALLY	115
ANGELL, EDNA E	102
ANGUISH, LAURA	3
ANKROM, MAGGIE	3
ANSEL, ELIZABETH	64
MAUD W	110
APPLETON, SUSAN	29
APPLEWHITE, LIZZIE	21
ARCHER, HAZLE	93
ARMSTEAD, EMMA BELLE	87
LETITIA	98
ARMSTRONG, ABBIE	22
DAISY M	49
ELIZABETH	33
EVE E	114
ISABELLE	185
MARGARET S	144
MARY A	146
ORA L	142
SARAH ALICE	160
SUSAN J	140
ARNDT, MARY H	14
ARNETT, ETHEL GRACE	57
ARNOLD, CLEO	89
EFFIE M	106
ELIZABETH	19
MARY GERTRUDE	60
MINNIE B	176
NAYOMA	66
PRICY A	45
SUSAN	8
ARTHUR, LENA	131
LUCINDA A	39
MARY A	130
NORA B	179
TELITHA F	189
ARY, JULIA A	93
ASBERRY, SARAH CATHARINE	62
SARAH E	156
ASBERY, FANNIE CAMPBELL	8
ASBURRY, EMMA	42
ASHBY, CLARA E	39
JOSEPHINE E	39
ASHER, MARY	188
ASHLEY, AMANDA	52
ASHWORTH, EARIE	188
CORA	79
MELVINA	176
OKEY	85
ASKEW, HARRIET	160
MARY J	104
ASTON, DULCEMA	74
ELIZABETH	66
ELIZABETH	98
HENRIETTA	55
MARIA	97
MARY A	102
MARY E	118
ATEN, LIZZIE JANE	178
ATKESON, VELLA	105
ATKINSON, BEULAH D	48
ELIZABETH A	124
MARY E	34
MARY F	179
ROXY A	170
VIRGINIA M	19
AUBERRY, (Mrs) ELLA	109
AUFLICK, JANE A	79
AUMILLER, AMA S	151
AMANDA	53
AMANDA M	141
ANNA MATILDA	170
CATHARINE	76
CATHARINE	125
ELIZABETH	47
FANNIE	19
HANNAH	149
LILLIAN M	105
MARY M	161
SARAH	53
SARAH	59
SUSANNA E	39
SUSANNAH	192
AUSTIN, ALICE A	176
DONLEY	12
EFFIE A	12
ELCIE	106
EVA A	154
KATHARYNE L	108
LAURA	177
LELIA O	137
LOTTIE C	185
LYDIA	141
MYRTIE L	153
NEVA I	36
PEARL	142
AUXIER, CARRIE	191
AYES, SALLIE C	88
AYLER, SARAH	184
AYRES, AURELIA J	3
LYDIA M	101
MARILLA T	3
SAVENA	103
BABBINGTON, SARAH A	32
BABER, EMMA C	147
BABLE, MARGARET ESTHER	14
BADGLEY, CATHARINE E	170
EFFIE	75
NELLIE	106
SAMARIA	159
SAMARIA C	151

Name	Page
BAHR, DESSIE D	182
BAILES, EMMA	42
EMMA	52
LUCETTA	16
BAILEY, ALICE P	86
ANNE	119
CATHARINE	104
ELLA	58
EMMA A	150
JULIA O	107
MARTHA A	63
MARY EVA	157
MARY J	148
MINNIE	40
NANCY E	31
SARAH	53
SARAH IDA	86
BAILS, MAGGIE B	75
BAIRD, DOLLIE	168
SARAH J	90
BAITY, EMILY	96
BAKER, ADDIE	190
CHRISTENA C	166
CLARA	3
CLARA	93
CLARA B	80
DELPHINE	103
E LOUISE	17
ELIZABETH	68
ELIZABETH J	71
ELLA L	150
ELLEN E	81
ELZENE	98
EMMA	140
HESTER H	49
ISABEL	156
JANE	132
LIZZIE	171
MALISSA	114
MARGARET	11
MARGARET	74
MARIA	26
MARTHA	168
MARTHELA MARGARET	142
MARY	59
MARY	158
MARY E	90
MARY FRANCES	70
MARY JANE	30
MARY JANE	120
MARY M	90
MINNIE E	26
MINNIE F	163
MINNIE FRANCES	115
MINNIE T	34
NANCY J	156
NANCY JANE	142
REBECCA F	74
SARAH ELIZABETH	76
TABITHA E	139
BALDWIN, MARY	38
RUTH	49
BALE, SARAH L	160
BALES, ELLA	14
LUSETTA	73
BALL, (Mrs) JULIA A	147
ABIGAIL	55
ALICE O	118
ANNIE	128
ARABELL R	154
CAROLINE	174
CATHARINE	153
CORA F	6
ELIZABETH T	177
ELSIE P	177
ERIE E	67
FRANCES E	112
LEOTI C	118
LURA M	156
MARGT E	83
MARTHA	129
MARTHA JANE	138
MARY A	135
MARY E	151
MARY ELIZABETH	169
MARY JANE	98
MARY L	147
MARY MATILDA	160
MEARLIE E	104
MILLIE CATHARINE	183
MINNIE E	92
MOLLIE	104
NANCY	117
OLIVE J	135
ORPHA E	91
ROSIE C	101
SARAH ELIZABETH	184
SUSANNAH	147
BALLENGER, SALLIE A	99
BALLINGER, RIXEY	6
BALTHASER, ADELINE L	33
BANKS, (Mrs) MARY ALICE	27
HATTIE	185
MAHALA FRANCES	99
MARY M	47
BANNASTER, MARIA	53
BANNISTER, ADACADE	161
BARBEE, ANN REBECCA	38
KATE L	111
MARY B	69
BARBER, ELIZABETH ELLEN	124
ETHEL	70
FANNY	124
LILLIE	41
MARTHA	129
SADIE	25
SADIE	115
VINIA	124
BARCUS, MARTHA MAY	126
BAREMORE, ANN	168
MARY E	97
BARGAR, IRENA C	116
BARGER, MARY A	4
BARKER, ALICE M	168
EDNA	5
EMILY	187
FLORIDA MAY	169
HARRIET A	125

VIOLA	78	SYNTHIA A	165
BARNES, (Mrs) PEARL	151	BARRET, JENNIE	31
BARNET, GOLDIA G	156	BARRETT, ANNA M	12
POLLY	48	LILLIE ALMA	112
BARNETT, ADA O	165	MARY E	11
ALTA	127	BARRETTE, NAOMA MIRTLE	43
ALZINA J	121	BARRINGER, LAURA L	114
BERTHA	182	BARROWS, AUGUSTA E	87
BETSEY	135	BESSIE E	8
CAROLINE	89	MARY E	19
DORA A	18	SARAH E	104
DORIS M	38	BARTLEY, MINERVA J	16
ELIZA JANE	86	BARTON, NEVA	155
ELIZABETH	157	BARTRAM, FANNIE	73
ELIZABETH JANE	152	FRANCES	129
ELLEN	26	GERTIE	175
ELLEN	172	BARTROM, JENNIE	179
ELLEN J	83	BARTRUM, (Mrs) ISADORA	155
EMILY	128	BARTZEL, MARY	62
EMILY M	75	BASS, (Mrs) FANNIE	119
EMMA S	155	(Mrs) MURREL	37
ESTHER	64	BERTHA MAY	73
EVELINE	47	CLARA	120
GEORGIANA	7	CLARA M	174
HADIE	191	ELCA M	13
HANNAH	184	ELIZA J	72
LILLIE F	114	ELIZA J	72
LOTTIE	86	EVA	120
MALISSA	111	EVA	125
MARGARET	163	FLORA	145
MARIA	170	FLORA A	73
MARY	92	HANNAH E	59
MARY	163	LAURA	144
MARY EDYSINE	63	LILLIE	47
MINNIE	78	LILLY MAY	19
NANCY A	122	LIZZIE	142
NANCY J	110	MAGGIE	138
PERMELIA F	121	MARY A	145
R FANNIE	67	MARY P	39
ROSANNA M	25	NETTIE	19
ROXY A	42	SARAH MATILDA	59
RUTH	44	VIRGINIA BELLE	152
SARAH	96	BATEMAN, ADA	41
SARAH	122	ANNIE M	68
SARAH E	28	BEATRICE	134
VIRGINIA F	153	BETTIE	84
BARNHEART, MARY JANE	175	ELIZABETH	132
BARNITT, ELIZABETH	7	EMILY C	135
HANNAH	33	IDELLA	6
MARY A	185	LUCY	68
BARR, BELINDA J	25	MAGGIE B	188
CHRISTENA	91	MARY A	135
DIANAH	6	MARY A	169
ELZA JANE	137	MARY L	109
ELZINA	118	MARY M	113
MALINDA	121	SARAH	109
MARY CATHARINE	151	SOPHIAH E	93
MARY ELLEN	127	SUSANNA	108
MAZILLA E	23	BATES, CARRIE O	122
NANCY B	6	ELSIE M	101
ROSETTA J	25	HORTENSE	166
SARAH M	156	LULU M	36
SOPHIA	23	LYDA E	48
SUSAN S	150	MARY	4

MARY ANN	137
VIRGIE L	5
BATTERSON, ANNA	64
ERMINIA D	64
ESTELLA	122
BATTRELL, CARRIE	151
MINERVA	28
VINNIE	52
BAUER, KATE	166
BAUM, ANNIE E	34
BAUMAN, MARY	108
BAUMGARTNER, BARBARA	181
BAXTER, ELIZABETH	137
LIZZIE	156
BEABOUT, CARRIE E	21
BEALE, CATHARINE M	122
ELEANOR MOORE	175
JULIA LEWIS	143
MARY M	66
SARAH E	8
BEALS, ELIZA M	64
BEAN, KATIE	167
BEARD, DELLA	108
EMMA	26
ETHEL M	167
ETHEL M	167
EVA A	68
LUCY C	3
MAGGIE	132
MARY A	63
MARY AMSY	6
ORA G	113
SARAH E	131
SOPHIA C	63
SOPHRONA	167
BEASLEY, ELIZA	183
BEATTIE, LAURA M	188
MAGGIE	6
MARY M	152
BEATTY, MARGARET	110
MELISSA	182
BEAVER, LORAINE M	143
MARIETTA	42
MINERVA	78
OLLA	5
ROSY	50
BEBEE, ANNIE	47
MARY ANN	163
ROSA L	130
SARAH M	167
BECHTLE, ELIZA S	87
NORA	67
VIRGINIA L	66
BECK, ANNIE M	49
EMILY	88
BECKETT, LUCY A E	60
BEHAN, GRACE	11
JANE	181
MARY F	187
BELCHER, MARY E	80
BELL, DELLA	109
JENNIE	81
LINNIE J	115
MARY	152
PEARL	15
BELLEE, SARAH	162
BELLER, MARGARET E	46
BENEDICT, OLLIE P	83
BENNET, JULIA	148
BENNETT, ANNIE GORDON	133
CORA	62
EDITH B	6
ELLEN	98
ELLEN	142
JENNIE A	112
JOAN	86
JOANNA	118
LAURA D	187
LOTTIE	101
LYDIA	155
MARGARET	112
MARTHA RACHEL	118
MARY	147
STELLA	55
BENNINGTON, CATHARINE	180
BENSON, MARY E	22
BENTZ, BERTHA M	151
BERGEN, MARY	151
BERGER, LAURA C	115
BERKLEY, MARTHA J	43
MARY M	179
BERRIDGE, OSA M	148
BERTHAL, MARTHA	130
BETHOULT, LEAH	117
BETTINGER, KATHARINE	6
LIZZIE	24
LOUISA	166
BETTS, BERTHA R	112
BEVAN, MAGGIE	62
MARY	48
BIBBEE, FANNIE	76
BICKEL, ANN ELIZA	151
DINAH E	59
MARY F	152
BIDGOOD, EMILY A	133
BILLINGSLEY, REBECCA E	137
BILLUPS, IDA	37
BIRCH, JOSEPHINE	31
BIRCHFIELD, CLARA	38
FLORA	179
LETIE A	126
NANCY E	47
REBECCA	175
REBECCA J	49
REBECCA J	55
REBECCA J	118
SARAH J	49
SONIA	57
VIOLA O	139
BIRD, ALMA F	122
ELIZABETH	111
ELIZABETH	1
EMILY	106
FANNIE CATHARINE	75
IDA C	40
JOSIE BELLE	106
SARAH D	4
BIRTHISEL, ELIZA	56

FRANCES J	145	BLAZER, ADA G	118
BISHOP, CAROLINE M	33	SONORA M	171
BITGOOD, RUTH E	191	BLESSING, ALTA AUGUSTA	130
BIXLER, LULU M	51	CHRISTINA M	139
BLACK, CATHARINE	32	ELIZA ANN	70
MALINDA	36	FANNIE L	15
MALINDA	125	JULIANN M	89
MARY	96	IDA MALINDA	106
MARY B	12	MAMIE A	177
OLLIE M	96	MARY ALICE	147
ROSE	33	MARY ANN	7
BLACKBURN, ELIZA M	171	PENELOPE	159
ELIZABETH CALISTA	44	SARAH C	144
SYLVIA GALE	5	SARAH S	112
BLACKSON, MAGGIE B	30	SAREPTA A	145
BLACKWELL, ADA	166	SEREPTA	170
CATHARINE A	183	VIRGINIA A	147
CORA	10	BLETNER, ELLEN MAE	13
LULU	36	BOARD, ADDA G	24
MARY	70	ANNA L	144
MINERVA	170	CORA	9
BLADEN, MARY JANE	114	ELLA G	13
BLADES, MARGARET	152	EMMA	171
BLAGG, BELVA L	159	FANNIE	99
HANNAH JENNIE	74	FANNIE B	169
BLAIN, CYNTHIA A	59	IDA M	47
LUELLA	132	KATE	136
MARY	17	LANORA	118
MARY J	3	LUCINDA ISABEL	54
MATILDA B	73	MABLE	168
MISSOURI	149	MARTHA A	24
VIRGIE	113	MARTHA E	51
BLAINE, (Mrs) WILLIE E	155	NANCY	21
BLAIR, CHARLOTTA	144	REBECCA	38
MARTHA	157	SARAH J	13
MARY	61	STELLA	43
BLAKE, (Mrs) EUNICE	25	SYLVIA N	21
(Mrs) JANE	60	BOARDMAN, EVA	98
(Mrs) JESSIE	131	HATTIE	131
ARAMINTA	189	JULIA	98
CORA B	188	MARY J	7
EMILY	110	BOBO, ELSIE	18
EMMA OLA	172	MARGARET	41
EVA M	130	BOGGESS, BEATRICE	145
GERTRUDE	72	JANE C	160
HESTER A	123	MARGARET A	96
LAURA B	29	MARTHA	103
LIZZIE	81	MARTHA J	60
LOUISA	155	MARY	160
MARGARET	37	MINNIE	59
MARY ANN	167	NORA L	133
MATILDA	78	OLIVIA D	103
ONEY E	153	VILINIA C	76
OSIE	18	VIRGINIA C	140
VIRGINIA L	116	RHODA	137
BLAKEMORE, MARGARET A	1	BOGGS, EDITHY V	64
BLAND, BETHLEHEM	135	BOHRAM, ELLA	42
BIRDIE	176	VELMA	64
LAURA A B	13	BOICE, ELIZABETH	57
SUSAN M	11	MARY	3
BLANKENSHIP, ELLA E	54	BOILES, DELIA MAY	104
MINNIE B	45	JULIA F	47
BLATCHLEY, MARY	190	BOLDEN, MARY E	143
MARY	190	BOLES, CARRIE	136

ELVA M	84
ISABELLA	186
MARY B	186
NELLIE	166
REBECCA	188
BONECUTTER, IDA	50
MINNIE	84
VIOLA	25
ZONA	118
BONNET, MARY	127
BONNETT, HARIET	105
LILLIE M	79
MARY	59
SUSANNA	128
BOOKER, IDA	24
MARGARET	184
MELINDA	15
BOON, MARY E	46
BOONE, MARY	80
BOORUM, EMILY	8
BOOTEN, MINNIE A	167
BOOTH, ANGELINA	63
ANN	96
BETHLEHAM	186
DORA E	191
ELIZABETH	49
ESTER	4
IVA M	153
LAURA S	60
LOUISA	61
LULA	108
MAGGIE E	143
MAYME	153
SARAH J	86
SUSAN	160
BOOTON, POLLY	51
RHODA	49
BORAM, LEATHY	67
TAZY	23
BORHAM, EVA L	126
BORING, CATHARINE L	140
BOSO, MARIE EDNA	136
BOSTER, COREVA	128
BOSTIC, ELMA C	101
LILLIE M	82
BOSTON, EDNA MAY	147
BOSWELL, JANE	24
BOTTRILL, BEATRICE V	138
BOUDER, MARY	108
BOWCOTT, NORA E	24
BOWDEN, JANE	142
BOWEN, (Mrs) RACHEL A	86
BEATRICE IMO	50
BETTIE	91
EDNA B	82
ELIZABETH	153
ELLA	155
EMMA B	120
ETHEL L	69
LAURA O	68
ROXIE	134
VIRGIE	102
BOWERS, CATHARINE	17
ELLEN	6
LAVINA	3
BOWLDEN, MARGARET	24
BOWLEN, LEVISA	90
BOWLES, EFFIE	20
ELIZABETH A	23
FRANCES	92
MATILDA	187
NANCY J	15
ROSELLA	30
BOWLEY, NANNIE	165
BOWLING, HATTIE E	172
JULIA A	40
BOWMAN, ELIZABETH	5
ELIZABETH	177
ELLA	15
HATTIE	120
MATTILDA	97
NANCY	177
WINNIE	77
BOWYER, HANNAH	41
MAGGIE	57
MAGGIE	137
NEIDA CHANCELLOR	111
BOYCE, ANNIE L	2
EMMA	82
ESTELLE JANE	97
HANNAH	91
SARAH	5
VIRGINIA	16
BOYD, ELEANOR	83
ISABELL	65
JESSIE	80
MATILDA	8
BOYER, IDA M	94
MARY M	10
BOYLES, CAROLINE	82
CORA	117
LOUISA G	4
SARAH	147
WILLIE E	117
BOZWELL, SUSAN	106
BOZZELL, ELIZABETH	22
BRADFORD, MARY A	139
BRADLEY , LOU	52
BRADLEY, CAROLINE	2
MARY	121
BRAGG, EMMA B	16
BRALEY, MORA ELIZABETH	178
BRANCH, BEATRICE	131
CORA M	80
MELVINA	119
BRANDY, ANNIE	122
BRANNAN, LENA MAY	75
MARY M	113
MATILDA C	127
NAOMI	100
BRANNON, MAGGIE L	93
MARY	188
SARAH E	93
BRATTON, AMY A	174
BREWEN, LAURA	186
BREWER, TINNIE	107
BRIAN, POLLY	15
BRICKLES, CYLASKIE	93

BRIDGET, MAUDE	35
BRIGHT, BERTHA ELLEN	74
EDITH E	110
ELLA B	187
FLORA M	141
LOUISA	124
LUELLA	6
LUELLA	17
LUVINIA S	102
MANDY V	171
MARY	73
MARY	88
MARY B	171
BRINKER, CAROLINE	103
FLORIDA	132
GERTRUDE	44
LUCIE V	107
BROFFERD, CATHERINE E	107
BROMFIELD, MAGGIE	89
BRONAUGH, MARY A	12
BROOKS, LIZZIE	125
MARY ELIZABETH	91
WINNY	48
BROWN, ALICE M	7
ADA B	79
AMANDA	65
ANNA F	5
ANNIE	126
ANNIE C	110
ANYTIS C	4
CAROLINE	16
CARRIE A	93
CLARA	23
CORA S	123
CYNTHIA C	121
DORA	154
ELLA	65
ELLA EUGENIA	70
ETHA	46
FANNY	100
FRANCES J	131
JENNIE	133
JENNIE E	47
JENNIE S	96
JINCY	157
LAURA	21
LAURA J	185
LIZZIE	59
LUCY M	22
MARGARET	44
MARGARET E	185
MARIA LOUISA	78
MARIAH SELINA	66
MARY	12
MARY	14
MARY	19
MARY	109
MARY	114
MARY	118
MARY	165
MARY A	174
MARY ANN	81
MARY C	86
MARY F	28
MARY I	137
MARY I	143
MATTIE VIRGINIA	60
NANCY	139
NANCY E	138
NETTIE A	129
PANELLA	35
REBECCA	102
REBECCA	19
SALLY	190
SUSAN M	154
VERLIE	15
VICTORIA	169
VIRGINIA H	4
ZENA	113
BRUESTLE, LILLIE F	82
BRUNER, EMMA	40
BRUNFIELD, EMRYNE	18
BRYAN, EVALINE	79
JENCIE	22
JOANNA ALICE	11
MARY	111
MARY E	86
NANCY	70
SALINA	34
SARAH A	13
SOPHIA	107
BRYANT, (Mrs) SARAH	31
BETTIE	78
JANE	26
JENEVIEVE E	20
SARAH	31
BRYMON, MARY ANN	58
BRYSON, PATSY	183
BUCK, MARY	173
MEDA	41
MILLIE	124
OLETHA	86
ROENA	165
BUCKALEW, CLARA E	152
BUCKALOO, REBECCA A	99
BUCKHANAN, EMMA L	32
BUCKLE, (Mrs) MARY	132
ALVIRA	99
JANE D	13
BUCKLEY, AUGUSTA	31
BUCKNER, (Mrs) JULIA	154
SUSAN C	183
BUDGET, MILDRED V	187
BUFFINGTON, ANNA M	125
ELLA B	39
MARTHA J	150
MARY B	77
ORPHALINA	181
BUGG, DORA	66
MIRTIE	40
ROSA	40
BULMER, ANN	106
BUMGARDNER, BETSY	33
BUMGARNER, (Mrs) EMMA C	192
ADA	163
CAROLINE	139
CARRIE B	19
EMILY S	184

EMMA	190	
ETHEL WINIFRED	78	
GEORGIA G	12	
HAGAR ELIZABETH	1	
IDA O	48	
JOSIE N	123	
JULIA ELIZABETH	190	
MARGARET	50	
MARGARET	184	
MARGORE	76	
MARTHA	23	
MARY CATHARINE	56	
MATILDA	175	
MILLIE B	77	
MINNIE	147	
MYRTIE	70	
MYRTLE	100	
NANCY	192	
OLEVA	132	
REBECCA E	54	
REBECCA JANE	142	
SARAH	63	
SARAH	128	
SARAH CATHARINE	56	
BURCH, ELIZABETH G	149	
ELOSHA	117	
EMILY	100	
MARY	38	
BURCHARD, ELLA F	74	
FLORA	13	
BURCHFIELD, ZOLA	23	
BURDETT, ARMINA	155	
DAINE M	84	
EMMA J	15	
ESTELLA M	64	
ETHEL S	121	
FLORA M	2	
JESSIE	149	
LELA E	179	
BURDETTE, LONA NAOMI	14	
BURFORD, EVA LUCINDA	182	
BURGER, LULA	162	
BURGESS, ALICE	68	
ANNE O	94	
NETTIE	102	
OATA	35	
BURGGESS, STELLA C	191	
BURGIN, LAVINIA	184	
LUCINDA	59	
BURGOYNE, REBECCA J	103	
BURK, MARY C	86	
BURKE, MARGARET M	175	
BURKLEY, EVELENA	170	
BURKS, BONNIE B	181	
MATTIE L	49	
BURNELL, ELIZABETH E	120	
BURNETT, L PEARL	182	
BURNS, (Mrs) FRANCES	169	
BERTHA	64	
BISHIE	67	
CATHARINE R	167	
EDITH M	144	
KATIE	126	
LEW ALICE	166	
MAGGIE	44
MARY E	124
MAYME BELLE	114
BURNSIDE, CLARIBULL	30
LUCY	166
MARY	9
BURRELL, LUCRETIA	178
BURRESS, SALLY	33
BURRIS, EDA	155
LOUISA	130
MARY L	111
MARY LEVENIA	104
ROSA B	168
SARAH C	106
SUSAN J	146
BURROWS, ANGELINE	74
ANGELINE	77
ARENIA M	45
AURILLA	109
EDITH	145
LAVINIA	62
MARTHA ELLEN	147
SUSIE	181
BURTON, HORTENSE	142
TACY	81
BUSH, BESSIE	65
BIRDIE	17
CAROLINE	23
DAISY T	151
DORA	23
ELIZABETH M	115
ELIZABETH R	129
FLOYA	113
HENRIETTA	25
LILLIE	12
LULA	14
MADGE	113
MARY JANE	96
MYRTLE D	11
NELLIE	146
SAMANTHA	57
SARAH A	186
SOPHIA E	169
BUTCHER, BERTHA H	102
CLARA	175
ELLEN	105
LENA L	176
LULA	126
LYDA J	6
MARY	174
NELLIE L	136
VIRGINIA	83
BUTIN, MAGGIE L	156
BUTLER, ANNIE L	48
ANNIE M	24
ANNIE MAY	156
CORDELIA E	183
ELLA C	178
FLORA B	162
MAYME	50
BUTRICKS, CLARA F	38
MARY M	135
BUTTRIX, SARAH E	154
BUXTON, ELECTA LODISA	118

MARY	20	ATTIE	124
BYBEE, ELIZABETH ANN	68	LELIE A	115
MARY ANN	161	MARTHA E	79
BYER, OMA B	133	CAMPBELL, ALICE BEATRICE	13
BYERS, CORDELIA A	111	CORNELIA D	172
HATTIE	163	ELIZABETH	9
JANE	171	ELIZABETH	114
KATE E	72	ELIZABETH	161
SALLIE N	1	EMMA F	153
BYRAM, MARTHA A	88	EVA M	67
BYRD, GARNETTE W	82	FANNY	141
BYRNE, ANNIE	62	ISABELLA	128
ANNIE E	19	LAVINIA	62
BETTIE HILL	87	LUCY A	189
MARY R	69	MARIETTA	188
BYUS, ETTA	161	MARY	8
KATIE	111	MATTIE	137
SALLIE M	189	MELINDA A	183
SIRENEA J	89	MYRTLE	148
CABLE, BESSIE S	22	NANCY E	140
BLANCH	113	ROSA B	68
HATTIE M	12	SARAH A	21
MARY E	136	SARENA A	107
CAHILL, MARGARET I	26	STELLA E	71
CAIN, (Mrs) JEANETTE	71	VIRGINIA A	191
ADALINE	110	CANADA, MARY	111
ALMA	165	CANSOL, VICTORIA	175
CHRISTENA	110	CANTER, ALICE	151
DEBORAH	130	BIRDIE	171
DELILAH	93	CINTHA	55
EDE A	32	MYRTLE	154
ELZINA	118	SARAH	148
JULIA	189	CANTERBERRY, ABIGAIL	165
LETITIA	84	ALTA A	133
LINDA	189	FLORENCE V	49
LULA	93	JULIA B	39
MARIAH	151	LOUISA	117
MARY	121	MARGARET J	64
MARY M	150	SUSANA	114
SARAH E	25	CANTERBURY, BETTIE E	67
VIOLA	121	MAYE	84
WILLIE A	166	CANTOR, NONA	81
CAIRENS, JESSIE ELLEN	112	CANTRELL, ELLEN J	117
CAISEY, JULIA E	189	GERTRUDE	92
CALDWELL, ANN	95	CAPEHART, ALICE ELLA	101
ANNIE	136	KELSIE F	147
CAROLINE	63	MAGGIE P	97
JANE B	139	MARY A	17
LAURA	96	MARY ANN	19
OLIVIA FRANCES	131	MARY M	156
REBECCA F	45	MATTIE A	123
SAMANTHA R	111	MINNIE	98
CALL, MARY L	108	OLIVIA J	159
SARAH J	49	ROSANE	179
CALLAGHAN, MARY	37	SALLY	142
CALLAHAN, SARAH	36	CARDER, LAURA A	190
CALLISON, NELLY	16	MAMIE M	165
CALLOWAY, LUCY	32	CARELL, MAGGIE	50
CALVERT, ELIZA P	66	CAREY, SARAH	32
CALWELL, RACHEL W	120	CARLETON, LIZZIE G	135
CAMDEN, EMMER M	134	CARLIND, SARAH J	174
MARY M	33	CARMAN, CORA E	51
CAMP, (Mrs) ELIZA JANE	151	CARNES, HANNAH	59
AMELIA	17	SARAH L	130

CARNEY, ANNA	162	
AROLE	154	
DELILAH	141	
MALINDA	170	
MARY F	179	
CARPENTER, DEBORAH	147	
ELLEN	65	
IDA M	27	
LAVINIA	153	
MARTHA FRANCES	48	
MARY	41	
MARY	27	
NANCY	154	
POLLY	172	
REBECCA	116	
SARAH E	123	
VICTORIA	85	
CARR, (Mrs) BLANCHE	21	
CARROL, PARTHENA	186	
CARROLL, ELLA	102	
KATHARINE M	90	
LILLIE J	161	
MAUD	55	
MERTY MELISSA	182	
NANCY	140	
NELLIE	97	
CARSEY, (Mrs) JANE	138	
CAROLINE	82	
IDA LUELLA	56	
CARSON, ADA	36	
CLARA P	60	
CORA B	39	
E LILLIAN	164	
ESTHA E	45	
MOLLIE R	112	
SARAH M	27	
CART, ELLEN J	100	
HARRIET C	174	
LYDIA	174	
CARTER, BESSIE J	125	
CLARA	129	
JENNIE	174	
LAVINIA M	25	
MARY E	8	
MATILDA A	119	
NANCY	7	
CARTMILL, ANNIE L	22	
ELIZABETH	119	
FANNIE	28	
IDA L	112	
JULIA M	168	
MARY C	68	
MINNIE	69	
NANCY J	62	
ORA E	59	
OTA B	192	
SARAH M	67	
CARTRIGHT, IRENE V	182	
CARTRITE, ELIZABETH	94	
MARY	62	
NANCY	172	
SARAH	75	
CARTWRIGHT, (Mrs) SABRA	161	
CLARA F	121	
EDITH	58	
EVA RUTH	117	
GRACE M	114	
HELEN RUTH	7	
MARIA A	179	
MARY SABRA	131	
STELLA MAY	79	
CASEY, BERTHA	190	
BESSIE	141	
EDNA	27	
EMMA F	131	
LENA	64	
LILLIE J	123	
LUCY	20	
LUCY J	178	
LULA	19	
MAHOLA V	9	
MARTHA A	16	
MARY ANN	73	
MARY F	52	
MINNIE	120	
MISOURI	159	
NANCY	82	
NEOLA	58	
RHODA A	44	
STELLA	112	
VIRGIE	150	
CASH, ANNIE M	15	
LUCY JANE	34	
WILLIE M	143	
CASON, JANE LUCY	89	
CASSADAY, SARAH	72	
CASTER, NANNIE M	134	
CASTO, ANNIE	55	
ANNIE B	61	
CLARA A	179	
CLARA E	155	
DELILA	92	
DELILAH	74	
EDNA	151	
FANNIE	120	
HARRIET	1	
JANE	150	
LILLIE	114	
LYDIA L	113	
MARGARET	37	
MARGARET E	124	
MARTHA J	91	
MATILDA F	38	
MINERVA J	25	
MINTA M	20	
NANCY	14	
RACHEL	80	
SARAH	111	
SARAH	182	
SARAH B	184	
UFANNIE B	110	
CAUFLE, ANNIE	88	
CAUFMAN, CYNTHIA A	44	
LOIS A	10	
CAVET, CLARA	126	
MARY	56	
NANCY A	38	
SARAH	185	

CAVETT, ADA	185
CAVIT, MARGARET A	170
SARAH	36
CAYLOR, LYDIA	83
MARY	16
CAZAD, AMY	61
CATHARINE	174
CAZY, CHARELLA	57
MARY	73
CENTERS, (Mrs) LINNIE	107
CHAFFIN, BLANCH	175
CASSEY	98
IDA CATHARINE	59
JESSIE	31
MALISA JANE	112
MATTIE LEE	69
CHAFIN, CLARA	21
LIDA	164
CHAMBERLAIN, CATHARINE	121
MARTHA E	179
MARY P	160
CHAMBERLIN, MARY F	153
CHAMBERS, KATHARINE D	72
LYDA	70
MATTIE	6
SALLIE	90
CHANCY, POLLY	97
CHANDLER, ELIZA MARGARET	115
FLORENCE	177
MALINDA	65
MARY E	115
MARY J	110
MELISSA	171
RENA	37
SARAH E	81
CHANNEL, N ESTELLA	154
CHAPMAN, ALMA	29
ANNIE	115
ANNIE	158
ANNIE	185
BERTHA P	85
CARRIE A	19
CORA A	78
ELIZABETH MARGT	85
ELVA	118
EMMA	111
FANNIE	50
FLORENCE M	181
FRANCES S	68
GENEVIA A	27
GEORGIA A	169
HELLEN	165
LEDIE	60
LEFAVOR	79
LIZZIE J	176
LOUISIANA	116
LUCINDA	165
LUCY A	25
LUCY L	180
MADLAIN MAY	18
MARGARET L	129
MARTHA J	27
MARTHA V	141
MARY	86
MARY	129
MARY	1
MARY ANN	40
MARY E	154
MARY F	33
MARY K	87
MARY L	65
MARY V	60
MAUD M	84
MAY	175
MILLIE C	191
MINERVA F	110
MINNIE	78
MINNIE M	33
NANNIE M	112
OLLIE M	147
RHODA	108
RUTHA J	151
SARAH	61
SARAH	115
SARAH C	12
SARAH E	109
SARAH L	144
URSULA J	149
VIRGINIA SOPHIA	176
CHARLES, EVA	83
JENNIE	171
MARY C	6
CHASE, KATHLEEN	71
MALINDA	141
CHATTEN, JULIA MARGARET	133
CHATTIN, ALMEDIA S	138
ELIZA G	48
FLORENCE E	68
MARTHA A	14
MARY	137
CHAVIS, PEARL A	176
CHEADLE, MERVANIA M	60
CHEESBREW, AILCY C	38
AUGUSTA L	134
CORA MAY	93
MARY S	25
NANCY E	98
CHEESEBREW, ARDELLA B	175
BARBARA A	127
BLANCHE	161
CICELY D	149
CORA M	44
EMILY JANE	122
ORA L	66
CHENEY, EMMA V	60
CHERINGTON, DELLA M	12
CHERRINGTON, ANNIE ELIZA	189
LILLIE	7
LULU	178
CHESLEY, LOUISA	82
CHESTER, ADDIE F	186
ELLEN A	127
EVA DELIA	97
CHEVALIAR, LILLIAN	152
CHICK, FEDILIA	15
GERTRUDE M	187
HARTIE F	24
JESSIE	180

CHILDERS, (Mrs) ADA	141		LULA A	80
CATHARINE	48		MARGARET	71
DANIE	42		MARY	155
ELIZABETH	140		MARY A	35
ELLEN	150		MARY C	62
JULIAN	115		MARY ELIZABETH	98
LUCINDA	71		MAY G	6
MARTHA	80		MINERVA	21
MARY A	155		ROSETTA C	167
MARY J	58		RUTH ADALINE	33
MATILDA C	150		SARAH	40
NELLIE	142		SARAH ALICE	162
REBECCA	85		SARAH M	98
SUSIE	93		VIRGINIA	130
CHILDS, FANNIE	119		CLARKE, ELLA	150
LIZZIE	168		KATHARINE R	71
CHISHOLM, MARGARET A	31		MARY ALICE	181
CHOEN, MARY ANN	67		NANNIE MARIE	129
MATILDA	3		CLARKSON, MARY E	97
CHRIST, CORDELIA	116		CLATTERBUCK, ETHEL L	27
JOSEPHINE	168		CLAXTON, (Mrs) GEORGIA	71
NANCY J	92		CLAYPOOL, MARY ELIZABETH	177
CHRISTOPHER, HARRIET	29		CLEEK, ANNIE B	38
CHRISTY, AMANDA	123		CHRISTIANE	155
JENNIE	61		NANNIE	170
MARY A	169		CLEMMENS, ELIZABETH	102
CHURCH, ELSIE	28		CLEMMES, CATHERINE	93
LOTTIE	31		CLENDENEN, ANN ELIZA	164
MARY	21		DELILAH O	190
CIRCKLE, STELLA	32		ELIZABETH E	111
CIRCLE, CHARLOTTE M	106		ELLEN M	134
ELLA	53		EMILY	160
FRANCES	188		JULIA	163
LINNIE M	41		LAURA C	133
LUTITIA	87		LUCENA	99
MAGGIE	49		LUCINDA L	4
MARGARET	64		MARY C	47
ROSA CATHARINE	168		NARCISSUS J	53
CLAGG, CORA B	191		RUTH A	56
DELITHA	116		CLENDENIN, ADA M,	160
HOLLIE ANN	187		ALICE R	51
LAURA B	48		ANNIE	33
MAGGIE	162		CELINA	178
MALINDA MIRAM	79		ELLA	45
MARY	36		FRANCIS MARGARET	139
MARY	122		IRIS	91
MARY F	39		JENNIE	187
MATILDA	81		LILLIE	135
NANCY	85		MAGGIE E	95
SARAH A S	5		MARGARET LUELLA	93
SARAH F	8		REBECCA	16
CLARK, AURILLA J	191		RUBY LEE	173
CHARLOTTE	30		SARAH	163
DESTA D	65		SARAH F	93
ELIZABETH	43		SOPHRONIA ELIZABETH	178
ELLA	127		CLENDINEN, JANE	186
ETHEL	69		MARY ANN	164
EVALINE	23		OZELLA	127
GLADYS E	149		SARAH U	87
HELEN M	2		CLICK, AMELIA	41
ISABELLA J	91		CHARLOTTIE	12
LAURA S	61		JENNIE	144
LENA	127		LELIA B	76
LORA	90		LILLIE	111

LIZZIE	42	ROSE B	172
LOUISA BELL	144	SARAH ELIZABETH	183
MARGARET	35	THINCY M	14
MARIA S	156	VIRGIE	183
MARY M	82	WINONA E	152
CLINDENEN, RACHEL S	164	COLINS, MARY J	39
CLINE, HANNAH	72	COLLET, KATIE	17
CLOCKSTON, ELIZABETH	69	PHEBE	152
CLONCH, ANNIE A	39	COLLIER, LAURA	114
BETSY J	182	NANCY E	110
DORA	117	COLLINS, ANNIE R	152
ELIZABETH	128	BERTHA	149
ELIZABETH	186	BLANCHE	1
EMILY MARGARET	128	CLARA M	151
MARTHA	11	ELIZABETH	5
MARY	153	ELVIRA V	58
NANCY J	80	METTIE	76
NANCY J	84	NEELY	188
RHODA F	171	SARAH	2
ROMA	131	SARAH	12
SARAH	184	COLSTON, MOSELLA H	5
CLUFT, HATTIE	124	COLVIN, MARGARET J	38
CLYSE, LILLIAN F	76	RACHEL A	61
COAL, ELIZABETH	97	COLWELL, ABBY R	94
COALMAN, ELLEN	171	CATHARINE	84
SARAH J	58	CORA LONG	155
COATES, ANGELINE	23	IDOMA	66
COBB, ELIZABETH MAY	141	LENA	130
ELLA	7	LIDDE	98
LAVINA	91	LULA	130
MARY	121	COMBS, SALLIE	95
RACHEL I	80	COMER, NONA J	34
SARAH	185	COMMONS, AUGUSTA B	169
COCHRAN, FLORA E	166	COMPSON, CLARA	102
MARY	97	MARY E	137
COFFMAN, KATE	28	COMPSTON, BERTHA	103
MARY M	137	LENA M	43
REBECCA	137	MAGGIE R	11
COLE, (Mrs) LUCINDA	185	COMPTON, VIRGIE	43
CINTHIA A	38	COMSTOCK, GEORGIA B	33
ISABELLA	63	KATHRYN VINCENT	181
LILLIE B	150	LULU G	69
COLEMAN, ANNIE	73	MARTHA CAROLINE	80
BESS	50	COMSTON, CORA E	76
CORDELIA E	97	CONDEE, MABELL	40
DELIA M	64	CONDIFF, RHODA C	123
DICIA	128	CONGROVE, HATTIE E	73
DORA	63	MATTIE E	35
ETHEL OLEVIA	44	NETTIE D	54
FLORENCE C	134	CONKLE, DORKIEST L	124
GEORGIA	191	NANCY	43
HATTIE	191	SARAH	106
IDA MAY	7	CONLEY, MARY	42
IVA	57	CONNARD, SARAH A	129
IVA	180	CONNER, ANN	34
JOANNA	44	CARRIE V	20
LIZZIE	72	HAZEL	88
MARGARET	86	MARY O	141
MARY	54	CONNOLLY, MARTHA R	157
MARY ANN	119	MAUD M	102
MATTIE	25	CONOWAY, FANNIE	9
MILDRED	137	CONRAD, ALMEDIA	78
NORA	134	BETTIE	158
RACHEL V	59	ELIZA A	103

	ELVIRA S	178
	EMILY	27
	JULIA B	54
	LELIA F	170
	NANCY	183
	ORPHA E	40
	RHODA	27
	STELLA	128
	VENA	85
	VIRGINIA	129
CONSOLL, IDA		100
COOK, CHARLOTTE		159
	MARTHA F	40
	MARY	71
	MARY M	157
COOKE, CELINDA		179
COON, ELMA		73
COOPER, EFFIE		107
	ELIZA	175
	ELIZABETH	165
	ELIZABETH E	174
	ELMIRA	84
	ETHEL	73
	FLORENCE A	71
	IDA	61
	LILLIE B	40
	LUCY M	86
	LUCY MATILDA	47
	MARGARET J	115
	MARGARET JANE	29
	MARGARET M	80
	MARY	134
	MARY PRISCILLA	111
	NANCY	156
	RACHEL F	9
	RHODA E	84
	SARAH E	169
COPAS, ALTA O		90
CORBETT, BETTIE		185
CORBIN, MARGARET L		42
CORBIT, JENNIE		54
CORDONIA, ALEXENIA		168
CORFEE, IDA		75
	LIZZIE	40
CORN, ANNA CAROLINE		188
	ELIZABETH F	57
CORNELL, ANNIE		178
CORNS, MARY		15
CORNWELL, MARGARET		60
	NANCY M	100
	NORA B	99
COSBY, MARY ANN		135
COSSEN, ALMIRA		133
COSSIN, (Mrs) MARY C		3
	BETHA M	150
	ELLA M	130
	GEORGIA	7
	LUCRETIA A	25
	MARY E	158
	MATILDA	9
	MOLLIE	134
COSTELO, MARGARET		148
COTHERN, NORA		112
COTTEREL, ANN		34

	MARY	111
	SARAH	34
	SARAH	34
COTTERELL, FLORA		81
COTTLE, DORA		23
	LUELLA G	21
COTTON, GRACE R		47
COTTRELL, BESSIE A		34
	CAROLINE	134
	PHOEBE A	85
COTTRILL, ESSTELLA M		48
	MARY C	122
	ROSE	14
COUCH, MARGUERITE		111
	MARTHA A	35
	SARAH F	45
	SARAH R	7
COUGHENOUR, TILLIE		152
COULTER, CATHARINE E		61
	MARY J	187
COURTS, JULIA A		15
COURTWRIGHT, MARY F		133
COVERSTON, MARIA		180
COVINGTON, LUCY V		18
COX, ELVIRA		42
	ERNESTINE	182
	JENNIE	38
	MARY E	103
	SARAH A	66
	SARAH E	157
	STELLA TENNESSEE	126
CRAFT, IRENE		122
	MARY	21
	NANCY ANN	14
CRAIG, ALICE		113
	ANNIE	1
	ANNIE	80
	BLANCHE	172
	EUGENIA	152
	GERTIE	82
	IDA MAY	124
	KITTY K	18
	LENNIE E	76
	LETTIE	3
	LULA J	74
	MARIA	101
	MARY	86
	MARY	126
	MARY A	86
	MATILDA	110
	MIRIAM	93
	ORA	86
	ORA	161
	SALLIE	1
	SUSAN	174
	VIRGINIA	125
CRAIGLOW, MARY A		170
CRAMENES, CATHARINE		48
CRAWFORD, HARRIET M		186
	JANE	37
	MARY	94
	OCTAVIA G	136
	VERDA ODESSA	115
CREASEY, MINERVA JANE		77

CREE, JERUSHA	98
CREECH, MARTHA ANN	111
CREIG, AMERICA	151
CREMEANS, ALICE	35
CUMA	178
ELIZABETH	54
ELIZABETH R	38
ELZA MINTA	100
HULDY	79
JULIA A	127
LUEZA	79
LYDIA	27
MARY	79
MARY E	96
MARY E	104
MATTIE J	27
NANCY	162
NARCISSA	50
PARTHENA	151
REBECCA J	12
CREMEENS, AMANDA	177
BERTHA D	6
BESSIE L	189
EFFIE	81
JENNIE F	188
MALINDA	116
MATILDA	85
MINTA	46
SARAH M	78
CREMENES, MARY	3
CREW, GUSTA	109
CRIG, PRUDY E	83
CRINE, PAMELIA	36
CRINER, ELLA MAY	18
LILLIE J	25
CRITES, ELIZABETH	187
CROOKHAM, ANNIE L	118
LUCINDA G	154
LUCY	187
LULA	8
MAUD M	86
SARAH	171
CROOKS, ADELIA L	24
AMY L	158
CROPLEY, MARY	171
CROSS, MARTHA	87
CROSSLEY, ELIZABETH	10
SARAH	187
CROUCH, MARTHA JANE	10
PAMELIA	73
SARAH E	10
SUSAN	31
CROUSE, MYRTLE	7
CROWDER, LENORA	129
CROWE, ELIVIRA	100
CROWN, ELIZA	60
CROY, BESSIE	47
CRUM, HATTIE E	177
CRUMP, ALLIE	44
BLANCH	189
EMMA E	57
HARRIET E	107
JENNIE	161
MARANDA	45
MARY	99
REBECCA JANE	99
SARAH	72
SARAH	131
CRUZAN, CATHARINE	101
HARRIET	107
SUSANNAH	93
CULLEN, ALLICE	45
ARTA	93
MARGARET	55
CULP, P LAURA	90
CULVER, M B	6
MARIA	156
CUMINGS, SARAH	162
CUMMINGS, LIZZIE	71
ROSA	137
CUMMINS, VIRGINIA	62
CUMPSTON, CORA	101
MARGARET	141
SALLY	24
CUNDIFF, AMANDA V	145
DAISY	191
IDA H	41
JESSIE	191
LOTTIE	155
MARY FRANCES	9
MELVINA C	180
MINNIE M	59
RHODA	50
RHODA M	170
SADIE	59
CUNNINGHAM, ANNA	155
ANNIE	67
BERTHA	146
BETSY ANN	147
CAROLINE	191
CARRIE	20
CLARA	77
CORA C	139
ELIZABETH	101
JOSIE	144
LYDIA MAE	74
MARTHA F	172
MARTHA L	77
MARY E	7
MARY M	77
MATTIE	141
MINA	105
TERISA MAY	77
VIRGINIA B	180
CURRY, CASSEY M	176
DELPHA	94
EMMER L	64
JANE	73
LENA	31
LILLIE B	180
LUELLA	74
MARY B	34
MAY	43
SARAH A	180
CURTIS, ELIZABETH	63
CUTCHALL, FLURRY	123
LOTTIE B	21
CUTLER, ANNA	63

Name	Page
CUTSHAW, REBECCA	162
SENA	124
DABNEY, ELIZABETH	177
GERTRUDE L	10
MARY E	9
MARY E	90
MARY V	142
MATTIE	24
NORA	108
ROSA M	74
DAIGH, ALICE	84
AMANDA	12
ANNIE	89
ELLA M	9
MINERVA	49
NANCY	167
DAILEY, EMMA	47
GRACE E	7
MAGGIE	47
DAILY, ELDA E	109
DAINS, LIZZIE M	99
DALTON, ELLEN C	1
MARGUERITE	10
SALLIE A	114
DANIEL, MINER	79
NANCY	50
DANIELS, ELIZA	85
LENA M	159
MARY A	29
DANKIN, TELITHA	54
DANNER, CARRIE	121
DANNIER, ALICE SAMANTHA	176
DARE, SUSANNA	24
DARNEL, OZELLO	30
DARNELL, AMERICA S	102
DARST, _____	190
ELIZABETH	121
HANNAH C	179
LYDIA M	120
MARGARET L	121
MARY AMANDA	155
MARY MAGDALENE	129
NANNIE MAY	107
PEARL	160
SARA D	3
DASHNER, MARY	62
MARY L	162
DAUGHERTY, CORA B	103
EMMA B	170
FANNIE	39
IVA	64
MARY	96
MARY ZELDA	164
VIRGINIA C	11
DAULTON, ELZANA	182
DAVAULT, CATHARINE J	102
DAVIDSON, LOUISE A	176
MARY	146
DAVIES, MARY	13
MARY	46
DAVIS, (Mrs) MARGARET E	141
(Mrs) NANCY ANN	154
ALMIRA	44
AMANDA J	92
ANN	172
ANN REBECCA	180
ANNIE E	166
ANNIE V	177
BELLE	56
BESSIE M	153
CARRIE	15
CLOE V	178
CYNTHIA	125
ELIZABETH	20
ELIZABETH	29
ELIZABETH	120
ELLA	184
EMELINE	16
EMILY J	166
EVA	105
FRANCES	62
FRANCES J	98
GEORGIA M	119
JULIA	98
LAURA B	89
LUCINDA	157
MAHALA	78
MAHALIA	114
MALINDA	182
MARGARET J	81
MARY	148
MARY A	83
MARY A	179
MARY ANN	177
MARY C	68
MARY M	21
NELLIE	75
OLIVE EDITH	1
OLLIE	181
ORA FLORENCE	29
ROSA	161
ROSA L	18
ROSANNA	182
RUTH E	171
SALVE	189
SARAH E	150
SARAH JANE	188
SYLVIA E	5
DAVISON, JENNIE R	61
DAWALT, ELIZABETH	122
DAWES, IRENE	9
DAY, (Mrs) J F	180
CARRIE H	10
ELIZABETH	155
EMILY	49
FRANCES M	157
LIDIA B	172
REBECCA J	52
SARAH LUCETTA	68
SUSAN C	34
DAYLONG, ANNA E	40
MARANDA	93
OCEA MYRTLE	50
SUSAN	149
DAYVALT, MARY FRANCES	128
DAYWALT, CATHARINE JANE	41
SARAH ANN	122
DAYWAULT, MARY	16

DEAL, CATHARINE	183
IRENA B	8
LEFAVOR	52
ORETHA	72
DEAMS, VIOLA E	151
DEARTLE, DELIA	48
DEBOLT, CHARITY A	182
DECKER, ELIZABETH	43
FANNY L	11
LIZZIE A	85
MINNIE M	140
ROSA L	139
DEEAN, KATE	24
DEEM, LETTIE L	85
MARY E	89
MARY M	10
NANCY	171
SUSAN	159
DEFENBACH, ELIZABETH	141
DEFFENBAUGH, CATHARINE	65
DEFOE, MARTHA ANN	136
DEFORD, HANNAH ANN	141
DELANEY, LEE D	7
DENBEL, E E	164
DENKENS, SUSAN	140
DENNEY, CYNTHIA	40
JOSEPHINE	55
NORA M	74
DENNIE, ALICE J	8
DENNIS, BERTHA	73
ETHEL F	64
KATHARYN	73
DENNY, CAROLINE	78
FRANCES	83
JESSIE FAY	143
LEONA M	185
MARY F	21
MINNIE A	20
ROSA	157
DENTON, ANNIE F	36
DERINBERGER, RUTH	130
DEVAULT, MARY H	38
SERENA ORA ETHEL	142
DEVOIR, ALICE	4
RACHEL J	67
DEVORE, MAUD A	44
ROSIE LEE	22
DEWEES, ELVIRA	160
FLORA A	80
MARTHA J	1
REBECCA E	130
RUTH	112
DEWEESE, ABIGAIL	187
ANNIE	77
CLARA	95
DIANAH	184
ELLA A	172
IDA C	95
LAURA M	2
LUCINDA J	156
LUELLA ABIGAL	95
MINERVA J	25
RACHEL	25
DEWET, LYDIA	141
DEWIT, CHARLOTTE	67
DeWITT, DAISE I	188
E GRACE	131
EDITH C	184
LEOTA JANE	61
NORMA C	142
DEWUEES, CATHARINE C	40
DICKEN, EVA MAY	53
MARY	125
MARY L	149
DICKINSON, BELLE	158
DICKS, CORA M	114
DIDGUS, EMMA A	105
DIEFENBACH, ANNA M	185
DIEFENBAUGH, LENORA	68
DIEHL, EMMA McCLAIN	141
LONA M	183
ROSA M	50
DILCHER, JOSEPHINE	132
DILL, CLARA M	168
JULIA	118
DINGEY, CHARITY A	41
RACHEL A	170
DINGY, CORA	10
DIVERS, LELIA	87
DIVES, LELIE	184
DIXON, (Mrs) MAUDE A	20
HANNAH B	109
MAGGIE	36
EDMONDS, SUSANNA MARY MARGARET THEODORA	172
DOBYNS, MARY A	26
DODSON, CAROLINE	47
CLARISSA	47
MARY I	99
OLLIE A	123
ROSE E	45
SARAH F	191
TENA	11
VIENNA	30
VIRGINIA F	30
DOLEMAN, MARIA	35
DOLMAN, ELLA	184
DONALLY, ABBY	189
LETHA	101
DONERY, EMILY	83
DONLEY, ROXEY A	69
DONNALLY, CORNELIA J	38
POLLY	162
DONOHEW, LYDIA	179
SUSIE	70
DONOHUE, ADALINE	3
EMMA A	16
LILLIE ROMA	50
MARTHA M	72
MARY LETTIE	168
DONOVAN, BRIDGET	134
DOOLEY, REBECCA J	1
DOOLITTLE, MARY C	112
DORNICK, MARY	21
SHUELLA	37
DORSEY, SALLIE	17
DOSS, ELLA	24
FLORENCE	108

LAVINA ANN	128
MARY E	25
ONA	28
PENELOPE SUSAN	22
DOTSON, MARY EVELINE	51
SARAH J	182
DOUGLAS, ALICE	92
MARY A	189
SAMANTHA E	114
DOUGLASS, MARY T	40
DOUTT, ROSALIE	116
DOW, NANNIE J	125
DOWELL, (Mrs) SARAH L	66
ALICE	183
BERTIE	81
MAGGIE	85
MARTHA E	156
MINERVA	180
MIRTIE M	67
SARAH	180
SARAH A E	38
SUSAN M	131
DOWER, JOSIE	14
MARY ELIZABETH	167
DOWNES, MARY ANN	127
DOWNS, BERTHA A	36
HANNAH	100
DRAKE, IRMA	46
MARY E	184
ZENIA	188
DRUMMOND, ALICE	141
DUDLEY, NANCY	102
DUFF, CASSIE R	139
DORA B	64
LAURA A	64
LOUISA L	32
ROSA L	143
SARAH J	43
SARAH J	143
DUFFER, MARGARET	158
SARAH	1
SUSAN JANE	113
DUFFY, ELLA	114
LILLIE B	186
DUFOUR, NETTIE	124
DUGH, REBECCA	72
DUN, JANE	135
DUNCAN, ALICE	9
BIRDIE F	45
CORA	54
CORA E	166
ELIZA	27
ELIZABETH L	109
FANNIE	44
FANNIE	190
HANNAH	180
HARRIET M	39
LUCINDA W	32
LURAY J	129
MAGGIE L	29
MARTHA	157
MARY J	189
MARY L	38
MATILDA J	97
NANCY C	133
NORA	151
ROSETTA M	66
SARAH	101
SARAH A	114
SUSAN M	80
DUNDESS, ROSIE L	179
DUNFIELD, ELIZABETH B	167
DUNHAM, ANTHE	166
IONA	118
MARY E	76
DUNLAP, ANGELINE	174
ANNIE	47
ELLA	44
EMMA	34
HESTER	32
DUNLOPP, SARAH B	50
DUNN, (Mrs) RHODA	72
ALICE	51
ALICE MAUD	68
ANN E	3
BERTHA	92
CORDELIA A	121
ELIZA J	12
ELIZA J	47
ELIZABETH	174
EMOGENE	152
LUTITIA BETTIE	191
MAGLINE	155
MARTHA REGINA	167
MARY A	74
RHODA C	73
SALLIE	55
STELLA MAE	179
DURST, ALICE H	143
ALTA	183
CHRISTENA	30
CORA A	113
ELIZABETH R	9
EMELINE R A	18
FANNY	30
HANNAH	50
LIZZIE A	11
LORA B	40
LULA M	126
MAE L	170
MARY	16
RILLA J	129
SUSAN	12
WILLIA H	163
ZILLIAN E	161
DUVALL, ANNIE	182
NANCY E	4
REBECCA J	14
DWYER, (Mrs) MARY A	148
DYE, ALBERTA	29
EMILY	44
MURL	14
DYER, ANN	185
ELMA G	127
MILA A	55
SUSAN	113
DYKE, LUCILE ESTHER	120
LYDIA M	168

PEARL	41
EADES, BERTHA J	137
ETHEL C	160
SARAH F	135
EADS, (Mrs) KATIE	73
ANGELINE	39
DELLA	183
DICIE ELLEN	147
IDA	21
KATIE	57
LAVINIA	93
MABEL RUTH	34
MAGGIE	42
MARY A	188
MARY F	190
MARY J	11
MARY J	25
MARY J	135
MINNIE ALICE	161
NANCY	108
NANCY	163
NANCY C	99
REBECCA	68
SALLY	57
SARAH E	111
EAGAN, MATTIE J	23
EAKIN, FANNIE E	90
EARWOOD, BETTIE	45
PEARLIE	18
EASTHAM, ALICE L	88
ANN	70
ELIZABETH	3
EMILY	103
LIZZIE F	15
LUCINDA	76
MARGARET	49
MARY KATE	34
EBLIN, NETTIE JANE	47
ECKARD, ALICE	139
ANN	45
ANN E	67
BARBARA	190
BARBARA C	133
CATHARINE	63
CLARA M	60
ELIZABETH	52
HENRIETTA	57
JANE	140
JOSEPHINE	98
LILLIAN	103
LUCH M	32
LUCY	140
LUCY J	184
MAHALA E	37
MALINDA	97
MARGARET	52
MARGARET ANN	190
MARTHA MATILDA	88
MARY	93
MARY	100
MARY ANN	140
MARY E	140
MARY ELIZABETH	97
MARY M	175
MATTIE B	113
MINNIE M	106
NAOMA	108
ORA ETHEL	134
SALLIE R	11
SUSAN	175
ECKART, BARBARA	144
EDEN, DORA MAY	189
FOREST	106
MINNIE	101
STELLA B	49
EDENS, MARY C	118
EDINGTON, BELLE	186
EVA	95
EDMONDS, JENNETTE F	36
MISSOURI	2
NEVADA	191
REGINA	171
ROXIE	188
SALLIE	94
SYBLE	66
EDMUNDS, CLARINDA	116
CORA	36
LUCY E	116
ORACY SIDNEY	79
SOPHIA J V	3
EDWARD, RESIA J	64
EDWARDS, (Mrs) ELIZABETH	177
(Mrs) PERMELIA ANN	71
ADA	141
ADA M	75
ALICE	124
ALICE	154
ALICE	162
AMA W	114
AMANDA	77
ARAMINTA JENNIE	171
BETSY	100
CARRIE	101
CHRISTINA M	165
CLARA	49
CORA	81
CORA	120
CORDELIA	85
CYRENA F	105
DELILA	3
DELILA	73
DRUZILLA	104
ELIZA	49
ELIZABETH	141
ELIZABETH	142
ELIZABETH	175
EMILY	122
ERCY	67
EVA LEE	17
FLORILLA	159
FLOSSIE J	141
FRANCES	30
FRANCES W	28
GERTIE M	111
HANNAH	175
HELEN J	126
HELLEN M	81
HENRIETTA	86

IDA	27	
IDA A	33	
IDA MAY	9	
JANE	20	
JANE	133	
JANE A	99	
JOSIE	192	
JULIA A	76	
LAURA	87	
LEAH	96	
LOTTIE	73	
LOUISA	25	
LUCY	100	
MAE	45	
MARGARET	96	
MARGARET	129	
MARGARET ANN	56	
MARIA A	30	
MARIA E	86	
MARTHA	120	
MARY	12	
MARY	54	
MARY	74	
MARY	120	
MARY C	149	
MARY CAROLINE	164	
MARY E	127	
MARY M	174	
MARY M	137	
MILLIE	166	
MINNIE	157	
MURIEL E	41	
MYRTLE M	142	
NANCY A	104	
NANCY V	99	
NARCISSA	107	
OLIVIA	92	
ORA M	3	
REBECCA E	36	
RHUAMA A	42	
SALLIE	16	
SALLY A	101	
SAMANTHA	23	
SARAH	47	
SARAH E	30	
SEREPTA A	57	
SULLA	100	
TILLIE	39	
VIRGINIA L	35	
EGAN, CORA JACKSON	12	
EGGENSCHWILLER, ANNA M	101	
LIZZIE	97	
MARY	189	
EGGENSWILLER, MILLIE	18	
EGGLESTON, HATTIE E	60	
EISHER, LYDIA A	3	
ELAM, MAGGIE	89	
ELIAS, JENNIE	106	
ELKINS, (Mrs) EFFIE M	97	
LIZZIE	36	
ELLENBACH, CAROLINE	151	
ELLENWOOD, ETHEL C	2	
ELLIOT, ANNIE V	136	
ELLIOTT, (Mrs) MANDA	189	
(Mrs) MARGARET A	146	
ALNORAH	131	
BERTHA	23	
CORA	107	
MARY	21	
MARY E	112	
MAUDE	147	
NANCY	33	
NANCY E	129	
SALINDA CATHERENE	13	
ELLIS, BERTINE	31	
KATIE	68	
LUCINDA ANNIE	56	
MARY F	172	
SUSAN ELIZABETH	1	
ELLISON, EDNA E	23	
EDNA E	134	
ELLSNICK, LILLIE	122	
ELLWANGER, FLORENCE	179	
ELMORE, MARY	101	
RHODA FRANCES	31	
ELY, ELLA	25	
EMMA M	64	
HULDAH M	56	
MINNIE A	160	
EMANUEL, ANNA B	138	
MARY M	45	
EMBLETON, IDA	178	
JENNIE	104	
MARY E	170	
SARAH	66	
EMBREE, (Mrs) BLANCHE	21	
EMORY, MARY JANE	56	
ENGEL, EDITH	169	
ENGLE, ROSE	149	
ENGLISH, EUNICE	114	
MARGARET LYNN	66	
MARY S	136	
ENIZE, ANNA	145	
ENTSMINGER, ELIZA	173	
MARGARET E	155	
ENTWHISTLE, MAGGIE M	171	
ENTWISTLE, NELLIE	70	
EPPLE, FREDA L	47	
EPPLEWHITE, (Mrs) DECIMAY	48	
ERETT, MARTHA	65	
ERRETT, JOSEPHINE	167	
MAY R	18	
VIRGINIA FRANCES	49	
ERVEN, JENNIE	79	
ERVIN, IDA	97	
MARIA	109	
REBECCA	110	
ERWEN, ELIZABETH	90	
MARGARET	90	
ERWIN, BARBARY	55	
NANCY	85	
NORA	115	
SARAH	79	
VIOLA	180	
ESHFIELD, MARY	103	
ESKEW, HESTER	156	
JULIA	172	
MARY	62	

VIRGIE L	187
ESTEP, AMANDA E	118
BESSIE L	147
GERTRUDE	145
ESTES, SARIAH	28
ESTILL, ALFORATA V	16
ESTIS, MARY JANE	76
EVANS, ANN	162
ANNA ETHEL	156
DEBORAH	29
ELIZABETH	185
EMOZETTE	43
LIZZIE	12
LORENA	108
LYDIA	102
MARY J	146
NELLIE	40
ONETA D	177
RACHEL L	175
SALLY	162
EVERETT, LUCY	127
POLLY	3
EVERETTE, JANE	104
EVRETT, JOSEPHINE	167
EWELL, MARY JANE	167
PRISCILLA	71
EWERS, MAGGIE	60
EWING, NINA FAYE	143
SARAH E	22
EWINGS, CORAH	133
EYLER, MARY	75
FADELEY, JESSIE A	94
KATE MISSOURI	93
MARY JANE	14
MITTIE A	115
FADELY, LYDIA M	47
MARY	164
FAIER, EMMA	72
FARGO, AMANDA	143
DELILA	125
EMILY C	90
HENRIETTA	47
IRENA	15
LUNA	53
FARLEY, ANNIE L	1
BESSIE	24
EASTER	115
FANNIE M	59
GRACE	27
GRACE	123
HELLEN G	46
HESTER	18
LAURA	180
MALINDA JANE	141
MIRTLE E	76
REBECCA	157
SIANDA	29
FARMER, MARY	117
FAUBER, JUDA J	36
FAUDREE, IDA R	129
SALLIE M	171
FAUVER, ALTIE J	168
FANNIE	22
NANCY A	33
FEENY, MARY A	104
FELLURE, DORA	49
FENIMORE, HANNAH E	94
HARRIET	142
KATE	107
FENTEN, ALICE	4
FERGUSON, E VANNA	28
ELLA	27
ELLA ELIZABETH	172
HESTHER	13
JUNIA	3
LEONA P	26
MINNIE	63
MINNIE	150
MYRTLE	84
FERRELL, FERNIE S	71
FETTY, BESSIE	27
CLAUDIE M	176
ELIZABETH A	115
EMMA	89
GERTIE	10
GOLDIE E	103
KATIE	176
LUCINDA J	127
MALINDA	115
ROSALIE	162
SARAH F	173
VERNA ELIZABETH	155
FIEDLER, VIOLA	58
FIELD, BERTHA MAY	38
BLANCHE	141
FIELDER, ANGELINE JOSEPHINE	107
ELIZABETH	26
ELIZABETH	88
GERTRUDE	98
MAMMIE	92
STELLA	139
FIELDS, ADIE F	188
FLORENCE M	144
FRANCES	173
IDA FLORENCE	19
IDA V	43
LILLIAN R	134
MARGARET A	105
MARY	10
MARY E	180
FIERBAUGH, LONA	20
FIFE, BETSY	143
ELIZABETH	124
FILSON, MYRTIE ROSS	122
FINDLEY, ALICE	136
BESSIE	137
ELIZABETH	28
MARTHA L	169
ORILLA	180
STELLA	140
FINICAL, ISIBEL	88
FINICAN, CATHARINE	77
FINICON, CLARA	113
FINNEY, ELIZABETH	110
FINNICUM, FANNY	66
FINNY, ANNIE L	53
CATHARINE	28
FIRST, LILLIAN V	61

MAY	22
FISHER, ADIE E	138
AMANDA	3
ARTA J	55
BETTIE L	101
CATHARINE	43
CATHARINE	111
CATHARINE E	162
CLARA A	126
CLARA LOVENIA	54
ELIZA	56
ELLA	145
EVALENA	54
FANNIE	30
FLORA L	17
HENRIETTA	14
IVIE L	20
JENNIE	67
JOSIE	90
JULIET J	77
LAVINIA A	54
LILLIE D	93
LUCY ANN	175
MARTHA ANN	140
MARY ANN	135
MARY B	162
MARY C	146
MARY L	190
MARY M	30
MATTIE	174
NANCY JANE	48
NINA M	130
REBECCA	156
ROSE B	175
RUTHA B	164
SARAH	127
SARAH	183
SARAH	54
SARAH L	175
SARAH S	42
SUSANNA	190
FITSGERALD, ELLEN	121
FITZSIMMONS, JULIA	52
FLAHARTY, RACHEL	151
FLAIG, EMMA	106
FLANAGAN, EMMA C	50
FLESHER, (Mrs) CATHARINE	166
GRACE	156
LIDIA	110
NANCY	83
RACHAEL	43
FLETCHER, ELIZABETH E	39
EMILY JANE	16
HATTIE	81
JUNE ADA	108
LEFAVOR	6
LILLIE M	125
MATTIE	125
MYRTIE	133
FLINT, LAURA E	76
MARY	175
REBECCA	43
FLORA, ANNIE	54
ELECTA	53
MARY A	124
THENORA	107
FLORAY, EFFIE LUCINDA	161
ISADORE E	5
JANNA J	185
FLORVA, PHOEBE J	41
FLORY, JENCIE	29
FLOWERS, (Mrs) VIRGINIA G	161
ANNIE A	28
DELIA	158
ELECTA A	161
EMMA	80
FANNIE	122
FANNIE	174
HATTIE A	84
MARY E	124
MIRIAM	189
RUHAMA H	57
SARAH	148
VIOLA	189
FOGLESONG, ALICE C	136
ELIZABETH	139
ELIZABETH J	139
FANNIE	175
JANE C	16
M MARGARET	139
MARGARET	63
MARTHA E	137
MARY J	140
MINNIE JANE	83
SARAH	139
SARAH F	135
VIRGIE L	111
FOLDEN, E F	101
HILDAH MAY	160
FOLDING, NANCY J	155
FOLEY, PRECILLA DUNLAP	152
FONLY, MARGARET	42
SARAH	8
SUSAN	8
FORBES, CATHARINE	154
CHRISTINA	65
ETHEL	164
EVA S	53
MOLLIE	2
FORBIS, ADA M	63
FANNIE	121
FORBUS, MARY M	184
OLA	118
ORA	94
VIOLA	86
FORD, ELDA	100
ELIZA	167
MARY ANN	32
FORDE, AMANDA CATHARINE	107
FOREMAN, LAURA M	146
MARY A	13
FORESHEE, MARY CATHARINE	112
FORREST, CATHERINE	18
ETHEL M	85
LILLIE	162
M MARY	85
MARY	169
MARY ELLEN	31

	MINNIE SABRIE	104
	ORENI	110
	SALLIE ELIZABETH	36
FORRESTER, JOANNA		132
FORTH, ANNA		42
	DELLA	85
	ELLA	78
FORTUNE, FRANCES N		154
FOSTER, CLARA L		79
	COLUMBIA A	40
	FANNIE A	124
	MATILDA G	84
FOUGHT, REBECCA		105
FOURCHE, JENNIE		57
FOURTH, ESSIE		61
	MADA	27
FOUT, LAURA		31
FOWLER, (Mrs) DAISY		19
	ADA	129
	ADDIE	174
	ANNIE	39
	ANNIE L	170
	BELVIL	23
	CORA	53
	DAISY L	138
	DORA ETHEL	82
	DORISCA	14
	EDNA	31
	EDNA	31
	ELIZABETH C	11
	ELLA	30
	ELNORA	45
	GEORGIA A	58
	GERTRUDE	126
	HARRIET	11
	HARRIET B	89
	HARRIET E	161
	INNEZ L	113
	LAURA C	20
	LENA FRANCES	144
	LETTIE M	95
	LILA	184
	MARGARET	186
	MARIA VIRGINIA	153
	MARY A	163
	MARY E	84
	MARY ELIZABETH	176
	MARY R	46
	MAY B	169
	NANCY E	72
	NANNIE	43
	ORILLA	42
	PAMELIA O	47
	REBECA E	17
	RHODA	43
	RHODA	29
	SALLIE	62
	SAMANTHA	70
	SARAH	51
	VICTORIA	12
	VIOLA	85
	WILLIE G	105
	WINNIE M	153
FOX, EMMA		164
	ETHELL	47
	LUCY J	22
	MARY	176
FRAKES, BERTHA		81
FRANCE, IDA E		101
FRANCES, ELIZABETH		41
	MARTHA	92
FRANCIS, EMMA		107
	KATIE	119
	MAMIE	46
	MARY	107
	MARY A	165
	SARAH	144
FRANKLIN, CELIA		119
	ELIZA	148
	FANNIE L	96
	LULU BLANCHE	172
	MARY C	82
FRANZ, MARY		96
FRASHER, LULA		2
FRASHIER, EDITH		88
FRAZER, MARGARET ANN		162
FRAZIER, (Mrs) REBECCA		74
	ARLI GERTRUDE	119
	CARRIE	96
	CLEMMIE	174
	HARRIET S	96
	LUELLA	181
	MARY E	94
	SARAH F	136
FREED, HARRIET		141
FREEMAN, ALICE		67
	CORA	24
	LUCY	122
	MARY S	181
	MIDE	114
FRENCH, ADALINE L		93
	ALICE	165
	AVA MARIE	60
	DELLA G	38
	ELNORA	17
	HATTIE	148
	MARY CATHARINE	134
	NANNIE J	79
FRESON, BETSY		81
FRIDLEY, BARBARA E		106
	LILLIE B	57
	REBECCA J	111
FRIEDMAN, PRUDENCE		132
FRIEND, AMANDA J		156
	ELLEN	24
FRINLEY, MAGGIE		91
FROIDVEAUX, MARY		82
FROST, ANNA		5
	FANNY	25
	FLORA A	117
	IDA	68
	JESSIE	72
	LENA	9
	MARY M	177
	MAUD	176
	PATSY	87
	SARAH F	60
	VEVA E	178

Name	Page
FROUNFELTER, CLEMMIE	60
FRUITH, ANNIE M	51
MAGDALENA	55
TILLIE	23
FRUTH, ANNIE	174
KATHARINE	102
NORA MAY	103
FRY, ALLIE M	13
ALMIRA	144
CHRISTENA	123
CLARA	139
DELPHA	147
EFFA M	8
ELIZABETH	122
ELIZABETH	155
ELIZABETH C	179
HANNAH F	13
HATTIE CLEMENTINE	21
IDA E	59
IDA F	144
INA M	1
IVA GENEVA	1
IVY M	6
LAURA A	59
LAURA L	139
LENA L	138
LIZZIE MAY	13
LONA	55
LOUISA	138
LYDIA E	51
MAGGIE L	91
MARTHA A	4
MARTHA J	175
MARY F	28
MARY M	147
MARY PHIDILLA	76
MATTIE E	115
MILLIE	144
MIRIAM A	168
NELLIE MAY	4
OLIVE	144
ROSA M	123
SARAH FRANCES	9
SARAH S	139
SHARON	180
STELLA	65
SUSAN C	81
SUSAN E	182
VINNIE R	152
FUGATE, MAYME	3
FUGETT, MARY A	94
FULKERSON, MARTHA W	134
FULLER, CLARA B	156
EMMA M	153
SARAH	85
FULLERTON, FLOSSIE	129
FULLMER, ELLA	117
FULLNER, MARY	190
FULTZ, MARIA H	107
MATTIE	114
RHEA PEARL	122
FUNK, ANN M	50
CYNTHIA	107
FURGET, NANCY C	125
FURGUSON, LIZZIE	164
MARY C	159
REBECCA	112
SARAH J	100
FURNELL, LIZZIE	162
FURTH, FRANCES	66
HENRIETTA	78
MARTHA	87
MARY	132
GABBERT, ADA F	52
ELLA C	72
ELLA C	182
ELMIRA D	40
ELMIRA D	79
NANNIE M	114
GAINES, MARY FRANCES	152
GALBREATH, AGNES S	84
GALE, SUE A	143
GALLAGHER, FANNIE	135
GALLASPIE, NANCY	55
GALLEHUE, LOUISE G	176
GAMBLE, CLARA E	126
GANDEE, LUCINDA E	58
MARY C	20
GANDY, JESSIE	113
GANNON, SARAH	38
GANO, PERMELIA	99
GARBY, LARINDA	98
GARD, CHRISTINA	38
MAGGIE	37
MARY	169
VIOLA	172
GARDNER, ALFRETTA	5
ANN	129
BESSIE A	53
CARRIE D	36
CLARA MELINDA	41
EFFIE COLLINS	76
EMALINE C	54
ESTELLA B	16
EVA	96
FRANCIS	122
HENRIETTA G	89
JANE	85
JOSEPHINE	60
JUDY WEST	16
LUCY	131
MARTHA	112
MARY	11
MARY A	22
MARY M	188
MARY S	34
NANCY ANN	98
OLIVIA J	103
SEVIE	120
GARLACH, ELIZABETH	96
GARLAND, ADA C	186
GARLIC, MATTIE E	153
GARNES, ALICE M	156
MALISSA ELIZABETH	30
GARNS, MARY	30
GARRISON, NANCY J	177
GARTON, FIDELIA M	43
FRANCES A	179

JUDY B	82	BERTHA A	18
MALVINA M	179	BESSIE	123
PATSY	129	BLANCH	97
PATSY	131	CARRIE	65
SARAH C	43	CATHARINE	98
GASKIL, ANNIE M	136	CHRISTENA CATHARINE	46
GASKINS, EFFIE A	135	DAISEY	122
JESSIE	175	DELLA	52
JUDA R	112	ELIZABETH	72
MARGARET S	156	ELIZABETH	124
MARIA J	116	ELVIRA	13
MINNIE C	57	ETHEL M	31
MINNIE M	45	EVA	71
NANCY	127	FANNIE F	62
RUBY M	104	FLORENCE E A	17
SARAH J	57	GENORA C	146
SEREPTA A	71	HANNAH E	87
GASTON, ANN	139	HANNAH L	106
MILDRED J	45	HATTIE K	28
GATES, CLARA	163	JULIA	37
MARY ANN	169	LAURA V	77
OLA	20	LILLIE	174
GEARHART, ANNA	191	LUCINDA B	175
CLARA A	141	LUCY	81
FANNIE	78	LUCY	81
GEBHART, EVA NORMA	184	LULA C	100
GEE, MARY M	156	MARGARET	176
PHEBE ANN	91	MARGARET JANE	47
GEHO, ANNIE C	156	MARIA	37
FRANCES A	104	MARIA EMMA	65
IDA IRENE	191	MARTHA	38
SARAH M	131	MARTHA	50
GENHEIMER, ADA	187	MARTHA C	33
GEORGE, ANNIE E	89	MARY C	27
ELIZABETH W	157	MARY C	110
JOSEPHINE	62	MARY CAROLINE	144
LYDIA L	73	MARY E	9
MARGARET ANN	102	MARY LOUISE	170
MARGARET B	17	MARY M	171
MARY ELIZABETH	70	MOLLIE	80
MARY F	7	MOLLIE D	100
NANCY	132	NANCY ANN	47
POLLY	50	NANCY V	46
SARAH ANN	187	NELLIE	69
SARAH M	53	OLIVIA J	141
GERLACH, HALLIE B	65	ORA M	94
LONA LEONORA	188	RACHEL FLORENCE	59
GERLICH, MARGARET	139	REBECCA	79
GERLOCK, DOROTHY E	181	REBECCA ANN	139
GERMAN, ELIZA J	46	ROMA E	69
LILLIE	112	ROSA	140
MARY	88	ROSANA	59
GESS, ALMIRA	137	SARAH	103
GIBAUT, (Mrs) ELIZABETH	190	SARAH A	59
GIBBEAUT, ANNIE	168	SARAH A	120
CELIA	93	SARAH ANN	14
MINNIE F	4	SARAH P	35
GIBBONS, ELLA J	50	SUSAN A	97
IDA K	122	SUSANA	77
LUCY A	168	UNIS	72
GIBBS, ADA A	15	ZELMA LEE	135
AMANDA E	77	ZUBY ANN	143
ANNA E	59	GIBEAUT, SARAH	143
ANNIE A	141	GIBSON, BIRTIE	25

EFFIE	110
ISABELLA BELL	67
LEVAGA E	177
LILLIE L	158
MARTHA VIRGINIA	116
MARY	99
MARY J	94
MISELLANA	126
SYLVIA MAY	191
GIDDER, AMELIA	74
GIFT, CATHARINE	124
GILBERT, CLARE	155
JULIA	26
GILES, LYDA K	172
MAGGIE	185
MILLIE	7
GILL, ANNA B	74
ELNORA	39
GARNET E	10
HARRIET A	105
LAVINA	14
VICTORIA	189
GILLAND, NANNIE	72
GILLASPIE, EMMA	14
MARTHA	134
GILLESPIE, EFFIE	142
ESSIE	115
MIRIAM	45
NORA	103
NORA C	64
SARAH J	66
GILLIAN, LYDIA	131
GILLILAND, SARAH J	113
GILLIS, ANN	31
CORA B	11
LIZZIE G	82
MARY ANN	96
GILLISPIE, ADA	78
CHARLOTTE G	68
DELLA	53
LUALLIE	57
MARTHA	66
OLLIE MAY	142
SARAH E	9
GILMORE, NELLIE B	44
CARRIE M	72
DORA B	124
EFFIE	101
ELIZABETH	108
ELLEN E	66
FLORENCE C	120
FRANKIE	80
LIDA F	27
MARY C	56
REBECCA	88
SHIRLEY M	108
VENICE	49
GILPIN, BLANCH	103
GRACE	166
HARRIET S	160
MARGARET	106
SARAH J	24
GILPON, GRACE	149
GILSON, ANN E	156
POLLY	127
GINDER, MARY	10
GINTHER, CAROLINE	99
ELIZABETH MARY	151
JENNIE L	117
GIPSON, MARY	115
GISE, ELIZA J	122
EMILY M	178
MARGARET	42
MARY ELLEN	45
REBECCA C	138
GIST, ELLA B	150
GLADYS E	24
MAY	2
GLASPIE, OLIVIA	119
GLASS, RACHEL	4
GLASSBURN, EMMA D	99
LULU M	97
MAGGIE C	12
MAGGIE C	77
GLEASON, (Mrs) KATIE	139
BARBARA ELIZABETH	125
MARY	31
GLENN, ANNIE E	143
IDA	92
MARY ELLEN	166
MAUDE E	150
SARAH E	146
GLISSPY, DORA E	5
GLOECKNER, HAZEL CLEO	148
MAGGIE	157
GLOVER, ANNIE L	46
ARTINSA	157
AUDLEY	124
CAROLINE	1
FANNIE M	164
NANNIE M	54
ROSE A	54
ROSINA	112
VIRGINIA	163
GLUESENCAMP, ANNIE	170
GOBE, LIZZIE A	20
GOBLE, VADIE	15
GODFREY, HELEN LOUISE	158
GODLEY, LAVINIA L	141
GOETING, LOUISE	61
GOLD, MARY MAGDALENE	148
GOODALL, SARAH A	109
GOODFELLOW, EMELINE	139
GOODIN, MARY DELLA	136
GOODNIGHT, LYDIA	191
SUSAN	62
GOODNITE, ANGELINE	21
DRUZILLA	21
ELIZABETH	120
GOODWIN, MATILDA	50
GORDAN, JESSIE	109
GORDON, (Mrs) MARY K	22
BERTHA	97
BESSIE M	62
ELIZA	61
GOLDIE	84
LOUISA	169
MYRTIE L	103

GORSUCH, EDITH	154	GREEN, AMANDA C	49
GOSNAY, ISABELLE	30	ELIZABETH	24
LOTTIE	3	EMMA A	42
MATILDA	24	JANIE	121
GOSSETT, EUNICE E	29	MARIA	60
LAVINIA FRANCES	191	MARY	113
GOUDY, MARIAMNE M	74	MARY A	96
GOULD, CARRIE	168	MARY J	2
ELLA	1	MINNIE	189
GOULDING, MARY A	128	MINNIE B	171
GOWER, LIZZIE	184	MITTIE	108
GOWIN, DORA L	68	ORA M	39
GOWLIN, NORA A	57	SARAH	61
GRADY, LORETTA	60	SARAH A	149
GRAHAM, ADDA A	94	GREENLEE, (Mrs) MAUDE	68
ALICE	25	ALICE	107
ALLIE	56	ANNA C	188
CAROLINE	46	BERTHA F	44
DELPHA R	88	CLARA B	88
DICIE E	16	DEBORAH	49
EFFA	65	ELIZA JANE	63
ELIZABETH J	16	ELIZABETH	137
ESSIE EDITH	34	ELIZABETH	138
HANNAH	157	ELIZABETH	138
HANNAH E	176	ELIZABETH	140
HETTIE E	65	ELLEN F	138
IDA	132	EMMA F	94
IDA B	3	FLORA	167
JESSIE	133	GEORGIE BELLE	17
MALINDA	84	HANNAH C	127
MINNIE F	27	HARRIET	14
NORA	23	HARRIET	50
RUTH E	37	HARRIET E	154
SARAH E	5	HATTIE	76
SARAH E	16	IDA E	88
STELLA M	94	INGABY	18
VICTORIA A	24	JANE	104
GRANDSTAFF, EDDETH ELDONA	85	JANE	123
EVETH ELZONA	39	JENNY	123
GRANT, LOTTIE	176	LELIA ANN	50
GRAY, CHARLOTTE	159	LENA	64
EFFIE E	59	LOUISA	2
ELIZABETH	69	LUCETTA	92
EMMA	166	LURETTA	32
FLORA B	158	MARGARET	15
HETTIE ANN	145	MARTHA	55
IDA A	94	MARTHA	148
JANE	186	MARTHA F	159
LINNIE A	139	MARTHA JANE	138
LYDIA M	160	MARY	76
MARY A	147	MARY	119
MARY E	100	MARY	13
NANCY	46	MARY ETHEL	95
NARCISSA	69	MARY J	10
RACHEL MARIA	14	MARY M	73
ROSANA	25	MARY S	63
RUTH	75	MELVINA	167
SARAH J	136	MYRTIE	169
SUSAN E	59	NANCY	152
VIRGIE E	160	NANCY	158
GRAYSON, LIDDIE M	60	NANCY C	167
GREASER, SARAH	162	NANCY M	147
GREATHOUSE, AMANDA	118	NELLIE ERMA BLANCHE	120
EMELINE	132	ORA O	45

PARETHA	49	
RACHEL	154	
REBECCA ANN	8	
SARAH	67	
SARAH	164	
SARAH C	5	
SARAH K	53	
SARAH M	139	
SUSAN	107	
VIRGINIA B	140	
VIRGINIA E	44	
GREENLEY, HANNAH K	58	
GREER, ADELIA	163	
CARRIE	64	
CATHARINE	33	
EMMA D	60	
ESSIE	120	
FLORA	170	
GARNET M	24	
IDA	63	
JANE	96	
JULIA	169	
LENA LEOTI	170	
LONA	64	
LYDIA J	61	
MARGARET I	104	
MARY M	163	
MARY T	31	
NANNIE B	32	
NANNIE M	103	
OLLIE	103	
OMA R	39	
ONIE	100	
SARAH C	134	
SARAH M	154	
SYLVIA L	127	
GREG, NANNIE S	131	
GREGGORY, EMMA B	97	
GREGORY, ALTHEA S	129	
ROSETTA	176	
SARAH M	88	
GRELLE, LEFA L	153	
GRESHAM, VIRGINIA	97	
GRESHEM, FANNIE	54	
GRESS, (Mrs) ATLINE	126	
ANNIE M	181	
LENA C	181	
MARGARET E	13	
GREY, CASSANDRA	40	
GRICE, MARY C	55	
VIOLA C	81	
GRIER, MARY W	30	
GRIM, ANGELINE	143	
CAROLINE	145	
CATHARINE	85	
CYNTHIA	49	
DELILA	174	
DORATHY	14	
LYDIA	146	
LYDIA MARGARET	131	
MARY F	151	
MATILDA A	46	
MELISSA J	46	
SARAH	145	
SARAH J	91	
GRIMES, BESSIE	142	
RHODA A	92	
GRIMM, AFFIE	74	
ALMEDIA	138	
AMANDA ELLEN	46	
CORDELIA A	123	
ELIZA JO	91	
EMMA R	62	
FANNIE	91	
FLORENCE	19	
FLOSSIE M	12	
IDA M	178	
ISABELLE	144	
LILLIE B	24	
MAGGIE	172	
MARTHA M	23	
MARTHA ROSE	145	
MARY C	146	
MARY J	186	
MAY	154	
OSA	113	
OSIE F	82	
GRIMMETT, MAGGIE J	16	
GRINSTEAD, IVA	56	
JULIA	105	
MARY F	5	
MARY G	121	
NANCY JANE	138	
SARAH	127	
GROGAN, MABEL L	106	
GROSS, MYRTLE	142	
GROVER, LILLIE MAY	23	
MITTIE	113	
NELLIE ANNIS	4	
PEARL SOPHIA	161	
SARAH C	168	
SUSAN MALINDA ELLEN	101	
VESTA	121	
VIOLA	152	
GROVES, BELLE	96	
MAGGIE J	49	
MARY M	155	
NANCY	76	
NANNIE G	78	
REBECCA J	43	
RUTH A	167	
GRUESER, ETHEL	64	
NEIDA M	165	
GUARD, JULIA A	87	
GUESS, ELLEN	101	
GUILD, EUPHEMIA	98	
GUN, NANCY	74	
GUNN, HARRIET A	178	
M ORA	39	
NANCY	115	
NANCY	52	
WILLIE MARY	77	
GUSTLER, NETTIE F	56	
GUY, (Mrs) MARTHA	182	
AMANDA M	60	
GWINN, AMELIA	55	
MARTINA	183	
MARY RACHEL	183	

MINNIE A	78
GWYNN, ANNIE	7
DESSA M	12
ELLA BELLE	95
MARY A	100
GYGAX, CAROLINE	173
HACKET, MARY F	109
HADDOX, ROSALIE	120
HADSELL, (Mrs) LUCIE	20
HAGEMAN, MAY	54
HAGER, ELLA	35
MATILDA	161
HAGERMAN, EVA S	100
HAINES, MARY J	118
HAINEY, MARY	114
HALBLEIB, MAGGIE	130
MITTIE	106
HALBLIEB, NAOMI A	45
HALE, CYNTHIA ANN	92
GRACE S	132
MARY	184
SALLY	71
SUSAN	152
HALEY, HARRIET	51
MILDRED	149
VERGIE H	2
HALFHILL, JULIA C	38
LOLA A	10
MINNIE	87
HALL, (Mrs) ELIZABETH	80
(Mrs) LUCY	88
ADELINE	33
ALLIE	119
ALMA F	87
CAROLINE	45
CATHARINE	70
CATHARINE	130
CLARA	114
CLARA	119
EDNA	49
ELIZABETH	37
ELIZABETH	66
ELIZABETH	161
ELIZABETH J	136
ELLEN V	154
EMILY	164
EMMA	109
ETTA	92
ETTA	161
FRANCES	188
GLENIA	178
GRACE	91
HAZELTINE	29
ISABELLE	78
IVA B	84
JANE	14
LAURA	79
LENNA	134
LEOTTIE	94
LILLIE	37
LURY ELLA	7
MABLE	145
MAGGIE A	73
MAGGIE MAY	69
MALINDA CATHARINE	9
MARGARET	155
MARIAM	126
MARIETTA	13
MARTHA ELIZABETH	191
MARY	98
MARY	134
MARY A	17
MARY A	171
MARY ANN	109
MARY JANE	183
MARY VIRGINIA	153
MATTIE	147
MATTIE A	160
MERAL	117
OLA L	132
OLLIE W	100
SARAH J	121
SOPHIA	113
VERNIA	85
HALLEY, BLANCH	113
HALSEY, ELLA	71
NANCY	21
HALSTEAD, ANN ELIZA	36
RHODA	41
HALSY, MARY M	106
HALTERMAN, MAUD	114
HAMAKER, KATE D	102
HAMBLEY, SUSAN P	173
HAMBRICK, ELLA	1
EMILY S	102
GRACE	1
KATE	78
LOUISE M	168
LUCRETIA	38
MINNIE	22
NORA E	57
HAMILTON, ALVINA	5
BLANCHE	16
LOUISA	40
MARGARET	185
MARY	82
HANDLEY, SARAH	92
HANDSHAW, VICTORIA	148
HANEH, CORA B	25
HANES, CATHARINE	85
LILLIE	86
HANING, CORA M	154
ELIZABETH J	70
LYDIA J	97
HANK, SARAH E	176
HANLEY, CAROLINE	50
HANLY, DORA	88
GRACE	16
MARY E	121
NANCY CATHARINE	59
ORETHA	92
VIRGINIA	74
HANN, BELLE	104
HANNA, ANNIE	123
FANNY	27
KATE V	80
MARY A	27
MILDRED NORRIS	123

HANNAH, MAGGIE G	148	HARNESS, ELZINA J	180
MARTHA	33	HARNSPACHER, SEVILLE	172
HANNAN, ADA PEARL	66	HARPER, AGNES	151
ALLIE	182	CATHARINE	110
BETTIE F	48	ELIZABETH	18
FRANCES A	178	FRANCES	87
JENNIE	109	IMOGENE	20
JENNIE B	116	JANIE	184
MARY E	13	MARGARET A	47
MIRIAM	74	MARTHA J	6
NANNIE	25	WILLIE B	154
NELLIE ELLEN	120	HARPOLD, ALICE V	192
SARAH	180	DRUZILLA	149
HANNIS, JENNIE L	1	ELECTA E	137
KATHERINE D	102	SUSSIE	24
HANNON, LEVENA D	27	HARPOLE, JEMESONA	16
MINERVA	161	MILLIE	37
HANSHAW, MARY	162	HARRAH, MAUDE M	66
HANSLEY, NANNIE	157	HARRIGAN, NORA	145
HANSON, MINNIE	102	REBECCA A	8
NELLIE	20	SARAH	15
HARBER, JANE	108	HARRINGTON, MYRTA	26
HARBOR, ANNIE	48	HARRIS, (Mrs) ANN	37
EFFIE G	143	ANNA M	87
LESTA	109	AURELLIA	174
MARY M	31	CARRIE L	79
HARBOUR, BERTHA L	106	CATHARINE	70
GRACE	138	CATHARINE	93
ISABELL	46	CATHARINE	100
MARY C	102	ELANOR	49
HARDEN, LOUISA ISABELLE	179	ELENOR	49
LUZETTA	169	ELIZA J	27
HARDIE, REBECCA	66	ELIZABETH	72
HARDIN, MARTHA JANE	87	ELIZABETH	103
HARDING, ELLA	58	ELIZABETH J	162
JESSIE E	34	ELLEN	157
HARDWICK, (Mrs) REBECCA A	153	ERSULA	148
BETTIE B	142	FRANCES	70
FRANCES S	25	FRANCES M	192
LEONER E	137	JENNIE	144
LURANEY C	93	JOSEPHINE	176
MARY JANE	138	LIZZIE	50
ORA	61	LOUISA	150
SARAH M	28	MAGGIE E	140
WILLIA A	188	MARY	159
HARDY, EMATELL	110	MARY	177
MARGARET A	11	MINNIE B	37
HARE, CATHARINE	141	MITTIE	178
HARKINS, ELLEN	42	NELLIE J	95
HARLER, MARGARET	29	ORA B	46
HARLESS, SARAH A	155	PEARL L	123
HARLEY, MARY E	50	POLLY	141
HARMAN, (Mrs) S B	21	REBECCA	184
CYNTHIA	161	SARAH	131
HARMON, ANN E	61	SARAH ANN	102
CLARA HELEN	106	SARAH C	178
CORA A	190	SARAH E	84
EFFIE	35	SOPHIA	65
LAURA MAY	71	SUSAN JANE	97
LEVENA D	27	SUSAN M	90
MAY	46	VIOLETTA	85
OMA	162	VIRGINIA	140
SARAH JANE	74	HARRISON, ALTA E	132
SEIGOUS A	102	ANN	149

CHRISTENIA E	54	
HARRIET	92	
JANE	140	
JENNIE	114	
MAGGIE	127	
MANDA A	75	
MARY	8	
MARY	25	
MARY	132	
MARY ANN	48	
MOLLIE	54	
NANCY	5	
OLETHA	159	
POLLY	74	
HARROLD, MARY E	183	
HARSCHBARGER, MINNIE	104	
HARSHA, MATTIE	130	
HARSHBARGER, LILLIE	165	
NANNIE E	104	
HARSHEY, NANCY J	130	
HART, ANNA C	181	
BLANCHE	114	
CATHARINE	162	
CATHERINE F	155	
CHARLOTTE	77	
CHARLOTTE	144	
DORA	29	
ELIZABETH	40	
ELIZABETH	192	
ELLA	94	
EMILY	63	
FANNIE	119	
FIDELIA	6	
HAZEL H	146	
ISABELLA R	190	
JANE	104	
JANNIE	60	
LAVINIA	51	
LORENA C	101	
LOUISA	159	
MARIA	5	
MARIA	139	
MARIA F	173	
MARION FRANCIS	158	
MARY	3	
MARY	77	
MARY M	28	
MARY M	59	
MAY	163	
OLGA	144	
RHODA	93	
RHODA E	104	
SARAH E	87	
VESTA	115	
VIRGIE AUGUSTA	51	
HARTINGER, EDITH	145	
HARTLESS, LIDE	183	
HARTLEY, BIRDIE	3	
MABEL	90	
HARVEY, (Mrs) LEUEMA	55	
MARTHA A	91	
MISSOURI	80	
HASKINS, ZERA M	76	
HATCHER, MARY	17	
HATHAWAY, LUCY	108	
HAUCK, MAGGIE	104	
HAVERTY, BLAYNE L	47	
HAWK, HELEN MARIE	49	
JENNIE	59	
LIZZIE M	149	
MARY JANE	123	
HAWKINS, ADA MAY	54	
ALICE	77	
ALICE N	104	
ALTHA	31	
BLANCH	136	
CATHERINE	23	
ELIZABETH	131	
ELIZABETH	180	
ELVIRA J	126	
GRACE P	45	
JANE ANN	15	
JANE T	94	
JOSIE	152	
JULIA E	18	
JULIA E	104	
JULIA M	66	
LAURA	11	
LILY J	136	
MAGGIE H	103	
MARTHA J	143	
MARY E	30	
MARY JANE	180	
MARY L	49	
NANCY	55	
ORTHA	172	
PERMELIA	49	
REBECCA FLORENCE	79	
VIRGINIA FRANCES	34	
ZERELDA C	4	
HAWLEY, MABEL	61	
HAWTHORN, ELIZABETH	108	
MARY	46	
MARY	108	
MARY C	78	
NANCY E	108	
ROSA M,	177	
SARAH E	37	
SUSAN	177	
HAWTHORNE, ELIZABETH	109	
KATIE	82	
HAY, VERA M	161	
HAYES, ANNIE B	161	
CORA	22	
CORA	47	
ELIZABETH	75	
ELLEN	173	
ERNA A	15	
LAURA M	175	
LEOTA	75	
LILLIE E	19	
MARY	99	
MINNIE	173	
SARAH	11	
SARAH C	85	
VIOLA	81	
HAYMAN, (Mrs) MINNIE R	122	
ADA	176	

ALMIRA	12	HENNOSY, MARY ELSIE	120
ANNA	163	HENRY, ADALINE	9
ANNIE	2	BARBARA ANN	159
ELIZABETH J	74	CORA	106
FLORA	106	ELIZABETH	125
FLORA R	106	ELLA	37
GEORGIA A	153	EMILY	76
HARRIET A	7	EMMA	57
IVABEL	181	EMMA	109
LETTIE A C	131	GARNETT MARIE	29
MARTHA C	14	IDA	177
MARY J	157	IVA	177
NANCY B	24	LILLY M	26
NANCY E	105	MAMIE FRANCES	4
SURA ANN	29	MARTHA F	178
HAYMON, ALMENIA	23	MARY	104
ALMERIA	23	MARY C	36
HAYNES, AURELIA B	28	REBECCA FRANCES	53
EARNIE	35	VINA	45
ELLA	73	HENSHAW, ELIZABETH	162
ELLA B	174	HENSLEY, ADELAIDE	133
LULU	184	ELIZABETH F	158
MARY J	41	MARY J S	181
HAYS, ETHEL	67	PARSENA	132
IVA G	7	HENSON, ELIZABETH	65
OLIVIA	76	GERMINIA	46
SARAH	98	LUELLA	36
HAYSE, LIDDIA	10	SARAH	6
LYDIA	12	SUSANAH	88
HAZLETT, LIZZIE	191	HENTHORN, MAHALA	156
HEAD, CARRIE	49	HENTHORNE, ANNIE E	165
HEARN, MURL W	155	HEPPLEWHITE, ANNIE	95
HEARSMAN, VIOLETTA F	29	HERDMAN, ALMEDA	55
HEATHERINGTON, HULDAH E	22	DORA	117
MABEL	92	MARTHA E	126
HECK, ELLA M	1	MARY J	96
HEDGE, ELECTA	52	NANNIE J	89
HEDRICK, MARIA J	113	HEREFORD, CATHARINE	34
HEIB, CLARA A	189	ELIZABETH CATHARINE	153
HEIN, JOSEPHINE A	91	ELIZABETH P	166
HELLAM, ROSELLA	6	ELLA E	168
HELLEMS, MARGARET	86	EMELINE C	58
HELPER, CLARISSA ANN	142	JULIET E	177
RACHEL	51	KATE	22
HELRICH, MARGARET	76	LAVINIA E	133
HEMSLEY, ELIZABETH F	170	M MARGARET	91
JANE A	48	MARIA C	32
HENDERSON, ANNA E	185	MARTHA	178
ELIZABETH	66	MARY A	8
HULDAH T	97	MARY EVELINE	187
JANE	80	SARAH C	189
KATIE	35	SARAH SANSON	115
MARIA E	179	VIRGINIA	119
MARY E	83	VIRGINIA E	13
MINNIE	97	HERLOW, BERTHA	127
NANCY	17	HERMAN, MURL	110
RHODA	68	HERN, LULU B	153
SALLIE A	58	MAY	98
SALLY	118	HERREN, MARTHA M	151
HENESEY, MARGARET	181	HERSHBARGER, (Mrs) RHODA S	33
HENKEL, MARY M	175	HERSMAN, EDITH	4
HENKLE, CAROLINE H	186	LUCINDA	95
HENNIGAN, NANCY J	18	MARY	22
HENNOSSY, KATE	160	HERTJE, BARBARA	129

HERZMAN, EDITH	152	CORA M	138
HESLOP, MARTHA	90	DIANA	113
SARAH E	152	EFFIE	35
SUE D	179	ELIZA J	189
HESS, EDNA L	49	ELIZA JANE	166
FRIEDA M	172	ELIZABETH I	189
LUCY L	186	ELLEN	14
LUCY L	173	FLORA	138
LUCY L	186	FORRIA	6
POLLY	128	GEORGIA	10
SARAH C	163	HANNAH M	26
HESSEN, TEXA ANN	12	HETTIE E	68
HESSON, BERTHA	55	HETTIE E	86
BERTHA M	37	IDA JANE	76
CLARA	86	JOSEPHINE	11
ELIZABETH	37	KEZIA	177
ELIZABETH	92	LENA R A	14
ELLA	13	LIZZIE	187
EMMA B	44	LOUISA	104
EVA	150	LOUISA J	93
JESSIE	144	LUCY	31
MARGARET ANN	24	M MAUD	77
MARY	122	MARGARET A	152
MARY A	71	MARGARET E	69
MERTIE	18	MARTHA ANN	7
MINNIE F	110	MARTHA J	140
HESTER, NANCY	37	MARTHA R	75
HEWIT, CAROLINE	6	MARY	31
HIBBARD, ADA	138	MARY F	144
HICKMAN, ELEANOR R	105	MARY M	5
EMILY J	136	MARY M	43
MARY E	141	MARY M	187
HICKS, ANNIE M	37	MARY O	26
ELLA	31	MEGGIE	121
ETHEL H	106	MELISSA	31
IDA	31	MINNIE	157
MARY J	93	MINNIE C	120
SUSAN	127	NANCY A	189
SUSAN A	140	NANCY B	42
HIGENBOTHAM, NANCY	125	NANCY G	187
HIGGENBOTHAM, ELIZABETH	99	NANCY J	71
HIGGINBOTHAM, EDITH L	167	NETTIE M	53
EVA G	35	OLIVE	121
EVA I	75	OLIVIA	151
MADALINE E	61	OMA O	140
MARY A	28	ORILLA	185
NANCY A	34	RACHEL M	176
WILLIE A	35	REBECCA J	133
HIGGINS, LAURA S	126	RHODA V	158
MARY C	80	RINNA M	86
HIGH, LUCINDA	142	ROSA	32
HIGINBOTHAM, LENIA	147	ROSA BELLE	41
LIZZIE	191	ROXY ANN	8
MARY	72	RUCY BELLE	8
SARAH ELIZABETH	111	SALLY	31
HILDEBRAND, CLARA	136	SALLY	104
HILL, ADDIE	135	SARAH E	135
ALLIE	100	SARAH M	152
AMERICA	164	SPICE A	28
ANNIE ELIZABETH	70	VENITIA E	8
BESSIE L	20	ZETTA M	27
BLANCH V	67	HINKLE, CARRIE	90
CHRISTENA	140	MARY S	153
CLARA MAY	173	HIPSHEAR, MARIA	52

HIRES, ELIZABETH	70		MARIA	113
HIVELEY, JENNIE	62		MARTHA M	160
HIVELY, LYDIA L	155		MARY F	103
HOBBS, BERTHA	8		MARY LUCINDA	49
BESSIE A	36		MARY LUCY	186
ELIZABETH	189		OLIVIA	66
HENRIETTA	130		OLLIE	174
IDA M	54		ORA	176
LEOTI	60		PATSEY	186
LUELLA	65		SARAH JANE	172
NINA J	41		SARAH L	18
SARAH E	32		HOGSETT, CLARA E	13
HODGES, EMMA J	178		FANNIE	78
STELLA M	21		ROSABELL	143
HOFFMAN, ALICE	134		HOIT, MARY M	92
ANNIE	174		HOLCOMB, GRACE	40
ANNIE G	42		HOLCTON, MALINDA	79
ARTIE M	139		HOLDEWAY, PEGGY	63
BARBARA	143		HOLDREN, ALMIRA	67
BERTHA E	30		LIZZIE	30
CAROLINE	146		MAHALA	58
CAROLINE	161		SADIE BELLE	26
CATHARINE	144		HOLEY, MATIE	168
CATHARINE	155		HOLLAND, ELMIRA	72
CLARA E	112		LELA	170
CORA	166		NELLIE G	11
DELIA	72		ODDIE	29
DORA	81		HOLLEY, ADDIE A	116
ELIZABETH	145		AMY	32
ELLA	36		BESSIE	170
EMALIZA	192		CAROLINE	20
EMELINE	37		DAISY	35
GERTRUDE B	158		DELLER	132
HANNAH	171		DORCAS	13
IDA	145		EFFIE M	78
IDA MAE	185		ELCIE	78
INA	18		ELIZA J	78
JENNIE F	117		ELIZA J	78
KATIE D	172		ELIZABETH	85
LAURA A	7		ELIZABETH B	35
LAURA B	139		ELLA	29
LUCY	59		EMMA	15
MAHALA	55		EVA	7
MALINDA	29		EVA	130
MARGARET	91		EVALINE	15
MARY M	51		FANNIE	35
MATILDA	170		GOLDIE S	152
MILLIE B	146		HENRIETTA	116
OLIVIA	106		HULDAH JANE	116
OLIVIA NORTON	191		JANE	25
OSIE	169		JINCY	52
RASILLA	57		LEFFLAVER	78
ROSETTA M	191		LIENARY	50
SARAH A	7		LILLY F	60
SARAH A	46		LINA	20
SARAH C	20		LOTTIE B	123
VENA	86		LOUISA FRANCES	36
HOGG, ARABELLA J	186		LYDIA E	46
DAISY L	54		MARGARET	132
ELIZABETH	77		MARTHA ETNA	39
ELIZABETH	186		MARY A	178
FLORA	189		MARY E	186
INEZ	45		MARY F	133
JULIA ANN	7		MARY JANE	100

MATIE	38	
MATTIE J	46	
MILLIE	33	
MYRTIE M	116	
ODA E	116	
ONA	162	
RENA	153	
RETTIE	78	
SARAH ANN	132	
SARAH M	46	
VERNIE	78	
ZELMA	36	
HOLLIE, MARY	102	
HOLLINS, MAUD	65	
HOLLOWAY, ANNIE M	108	
BETSEY A	60	
HOLLY, ADA	177	
ARIZONA	116	
BETTIE J	104	
CAROLINE	29	
CATHARINE	79	
CHARLOTTE M	176	
CORA FRANCES	85	
DELILA J	79	
ELIZABETH	50	
ELIZABETH R	121	
ELIZABETH S	133	
ELLEN FRANCIS	38	
EMMA C	153	
ESTER MAY	78	
ETTIE V	12	
FANNIE	78	
HULDAH A	158	
IDA A	100	
LOUISA F	115	
LUCINDA	33	
M ELIZABETH	96	
MALINDA	116	
MALISSA ANN	115	
MARTHA JANE	116	
MARY	29	
MARY	13	
MARY A	26	
MATILDA	115	
MATILDA C	116	
MAUD A	100	
MAUD E	46	
NANCY	102	
OULTA E	116	
SALLY	116	
SUSAN	116	
HOLMES, EDNA B	126	
VERNA	115	
VERNA C	79	
HOLSEY, HATTIE	137	
HOLSTEIN, MARCY ELLEN	63	
HOLT, BARBARA	95	
JANE	160	
JENNIE	162	
LILLIE	94	
MARY E	159	
MERREL	172	
HOLTE, AUDREY	53	
HONAKER, ADA L	101	
HONSHELL, ANNIE	169	
HOOD, BESSIE	50	
MARY P	19	
PEARL MAY	47	
HOOFF, JENNIE MOORE	149	
MARY F	4	
HOOP, HARRIET E	31	
HOOPS, MARY	128	
HOOTON, EDNA L	50	
HOOVER, BETTIE	95	
DORA	181	
ELIZABETH F	80	
JENNIE	48	
MARY	183	
HOPE, AURILLA J	122	
ELIZABETH M	161	
ELLEN	149	
IONA B	51	
MARY	59	
MATILDA F	108	
MATTIE C	60	
HOPKINS, JOSIE V	135	
LAURENA	188	
NANNIE	186	
HOPLITE, BERTHA E	99	
HOPSON, ADALINE	28	
MARY A	72	
SOPHRONIA	62	
HORNBY, MANERVA	188	
HORNER, MARY W	109	
HORTON, ELIZABETH	186	
HOSCHAR, ATHENIA J	59	
CATHARINE	175	
ELIZABETH	131	
JANE C	131	
LUCRITIA G	63	
MARGARET A	140	
MARTHA F	114	
HOSKINS, AURILLIA	89	
HOVER, (Mrs) MARY	9	
NETTIE M	174	
HOWARD, AUGUSTA E	125	
BERTHA M	181	
CASSIE	136	
MARILL K	11	
MARTHA J	136	
MISTA M	14	
NANNIE HELEN	184	
NELLIE	170	
HOWELL, BERTHA V	104	
CASANDA	158	
DOROTHY E	104	
ELIZA JANE	40	
ELIZABETH	3	
ETTA	16	
FRANCES	53	
FRANCES E	101	
HANNAH B	64	
JANE	62	
LORA B	128	
MARTHA A	117	
MARY A	19	
MARY B	124	
SARAH	45	

SUSA	73
HOWLES, ANN	120
HOY, CATHARINE	157
HUCHINSON, ELIZABETH A	179
HUDLIN, FRANCES H	95
HUDNALL, LILLIE B	16
HUDSON, ALTA JANE	67
ANN GEMIMA	179
ANNA	5
CARIE M	68
CATHARINE	109
DASEY	72
DELLA	124
DOSHIA K	62
ELIZABETH	131
HESTER A	97
LAVINIA E	85
LETHA A	53
LINNIE	126
LIZZIE	55
LIZZIE E	29
LUELLA	50
MAGGIE	137
MARTHA JANE	144
MARY A	128
MARY E	29
MARY OLEVIA	90
RILLA	163
SARAH A	42
SARAH A	170
SARAH F	20
HUFF, EMMA	152
HENRIETTA	43
HUFFMAN, ELIZABETH	168
LILLIE	162
LUCINDA	145
MARY	142
NANCY	106
HUGGINS, RETTA MABEL	162
HUGH, ANNA	52
HUGHES, ADDIE	180
AMANDA	48
ANNIE	81
ANNIE ROSETTA	8
BETTIE	183
CALLIE M	153
CATHARINE	73
CORA	189
DIANAH M	52
DORA	143
ELIZABETH W	11
EMMA	154
HARRIET	156
IDELLA	76
ISABELLE	157
JEMIMA B	52
JEMIMA R	101
LAURA	44
LAVINA A	24
LIZZIE	86
LYDIA	44
MAHALA	168
MALINDA	180
MALINDA R E	74
MAMIE V	167
MARGARET B	61
MARIETTA C	151
MARY	3
MARY E	154
MARY ELLEN	119
MARY F	108
MAY	60
MAY	72
MAYMIE V	165
MAZELLA J	69
MELINDA	104
MIRTIE	74
NANCY A	116
NELLIE B	16
NORA A	44
OSA L	75
REBECCA	52
SARAH	52
SARAH	178
SARAH A	81
HUGHS, CELIA	140
DELILAH	149
ELIZABETH	94
ELIZABETH	111
GRACE	102
HARRIET A	166
LUCY	55
MARGARET E	108
MARTHA	31
MARY	37
MARY	82
NANCY	93
PARMELIA	110
SUSANNA	3
HULBERT, IRENA	41
MARY E	179
HULL, CLARA E	80
FRANCES C	108
IVA	72
LILLIE MAY	66
MARGARET JANE KYLE	111
MARY C	55
NETTIE	72
NETTIE	163
SARAH F	179
HUMMEL, ELLEN EUGENE	71
HUMMELL, MARY A	95
HUMPHREY, MARTHA	58
NORA	182
HUMPHREYS (Mrs) ORA	182
MELVIRA ANN	69
E GRACE	13
ELIZABETH	12
EVELINE W	66
LETHA E	69
LOUISA	103
HUMPHRIES, LOUISA	157
LUCY M	149
MARY	20
HUMPREY, MARY E	129
HUNDLEY, MARTHA S	87
HUNNELL, DORA	65
HUNTER, ANN	91

ANNA J	93	
CATHARINE	88	
ELIZABETH	82	
JULIA	95	
LAKIE M	132	
LAURA J	24	
MARY F	19	
MARY M	166	
HUPP, REBECCA	188	
HURDMAN, MARY MARGARET	82	
HURLOW, LIZZIE	51	
MARGARET ANN	139	
HURSHMAN, MARTHA	33	
HURST, EDITH	67	
HUSTON, IDA M	176	
MARY ELIZABETH	153	
HUTCHINSON, AMELIA	27	
BELLE MARY	27	
ELLA	118	
JANE	39	
HUTSON, PERMELIA	192	
HUTTON, MADALINE R	141	
VIOLA	169	
HYATT, ANNA B	158	
B ELLNORA	74	
BELLE	75	
CELIA	95	
ELIZABETH	58	
ELLEN J	119	
REBECCA J	139	
REBECCA JANE	7	
HYATTE, ELLENOR	38	
HYDE, DELILA	66	
HYLTON, BERTHA E	192	
HENRIETTA	158	
JESSIE C	149	
MARY D	192	
HYSEL, DINAH	132	
HYSELL, GARNETT	148	
JENNIE	143	
LILLIE B	39	
LUCINDA	43	
MAGGIE	2	
MARY E	97	
SYLVIA	156	
ICENHOWER, ELIZA F	53	
IHLE, CORA M	86	
INAW-WOCKHWOE, PRAIRIE FLOWER	5	
INGHAM, ROMIE R	190	
INGLES, ELIZABETH	60	
INMAN, ADA D	164	
URNA F	105	
INVERN, VIELLA	22	
IRNES, MARY E	161	
IRVIN, ELIZA	90	
ELLA MAY	1	
LORA E	166	
NOLA	48	
ROSIE	12	
IRWIN, ANNIE J	166	
MARY I	62	
NANCY J	79	
ISAACS, MALINDA	17	
JACKSON, ALICE	60	
ANNIE	10	
BELVA D	30	
E ETHEL	125	
EDA E	174	
HENRIETTA	45	
JENNIE	61	
JENNIE	169	
LILLIE M	187	
LULLA MAY	47	
MAMIE	164	
MARGARET	47	
MARY	124	
MARY E	171	
SARAH M	138	
JACOBS, DELIA	121	
LIZZIE	92	
LUTITIA	92	
NESSIE R	134	
SARAH J	149	
VIRGINIA	2	
JAMES, AMANDA	89	
CATHARINE	91	
ETHEL B	65	
LAURA	24	
MARY E	108	
MARY MAGDALEN	161	
MYRTLE B	8	
JANET, MARY E	56	
JAQUES, MAGGIE	40	
SUSIE	28	
JARROT, MATTIE L	120	
JARROTT, AURILLA J	74	
SADIE FRANCES	148	
JARRY, LYDIA	65	
JARVIS, IDA M	118	
STELLA	13	
JEFFERS, AMANDA E	28	
AMY	70	
ANALIZA	151	
ANNIE E	134	
ARTIE	172	
DORA	54	
ELIZA	23	
ELIZABETH	125	
ELLEN	36	
ESTHER	33	
FANNIE	17	
FLORA J	178	
HARRIET E	130	
IDA MAY	54	
IMAGENE	88	
JENNEVA	99	
JESTA	135	
KATIE	109	
LILLIE MAY	101	
LIZZIE	54	
MARTHA	14	
MARY	134	
MARY E	94	
MARY E	130	
MARY JANE	84	
MARY M	122	
MODJESKA	158	

NAOMI FRANCES	56	ROXY	159
OMA	14	JOACHIM, ELIZABETH	149
OTTIE M	181	JOBE, CORA E	77
PEARL	25	JOCHIM, BETTIE	191
RACHEL	85	JOHNSON, ANNIE	29
RHODA C	41	ANNIE	61
RUBY	126	ANNIE G	142
SARAH	35	AURILLA R	155
SARAH E	21	BELLE	56
VIRGIE	98	BERTHA E	171
VIRGINIA C	76	BETSY E	40
JEFFERSON, CORA	190	CAROLINE V	118
MARIE	83	CLARA E	14
JEFFRESS, ELIZABETH	43	CLARISSA J	191
MAHALIA	90	CORA	15
MARY	98	CORA B	174
JEFFRIES, CORA	76	CORA E	69
MAHALIA	90	DORA F	155
POLLY	98	EDITH L	67
JENKINS, (Mrs) NANCY	116	EDNA	181
AROLLA	116	EDNA ADA	20
CORDELIA CATHARINE	64	EDNA O	170
ELIZABETH	41	EFFIE L	40
GWINNIE	105	ELA	66
IRENE E	115	ELIZA	38
JULIA F	36	ELIZABETH F	117
LUCETTA C	41	ELLA	113
LUCY M	117	ELLEN	87
MAGGIE	181	ELLEN	103
MAGGIE ELLEN	95	FANNIE	35
MARTHA J	147	FANNY	29
MARY ELIZABETH	57	FRANCES	29
MATILDA A	78	FRANCES	64
NANCY SUSAN	35	GEORGIA E	58
PRUCILLA	116	IDA	149
ROSA MAY	116	IDA M	45
SUSAN MALINDA	118	IDA MAY	86
JENKS, ETHEL	132	JANE	118
JENNINGS, ELLA	45	JULIAN	180
IDAH B	48	KATE E	119
MYRTLE M	175	LAURA	131
VERNA LILLIAN	143	LAURA J	41
JEWELL, MARY C	180	LAURIE ELLEN	12
JEWETT, ANNIE FLORENCE	40	LETHA J	124
JIBEAUT, EVALINE	83	LILLIE F	13
JINKINS, JENNIE	137	LIZZIE	89
JIVEDEN, MARY JANE	66	LIZZIE K	134
JIVIDEN, ANNIE	179	LUCINDA	4
AUDREY A	154	LUCY	189
BERTHA	150	LUTITIA	159
CORA A	151	MAGGIE	149
EASTY	24	MALISA JANE	84
ETHEL MABEL	187	MARGARET	102
GLENN M	69	MARGARET A	165
IDA	130	MARGARET J	31
INA	167	MARY	62
JOSEPHINE	152	MARY	119
LAVENIA M	48	MARY	168
LIZZIE	102	MARY A	112
LUCINDA A	34	MARY E	156
LUVERNIA	14	MARY ELIZA	57
MARGARET J	178	MARY JANE	28
MARY A	76	MATTIE	179
MINNIE	76	MAUD	85

MAY	53		JANE	97
NANCY	164		JANE	148
NETTIE	95		JENNIE	32
NORA	91		JENNIE	53
OELLA	58		JENNIE WASHINGTON	52
ORA	19		JETTIE	89
ORA	19		JOSEPHINE	11
PHOEBE ANNIE	184		LAURA ALICE	61
REBECCA	58		LOUISA M	23
ROSETTA	82		LUCETTA	113
RUBY	92		LUCY	111
SALLIE	3		LUELLA	127
SARAH	71		LUELLA	157
SARAH E	74		MAGGIE	165
SARAH MARGARET	159		MARTHA	15
SUSAN	177		MARTHA	26
VERNICIA	19		MARTHA ANN	112
VIRGINA A	142		MARTHA JANE	141
VIRGINIA	185		MARY	2
JOHNSTON, (Mrs) LOUISA	3		MARY	10
BERTHA E	60		MARY	73
MARGARET	76		MARY ADDIE	66
MARGARET F	25		MARY J	53
MARY	102		MARY JANE	163
SARAH	51		MATTIE LEE	43
JOHNSTONE, MAGGIE M	138		MINNIE	67
JOLLEY, ELIZABETH	58		MINNIE	86
JOLLY, ANGELINE B	119		NANCY	130
NORA	27		NETTIE	2
JONES, (Mrs) IDA V	106		OLIVIA	14
(Mrs) JANE	38		OLLIE	185
AGNES	89		OMA	42
ALICE	181		ORETHA	39
ANAMA ELIZABETH	17		PEARL D	28
ANNA G	50		PERLINA A	74
ANNIE	98		POLLY	44
ANNIE B	36		RACHEL E	151
ANNIE E	142		REGINA VIRGINIA	51
ANNIE ELIZABETH	148		RETHA A	183
ARLA	93		ROSELLA	36
ARNA	49		SARAH E	148
BETTIE	109		SARAH W	173
BIRDIE	130		TIRZAH A	48
BIRDIE	175	JORDAN, A L		22
CHRISTINA	100		ALICE	19
DELPHIA E	80		AMERICA	169
EDITH MAY	106		ARIZONA E	173
ELIZABETH	7		BESSIE S	67
ELIZABETH	36		CAROLINE	189
ELIZABETH ANN	7		CLARISSA	4
ELIZABETH G	19		CYNTHIA	53
ELIZABETH G	67		EDITH M	189
ELLA	57		ELIZABETH	21
ELLA	57		ELIZABETH	92
ELSIE J	125		ELIZABETH	121
EMILY	113		ELIZABETH E	83
EMILY B	150		EMAZETTA M	90
FRANCES	67		FLORA	143
FRANCES	133		FRANCES	153
GENEVA SUSAN	107		GEORGIANNA	87
GERTIE	55		HATTIE N	161
GERTRUDE	55		IDA	136
INA	98		JENNIE P	21
INEZ	11		JESSIE	170

Name	Page
JESSIE BLANCHE	23
LILLIE B	52
LORA	162
MAGGIE	61
MAGGIE	187
MAGGIE M	7
MARGARET	43
MARGARET EMEZETTA	22
MARY E	81
MARY J	68
MARY JANE	48
MARY M	156
MINNIE R	72
MIRTIE	51
MURTLE L	9
RILLA	102
RODIE	170
ROSA	3
SARAH MARGARET	85
VIRGINIA P	136
JORDEN, AURRILLA	173
ELIZA EMILY	106
ELIZABETH JANE	160
HANNAH	3
LEAH MARGARET	169
MARY M	58
MARY N	167
NANCY	22
PENELOPE	34
JOSEPH, NETTIE	165
JOUMELL, (Mrs) MARSHALINE	95
JOURDEN, NANCY SUSAN	42
JULICK, MARY ANN	174
KANOUS, ELLIE E	125
KAPP, ANNIE L	139
CHARLOTTE	55
LOTTIE	53
LOUISA	30
KARNES, ROSA	140
SARAH	139
KARRICK, JENNIE M	182
KASIE, ELLA J	52
KASTER, ADDA L	149
KAUFF, BESSIE M	34
EVA M	50
REBECCA	59
KAUFLEY, ROSEY	98
KAUFMAN, MARTHA ANN	125
KAULBERCH, CHRISTENA	173
KAY, ELIZA DOVE	65
ELIZABETH A	59
EMMA JENNINGS	143
EVA C	6
HANNAH	22
MARGARET L	5
KAYLOR, MARY	88
MINNIE	91
SARAH	76
KEAN, EMMA FLORENCE	41
KEARNS, (Mrs) MARGARET	146
ELLA	70
JENNIE SCOTT	138
LIZZIE M	97
MAGGIE	186
MAHALA B	15
MALINDA C	140
MARGARET	17
MARY ANN	58
MATTIE N	164
NANNIE	163
NANNIE A	143
NETTIE E	96
ORA ELLEN	189
SARINA C	45
KECK, ATTIE A	61
KEEFER, ANNIE J	75
DORA ELLEN	157
GUSSIE	1
ISABELLA	91
JANE	128
LAURA M	26
LIZZIE MAY	174
MENERVA LOUIZA	185
MINNIE ALICE	77
SARAH LIZZIE	2
KEEVER, ELIZA J	119
KEISER, ANTOINETTE	186
KEISTER, LILLIE J	115
LIZZIE F	107
KEITH, LUCETTA	83
KELL, ANNIE	107
ELIZABETH	129
MAGGIE	179
KELLEY, JULIA A	6
KELLY, IDA E	183
LAURA E	172
MARGUERITE	26
SAMANTHA J	169
SARAH E	180
KEMPER, CARRIE L	143
ORMA	145
KENEDY, NELLIE	53
KENNEDY, ANTOINETTE OSBORNE	105
ELIZABETH R	182
MAGGIE L	181
KENNEY, DORA	18
MARY L	187
KENNY, MARGARET	67
KENT, MALINDA A	102
URMA E	87
KENTZLER, MARY	40
KERBEY, ELLA	50
KERN, MARGARET	62
KERNS, MAE E	148
KERR, SADIE M	96
KERWOOD, BERTHA HILDA	77
CARRIE M	33
EDITH M	41
EFFIE	98
ESTELLA A	38
FLORA M	17
GRACE B	174
KATE	151
LAURA G	178
LIDA	32
MARGARET I	92
MARY	79

MARY A	87
PEARL E	122
PRISILLA	30
SARAH E	158
KESSEL, LUCY	184
LUTITIA	164
PEARL	167
KEY, MELINA (MALINDA)	28
KEYS, LIZZIE	93
KIDDER, (Mrs) HARRIET A	101
KIDWELL, KATIE MAY	28
KIESLING, MINA	15
KIESTER, WILLA E	187
KIESZLING, MAGGIE M	50
KIGER, ARABELLA	156
KILE, JANE C	73
KILLEEN, KATIE	43
THRESA	68
KIMBERLIN, RUTH	137
KIMBERLING, (Mrs) ALICE	48
ANYTIS	120
BELINDA	28
ELIZA A	71
ELLEN	50
EVA B	126
FANNIE M	135
FRANCIS J	153
GERTRUDE	172
HARRIET	3
JOANNA	11
LUCETTA	159
MARIA	63
NANCY	97
NANCY	172
NANCY	184
PENELOPE	124
PRUDENCE	84
RACHEL JANE	75
SALLIE A	16
SARAH F	184
SARAH HARRIET	121
VICTORIA B	84
KINARD, CATHARINE VICTORIA	75
KINCADE, ADA FRANCES	113
ANNIE AGNESS	139
BLANCHE	111
DELLA M	135
ELIZABETH	97
ELLEN	21
ISABELLA	190
JANE	188
JOSIE E	165
LENA	99
LOUISA	183
MARY A	53
MARY MARTHA	10
MINNIE MAHALA	53
OTTIE L	30
SARAH	30
VIRGINIA	99
KINCAID, ELIZABETH	119
NANCY	21
KINDER, LUARY	181
MAUD LULU	124
KING, ALICE M	166
ANN E	183
BESSIE M	161
BESSIE P	159
CATHARINE	38
CHARITY	190
CLARA MABEL	188
CORA E	104
CYNTHA J	121
CYNTHIA ANN	72
DORA	22
DORA	171
DORA E	161
ELIZABETH	24
ELIZABETH	77
ELIZABETH	102
ELLA F	94
EMMA M	56
FLOSSIE E	15
FRANCES E	124
JANE	4
JANE	42
JEMIMA MAY	166
JESSIE A	69
JUDY	96
KITTY	140
LIEARENA	180
LILLIE F	103
LUCINDA	41
LURANY C	151
MARIAH	110
MARIAH	155
MARTHA	90
MARY	103
MARY	147
MARY A	35
MARY A D	142
MARY A D	172
MARY C	172
MARY E	2
MARY J	34
MARY JANE	39
NANCY	150
NANCY J	94
NELLIE	157
OMA N	158
REWAMA	91
SARAH	74
SARAH	147
SARAH E	5
STELLA	31
STELLA	64
SUSAN	10
SUSIE	21
VIOLA F	171
VIRGINIA L	111
WAVIE J	162
KINGRY, NANCY ELIZABETH	186
KINNEY, CATHARINE	33
KINSER, NANCY	167
KINTZEL, ELMIRA	190
FLORA	49
MAGGIE D	5
KIRBY, ELIZABETH	121

HENRIETTA	2
NAOMI	146
ODESSA M	123
KIRK, ELIZA M	44
MARY F	32
MILLIE M	122
NANCY C	36
SARAH	26
TABITHA C	45
KIRKENDALL, EVA	169
SADIE A	97
KIRKER, (Mrs) LENA M	155
BIRDIE	18
CARRIE	57
JESSIE	190
MAGGIE R	57
KIRKPATRICK, CHARLOTTE	163
ELIZABETH S	70
JULIAN	62
MARTHA	126
MARTHA E	8
MARY F	76
MARY J	53
MARY JANE	126
KIRKWOOD, SARAH JANE	161
KIRNES, SHALLIE	112
KISAR, MAUD	160
KITE, GEORGEA	56
KLASS, ALICE E	9
KLEENE, MAGGIE	73
KLEIN, EMMA	65
KLICKER, ELLA	125
KLINE, LAURETTA N	81
KLINGENSMITH, ELIZABETH J	130
LEAH ANN	138
LOUISA	135
KLINGER, ELLEN	22
KLINGINGSMITH, ANNIE	59
KATE	138
KNAP, MARGARET	63
KNAPP, ALICE	94
ALMIRA	16
ALMIRA	159
ANNIE S	144
BETSEY	190
BETSY	190
BETTIE	82
CAROLINE	3
CARRIE	131
CARRIE ESTELLA	111
CATHARINE	119
CHARLOTTE A	163
CHARLOTTE M	127
CHRISTINA	165
DRUSILLA	131
EFFIE E	20
ELLA MAY	28
ELLORA V	142
EMELINE	63
EMMA	34
EMMA F	127
ERMA A	20
ETHEL	92
FANNIE	75
FLORENCE	191
HANNAH	154
HANNAH	171
IDA	127
LILLIE	125
LORA L	104
LUCY	95
MAKE	110
MARGARET ANN	130
MARGARET VIRGINIA	48
MARTHA L	82
MARY J	22
MARY J	113
MARY M	105
MILLIE BERTHA	119
MYRTIE E	152
NELLIE	22
NEVA A	125
NEVA A	189
PALMYRA	190
REBECCA J	58
REBECCA J	62
ROENA	86
ROSA J	118
ROSY	21
RUTH E	42
SARAH A	75
SARAH E	100
SARAH J	47
SOPHIA	41
STELLA A	135
SUSAN VIRGINIA	22
VIRGINIA	22
KNAPPENBERGER, DORA	163
EFFIE E	163
ELIZABETH	81
FLORENCE	124
KNICKLES, MANDY	129
KNIGHT, (Mrs) OAKLEY	91
(Mrs) SARAH JANE	21
ARTIE M	103
BLANCHE E	37
CLARA	181
EVA L	133
IDA M	58
IRMA LOUISE	3
KATE	18
LAURA S	128
LILLIE B	16
MAGGIE	152
NORA	60
REBECCA	18
REBECCA	184
SALLIE F	37
SARAH L	117
SUSAN	77
SUSIE	173
KNOP, LUCINDA	143
KNOPP, AMANDA	149
ANNIE L	12
CATHARINE C	30
DORA	57
FANNIE S	170
JESSIE E	107

KATE	70	LANGLEY, (Mrs) F P	133
LENA M	179	LANGTREE, ANN	35
MARTHA A C	26	LANGTRY, CATHARINE	35
MARY L	57	CATHARINE M	115
MARY M	44	LANHAM, ADIE ELIZABETH	44
ROWENA	22	ANNIE	143
SARAH ELIZABETH	160	MATTIE B	129
KNOTT, EMMA	171	NORA M	58
KNUCKLES, ROSA	111	LANIER, CHARLOTTE	124
KOBLENTZ, ANNIE	131	DELLA	124
ELIZABETH	173	DIANAH G	45
KOELER, MARY H	153	HATTIE MAY	62
KOLBE, CLARA L	43	IDA	44
KOONTZ, SABINA	51	JESSIE P	168
KOPP, KATIE	182	LETHA M	84
KOSTER, MARY	92	LOUISA E	190
KOUNS, MARY	34	LOVENIA	93
KRAFT, CLARA E	3	LUELLA	14
ELLA E	45	MARIA Z	10
MARY E	58	MARTHA N	73
KRANSZ, BARBARA	90	MARY	80
KRAUS, DELLA E	164	MARY A	180
KRAUSE, CATHARINE	119	MARY S	108
KRAUTER, BARBARA	103	MATILDA JANE	17
KRAUTHER, ELLEN	151	ROMA G	153
KRAUTTER, ANNIE	129	SARAH A	188
LAURA	151	SUSAN F	184
KREBS, CLARA B	25	VIRGINIA C	124
MAGGIE	166	LARIMER, LYDE E	2
MARY E	154	ROSE	179
KREPPS, EDITH M	137	LARUE, FLORENCE	64
MALINDA JANE	117	LARWOOD, (Mrs) ANNA L	172
KRIBS, CLARA B	187	LASHER, ELIZABETH SUSAN	151
KRIEG, (Mrs) EVA	163	LASLEY, HATTIE E	16
KUHN, NINA A	11	LATHEY, LEOLA	133
KUPPINGER, BARBARA	117	MARY	175
LaCOLLETT, FRANCES	65	MAUD	165
LAINE, LILLIE	6	LAVENDER, (Mrs) ADDA M	12
LAMBERT, DELIA	95	ELLEN J	108
EDITH GOLDIE	166	MINA	136
EDNA	170	SARAH	105
EMILY B	143	LAW, CATHARINE	100
ETHEL OLEVA	72	MARY JANE	125
IDA M	162	LAWRENCE, CORA E	34
IDA MAY	60	DARTHULA C	81
JENNIE	150	SARAH E	117
JENNIE M	44	LAWSON, AMANDA	2
LAURA C	106	EDNA	148
MARY S	136	ELIZA ANN	122
MINNIE	27	EVA A	8
PRISCILLA	20	ISABELLA	131
SALLIE B	54	JESSIE L	84
SARAH E	58	LYDIA J	37
SARAH J	95	MAGGIE	160
LANDSTUFFER, NANCY	119	MARY LEVINIA	105
LANE, ANN ELIZA	88	SADIE MAY	144
ELIZA	91	SARAH JANE	165
ELIZABETH	96	LAYNE, ELLEN F	89
LUCY	148	SARAH A	155
LYDIA	67	LAYONS, CATHARINE	37
MARY	139	LAYRUE, MABLE	28
MARY F	112	LEACH, BESSIE	53
PENELOPE	99	EMMA L	53
ROSETTA	82	LILLIE D	119

Name	Page
MARY E	93
LEADMAN, RICEY JANE	37
LEARY, MARY L	55
LEDERER, KATHREN	58
LENA	2
LEE, (Mrs) MARY JANE	76
BETSY	125
ELIZABETH	125
ELIZABETH A	118
ELLA	169
ELLEN O	138
ESTELLA H	17
EVIE	44
FRANCES	180
GERTRUDE	175
GRACE M	17
HANNAH B	28
HATTIE	72
IDA	86
JEMIMA C	138
JENNETTE	107
KATIE	15
LUCINDA	134
MARTHA F	149
MARY D	74
MARY E	82
MELISSA	25
MINERVA	150
NANCY	135
NANNIE M	39
SALLIE ELIZABETH	174
SARAH	83
SUSIE	128
LEG, RUTH	111
LEGG, ANNIE L	173
ANNIE LAURA	128
ERNA	173
JANE ANN	179
JUNIA	35
MATTIE	19
SARAH F	183
LEGGE, EMMA	125
LEGUE, ELNORA C	183
LELA	125
MURT	76
NANNIE Z	180
NORA	180
SARAH L	31
LEHEW, MABEL G	71
LEIGHTON, NANCY A R	118
LEITWILER, MARY M	144
LEMASTER, ANNIE R	171
ARABELL	7
BLANCH	11
CATHARINE	4
CORNELIA F	93
DRUZILLA C	137
ELIZABETH	189
EMMA	117
FANNIE	107
JULIA	133
LIZZIE	61
LOUISA	14
LUCETTA	137
LULA	127
LUTITIA	71
LUTITIA	93
MARGARETTA	45
MARGARETTA L	17
MARTHA A	117
MARY	42
MARY A	17
MARY E	25
MARY ELIZABETH	33
NANCY ANN	124
SARAH ANN	46
SOPHIA	134
LEMASTERS, ANNA	103
JANE CATHARINE	117
MARY	10
NORMA MAY	9
PRISCILLA	47
RHODA	112
LEMLEY, MINNIE	181
LEPORT, ADDIE	73
EUNICE J	128
FRANCES	178
JENNIE	13
JENNIE	1
JENNIE B	160
POLLY	183
SALLIE	121
LERNER, ANNA M	143
LEVISAY, FANNIE	128
LEWIS, ADA E	28
AGNES	152
AGNES E	29
AGNES S	152
ALICE B	48
ALICE M	101
AMERICA	11
AMERICA	51
BELL	35
CASANDER	165
CASSIE	137
DAISY L	102
DELILAH	175
DELILAH S	186
DELLA D	81
DORA	165
ELIZA ANN	148
ELIZA J	83
ELIZA JANE	125
ELIZA S	66
ELIZABETH	67
ELIZABETH	76
ELIZABETH	171
ELIZABETH	127
ELIZABETH A	3
ELIZAGETH	30
ELLA L	164
ELVIRA	89
EMILY J	54
EVELINE	163
FANNIE	48
GOLDIE E	4
HANNAH	16
HANNAH	151

HARRIET R	174	LILLICH, EMMA	58
HULDA CATHARINE	79	LILLY, MARY	70
JENNET	16	LINCOLN, JESSIE D	87
LAURA	188	LINDSAY, IDA	116
LAURA S	160	LINDSEY, HELEN BROWN	148
LAVINA F	79	LINKFIELD, ALICE	108
LETITIA	35	ALICE	121
LILLIE	14	IDA	177
LILLY E	107	MARY	138
LIZZIE	70	LINKHART, ANNI C	34
LIZZIE B	77	CATHARINE	191
LUCINDA	142	MARY	52
LUELLA	147	LINKINHOGAN, EMMA	76
LURA	56	LINNELL, EMOGENE J	150
MARGARET S	176	LINSCOTT, EMMA E	85
MARTHA A	81	LIONS, ANNA	173
MARTHA R	20	NANCY JANE	126
MARY	36	LITCHFIELD, BESSIE LEE	5
MARY	164	ELIZABETH	52
MARY C	26	LUCINDA	16
MARY C J	84	MARY	37
MARY J	63	NANCY	116
MARY JANE	6	SADIE	84
MATTIE A	21	SARAH E	72
MAUD	38	LITTERELL, EMILY C	178
MEDORAH	189	LITTLE, ELIZABETH	8
MINERVA	33	ELVA	86
MYRTIE	7	FREDA	86
NANCY	73	IDA	150
NONA	172	LONA	176
NORA	172	ROSA E	31
OLGA	146	LIVEZEY, ELVIRA C	58
PLENORA S	87	FANNIE M	182
PRISCILLA	8	LIVING, MARY E	123
RACHEL G	63	LIVINGSTON, (Mrs) MALINDA	35
REBECCA	30	EDITH L	133
REBECCA	134	ELIZABETH	68
ROSA	25	ESTER	182
ROSA B	123	LOUISA	81
ROSE E	95	MARY E	74
ROSIA A	79	MINLINDA	90
SARAH	83	TACY C	6
SARAH	131	LIVINGSTONE, CHLOE	171
SARAH	155	LLOYD, MAGGIE A	15
SARAH A	111	LOCK, DELILAH E	177
SARAH C	178	JULIA A	6
SARAH E	23	MARGARET J	65
SARAH FRANCES	35	LOCKE, IVA E	62
SARAH L	96	MARTHA M	92
SEJUS ALMEDA	3	SILOTA B	108
SUSAN	174	VIOLA S S	114
SUSANNA	134	LOCKETT, ANNIE	148
UNA Z	118	LOCKHARD, MARY ANN	187
LIETWILER, MILLIE	146	LOCKHART, DORIS	187
LIEVING, ADDIE	19	EMMA	12
CLARA	150	JENNIE F	40
FANNIE EMELINE	150	KATE C	12
FREDRIECA	126	LOGUE, MARY EMMA	78
RETTA V	146	LOHR, MARY ANN	40
LIKEN, SARAH C	62	LONG, (Mrs) MARGARET A	138
LIKENS, EMILY D	121	ALICE S	53
MARY M	38	AMANA C	52
NANCY A	151	AMANDA	83
LILICH, CARRIE	23	ANN E	154

ANN ELIZA	103
ANNETTE K	166
CAROLINE	125
CATHARINE R	37
ELIZABETH	164
ELIZABETH	18
ELIZABETH	4
ELIZABETH E	161
ELLA	64
ELLA	137
ELLEN V	159
EMILY SUSAN	18
EVA K	143
EVALENE	109
EVELINE E	43
FANNIE	57
FRANCES E	55
IDA	163
ISABELL	114
JULIA F	25
JULIA M	40
LEARNER	9
LILLIE	21
LIZZIE	96
LOUISA	22
LUCINDA	68
LUCY E	2
MALINDA	77
MARGARET M	188
MARTHA J	123
MARY	29
MARY A	45
MARY CATHARINE	42
MARY E	187
MARY J	160
MARY M	18
MINNIE	138
NANCY	108
NANCY E	2
NOLA	25
SARAH C	88
SARAH E	120
SARAH H	69
STELLA	136
LONGLUTZ, BARBARA	191
LOOMIS, CLARA M	82
ELLA M	117
MARY A	172
LOTTRIDGE, MERLE E	138
LOUDEN, FLOSSIE A	154
JESSIE E	44
LOUDENSLAGER, M A	63
LOVE, ANNETTA	5
CAROLINE	130
DELLA	119
DORA E	144
ELLA	112
ELVA J	63
EMMA C	97
FANNIE A	56
FLORA	52
GEORGIANNA	27
IDA F	160
IVA I	82
IVY	82
LILLIE	120
LUCINDA	160
LUTITIA	127
MABEL IRENE	59
MAGGIE E	139
MAGGIE L	122
MARTHA ANN	6
MARTHA J	123
MARTHA JANE	112
MARY	39
MARY A	185
MARY ISABELLE	14
MARY V	17
NORA L	114
OLIVE M	4
ORA	66
OSCEOLA	145
PAMELA	55
PERMELIA	99
POLLY	152
REBECCA A	141
SARAH JANE	136
SARAH KATHARINE	62
LOVET, (Mrs) MARY ANN	140
LOVETT, PHEBE	8
PHEBE	20
LOWE, MARY	70
MARY A	159
LOWERY, ALLIE U	82
LOYD, RICHMOND	15
LOZIER, MELVINA M	104
LUCAS, CAROLINE	118
LUCKADOE, SALLIE	35
LUCKEY, HAZEL	75
LUELLEN, MYRTIE	5
LUH, IDA	86
LUNSFORD, MABEL J	71
MALINDA	79
LUSE, CARRIE B	42
CYNTHIA J	51
LUSHER, BONNIE ELIZABETH	10
MAE C	38
LUSK, MARY E	132
LUTE, SARAH E	3
LUTTON, CORDELIA J	46
MARY	184
MARY ELEANOR	103
REBECCA J	64
SALLIE	77
SALLIE M	54
SOPHIA	190
VIRGINIA	175
LUTZ, MARY A	191
LUTZE, EMMA	30
LYDA, MARTHA LAVINIA	162
LYER, BARBARA	97
LYKENS, EMMA	116
MIRIAM	83
LYKINS, ROSETTA	85
LYNCH, JUANITA	158
MAE ELIZABETH	17
LYNN, POLLY	36
LYON, CORDELIA A	65

LYONS, CHARITY	162	CAROLINE E	68
EMELINE	44	CATHARINE	97
EVA L	171	CLARA	50
FLORA ALICE	49	DORA	5
JENNIE	171	ELIZABETH	134
LAURA	146	ELIZABETH M	8
LILLIE M	154	EMMA F	192
LINNIE L	75	FANNIE J	30
LUANA	104	FLAVIA	57
LUCRETIA	70	HATTIE L	148
MAGGIE A	65	HELEN H	120
MYRTLE	154	HENRIETTA J	33
LYRE, MAGGIE	101	IVA M	96
MABE, CYNTHIA M	181	JANE	167
MacDANIEL, CATHARINE	176	KATE	188
MACE, MARTHA J	106	LAURA	189
MACHIR, CARRIE F	186	LENA A	117
FANNIE S	105	LILLIE A	164
LAURA V	105	LIZZIE L	122
MACKLEY, ANN	16	LOU	160
BARBARA	82	LUCY F	15
MARY F	55	LULA	84
NELLY	113	LULIE	107
POLLY	84	LYDIA J	185
VIRGINIA M	170	MARGARET	69
MACKLY, VIOLA	28	MARGARET A	110
MACRIA, ELIZA	172	MARIA	33
MADDOCK, HANNAH	177	MARY	21
MADDY, OLIVE ELIZABETH	176	MARY	107
ORILLA	168	MARY A	8
MAERZ, JESSE H	59	MARY ANN	132
MAHAFFY, SALLY	17	MARY CATHARINE	177
MAIGE, DAISEY	132	MARY D	73
MALLORY, ELLEN M	67	MARY J	153
MALONE, ANNIE K	55	MARY M	9
ELIZABETH	155	MATILDA A	120
MARY S	26	MINNIE B	31
NELLIE L	132	NORA	90
TERESA	137	NORA C	12
MALONEY, MARY ELIZABETH	27	OLIVIA	177
MANICK, SARAH	47	PEARL	55
MANLEY, ANNA	39	REBECCA	60
ELIZABETH	55	THIRSEY	110
RETTIE	44	VERNIE L	83
MANLIE, IDA	38	MARTINE, GEORGIA L	83
MANNING, LILLIAN D	102	MARVEN, CATHARINE	181
MANNON, LAURA	152	MARY, ELIZA	98
MARAN, MARY	111	MASH, BETTIE I	99
MARKHAM, MARY	50	HATTIE	18
MAUD M	84	LUCY L	129
MARKUM, MAUD	50	MATILDA	115
MARLIN, HARRIET E	128	NETTIE	99
MARRIS, MARGT J	41	ROSA MAY	41
MARRS, ANNIE	35	SARAH FRANCES	39
MARSH, RUBY	58	VICTORIA JANE	78
MARSHALL, MARY A	112	MASON, (Mrs) HELEN	37
SAMANTHA M	173	(Mrs) MARY	84
SARAH M	75	BIRTA D	181
MARTENESS, EMMA E	158	CATHARINE A	36
MARTIN, ADDA	10	FANNIE L	135
ANNIE L	87	FRANCES M	33
BESSIE A	188	HANNAH	183
BRIDGET	167	ISABELLA	21
CAROLINE	65	LENORA	91

MARGARET	5	
MARGARET	1	
MARIA	82	
MARY	21	
RACHEL	54	
VIRGINIA	113	
MASTERS, MARY E	84	
MASTERSON, MARTHA	65	
MATHENY, ANNA	52	
ANNIE	68	
CORA	170	
DORA F	151	
ELIZABETH	74	
MARY A	84	
MATHEWS, ELIZABETH M A	108	
MATHEWSON, JANE H	23	
MATSON, MARY J	123	
MATTHEWS, BIRDIE	81	
CLARA INDIA	148	
EVA MAE	157	
MATTHEWSON, LEONA M	93	
MATTHIS, MARY	177	
MATTOX, BARBARA	111	
BARBARA ELIZABETH	137	
CORA	77	
EMMA	72	
HANNAH	139	
NANCY UNORA	95	
SUSAN	128	
SUSAN C	55	
MAUPIN, AMANDA M	76	
COLUMBIA A	53	
ELIZABETH	109	
ELIZABETH J	127	
EVELYN L	99	
JENNETTE A	31	
JULIA J	13	
MARY M	176	
MILDRED V	132	
SALLIE G	2	
MAXWELL, MEHALA	55	
MAYES, ANN E	126	
ANNA	61	
ELIZA Y	94	
ELIZABETH J	80	
EMMA D	28	
LAURA	65	
LILLIE E	120	
LOTTIE M	115	
LUTITIA ELLEN	163	
MARGARET	177	
MARTHA J	3	
MARY A	40	
MARY M	32	
MINNIE	8	
RETHA ELLEN	6	
RETHA ELLEN	72	
ROSA B	153	
ROSSETTA	4	
ROZETTA	173	
RUTHY ANN	170	
SETTIE	81	
STELLA MARIE	40	
VANSIE	4	
ZOLA	74	
MAYFIELD, OLIVE B	99	
MAYS, ELIZABETH J	45	
ELIZABETH J	108	
IDA	4	
MARY	93	
MARY J	44	
NANCY	105	
RUTHY ANN	170	
MAYSE, ELIZABETH T	9	
EMMA E	38	
MARY B	38	
MAYZE, REBECCA	89	
MAZE, PATSY	128	
McADAMS, CHRISTINA M	182	
McALLISTER, BETSY	89	
McBRIDE, AMANDA M	107	
CAROLNE	168	
MINA F	44	
McBRIEN, JANE	9	
WILHELMINA	130	
McCALISTER, VIRGINIA	48	
McCALL, DESSIE	19	
LAURA	183	
MAGGIE MAY	109	
MIRTIE	35	
MURTIE	173	
McCALLISTER, AMRY F	46	
ANN	88	
ANNA E	187	
ELIZABETH	4	
EVA	125	
IDILLA	9	
MARIAN	48	
MARY	183	
OLIVIA	125	
ORPHA	6	
SARAH M	191	
VIRGINIA	115	
McCANY, MARY E	104	
McCARL, KATHRYNE	64	
McCARLEY, ELLA	23	
McCARNY, ELLEN	89	
SUSAN	30	
McCARTHY, MARGARET E	186	
McCARTY, BERTHA M	34	
JULIA	88	
MARY	67	
MARY A	92	
MYRTIE E	27	
NANNIE	17	
McCAULEY, ELLA B	112	
ELLA B	112	
FANNIE M	104	
IDA M	5	
MARTHA J	107	
PLEASANT U	158	
McCLAIN, ELIZA ANN	33	
MARGARET J	13	
McCLAINE, EMMA F	91	
McCLARA, LAURA	168	
McCLELLAN, BERT	87	
McCLOUD, ANNA	81	
DELIA	124	

ETHA	102
MALINDA J	102
MARY	148
MARY C	109
VERNA	91
McCLURE, EMILY J	183
LILLIAN	31
LIZZIE E	151
MAGGIE C	6
MARY E	27
SARAH J	133
McCOLLISTER, AMANDA E	128
ELLEN	182
MARTHA	18
MARY A	152
MARY J	13
MARY J	84
MARY J	191
VIRGINIA S	81
McCOMB, MALINDA J	1
VIOLA P	177
McCOMBS, ELIZABETH M	99
McCONIHAY, ELLA	167
MARY S	152
MATTIE	45
McCOWN, MARY JANE	48
McCOY, ADELPHIA A	74
ANGELINE	11
ANNIE C	120
BESSIE	136
BETSEY ANN	98
BETZY ANN	98
CASIE	64
CATHARINE	69
CATHARINE	85
CATHARINE MARGARET	89
CHRISTENA F	137
CHRISTENIA F	184
CORA	48
CORA	69
DELIA	190
EDDA	14
ELIZA A	85
ELIZA F	90
ELIZABETH	173
ELIZABETH	183
EVA M	66
EVELINE	108
HADIA E M	73
HANNAH	31
HARRIET	121
HATTIE M	158
IBELIZA	82
IDA	98
JANE	77
JANE ANN	90
JANNIA	80
JESSIE	93
LAVINIA	24
LORENA	136
MAGGIE MAY	66
MALINDA	85
MARGARET	38
MARTHA C	42

MARY	68
MARY	89
MARY ELLA	116
MENA	10
MINNIE	129
MYRTLE	91
NANCY	90
OMA	94
ORA	86
SALLIE	84
SAMANTHA	32
SARAH	98
SARAH	181
SARAH F	1
SARAH J	28
McCRONEY, MARY	148
SARAH	101
McCULLOCH, CHARLOTTE BYERS	163
JANET	22
KATE LOUISE	161
LYDIA ANNIE	30
MARGARET P	100
MARTHA OLIVIA	100
MARY E	120
SALLIE LEWIS	163
SARAH V	17
McCULLOCH, MARY E	63
McCUMBER, JENNIE R	75
LIZZIE	178
LYDIA	83
NORA B	29
McCUNE, RACHAEL	190
McDADE, BELLE	52
DORA A	110
EVELINE	82
GRACY	157
HARRIET I	165
JANE	121
MARGARET	119
MARMA	44
MARTHA E	74
MARY M	110
MARY MARTHA	164
MIRAM	185
NANCY	26
SEANY	105
SELUDA E	64
SUSANNA	25
McDANIEL, (Mrs) MARY	122
ADALINE	128
ALICE R	121
ANN ELIZA	151
ANNIE	16
BELLE	43
BIRDIE	94
CAROLINE	16
CORA BELLE	126
CORNELIA	138
CYNTHIA	99
DEBORAH	164
ELLA	115
ELLEN E	70
ETTA	105
FANNIE	58

	FANNIE	160	McFANN, (Mrs) LIZZIE	178
	FRANCES C	146	McFARLAND, ANN ELIZA	29
	GRACE L	112	ANNA MARIA	180
	HANNAH	98	SUSAN I	151
	IDA	149	McGARVEY, ELIZA	95
	IDA MAY	159	LUCINDA	9
	LILLIE B	92	MARY	163
	MADALINE	165	McGEE, MARGARET	104
	MARGARET E	182	McGHEE, KATIE	32
	MARTHA	16	McGILL, VIRGINIA LEE	104
	MARY ANN	188	McGINNIS, JOANN P	45
	MARY E	121	McGLAUGHLIN, NARSISSES	178
	MARY J	105	McGLOTHLIN, LAURA	145
	MINA	69	SABINA J	176
	MINNIE J	135	McGLOUGHLIN, OLIVE J	124
	NANCY	108	McGRADY, ELIZABETH	109
	OLLIE MAY	35	HETTY	110
	RACHEL	135	MARGARET	109
	REBECCA	44	McGRAIL, SARAH J	162
	REBECCA	123	McGRAW, BETTIE	148
	SARAH	95	GEORGIANNIE	1
	SARAH	127	HENRIETTA	156
	SARAH E	19	IVY	187
	THENA H	117	LILLIE	169
	VIOLA FRANCES	13	LUCRETIA A	157
	VIRGINIA	180	MAGGIE MAY	150
McDERMIT, CYNTHIA		26	SARAH	162
McDERMITT, ALTA MAY		151	McGREERY, CATHARINE	77
	ANNIE LAURA	166	McGREW, IDELLA	8
	ANNIE R	99	ISABEL	129
	BLANCH	124	McGUCKIAN, MARY	80
	CHLOE A	9	McGUCKIN, ELLA	136
	CLARISSA ANN	143	McGUFFIN, ANNIE L	152
	EMMA	73	EMMA J	103
	HARRIET	47	IDA M	106
	JOSEPHINE C	170	LILLY B	29
	KATIE M	173	LUCY MENTOR	59
	LAVINA	64	MARY M	76
	LOTTIE	183	ORA A	34
	LUCINDA J	53	McGUIRE, (Mrs) JANE	110
	MAE	154	ANN	6
	MAGGIE B	51	ARMEDA A	189
	MALINDA	150	DIMMIE	191
	MARY J	74	ELIZA A	102
	MARY M	163	ELIZABETH	1
	MARY SUSAN	119	ELIZABETH	85
	MATILDA	140	ELIZABETH J	118
	MAUDE E	149	MARY	84
	MINNIE B	63	MARY	156
	OSA	128	NANCY M A	127
	RACHAEL	136	RACHEL	158
	RACHEL	63	SARENA C	69
	REBECCA J	170	McGUNIGAL, ANNA	61
	RHODA	28	McHONE, MARY	18
	ROSE ANN	163	McILVEEN, MARY	16
	SARAH	134	McINTIRE, MARY	184
	SARAH L	106	SARAH	26
	SUSAN	117	McINTOSH, LOUISA M	134
McDONALD, ALEXY		173	NONA A	140
	MARGARET	69	McKEE, MARGARET	181
McDOWELL, MARIE A		83	McKEEVER, GEORGIANA	138
McELVAIN, JULIA A		6	McKEOWN, MARY E	189
McFADDEN, MARY A		32	McKERN, BARBARA E	16
	SARAH C	4	McKIAG, ALICE	137

Name	Page
McKIBBEN, WILD R	177
McKINDLEY, ADA B	154
ORA L L	140
McKINEY, ANNA B	84
DESSIE M	94
ELIZA J	24
LILLIE	34
MARY	131
MINNIE	59
MYRTIE	174
NANCY J	163
McKINNEY, EMMA	134
MARTHA J	63
McKINNY, MIRANDA	185
McKITRICK, CAMMIE A	180
McKNIGHT, MARY E	184
McKOUN, ANNIE J	190
McLANE, LOUISA A	174
McLEOD, CHRISTIE	2
MATTIE	120
McMAHAN, AGNES	73
ROSE	44
McMAHON, KIZZAIAH	98
McMANAWAY, MAY	142
McMANN, HANNAH	4
McMARRY, MARGARET	127
McMILLEN, ANGIE	145
ANNIE	192
ELMA	88
GARNETTE L	74
JANE	90
JENNIE	19
LUCY B	67
LUSETTA	54
MAGGIE ALLAH	56
MARGARET ELIZABETH	51
MARY S	150
MATILDA	141
SARAH FRANCES	51
McMILLIN, (Mrs) REBECCA ANN	78
BERTHA	83
ELIZABETH	139
MARGARET	19
MILDRED E	84
McMILLON, SARAH M	191
McMULLEN, CATHARINE	68
ELIZA	30
POLLY	35
McMURRAY, RACHEL	147
McNAUGHTON, HANNAH L	147
SARAH V	182
McNEAL, TABITHA A	64
McNEALEY, DELLA M	49
MAGGIE	67
McNEALY, RHUA	102
McNEAR, LINA E	110
McNEILL, BESSIE A	94
WILLIE R	78
McNERRY, MARY	34
McNICHOLE, CYNTHIA	119
McPHERSON, ADELINE	42
McQUAID, LILLY	45
MARY E P	6
McTHENY, (Mrs) SUSANA	34
McVEY, ERSA	44
McWHORTER, AMANDA	110
JENNIE	90
NETTIE	78
NORA F	78
McWHORTOR, MARGARET F	26
McWILLIAMS, EXEVERIA	191
MEAD, BETTIE	79
NANNIE L	163
MEADOWS, (Mrs) IDELLA	116
ABIGAIL	6
ADA	46
ADIE	116
ALICE	176
AMANDA	46
ANGELINE	36
BERTHA	96
CARA MABEL	25
CATHARINE ANN	79
CLARINDA J	117
CYNTHA A	176
CYNTHIA ANN SUSAN	49
DAISY	13
EDITH	68
ELCIE	85
ELIZA M	68
ELIZABETH	23
ELIZABETH	40
ELLA	177
ESSIE A	163
ETHEL JEANNESS	2
EVA W	78
GUSTIE E	23
IDORA D	50
ISABEL	79
IVA M	142
JENNIE	168
JENNIE A	27
JENNIE CATHARINE	46
JULIA J	26
LENA	42
LETTIE O	53
LONA MAY	104
LORNA	169
LOTTIE	71
MAHALA A L	1
MALINDA SUSAN	188
MANDY B	33
MARTHA H	166
MARY A	149
MARY A F	85
MARY E	133
MILLIE P	116
MINERVA	167
MINNIE C	116
MINNESOTA	101
NANCY J	29
OCIE O	23
OLIVIA	109
OLLIE	109
ONA	36
PARTHENIA E	26
ROSA M	85
ROZELIE	36

Name	Page
SALLIE	178
SARAH C	5
SARAH E	32
SARAH E	46
SELAH	58
SEMINET	50
SINA B	39
SOPHIA	80
SOPHIA M	116
TELITHA ANN	69
VINIE	55
MEDLEY, MARY	157
MARY ELLEN	130
SALLIE	2
MEDORS, BLANCHE	158
MEEK, ELENOR	61
ELSIE	66
NANCY	99
MEEKS, ADDIE M	170
BETTIE	75
LILLIE A	72
NANCY J	26
OLLIE	43
SADIE	95
SOPHIA	192
MEES, ANNA MARGARET	11
BERTHA S	98
ELIZABETH	41
SOPHIA	57
MEHEN, MARGARET J	127
MEHONE, ELIZA ANN	113
MEIGS, PARSHONEA	18
MELTON, AMANDA	51
ELIZABETH	83
LAURA	144
MARY M L	61
SARAH E	89
MENAGER, HENERIETTA B	116
IDA L	23
MARIA L	104
MARY E	120
MERCHANT, GARNETTE BELLE	65
MERITT, GOLDA	143
MERRITT, DELLA B	154
MATILDA M	94
MESSICK, ELIZABETH C	183
ETHEL M	15
MESUSAN, CATHARINE	154
LYDIA	133
METHENA, ELSIE	182
MEYER, FREDA	73
MICHAEL, MARY JANE	174
MIDDLECOFF, ADELINE	178
ANNETTA B	186
CORNELIA A	134
EMELINE R	78
IDA	19
KATE L	59
MARGARET S	173
MARY JANE	108
MARY MARGARET	61
SARAH E	185
MIDDLETON, ELIZABETH	87
SARAH E	90
MILAM, MARY R	57
SARAH	169
MILES, LULIE J	123
MILLER, (Mrs) MARY C	79
(Mrs) MARY C	160
AGENORA	85
ALICE	184
ALICE JORDEN	79
ALMA G	172
ALSONA	19
ANN E	112
ANN ELIZA	19
ANNIE	160
ATLANTIC O	120
BLANCHE C	183
CAROLINE H W	94
CHARLESANNA R M	17
DELIA	36
DELTA V	6
DORA	28
DORA	157
EDITH C	163
ELIZABETH	175
ELIZABETH PEARL	128
ELLA	161
ELLENOR B	19
ELLOURIA	163
EMMA	47
EVA D	15
FANNY E	182
FLORENCE	135
HANNAH JANE	118
HELEN E	50
HELEN E	172
IDA C A	39
JEANNETTE	49
LAURA JOSEPHINE	79
LINDA	78
LIZZIE	179
LUELLA G	76
MAGGIE	95
MALINDA R	33
MAMIE BELLE	23
MARGARET E	97
MARGARET E F	39
MARGARET J	3
MARTHA E	83
MARY	105
MARY	160
MARY B	36
MARY C	26
MARY D	91
MARY ELLEN	164
MARY JANE	164
MARY M	94
MARY S	16
MATTIE L	33
MINERVA G	124
MINNIE	42
MINNIE	55
MINNIE J	12
MONIE	113
MYRTLE	49
MYRTLE	93

NANCY	53		SOPHIA JANE	120
NANCY L	176		SUSAN	186
NANCY R	15		MITCHELTREE, ELIZABETH	56
NELLIE	174		SARAH F	192
RACHEL	49		MOBLEY, AUGUSTA	128
RACHEL E	92		BERTHA A	135
REBECCA	79		LUCY A	161
RHODA J	26		NANCY JANE	74
ROSA	46		MOBLY, MARGARET E	57
SALLIE V	34		MOCK, BLANCHE I	157
SALLY	128		EMMA	83
SARAH E	85		MOLDEN, EMMA	21
SARAH E	86		VALLIE V	62
STELLA M	121		MONK, ELIZABETH	98
VICTORIA V	154		MONROE, ETTA M	124
WILLIE A	45		FRANCES	179
MILLS, ANN	48		GEORGIA A	61
ANNA	90		MARTHA W	127
ELLA	162		VIRGINIA	11
ELLEN	9		MONTGOMERY, ELLA	148
JENNIE	90		GRACE	148
MARTHA B	49		IDA	47
MARY	36		NAOME	190
MINICH, ELIZABETH	76		RUBY	46
SOPHA	163		MOODESPAUGH, ELIZABETH	114
MINICK, JANE ANN	112		KATIE	21
MINIS, MINNIE	118		MOODY, CELIA	181
MINK, ALICE	148		EDITH A	53
GERTIE	120		JESSIE	111
GIRTIE	17		MAGGIE M	134
HANNAH	162		MOOR, JANE	9
MINKS, MARY ALICE	117		MOORE, (Mrs) ANN	165
MINNICK, MARY J	55		(Mrs) NANCY ANN	106
SARAH	127		ANN	84
MINNS, MARY A	24		ANNIE	54
MINTURN, DELILAH	37		BIRD	134
ELLEN A	148		DULCIE E	27
FRANCES	150		ELIZABETH	9
JANE	88		ELLEN	76
LENA J	88		FLORA	59
MARION	70		FLORENCE V	159
ROXA	185		FRANCES HANNAH	164
SARAH A C	46		FRANCES R	13
MISNER, ELIZA JANE	57		HENRIETTA M	66
ELIZABETH M	32		IVY A	88
MITCH, EDDA	85		JENNIE	175
MITCHELL, ALTHA	143		KATIE	138
ANGELINE	28		LAVINA	10
ANNA LAURA	165		LEAH	39
CATHARINE	48		LUCRETIA H	167
CATHARINE M	156		LYDE MAY	43
DORA	187		MARTHA	97
EDNA	128		MARY	109
ELLA	72		MARY L	174
EMMA	72		MARY MARGARET	120
EVA LOUISE	65		MARY S	158
FLORENCE V	138		MATTIE A	10
MARGARET	186		MERLEY	9
MARGERY	19		NANNIE	162
MARIA	37		NORA F	26
MARY E	186		OLIVIA M	147
MARY M	118		RHODA JANE	82
MAUD	36		ROSA	101
NANCY	160		ROSIE	66

SALLIE E	110
SARAH E	163
SARAH M B	124
MORARITY, BIDDIE	105
MOREDOCK, JENNIE S	124
MOREHEAD, ANNIE E	179
LUCINDA	4
MARY	135
MORGAN, ELIZABETH	184
EMMA K	119
KATHRYN JANE	180
MARGARET T	171
MARY JANE	71
MINA L	43
OLIVE	152
RACHEL	28
MORIARITY, KATIE	127
MORIARTY, ELLEN	176
MORNING, SARAH	9
MORRIS, ANN M	38
ARRETTA E	27
CATHARINE A	22
CORA E	61
ELLEN S	132
ELVIRA	187
EMILY	131
JESSIE F	30
LAURA	150
MARIA E	68
MARY	191
MARY	18
MARY S	175
MINERVA	137
MINNIE B	20
NANCY	51
PANTHA	63
SARAH JANE	187
SUSAN	94
SUSAN M	129
MORRISON, ALDA B	43
BETSY	181
CLEE O	190
DORA J	90
EARLY JANE	63
HANNAH E	69
JENNIE	48
LOUISA	105
LULU	178
MAY	187
MOLLIE	170
REBECCA L	184
SALLIE	187
SARAH ANN	124
VELLA M	110
MORRISTON, ARAY A	38
LETHA J	46
MELISSA	100
NANCY E C	117
MORROW, ALICE CLARINDA	1
DOLLIE A	115
EMILY J	9
JEANETTE	97
LILLY	155
MARY J	123
MELINDA	177
NANCY F	129
OLIVE	186
REBECCA	177
SARAH	154
SOPHRONIA J	178
VIOLA	34
MORSE, IDA M	18
MORTON, BLANCH A	69
MOSBARG, BETSY	28
MOSES, EMMA	29
MOSGROVE, ANNA	106
MOSIER, JULIA E	157
MOSLEY, MAGGIE	88
MOSS, CYNTHIA	154
MOTT, SARAH	169
MOTTS, GERTRUDE	104
MOULDING, LUCY M	83
MOURNING, EDITH G	45
ELIZA	73
EMILY J	44
LAURA ELLEN	125
LUELLA BLANCHE	3
NANCY J	139
ORA E	86
REBECCA N	59
SARAH C M	175
MUGRIDGE, MINNIE MAY	97
MULFORD, AMY I	188
JANE	86
LUCINDA	172
LYDIA	41
MARY J	13
MATTIE	40
VERNA MAY	128
MULLAN, NETTIE C	119
MULLEN, ARTIE	93
ETTA	154
KATIE A	109
MULLIN, ANGELINE	35
BERTHA	97
BRIDGET	38
MULLINS, MARGARET	33
MUMAW, (Mrs) MARY FLORENCE	69
ELIZABETH SEICHRIST	13
LYDIA	181
MUNDELL, MALINDA	83
RACHEL	102
MUNFORD, FLORENCE MAE	166
MUNSELL, CLARINDA	178
MURDOCK, CATHARINE M	176
MURPHY, NORA	107
MURRAY, ALICE	168
MAUDE	7
MURREY, MARGARET M	149
MURRY, MARY	131
MARY A	181
NANCY	56
SARAH A	90
MUSGRAVE, ANNIE LEE	60
CLARA BELLE	61
EMMA C	25
MARY C	147
MARY E	92

MARY L	52		NEIGHBORS, ELIZABETH	179
MYERS, (Mrs) NELLIE ANN	22		NANCY M	149
BELLE V	176		NELSON, BERTHA E	48
BERTHA C	49		ELIZA JANE	167
ELIZA M	165		LUCINDA A	46
ELIZABETH	162		NORA	120
HATTIE R	31		ORA E	61
LOUISA	47		NEMMO, MARY E	116
LYDA ANN	29		NESSELLROOD, BERTHA	129
MATILDA	116		NESSELROAD, MARGARET L	162
MATILDA A	133		NETROSS, ELLENOR T	162
NETTIE F	32		NEVILLE, (Mrs) MARY D	21
PHOEBE	41		HANNAH M	119
SOPHRONIA C	10		NORA B	118
NANCE, LANEY A	191		SAMANTHA J	9
NEAL, ALICE	89		SARAH	131
KATIE MARGARET	85		NEWAL, DRUSILLA	119
MARY N	166		NEWBERRY, (Mrs) IDA	151
MARY SUSAN	141		NEWBRAUGH, ADDIE R	117
SARAH ANN	89		NEWBY, FLORENCE A	39
VERA CRUZ	68		MARGARET E	48
NEALE, CATHARINE M	99		NEWEL, SARAH	128
E V	50		NEWELL, ANNIE L	38
EMMA E	26		BARBARY	99
FLORENCE	189		BERTHA	82
FLURY	141		ELIZABETH	75
IDA	154		ELIZABETH	105
JENNIE C	166		EMILY J	84
LOU	11		EVA	31
LUELLA	97		FLORA	54
MARGARET LEWIS	12		GERTRUDE	57
MARY A	43		LELY	69
REGINA	5		MARGARET	103
NEALY, REBECCA	104		MARTHA F	81
NEASE, (Mrs) CHRISTINA	70		MARY	88
(Mrs) MARTHA MATILDA	192		MARY A	66
BERTHA E	145		MYRTLE B	149
CATHARINE	145		OLEVIA	92
EFFIE L	147		RHODA	176
FRANCES ELIZABETH	75		SADDIE	164
LAURA L	179		SARAH ELIZABETH	136
LORETTA C	144		NEWLAND, LAURA	75
MARY A	146		NEWLON, LUCY A	115
MELVINA	84		NEWMAN, FRANCES	91
MINNIE FRANCES	42		FRANCIS	133
NANNIE	39		MARGARET E	7
NANNIE LOUISE	110		MARTHA M	8
SABINA S	73		MARY C	89
SALOME	56		MARY CATHARINE	75
SARAH E	101		MARY E	178
SARAH F	191		MATILDA H	55
SUSANNA	191		SUSAN M	143
NEEDHAM, ELIZABETH	101		NEWTON, MARY F	148
LILLIE	108		NIBERT, ALTA	17
MAGGIE J	52		BERTHA M	44
MARY CATHARINE	48		ELIZA J	97
MATILDA J	169		GRACIE	96
VIRGIE M	116		IDA	79
NEEL, SOPHIA	30		KITTIE	89
NEFF, HATTIE R	105		LUCRETIA	189
NEIBERT, JEMIMA	26		MARY	126
NEICE, LOUISA	100		MARY E	155
NEIGHBERT, NANCY	187		MARY H	72
NEIGHBORGALL, ANNIE	157		NANCY	73

TINA LURE	96	
VERNA M	73	
NICHOLAS, MARIAH	82	
NICHOLL, MAGGIE MAY	63	
NICHOLS, ABBY	35	
EVA	175	
JANE	110	
SALLIE	177	
SIMMERIAN C	77	
NICHOLSON, BESSIE	192	
JAINIE DANEAL	91	
ROENA E	25	
SARAH A	105	
NICKLE, JANE	112	
MARY	158	
MARY R	158	
NIECE, EMILY VIRGINIA	94	
NIEMEYER, CATHARINE S	40	
NIZELY, MAHALA	69	
NOARK, MINNIE	3	
NOBLE, AGNES ORA	66	
ANN ELIZA	138	
BERTHA M	138	
ETTA F	28	
RACHEL A	96	
ROSANA	81	
SARAH E	85	
NOBLES, ELIZA J	46	
NOE, ELIZABETH	15	
NORMAN, DAISY	41	
NORRIS, CARRIE D	147	
E C	69	
MARY C	61	
NORTH, MARY ELIZABETH	153	
NORTHUP, VIVIAN L	114	
NORTON, ANNA	32	
NORVELL, ANNIE	106	
NOTT, LEOTA	63	
NOTTER, NETTIE E	122	
NOTTINGHAM, LELA M	72	
NOWLIN, GARNETT	106	
RUBY PEARL	78	
NUCKLES, MARTHA	110	
MARTHA	184	
MARY L	130	
MARY R	137	
NUMAN, SARAH J	35	
NUNLEY, MARTHA L	54	
NUTTER, LEOTA L	64	
ROSA	23	
TOLA	2	
O'CONNOR, (Mrs) ALICE J	48	
JOSIE	153	
O'DONEL, BRIDGET	122	
O'HARE, MARY A	70	
O'LEARY, ANNA C	99	
CATHERINE	135	
MARGARET	22	
NANNIE	39	
NORA	158	
O'NAIL, INGARY	65	
MARY A	69	
O'NEAL, ANN	47	
FLORENCE	153	
JANE	51	
O'NEILL, ALICE	95	
CLARA E	11	
OAKS, JULIA E D	117	
OHLINGER, ADDIE E	161	
ANN B	123	
DOLLY	158	
EMMA	105	
FLORENCE MAY	157	
LUELLA B	101	
LYDA M	146	
LYDIA	81	
MARY L	13	
MARY V	145	
NANCY	40	
RUBY J	113	
SARAH	16	
VESTA M	144	
OLDACRE, CELIA	69	
CYNTHIA	177	
JANE	11	
OLDAKER, IDA M	74	
JANE	111	
JEMIMA	115	
LAVINIA	133	
LILLIE B	177	
MARGARET	11	
MARY	23	
MINNIE A	1	
URENIA	129	
OLDAKERS, DEBORAH	20	
FRANCES C	70	
REBECCA ANN	7	
VIANA V	171	
OLDFIELD, JEMIMA	80	
MINNIE B	32	
OLINGER, BARBARA ANN	157	
CAROLINE	186	
MARY C	187	
STELLA E	56	
SUSANNAH	109	
OLIVER, (Mrs) JULIA	69	
ALICE	54	
AMANDA M	107	
ANNA GRACE	25	
ELIZABETH	144	
ETHEL PEARL	11	
EVA B	107	
FANNIE	60	
GEORGIA ANGELINE	162	
HANNAH M	170	
HARRIET	97	
JANE	163	
JANE ANN	67	
LELIA V	94	
LENA B	44	
LILLIE B	71	
LULU	150	
MAGDALINE	60	
MAMIE	189	
MARY	21	
MARY	47	
MARY	92	
MARY	167	

MARY A	132	
MARY ANN	19	
MARY C	103	
MARY E	5	
MAUDE E	112	
MAY	87	
NANCY	5	
SARAH LOUISA	161	
SARAH VIRGINIA	71	
SUSANNAH	47	
VIRGINIA F	70	
ONEAL, ANN	47	
ORD, ADDIE F	188	
ELLA	24	
MARY	83	
ORONIGS, IDA V	120	
ORR, EVA C D	11	
ORRINGTON, IDA M	33	
OSBORN, SUSANNA	100	
OSHEL, LENNA G	34	
OTER, ELIZABETH	93	
OUSLEY, ANNA L	119	
OVERSHINER, ELISA A	182	
MARGARET	10	
SARAH	159	
OWENS, ELIZA	35	
MARY ELIZABETH	139	
PADEN, ALICE	191	
EMMA	106	
PAGE, EMILY E	76	
EMMA	3	
HARRIET	185	
JANE E	68	
LUCINDA J	27	
MARGARET	186	
MARTHA F	39	
MILDRED A	118	
NEVADA MAY	2	
SARAH E	120	
SARAH F	155	
PAIN, ELIZABETH	17	
MARY	168	
PAINE, SOPHA	184	
SOPHIA	184	
PAINTER, EFFIE	50	
ISA	6	
VIRGIE L	115	
PALEY, HARRIET	67	
PARISH, DORA	56	
PARK, (Mrs) MALINDA A	107	
ALICE	165	
CAROLINE	159	
EDITH	23	
MARY A	96	
PARKER, (Mrs) MATILDA	167	
ANNA	56	
CHARLIE ANNA	131	
KATE A	181	
LAURA M	87	
MARTHA	20	
MARY	143	
MARY ANN	18	
VIRGINIA	176	
PARKS, ELIZABETH	130	
PARMER, (Mrs) ELLA	107	
PARRISH, ROSA E	168	
VIRGINIA	169	
PARRY, HANNAH	192	
REBECCA	42	
PARSINGER, JANE	113	
PARSON, CATHARINE	187	
MARY A	50	
PARSONS, (Mrs) LUCINDA	28	
ADELPHIA M	156	
BERTIE	62	
BIRDIE	172	
DELPHA	154	
EFFIE J	25	
ELIZABETH	14	
ELIZABETH	14	
ELIZABETH	159	
EMMA L	40	
ESTELLA	50	
ESTHER L	135	
FRANKIE	143	
HANNAH	134	
HANNAH	173	
HAZEL	158	
INA MAY	82	
ISABELL	43	
JENNIE M	161	
JESSIE	187	
KITTY B	16	
LETHA ANN	175	
MARGARET	152	
MARIA	171	
MARTHA	191	
MARY	167	
PEARL	88	
REBECCA	124	
ROSA L	128	
SARAH	63	
VESTA J	43	
PASIN, CATHARINE	128	
PATCHAL, NANCY A	32	
PATRICK, MAGGIE	21	
PATTERSON, (Mrs) EMMA	144	
AMANDA C	178	
AUGUSTA A	57	
BARBARA A	103	
DAISY	15	
ELIZA	57	
HULDA	127	
JENNIE	91	
MAHALA	4	
NANCY	75	
NANCY	128	
OLLIE	35	
PARTHENA	102	
POLLEY A	106	
ROSA	31	
PATTON, MINNIE L	50	
PAULIN, LILLIE M	115	
MARY J	187	
PAULY, (Mrs) TERESA	22	
PAYNE, LUCINDA	88	
MARY	79	
PAMELIA	5	

PAMELIA	5
PEAL, MINNIE	80
PEARSON, ELIZABETH J	49
FLORENCE	96
HERMA	170
IDA	172
IRS	164
KATIE	161
LELA A	83
LILLIE	166
MINNIE	134
ORA E	2
SARAH C	153
SOPHIA R	181
PEASE, ELIZABETH	77
ELIZABETH	182
MARY JANE	3
PECK, ANNA	62
CARENA C	117
CAROLINE	95
CYNTHIA	54
DEBORAH J	166
ELLA	126
EMILY M	78
ETTA MAY	127
GEORGIA	128
ITLEY V	55
LAVINIA	21
LETITIA H	78
MALINDA A	141
MARY	57
SARAH HAMILTON	135
SUSAN J	70
VIRGIE	185
WILLIE	55
PEDEN, ALICE	191
CLARA	69
PEGRAM, MAGGIE	45
PENCE, MARTHA E	87
RACHEL	132
PENNEABAKER, FLORIDA B	51
PEOPLES, ALFRETTA	66
PERDUM, DAISY M	119
PERRY, CELIA	69
ELIZABETH	5
ELIZABETH A	33
GRACE	87
LULA MAY	104
MARGARET	6
MARY ELIZABETH	107
MARY S C	2
MAY	179
ROSE B	19
PERSINGER, ALTA MAY	73
MARTHA SUSAN	43
VIRGINIA	129
VIRGINIA F	73
PETERSON, MARY	155
PETTY, ALICE L	115
GLADYS	159
IDA L	18
SARAH J	167
PEYTON, MARY E	120
SUSAN F	17
PFADT, LIZZIE	153
PHELPS, FLOSSIE LENORA	82
MARY E	24
NANCY	31
NANCY A	56
PHILIPS, BESSIE	25
CYNTHIA ALICE	109
MARGARET	133
SADDIE	17
PHILLIPS, CORA MAY	134
EMILY J	130
KATE	31
MARY W	190
MINNIE A	176
MINNIE L	148
RACHEL LORINDA	123
PIATT, CATHARINE	123
SARAH	136
PICK, HARRIET LUCINDA	68
PICKARD, MARY L	144
PICKEN, THEODOSIA	34
PICKENS, ADALINE	22
ALLIE M	13
ALMA	146
AURILLA	165
BERTHA ALICE	93
BERTIE V	7
CHRISTENA	152
CLARA B	93
DELINDA	140
DELLA PEARL	87
DOSHEY	76
ELIZA A	108
ELIZABETH B	172
ELLEN	82
EMMA	53
IVA ELLEN	1
KIZZIAR	145
LAURA	91
LOAH A	159
LONA	71
LUCINDA E	146
LUCY E	144
MAGGIE	118
MAHALA J	160
MARGARET	103
MARY	141
MARY M	22
MATTIE	75
MAUDE R	34
MELISSA M	105
MINNIE	188
MISSOURI B	63
OMA	70
RUTH ANN	51
SARAH	63
SARAH MARGARET	51
SEVILLEY A	138
VICTORIA	15
VIOLA	8
WINONA	29
PIERCE, ALLIE	102
BESSIE MAUD	114
BETTIE	111

BLANCH I	33	
DEBBIE K	57	
ELIZA	117	
ELLEN	4	
EMMA	158	
EMMA L	180	
FANNIE	88	
KATE	77	
MARY	8	
MARY F	125	
MARY JANE	105	
MARY MAGDALANE	26	
PIERCY, DELILA	141	
ELIZABETH	72	
ELIZABETH	13	
HESTER	28	
NANCY	58	
PIERSOL, (Mrs) LEOTA	16	
ANNIE B	92	
PIERSON, BERTHA	172	
BLANCHE	170	
CATHARINE A	69	
EFFIE M	12	
HANNAH	184	
RACHEL	120	
PIKE, EMMA	141	
LUCINDA	133	
MARY A	52	
PILCHARD, ANNIE	113	
NANCY E	154	
PILES, ANNIE	125	
EMILY J	17	
MARY	101	
PILLOW, ANNIE M	176	
LAURA	111	
PILLOWS, OLEVIA J	171	
SALLIE S	189	
PINE, MARY A	135	
PINNELL, ELIZA M	55	
PINNICK, MARTHA E	6	
MARTHA ELIZABETH	6	
PITRAT, HARRIETTE BENOITE	122	
PLANTS, ADA	132	
ANNIE E	66	
DONA	83	
EFFIE	119	
ELLA	131	
LUCY ELLEN	58	
MARY F	98	
MARY J	108	
MARY J	16	
NANCY ANN	4	
NANCY E	63	
NANCY JANE	108	
OLLIE	21	
RHODA E	80	
ROSA	169	
ROSA B	169	
SUSIE	2	
VICTORIA	138	
PLANTZ, MAGGIE	181	
PLATT, CHARLOTTE E	25	
MATILDA	6	
PLYMALE, BEATRICE	132	
POFFENBARGER, HATTIE G	73	
JEANNETTE	2	
RACHEL	57	
SALLIE	76	
VIRGINIA	185	
POLK, ETTA	27	
ETTIE	12	
POLLOCK, MARIE	54	
MINNIE	173	
POLLY, EMMA RILLA	22	
POLSLEY, AUGUSTA	79	
ELIZA M	36	
ELIZA V	12	
EMMA GERTRUDE	135	
HARRIET B	159	
HARRIET S	126	
KATE ALICE	18	
POMEROY, FANNIE SEHON	117	
PONTSLER, REBECCA	40	
PONTZLER, ALICE	53	
ALMIRA	117	
ELLEN	172	
MARGT	62	
POOL, EMMA	107	
PORE, CYNTHIA A	189	
MAGGIE E	31	
SARAH	82	
PORTER, ANNIE AGNES	80	
ESTHER	164	
MARTHA	37	
MARTHA	137	
MAYME	182	
POSEY, KATY	161	
POST, ELDA	50	
LAURA E	96	
POSTLETHWAIT, ELIZA	82	
POSTLEWEIGHT, LUCINDA	107	
RHODA J	162	
POSTON, AUGUSTA E	156	
LUELLA B	40	
MARY C	77	
PLEASANT	55	
POSTTLEWEIGHT, SARAH E	166	
POTTS, ANNA	130	
BELLE	127	
DORA	11	
MARGARET ANN	190	
MARY	102	
SOPHRONIA	132	
POUND, RACHEL	144	
POUNDS, ANN	137	
ARLETTA	146	
LYDIA	144	
LYDIA	145	
RACHEL EVELENE	71	
SARAH E	145	
SUSANA	113	
POUR, ELIZA A	169	
POWEL, ARIMINTY	169	
CAROLINE	112	
CAROLINE	164	
MARY	74	
POWELL, ABIGAIL	180	
AMANDA	131	

AZERAH B	37	
CASSIE	180	
EMELINE	159	
EMMA J	160	
FANNIE BELLE	12	
LALLAH	5	
LELIA	31	
LENA N	41	
LYDIA	118	
MALINDA	180	
NORA	188	
REGINA	152	
ROXY A	89	
SUSAN	78	
TESSA	11	
POWER, BRIDGET	122	
POWERS, BARBARA CATHARINE	89	
JEMIMA	43	
LOUISA F	45	
MABEL	168	
MARGARET A	137	
MARTHA	35	
PRATT, LUCRETIA	165	
PREDY, MARY M	172	
PREWETT, EMILY	149	
PREWIT, FRANCES	63	
PRICE, CARRIE G	137	
GARNET	138	
GOLDIE M	166	
KATIE	104	
LEAH K	128	
MINNIE B	55	
MINTORA	87	
ROSSETTA	178	
STELLA	86	
PRICHARD, JANE	151	
PRICKETT, PATSY	136	
PRIDDY, ADDIE	170	
ALLSONA M	186	
ANNIE E	100	
ELIZABETH C	72	
ELLA	72	
LANA L	105	
LAVINIA F	163	
LUCY	131	
LUCY JANE	58	
LUCY JANE	58	
MARTHA	172	
MARY	126	
MONA G	166	
VIRTIE M	66	
PRINCE, FRANCES E	68	
PRIODE, IDA M	143	
LENA J	58	
SOPHIA E	67	
PRIOR, ELIZA	176	
PRITCHARD, LIZZIE	137	
MARY	149	
SARAH E	127	
PRITCHETT, PHEBE	91	
PRITT, DOLLIE	166	
ORA E	166	
PROFFITT, FRANCES	112	
MARGARET A V	16	
MARTHA J	140	
MARY E F	103	
SOPHIA A	140	
SOPHIA J F	16	
PROSE, JENNIE	182	
PROSSER, DORTHY	160	
ELIZABETH	95	
ELIZABETH J	101	
MAHALA M	43	
MARY H	80	
PUGH, LULU	153	
PULLEN, NELLIE	35	
PULLIN, DAISY	164	
DORA M	168	
ESMERALDA	33	
GRETCHEN	185	
JANE A	112	
LENORA M	114	
MARGARET	47	
MARGARET B	114	
MARY	34	
MARY E	136	
MINNIE ELLEN	104	
NANNIE E	62	
NELLIE L	170	
SELMMA L	101	
PULLINS, ANN	100	
FRANCES	52	
JENNIE M	119	
NANCY	33	
SARAH A	97	
PUMPHREY, MARY EMMA	131	
PURDY, ANNIE	154	
CORNELIA M	10	
PURVIANCE, ALTA MAY	149	
PUSEY, LAURA F	81	
PUTNEY, MARY E	43	
MINNIE E	103	
SARAH C	84	
PYLES, LOTTIE MAY	66	
QUEEN, OCTA E	32	
QUICKEL, (Mrs) MARY J	91	
QUICKLE, KEARLIE	105	
NELLIE M	160	
WILLIE	119	
QUILLEN, ANNA	147	
EVA G	144	
HARRIET LURA	190	
MATTIE C	8	
MOLLEY	102	
SADIE N	147	
VINNIE	144	
QUILLIN, BIRDIE LELIA	138	
MATTIE	58	
OLIVIA	144	
QUILLON, ELLENOR	152	
QUINBY, FANNIE	94	
JANE	102	
RABB, LOUISA	73	
RADER, POLLY	135	
SUSAN	133	
RADFORD, SUSAN C	133	
RAINER, ANNA	165	
RAINEY, CORA INEZ	44	

LIZZIE S	121	
MARGARET V	142	
OLLIE	108	
VINA F	142	
RAIRDEN, HANNAH	42	
IDA M	150	
MARY E	113	
RAMBOW, DORIS S	20	
RAMSEY, ELIZABETH	73	
IDA B	161	
LOUISA	36	
MAY	101	
RANDALL, ALICE	146	
RANEY, MARY E	142	
RANSON, PAULINA A	70	
RAPP, DORA	130	
RAPPOLD, (Mrs) ADDIE MAY	29	
RARDON, CARRIE	89	
RATHBURN, SARAH	148	
RAWSON, CATHARINE M	49	
RAY, ELIZA E	13	
FANNIE L	56	
LELIA A	33	
LILLIE B	66	
MARY	6	
OSA	10	
RETHIE	1	
SARAH ANN	189	
STELLA DEL	18	
RAYBOULD, ANNA E	9	
LUCY J	188	
MARY M	108	
RAYBURN, ALICE C	157	
ANGELINE R	51	
ANN	59	
ANNIE	139	
ANNIE B	174	
ANNIE J	190	
ARABELLA	45	
BETSEY	8	
CAROLINE	93	
CAROLINE	102	
CATHARINE	100	
CLARA, B	27	
DELLA P	146	
DIANA	103	
ELIZABETH M	22	
ELLA	186	
ELLA FRANCES	174	
ELSIE M	32	
EMMA	5	
FRANCES	51	
GOLDIE O	121	
HANNAH	112	
HATTIE M	103	
IDA	173	
IDA E	59	
JENNETTE	5	
JENNIE V	136	
LILLIAN ANN	110	
LUCINDA	75	
LUCY C	13	
MARGARET	147	
MARTHA A	78	
MARTHA J	112	
MARY	182	
MARY E	61	
MARY E	103	
MATTIE B	98	
MATTIE S	18	
NANCY	135	
OLIVIA J	141	
POLLY	54	
ROXY	158	
RUTH	33	
RUTH	179	
RUTHA F	14	
SARAH C	51	
SARAH E	106	
SUSAN	113	
VIOLA B	23	
RAYNOR, GRACE L	43	
REA, MARTHA A	157	
SARAH J	27	
READ, MARGARET	68	
RECE, MILLIE	150	
REDMAN, NANNIE	163	
OLIVIA A	125	
POSEY	155	
REDMOND, MARY LIZZIE	170	
REECE, ETHEL	167	
REED, IDA FRANCES	182	
LIZZIE	123	
MAGGIE	162	
MARY ANN	52	
MARY W	77	
RUBY E	97	
REES, ANNIE B	99	
REESE, LUNA	52	
MARGARET	85	
REEVES, EMMA L	41	
HARRIET L	99	
REFSNYDER, ERMA	8	
REITMIRE, ANNA	186	
REOECH, CATHARINE	98	
REUTHER, ANNIE M	117	
REYBURN, ELIZABETH	132	
REYNOLDS, ADALINE	62	
BESSIE M	165	
CHRISTINA	23	
CORA L	105	
FLORENCE B	105	
HATTIE A	75	
IDA M	152	
JULIA	31	
LOUISA ANN	92	
MARIA	60	
MINERVA	2	
NARCISSA J	45	
VIRGINIA E	133	
RHEY, PERMELIA J	32	
RHOADES, FANNIE	183	
MAUD	5	
MYRTLE	71	
SARAH A	67	
RHOADS, ARIZONA	51	
EMELINE	111	
MAGGIE	73	

MARGARET	163	
MARTHA ADALINE	76	
MARY S	111	
RHODES, ANNA	172	
BARBARA J	56	
CARRIE	90	
ELIZABETH	167	
ELIZABETH	80	
FRANCES	18	
JENNIE D	146	
MARINDA	99	
MARY A	99	
MARY A	166	
MINERVA	98	
MINNIE C	101	
RACHEL	84	
RHUSS, TRYPHENA	13	
RIARSON, ELIZABETH	114	
RICE, ALMEDA	65	
CARRIE	185	
CATHARINE	168	
CLARA H	151	
CORA MAY	24	
DAISY A	46	
ELIZABETH C	23	
ELLA	72	
ELLA	187	
ELLA B	24	
ELSIE	47	
FANNY	148	
HATTIE E	13	
IDA	25	
JESSIE H	136	
JONNIE EARNEST	54	
KATIE M	36	
LELIA J	64	
LIDA	100	
LUCETTA C	178	
LUCY H	150	
MAGGIE M	94	
MARGARET L	151	
MARIA	161	
MARIETTA	47	
MARY E	91	
MINNIE B	152	
NANCY	165	
ORA E	54	
RHODA MARGARET	140	
SARAH E	54	
SARAH F	121	
SARAH LILLIE	135	
RICHARD, MARY	120	
RICHARDS, ADELINE M	80	
HANNAH	162	
JANNETTE	49	
RICHARDSON, ELIZA H	11	
RICHEY, RUBY B	106	
RICHIE, DANIE	86	
RICKARD, ALICE M	80	
ANGALINA	130	
ANNIE	77	
BARBARA E	9	
BERTHA	181	
BERTHA K	151	
CATHARINE	59	
CLARINDA	145	
DELPHA	27	
DORA	54	
ELIZABETH	168	
ELIZABETH A	115	
EMMA F	171	
HATTIE	50	
HATTIE M	126	
MARGARET A	147	
MARGT	18	
MARY	25	
MARY	70	
MARY C	9	
MARY C	130	
MARY V	37	
NANCY	115	
NANCY CATHARINE	64	
OMA L	146	
RHODA A	77	
ROSA	164	
SARAH CATHARINE	45	
SAVANAH FRANCES	122	
SEVILLA B	47	
SEVILLA MARY	71	
SUSAN	135	
SUSANNA	13	
VERNISHIA	173	
VIOLA	37	
RICKART, MALINDA	126	
MARGARET	144	
SARAH	175	
SUSAN	144	
RIDDLE, SARAH A	114	
RIDER, MARY D	165	
RIDGEWAY, SUSAN	90	
RIEHL, IDA MARY	41	
RIFE, MARY A	27	
MILLIE	133	
RIFFLE, ADDA	63	
ALICE	82	
ANN MAGDELENA	175	
ANNER L	26	
ANNIE	130	
BARBARA	57	
BARBARA	141	
CATHARINE JANE	139	
CARRY F	173	
CATHARINE	16	
CATHARINE	64	
CHRISTENA	159	
CORDELIA F	45	
CYNTHIA F	30	
ELIZABETH	45	
ELIZABETH	80	
EMMA	52	
EMMA	136	
EMMA E	62	
ESTELLA	43	
EVELINE	183	
FANNIE	14	
FLORA C	164	
HATTIE M	149	
HESTER	170	

IDA	52	ANNA	138
IDA MAY	23	LINNIE MAY	188
JANE	140	MALINDA V	58
JENNIE FRANCES	136	MARTHA A	32
KATE	57	MARY E	23
KATHARYN	40	NANCY M	149
LAURA SUSAN	37	RINGS, LIZZIE	94
LAVINIA	14	MARY M	50
LINNIE V	138	MENA	23
LIZZIE	171	RIPLEY, ANNA	8
LOUISA J	44	GERTRUDE	180
LUCY LUELLA	146	MARTHA J	189
LYDIA	183	MARY ANN	133
MAGGIE	157	RISER, ELLA	77
MAHALA	171	JOSEPHINE	145
MAHALA E	165	SAMANTHA	173
MALINDA	21	RISK, MARY JANE	171
MARGARET ANN	190	SARAH ELIZABETH	172
MARTHA F	96	RISLEY, EMMA	168
MARY B	63	RISON, GUSSIE	2
MARY E	160	ROACH, MABEL M	93
MARY JANE	186	MARY	45
MARY S	42	MARY J	59
MARY S	63	MARY R	47
MINA L	37	SARAH	161
MINNIE	30	SARAH	163
MIRIAM	28	SOPHIA V	87
MOLLIE A	187	ROADES, MARTHA E	70
NANCY R	140	MIRRAM	142
NELLIE J	11	ROADIAMOUR, EMILY C	172
OLIVIA	152	ROBBINS, FLORENCE	121
PEARL	158	HARRIET A	92
POLLY	175	ROBERTS, CLARINDA	121
SADIE	11	EFFIE E	129
SADIE V	29	ELIZA	173
SARAH	165	ELIZA J	6
SARAH A	80	FANNIE F	168
SARAH A	154	FLORELLA M	70
SARAH E	63	FLORENCE	82
SARAH E	105	HATTIE BELLE	155
SARAH M	8	IDA	98
VIRGIE	24	JULIA C	176
VIRGINIA	51	LILLIE M	131
RIGG, GEORGIA F	68	LOUISA	9
IDA A	115	MARY E	99
NANCY J	153	MARY L	173
WILLIE A	71	MARY R	175
RIGGS, HARRIET D	144	MINNIE	141
LELIA M	62	MINNIE F	40
LULA B	148	PEGGY	45
LULA F	97	VIRGINIA E	143
MARTHA ANN	75	ROBERTSON, ELIZABETH	49
MARY J	184	ROBINETTE, MAUDE G	104
MINNIE	65	ROBINSON, (Mrs) MAUD	7
MINNIE R	94	CATHARINE	132
ROSA E	58	CHARLOTTE O'DELL	158
SUSAN E	129	CLARISSA A	112
RILEY, CORA P	130	ELIZA A	82
ELLA	138	ELIZABETH	12
LELA A	127	ESTELLA	148
RIMMEY, IDA McK	56	FANNIE G	101
LILLIE D	35	FRANCES A	107
PEARL R	166	GRACIE	117
RINE, ADDIE	185	IDA F	191

JULIA FRANCES	117	
KATIE	119	
LIZZIE	110	
LIZZIE	173	
MAY O	137	
SARAH	37	
SARAH J	58	
SUSAN	56	
WILLIE	144	
ROBISON, FLORA I	90	
MARY	81	
ROBSON, ANNIE	32	
ELIZABETH	87	
ELLA R	117	
GOLDIE M	5	
ISABELLA	18	
LIZZIE	54	
MARGARET	173	
MARIETTA	125	
SUSAN	79	
ROCK, ALMA	182	
RODES, DELLA	25	
RODGERS, ALMIRA E	97	
EFFIE	153	
EFFY S	59	
ELIZABETH	129	
HATTIE E	29	
LENNA	176	
LINA	149	
LUELLA E	44	
MARGARET	57	
MATTIE L	57	
MINA F	54	
NANNIE A	80	
NELLIE F	33	
SARAH	45	
SUSAN M	28	
VADA G	74	
ROE, ALICE	83	
ROGERS, ANNA LEE	189	
BERTHA E	2	
DELIA V	33	
GRACE	79	
IDA E	22	
LULU J	166	
MARY JANE	123	
NANCY E	141	
SALLIE S	109	
STELLA	129	
ROHBAUGH, SUSAN	27	
ROHNAN, ELIZABETH J	69	
ROHRABAUGH, EFFIE	1	
MARY	156	
MILLIE LOURAS	19	
ROLAND, MARTHA A	89	
ROLLAR, CATHERINE	150	
ROLLER, EVA C	109	
MARY C	192	
MINA M	128	
ROLLINGS, ALCINDA	185	
ROLLINS, ADA	44	
ADALINE	55	
ADDA VIRGINIA	146	
ANGELINE	12	
CHRISTENA A	62	
DOROTHY E	61	
ELIZABETH	111	
ELIZABETH A	65	
ELIZABETH C	64	
ETHA J	13	
ETTIE	75	
HATTIE A	134	
INA	188	
ISA DORA	191	
LAVINA CATHARINE	100	
LILLIE B	51	
LOUISA EVALINE	12	
MAGGIE E	124	
MARY	104	
MARY M	134	
MARY MALINDA	164	
MARY VIANA	138	
MINNIE F	185	
MOLLIE	171	
NANCY	182	
ORA	163	
REBECCA	103	
ROSA E	170	
SARAH E	2	
SARAH M	140	
VICTORIA F	91	
VINNIE	68	
VIRGINIA	127	
WILLIA VERNENA	120	
ROLLISON, ANNIE	91	
ROLMAN, ELIZABETH J	69	
ROMINE, CLARA B	41	
JULIA A	66	
ROOD, BLANCHE A	145	
ROOT, ANNETTE	11	
ROSE, ALICE J	109	
AMANDA	50	
ANNA B	18	
ANNA M	89	
AUGUSTA ROMAINE	30	
ELIZABETH A	5	
LORETTA J	162	
LUCY	66	
LUCY	102	
MARY	124	
MIME E	66	
MINNIE DAY	156	
POLLY	35	
PRISCILLA	136	
RUTH	34	
ROSEBERRY, ANN	159	
CORA L	128	
EFFIE F	160	
ELIZABETH	174	
ELLA	28	
ELVIRA	26	
EMMA C	122	
FLORA	149	
FLORA A	88	
FLORA A	183	
GEORGIA A	41	
HANNAH D	190	
JANE	61	

JANE	119	CATHARINE	32
JENNIE	168	CATHARINE	145
LENA LORENA	117	CORA	140
MAGGIE M	82	DELILA	61
MARGARET JANE	160	DELLA F	130
MARTHA J	174	DOLLY	126
MARY J	121	DORCAS	75
MARY M	70	DRUSILLA	138
MARY MARGARET	88	EDA	21
MAUDE	128	ELECTA A	94
MINNIE	126	ELIZABETH	70
NETTIE A	24	ELIZABETH	128
ROSALIE	10	ELIZABETH	174
SARAH A	57	ELIZABETH	181
SARAH C	70	ELIZABETH	185
TESSIE A	56	ELLA	140
ROSS, (Mrs) LIZZIE	138	ELLA M	146
ANNA A	95	ELSIE	17
B LILLIAN	69	ELVIRA	149
ELIZABETH J	114	ELZADIE	21
VIRGINIA	102	EMMA L	20
ROTENBERRY, LUCY	52	ETTA	145
ROTHGEB, NANCY J	17	EXEVERIA	89
TENA	85	FANNIE E	126
ROUSCH, CATHARINE	155	FRANCES E	191
REGINA	143	GENORA	188
SARAH	103	GEORGETTIE	115
ROUSE, BERTHA M	98	HANNAH	70
SARAH ANN	122	HANNAH	182
SARAH F	11	HESTER	69
ROUSH, (Mrs) BERTHA E	95	HOUMA	32
(Mrs) JOSIE	147	ICIE	13
	144	ICY	39
ADA F	171	IDA	62
ADA M	125	IDA F	80
ADA Z	187	IDA F	126
ADALINE B	115	IDA F	185
ADUTH E	62	INEZ	158
ALICE	51	ISABEL	62
ALICE A	56	IVA ELIZABETH	56
ALICE S	15	JANE	77
ALMA	105	JEANNETTE	46
ALMERIA	19	JEMIMA	127
AMANDA E	172	JENNIE B	40
ANGELINE	56	JENNIE B	81
ANGELINE M	142	JESSIE C	123
ANN E	91	JOSEPHINE	157
ANN R	72	JOSIE	147
ANNA	56	JULIA E	84
ANNA	97	KATHERINE M	146
ANNA L	56	KATIE	154
ANNA R	101	LAURA	9
ANNIE	74	LAURA	149
ARLETTA	180	LAURA A	113
ARTA	19	LAURA A	138
AURILLA	65	LIZZIE	145
BARBARA	8	LIZZIE F	20
BARBARA	81	LIZZIE M	30
BIRDIE M	4	LOUISA	41
CALLIE	21	LOUISA	138
CARIE	19	LOUISA C	126
CAROLINE	130	LULU	29
CAROLINE A	81	LYDIA	115
CARRIE E	91	LYDIA	132

LYDIA	146		SALLY	139
MAHALA	99		SAMANTHA	74
MAHALA	180		SARA A	19
MARGARET	109		SARAH	19
MARGARET	145		SARAH	72
MARGARET	146		SARAH	102
MARTHA	8		SARAH	136
MARTHA	129		SARAH	142
MARTHA A	165		SARAH A	42
MARTHA J	130		SARAH ANN	61
MARTHA SUSAN	83		SARAH ANN	126
MARY	26		SARAH C	44
MARY	51		SARAH C	56
MARY	70		SARAH E	90
MARY	126		SARAH J	40
MARY	146		SARAH J	41
MARY	146		SARAH M	131
MARY	174		SARAH M	161
MARY A	86		SARAH M	113
MARY C	84		SARAH S	56
MARY E	113		SARAH V	173
MARY E	180		SARAH VIRGINIA	77
MARY ELLEN	143		SAREPTA	145
MARY F	180		SERENA F	62
MARY FRANCES	127		SEREPTA	65
MARY IZETTIE	42		SEVILLA E	13
MARY L	123		SUSAN	37
MARY M	43		SUSAN	81
MARY M	51		SUSAN	145
MATILDA	133		SUSAN E	65
MATILDA	154		SUSAN J	144
MATTIE V	76		SUSANNAH	142
MAUD M	93		SYRENA C	56
MERTIE C	65		V J	187
METTIE E	33		VINA E	136
MILLIE	87		VINA MAY	51
MILLIE E	132		VIOLA V	37
MILLIE S	126		WYOMA	17
MINNIE V	128		ROWLEY, (Mrs) LULA MAUDE	137
MYRTLE A	138		ANNIE	174
NANCY	38		DELIA	33
NANCY	93		ELIZABETH	142
NANNIE R	161		ELLA	64
NETTIE	20		FRANCES E	168
NETTIE M	4		HANNAH	53
NORAH	20		LAURA G	53
OLIVIA J	62		MARTHA G	73
ORILLA	62		NELLIE	175
ORILLA C	190		ROWSEY, DELILAH M	12
PHEBE	106		ELLEN FRANCES	10
PHEBE JANE	62		ISADORE B	158
REBECCA	145		MARGARET	156
REBECCA	81		MYRTLE M	7
REBECCA A	17		PERLINA ANN	60
REBECCA ANN	140		ROY, ALICE MAY	52
RHODA	37		MARY A	94
ROSA	9		MINNIE	78
ROSA	111		RUCKER, FRANCES E	147
ROSANNA	100		MARY J	90
ROSANNA	74		RUGGLES, ELIZABETH	21
ROXA	130		RUGH, CLARISA	14
RUTH V	61		RULEN, FANNIE	158
SALLIE M	2		LUCINDA	128
SALLY	77		RUNION, CHARLOTTE	98

CHARLOTTIE	78
HATTIE	12
MYRTLE S	171
SOPHA	74
RUNNION, BETSY	86
MARTHA J	10
MARY A	188
RUPERT, CAROLINE E	73
RUSH, MARY A	63
RUSK, ETTIE	181
OLLIE E	101
SUSAN L C	2
RUSSELL, (Mrs) L MARGARET	23
ANNIE	46
BERTHA H	83
ELIZA	135
ELIZA	188
ELMIRA J	83
ELVIRA	81
ETTA	124
EVE MAY	118
FLORENCE R	41
GRACE	77
HATTIE B	127
JESSIE	15
JETTA L	148
LOUISA	99
LUCRETIA	39
LUELLA	89
MAGGIE	175
MAY	174
OLLIE H	186
ORA	21
RUTH M	41
SAMMA DALE	109
SARAH	32
RUTHERFORD, MAUDE	182
RUTSCHMIER, MARY A	96
RUTTENCUTTER, MAGGIE	51
MARTHA K	53
WILHELMINA F	18
RUTTER, MARY E	125
RYAN,	
JANE	71
MARY	5
MOLLIE CLEOPATRA	24
RYNE, CATHARINE	42
SADDLER, CYNTHA	52
SALLAZ, LULA O	30
SALMONS, ROENA	85
SAMPLES, DELIA A	32
KATE M	56
SANDERS, CATHARINE A	18
FANNIE E	46
GERTIE B	183
JANNETTE	67
KATIE	52
LIZZIE E	95
MAGGIE	9
MARIETTA	180
MARY	117
MARY	184
MARY J M	71
NANCY	185
QINNIE D	62
REBECCA	65
SANDS, AGNES	91
AGNESS	91
CORDELIA C	161
EFFIE E	45
FRANCES B	108
GEORGIA E	91
LOUISA	155
MARY	157
MATTIE L	84
SANFORD, FLORA E	92
SANNS, NETTIE MASON	10
SANTEE, ELIZA	114
SARGENT, IDA F	48
MARY D	7
SATTES, LUTITIA A	31
MARY FRANCES	65
SAUER, EDITH MAY	11
SAULSER, LUCINDA	125
SAUNDERS, ALICE	17
BERTHA M	36
ELIZABETH F	89
EMELIA	181
FLORENCE	80
GARNETT	80
JANE A	126
JESTIE C	80
LUCINDA	150
MARY E	152
RUBY E	29
SARAH A	46
SAVINE, HANNAH	183
SAWYER, JENNIE	166
SAXTON, BERTHA F	89
CAROLINE	22
CLARA	134
ELLA	169
LAURA	60
MARY	148
MATTIE	31
MIRTY	7
SALLIE	134
WILLIE	85
SAYER, MAY	19
SELIA	158
SAYLOR, CATHARINE A	186
SAYRE, (Mrs) ELIZABETH	154
(Mrs) IVA M	12
(Mrs) L N	28
(Mrs) ORILLA R	87
ADALIZA M	138
ALICE	139
ALLIE BELLE	118
ALZINA	52
AMANDA M	54
ANNA	134
ANNIE	181
ANNIE BELLE	88
AUGUSTA A	132
BERTHA E	136
CELIA A	146
CLARA A	60
CORA A	179

CORA D	184		RACHAEL		69
CORDELIA E	175		REBECCA		89
CYNTHIA	159		ROSA		20
DELILA	54		ROSA		163
DELILA	111		SARAH		16
DELLA	145		SARAH		85
EFFA E	17		SARAH		180
ELECTA FLORENCE	75		SARAH A		52
ELIZABETH	89		SARAH A		155
ELIZABETH F	2		SARAH ANN		156
ELIZABETH E	56		SARAH H		65
ELLA	41		SYDNEY		29
ELLA	146		SYLVIA		6
ELLEN	52		VETRICE		109
ELLEN	184		VIRGIE F		114
ELZINA	144		VIRGINIA H		17
ELZINA	154	SAYRES, MIRIAM			175
EMILY J	172		R		128
EMMA	146	SCANTLING, MARGARET			7
EMMA	155		MARY A		159
EMMA R	159		NANCY		150
ESTELLA	32		RHODA A		53
ESTHER J	117	SCARBERRY, EFFIE			159
EVA	10		ELLA FRANCES		136
EVA	40		HANNAH E		114
EVA	103		JEANETTE		47
FANNY	118		JULIA E		21
FLORA	103		LOUISA A		43
HANNAH	34		MARTHA J		6
HANNAH	135		REBECCA		113
HARRIET E	79	SCHLAGLE, ROSINA B			156
HARRIET E	110	SCHLARB, EMMA R L			128
HATTIE	146	SCHMANFER, INEZ			22
KATHERINE	10	SCHMIDT, LOUISA T			120
LENORA	32	SCHMITH, MARIANN			151
LIZZABETH J	83	SCHNEIDER, ANNA C			61
LIZZIE	154		ANNE M		165
LIZZIE JANE	116		FLORENCE E M		78
LORA	65	SCHOLL, FRANCES VIRGINIA			37
LOUISE	110	SCHOLL, SARAH E			144
LOUISE MARIE	89	SCHOLZ, ELLENOR			15
LUCENA	75	SCHOMEHL, EMILY			137
LUCY LUELLA	139	SCHOOLS, ANNIE BELL			98
LUVERNA	63		BESSIE		18
MARY	26		LOVINE F		8
MARY	164		LUCINDA C		68
MARY	176		LULA E		182
MARY	184		REBECCA BLANCH		139
MARY ANN	151		ADIE L		140
MARY M	164	SCHOONOVER, ADDA I			127
MATILDA	157		MARY PEARL		43
MAUDE E	136	SCHRAY, MARY			37
MAY	88		MARY		156
MINERVA J	81	SCHRUGG, ANNIE			179
MIRAM F	75	SCHULL, MARGARET			58
MIRIAM VICTORIA	107	SCHULTZ, MINNIE			75
NANCY B	158	SCHWARTZ, BARBARA			104
NANCY D	74	SCHWARZ, JOSIE A			181
NORA A	32		MARTHA JOSEPHINE		182
OLA	105	SCOLLARD, ROSA			122
PAMELA	140	SCOTT, ALLENA L			175
PEARL	192		ANNIE L		1
PEARL F	67		EFFIE E		168
PHILENA	154		ELIZA JANE		167

FLARA ETTA	165	
HARRIET	35	
LUCY	120	
MARY B	103	
MAUDE F	56	
MINNIE	121	
SCOYC, ALICE	26	
SCURLOCK, IDA MAY	132	
SEAL, IDA P	131	
SEAMANS, LIZZIE G	24	
SEARLS, BESSIE F	38	
M J	86	
SARAH C	87	
SEBRELL, BETTIE J	71	
BLANCHE	8	
BLANCHE PRESTON	106	
JOSIE	135	
MARGARET	190	
SARAH ANN	178	
SEBRIEL, BETSEY	190	
SEE, ELIZABETH	154	
EMMA	19	
LIZZIE	32	
MAGGIE	55	
MAGGIE	157	
MALVINA	158	
SEELY, BLANCHE	163	
SEGRIST, CAROLINE A	23	
SEHON, FANNIE	132	
SELBY, ADALINE	176	
ARIE E	117	
BETHA L	24	
ELEANOR	64	
ELIZA	77	
ELLA	104	
EMILY MARIA	117	
IVA E	14	
LAURA	64	
MARTHA	170	
MINNIE	183	
ORA	70	
ORILLA	163	
ROXY	98	
SARAH JANE	109	
SENNITT, FRANKIE O	14	
SENTERS, JOSEPHINE M	106	
SERGEANT, (Mrs) CATHARINE	145	
SETTLES, BESSIE E L	190	
GERTRUDE	100	
SEWELL, AMANDA	2	
CARRIE E	103	
IDA E	153	
SHAEFER, ANNIE C	90	
SHAFER, MARGARET	92	
SHAFFER, EMMA F	88	
SHAHAN, ZENNA E	124	
SHAIN, IDA	86	
SHAMBLIN, MARGARET	156	
SHANG, PRILLA	89	
SHANK, CARRIE F	34	
ELIZABETH	90	
ELLA F	19	
EMMA E	109	
EUGENE M	113	
EVA F	19
GRACE E	179
KATIE	157
LELIA M	117
MARY E	134
MARY F	49
MARY J	89
MINA M	12
NANCY J	27
OCTAVIA V	114
OLIVETTI F	172
VIRGINIA R	75
ZUA M	23
SHANNAN, ANNIE	121
SHARON, MAY	119
SHARP, (Mrs) EMMA	171
ELITHA	175
FLORENCE	24
JENNIE	167
MARTINNIE	40
WILLIE PEARL	40
SHARROCK, ELIZABETH	62
SHATO, BESSIE B	30
SHAVER, MATILDA	153
SHAW, ANN A	175
BLANCHE	91
JUDITH E	147
MARIA S	105
MARY B	24
MATTIE J	118
REBECCA T	24
SHAWN, MATILDA	136
SHAY, MARGARET	116
MARY	32
SHEARER, LOUISA JANE	70
SHEETS, (Mrs) MARIA	50
ANNA M	118
SHELINE, ANNA	141
CATHARINE	141
CATHARINE E	107
CATHARINE E	129
CLARA B	157
EFFIE	155
ELIZA Z	4
HULDAH	128
MARGARET A	70
MARY	12
MARY J	134
MINNIE	121
NELLIE	72
RONA	160
ROSABELL	99
RUTHIE	4
SYBILL D	10
SHELL, EMILY MAY	164
SHELTON, JOANA	18
LUCY ANN	133
MARY	161
SHEPHERD, MARGARET	99
SHEPPARD, BLANCH	118
VERNA LOUISE	83
SHERWOOD, PARMY	47
SARAH	96
SHIELDS, (Mrs) CATHARINE	65

ADDIE	101
DELLA M	42
ELIZABETH	38
ELLA	184
EMMA	160
MARGARET	140
OLIVIA	114
SARAH E	9
SUSAN	156
VIOLA	140
SHIELS, VIRGINIA	50
SHIFLET, ELVERETTA FRANCES	102
IDA	4
SHIFTLETT, ELLA	15
SHILTS, JANIE	125
SHINN, CLARA J	95
LONA	22
VESSIE	22
SHIPLEY, ELLA	24
FRANCES	144
MARY JANE	180
SHIRLEY, ABBIE E	181
BERTIE	159
BESSIE	139
CAROLINE E	168
FLORIDA FRANCES	15
FORREST	44
JOSIE J	152
LORENA	186
LUANA	141
MARY E	44
MARY R	112
MATILDA	146
SHIRLY, EMILY J	140
SHIVELEY, LEONA B	100
MARY F	31
NANCY E	46
NANNIE	148
SHIVELY, ANGELINE	118
EMMA	12
HENRIETTA	181
MELVINA	72
ORETHA	67
SHOEMAKER, ADALINE	162
HATTIE	185
JOANA B	164
MARTHA E	161
SHOLL, ELLEN	185
SHOOL, FRANCES MOORE	37
SHORT, ELIZA J	137
ELIZABETH A	121
MARY A F	89
PAMELA	47
SHORTER, JENNIE	137
SHOWALTER, ELIZABETH	182
SHOWALTERS, ROSA	125
SHREWSBURY, HATTIE C	7
SHULER, NANNIE G	147
SAMARIA	10
SAMARIA	10
SHULL, ELIZABETH	47
SHULTZ, HARRIET	15
SHUMAKER, MARY	64
SARAH V	162
SHUMARD, VIRGINIA MARGARET	183
SHUMATE, JANE	53
VIRGINIA C	166
SHURZ, DARLIE D	60
SHY, RUCY HELLEN	38
SIDEBOTTOM, MARY E	167
SIDENSTRICKER, MARY H	168
SARAH J	32
SIDERS (Mrs), JULIA C	51
ANNA	115
EMELINE	41
FANNIE	129
JESSIE A	188
JESSIE ATLANTIC	76
L MARGARET	22
LISETTA	6
LOUISA M	22
MAGGIE M	29
MARIETTA	52
MARY	68
MARY L	26
NETTIE	37
REBECCA S	131
SARAH E	23
SUSAN	80
SIEGRIST, HANNAH M	23
MARGARET	145
POLLY	73
SARAH A	142
SERENA L	83
SIGMAN, MALISSA	95
SIM, ROSA V	96
SIMMONS, KATE F	181
LONA MAUD	109
SARAH	76
SIMMS, ELLA	4
KATIE E	189
LOUISA H	147
SIMPKINS, LAVENIA	112
LEATHA	106
MAGGIE	133
NANCY S	44
SARAH R	17
VIRGIE F	80
VIRGINIA S	129
SIMPSON, ELLA	116
LIVIA N	131
MARY MARGARET	19
NANCY E	111
SUSAN	39
SUSANNA	15
SIMS, ELVA MAY	59
MABEL A	171
SINES, ABIGAIL	183
ALMEDA	190
ARAMINTA	173
CASSIE	104
CATHARINE L	105
ELIZABETH	131
ELLEN V	14
EVA	60
EVA M	179
LONA	159
LYDIA M	142

MARY C	142	
MARY E	20	
MARY ELIZABETH	96	
NINIE M	44	
SARAH M	101	
SINGLETON, ANNA	69	
SINGLETON, MAUDE CELESTINA	79	
SISSELL, ELLA	93	
SISSON, ELLEN L	185	
FLORENCE M	41	
MARIA E	22	
MARTHA	167	
MARTHA R	158	
OLIVE H	137	
SIZEMORE, ROSA A	103	
SKEEN, MARY	77	
POLLY	94	
SKEENS, ESTELLA	128	
SKEIN, MAHALIA	146	
SKILES, ELLA MARGARET	156	
SKINNER, AUGUSTA	55	
GRACE G	84	
SKINNIN, ROSE	43	
SKIVERS, SABRA	25	
SLACK, BELLE B	134	
ELIZABETH	49	
JESSIE P	81	
MARY	90	
MARY M	99	
NANCY	89	
NANCY	122	
SARAH A	97	
SARAH ELIZABETH	173	
SLADE, HARRIET	5	
SLAUGHTER, LEVERNIA T	156	
RUTH	150	
VIRGINIA E	52	
SLAYTON, BLANCHE A	38	
OLA	169	
SMALL, HARRIET	149	
SMART, AURILLA	146	
ETTA	58	
LAVINIA	97	
SMELTZER, LAURA GENEVIEVE	70	
SMITH, (Mrs) ANNIE	4	
(Mrs) EMILY A	134	
(Mrs) MARY R	36	
A ELLEN	37	
ADA	116	
ADA	51	
ALICE M	188	
ALMA K	44	
ALMIRA	50	
ANNIE	12	
ANNIE	95	
ANNIE E	167	
ANNIE M	114	
ANNIE MARGARET	32	
ANNIE O	70	
ARRIENA	134	
AUGUSTA E	77	
BESSIE M	44	
BESSIE RUTH	183	
BETHA	120	
BETTIE W	158	
BLANCHE	79	
CARRIE B	157	
CASSANDRA J	71	
CATHARINE	137	
CATHERINE	96	
CHRISTENA E	5	
CLARA	166	
CLEMANTHA J	87	
CORA	90	
CORA A	26	
CORA BELL	153	
CORNELIA	142	
DIMMA S	94	
EDITH M	83	
EDITH M	161	
ELENOR JANE	164	
ELIZA J	125	
ELIZABETH	123	
ELIZABETH	172	
ELIZABETH	28	
ELIZABETH R	143	
EMELINE M	64	
ESTELLA E	101	
ETHEL F	27	
EVA L	38	
EVA VAN VATRE	164	
EVALINA	11	
FANNIE	78	
FANNIE B	78	
FANNIE M	96	
FANNIE S	100	
FANNY	11	
FININE A	39	
FLORA A	88	
FLORA D	39	
FRANCES A	133	
FREDA	157	
GRACE	13	
HANNAH J	169	
HARRIET	139	
HARRIET B	24	
HATTIE	137	
HELLEN M	81	
IDA	116	
ISABELLA A	142	
JANE	25	
JESSIE	87	
JESSIE MAY	118	
JOSEPHINE C	112	
JULIA	2	
JULIA M	171	
KATE	92	
KATIE	59	
LAURA JANE	191	
LAURA MARGERY	72	
LEATHA ANN	97	
LELA	85	
LELIA NYE	150	
LINNIE	86	
LIZZIE MAY	103	
LODICIE A	114	
LONA	96	
LOUISA	163	

Name	Page
LOVICA JANE	189
LOVIE	170
LUCY	157
LUCY A	65
LUELLEN	60
LUSETTA	111
LYDIA	42
MALISSA	82
MALISSA	106
MAMIE E	88
MANERVA	110
MARGARET	102
MARGARET	116
MARGARET	185
MARGARET E	34
MARIA L	133
MARTHA	60
MARTHA A	79
MARTHA J E	10
MARY	5
MARY	120
MARY	171
MARY A	58
MARY A	95
MARY E	71
MARY JANE	41
MARY L	34
MARY M	157
MARY MARGARET	104
MARY MARIA	131
MARY T	123
MARY VIRGINIA	133
MAY	92
MAY O	4
MINERVA J	152
MINNIE BELLE	186
MINTIE L	122
MOLLIE	96
MOLLIE	178
NANCY	113
NANCY	20
NANCY E	17
NANCY J	159
NANNIE	41
NELLIE DELANCY	116
NINA E	40
NITA JANE	57
NIZA	71
NORA B	120
OLIVIA E	155
PAULINA CATHARINE	164
PHEBE I	171
PLEASANT W	83
RACHAEL	95
RACHEL	6
RACHEL	42
RACHEL	114
RACHEL	133
RACHEL ELLEN	150
REBECCA	9
REBECCA A	24
REBECCA JANE	29
ROSA A	159
SAMANTHA	95
SAMARIA	66
SARAH	11
SARAH	36
SARAH A	191
SARAH B	156
SARAH C	20
SARAH C	126
SARAH E	190
SARAH JANE	66
SARAH MARGARET	5
SUSAN	124
VIRGINIA	77
SNELL, ELVIRA	127
MARTHA ANN	111
MILDRED A	48
NANNIE	182
SNIDER, BERTHA L	130
CHARLOTTE E	174
MARY C	129
SNIFF, MARY	96
SNOW, INGRY	171
LILLIE	161
SALLY	103
SNYDER, (Mrs) EMMA	123
AGNES N	178
AMANDA J	161
CARRIE	151
CORA	65
DOMINE V	32
DRILLIE	21
EFFIE S	142
ELIZABETH	147
EMMA B	92
ETHEL O	179
FLOSSIE MAY	90
GRACE	34
HETTIE	138
LOLA	55
LOUELLA	154
LUCINDA	130
SARAH	160
SARAH B	184
ZONA	167
SOMERS, VIRGINIA	153
SOMERVILLE, (Mrs) CATHARINE	111
ADA ROSE	153
ALTA M	64
ANN	23
ANNIE L	192
BARBARA	119
CATHARINE B	19
CORDELIA	100
ELIZABETH BLANCH	107
ELLA B	160
ELSIE C	143
EMMA LORENA	146
JANE ANN	102
JULIA A	100
LUADA E	180
MARTHA ANN	179
MARTHA S	152
MARY ANN	7
MARY E	56
MARY L	115

MARY MARGARET	168
MATILDA R	117
REBECCA	14
REBECCA	109
REBECCA J	123
SUSAN J	73
VINNIE M	145
VIRGINIA B	95
SOMMER, CLARA	26
MARY CATHARINE	113
ROSE E	30
VIOLA	185
SONDERS, EDNA	58
SOULSBY, BESSIE	153
JANE	142
SOVINE, ELLEN O	163
SOWASH, BLANCHE J	34
SOWERS, (Mrs) VINA	188
DOLLIE	33
SPANN, BERTHA	20
SPAUN, WINNIE MAY	129
SPEARS, BETTIE	123
KATE	124
LUCINDA	35
MATILDA	96
NORA	101
OLLIE	160
VICIE B	93
SPENCER, ANNIE M	57
BESSIE	68
CATHARINE	97
EDITH F	157
ELLEN A	11
HARRIET M	137
JANE	106
LESTA A	145
MAGGIE	57
MARY A	129
NANCY	121
SARAH C	108
SUSANAH	57
SPENGLER, ELIZABETH H	102
SPIES, CARRIE M	191
SPIRES, ANNA	186
SPOUNIGAL, MARY	80
SPRADLING, BESSIE J	130
SPRAWLS, ETHEL	124
SPROUSE, ETHEL M	43
NANCY E	86
SUSIE	98
SPROUT, ADELINE	56
SARAH	146
SPURLOCK, LILLIE M	114
LOLA	110
LOUISA	27
LUNA	71
MARIAH	122
MARY	185
MARY C	189
MARY ELIZABETH	147
VICTORIA	22
SQUIER, SARAH A	30
St CLAIR, MARGARET S	148
MARY A	54

ROSE W	79
St CLARE, JOSEPHINE	16
STAATS, ADDIE	59
CYNTHIA	92
MARY F	46
MARY L	130
REBECCA C	98
STAGG, EMMA R	39
STALDER, MYRTLE	102
STALEY, MARY A	48
STALNAKER, FANNIE	144
LIZZIE	33
MURREL M	28
STANFORD, MARGARET	100
STANLEY, BRIDGET	104
DAISEY	113
EDY	150
ELIZA	162
GEORGIA	20
HANNAH	10
JENNIE M	82
LEONA	109
LIZZIE	20
LUCY	25
MAGGIE B	67
MANISE	53
NANCY	3
NETTIE E C	49
STANSBERRY, SALLIE V	127
STARBURGH, CLARA	43
STARCHER, ANNA	82
CATHARINE	132
MARGARET	180
STARKEY, ANNIE M	182
ELIZABETH	110
SUSIE	101
STATEN, HENRIETTA	157
ROZELLA	7
STATON, ADALINE	157
ANNA B	76
ELIZA C	168
JULIA M	136
STATTS, CLARA	145
ELIZABETH	94
HANNAH	1
MARY	49
MELINDA	150
NANCY	156
SARAH	101
STEADMAN, (Mrs) MARTHA J	148
STEEL, (Mrs) MARY	15
CATHARINE	112
ELIZABETH	68
ELIZABETH	112
HARRIET	59
HETTIE	74
JANE	8
JANE C	99
JOSEPHINE	143
LOUISA	61
MARGARET	35
MARY ANN	177
NANCY S	140
REBECCA	175

SARAH A	112
STEELE, ABBIE G	28
ALICE	109
ANNA M	131
BELLE	63
BESSIE	167
ELIZABETH J	82
HATTIE	107
LILLIE M	8
MARY M	8
MARY M	68
MINNIE	32
NANCY E	191
SALLIE ANN	10
STEENBERGEN, CAROLINE	117
CATHARINE	123
ELIZA	99
ELLEN D	10
FRANCES	86
MARY E	111
SARAH ANN	34
SUSAN V	161
STEINBACH, KATHERINE LEONORA	11
STEINMETZ, EMMA	113
STEPHEN, ELIZA	48
SARAH M	36
STEPHENS, AMANDA	185
CLARA B	179
EDITH M	176
FANNIE	164
JANE	104
LAURA B	31
MARIA	76
MARY C	164
MARY JANE	70
MINERVA J	28
PARMELIA	6
REBECCA ANN	105
STEPHENSON, BETHA C	36
ELEANOR JANE	59
JULIA	127
LENA LEOTIE	21
MARTHA E	30
MARY	150
MARY J	150
MINNIE	142
NANCY	163
NANCY J	63
SALLIE	178
SARAH	174
SARAH C	64
SUSANNA	59
VIOLA T	180
STERLING, EDITH M	160
STERNE, GUSTA O	165
STERRETT, EVELINA M	164
HELEN V	80
STERRITT, AGNES T	30
MARY E	133
STEVENS, ANN E	73
CAROLINE	148
ISABEL	14
MALINDA	140
MAUD	71
NANNIE	51
WILLIE B	134
STEVENSON, ALICE L	153
LUCY	173
MARY F	55
STELLA	116
STEWARD, FLOE L	42
M CATHARINE	168
NANNIE E	86
STEWART, ADDA B	18
ALBERTA	171
ANNA	48
ANNA P	30
AURILLA F	168
BERTHA I	83
BLANCH E	110
CLARA	163
CLARISSA J	91
CORDELIA F	57
DELLA	138
DIEMMA	125
EDNA	126
ELIZABETH	112
ELIZABETH	139
ELLA J	153
GEORGIA A	148
IDA	139
JULIA A	98
JULIA H	175
JULIANN	71
LAURA	140
LENA E	93
LIZZIE	158
LONA	140
MADLEN	158
MARIE E	50
MARTHA M	91
MARTHA R	53
MARY E	165
MARY M	174
MARY M	91
MAUDE B	174
MAY BELLE	97
MYRTLE M	184
NELLIE	7
NETTIE L	147
OLLIE	110
RACHEL A	187
ROEANNA	158
RUTH A	58
SARAH C	110
SARAH C	121
SARAH E	93
SARAH J	175
SARAH JANE	95
SUSAN	28
SUSAN	71
VICA M	53
VILETTA	19
WYNNE B	28
ZILPHA	91
ZILPHA R	182
STIDGER, KATE E	55

Name	Page
STILES, BLANCHE	23
GARNETTE L	151
STIMBLE, ELLA	81
STIVERS, EMMA	192
STOKELY, BLANCHE	59
ISABEL	87
MARY	145
STOKLEY, MABEL M	139
STONE, (Mrs) ANN ELIZA	166
ALICE M	113
BELLE I	7
BESSIE	66
BLANCHE C	133
BLANCHE L	181
EDITH J	175
EFFIE	75
ELIZA J	34
EMMA ALMIRA	118
FANNIE	174
FRANCES	95
FRANCES J	96
HATTIE MAY	48
LINNIE M	114
LIZZIE	44
LIZZIE	100
LUCRETIA F	150
LUCY	133
MARY ELIZABETH	120
MARY G	169
MARY J	90
MARY J	166
MARY M	81
MYRTLE B	121
ORA	6
PERMELIA	27
SARAH MINERVA	112
STONEKING, JULIA A	26
STONEROCK, MATTIE M	60
STORTZ, ANNIE B	53
MARY	130
STORY, MANTIE	60
STOUT, LUCINDA C	180
MARTHA J	1
STOVER, (Mrs) EMMA JANE	93
ADALINE	160
ALZINA	53
ANNIE	34
ANNIE A	156
ARIZONIA	54
CATHARINE J	170
DORA	43
DOSHA O	156
ELLA	43
ELLA E	151
EMILY J	134
IDA M	129
IVA MAY	104
IVEY L	22
JULIA A	151
LIVY	179
LUVENIA	111
MALINDA A	66
MARY CATHARINE	7
MARY L	122
MARY M	167
MINNIE	68
MINNIE E	68
MIRTIE BLANCHE	1
NETTIE	111
OLLIE M	94
SARAH ESTHER	62
STOVERS, NANCY BELLE	35
STOW, ALICE K	24
STOWERS, VIRGIE MAY	77
STRAIGHT, ALMA C	22
STRAIT, (Mrs) LILLIE	118
CORA D	31
MARY	110
MARY BLANCHE	167
STRATTON, LUCY M	67
STRAUGHN, PEARL M	68
STRAUTHER, SYNTHA	34
STREIGHT, JEMIMA	39
STRIBLING, IDA V	88
MARY	35
MATILDA J	176
NANCY T	159
RACHEL	62
SALLIE A	115
SARAH	17
SARAH MALINDA	172
STRICKLAND, JULIA MAY	19
STRIMBACK, MARY M	108
MATILDA	107
STROBLE, CLARA E	27
STROSNIDER, MAGGIE	167
STUART, MARGARET	111
MARY	111
STUMP, MARGARET J	124
MARY ANN	155
STURGEON, AMANDA	72
ELIZABETH	169
MARGARET	147
MARTHA	98
MARY	182
ROSA	51
STUTLER, CLARA B	33
MINNIE	10
SULLIVAN, ADA BLANCH	22
BESSIE L	122
CLARA	139
DELILA L	168
FANNIE L	39
FLORENCE E	108
GEORGEANNA	187
HANNAH	176
LURETTA	63
MAGGIE	142
MAGGIE F	8
MARIA A	28
MARY JANE	124
MINA D	166
REBECCA	107
SALLIE J	41
VIRGINIA	75
SUMMERS, (Mrs) L M	189
AMANDA	13
MARY M	173

SAMANTHA	96
SOPHRONIA	74
SUSAN ANN	13
VIRGINIA	186
SURGEON, BLANCH	145
SARAH ELIZABETH	37
SURRATT, GEORGIA	151
SUTTON, MELISSA ANN	85
MARIA	33
SWAIN, GOLDEN	95
SWALLOW, MARY E	126
MATTIE E	13
SWAN, SARAH C	63
SWANN, ANNIE G	86
MAUD O	3
SWARZ (Mrs), ETTIE	51
SWICK, BLANCHE	170
SWINK, AUGUSTA V	188
SWISHER, BELLE F	138
BERTIE LUELLAN	30
CARRIE	169
ELLA	12
LUELLA	89
MARY L	39
ROSA	155
SWON, CLAUDIA V	190
JEANNET	164
LOUISA	95
MATTIE L	115
OLIVIA	92
SARAH	8
SYDENSTRICKER, CLEMMA	132
ELECTA	39
NANCY E	169
SYRUS, CATHARINE	168
TACKETT, ROSE E	78
TALAFERO, ANNIE MAY	180
TALAFERRO, BARBARA M	52
TANNER, JEMIMA	157
NORA	15
TATE, ADDIE	182
ALCINA C	132
ARABELLA A	168
EDNA M	120
ELIZABETH	153
LUCY O	91
SARAH	39
TAYLOR, (Mrs) ELZAMINTA	102
(Mrs) M J	149
(Mrs) MOLLIE	183
(Mrs) RACHEL	162
AMANDA	95
ANGELINE	20
ANN	3
ANN M H	78
ANNIE L	108
AUGUSTA	141
CATHARINE	56
DORA	71
EDY ANN	51
EFFIE	41
EFFIE	148
ELECTA V	16
ELIZABETH	183
ELIZABETH F	115
ELIZABETH F	178
ELIZABETH J	169
ELIZABETH JANE	78
EMMA	61
EVA L	128
FANNIE M	174
FRANCES	182
IZETTA	51
JULIA ANN	130
LAURA	92
LAURA	125
LUCY J	4
MAGGIE	69
MARGARET	145
MARTHA A E	169
MARY	123
MARY	130
MARY A	2
MARY B	63
MARY C	36
MARY DELILA	33
MARY E	17
MARY E	32
MARY E	136
MARY E	176
MARY ELLA	116
MARY F	90
MARY H	38
MATILDA E	96
NANNIE	2
NEVADA	149
REBECCA	169
RENA	66
SARAH	83
SARAH	188
SELAH D	2
SELENA L E	182
SUSANAH	116
TEETERS, ANNA G	88
TEFORD, MARY J	20
TEMPLES, HANNA J	12
TEMPLETON, ADALADE	15
ELIZABETH	89
LUCINDA	140
TERRY, ANNIE L	168
ELIZA C	101
LYDDIE	79
MARY B	186
MARY F	167
SARAH C	9
SARAH C	127
SARAH E	154
TEWKSBURY, MINTIE	64
THACKER, EMMA M	48
THARP, BELLE	126
MARY	159
THAXTON, MAY	68
VALLEY	27
THEVENIN, EDITH A	68
EMMA	11
THIVENER, CARRIE I	1
THOMAS, ADER MAY	161
AMELIA	118

ANN	131	NAOMA	181
ANNA B	64	NORA	1
ANNIE	32	THOMSON, M A G	7
BLANCHE	130	THORN, CLARA M	119
DELLA B	144	THORNE, MARY M	53
DELLA MAY	142	THORNTON, ADALINE	95
DOLLIE MARIE	70	BELLE	150
EDNA	118	CATHARINE M	170
EFFIE J	5	CHRISTENA	42
ELIZABETH	11	CORA	176
ELIZABETH	74	DELLA	181
ELIZABETH N B	153	DELPHIA	40
ELLA	42	DESSIE L	160
EMMA	107	EDDIE	152
ESTHER C	155	EFFIE	143
HANNAH M	105	ELIZABETH A	80
IDA M	57	ELIZABTH	153
LANIE	36	EMMA J	58
LIZZIE S	73	ESTHER	62
LUCRETIA J	178	GEORGIA	37
MABEL G	132	IVA M	80
MAGGIE A	92	JANE	167
MALINDA	101	JULIA CAROLINE FRANCES	125
MARGARET	88	LAURA A	39
MARGARET	104	LETITIA	163
MARIA L	158	LIEUVANA A	39
MARTHA J	158	LUCINDA	181
MARY	99	LUCINDA	75
MARY	120	LUCY M	146
MARY	171	LUELLA	159
MARY J	129	MARY	4
MARY P	158	MARY	34
MAY B	38	MARY E	138
MYRTLE	149	METTA	70
NORA	12	MISSOURI	105
SARAH	189	NANCY F	140
SARAH A	68	NORA	184
SARAH MARGARET	106	ODA A	88
SAVILLA	22	RACHEL F	167
SEREPTA J	46	RACHEL J	149
STELLA L	64	REBECCA	75
SUSANNAH	51	RHODA B	135
VIRGIE	9	SALLY	69
THOMPSON, ADDIE	46	SARAH J	39
ALBERTA	94	SUSANNAH F	170
ANNA	125	TENA	39
CAROLINE	32	THRASH, VERA	137
CARRIE	54	TIBBS, VIRGINIA L	166
CARRIE W	149	TICE, WILLIE	184
CLYDE E	80	TIDROW, LYDIA A	83
CORA E	120	TILLA, HANNAH	134
CORA E	178	TILLIS, (Mrs) NANCY	34
ELIZA L	163	ALICE	184
ELIZABETH	185	ANN	75
ELMA L	101	CARRIE ALICE	159
ESTELLA	51	ELLEN	89
EVA L	164	ELZINA	98
HARRIET	91	HANNAH	75
HATTIE M	48	HARRIET	159
IDA	139	IDA JANE	41
JENNIE V	141	KIZZIE	98
LOUISETTA	92	MALINDA E	28
LUELLA MARGARET	148	MARTHA	32
MARGARET S	3	MARY M	78

MELINDA	182
OLIVE B	149
REBECCA	173
SOPHIA	70
WADIE K	79
TINGLE, NANCY	133
TIPPETT, EDITH BLAIR	83
GEORGIA A	73
KATE L M	48
TIPTON, PERLIE A	124
TOBIA, ALTHA	66
TODOFF, LOUISA	169
TOLDS, ELIZABETH	110
TOLES, JANE	88
MARY	141
TOLIVER, REBECCA J	52
TOLLIVER, EVA	13
TOMLINSON, BLANCHE	30
MAUD	80
TONEY, CORA	41
TORRENCE, ANNA M	2
TOTH, ALMIRA	150
TOTTEN, GOLDIE	135
TRANOR, GRACE	135
TRIBBLE, MARY E	179
TRIPP, LINNA	118
TRISLER, SARAH	115
TROBAUGH, MARY	88
TROEGER, JULIA	151
LORENA	181
ROSA MAY	38
TROSCHKE, MATTIE E	122
TUCKER, ALCEY A	121
ALTA	183
ARNITIS	75
CAROLINE M	60
CLARA	71
CYNTHIA J	173
DEARNIE	75
ELIZABETH	90
ELSABELL	35
EMILY ELIZABETH	185
EMILY L	30
ETHEL L	34
MADDY	5
MAHALA ELIZABETH	183
MARY	167
MARY	183
MINNIE M	73
NANCY	126
OLIVE J	109
ROSETTA B	49
SARAH E	133
SARAH E	137
VEVA I	23
WYNONA B	152
TULLER, ANN M	146
TULLY, ANNIE	21
CATHARINE	160
LIZZIE G	19
LUCY	115
MINNIE	42
RUBY MAY	169
VIRGINIA E	143
TURLEY, ALLIE M	71
ANNIE	79
DELIA	165
EDNA O	74
EMELINE	77
HESTER JANE	117
JENNIE C	37
MARY	119
MARY E	14
NANNIE	185
NANNIE F	173
SARAH M	122
TURNBULL, ELIZABETH A	74
ELLEN	173
HANNAH	131
JESSE B F	145
LARAHAN	85
MARY A	192
MARY E	29
MARY J	67
MAUDE M	77
WILLIE M	21
TURNER, ANNIE	148
BELLE	169
CLARINDA	20
ELIZA M	107
ELLA MAY	81
GRACE P	71
IDA M	63
LEVINA	128
MARY	62
MARY	152
M F	132
POLLY ANN	50
TWYFORD, ADDA Z	152
TYLER, CHARLOTTE BEVERLEY	96
MARGARET LEE	105
MARY F	108
UHRIG, LOTTIE M	181
ULRICH, ANGELINA	122
UPTON, VIRGINIA M	80
UTERS, ALICE	171
VAIL, CAROLINE	70
VALE, LEONA DARE	176
VAN KIRK, LYDIA	139
VAN MATRE, MARY M	77
VAN MATRE, (Mrs) ANNA E	113
ALFRETTY	153
ALICE	39
ANNIE E	146
ANNIE I	105
ANNIE J	150
ANNIE L	68
CARRIE C	64
DESSIE	148
EDNEY F	87
ELIZA	31
EMMA C	168
FANNIE FRANCES	77
IDA	157
IDA L	145
IDA MAY	192
JENNIE	80
JESSIE	25

KATE	159
LAURA	54
LILLIE	147
LIZZIE E	4
LOTTIE MAY	46
MARGARET ANN	144
MARTHA	8
MILLIE	132
MIRIAM JANE	155
MOLLIE	32
NORA E	87
PAMELIA ANN	47
RUTH V	168
SARAH AMANDA	98
VIOLA E	24
VAN METRE, LIZZIE	165
LORENO	29
VAN SICKLE, BETTIE	29
DELLE	129
MARTHA S	135
NANCY E	92
VAN SICKLES, KATIE M	93
NANNIE F	135
SARAH C	52
SARAH E	149
VANCE, LEOLA	10
MARY S	150
SUSAN EMILY	107
VANMATER, MARIA	3
VANMATRE, AGNESS E	165
ELIZABETH	51
HARRIET	127
MAHALA	46
MARGARET	88
MARGARET ANN	100
MARIA	59
MARIA JANE	186
MARY	40
MARY	146
MARY	148
MARY E	159
MARY MAHALA	185
NANCY	179
PATSY	76
PRISCILLA ANN	122
REBECCA	33
REBECCA SUSAN	46
SARAH	26
ZEBA ANN	122
ZELPHA	83
VANMETRE, ANNIE M	87
VANSICKLE, BESSIE	100
CHRISTENA	177
HANNAH	52
MAGGIE E	106
VANSICKLES, ROSANNA	63
VARIAN, CARRIE M	123
CLARA M	174
FREDA	154
HANNAH ELIZA	150
IVA	150
JOANNA	187
MABEL L	92
MARTHA MALINDA	187
MARY LEOTA	185
MATILDA	61
MATILDA	150
MINNIE	52
ORA V	18
REBECCA J	136
URENA CLACK	171
VARNER, MALINDA	175
VARNEY, BERTHA	135
VAUGHAN, NANCY E	31
VAUGHN, BERTHA	166
LUDA	116
MALINDA	73
VAZEY, MARY	84
VEITH, LIZZIE MAY	71
VENNOY, RACHEL	168
VENOY, ELECTA	182
VERHOLTS, MARY D	141
VEST, ELLA M	75
LILLIE A	64
VIA, MIRANDA	135
VICKERS, (Mrs) LOUISA	105
ANNIE FLORENCE	113
CARRIE E	65
HELEN Z	142
LOUISANA	126
LUCY M	123
MAUD	17
SUSAN A	132
VIERS, SARAH F	52
SUSAN S	51
VILLARS, LORA L	35
MARY A	99
ONA A	188
ROSESRUTHEY	27
VINCENT, AMANDA V	67
BERTHA O	51
EMILY C	97
MARANDA	65
MARY	37
MARY	133
MARY	143
MINNIE	142
RUTH	117
VINEY, AUGUSTA	183
VIRCA, ELIZABETH	129
VIRON, MARY L	179
VOLENTINE, LUCY ELIZABETH	126
VOLKERT, SARAH	150
VOLLBURN, CAROLINE	61
VOLLERT, LOUISE C	126
PAULINE C	132
SOPHIA B	90
WADDEL, MARY	122
WADDELL, IRENE	61
KATIE	129
MARTHA A	30
WADDLE, MARY	52
WADE, ELLA	34
MARTHA	26
MARY C	75
MARY J	26
RUTH E	177
SARAH JANE	119

Name	Page
WAGGENER, ATTARAH B	123
HANNAH L	119
HELEN V	123
LAVINA	38
MARY B	42
MILLY	7
WAGGONER, HELEN	34
WALDEN, JULIA A E	35
WALKER, AMELIA M	9
ANGELINE	132
ANGIE	81
CARRIE	15
CARRIE I	83
EMILY	184
EMMA R	154
ETTA	24
FANNIE	94
JENNIE	92
JULIA E	39
KATIE	33
LAURA	8
LORA L	31
LULA B	165
MARIA	167
MARIA A	27
MARIAH	38
MARTHA J	132
MARY	173
MARY E	156
RHODA	20
ROSE O	65
SOPHRONIA	71
WALKUP, ELIZABETH	33
WALLACE, ABIGAIL	172
ANNA	58
BETTIE	114
CARRIE E	1
EMEZETTA	114
EMMAZETTA	190
EVA	170
MARGARET E	114
MARTHA A	55
MARY C	38
MEDA	60
NANCY	66
NANCY	177
NORRIS L	107
OTI	160
PATSY	20
PATSY	20
ROSA BELLE	32
SALLY	60
SARAH ANN	187
VIRGINIA E	58
WALLAHAN, ESTER JANE	162
WALLER, SARAH	187
WALLIS, ALMA	103
CATHARINE	27
CYNTHIA ANN	94
ELIZA	173
ELIZABETH	42
ELLEN	101
EMMA	153
FLORENCE EMILY	18
JANE A	82
LAURA M	36
LULLA	4
MARGARET J	94
MARGARET J	188
MARTHA	53
MARTHA A	82
MARY E	32
MARY J	81
NANCY E	125
NANCY J	89
RUSHIA A	35
SARAH E	6
SARAH J	52
SIDENA	167
WALTER, ENOLA	99
LOTTIE L	166
WALTERS, LIZZIE	165
WAMACK, LUCINDA B	180
WAMSLEY, ANNIE	14
ELIZABETH	131
HATTIE	84
MARY ALICE	4
MARY ALICE	8
MAUDE E	2
MITTIE	157
NANCY M	9
NANCY M	121
NOLEY M	84
REBECCA ANN	121
SOPHRONIA	153
VIETTA	133
WILLIE B	29
WARD, BERTHA ALAMEDA	18
BINA	114
BLANCH	60
ELIZABETH	10
EMMA	124
FLAVIA O	98
GERTIE	76
GINSY	153
HANNORAH	56
LECTA M	44
MAGGIE MAY	28
MARGARET SUSAN	176
MARY	18
MARY	175
MARY	91
MARY E	60
MARY E	186
NANCY	3
ORAH	41
ORETHA	106
RENA	148
SARAH E	35
VIRGINIA F	115
WARDEN, AMANDA	76
CUMA	149
EDITH E	29
ELIZA	67
LILLIE MAY	177
ORPHE BELLE	29
VIRGINIA E	187
WARNER, AMY	5

BELLE	86	
BESSIE	61	
CHARLOTTE	64	
CLARISSA C	68	
CLEO P	82	
DORA	26	
ELLA	133	
ELLEN L	6	
EMMA	101	
EMMA L	36	
ETHEL	101	
HALLIE N	5	
HARRIET	159	
HATTIE DEEM	75	
IVA	107	
JANE	29	
LUCY	66	
LUCY B	121	
MAGGIE	190	
MARIETTA D	149	
MARTHA F	5	
MARY A	159	
MARY A	117	
MARY M	71	
NORA	150	
POLLY	70	
RUBY E	2	
SUSAN	107	
VERNA S	107	
WARNER-HALL (Mrs), LUCY	42	
WARTENBURG, CORA M	12	
WARTH, ELIZA	100	
HANNAH	48	
MARY	48	
WASHINGTON, EMMA	88	
FANNIE	19	
FLEETA	44	
JUDITH R	160	
MARGARET	163	
MARY LOUISE	190	
MINA M	87	
VIRGINIA S	133	
WATERS, ELIZABETH	134	
WATERSON, JENNIE	78	
LIZZIE M	137	
MARIA	61	
WATKINS, ELIZABETH	109	
ELIZABETH	123	
HATTIE	122	
JANE	186	
JULIA A	15	
MAGGIE	7	
MAGGIE	17	
MARY	152	
VIRGINIA C	149	
WATSON, (Mrs) MARY L	58	
BESSIE	129	
CHARLOTTE EMMA	16	
CORA E	111	
DORA A	111	
JENNIE L	164	
JULIA	121	
MARGARET	59	
MARY E	32	
WATTERSON, BERTHA	43	
EDITH A	177	
FLOSSIE J	51	
LAURA M	180	
LIZZIE	88	
SARAH E	147	
WATTS, MARY E	84	
WAUGH, ALICE	89	
AMANDA	71	
CATHARINE	187	
DORA	22	
ELIZA	189	
ELIZABETH	189	
ELIZABETH S	71	
FANNIE H	54	
JANE	22	
MAHALA	178	
MANDA	157	
MARTHA	178	
MARTHA	178	
MARTHA JANE	40	
MARY	13	
MARY A	36	
MARY LEVINA	119	
MARY M	189	
METY	16	
NANCY CATHARINE	2	
NANCY E	82	
ROSA	45	
ROSA	177	
ROWANNA	189	
SARAH A	179	
SARAH E	33	
SARAH ELLEN	6	
SOPHA A	16	
VINA C	173	
VIRGINIA B	86	
VIRGINIA G	108	
WAYBRIGHT, MERLIA F	77	
WAYLAND, MARY W	147	
WEAKLEY, ANNIE	39	
WEARS, (Mrs) LILLIE	97	
MALVINA	177	
MARTHA	62	
MINERVA J	156	
NORA	20	
WEATHERS, DAISY	8	
WEAVER, ANGELINE	146	
ANGELINE	152	
BELLVINA	140	
CASSY	135	
CHRISTENA	132	
CLARA T	92	
DOROTHY	1	
DORTHA S	1	
ELIZA	96	
ELIZABETH	96	
ELIZABETH	141	
ELLA M	26	
ELLEN	84	
ETTA	69	
FRANCES EVELINE	83	
LAVINA	73	
LYDIA	146	

MARGARET	155
MARGARET E	145
MARIA TERESA	42
MARTHA E	129
MARY V	12
MINA E	146
ROSETTA	147
ROXANA	125
SARAH	58
VERINITIA	145
WEBB, HATTIE	49
MARY MELISSA	184
WEBBER, ORA E	100
WEBSTER, GEORGE ANNA	108
JENNIE B	109
WEDGE, MEARLA	183
NANNIE	118
WEEKLY, RUBY	108
WEEKS, MELINDA J	41
WEERS, ABIGAIL	177
WEES, EDITH L	51
MABEL F	78
WEETHEE, ROSABELL	130
WEIGAND, ABBIE E	17
ANNIE	65
ARTIE E	14
EUNICE	103
GERTRUD M	13
JESSIE	81
KATIE M	170
WEIRS, ANN	7
JEMIMA	82
MARY J	130
MARY L	14
WELCH, DORA	68
IDA	162
WELLS, MAY G	103
SUSAN A	43
WELTON, ELLA M	45
MOLLIE	40
WENDELAND, CATHARINE	136
WERNER, EMMA	19
MOLLIE	142
OLEVIA	181
SUSIE P	59
WESBAY, SARAH C	159
WESSEN, MINERVA	17
PAULINA B	115
WESSON, EMMA B	192
WEST, BESSIE	112
BETHLEHEM	33
CLARA	83
WESTBAY, ELIZABETH A	15
WESTFALL, IVA	128
WETZEL, ELIZABETH	100
EUPHRASIA A	123
MARGUERITE	89
MARY JANE	143
RACHAEL	159
REBECCA J	42
SOPHRONIA B	114
WHALEY, ESTELLA M	149
FANNIE	113
MARY J	56
MARY L	113
MAUD K	24
NELLIE F	87
WHARFF, STELLA FAYE	84
WHEATLEY, MARY	83
WHEATON, HATTIE E	116
LOUESA	167
MARY	65
MAUD	111
WHEELER, ELLEN	9
ELLERDEYER	159
IVA	109
MAHALA	14
REBECCA	69
WHETSTONE, MARY S	35
WHITAKER, FLORENCE	158
WHITE, (Mrs) ELIZABETH D	159
ALMA	3
CLARA H	173
CORA	74
CORA BELLE	119
DEMARRIS L	94
ELIZABETH	132
LOTA MAY	128
MARGRETTIE T	185
MARINDA	58
MATILDA J	86
MAUD	95
MINTIE	126
RUTH L	95
SUSAN	57
SUSAN F	190
WHITEHEAD, COLUMBIA JANE	90
DIANA G	47
WHITESIDE, MARTHA ELIZABETH	165
MAUD	34
MINNIE F	58
WHITMORE, MINNIE	112
WHITNEY, MARY	2
WHITT, ALMA L	106
AMISHA	64
EMMA L	42
FRANCES	130
HETTIE G	89
MARTHA F	19
SARAH A	88
SUSANNA M	10
WHITTAKER, LAURA E	2
WHITTEN, ELIZABETH	75
FRANCES	108
SARAH M	184
WHITTENDON, MARTHA J	59
WHITTINGTON, ALICE	173
BESS	86
BETTIE	9
CARRIE	43
CLARISSA	122
DAISY	107
ELLA	94
FLORA M	188
FRANCES L	52
IDA	180
MAMIE	94
MARIA	109

	MARTHA A	133	ANGELINE	72
	MARTHA JANE	105	ANNABELLA	8
	MARY B	131	ANNIE	27
	MINNIE O	173	BETSY	108
	NANNIE A	1	CATHARINE	127
	RHODA	20	CORA	179
	SARAH	89	CYNTHIA R	83
WILCOXEN, SALIMA		144	DORA	165
WILDMAN, LIZZIE		167	ELIZA	23
WILES, AMELIA FRANCES		88	ELIZA	31
	MARY A	63	ELIZA F	188
	MOLLIE	135	ELIZABETH	152
WILEY, AMERICA J		186	ELLA	56
	CATHARINE	3	ELLENORA	53
	CHARITY ANN	157	ELSIE	169
	GERTIE	65	EMMA L	42
	JANE R	10	EVA L	169
	JENNIE	83	GOLDIE	162
	JULIA W	69	GOLDIE L	190
	MALINDA ANN	128	HANNA	10
	MARGARETTA	191	HELLEN P	111
	VIRGINIA W	127	ISABELLA	152
WILKINSON, ELIZA		95	JANE	42
WILKS, MALINDA		41	JANE	57
WILL, JENNIE M		165	JENNIE	90
WILLARD, ELIZABETH		137	JERUSHA	110
WILLIAMS, ANNIE L		45	LEANAH	54
	ALBERT CHRISTENIA	91	LOUISA	171
	BLANCHE	67	MARGARET E	105
	ELIZABETH	43	MARY	60
	ELLA MARIA	88	MARY A	190
	FRANCES E	4	MARY C	74
	GWENDOLINE	20	MINNIE O	72
	JENNIE	46	NANCY	143
	JOSEPHINE	13	NANCY C	14
	L DORAH ANN	155	ROSELLE	142
	LELIA	170	SARAH	15
	MALINDA S	100	SARAH A	188
	MARTHA J	96	SARAH J	130
	MARY	51	SARAH V	20
	MARY	113	VIRGIE	119
	MARY	184	VIRGINIA	69
	MARY C (BURNELL)	11	WIMER, IDA	41
	MARY JANE	169	WINDELS, BERTHA	112
	MARY M	87	WINDLE, BERTHA	188
	MARY M	88	REBECCA	186
	NELLIE	150	SARAH	101
	PATSY	87	WINDON, ADA DAY	136
	REBECCA	110	ANNIE R	121
	REWHAMA J	155	CLARA E	176
	RHODA	4	ELIZABETH A	95
	ROSA	179	EVA BELLE	43
	ROSA	185	HARRIET JANE	141
	SALLIE	53	HATTIE M	79
	SARAH M	55	KATHRYN L	141
	STELLA	15	LELIA EDITH	172
	TABITHA	69	MARY E	160
WILLIAMSON, ELIZABETH		10	MARY JANE	136
	FLORA A	58	MATTIE J	186
	INEZ	165	NANCY C	80
	MAUD B	122	NANCY M	28
WILLIS, MARY ANN		183	RHODA J	186
	SUSAN F	95	ROSA D	131
WILSON, ALLIE		96	ROSANA	161

SARAH F	30
SUSAN M	18
WINDSOR, MABLE	30
WINEBRENER, FLORENCE	164
WINER, FANNIE	43
WINES, NELLIE	114
WING, HATTIE	43
WINGER, MARY J	26
WINGET, ALMA	8
MINTIE	75
WINGO, GILLEY FRANCES	152
WINKELBACK, ELIZABETH JANE	26
WINKLEY, ADA O	87
BEDA A	190
HARRIET B	92
WINSHIP, HANNAH	132
WINTER, ANNA M	173
DENA	158
EMMA	192
WIRES, MARY	68
WISE, MAUD	4
MAUD	99
REBECCA J	191
WISEMAN, MARY	28
MARY	191
MARY J	119
NANCY L	95
WITHERS, BERTHA	123
CATHARINE	132
EDNA A	4
EFFIE	71
ELIZA	178
ELIZA F	105
ELIZABETH A	116
GRACE	74
IDA	169
JENNIE	38
LULA	148
LULA MARICE	36
MARTHA	64
MARY C	102
MARY C	119
MARY JANE	9
MINERVA C	27
NELLIE B	125
SARAH	177
SARAH J	106
SARAH L	11
VIRGINIA	177
WITHROW, LEONA	26
WOGAN, (Mrs) EMMA	131
WOLF, BARBARA	187
DOROTHY	184
EMILY JANE	37
EVA	162
FLORENCE	147
IDA	158
JANE	73
JULIA CATHARINE	85
LIZZIE	13
MARGARET	61
MARTHA	76
MARY A	46
MARY JANE	72
NORA	4
REBECCA	24
VIRGINIA	5
VIRGINIA	5
WOLFE, AMERICA	134
ELIZABETH A	145
LUELLA MABEL	103
MAGGIE I	48
RUBY B	106
WOLFORD, EUSTASIA L	26
REBECCA V	46
RHODA E	68
WOMELDORFF, MINNIE E	47
WOMELSDORFF, HENRIETTA	160
WOOD, ALLIE L	129
ANNIE E	11
EFFA B	19
EMMA M	53
JEANIE D	83
MARY	67
ROSA V	110
SARAH JANE	112
SUSAN	72
SUSAN	118
SUSAN	178
WOODALL, CORA	92
JENNIE	83
MARY E	94
REBECCA J	183
SARAH	90
WOODARD, AMANDA	139
BERTHA SELL	148
OLEVIA	54
WOODLEY, EMMA	16
WOODRUFF, FANNY	128
RACHEL	162
WOODRUM, BLANCHE	48
CORA A	72
EVA	57
EVA L	111
IDA M	79
SARAH ELIZABETH	156
WOODS, ELANORA	174
ELEANORE BAIRD	41
ELIZA	181
FLORENCE	20
LETHA M	7
MARGARET T	52
MARY	140
MARY A	178
MARY ANN	190
MARY JANE	98
VIOLA KATHARINE	108
WOODWARD, ALMIRA	112
CAROLINE	
MARY JANE	84
WOODY, CARRIE	29
ELIZA	42
LUCY J	168
MAMIE AUGUSTA	9
VIOLA	6
WOODYARD, LOTTIE	131
MINERVA S	169
SARAH	184

WOOLFINGBARGER, LAURA B	145	SARAH	142
WOOMER, (Mrs) ALICE	25	SARAH	145
WOOTEN, LUCRETIA	182	WURNEL, JANE	18
MARY MARGARET	89	YAUGER, BYANTHA	6
MATILDA	187	DOROTHY	134
MAUD	22	EVA	122
WORELL, ELLA	128	JENNIE	47
WORK, EMMA A	80	LEUCRETIA E	156
GRACE A	125	LETTIE	147
MARGARET E	166	MARY	67
MARY E	77	MARY FLORENCE	182
WORKMAN, AMANDA	46	NANCY J	92
CAREY M	45	RACHEL	61
CLARA C	61	RACHEL	131
CLARA CATHARINE	67	SARAH	17
CORA	164	SARAH C	58
EFFIE	153	SOPHIA	156
ELIZABETH E	67	YEAGER, ALBERTA	14
ELIZABETH J	100	ALICE	39
FANNIE	186	ANN ELIZA	162
MARY	15	ANNA	82
MARY M	15	ANNA L	7
VENA E	44	BARBARA	61
WORLEY, LUCY M	147	BERNETIA	67
WORRELL, CARRIE E	116	CATHARINE	86
LOUISA	139	CATHARINE	143
MINNIE J	95	EDITH E	65
SABRE	107	ELIZA	14
WOYAN, BARBARA	185	ELIZA J	174
MAGGIE MAY	1	ELIZABETH	30
MINNIE MONA	60	EMELINE	126
WRAY, ARAMANTHA F	94	EMMA B	53
EMMA ELLA	68	ETHEL V	56
JANE	125	FLORA C	156
LENA M	124	JANE	55
LUCY J	90	LUCINDA	158
MARGARET V	4	MAGGIE LEE	86
MARY F	81	MARGARET	30
MARY JANE	42	MARGARET MERTILLA	177
NANCY V	94	MARY	19
SADIE F	7	MARY	127
SADIE F	7	MARY	188
WRIGHT, LIZZIE C	45	MARY C	40
BERTHA	189	MARY M	143
BESSIE MAY	125	MATILDA	9
CHARLOTTE	1	POLLY	122
DAMIE J	87	REBECCA	146
DEBBIE E	119	SARAH	17
ELIZABETH A	117	SARAH ANN	31
EMMA	190	SARAH C	149
ETHEL G	156	SARAH M	146
LILLIAN	54	STELLA E	160
LOU	124	SUSANNA	29
LUCINDA	26	YERTY, MARTHA ELIZABETH	179
LYDIA A	125	YOHO, MARGARET	135
MARY	10	MARY E	188
MARY E	48	YONKER, ELIZABETH ANN	145
MARY ELIZABETH	27	ELLEN J	191
MYRTLE E	55	EMMA F	62
NANCY A	69	FANNIE	67
POLLY	25	HATTIE G	136
RHEUAMA	49	LAURA E	123
RHODA	88	LAVINA FRANCES	37
RUTH	135	LOVINA	191

MABLE BONNER	130	
SARAH F S	102	
YOUNG, (Mrs) ANNIE	64	
(Mrs) MARGARET	100	
AGNES	14	
AGNES C	126	
ALICE R	32	
ANNA BLANCHE	117	
ANNIE	69	
ANNIE M	15	
ARDENA A	165	
ARTIE MISHA	102	
CAROLINE	23	
CARRIE	167	
CLARA	48	
CORY OCIAL	36	
DERTHA R	109	
ELIZABETH	79	
ELIZABETH	173	
ELLA	23	
FLORA ELLEN	113	
HANNAH A	2	
JESSIE	105	
KATHRYN A	1	
LILLIE OLIE	110	
LINNA DROWN	131	
MAGGIE	153	
MARGUIRETTA	151	
MARY DORCAS	187	
MAUDE	135	
MINNESOTA	116	
MINNIE M	142	
MINNIE T	110	
NEVADA	30	
SADIE S	154	
STELLA	165	
SUSAN J	110	
TREACY	59	
VIRGINIA E	105	
VIRGINIA F	48	
YOUSE, ANNIE A	129	
ZAPF, BARBARA	4	
BARBARA	151	
ELIZABETH	141	
MARY	136	
ZEARLEY, MINERVA	159	
ZEARLY, FRANCES J	158	
ZERCKEL, HANNAH MARY	86	
MARGARET A	47	
REBECCA	136	
SARAH J	62	
ZERCKLE, FRANCES V	126	
REBECCA J	147	
SARAH	18	
ZERCLE, ELIZABETH	56	
ELIZABETH	56	
ZERKEL, AMANDA M	93	
BARBARA	144	
CHRISTINA	123	
JENNIE	82	
L B	76	
LANORA	87	
LAURETTA C	56	
LUELLA	87	
NANCY	123	
ZERKLE, ALMIRA S	134	
ANNIE E	23	
CORA B	173	
EDNA E	174	
ELIZABETH	144	
ELNORA	4	
IDA	122	
LUNIA V	150	
ZIMMER, MARGARET	141	
ZIMMERMAN, MEDIA A	27	
ZIRCKEL, MARY	56	
ZIRCKLE, ADA V	25	
DORCAS M	191	
ZIRCLE, CHRISTENA	81	
MARGARET E	173	
ZIRKEL, BERTHA	77	
EMMA B	137	
ORRILLA	24	
SARAH E	142	
SARAH F	178	
SUSANNAH	147	
ZIRKLE, ADDIE L	15	
CATHARINE	37	
ESTA E	123	
MARY ELLEN	179	
SUSIE	114	
ZURKLE, CANILLA	9	
ZUSPAN, ANNA E	57	
ANNA E	58	
CARIE L	135	